ISBN 978-0-483-33304-8
PIBN 10500969

This book is a reproduction of an important historical work. Forgotten Books uses
state-of-the-art technology to digitally reconstruct the work, preserving the original format
whilst repairing imperfections present in the aged copy. In rare cases, an imperfection in
the original, such as a blemish or missing page, may be replicated in our edition. We do,
however, repair the vast majority of imperfections successfully; any imperfections that
remain are intentionally left to preserve the state of such historical works.

PUBLICATIONS

OF THE

ŇARRAGANSETT CLUB.

(First Series.)

VOLUME V.

PROVIDENCE, R. I.

MDCCCLXXII.

Providence Prefs Co., Printers.

Providence Prefs Co., Printers.

INTRODUCTION.

———o———

OGER Williams for well nigh a quarter of a century after the publication of *The Bloody Tenent yet more Bloody*, refrained from "ufing the help of printer men." In the year 1676, and when nearing the fober limit of fourfcore, he made his final appearance as a controverfial writer in the Treatife which is here reprinted for the firft time. The circumftances which led him to affume an attitude fo unlike that maintained during the earlier portion of his career, form an interefting epifode in the early hiftory of Rhode Ifland.

At the time when "the People called Quakers,"[1] were excluded by harfh enactments from the other New England Colonies, in Rhode Ifland alone they were received with fympathy and kindnefs. While the fecond party of Quaker miffionaries that had arrived in Maffachufetts were languifhing in Bofton gaol, Samuel Gorton, though dif-

---

[1] This name, which has come by ufage to be the familiar defignation of the followers of George Fox, was firft applied to them in 1650, by Gervace Bennet, a magiftrate of Derby, "who was the firft that called us Quakers, becaufe I bid them tremble at the word of the Lord." *Journal of George Fox*, 3d edit. 1765, p. 35. The explanation given by Williams on page 41, *infra*, Fox in his reply denies, (*A New-England-Fire-Brand Quenched*, Part i: p. 26;) repeating the account given in his *Journal*. In the following pages I have ufed, for convenience, a term that has long ceafed to convey reproach.

B

fering with them in principle not lefs than he differed
with Roger Williams, found the means of conveying to
them the affurance of his Chriftian fympathy. Had his
benevolent projeft been carried out, this little company
would have been the earlieft apoftles of the new faith on
the fhores of the Narraganfett. He propofed, if he could
be informed what time the fhip would fail, "to have a
veffel in readinefs," to take them in, and fet them where
they might enjoy their liberty. In their reply, they ftated
that the mafter of the veffel had been placed under fuch
heavy bonds "to fet them afhore in England," as to render the undertaking hopelefs.[1]

At their annual meeting in September, 1656, the Commiffioners of the United Colonies, refolved to "propofe to
the feveral General Courts, that all Quakers, Ranters, and
other notorious heretics, fhould be prohibited coming into
the United Colonies, and, if any fhould hereafter come or
arife, that they fhould be forthwith fecured, or removed
out of all the jurifdictions."[2] Each of the four confede-
rated colonies enacted laws in accordance with this recommendation. After an experience of two years rendered it
plain that thefe meafures had failed of the defired effect,
the Commiffioners, under the prefidency of Endicott,
"ferioufly commended to the feveral General Courts, to
make a law that all fuch Quakers formerly convicted and
punifhed as fuch, fhall, (if they return again,) be imprifoned, and forthwith banifhed or expelled out of the

---

[1]This interefting correfpondence was
publifhed by Gorton in 1657, as an Appendix to his *"Antidote againft the Common Plague of the World." R. I. Hift.
Coll.* ii: 16. The letter refutes the
remark of Palfrey that his motive was
to annoy Maffachufetts. *Hift. N. E.* ii:
464.

[2]Hazard's *State Papers,* ii: 349.

said jurifdiction, under pain of death; and if afterwards they prefume to come again into that jurifdiction, then to be put to death as prefumptuoufly incorrigible, unlefs they fhall plainly and publickly renounce their curfed opinions."[1] To Maffachufetts belongs the diftinction of being the only one of the United Colonies to carry this advice into full effect. It was under a ftatute paffed by the General Court in compliance with the foregoing recommendation, that William Robinfon, Marmaduke Stevenfon, Mary Dyer and William Leddra were hung on Bofton Common.[2]

Almoft from the beginning Rhode Ifland became an afylum for the "curfed fect." In the autumn of 1656 Nicholas Upfall a "weakly old man," for "reproaching the honored magiftrates, and fpeaking againft the law made and publifhed againft Quakers," was fined twenty pounds, and fentenced to "depart the jurifdiction within one month."[3] Upfall having been denied a refting place in Plymouth Colony, at laft found refuge in Rhode Ifland.[4] Although a member of the Bofton Church, Upfall had adopted Quaker principles, and feems to have been the firft of that perfuafion who fought fhelter in this Colony.[5] The number, however, foon increafed. Little more than a year had elapfed from the landing of the firft Quakers before the Commiffioners of the United Colonies, "being

---

[1] Hazard ii: 399.

[2] Bifhop, *New England Judged,* 114. John Winthrop, of Conn., who fubfcribed to the vote of the Commiffioners "as a query, and not as an act" tried to fave the lives of Robinfon and Steveufon. See Letter of Wm. Coddington to J. Winthrop, Jr., June 29, 1672.

Mass. Hift. Coll. 4th feries, vol. vii: p. 287.

[3] *Mass. Rec.* iv: (1) 277, 280. Bifhop, *New Eng. Judged,* 39.

[4] Bifhop, 40, 161. Whiting, *Truth and Innocency Defended,* 15.

[5] Bifhop, 39. Burnyeat, *Truth Exalted,* 49.

informed that divers Quakers are arrived this summer at Rode Island, and entertained there, which may prove dangerous to the Colonies," addressed a letter to the Governor, requesting that measures might be taken for removing those Quakers who had already been received, and for prohibiting their coming in the future.[1] In reply, the authorities of Rhode Island declared that while desirous of maintaining a "fayre and loveing correspondence and entercourse with all the collonys," and while ready at all times to return "such as fly from the hands of justice, for matters of crime," they had no law "whereby to punish any for only declaring by words, &c., their minds and understandings concerning the things and ways of God, as to salvation and an eternal condition."[2] At the same time they expressed their willingness to commend the consideration of any "extravagant outgoings" on the part of the Quakers to the next General Assembly. At the next meeting of the Assembly, at Portsmouth, March, 1658, a letter was addressed to Massachusetts, affirming that freedom of conscience was "the principal ground of their Charter," and was still prized by them "as the greatest hapines that men can possess in this world," but that in case the Quakers should refuse to subject themselves to ordinary duties, "as members of civill societies, for the preservation of the same in justice and peace," the matter would be laid before the authorities in England, "humbly craveing their advice and order, how to carry ourselves in any further respect towards these people soe that therewithall theire may be no damadge, or infringement of that chiefe principle in our charter concerninge freedom of consciences."[3] From

[1] Letter of Com. of the United Colonies, Sept. 12, 1657. Hazard, ii : 377.

[2] Hazard, ii : 552. *R. I. Rec.* i : 377.
[3] *R. I. Rec.* i : 378.

this "chiefe principle" nothing could force them to fwerve. Even the further threats of being excluded from trade with their fifter colonies, only led in the following year to an appeal to the Protector that they "may not be compelled to exercife any civill power over men's confciences, foe longe as humane orders in poynt of civility are not corrupted and voyalated."[1]

This confiftent liberality of the Colony of Rhode Ifland appears in a ftill more ftriking light when the fact is borne in mind that the doctrines advocated by the Quakers at this time, were far from receiving a general affent. In the Reply of the Authorities to the Commiffioners of the Colonies their diflike of the new comers is uttered in very decided terms : "We moreover find" they write, "that in thofe places where thefe people aforefaid, in this coloney, are moft of all fuffered to declare themfelves freely, and are only oppofed by arguments in difcourfe, there they leaft of all defire to come, and we are informed that they begin to loath this place, for that they are not oppofed by the civill authority, but with all patience and meeknes are fuffered to fay over their pretended revelations and admonitions, nor are they like or able to gain many here to their way ; furely we find that they delight to be perfecuted by civill powers, and when they are foe, they are like to gain more adherents by the confeyte of their patient fufferings, than by confent to their pernicious fayings. And yet we conceive, that theife doctrines tend to very abfolute cutting downe and overturninge relations and civill government among men, if generally received."[2]

Notwithftanding, however, the opinion here expreffed

[1] *R. I. Records,* i : 398.   [2] *R. I. Records,* i : 377.

with regard to the probable growth of the sect, the facts go to show that the number of Quakers in Rhode Island constantly increased. Horred Gardner, who was flogged and imprisoned by the authorities at Boston, in May, 1658, was "an Inhabitant of Newport in Rhode-Island."[1] Thomas Harris, who was imprisoned and repeatedly flogged in the following month, had moved from Barbadoes to Rhode Island.[2] Catherine Scot, who was imprisoned for two weeks, and publicly flogged, in the autumn of the same year, was wife of Richard Scot of *Providence.*[3] William Robinson, the first Quaker put to death, had been "moved of the Lord to go from Rhode Island" to bear his testimony in Massachusetts.[4] His companion at the gallows, Marmaduke Stevenson, came by way of Rhode Island from Barbadoes.[5] Mary Dyer, the only woman put to death, was wife of William Dyer, Secretary of *Providence Plantations.*

While Rhode Island lacked the allurement of persecution it still furnished an inviting field to the Quaker missionary. It had been settled mainly by Baptists, and it was from among the Baptists that many, if not most of the early converts to Quakerism had been gained. Many of the doctrines, and much of the discipline afterwards adopted by the Quakers can be traced directly to a Baptist source. The most striking resemblance is presented by the General Baptists, who existed as a distinct body forty years before the founder of Quakerism began to preach. Like the Quakers, the Baptists had claimed that the church was

---

[1] Bishop, *New Eng. Judged,* 60.
[2] Bishop, 61.
[3] Bishop, 95.
[4] Bishop, 114.

[5] Marmaduke Stevenson's *Paper of his Call to the Work and Service of the Lord,* in *New England Judged,* 133.

a fociety of equals; they held that the ordinances of the
Old Teftament were abolifhed; they were inclined to lay
ftrefs on inward revelations; they faid that allegiance was
due the civil government only in temporal things. Like
the Quakers the Baptifts had permitted women to preach
in public; they had the fame fcruples about ufing the pagan names of months and days; they had protefted againft
the neceffity of a learned miniftry; they had oppofed any
regular minifterial fupport; they had expreffed the fame
repugnance to taking oaths. Both Baptifts and Quakers
held their monthly, quarterly and yearly church affemblies
and both termed them "meetings for difcipline." The
"brother confirmed" of the Baptift was but another name
for the "acknowledged minifter" of the Quaker. The
method of folemnizing marriages adopted by the early
Baptifts was nearly identical with that followed by the
Quakers. Both bodies were much exercifed by their members "marrying out of church." Many of the early Baptifts ufed the fingular pronoun "thou" and "thee" in addreffing individuals.[1] George Fox indeed added little beyond boundlefs enthufiam to the views which the Baptifts
had already advanced. He had an uncle who was a Baptift; one of his earlieft fermons was preached at "a great
meeting of the Baptifts at Broughton;" when he went
into Leicefterfhire "there were fome Baptifts in that
country" whom he defired to meet.[2] The firft perfon
in *Providence* who embraced the principles of George
Fox, according to tradition, was Richard Scot,[3] who

[1] On this unexplored fubject fee *George Fox, the Friends, and the Early Baptifts.*, By William Tallack, London: 1868.
[2] Fox's *Journal*, p. 3, 12, 26, 99,
&c., compare Edmundfon's *Journal*, p. 34, 35.
[3] Staples' *Annals of Providence:* 420.

like Roger Williams, had been for a time connected with the Baptifts.[1]

In a fhort time the number of Quakers muft have confiderably increafed, for when the General Meeting was "fet up" at Rhode Ifland, in the fpring of 1661, the concourfe was fo numerous, that in Maffachufetts grave apprehenfions were aroufed "that the Quakers were gathering together to kill the People, and to fire the town of Bofton."[2] As early as 1665 the Quakers had been reinforced by men as prominent as Coddington and Eafton, fince in March of that year thefe two prefented a memorial to the Royal Commiffioners in behalf of their fellow-religionifts. The greatly increafed influence of the Quakers in Rhode Ifland at this time may be ftill more conclufively inferred from the fact that when the Commiffioners required that an "oath of allegiance" fhould be adminiftered to "to all houfeholders inhabiting the colony," the General Affembly fubftituted "an engagement," in favor of "fuch as made a fcruple of fwearing."[3] According to the account of Richard Scot, when two of the Commiffioners were at Providence, "being in the Houfe of Thomas Olney, Senior, of the fame Town," Roger Williams propounded to them the following queftion: "We have a People here amongft us, which will not act in our Government with us; What courfe fhall we take with them?" "Then George Cartwright, one of the Commiffioners afked him, What manner of Perfons they were? Do they live quietly and peaceably amongft you? This they could not deny; Then he made them this Anfwer; If they can

---

[1] Letter of R. Scot in *New-England-Fire-Brand-Quenched*, Part ii : 247.

[2] Bifhop, *New England Judged*, 351.
[3] *R. I. Rec.* ii : 110–118.

Govern themfelves, they have no need of your Government."[1] This is the earlieft indication of Roger Williams' attitude with reference to the Quakers.

The firft Quaker miffionary of eminence who vifited Rhode Ifland, was John Burnyeat, who having fpent fome time at New York "in the *fourth month* 1666," then "took fhipping for *Road Ifland* in *New England*, and there fpent fome time in vifiting Friends, and their Meetings."[2] He next vifited Bofton and the towns in Eaftern New England, and returning to Rhode Ifland in the winter and ftayed for fome time; "for there was no going off the Ifland unto the Main, the Snow was fo deep."[3] In the latter part of March, 1667, he failed for Barbadoes, and in the autumn returned to England. In July, 1670, he again left England for Barbadoes and having remained there fix months, failed for New York, in April, 1671. Having

[1] Letter of R. Scot in *New-England-Fire-Brand Quenched*, p. 248. "This was told again by a Woman of the fame Houfe (when the Speech was fpoken) to another Woman, whom the Complaint with the reft was made againft, who related it to me."

[2] *The Truth Exalted in the Writings of that Eminent and Faithful Servant of Chrift John Burnyeat*, p. 35. Burnyeat was born about 1631, at Crabtreebeck, parifh of Lowfwater, in the county of Cumberland, "where his Parents were of good repute, aud his Education was according to his Parentage." See *Teftimony concerning the Life and Death of John Burnyeat* prefixed to *Truth Exalted*. He became a difciple of George Fox in 1653. In 1657 the Lord "began to ftir in his heart by his Spirit to go forth in the ftrength of his Word." After preaching for a time in England in 1658, he preached in the northern and weftern parts of Scotland. In 1659 he vifited Ireland, where he "travelled aud labored in the Gofpel for *Twelve Months*." Early in 1662, he was "moved by the Lord to go to *London* to George *Fox*, and others of the Elders, and acquaint him with what was upon me from the Lord to go to *America*." Circumftances, however, delayed his going for two years. "About the *Seventh Month*, 1664," he "took fhipping at *Galloway* in *Ireland* for the *Barbadoes*." He then vifited Virginia and Maryland, and in June, 1666 went to New York. See *Truth Exalted*; p. 1, 16, 26, 29, 32, 35.

[3] *Truth Exalted*, p. 35.

spent some time on Long Island he "took shipping for *Road Island,* and was there at their Yearly Meeting in 1671, which begins the *ninth* of the *fourth month* every Year, and continues for much of a Week, and is a General Meeting once a year for all Friends in *New-England.*"[1] After going East as far as Piscataway he "came to Road-Island again, and there spent some time, and went up to *Providence,* and did visit Friends there."[2] The winter of 1671 was spent at the South. Returning to Long Island he "then set Sail for *Road-Island* the 29th of the *third Month,* (1672) and arrived at *Road-Island* the *thirtieth of the same,* and there stayed till the *Yearly Meeting,* which began the *eighth day* of the *fourth Month,* which was the sixth day of the next Week following; and at that *General Meeting* there were many Friends from most places in *New-England,* where Friends dwelt, and abundance of other *People* came into our Publick Meetings. And we had Meetings for *eight days* together, every day a Meeting, some publick and others *Men-*and *Womens-Meetings* for settling the affairs of the Churches in the Order of the Truth; that all things might be kept sweet, clear, and well. And when all was over, and the Service of the Meetings finished, I took my Journey *Eastward,* to go through the Meetings in the *Eastern Parts* of *New England,* and with me went *John Cartwright* and *George* Pattison, and several other Friends to accompany us; and we left G. F. *upon the Island,* and he went to *Providence* and the *Narraganset Country.*"[3]

The visit of George Fox, to which allusion is here made, was an event that could not fail to fix the attention of the

---

[1] *Truth Exalted,* p. 40.
[2] "   "   p. 41.
[3] *Truth Exalted,* p. 47 : compare Fox's *Journal,* p. 443.

whole community.[1] If Fox may not, with ſtrict truth be called the founder, he was certainly the recognized leader of the ſect.[2] He was the foremoſt repreſentative of its doctrines during the firſt period of its hiſtory. For a quarter of a century he had been laboring with tireleſs zeal to commend them to his countrymen. His name was now familiar wherever the Engliſh language was ſpoken. Thoſe who oppoſed his teachings were everywhere filled with alarm when it was announced that "the man in leathern breeches had come."[3] Beneath an external garb of wild and coarſe fanaticiſm he poſſeſſed an unuſual ſhare of prudence, great ſhrewdneſs, and an indomitable courage that commended him highly to the fierce religioniſts who had been trained in the Civil War. In perſon he was large ; his eyes were bright and piercing, and his voice pow-

[1] " I was born in the month called July, in the year 1624, at Drayton in the Clay, in Leiceſterſhire.   My father's name was Chriſtopher Fox. He was by profeſſion a weaver, an honeſt man, and there was a ſeed of God in him.   The neighbors called him Righteous Chriſten.   My mother was an upright woman ; her maiden name was Mary Lago, of the family of the Lago's, and of the ſtock of the martyrs." *Journal* of George Fox, p. 1. When towards nineteen, "at the command of God" he left his relations and broke off all fellowſhip with young or old. Some adviſed him to marry ; one " ancient prieſt " bade him take tobacco and ſing pſalms." The Lord ſhowed him clearly " that he did not dwell in theſe temples which men had commanded and ſet up, but in peoples hearts." After he had received the " opening from the Lord

that to be bred at Oxford or Cambridge, was not ſufficient to fit a man to be a miniſter of Chriſt," he " regarded the prieſts leſs and looked more after the diſſenting people." But ſoon he " left the ſeparate preachers alſo." He began his extraordinary career as a preacher in 1647. *Journal*, p. 6.

[2] "Fox was rather the *organizer* or *completing agent*, than the founder of Quakeriſm." Tallack, *George Fox*, p. 67.

[3] " Perhaps the moſt remarkable incident in Modern Hiſtory is not the Diet of Worms, ſtill leſs the *Battle* of Auſterlitz, Waterloo, Peterloo, or any other *Battle* ; but an incident paſſed careleſſly over by moſt Hiſtorians, and treated with ſome degree of ridicule by others : namely, George Fox making to himſelf a ſuit of Leather." *Sartor Reſartus,* B. iii : Chap. I.

erful enough to command the attention of the moſt tumultuous aſſemblage. According to the teſtimony of Thomas
Ellwood, who did not meet him till the year 1660,
but who "from that time till the time of his death knew
him well, converſed with him often, obſerved him much,
loved him dearly, and honoured him truly," he was
"graceful in countenance, manly in perſonage, grave in
geſture, courteous in converſation, weighty in communication, inſtructive in diſcourse, free from affectation in
ſpeech or carriage."[1]

In 1671 it "was upon him from the Lord to go beyond
ſea, to viſit the plantations in America." Accordingly with
twelve companions, among whom were William Edmundſon[2] and John Stubbs,[3] he ſailed from Graveſend, Aug.
13th, "in a yatch, called the Induſtry." "The third of
the eighth month" he reached Barbadoes. In March,
1672, he landed in Maryland. Continuing his journey
through the Jerſeys and Long Iſland, he waited at Oyſter
Bay for a wind to take him to Rhode Iſland. His *Journal*
thus continues :

[1] Ellwood's *Account of Fox*, prefixed to Fox's *Journal*.

[2] William Edmundſon was born at Little Muſgrove, in Weſtmoreland, in 1627. His mother died when he was four years old, his father when he was eight. He was brought up by an uncle who "uſed him hardly." As a child he was greatly exerciſed "concerning his Salvation, alſo about Election and Reprobation." He entered the army, and in 1650 ſerved in Scotland under Cromwell. Returning to England the next year he heard two Quaker women preach, "and the more he heard of this people the better he loved them." In 1652 he married, and in 1654 began to preach. *Journal* of William Edmundſon, p. 1–15.

[3] John Stubbs was an old ſoldier of the Commonwealth who had been diſcharged from the army becauſe he would not take the oath of allegiance to Cromwell. He became a convert to Quakeriſm in 1653. In company with Samuel Fiſher he preached in the Low Countries and Germany. Afterwards he viſited Rome. When George Fox came to America, Stubbs, in company with Edmundſon and others came with him. George Fox's *Journal*, p. 113, 139, 426. William Edmundſon's *Journal*, p. 60, Biſhop, *New-England Judged*, p. 16, 17.

"As foon as the wind ferved we fet fail, and arrived in Rhode Ifland the thirtieth of the third month; where we were gladly received by friends. We went to Nicholas Eafton's,[1] who was governor of the Ifland; where we lay, being weary with travelling. On firft day following we had a large meeting; to which the deputy governor[2] and feveral juftices came, and were mightily affected with the truth. The week following the yearly meeting for friends of New England, and other colonies adjacent, was held in this ifland; to which, befides many friends who lived in thefe parts, came John Stubbs from Barbadoes, and James Lancafter and John Cartwright from another way. This meeting lafted fix days. The firft four were fpent in general publick meetings for worfhip; to which abundance of other people came. For having no priefts in the ifland, and no reftriction to any particular way of worfhip; and the governor and the deputy-governor, with feveral juftices of the peace, daily frequenting meetings; it fo encouraged the people, that they flocked in from all parts of the ifland. Very good fervice we had amongft them, and the truth had good reception. I have rarely obferved a people, in the ftate wherein they ftood, to hear with more attention, diligence, and affection, than generally they did, during the four days; which was alfo taken notice of by other friends. Thefe publick meetings over, the men's meeting began, which was large, precious and weighty. The day following was the women's meeting, which alfo was large

---

[1] Eafton, like Coddington, was a convert to Quakerifm from the Antinomians. More than thirty years before this Winthrop fpeaks of him as " man very bold, though ignorant." Winthrop's *Journal*, i: 338; 2: 48.

[2] John Cranfton. The degree of "Doctor of phiffick and chirrurgery" was conferred upon him by the General Affembly in 1664. Arnold, *Hift. R. I.* i: 303.

and very folemn. Thefe two meetings being for ordering the affairs of the church, many weighty things were opened and communicated to them, by way of advice, information and inftruction in the fervices relating thereunto; that all might be kept clear, fweet, and favoury amongft them. In thefe, feveral men's and women's meetings for other parts were agreed and fettled, to take care of the poor, and other affairs of the church, and to fee that all who profefs truth walk according to the glorious gofpel of God. When this great general meeting was ended, it was fomewhat hard for friends to part; for the glorious power of the Lord, which was over all, and his bleffed truths and life flowing amongft them, had fo knit and united them together, that they fpent two days in taking leave one of another, and of the friends of the Ifland; and thefe being mightily filled with the prefence and power of the Lord, they went away with joyful hearts to their feveral habitations, in the feveral colonies where they lived."

"When friends had taken their leave one of another, we, who travelled amongft them, difperfed ourfelves into our feveral fervices, as the Lord ordered us. John Burney-eate, John Cartwright, and George Pattifon went into the eaftern parts of New England, in company with the friends that came from thence, to vifit the particular meetings there;[1] whom John Stubbs and James Lancafter intended to follow a while after, in the fame fervice; but they were not yet clear of this ifland. Robert Widders[2] and I ftaid longer upon this ifland; finding fervice ftill here for the Lord, through the great opennefs, and the

[1] Compare *Truth Exalted*, p. 47.
[2] Cartwright, Pattifon, Lancafter and Widders had accompanied Fox from England. See Fox's *Journal*, p. 426.

daily coming in of frefh people from other colonies, for fome time, after the general meeting; fo that we had many large and ferviceable meetings among them."

"During this time, a marriage was celebrated amongft friends in this ifland, and we were prefent. It was at a friend's houfe, who had formerly been governor of the ifland;[1] and three juftices of the peace, with many others not in profeffion with us, and friends alfo faid, they never faw fuch a folemn affembly on fuch an occafion, fo weighty a marriage and fo comely an order. Thus truth was fet over all. This might ferve for an example to others; for there were fome prefent from many other places."

"After this I had a great travail in fpirit concerning the Ranters in thofe parts who had been rude at a meeting which I was not at. Wherefore I appointed a meeting amongft them, believing the Lord would give me power over them, which he did, to his praife and glory; bleffed be his name forever! There were at this meeting many friends, and divers other people; fome of whom were juftices of the peace, and officers, who were generally well affeded with the truth. One, who had been a juftice twenty years, was convinced, fpoke highly of the truth, and more highly of me than is fit for me to mention or take notice of."

"We had a meeting at *Providence*, which was very

---

[1] Coddington writing to John Winthrop, Jr., under date of June 29th, apparently refers to this; "and Geo. Fox being at my howfe (who faw thee in England) fpake to me to write to thee, viz: that Samuell Winthrope, thy brother, was with him at Barbadoes, came thither to vifit him, and G. F. could wifh that thou was like him, and that thou would ftaue of perfecution in thy day, in thy Jurifdiction, that thou mayeft not be numbered amongeft perfecutours, and thee wicked, whofe names fhall rote." *Mafs. Hift. Coll.* 4th feries, vii: 288.

large, confifting of many forts of people. I had a great
travail upon my fpirit, that it might be preferved quiet,
and that truth might be brought over the people, and might
gain entrance and have place in them ; for they ewer generally above the priefts in high notions ; and fome came
on purpofe to difpute. But the Lord, whom we waited
upon, was with us, his power went over them all ; and his
bleffed Seed was exalted and fet above all. The difputers
were filent, and the meeting quiet and ended well ; praifed
be the Lord! The people went away mightily fatisfied,
much defiring another meeting. This place (called *Providence*) was about thirty miles from Rhode Ifland ; we
went to it by water. The governor of Rhode Ifland, and
many others, went with me thither ; and we had the
meeting in a great barn[1] which was thronged with people,
fo that I was exceeding hot, and in a great fweat ; but all
was well ; the glorious power of the Lord fhined over all,
glory to the great God forever."

"After this we went to Narraganfett, about twenty
miles from Rhode Ifland ; and the governor went with us.
We had a meeting at a juftice's, where friends never had
any before· The meeting was very large, for the country
generally came in ; and the people from Connecticut, and
other parts round about. There were four juftices of
peace. Moft of thefe people were fuch as had never
heard friends before ; but they were mightily affected, and
a great defire there is after the truth amongft them. So
that meeting was of very good fervice ; bleffed be the Lord
forever! The juftice, at whofe houfe it was, and another

---

[1] The " fair large meeting houfe " in
Providence was not built till 1703 or
1704. Staples' *Annals*, p. 424. The Quakers feem to have increafed flowly, fince
they are defcribed at that time as " cou-
rageous and noble being but few."

juftice of that country, invited me to come again ; but I was then clear of thefe parts, and was going towards Shelter Ifland. John Burnyeate and John Cartwright, being come out of New England into Rhode Ifland before I was gone, I laid this place before them, and they felt drawings thither, and went to vifit them.[1] At another place, I heard fome of the magiftrates faid among themfelves, ' if they had money enough, they would hire me to be their minifter.' This was, when they did not underftand us, and our principles : but when I heard of it, I faid, ' It was time for me to be gone ; for if their eye was fo much to me, or any of us, they would not come to their own teacher.' For this thing (hiring minifters) had fpoiled many, by hindering them from improving their own talents ; whereas our labour is, to bring every one to their own teacher in themfelves."[2]

From Rhode Ifland Fox returned to Shelter Ifland, where he met William Edmundfon on his way North from Virginia.[3] Burnyeat, Stubbs, and Cartwright remained

---

[1] According to Burnyeat this vifit to Narraganfett was in company with Stubbs, and after the difcuffion with Williams. " So after fome time together upon the Ifland, *John Stubbs* and I went over, with feveral Friends that did accompany us, to *Narraganfet ;* and then we had a Meeting the *four and twentieth* of the *fixth month* at one *Richard Smith's ;* and *next day* took our journey towards *Hartford*." *Truth Exalted,* 54. Compare Edmundfon's *Journal,* 76.

[2] Fox's *Journal,* pp. 442–444.

The above account of the memorable vifit of George Fox to Rhode Ifland, is taken from the third edition of his *Journal,* London : 1765. The remark of

Macaulay fhould be borne in mind : " This Journal, before it was publifhed, was revifed by men of more fenfe and knowledge than himfelf, and therefore, abfurd as it is, gives us no notion of his genuine ftyle."—*Hift. Eng.* iv : p. 22. Yet Macaulay's account of Fox can hardly be regarded as any thing more than caricature. While his eccentricities are vividly depicted, the true fource of his great influence is unnoticed. The leader of fo marked a religious movement muft have been fomething more than a man " too much difordered for liberty, and not fufficiently difordered for Bedlam."

[3] " From thence (Long Ifland) I went to Shelter Ifland, where I met with

behind, and what followed is thus narrated by the former :
" J. S. and I went up to Providence, had a Meeting
there ; and as we returned, we had a meeting at *Warwick*,
where none had been before ; and feveral were Convinced
and did own the Truth.   And there we had to do with one
Gorton, and his Company, who were by other People then
called *Gortonians*, but they called themfelves *Generalifts*.
They were of Opinion, *all fhould be faved*.   But they were
in reality *Ranters :* for in our Difcourfe they would maintain, and fay, *No Creaturely actions could be Sin ;* and would
have no *Whoredom*, nor *Drunkennefs*, not the like to be *Sin,*
but what was fpiritual ; the outward action was but creaturely.   And thus in their filthy, unclean Spirit, they like
the old *Ranters,* made merry over the reproof of God's
Spirit."[1]

"So from thence we came down again to *Road-Ifland,*

George Fox again, and feveral *Friends*
with him, coming from *New England*
and going to *Virginia*.   I told him of my
Travels and Service for the Lord, at the
Hearing of which he was glad, and we
praifed the Lord for his Goodnefs; I
told him I was much preft in Spirit to
haften for *Ireland :* he told me *That
Friends in New England had heard of
me, and they expected I would vifit them,
and befides, the Paffage of Ships from thofe
Parts were ftopped, by reafon of Wars between* Holland *and* England."—Edmundfon's *Journal,* p. 73.

[1] When Prefident Stiles was in Providence, Nov. 18, 1771, he vifited Mr.
John Angell, then eighty years of age,
and the laft furviving follower of Gorton.   "I afked him if Gorton was a
Quaker ; as he feemed to agree with

them in rejecting outward ordinances.
He faid, no ; and that when George Fox,
or one of the firft *Friends*, came over,
he went to Warwick to fee Gorton, but
was a mere babe to Gorton.   The Friends
had come out of the world, in fome
ways, but ftill were in darknefs or twi-
light, but that Gorton was far beyond
them, he faid, high way up to the difpenfation of light.   The Quakers were
in no wife to be compared with him. He
faid, Gorton was a holy man; wept day
and night for the fins and blindnefs of
the world.   He was univerfally beloved
by all his neighbors, and the Indians, who
efteemed him, not only as a friend, but
one high in communion with God in
Heaven, and indeed he lived in Heaven."
R. I. Hift. Coll. ii : 20.

and there we fpent fome time, and had a long Difpute with one *Roger Williams*, that fent us a *Challenge* from *Providence*, with *fourteen Propofitions*, as he called them, but they were *Charges*; and he engaged to maintain them againft all Comers; the firft *Seaven* to be difputed on at *Road-Ifland*, and the latter *Seven* at *Providence.*"[1]

Roger Williams, never indifferent to novelties in religion, had watched with intereft the rife of Quakerifm. He had "long heard of the great name of G. Fox," and "fome years" before Fox came to Rhode Ifland had "read his book in Folio."[2] He was familiar with other Quaker writers.[3] He had alfo examined "above *fix fcore Books* and *P*apers written by pious and able pens againft them." But notwithftanding a marked coincidence on fome minor points, he was never inclined to their more peculiar notions. In a letter to the younger Winthrop, he notes with evident fatisfaction that Catherine Scott, one of the firft to fuffer for the new faith, had been led in part to renounce it.[4] When Burnyeat made his vifit to Newport in 1671, Williams attended the General Meeting, where was a "great *Concourfe*," and attempted to hold a difcuffion with them, but was ftopped by "the fudden praying of the

---

[1] *Truth Exalted*, p. 53.

[2] p. 1, *infra*. The title of this work was "*The Great Myftery of the Great Whore unfolded; and Anti-Chrift's Kingdom revealed into Deftruction;*" By Geo. Fox. London, 1659· cf. p. 53, *infra*. The writings of Fox were very numerous. For a full lift fee "*A Defcriptive Catalogue of Friends' Books*," by Jofeph Smith. 2 vols. 4to, London: 1867, pp. 644–697.

[3] p. 277, *infra*.

[4] "Sir, my neighbor, Mrs. Scott, is come from England; and what the whip at Bofton could not do, converfe with friends in England, and their arguments, have, in a great meafure drawn her from the Quakers, and ufually from their meetings. Try the fpirits. There are many abroad, and muft be, but the Lord will be glorious, in plucking up whatever his holy hand hath not planted." Letter of Williams to John Winthrop, Jr.: Sept. 8, 1660.

Governour's Wife," and by the fummary action of Burnyeat in difmiffing the affembly.[1] Warned by this experience
although Fox was "feveral weeks at Rode Ifland,"[2] Williams fought no opportunity of feeing him at any of the
ordinary meetings of the Quakers. Even when Fox was
in Providence, Williams did not vifit him.[3] "Tis true G.
Fox was at *Providence* fome few dayes before, and fpake
publickly; and it was free for me publickly to have heard
him and oppofed him; But going the laft year to one of
their general affemblyes at *New-Port,* and having begun
to prefent to them fome Confiderations about the *True
Chrift* and the *falfe,* the *True Spirit* and the *Falfe,* and being
cut of in the mideft, by the fudden *Prayer* of one, and the
Singing of another, and then by the *Prayer* of another,
and the fudden diffolving of the Affembly, I refolved to try
another way, and to offer a fair and full Difpute, according
to *Ed. Burrowes* (and therein G. *Foxes*) Offer in his large
Epiftle to Foxes Book."[4]

In accordance with this refolution, Williams drew up
the Fourteen Propofitions which gave rife to the difcuffion
narrated in the volume now reprinted.[5] But inftead of

[1] p. 12, *infra.*

[2] Fox arrived at Newport, May 30,
1672, and "was fome hours departed"
when the letter of Williams was brought
to Cranfton, July 26.

[3] "For he had not fo much *Civility,*
as to fpeak to G. *F.* when he was at
Providence; but fnarling behind his back,
Bafe and Un-warlike." *New-England-
Fire-Brand-Quenched,* Pt. i: 183.

[4] The *"Epiftle to the Reader,"* prefixed to *The Great Myftery of the Great
Whore unfolded,* was written by Edward
Burrough, and contained a challenge to
"any unfatisfied ftill in the matter," to

a public difcuffion, "with the confent of
the chief in authority that have power
in this nation, who may preferve peace
and fafety among people, and thereby
ftop all jealoufies." George Fox's *Works,*
iii: 25.

Thus it appears that the courfe adopted by Williams of fending the Propofitions to Cranfton, was ftrictly in accordance with the fuggeftion of Burrough
himfelf. The "Epiftle" is dated London, the Ninth Mo, 1658.

[5] Thefe are given in full on pp. 4, 5,
infra.

being fent directly to Fox, they were inclofed in a letter to
Captain Cranfton, the Deputy Governor of the Colony.
Had the contents of this communication not been divulged
it would doubtlefs have reached its deftination in feafon.
Unfortunately, however, for his purpofe, before the boat
which was to carry the letter to Cranfton had failed, Williams furnifhed a copy of the Propofitions to a neighbor
whom he knew to be inclining to Quakers views.[1] This
copy was read at a meeting of the Quakers, and in that
way the purport of the letter became known to the master of the boat, who was alfo a difciple of Fox.   Thus the
plan of Williams was difclofed before the letter had been
delivered to Cranfton, and according to Williams, "in
the *Junto* of the *Foxians* at *Newport,* it was concluded for
Infallible Reafons, that His *Holinefs* G. *Fox* fhould withdraw."   Accordingly they arranged that the letter to Cranfton fhould not be delivered until Fox had gone.   The
Propofitions had been enclofed to Cranfton in order "that

<hr>

[1] Williams feems to have taken confiderable pains to circulate information
of the propofed difcuffion. Under date
of Aug. 23, 1672, Coddington writes to
J. Winthrop, Jr., "fence whofe depar-
tuer (Fox,) even that daye, in a letter
incloffed to John Cranfton, our Deputie
Governour, was inclofed 14 propofitions
to George Fox or other of his Coun-
triemen at Newport, on Rode Ifland, who
fay they are apoftles or meffengers of Jefus Chrift, which he offered againft all
comers to maintaine in publicke, the firft
7 at Newport, the other 7 at Providence. I fhall not neede to trouble thee
with further relation conferneing them,
(he had difperced them into the Maffachufetts,) but refere thee to thee berer
herof."—4 *Mafs. Hift. Coll.* 7 : 291.

Among the archives of the State of
Connecticut, is preferved a copy of the
14 Propofitions in the handwriting of
Williams and bearing his fignature. It
is ftyled *Mr Wms Q againft ye Quaker,*
and, in addition to fome unimportant
verbal differences, is dated "ye 15th"
inftead of the 13 of July. Poffibly this
is one of the copies which Williams "had
difperced." It is printed in the *Hiftorical
Mag.* ii : 56. In the courfe of the third
day's difcuffion, Williams refers to "one
copy" of the Propofitions that did not
ftrictly agree with that fent to the Quakers ; p. 137 *infra.* With regard to
dates Williams was a little carelefs as
appears from his Second Letter to J. T.
p. 17 *infra.*

being fuch a public perfon, he might timely be informed
of fuch a publicke Affembly, and as alfo might vouchfafe
(as afterwards he carefully did) to afford his *Countenance
and Affiftance* to fuch *Peaceable* and *Pious Exercifes.*" Cranfton "did publickly teftifie" that the letter of Williams,
dated July 13th, was not delivered until the 26th of the
fame month, "and untill G. *Fox* was fome hours departed."
Williams did not hefitate to accufe Fox of complicity in
this tranfaction : "G. F. fuppofed I would be forced to be
as plain in my *Proofs* as I was in my *Pofitions.* He knew
that I was furnifhed with Artillery out of his own *Writings.* He faw what *Confequences* would roll down the
mountaines upon him from his proud and Infolent, yet
poor and bald *Writings;* and how far fome of his prefent
practices were fallen out with his *Writings,* and therefore
this old *Fox* thought it beft to run for it, and leave the
work to his *Journeymen* and *Chaplains* to perform in his abfence for him."[1] This accufation Williams brings forward
ftill more confpicuoufly on the title page of his book.[2]

The charge, that he thus purpofely avoided Williams,
Fox denies in the moft emphatic language. Of the 14
Propofitions he declares that he "not only never received,
but never faw, nor fo much as knew of them;"[3] he "*knew
nothing* of his Accufations, or pretended proof, which *R.
W.* vainly calls his *Artillery;* nor that he ever read, much
lefs objected anything againft G. F.'s Book."[4] To the
affertions of Williams that Fox "run for it;" that he arranged that the 14 Propofitions fhould not be delivered till

---

[1] p. 7, *infra.* Compare the prelimi-
nary letter " *To the People called* Quakers."

[2] (*G. Fox* flily departing.)

[3] *New-England-Fire-Brand-Quenched,*
Pt. i: 1.

[4] *New-England Fire-Brand-Quenched,*
Pt. i: 2.

after his departure; that he did this that he might fay he never faw the paper; and that he knew the fubftance of the Propofitions perfectly before his departure; Fox re-joins; "Thefe are *four great Lies :* for G. F. knew not what was in thy *Papers Roger*, neither had G. F. feen the *Copies* of thefe *Propofals ;* neither did G. F. hinder their being delivered to the *Governour.* Nor did G. F. ever receive any letters from R. W., or go away for fear of him or them; nor was it a likely thing, that he fhould, when he knew nothing of them: for as I faid before, when I was at *Providence,* where this *Roger* lives, he came not at me. And if he had anything to have fpoken to me, he might eafily have done it, or have written to me, and have fent the fame copies to me, he fent to Captain Cranfton; and not have made a clamour againft me, belying of me to the world behind my back, when I was gone. But this is like the *Fruits of his Spirit,* but not the Spirt of Chrift, and his Difciples."[1]

---

[1] *New-England-Fire-Brand Quenched,* p. 9. To fhow that Fox was not lefs fkilled than his opponent in the ameni-ties of religious controverfy, I fubjoin the following fpecimens of his ftyle : "a Lying, Slanderous Book :" "How dare *R. W.* to Dedicate fuch palpable Lies to the King :" "Oh how dareft thou *Ro-ger* Williams, publifh fuch *falfe lyes* to the World, when thou knoweft in thy Confcience, that *G. F.* had never any *Writing, or Letter or Propofals* from thee: neither did he ever exchange a word with thee. The Lord God of Heaven knowes it, and the *Deputy Governour* knowes, that I received none of thy Writings or Papers of Propofals by him. Behold all fober people the foundation of this mans Attempt, the beginning of his work; and fince the foundation of thy Book is a *notorious lye,* the building upon fuch a *foundation of lyes* is not like to be otherwife: which *lyes* thou haft made thy *refuge ;* as throughout thy Book may be evidently feen. For except a man had fold himfelf to work falfehood, and make lyes; he could not have done more wickedly, and have uttered felfer charges than thou haft done. But the Lord God which knows them, and fees thy evil defign in them, will *fweep them away with the Befom of Deftruction,* and clear his people from thy manifeft falfe tongue. And I doubt not but the *Dep-uty Governour* will teftifie for me, that I am clear of this charge; and that I never

That Williams fent the Propofitions in good faith, and
that he defired the controverfy with Fox, cannot be for a
moment doubted. The reafons that he affigns for not feeking
his opponent at any of the public meetings of the Quakers, and for not addreffing his letter to Fox directly, remove any fufpicion of intentional evafion.[1]   On the other
hand it feems not lefs certain that Fox never faw the letter.   Not only do we have his own repeated denial that it
ever reached him, or that its contents ever were known
to him, but Burnyeat profeffed "that he knew nothing of
the detaining of the Letter, only he knew that G. *Fox*
never faw the Papers,"[2] and Williams concedes that "probably, as afterwards in the difpute, he fpake honeftlie not
knowing the Myftery."[3]   There feems, therefore, no
ground whatever for the charge made by Williams that
Fox "flily departed."   No characteriftic of Fox was more
marked than felf-confidence.   At no time did he ever
fhrink from meeting an adverfary; he was now in the
prime of life, and in the full flufh of his career as prophet
of a new fect.   No reafon can be conceived why he fhould
have been unwilling to meafure his ftrength with Roger
Williams, a man paffed three fcore and ten, and wield-
ing at this time, but little influence.[4] As little does it feem

---

faw, nor knew that which *R. W.* writ,
and lent to him." **N. E.** *Firebrand
Quenched*, Pt. i : 2.   .

[1] Fox makes this charge. **N. E.** *Fire-
Brand Quenched*, Pt. i : 23.

[2] p. 7 *infra.*

[3] p. 35 *infra.*

[4] " And why cannot this Man be *quiet*
with his own *Liberty* in his own *Opinions* and *Imaginations*, but he muft *grudge*
at others ? but the *Governors* have not
grudged at him for *his;* but he may

preach as long as he will, if people
will go to hear him ; but I think he is
an *Old Doting Man,* and few mind
him ; for I did not hear, that he
preached to any, when I was at *Providence.* And he may think by publifhing
this *Book* of *Lies* to get fome *Followers:*
Its like, he may get *fuch, as are given up
to believe Lies,* but none that fear God
and follow Chrift *Jefus.*" *New-England-
Fire-Brand-Quenched,* Pt. i : 25.

likely that " in the Junto of the Foxians at Newport," as Williams alleged, it was arranged that Fox should withdraw, for not only did Burnyeat know nothing of the matter, but it is difficult to understand why, if the difcuffion was to take place, one party should wish to have their strongest man out of the way. The more probable conclusion seems to be that some personal enemies of Williams in *Providence*, detained the letters, unwilling perhaps that he should gain any credit from the controversy. This seems likely from the fact that Throckmorton,[1] to whom a copy of the papers was furnished, wrote to Williams advising him "to refrain any further publishing thereof;" and Croffman, mafter of the boat, infulted Williams "in the open ftreet," becaufe he " durft fend 14 Lyes to fuch a man as G. *Fox.*"[2]

The departure of Fox[3] did not interfere with the propofed difcuffion. A few days after Cranfton had delivered to the Quakers the fourteen propofitions of Williams, Stubbs, Burnyeat and feveral others, went to *Providence* and made an agreement to meet their opponent at Newport on the ninth of Auguft.[4] As fome of the neighbors

[1] That his " former antient Neighbor and friend *J. T.*" to whom Williams fent a Copy of his pofitions, cf. p. 6, *infra*, was John Throckmorton, appears from the Letter of Richard Scot, *New-England-Fire-Brand Quenched*, Pt. ii : 249. Throckmorton was one of the original fettlers of Providence, and in the affignment of " home lots," his was located next fouth to that of Williams. Staples' *Annals of Providence*, 35.

[2] pp. 6–8, *infra*.

[3] The day before he left Fox addreffed a communication to two citizens of Providence, Thomas Olney, jr., and John Whipple, which makes no allufion to the difpute with Williams, but deferves notice for fome of its practical fuggeftions. Among other things he recommends a " law againft drunkennefs, and them that fell liquors to make people drunk," "a market once a week, and a houfe built for that purpofe," and " in every town and place in all your colony, one to receive all your births, marriages, and them that die." The letter is printed in the *Philadelphia Friend*, vii : 55.

The earlieft Regiftration Law in R. I., was enacted in 1708.

[4] p. 35, *infra*.

of Williams were "grieved that the *Conference* fhould be carried away from *Providence* to *Newport*," it was further agreed that after the firft feven propofitions had been difcuffed at Newport, fome of the Quakers fhould meet Williams at Providence. Having thus arranged the preliminaries Williams promifed that he would not fail to meet them, "and God" he fays "gracioufly affifted me in rowing all day with my old bones fo that I got to *Newport* toward the *Midnight* before the morning appointed."

The place of difcuffion was the Quaker Meeting Houfe at Newport, the fcruples of thofe who hefitated about entering fuch a place having been overcome by the argument of Williams "that it was one thing to goe into a *Jews Synagogue*, or a *Popifh Chappell* to worfhip, or countenance. their Worfhips; another thing to Profefs and Inteft againft them." The aged Governor, Eafton, and feveral other Magiftrates, who had adopted Quaker views, were prefent, affording the affurance that no unfeemly difturbances would interrupt the debate.

When Williams made his appearance at the hour appointed, he found his three opponents "fitting together on an high Bench." The diftinctive characteriftics of thefe whom he terms "able and noted preachers," are fketched in a few words. He had heard that John Stubbs "was learned in the *Hebrew* and the Greek," and found him fo. On the fecond day, Stubbs brought with him his Hebrew Bible, and Williams fays, "it may be he underftands the *Hebrew* and the *Greek* and other Languages as well as myfelf and better too."[1] So Burnyeat he found "to be a mode-

---

[1] p. 95, *infra*. Stubbs was affociated with Benjamin Frisby in compiling the book called the "Battledore," "which was written to fhow that in all languages Thou and Thee is the proper and ufual form of fpeech to a fingle perfon. This

rate *Spirit,* and a very able Speaker."[1] But Edmondſon ſeems to have arouſed his ſpecial diſlike. While Stubbs and Burnyeat were "civil and ingenious," Edmundſon "was nothing but a bundle of Ignorance and Boiſterouſneſs." He "would frequently and inſolently interrupt;" he was "very ignorant in the *Scripture* or any other Learning;" he "had been a ſoldier in the late warres, a ſtout, portly man of a great voice, and fit to make a *Bragadocia;*" he is termed " *a Pragmatical and Inſulting Soul.*"[2]

was ſet forth in examples or inſtances taken out of the Scriptures, and out of books of inſtruction in about thirty languages."—Fox's *Journal,* p. 328.

Fox himſelf added ſome things to the book. Cotton Mather ſays "it was afterwards found that certain Jews were hired to do that work, and had fourſcore pounds for their pains, and a dozen bottles of wine over and above."—*Magnalia,* ii : 527. But Whiting denies this : "And what if a *Jew* was hired to help in ſome part of that Work, was that any Crime ? It was known, that John Stubbs, the Chief Author of it, was a very learned Man, and had thirty Languages (almoſt as many as are in that Book) as *C. M.'s* Champion, *Roger Williams,* confeſſed."—*Truth and Innocency Defended,* p. 113.

Coddington writing to J. Winthrop, jr., under date of Aug. 23, 1672, ſays of Stubbs ; " he is a larned man, as witneſs the battele dore in 35 languages."—4, *Mass. Hiſt. Coll.* vii : 292.

[1] Fox ſays of Burnyeat: "He travelled and Preacht the Goſpel in Ireland, Scotland, Barbadoes, Virginia, Maryland, New Jerſeys, Long-Iſland, Road-Iſland, and up and down in New England; and

had many Diſputes with many Prieſts and Profeſſors, that oppoſed the Truth ; but the Lord gave him Dominion over all, and to ſtop the mouths of the Gainſayers, and he turned many to the Lord, and was a *Peacemaker ;* and he preacht in his *Life* and *Converſation,* as well as his *Words.*"—*Fox's Teſtimony in Truth Exalted,* p. 1. "His *Innocent Deportment* and blameleſs Converſation preached wherever he came." " And the Lord Cloathed him with *Humility* before all, as became the *Goſpel* he preached."—Teſtimony of Friends in Cumberland, do. pp. 6–7. " He was *meek* and *gentle* and of a healing *Spirit.*"—Teſtimony of Friends in Ireland, do. p. 16.

[2] p. 99, *infra.* With this deſcription of Edmundſon it is intereſting to compare the ſtatements of his friends : "He was a man of uncommon Courage, and the Truth invigorating his underſtanding, made him as bold as a Lion ; he was early convinced of the everlaſting Truth, and ſoon after was publickly engaged in its Service; he had a great Share of natural Parts, though not much outward Education ; and he who enabled *Gideon* of old, though but of a mean Tribe and Family, and advanced him to

Taking his feat at the oppofite end of the houfe, Williams began by calling God to witnefs that he had not been prompted to the difcuffion by any perfonal or interefted motives. Like the Quakers he had acted from a "motive within," and his end was threefold;[1]

1st, to vindicate the moft holy Name of God, trodden in the dirt by Fox and his difciples.

2d, to vindicate the Colony of Rhode Ifland which on account of receiving the Quakers was liable to be reckoned among their abettors.

3d, to make a practical application of the leffon to be derived from the dying outcries, while drowning, of a well-known Quaker, Mr. Nicholas Davis.[2]

The Debate which followed confumed three days, the 9th, 10th and 12th of Auguft. On the 11th which came of a Sunday, it was fufpended, not as Williams averred, becaufe the Quakers "cordially owne that day,"[3] but

<hr />

be a great General of the Hoft of *Ifrael*, making him a Deliverer of his chofen People when in Diftrefs, the fame Almighty Power raifed this our dear Friend, and led him from an outward to a fpiritual Warfare, in which the Lord his God was with him, covering his Head as in the Day of *Battle*, and *teaching* (according to the Words of the Pfalmift) his Hands to war and his Fingers to fight." A Short Teftimony concerning Wm. Edmundfon, prefixed to *Journal*, p. 12. "Indeed to me he feemed to be as a *Boanerges*, or *Son of Thunders*, his Miniftry was fo powerful in the Demonftration of the Spirit "—Teftimony of Chriftopher Wins, lxvii.

[1] p. 39, *iafva.*
[2] Davis was from Barnftable in Plymouth Colony. He joined Stevenfon

and Robinfon at Bofton, and was banifhed with them and Mary Dyer.—Bifhop, *New England Judged*, 114. Williams makes no further allufion to Davis in the courfe of the difcuffion, but enforced the leffon in his Second Pofition, that the inward Chrift of the Quakers was not the true Chrift.

[3] Fox replies to this; "But we Meet together on the *Firft Day* of the Week, as the *Primitive Chriftians* did; and fo beftow it better, than to *Hear thy Lies* and Blafphemies: any other *day* would ferve *R. W.* But we do not underftand that *R. W.* maketh any *Confcience*, or hath fuch a *Zeal* either for *God* or that *Day*, as to *Meet* to Worfhip God upon that *Day*."—*N. E. Fire-Brand Quenched*, Pt. i: 68.

"they wifely refolved to have the whole firft day with the *People* to make up their *Breaches*, ftop *Leakes*, drefs the wounds that might be in the foregoing *Agitations* againft their *Confciences* & *Credits*." But it is more likely that when the Quakers fixed upon the 9th they did not anticipate that their opponent would confume fo much time in the difcuffion. They repeatedly complained of the unreafonable length to which his argument was extended. Each Propofition was read aloud by the Quakers as the debate proceeded.[1]

The firft day was devoted wholly to the Firft of the 14 Propofitions; *That the People called Quakers are not true Quakers according to the Scriptures.* Williams argued that the Quakers were "but a new upftart party,"[2] and that their "horrid and monftrous motions" were not fuch trembling as the Scriptures enjoined, but the "workings of Sathan upon his fervants."[3] Throughout the day Williams made conftant reference to Fox's "book in folio," fo that the latter, though, not prefent, was in faĉt a leading party to the controverfy. The three aĉtive participants on the Quaker fide did little more than defend the pofitions of their leader. Notwithftanding the precaution taken to preferve order, feveral befides the regular champions entered the lifts, "fome in favor of, and fome againft the

---

[1] p. 137, *infra.*

[2] Fox comments fharply on the contradiĉtory affertions of Williams, that "the Quakers were but a new upftart party rifen up little above 20 years fince," p. 42, *infra;* that "their ugly Child and Daughter Rantifme rofe from their Bowels," p. 43; and that he had known the Ranters "almoft fixty year," p. 243,

"fo he hath made the Child, according to his own Knowledge, nigh 40 *years* Elder than the *Mother*."—*N. E. Fire-Brand Quenched*, Pt. i: 177.

For an account of *Theora John*, whom Williams incorreĉtly reprefents as a Quaker, fee Burton, *Cromwellian Diary* i: cxxvi.

[3] p. 45 *infra.*

Quakers." Among the reft, a brother of Roger Williams, "Mr. _Robert Williams_,[1] School-Mafter in _Newport_," fub-mitted a paper which the Quakers very properly declined to receive, as not included in the original propofitions. The difcuffion naturally became quite difcurfive, the ufe which the Quakers made of Scripture becoming a fubjeƈt of warm difpute. Both Coddington and Eafton fpoke, the latter " fharply," but throughout the day Williams paid chief attention to his principal antagonifts, who were placed "on high in their Defks againft him."[2] "_John Stubs_ and John _Burnet_ were more fober and manly, but W. _Edmundfon_ (who was the junior of three) would fpeak all like _Solomon's_ foolifh woman, loud and _clamorous, fimple_ and _knowing nothing_, being in truth nothing but a _flafh_ of wit, a _Face of Brafs_ and a _Tongue_ fet on _fire_ from the _Hell of Lyes and Fury_."[3] In one inftance Edmundfon was called to order by Cranfton. When, near the clofe of the day, he inveighed againft Williams for flandering the Quakers, the latter retorted by adducing the Quaker praƈtice of going ftark naked into public affemblies,[4] which led to a long difcuffion of the doƈtrine of Figures and Signs. In the

---

[1] The name of Robert Williams ftands firft in the lift of thofe to whom "home lots" were affigned at the fettle-ment of Providence. It is alfo fub-fcribed to the agreements of 1640 and 1647. He was living in Providence as late as 1655.—Staples' _Annals_, pp. 35, 43, 112. In a letter to J. Winthrop, jr., dated Sept. 8, 1660, Roger Williams writes: "My brother runs ftrongly to Origin's notion of univerfal mercy at laft, againft an eternal fentence."— Knowles' _Life_, 314.

Befides Robert, Roger Williams had

another brother "a Turkey-Merchant," p 146, _infra_.

[2] Fox denies this, and fays: "It was but upon a _Common Seat_ as was at the other End."—_N. E. Fire-Brand Quenched_, i : 32.

[3] p. 57, _infra_.

[4] "We told thee then, we own'd no fuch _Praƈtice_ in any, unlefs they were called into it by the Lord, as a _Sign_ of the _Nakednefs_ of the _Profeffors_ of _Our Ages_, who want the _Covering of the Spirit_."—_N. E. Fire-Brand Quenched_, i : 28.

midft of the debate the fun was eclipfed, an event which Williams interpreted as betokening that the true Sun of Righteoufnefs would only be for a time obfcured by Quaker errors; but fo far as the arguments on either fide were concerned, the firft day clofed with no decifive refult. Both fides were difappointed becaufe the whole difcuffion was not ended.

The fecond day found Williams more inclined to keep his bed than to go forth to a frefh difpute. Loud fpeaking the day before, and wet feet, the refult of a heavy rain that followed the eclipfe, had combined to make him very hoarfe. He choofe a middle feat, nearer his three antagonifts, fo that he might be heard with lefs ftraining of his voice. On the fecond day there was again a "great Affembly," and as on the firft the difcuffion continued until evening. The phyfical difability of Williams gave occafion to a flander, circulated in private, that he was drunk, but he ftates that though his daughter kindly offered him a dram for his illnefs, he declined it left it might curdle the milk he had taken at breakfaft.[1] The incident deferves notice only as illuftrating the bitternefs which the controverfy had created. The day was devoted to the difcuffion of the Second of the 14 Propofitions, *That the* Chrift *they profefs is not the* true Lord Jefus Chrift. The main point on which Williams infifted was that the Quaker doctrine of the Chrift within tended to obfcure or deftroy the Chrift without.[2]

---

[1] p. 67, *infra*. Fox makes no allufion to this report.

[2] Fox earneftly repudiates this charge, "As for his *Ungracious, Unfavoury* words, they are not worth mentioning: let the *Reader* fee, if *G. F.* ever denied *Chrift* (*that died at* Jerufalem) in any of thefe *pages*, that he hath wrought, or any of the *Quakers* Writings?"

"*Roger*, thou addft *Lie* with *Lie*. For that Chrift, *that died at* Jerufalem *bodily*, we own."—*N. E. Fire-Brand*, Pt. i: 49.

The argument turned, even more than on the day before, upon the teachings of Fox, whofe " Book in folio " was in conftant requifition. Burnyeat held a copy in his hands, and followed Williams clofely in all quotations. " Ever and anon," in the midft of this examination, Williams " made fallies out upon them, and had fome *Skirmifhings* and fometimes fharp *Difputes*." He charged that the Qua-kers' notion of Chrift was "Frantick and Whimfical; Grofs and Blockifh." Although Williams defired to com-plete the difcuffion of the firft feven pofitions on the fecond day he was prevented by two long harangues which Edmundfon and Stubbs were moved to addrefs to thofe prefent. When they had ended Williams complained with juftice that a mutual difputation had been turned into a preaching fervice.[1] He clofed the day's debate by fhowing that the denial of the " Chrift Without " involved the denial of the vifible Church. When, at this point, Wil-liams was taunted with " not being in Church ordinance," himfelf,[2] he briefly explained his own peculiar pofition with refpect to Church communion. After complaints on both fides about the time already confumed, the Quakers agreed to meet Williams "on the fecond Day following *at nine in the Morning*, only they would not endure any long and tedious Difcourfes."

[1] Fox rejoins: "And when *W. E.* did *Appeal to the People*, thou haft not fhewed, that the people was diffatisfied with *W. E.'s Appeal*; and were not *W. E.'s* and *J. S.'s*, their *Speeches* (which thou fcoffingly call'ft Sermons) to the Matter of the *Falfe Charges*, which thou could'ft nct make Good?"--*N. E. Fire-Brand*, Pt. i: 59.

[2] "*J. Stubs* had *Good Reafon* to ask then this *Queftion*, feeing thou liveft not in the *Practie*, nor under the *Exercife* of none thyfelf, as we underftand. And whom hath *R. W.* Fellowfhip withal? or of what *Church* is he a *Member* of? but is not *R. W.'s* (like wild *Ifmael*) his *Hand againft* every man?"—*N. E. Fire-Brand*, Pt. i: p 63.

On the third day, it was agreed that Williams fhould devote but fifteen minutes to each Propofition, in order that the remaining five might be defpatched at a fingle feffion. In confequence of this he was obliged to omit the reading of many paffages from Fox, but thefe have been fupplied in his account of the debate. Before he began to fpeak a fealed letter was handed to him directed in the handwriting of his brother Robert. The letter was not read but is printed by Williams.[1] While it appears that Robert Williams did not approve of the manner in which his brother had affailed the Quakers, whom he recognizes as " fervants of the Lord," and falutes as " Loving Friends," he complains of their rudenefs in conftantly addreffing their opponent as " Old Man,"[2] and of their unfairnefs in reproaching him with wafte of time when it was their own fault that the arguments had fo much exceeded the anticipated bounds.

Putting the letter unopened into his pocket, Williams proceeded to his third Pofition ; *That the Spirit by which they acted was not the true Spirit of God.* On this point he argued that the ordinary operation of the Holy Spirit was " by means," while the Quakers claimed that it was immediate.[3] Before, however, he had fpoken for the ftipulated fifteen minutes he was interrupted, as ufual, by the other fide. In the warm debate that followed, Williams

---

[1] p. 111, *infra.*

[2] " But as to our faying OLD MAN to thy Brother, it was not in *Difrefpect* to his *Perfon,* nor to fet at nought his *Old-Age* (for we have learned better ;) but it was a True Title to him, and not *Difhonorable,* nor by us given in *Derifion,* though thou and thy Brother take it fo."

N. E. Fire-Brand Quenched, Pt. i : 73.

[3] p 120, *infra.* Fox replies : " But we never denied the *means* of the *Spirit* of God to work withal ; but your *Means,* which are without the *Immediate Spirit* of God, and the *Light* of Chrift *Jefus,* which thou *Blafphemoufly* calleft an Idol."

N. E. Fire-Brand, Pt. i : 74.

was accufed by Edmundfon of uttering blafphemy, but Cranfton declared that his meaning had been miftaken. As one proof that the Quakers were not led by the true Spirit of God, Williams adduced " their monftrous way of Singing and Toning and Humming many at once, as they often do, and notorioufly did at *Portfmouth*, in *Rhode Ifland* this laft year."

"After fome few interchanges and altercations," the fourth Pofition was taken up ; *That the People called Qua-kers did not own the Holy Scriptures.* On this point Wil-liams argued that the doctrine of the Inner Light, as held by the Quakers, was no lefs fatal to the authority of Scrip-ture than the Papal theory of Infallibility. He ftood ftrictly on the common Proteftant ground. There was no middle courfe between "fubfcribing to the Papifts," or with Luther and Calvin "fearching the originals alone.[1] He maintained that a pure Chriftianity had always been marked by "Love to the *Holy Scriptures.*" It was no wonder that the Quakers " cried out fo fiercely againft the Schools of Learning in *Old* and *New England*," fince " the right and regular propagation of natural, of civil, and efpecially of *Divine Knowledge* fcatters the thick Fogs of the *Quakers* affected hellifh ignorance."

The fifth Pofition was that their *Principles and Profef-fions are full of Contradictions and Hypocrifies*, which Wil-liams explained to mean not that the Quakers knowingly deceived, but that they were " *blind Guides or Followers.*"[2] On this point he claimed that the ftatements of the Qua-kers refpecting Chrift, the Church, the Scriptures, and the

---

[1] p. 142, *infra.* "*R. W.* may *fub-fcribe to the* Papifts. How can he *fearch the Scriptures and ftudy the Originals* without the *Light* of Chrift ?" *N. E. Fire-Brand*, Pt. i: 92.
[2] p. 164, *infra.*

power of the Civil Magiſtrates were at variance. He quoted Fox to prove that the Quakers owned no magiſ-trates but ſuch as were godly in their ſenſe.

With regard to the ſixth Poſition, that *The Religion of the Quakers is not only an Hereſie in the matters of Gods holy worſhip, but alſo in the Doƈtrines of Repentance, Faith*, &c., Williams claimed that as to worſhip, they denied the Viſible Church and its Ordinances ; and as to Repentance, a true ſorrow for ſin and godly contrition. They were haunted for the moſt part by "a ſoure, proud, and melancholy"[1] ſpirit ; while they talked of Faith in Chriſt they turned him into a "meer Fiƈtion."

At laſt, "by God's merciful help," Williams reached the ſeventh and final Poſition to be diſcuſſed at Newport, that *Their Religion is but a confuſed mixture of Popery, Armine-aniſme, Socineaniſme, Judaiſme, &c.* As Williams was pro-poſing to return to Providence by boat the ſame night, he was here compelled "not to exceed his quarter glaſs," but in the printed account he gives his argument more fully. He declared that the Quakers "were *downright Papiſts* in many points."[2] They both agreed in denying Total Depravi-ty ; in maintaining "that *dolefully, uncomfortable*, and *deſ-*'*perate Doƈtrine* of falling away from *true* and *ſaving grace*;" they "were *great Confederates* in their endeavours to raze the *Records of Heaven*;" they "ſhake hands in the moſt *hel-*

---

[1] Compare the ſtatement of Evelyn. At Colcheſter, July 8, 1656, he writes : "I had the curioſity to viſit ſome Quakers here in priſon ; a new fanatic ſeƈt, of dangerous principles, who ſhow no reſ-peƈt to any man, magiſtrate, or other, and ſeem a melancholy, proud ſort of people, and exceedingly ignorant."—

Evelyn's *Diary*, i: 315. So Henry More ſpeaks of the "Phariſaical Sour-*neſs*" of the Quakers, and ſays, that they "undoubtedly are the moſt *Melan-oboly Seƈt* that ever was yet in the world."—See *Theological Works,* 371 ; *Enthuſiaſmus Triumphatus,* 19.

[2] p. 196, *infra*.

lifh Doctrine of Juftification by what is within us;" they "arrogate Infallibility;" agree in the "lofty Conceit of their *Perfection*;" in their notion of "Revelations;" and in various other matters of belief and practice.[1] Their agreement with Arminians and other fects was alfo not lefs fully infifted upon.

Thus ended the three days' debate at Newport, and the difcuffion of the firft feven of the fourteen Pofitions which Williams had advanced. The unufual fpectacle had drawn together a great number, who had watched, with eager interest, the fortunes of the ftrife. During the courfe of the debate, they had, from time to time, freely expreffed their views, and their judgment feems to have been divided. Even thofe who fympathifed with Williams, were not wholly fatisfied with the manner in which his felf-impofed tafk had been accomplifhed. The only full report of the proceedings is from his pen, and from the pains which he took to preferve and publifh this account it is evident that, in his own opinion, he had vanquifhed his opponents. They naturally took a very different view. The fecond day after the difcuffion at Newport clofed, John Stubbs, in a

---

[1] The coincidence of the Quaker doctrine with the Roman Catholic was early noticed. One of the firft publications of Penn, was a Reply to Clapham's *Guide to the True Religion*, in which Papifts, Socinians and Quakers had been claffed together. In a public difcuffion about the fame time, (1668) Penn was called a Jefuit.—Clarkfon's *Life*, i: 39. In his addrefs before the Houfe of Commons, during the excitement occafioned by the Popifh Plot, he fays, "for a long time I have not only been fuppofed a Papift, but a Seminary, a Jefuit, an emiffary of Rome, and in pay from the Pope," *do*: 215. An opponent of the Quakers, Leflie, declared, "The *Quaker Infallibility* was contrived on purpole to bring men back to the Infallibility of the *Church of Rome.*"—*The Snake in the Grafs*, p. 188. Barclay defended the Quakers in *The Anarchy of the Ranters; the Hierarchy of the Romanifts; equally reproved and refuted.*" 1674.

letter to Margaret Fox,[1] the wife of George, gave this curious account of the proceedings.

John Stubbs to Margaret Fox, at Swathmoor Hall.[2]

Newport in Rhode Iſland, yᵉ. 14: 6: 1672.

"Since thy huſband's departure from this place we have had a diſpute with one a great linguiſt & a Scholler, an Orthodox man ſoe called, who lives at a place called providence about 30 miles from this place ; he ſent a challenge to this place to thy huſband or any of his Countreymen to Argue with him in 14 poſitions which he would maintaine ag: all commers. Wee could not avoyd it but to give him a meeting, the firſt Seaven he was to performe at this place and the others at providence. Soe yᵉ laſt ſixt day being ye 9ᵗʰ of this inſtant we gave him a meeting and yᵉ Countreys adjacent came in from all parts ſoe that there was a very great congregation of high and lowe ; and before he began we laid it upon him to prove all his charges againſt us by the Scriptures, and Soe he be-

---

[1] Margaret Fox was the widow of Judge *Fell*, of Swathmore Hall. "A convincement of the Lord's truth came upon her" early in *Fox's* miniſtry. Fell remained a Churchman, but favored the Quakers. In 1669, eleven years after his death, Margaret married Fox, ſhe being fifty-five and he ten years younger. He writes in his *Journal:* "I had ſeen from the Lord a conſiderable time before, that I ſhould take Margaret Fell to be my wife ; and when I firſt mentioned it to her ſhe felt the anſwer of Life from God thereunto." At the marriage "in the public meeting-houſe at Broad Mead

in Briſtol," "living and weighty teſtimonials were borne thereunto by friends in the movings of the heavenly power." *Fox's Journal,* pp. 71, 412.

[2] Swathmoor Hall, the ſeat of Judge Fell, was near Ulverſtone, in Lancaſhire, juſt north of Morecambe Bay. After his wife had adopted the views of Fox, the Judge gave the Quakers permiſſion to hold a regular meeting at the Hall. This continued to be held until 1686, when Fox built a meeting houſe adjoining the Hall, which is ſtill uſed.—Tallack, *George Fox,* p. 110.

gan about yᵉ Ninth houre in yᵉ morning and continued
till about 6 in the afternoone, and could not prove yᵉ firſt
charge, for we would not let him proceed to a ſecond till
he had proved the firſt, or if he could not, then to acknowledge the wrong to us; but nothing he could prove neither
from Scripture nor Argument nor Example. He could
give Satisfaction noe not to his owne friends wh. conſiſted
moſtly of Baptiſte and ſome other Separated people, for yᵉ
Baptiſts here were full of rage agt. us,[1] ſoe the night in a
manner put a period to yᵉ firſt dayes Diſpute. And the
next day being yᵉ ſeaventh day of yᵉ week, about yᵉ 9ᵗʰ
houre in the Morning we begunne againe: and then wee
deſired him to be as full and as ſhort as he could in things,
and if the Scriptures of truth would not beare us out in
our principal Doctrines and practice then let us fall with
ſhame. And ſoe we deſired him to proceed to yᵉ·Second
ſeing in a whole dayes time before he had made nothing
of the firſt to to prove anything but had altogether diſat-
isfied yᵉ Auditt. Soe then he told us he would be as
Briefe as he could. And he had the day before ſpoken of
ſuch & ſuch greevous errors and Blaſphemies &c, by Such
& Such, & in Such & Such Bookes of ye Quakers & moſt
Eſpecially in a Book of Georg ffox's in folio and this he
mentioned the day before, and ſoe the ſecond dayes diſcourſe in yᵉ beginning of yᵉ diſcourſe as was Said before
we deſired him to be as full and as Briefe as he could, and

[1] The ſtriking reſemblance between the views of the Quakers and the early Baptiſts which has been before referred to, and the fact that George Fox and other preachers were ſo often " moved by the Lord " to go among them, natur- ally made ſuch Baptiſts as did not adopt his views eſpecially bitter in their oppo- ſition. Edmundſon's *Journal* atteſts his deſire to meet the Baptiſts, and the min- gled favor and oppoſition with which he was received. pp. 35, 95, 102.

whereas yᵉ day before in yᵉ Audience of yᵉ people he had
fpoken much of Errors in Bookes and Efpecially in a Book
of folio of Georg ffoxes we bid him read thofe errors to
yᵉ people yᵗ all yᵉ Congregation might hear him and
judg of them, and foe he began and read w'hout interruption and gave his own inferrences and continued reading
and giving his inferrences all yᵉ day almoft, for he had
noted (as he conceived) abundance of errors in yᵉ Book in
near 40 pages, and Soe is faid before he read diftinctly to
yᵉ Auditt. yᵉ Preifts and yᵉ Profeffors principles & G. F.;
anfwers in thofe heads yᵗ he had noted for Errors. And
truly thofe wh. he had marked wh. they came to be read
proved quite contrary to his Expectations for yᵉ people
generally faw and were fully fatisfied yᵗ thofe places wh.
he alledged out of yᵗ Book as great Errors and Soe to
make for him agᵗ us, but as I faid before it proved quite
contrary, for indeed when ᵗhat wh. he called errors were
read Generally peoples Eyes and eares were opened and
their hearts and minds fatisfied[1] wh. made us greatly rejoyced w'hin ourfelves when we faw how the Lord vindicated his own caufe and how the crafty was caught in his
own fnare, and yᵉ innocent delivered ; and Soe moft of
yᵗ Second dayes difpute was ended in turning over from page
to page in yᵗ prementioned Book wh. proved better fervice
for the truth than my tongue or pen can demonftrate, and
then wⁿ the night ended yᵉ dayes worke, he defired to
have another day, and foe we told him we would give him
3 houres time upon yᵉ fecond day of the ffollowing week,

---

[1] "And did not a *ftranger* fpeak aloud
then, and faid ; *I am no* Quaker ; *yet I
fee, that* Mr. Williams *hath rather proved*
againft himfelf, *and not for himfelf.*"—*N.
E. Fire-Brand Quenched*, i : 73.

and w[n] he came he made a preamble and proceeded on in the Book ag[n] in some other pages and foe continued some houres, and y[e] Book vindicated itfelf ftill ag. him and for us. And then the man began to be much confounded and amazed in himfelf when he underftood his friends were diffatisfied[1] & every thing made ag.[t] him foe 'y[t] not any one of y[e] firft 7 propofitions he could make good. Soe W[m]. Edmundfon ftood up and fpoke a pretty while to y[e] people very well, and then Jn[o] Burnyeat, and the truth came over all, Bleffed be the Lord for it. And now the next Seventh day, wh. is the 7th of this inftant W[m] Edmundfon and I are to goe to providence to give him a meeting about y[e] laft 7 propofitions and the day following, if y[e] Lord will, to have a meeting for y[e] Town for there is a great opennefs in thofe parts of late."[2]

[1] All were not, for as Williams was ftepping down to the boat the Lord "opened the mouth" of Elizabeth Williams, his brother Robert's wife, " one of the Society of the *Baptifts* in *Newport*" to declare that he had "fully proved" what he undertook.—p. 213, *infra.*

[2] The original of this letter is in the Cabinet of the R. I. Hift. Society.

Of the proceedings at Newport, Edmundfon, who as we have feen met Fox at Shelter Ifland, gives the following account:

. "After fome Day's Travel by *Narraganfet* and those Parts, I came to *Rhode-Ifland*, where I met with *John Burnyeat*, *John Stubbs* and *John Cartwright*; then one *Roger Williams* an old Prieft and an Enemy to Truth, had put forth fourteen Propofitions, as he called them, which he would maintain againft any of the *Quakers*, that came from *Old-England*, and challenged a Difpute of feven of them at *Newport* in *Rhode-Ifland*, and the other feven at *Providence*."

"I joined with Friends in anfwering the Challenge, at the Time and Place appointed for the Dispute, which was to be in Friends' Meeting-houfe at *Newport*; thither a great Concourfe of People of all Sorts gathered. When thofe Propofitions, as he called them, came to be difcourfed of, they were all but Slanders, and Accufations againft the *Quakers;* the bitter old Man could make Nothing out, but on the contrary they were turned back upon himfelf; He was baffled, and the People faw his Weaknefs, Folly, and Envy againft the Truth and Friends."

"There were many prejudiced Baptifts who would fain have helped the old Prieft againft Friends; but they durft not undertake his Charge againft us, for they faw it was falfe and weak. So the Tef-

On the feventeenth of Auguft, the difcuffion, according
to agreement was continued at Providence ; as at Newport there was a very large affemblage. Of the place
where it was held no tradition has been preferved.[1] Poffibly it was the "great barn" in which Fox had fo copioufly
perfpired. In Rhode Ifland, it muft be remembered, the
meeting houfe was not, as in Maffachufetts, the nucleus of
each new fettlement. Providence had been founded for
more than two generations before any place of public
worfhip was erected. By adhering to the fifteen minutes
rule the remaining feven Propofitions were difpatched in a
fingle day.[2] On the fide of the Quakers, only Stubbs and
Edmundfon appeared ; but, as in Newport, the debate was
not confined to the principal antagonifts. At the outfet,
Thomas Olney, "an able and *Leeding man* amongft the People called *Baptifts* at *Providence*," Captain Holden, Captain
John Green, and Mr. Caverly, of Warwick, all made
themfeves heard, the latter urging that a Moderator fhould
be chofen. When the firft Pofition, *that the Quakers in
Effect held no God, no Chrift, no Spirit, &c., but what was in
Man*, had been a little while debated, Samuel Gorton defired to fpeak. He argued that if the foul, as Fox held,
was "a part of God," the argument of Williams was con-
clufive. In the application of Scripture he proved himfelf
more than a match for Stubbs.[3] As the fhort time allowed

timony of Truth in the Power of God
was fet over all his falfe charges, to the
great Satisfaction of the People."—Edmundfon's *Journal*, p. 73.

[1] Staples' *Annals*, p. 422.

[2] It would feem from a difpute about
time, that Williams was not the owner
of a watch.—p. 106, *infra*.

[3] Gorton like Williams had received a
good claffical training. His religious
views at this period of his life may be
found in an interefting letter to John
Winthrop, jr., dated Warwick, Oct. 21,
1674.—4 *Mafs. Hift. Coll.* vii : 604
He feems never to have inclined to the
Quakers.

him did not enable Williams to bring forward all his quotations from Fox, he has commented upon them more freely in his printed account.

The remaining Pofitions difcuffed at *Providence* related not to doctrine fo much as to matters of perfonal opinion. Williams muft have had uncommon confidence in his own powers if he ever cherifhed the remoteft expectation that his opponents would be brought to acknowledge that their religion required no more than a reprobate might eafily attain to ; that the Popes did not fwell with a greater pride ; that their belief was more deftructive to falvation than moft religions extant ; that their books were poor and made up of boafting and vapor. Burnyeat was right in faying that thefe were charges rather than propofitions to be debated. At length Williams clofed, with his 14th Pofition, in which the fpirit of Quakerifm was affirmed to tend to Barbarifm ; to arbitrary Government ; to Affaffination and to Perfecution. In point of breeding the Quakers, he declared, were worfe than the Indians ; for the latter would return a falutation,[1] and did not fhow themfelves ftark naked in private houfes. This latter imputation caufed great irritation. Stubbs afferted that in nineteen years experience as a Quaker he had never feen a woman naked, and fome among the Quakers, who had been Williams' friends, were fo enraged that he deemed it expedient to drop the fubject. That Quakerifm would logically refult in arbitrary government Williams argued on the ground that thofe acting from the immediate in-

---

[1] Fox replies : "It is alfo falfe, that even the *Quakers* were againft *Taking by the Hand*, or true *Courtefy ;* though to *Bow*, and *Uncover the Head* (whether *half* or *whole*) they are againft, and loft upon us in *Apoftacy*, if done by any of them."— N. E. *Fire-Brand Quenched,* i: 222.

fpiration of Grace would not need to be "cumbered with Lawes." An aged man, Thoma, Arnold, "though much of late adhering to the *Quakers*," thought there was weight in this reafoning. With regard to the charge that the "Quaker Spirit tended to the fudden cutting off of People," Williams acknowledged that he had no facts to bring forward, and that he only charged them "with a tendency." Ravaillac, the affaffin of Henry IV, "that famous and wonderful man," had claimed to act as the inftrument of God, and a Quaker might do the fame. At this point Edmundfon retorted by accufing Williams of having approved the execution of Charles Firft. William Harris handed Edmundfon a book from which to fubftantiate this charge, but Captain Green, a Magiftrate, interfered, and the book was laid afide. The paffage, as Williams explains, expreffed fome approval of Parliament, but had no reference to the King's death, "which God knows I never approved to this day." Williams did not forget the part played by Harris in this epifode, and in the account of the difcuffion devotes to him a bitter paragraph.[1]

---

[1] p. 316, *infra.* William Harris was one of thofe who joined Williams at Seekonk. With John Throckmorton and others he is named in the "Initial deed" of the territory on which Providence was fettled. On the "Towne Street" his lot was next to Throckmorton's. When the town made its firft remove from pure democracy, in 1640, he was one of the four to whom the adminiftration of affairs was entrufted. In the winter of 1654–5 he feems to have been concerned, with Robert Williams and others, in fome difturbance. In confequence of this a paper was fent to the town afferting "that it was blood-guiltinefs and againft the rule of the gofpel, to execute judgment upon tranfgreffors againft private or public weal." For afferting this doctrine Harris, two years later, was arrefted for high treafon on a warrant iffued by Williams in his capacity as Prefident of the Colony. The matter was referred to the Agent of the Colony, and feems to have been carried no further, but it was the beginning of a feud between Williams and Harris that only clofed with death. In 1660, Harris was one of the Commiffioners from Providence, and alfo in 1662 and 1663,

The laſt point of the 14th Poſition, *that the Quaker Spirit tended* to *Perſecution*, Williams did not urge, as he had already touched upon it at Newport, and was wearied with the long debate. After he had withdrawn, Captain Green deſired to return to the more ſtrictly theological queſtions, whether revelations were immediate, and whether the ſoul was a part of God, but the Quakers waved them as too abſtruſe. Then *Pardon* Tillinghaſt, "a leading man among the *People* called *Baptiſts*," raiſed the queſtion of Ordinances. After a brief diſcuſſion Edmundſon "fell to prayer," when Tillinghaſt alſo withdrew, declaring "that he was free to diſcourſe with them, but not to join with them in worſhip."[1] Thus ended the diſcuſſion at Providence, much in the ſame way that the previous one in Newport had ended, each ſide apparently well ſatisfied with the reſult. From Providence, Stubbs and Edmundſon went to Warwick, where the next day they had a meeting in which "the Lord's Power and Preſence were largely manifeſted."[2]

---

facts which go to ſhow that the charges of Williams was not endorſed by the majority of the community. In 1667, Harris brought a charge againſt Arthur Fenner for riot, but Fenner was acquitted and Harris fined fifty pounds for cauſing the Aſſembly to be called without cauſe. Yet afterwards the General Aſſembly remitted the fine. A ſtatement of the facts was drawn up by order of the town, and ſent to other towns of the Colony in which Harris was deſcribed as a "Firebrand." Notwithſtanding this, Harris was reëlected Aſſiſtant in May following, when the town addreſſed to the Governor and Council a ſecond remonſtrance, in which Harris was ſeverely denounced. The circum-

ſtance that rendered Harris unpopular was his uſually acting as the attorney of Connecticut in the frequent diſputes between that Colony and Rhode Iſland. He ſeems to have been the more ſucceſsful before courts of law, while Williams had the greater influence with the community. Staples'*Annals*, pp. 20, 40, 143, 147. Arnold, *Hiſt. R. I.,* i: 254, 262.

[1] The Baptiſts ſeem to have been very ſtrict upon this point. As late as May 25, 1732, the Church in Providence agreed, "that if any brother or ſiſter ſhall join in prayers without the bounds of the church, they are liable to be dealt with by the church for their offending their brethren."—Staples' *Annals*, 413.

[2] Edmundſon's *Journal* p. 75.

Thence Stubbs went to Narraganfett, while Edmundfon returned by boat to Newport.[1]

The following narrative of the difcuffion, though not publifhed by Williams until four years later, was drawn up, as appears from the title, foon after the debates took place. In preparing it he feems to have had no help beyond his memory; he endeavored to procure a fhort-hand writer, but could not.[2] In this refpect his opponents were better provided, for when a difpute arofe, during the third

[1] Of the proceedings in Providence Edmundson gives the following account:

"When this Meeting (i. e. in Newport) was ended, which lafted three Days, *John Stubbs* and I went to *Providence*, accompanied with many Friends, to hear the other feven Propofitions, which lafted one Day, *John Burnyeat* and *John Cartwright* going another Way in Truth's Service. Now at *Providence* there was a very great Gathering of People, both *Prefbyterians*, *Baptifts* and *Ranters*. *Roger Williams* being there, I ftood up and told him in Public, We had fpent fo many Days at *Newport*, where he could make Nothing out agreeable to his *Challenge*; but on the contrary manifefted his Clamour, rash and falfe Accufations, which he could not prove againft us; that I was not willing to fpend much Time in hearing his Clamour and falfe Accufations, having other Service for the Lord, therefore would only fpend that Day. So he went on, as he had done at *Newport* in *Rhode-Ifland*. We anfwered to all his Charges againft Friends, and difproved them."

"Now the old prejudiced Man was filenced; then the Profeffors defired to know our Belief, *What the Soul of Man was made of?* I told them, I believed what the Scriptures faid, that when God made man, he breathed into man the breath of Life, and he became a living Soul; and that it was fufficient for me to know Chrift Jefus who redeemed my Soul. But if any of them, that were great Profeffors and old Difputants, would undertake to fhow, what God made the Soul of man of, he might. Then one that was an ancient leading Man among them faid, *He would not meddle with it:* This ended the Difpute. Then we had a feafonable Opportunity to open many Things to the People, appertaining to the Kingdom of God, and Way of Eternal Life and Salvation. The Meeting concluded in Prayer to Almighty God, the People went away fatisfied and loving."—Edmundfon's *Journal*, p. 75.

Soon after this Edmundfon returned to England. In 1676, directly after the excitement occafioned by King Philip's war, he again vifited Rhode Ifland. He had "many bleffed and heavenly Meetings," but makes no further mention of Roger Williams. do. p. 93.

[2] See his Addrefs *To the People called Quakers, infra.* Short-hand was much ufed in the 17th century.

day's difcuffion at Newport, refpecting the precife words
ufed by Williams, Edmundfon infifted that thefe words
fhould be read by "one of theirs," who had taken them
down in fhort-hand.[1] But while Williams was thus compelled to rely upon his memory, Fox and Burnyeat, in
their Reply, although bitterly denouncing his ftatements,
do not queftion the general accuracy of his report.

Not only was the manufcript prepared, but the book
feems to have been actually in print before the fpring of
1673, fince in the addrefs *To the People called* Quakers,
the author refers to the pages as they now ftand. Why
the publication fhould have been fo long delayed does not
appear. Although Williams had affigned as a principal
motive in propofing the difcuffion the vindicating of Rhode
Ifland, much intereft feems to have been manifefted in
the work by prominent perfons in the neighboring colonies. Governor Leverett, of Maffachufetts, declared that
he would give twenty pounds rather than that the book
fhould not be printed, and to this the Governor of
Plymouth offered to add five pounds more.[2] Williams'
himfelf attached fo much importance to the difcuffion,
that had he failed to fecure a publifher on this fide the
water, he had "great thoughts" of having his "large narrative of all thofe four days' agitation" printed in England.[3] He fpared no pains to fecure for his work the moft

[1] Burnyeat fays : "There is a Book in
Manufcript, of what was taken in *Short-
hand* of the Difcourfe at that prefent."
Truth Exalted, p. 54.
[2] Coddington's letter to Fox, in *New-
Eng. Fire-Brand Quenched*, Pt. ii : 246.
[3] See his letter to Samuel Hubbard, in
Backus, *Hiftory of the Baptifts* i : 511.

Williams feems to have had lome difficulty in getting his later works printed.
In a letter to Governor Bradftreet, in
May, 1662, referring to a propofed volume of his fermons preached to the Narraganfett Indians, he writes : "For printing, I am forced to write to my friends
at Maffachufetts, Connecticut, Plymouth,

favorable reception. It was prefaced with an "Epiftle Dedicatory" to Charles the Second, a monarch whofe name ftands in odd connection with fuch a controverfy, but whom Williams thus addreffed becaufe His Majefty had been liberally provided with Quaker publications. Barclay's *Apology*, which appeared in 1676, was alfo dedicated to the King but in a ftrain of fober eloquence, for which we fhall fearch in vain the pages of the following work. For writing this Dedication, Fox charged Williams with " manifefting a temporizing fpirit,"and with now flattering the King as he formerly had flattered the Parliament.[1] But if Williams laid himfelf open to the charge of flattery in his Dedication to the King, he certainly guarded againft any fuch accufation in the brief addrefs which follows, *To the People called* Quakers. He here accufers the Quakers of denying the fundamental doctrine of Proteftantifm ; repeats in offenfive language his charge that Fox purpofely avoided meeting him at Newport; and affirms that fpiritual pride was the "Root and Branch" of the whole Quaker religion. His aim was "to give teftimony in his generation," with the expectation, as he confeffes, that few would be influenced by his arguments. While, however, hoping little from the Quakers, Williams

and our own colony, that he that hath a fhilling and a heart to countenance and promote fuch a foul-work, may truft the Paymafter (who is beforehand with us already) for a hundreth for one in this life."—Knowles' *Life*, p. 353.

[1] "And *R. W.* who hath now fo much flattered the *King* in his Epiftle (in his Book 1676) and would have us to be *punifhed;* but let *R. W.* read his *Book* called *The Bloody Tenant,* &c. (1652,) and his Epiftle to the *High Court* of *Parliament,* what he faith then of the *King. R. W.'s* words are, as followeth: *The late King* Charles *his* Confcience, to *opprefs the* Confcience *of others, no fmall* Occafion *of the Ruin of him and his.* So *Roger,* read thy words in thy Book (1652) and thofe in thy Epiftle to the *King* now (in 1676) againft the Quakers." N. E. *Fire-Brand Quenched,* Pt. ii: 241.

was anxious to conciliate the favorable judgment of another clafs. Accordingly he added a third Epiftle, to the "*many* Learned and Pious Men" whom Fox had attacked, efpecially Richard Baxter and John Owen.[1] Thefe Epiftles all bear the fame date, and were written after the body of the work had been put to prefs. Appended to the account of the Difcuffion was a copious collection of Proofs of the Thirteenth Pofition, confifting of paffages from Fox's book.

The origin of the punning title of the book, Williams explains as follows : During the firft day's difcuffion at Newport, Edmundfon reproved him for fpeaking of Fox and Burrowes "in fcorn and derifion," underftanding him to fay "Fox in his Burrowes." Williams protefted at the time that he had ufed no fuch language, but afterwards, when he came to write his narrative, he wittily followed the hint of his antagonift, feeing in it "the finger of God directing and pointing him to fo proper and pertinent an ufe and application.[2]

However favorable in fome quarters may have been the impreffion made by the book, among the Quakers of Rhode Ifland it aroufed the moft bitter rage. William Coddington, like Roger Williams long paft three fcore and ten, wrote to George Fox denouncing the author in unmeafured ftrains. Richard Scot, a neighbor of Williams for nearly forty years, wrote to the fame effect, and

---

[1] The impreffion made by the work upon the orthodox party may be inferred from the remark of Cotton Mather, in his account of Roger Williams : "And againft the Quakers he afterwards maintained the main principles of the Proteftant religion with much vigour in fome difputations ; whereof he afterwards publifhed a large account, in a book againft George Fox and Edward Burrowes." *Magnalia,* ii : 499.

Mather, charitably remarks of Williams "that many judicious perfons judged him to have had the 'root of the matter' in him."

[2] p. 53 *infra.*

¹ Thefe letters are interefting as illuf-
trations of contemporary opinion. Coddington under date of June 25, 1677,
writes of Williams; "He began with a
Thunder, and had *Three Days* time to be-
wilder and befool himfelf, and fo ended
in a great *E lips* of the *Sun* (which was
taken notice of.) I have known him
about 50 Years, a meer *Weather Cock*,
Conftant only in Unconftancy; Poor
Man! that doth not know, what fhould
become of his *Soul, if this Night it fhould
be taken from him*. He was for the
Priefts, and took up their principles to
fight againft the *Truth*, and to gratify
them and bad *Magiftrates*, that licked up
his *Vomit*, and wrote the faid *Scurrilous
Book*: and fo hath tranfgreffed for a
Piece of *Bread*."

"*Dear* G. F. I may yet more prove,
what I have faid. One while he is a
Separatift at *New-Plymouth* in *New England*, Joining with them till they are weary of him (as from *Morton's Memorials*
in Print dcth appear:) Another time
you may have him a *Teacher* or Member
of the Church at *Salem* in *New England*: O! Then a great deal of Devotion is placed in *Women wearing of Vails*

in their Affembles, as if the Power of
Godlinefs was in it; and to have the
Crofs out of the *Colors*: and then be
againft the *King's Patent* and Authority;
and writeth a large Book in *Quarto*
againft it. And another time he is Hired
for *Money*, and gets a *Patent* from the
Long Parliament; fo that it is not long,
but he is *off* and *on* it again; One time
for mens wearing C̸ ᷍s and not *Hats* for
Covering their *Faces*; and again *Hats*
and no *Caps*: One time for *Water-Bap-
tifm*, Men and Women muft be *plunged*
into the *Water*; and then throw it all
down again. So that Cotton (who in
his day did know the Power of God to
Salvation) faid of him, That he was a
Haberdafher of fmall Queftions againft
the Power." *N. E. Fire-Brand Quenched*,
Pt. ii: 216.

Scot writes: "Concerning the Converfation and Carriage of this Man *Roger Williams*, I have been his neighbor
thefe 38 years: I have only been Abfent
in the time of the Wars with the *Indians*,
till this prefent. I walked with him in
the *Baptifts* way about 3 or 4 Months,
but in that fhort time of his Standing I
difcerned, that he muft have the *Order-*

H

nyeat,[1] drew up the work which was publifhed in 1678, "*A New-England Fire-Brand Quenched,* Being Something in Anfwer unto a Lying, Slanderous Book, Entitled *George Fox Digged out of his Burrowes* &c. Printed at Bofton in the year 1676, of one *Roger Williams* of *Providence* in *New England.*"

The Reply of Fox was in two parts. The firft contained an examination, page by page, of the narrative which Williams had given of the difcuffions at Newport and Providence. The quotations that have already been made from this portion of the work, renders fuperfluous any further illuftration of its method and temper. The fecond part was an anfwer to the Appendix, with which Williams had reinforced his narrative. To the fecond part was added a "Catalogue of *R. W.'s* Envious, Malitious, Scornful *Railing Stuff,* falfe Accufations and *Blafphemies,* which he *foully* and Un-*Chriftian-like* hath Scattered and Difperfed throughout his Book, and calls it *Scripture-Language.*" The Letters of William Coddington and Richard Scot, to which reference has already been made, were alfo

---

ing of all their *Affairs,* or elfe there would be no Quiet Argument amongft them. In which time he brake off from his *Society,* and declared at large the Ground and *Reafons* of it: That their *Baptifm* could not be right, becaufe it was not *Adminiftered* by an Apoftle. After that he fet upon a Way of *Seeking* (with two or three of them, that had diffented with him) by way of *Preaching* and *Praying;* and then he continued a Year or two, till *Two* of the *Three* left him."

"That which took moft with him, and was his Life, was, *To get honor amongft*

men, efpecially amongft the *Great Ones.*" *N.E. Fire-Brand Quenched,* Pt. ii : 247.

[1] "I ftaid at Worminghurft about three weeks, in which time John Burnyeat and I anfwered a very wicked and envious book, which Roger Williams, a prieft of New England (or fome Colony thereabouts) had written againft truth and friends."—Fox's *Journal,* p. 500.

From the circumftance that this reply was written at Penn's houfe, his biographer thinks it probable that Penn affifted in preparing it.—Clarkfon, *Life of Penn,* i : 177. But would not the fact have been ftated?

included in the volume. The example which Williams himfelf had fet of reforting to invective in place of argument, his Quaker opponents were not flack in following. Amply fupplied as his vocabulary was with the language of perfonal vituperation, it muft be confeffed that, on this occafion, he was fairly beaten with his chofen weapons.

It is well for the fame of Roger Williams that it does not reft upon his lateft work. Compared with his earlier productions it leaves the impreffion that what Cotton Mather terms "the long winter of his retirement" had as little promoted his fpiritual as his intellectual growth. Forty years inceffant contact with the petty animofities of a fettlement fingularly rich in difputes of every fort, ifolation from all external religious communion, bitter perfonal feuds with his neareft neighbors, had neither enlarged his underftanding nor fubdued his temper. The hot Welfh blood that courfed through his veins did not lofe any of its fire till his heart ceafed to beat. In his old age he is as quick to hurl denunciations againft thofe who differed with him as when forty years before he had queftioned the validity of the Maffachufetts charter. For one who had laid fo much ftrefs upon fpiritual liberty, he is fingularly harfh in his treatment of fuch as had exercifed that liberty in arriving at conclufions not coincident with his own. As an examination of the theological fyftem of the Quakers the prefent work is inconclufive and unfair. Not only does Williams fail wholly to detect, beneath wild eccentricities of fpeech and action, the "effence and marrow" of this great proteft againft the formal orthodoxy of the age, but in urging particular objections he continually forces the meaning of his opponents' language, and infifts upon drawing conclufions againft which they ftrenuoufly protested. Much of the argumentation, if it may be so called, is weak and quibbling. We search in vain for any searching, dispassionate discussion of the real principles of difference between the Quakers and their opponents. It may be urged, and with truth, that the first generation of " old Foxian-Quakers" differed from the more moderate disciples of Penn and Barclay, yet surely his own experience should have taught Williams to treat with greater forbearance follies which, for the most part, had been provoked by harsh persecution. And when reproaching the Quakers for rudeness of manners, he might have remembered his own former scruples about taking off hats.[1]

But while the present work possesses no value whatever as a theological treatise, it is the most interesting of all the author's writings for its local and personal coloring. There is no book that throws so much light upon the heterogeneous society then struggling into being along the shores of the Narragansett. We find nowhere else the character and opinions of Williams himself so clearly revealed. His love of disputation is illustrated on every page. His vehement and inaccurate habit of speech is not less apparent. His tenacious recollection of real or imagined injuries is shown in the evident satisfaction with which he turns aside from George Fox to deal a blow at William Harris;[2] and his readiness to jump at erroneous conclusions, in his repeated charge that Fox had " slily departed." Yet, at the same

---

[1] "And he that could not put off his *Cap* at *Prayer* in his *Worship*, can now put it off to every Man or *Boy* that puls off his *Hat* to him." Letter of R. Scot, *N. E. Fire-Brand Quenched*, Pt. ii: 247.

[2] That Williams did not regret this part of his work is shown in his letter to the Commissioners dated Oct. 18, 1677: he says of Harris; "I have presented a character of him to his Majesty, (in defence of myself against him) in my narrative against George Fox, printed at Boston."—Knowles, *Memoir of Roger Williams*, p. 498.

time, it fhould be remembered that the perfonal peculiarities so confpicuoufly fhown in the prefent work do not reveal the whole man. Reading this alone we fhould be at a lofs to underftand how he retained, till the day of his death, the affection and efteem of the beft men in Connecticut and Maffachufetts.

Perhaps nothing is more ftriking in this volume than the very flight difference which it reveals between the views of Roger Williams and the prevailing Calvinifm of his day.[1] We habitually think of him as "having a windmill in his head," but he was a confervative in religious opinion, and on nearly all fundamental points of belief was fully in accord with the churches of New England. Nothing can be more hearty than his commendations of their doctrinal purity. On one point alone did he radically depart from them, in refufing to be connected with any vifible body of believers. Still on this point he agreed as little with the Quakers. They denied that there was any Vifible Church, and held that external ordinances had been forever done away; Williams, on the other hand, profeffed belief in a Vifible Church; and rejected the miniftry and ordinances of his own day, fimply becaufe he deemed them unauthorized.[2] For the earneftnefs, indeed, with which he infifts upon a regular adminiftration of the facraments, he almoft deferves to be reckoned a High Churchman. He condemned as "unnatural" the preaching of women in public,[3] a practice which not only the Quakers but the Baptifts encouraged. For a very brief

---

[1] "This is the main ground of my controverfy with the proud Quakers, they flie up in their Illuminations in themfelves, and Condemnations againft others, but they magnify (with the *Papifts* and *Arminians*) Curfed rotten Nature."—*infra*, p. 343.

[2] Compare *Hireling Miniftry*, p. 4, and Winthrop's *Journal*, i: 307.

[3] *infra*, p. 134.

period, three or four months, Williams had "walked in the Baptift way,"[1] but while in the prefent volume he repeatedly refers to "the People called Baptifts," it is plain that he did not regard himfelf as having the leaft connection with them. He denies that the doctrine of Baptifm is one of the "great fundamentals" of the Chriftian Religion.[2] It is no lefs plain, that as years had leffened the bitternefs of his early fufferings, he had come to look with a far more kindly feeling upon the Churches of the Bay. He commends the "heavenly Principles" of the "*Leaders* and *Corner Stones*" of the New England Colonies; he confiders that holding as they did to the neceffity of fome evidence of an inward change, they "came nearer than others to the *firft primitive Churches,* and the *Inftitutions* and *Appointments* of Chrift Jefus."[3] It is alfo to be noted that neither does Fox, nor the three Quakers who managed the difpute at Newport, affociate Williams in any manner with the Baptifts, on the contrary they repeatedly defcribe him as a "New England Prieft."[4]

For thus bitterly denouncing the Quakers, Williams has been charged with inconfiftency, but this is an entire mifapprehenfion of his pofition. He fimply difcuffed their doctrines; he did not feek to exclude them from the Colony, nor did he invoke againft them the interference of the civil power. It was becaufe of the full toleratiou extended to them that he deemed it neceffary to "vindicate the Colony" from the reproach of being counted their abettors. The only ground for the charge, which was firft urged by Fox, was the declaration of Williams "that a due

---

[1] Letter of Richard Scot.
[2] *infra,* p. 177.
[3] Compare *infra,* pp. 103 and 343.

[4] Edmundfon's *Journal,* p. 74. *N. E. Fire-Brand Quenched,* Pt. i: 36, Pt. ii: 177, &c.

and moderate reſtraint and puniſhing of incivilities" was not perſecution.[1] Williams has reference here ſimply to breaches of ordinary decorum. The poſition he takes does not differ from that ſtated with ſo much clearneſs in his Letter to the Town of Providence.[2]

In point of ſtyle the preſent volume is inferior to the author's earlier compoſitions, a circumſtance no doubt in part to be explained from the nature of the work. Yet it is throughout characteriſtic of the writer. A feature which deſerves attention is the marked preference, ſhown in all his writings, for metaphors drawn from his experience of ſea life. Thus in addreſſing the King, he ſpeaks of Charles V. as having his "Trick at Helm;" he tells Baxter and Owen "that many able and honeſt Sea-men differ in their Reckonings;" he terms the declaration of the Quakers "an Engliſh Flag in an Enemies Bottome;" in his argument he was "glad to *hale* his *Tacks* and *Bolings* cloſe home, and now and then *loof* up into the wind;" of Edmundſon he ſays, "upon a ſudden, a violent, tumultuous, diſorderly *Wind* filled all his ſails;" to one of Fox's anſwers he rejoins, "may not half an eye ſee what a *ſimple* Sophiſter this is, to make ſuch Yaws as not to come near the Ships Courſe and point in hand." Theſe inſtances ſhow how much force ſhould be attached to the phraſe "ſteered my courſe," in proof of the theory that Roger Williams came from Salem to Seekonk by water.[3]

In this reprint the NARRAGANSETT CLUB has made uſe of a copy of the original work, courteouſly placed at their diſpoſal by Charles Deane, Esq., of Cambridge. But

[1] *infra.* p. 307.
[2] Knowles' *Memoir*, p. 279.
[3] *Pub. Narr. Club*, vol. i. Biog. Introd. p. 33. Fox ſays of Williams that he "went to the woods."—*N. E. Fire-Brand Quenched*, Pt. i: 172.

throughout, the volume has been carefully collated with a
copy in the Library of Brown Univerfity, which contains
marginal corrections in the handwriting of the author. Unfortunately this volume is not perfect, the firft thirty-two
pages, pages 97 to 104 inclufive, and the laft feventeen pages,
having been reprinted from the copy in the Library of
Harvard College.   In the *Prince* Collection there is a one
in all refpects like that belonging to Harvard College,
while the Bofton Athenæum has another in which the title
reads G. Fox, and the Letter to Baxter and Owen precedes
the Addrefs to the King. The latter change feems, however,
to have been inadvertently made when the volume was re-
bound.   As the paper and watermarks in all the copies are
fimilar, it is probable that the flight change on the title
page was fimply to improve the typographical appearance.

J. L. D.

Providence, October 15, 1872.

George Fox

Digg'd out of his

Burrovves,

Or an Offer of

DISPUTATION

On fourteen *Propofalls* made this laft Summer 1672 (fo call'd)
unto *G. Fox* then prefent on *Rode-Ifland*
in *New-England*, by *R. W.*

As alfo how (*G. Fox* flily departing) the Difputation went on
being managed three dayes at *Newport* on *Rode-Ifland*, and
one day at *Providence*, between *John Stubs, John Burnet,* and
William Edmondfon on the one part, and *R. W.* on the other.

In which many *Quotations* out of *G. Fox* & *Ed. Burrowes* Book
in *Folio* are alleadged.

WITH AN

APENDIX

Of fome fcores of *G. F.* his fimple lame Anfwers to his Oppofites in that Book, quoted and replyed to
By R· W. of *Providence* in N. E.

BOSTON

·Printed by *John Fofter,* 1 6 7 6 .

TO

The KINGS MAJESTY

Charles the IId: &c.

Whom the King of Heaven long and eternally Preferve.

Royal Sir.

THE Moft High hath adorned you with an *High Birth*, with a *gallant Temper*, and Endowments of Nature, with *Princely Education*, and *rare Experiences &c.* The *Crown* of all, the *Sanctifier* of all muft be *L'efprit de Djeu*, or elfe all that is under the Sun *in fumum abeunt*.

Touching this moft *holy Spirit*, and other heavenly *Points* in difference between the *Proteftants* and the *Quakers*, I prefent your royal eye with a *Lantfkip* of a *Battle* fought this laft Summer in your Majeftyes *New-England*, between fome of the eminenteft of the *Quakers* and my felf, three dayes at *Newport* on *Rode-Ifland*, and one at *Providence* on the *Main* in the fame *Colony*.

1   I am

I am humbly bold to preſent it to your *Royal Hand,*

1.   That your own precious *Soul* (infinitely more precious then thouſands of *Brittains* or *Worlds* may ſee the *Grounds* and *Roots* of theſe *Proteſtant Diſquiſitions.*

2.   That your *Majeſty* may ſee what your *New-Engliſh Subjects* are doing under the gracious *Wing* of your wonderfull *Favour* to us &c

3.   Becauſe your Majeſtyes *Name* is often mentioned and concerned in theſe *Concertations.*

4.   Becauſe it was affirmed by ſome of my Oppoſites in publick, that there were ſcarce any of their *Books* came forth, but the *King* had one: I thought it ſome obligation on me, to preſent the *Proteſtant Truth* (thus publickly and ſolemnly aſſerted) more juſtly then my *Popiſh* and *Arminian Oppoſites* to offend your Royal eyes with Smoak out of the *Deep Pit.*

Gracious Sir, I know your precious *Spirits* and *Minutes* are exhauſted in managing your *Warrs* abroad, and in preſerving your Dominions in *Peace* at home; I cannot therefore hope for one *glance* of your eye upon any more then this poor *Epiſtle.*

Charles the Great was one of the greateſt Princes of that name in the world.   And *Charles* the fifth (both Emperours) had his wonderfull *Trick at Helm* alſo; but both (and all) turn into the *Cabbin* & *Pit* of *Rottenneſs. Charles* the 5*th.* in his 58*th.* year, *Charles* the *Great* in his 72*d.* year: But were every *drop* of water between your *Old-England* and *New,* a million of years, yet *Mors ultima linea,* and tis but *Momentum unde pendet Eternitas.*

By Gods moſt wiſe and righteous Permiſſion, the *Pope* and *Quakers* pretend their *Enthuſiaſmes* and *Infallibilityes:* I know and have detected much of both of their *Impoſtures,*

and

and I befeech him who is the eternal *Pater Luminum,* to preſerve your *Royal Spirit* from both their *Cheatings,* that is from the *Oracles* of *Hell* in their mouths.

And I humbly importune your *Majeſtyes continued Grace* and *Patience* to this poor *New-England,* which (though a miſerable, cold, howling Wildernefs, yet *L'eternel* hath made it his *Glory,* your Majeſtyes *Glory,* and a *Glory* to the *Engliſh* and *Proteſtant Name*: and if the moſt High pleaſe, *Old* and *New-England* may flouriſh when the *Pope* and *Mahomet, Rome* and *Conſtantinople* are in their Aſhes.

Providence in *N-England,*
March 10th. 167$\frac{2}{3}$.
(*ut Vulgò,*)

Your Majeſtyes moſt loyal and affectionate Orator at the Throne of Grace.

Roger Williams.

To the People called Quakers.

Friends & Country-men:

1. THe occafion of thefe *Difcourfes* you may fee in the firft *Page*: the 14 *Propofals* in the fecond Page, and the occafion of the Title in the 34.

2. The truth is (as *Edmund Burroughs*, and others of you fay of your felves) from my Childhood (now above three-fcore years) the Father of *Lights* and *Mercies* toucht my Soul with a love to himfelf, to his only be-gotten, the true *Lord Jefus*, to his *Holy Scriptures*, &c. his infinite Wifdome hath given me to fee the City, Court and Country, the Schools and Univerfities of my *Native Country*, to converfe with fome *Turks, Jews, Papifts*, and all forts of *Proteftants*, and by Books to know the *Affairs* and *Religions* of all *Countries*, &c.

3. My Conclufion is, that *be of good chear thy fins are forgiven thee*, Mat. 9. is one of the joyfulleft founds that ever came to poor finful Ears: how to obtain this found from the mouth of that Mediatour that fpoke it, is the great difpute beween the *Proteftants* and the bloody *Whore of Rome*: this is alfo the great point between the true *Proteftants* and your felves: as alfo (in order to this) about what man is (to the utmoft) now by nature, what the true Lord Jefus Chrift is, and all other controverfies (difcuffed in this Book, not unworthy this your ferious weighing (as *Mary* did) in the hearts and fpirits, &c.

4. Bear with me while I fay, that as the *Jefuites* pre-tend to deifie the *Pope*, but it is known, the end is to deifie themfelves under the cloak of the *Popes* Name: fo Satan

pretends

pretends to exalt and deifie you, under the name of *God*, and *Chrift*, and *Spirit*, &c. but his end is as *Peter* tells us, to exalt himfelf, and fill his hellifh *Paunch* with Souls.

5. I endeavoured, but could not procure a Short-hand writer, fo that I am forced to recollect Tranfactions from my Memory, and I believe (as in the holy prefence of God) that I have not failed to prefent the true fubftance of paffages without advantage to my felf, or difadvantage to my Oppofites.

6. I have ufed fome fharp Scripture Language, but not (as commonly you do) paffionately and unjuftly: I fometimes call you *Foxians*, (as *Nicolaitans* from *Nicholas*) becaufe *G.Fox* hath appeared the greateft Writer, and the greateft *Preacher* amongft you, and the moft deified that I can hear of, fure it is that here he fubtly run for it: he ordered that my Letters to our Deputy Governour Captain *Cranftone* (in which my Propofals to *G.F.* were, fhould not be delivered to the Deputy, until G. F. was fome hours under fayle, that he might fay he never faw my *Paper*, though it is as clear as noon-day that he knew all matters by Copies, Letters and Relations, perfectly many dayes before his departure.

7. My difadvantage (in our Contefts (efpecially at *Newport*) were great and many: for though *J. Stubs.* and *J. Burnet* were more civil and ingenious: yet *W. Edmondfon* was nothing but a bundle of Ignorance, and Boifteroufnefs, he would fpeak firft end all (though all three were conftantly on me at once) no man might fpeak at all in favour of my Pofitions: any might freely fpeak againft them: they fat in the midft of the Governour & Magiftrates (of their Opinion) and the whole Affembly (of their way) *W. Edmundfon* (though *J. Stubs* twice faid in publick, that I had not inter- interrupted them) yet *W.Edmundfon* would frequently and infolently interrupt me: fo that I was not only
                                                              forced

forced to bear patiently (through Gods only help) but to
ſuppreſs my thoughts, which here I have added in ſome
places. 8. I know that a great weight of your Opinions
and Actings lye upon your believing your ſelves guided by
the immediate Spirit of God: but I believe that I have
proved that it is no more the holy Spirit of God, that
ſpeaks and acts in you, then it was the true *Samuel* that
ſpake ſuch heavenly words in the appearance of *Sam.*
Mantle amongſt a cloud of other witneſſes you ſhall never
perſwade Souls (not bewitched) that the holy ſpirit of God
would perſwade your Women and Maidens to appear in
publick (ſtreets & aſſemblies) ſtark naked, &c. of which I
have ſpoke more particularly in our diſputations. 9. It is
hard to perſwade a Fox or a Wolf that he is ſo, &c. or
that he doth Rob or Steal, or Murther; it is hard to perſwade a man while he dreams that he is in a Dream : yea
though he be a filthy Dreamer as Gods Spirit ſpeaks: In
our Dreams we believe lyes and impoſſibilities to be true
as that we.are many thouſand miles of, that we talk with
dead men, &c. that we are at Marriages or Burials and are
Kings and Queens. &c.

10. All that I can hope for (without Gods wonderfull
mercy) is to give my Teſtimony in my generation: for (as
Solomon ſpeaks of the Whore) few or none of you return.
Yet I know Gods foundation is ſure he knows who are his
amongſt you as amongſt other perſwaſions. I have proved,
and will prove (if God pleaſe) that ſpiritual *Pride*, that is
Pride about ſpiritual matters, is the Root and Branch of
your whole Religion, and that the King Eternal, who did
caſt out proud Angels out of his *Palace*, will hardly open
his Gates to proud and ſcornful Duſt and Aſhes:

Providence, March 10.   *I am one of your beſt Friends, R.W.*

1 6 7 $\frac{2}{3}$ (ſo called)

To *thofe many Learned and Pious Men, whom*
G. Fox *hath fo fillily and fcornfully anfwered*
in his Book in Folio

Efpecially to those whofe Names I have been bold to mention in the *Narrativt* and *Apendix,*

Mr Richard Baxter, *Mr* Iohn Owen &c.

Sirs,

THrough *your fides the Devil by the Clawes of this*
wily Fox, *hath tore at the heart of the* Son of God;
it is no wonder then if he tear at the Heart of his
Love-Letters, *and Inftitutions, and the true Pro-*
feffors of his name, who are innumerable in Abrahams Bofome, *and the reft travelling uprightly thither.*

For Brevity *fake I was forced to omit many excellent*
Paffages, felected by Fox *out of your Writings & to felect*
fhort Sentences of yours unto which he gives fhort Anfwers.
As to matters in Difference *between yourfelves and me, I*
willingly omitted them, as knowing that many able and honeft
Sea-men *in their Obfervations of this* Sun (*one picture of*
Chrift Jefus*) differ fometimes in their* Reckonings, *though*
uprightly aiming at, and bound for one Port *and* Harbour.

Eternally *praifed be the* Father of Lights, *and mercyes,*
that we are one in that moft glorious ever fixed Cynofura
(*about whom his true Prophets & Meffengers ever have and*
doe and fhall move: and he boldeth them in his right hand.

I humbly *beg of you.* 1. *That you will more and more*
earneftly, candidly and chriftianly ftudy the things that differ
without reflecting upon Credit, Maintenance, Liberty *and* Life
it felf, remembring who it was that faid it; He *that loves*
his life fhall lofe it. 2. *More and more to ftudy the Prophefies*
and the Signs of the Times, You know when it was that five

2   *Bifhops*

Bishops, twenty-two Ministers & almost three hunared other precious Believers in the true Lord Jesus, were sacrificed in the Flames, for his ever‿blessed sake, against that monstrous Man of Sin and bloudy Whore of Rome. These Foxians fancy is but a feather to to those high Pico's and Tenariffs, the Pope and Mahomet whom some of you may live to see flung into the Lake that burns with Fire and Brimstone.

Were it not that the infinite Compassions of Heaven had made our gracious Sovereign the Breath of our Nostrills, the fiery Fornace had certainly burnt seven times hotter against Hananiah, Mishael and Azariah : Surely as for Conscience sake we ought to obey, so for Conscience sake we ought to be Instant and Constant at the throne of Grace for his Royal Preservation and Salvation.

Prov. March 10, 167$\frac{2}{3}$. I am unworthy to be yours R. W.

A Narration of

A CONFERENCE

OR

DISPUTE,

This laſt *Auguſt* 1672 (ſo called) in the
Colony of *Rode-Iland* and *Providence*, Plantations in
N.ENGLAND, between *Roger Williams* of *Provi-
dence* (who Challenged *Fox* by writing (which fol-
lowes) and all his Friends then met on *Rode-
Iland*, (and *G. Fox* withdrawing) *John
Stubs*, *John Burniat*, and *William
Edmundon* (three of their ableſt Apoſ-
tles) on the other, that is, (on the
pretended *Quakers*) Party.

Having long heard of the great name of
G. *Fox*, (a man cried up by the Peo—
ple called *Quakers*) and having read The Occa-
his book in Folio (ſome years ſince) ſion of the
Diſputa-
againſt, as I think above *ſix ſcore Books* and *Papers* tion.
(written by pious and able pens againſt them) and
now this Summer hearing of his coming into theſe

Parts

Parts of *N England*, and the poor cheated Souls the *G. Fox* his *Quakers* with joy expecting his coming, as the Book in *Folio* weighed. coming of *an Angel of light* from Heaven: I read over his Book afresh (as in the holy presence and eye of God, (with a single Eye and Heart) and more clearly finding his *Answers* so weak and silly, so Anti-Christian and Blasphemous, and yet so Imperious and Scornfull, so Cursing and Censorious, [2] Damning and Reprobating all that bow not down to their new *Upstart Image*, my Spirit rose up within me, and I believe the holy *Spirit of God* (in answer to my poor *Petitions* and *Meditations*) resolved and quickened my Spirit to the present *Undertake* and Service. And therefore for his most holy Names sake, and the name of his most holy only begotten, the true *Lord Jesus* the *God-Man* and *Mediator* &c, And for the honour of the most holy *Spirit of God* (so horribly torn in pieces by this foul *Spirit of the Quakers*) For the vindicating of many of the precious Truths of the old *Christian purity*, and for the sake of so many precious Souls lying slain and bleeding before me, I made this Offer following to G. *Fox*, and any or all his Followers or Associates, then together at *New-port* on *Rode-Iland*. Tis true G. *Fox* was at *Providence* some few dayes before, and spake publickly; and it was free for me publickly to have heard him, and opposed him; But going the last year to one of their general Assemblies at *New-Port*, and having begun to present to A Spirit of Confusion in the Quakers Meetings. them some Considerations about the *True Christ* and the *false*, the *True spirit* and the *False* and being cut of in the midest, by sudden *Prayer* of one, and the

Singing

Singing of another, and then by the *Prayer* of another and the fudden diffolving of the Affembly, I refolved to try another way, and to offer a fair and full *Difpute,* according to *Ed. Burrowes* (and therein G *Foxes*) Offer in his large *Epiftle* to *Foxes* Book. To this Purpofe I drew up my thoughts into fourteen *Propofitions*; and knowing that *New-Pòrt* was the chief Town on *Rode–Iland* and *Provi-dence* on the *Main,* and that G. *Fox* had fpake at both places and *bewitched* many with his *Sorceries,* I fent this Paper following to G. *Fox* at *Newport,* viz,

My Offer
of Difp. on
14 Propofi-
tions.

TO G. Fox *or any other of my Countrey–men* at New-Port *who fay they are the Apoftles and Meffengers of* Chrift Jefus, *In humble Confi-dence of the help of the* Moft High, *I offer to maintain in Publick, againft all* Comers, *thefe* 14 Propofitions *following, to wit, the firft feven at* New-Port, *and the other feven at* Providence: *For the time* When, *I refer it to* G. Fox *and his Friends at* New-port.

Only I defire

1 *To have three dayes Notice, before the day you fix on.*

2 *That without* Interruption (*or many fpeak-ing at once*) *the* Conference *may continue from* Nine *in the morning till* [3] *about* four *in the afternoon.* and

· 3 *That if either of the feven Propofitions be not finifhed in one day, the* Conference *may con-tinue and goe on fome few hours the next day.*

· 4 *That either of us Difputing fhall have free uninterrupted*

uninterrupted liberty to speak (*in* Anſwers *and* Replyes)*as much and as long as wee pleaſe, and then give the* Oppoſite *the ſame* Liberty.

That the whole may be managed with that *Ingenuity* and *Humanity*, as ſuch an *Exerciſe*, by ſuch *Perſons* in ſuch *Conditions*, at ſuch a *Time*, ought to be managed and performed, the *Propoſitions* are theſe that follow.

Firſt   *That the People called* Quakers *are not true Quakers according to the holy* Scriptures.

2 *That the* Chriſt *they profeſs is not the* True Lord Jeſus Chriſt.

3 *That the* Spirit *by which they are acted is not the* Spirit of God.

4 *That they doe not own the holy* Scriptures.

5 *Their* Principles *and* Profeſſions, *are full of* Contradictions *and* Hypocriſies.

6 *That their* Religion *is not only an Hereſy in the matters of* Worſhip, *but alſo in the Doctrines of* Repentance Faith. *&c*

7 *Their* Religion *is but a confuſed mixture of* Popery, Armineaniſme, Socineaniſme, Judaiſme *&c.*

8 *The People called* Quakers (*in effect*) *hold no* God, no Chriſt, no Spirit, no Angel, no Devil, no Reſurrection, no Judgment, no Heaven, no Hell, *but what is in man.*

9 *All that their* Religion *requires (externall and internall) to make* Converts *and* Proſelites, *amounts to no more than what a* Reprobate *may eaſily attain unto, and perform.*

10 *That the Popes of Rome doe not ſwell with, and*
exerciſe

exercife a greater Pride, *then the* Quakers *Spirit hath exprest, and doth afpire unto, although many truly humble Soules may be captivated amongst them, as may be in other* Religions.

11 *The Quakers* Religion *is more obftructive, and deftructive to the* Converfion *and* Salvation *of the Souls of* People, *then moft of the Religions this day extant in the world.*

12 *The* Sufferings *of the* Quakers *are no true evidence of the Truth of their* Religion.

13 *That their many* Books *and* writings *are extremely Poor, Lame, Naked, and fweld up only with* high Titles *and words of Boafting and* Vapour.

[4] 14. *That the Spirit of their* Religion *tends mainly,*

1 *To reduce Perfons from* Civility *to* Barbarifme.

3 *To an* Arbetratry Goverment, *and the Dictates and Decrees of that* fudden Spirit *that acts them,*

3 *To a fudden cutting off of* People, *yea of* Kings *and* Princes *oppofing them.*

4 *To as fiery* Perfecutions *for matters of Religion and Confcience, as hath been or can be practifed by any* Hunters *or* Perfecutors *in the world.*

Under thefe forementioned Heads (*if the Spirit of the* Quakers *dare civilly to Argue*) *will be opened many of the* Popifh, Proteftant, Jewifh *and* Quakers *Pofitions, which cannot here be mentioned, in the Difpute* (*if God pleafe*) *they muft be alleadged, and the* Examination *left to every perfons* Confcience, *as they will anfwer to God,* (*at their own Perills*) *in the great day approaching.*

Roger Williams.
This

THis *Paper* above-faid I fent inclofed in a Letter to my kind friend *Capt. Cranſton* Deputy Governour of the *Colony*, that being ſuch a publick perſon, he might timely be informed of ſuch a publick Aſſembly, and as alſo might vouchſafe (as afterwards he carefully did) to afford his *Countenance and Aſſiſtance* to ſuch *Peaceable* and *Pious Exerciſes*. But before the *Boat* went down with the Letter aforeſaid from *Providence* to *Newport*, I ſent a Copy of my Poſitions to a Neighbour *J T.* whom I heard was inclining to them. He takes a Copy of them and reads them in their Meeting, before *John Croſman* Maſter of the Boat (one of them alſo) who preſently the ſame hour, called me *Blind Sot* in the open *Street*, upbraiding me, how I durſt ſend my 14 *Lyes* to ſuch a man as G. *Fox* (one of them called him) *the eternall Son of God*; ſo that before my Letter went to *Newport* (which *Croſman* carried) by Letters, & *Croſman* his and other Relations, all was known, even long before my Letters were opened, or delivered to the Deputy Governour: For in the *Junto* of the *Foxians* at *Newport* it was concluded for *Infallible Reaſons*, that His *Holineſs* G. *Fox* ſhould withdraw, ſeeing there was ſuch a Knot of the Apoſtles of Chriſt Jeſus now at *Newport* together, (eſpecially *John Stubs*, a man knowing the *Greek* and *Hebrew*) Therefore that it might appear that ſuch a Nehemiah as he would not fly, it was [5] agreed that my Letters ſhould not be delivered to the *Deputy Governour*, untill G. *Fox* was gone; ſo that it might be truly ſaid, that he never ſaw the *Paper* which I ſent unto him. h I

ad

The firſt uſage to the Author & his Propoſals.

The deceitfulneſs of Fox & Foxians.

had a touch of this *Leger de main* trick in our Dif- one of the
pute at *Newport,* and the *Deputy Governour* did pub- subtil
lickly teftifie that my Letters to him were dated this subtil
the 13 of *July* (which he faid he wondered at) but *Fox* viz. to
were not brought to him untill the 26th of the faid fomly from
Moneth, and untill G. *Fox* was fome hours departed. the *Difpute*
John Burniat profeft that that he knew noth- & yet not
ing of the detaining of the Letters, only he knew all to run
that G. *Fox* never faw my *Paper.* G. F. fuppofed for it.
I would be forced to be as plain in my *Proofs* as I
was in my *Pofitions.* He knew that I was furnifhed
with *Artillery* out of his own *Writings.* He faw
what *Confequences* would roll down the mountaines
upon him from his proud and Infolent, yet poor
and bald *Writings*; and how far fome of his prefent practices were fallen out with his *Writings,* and
therefore this old *Fox* thought it beft to run for it,
and leave the work to his *Journey-men* and *Chaplains* to perform in his abfence for him.

Before I come to Tranfactions between thofe
three left behind him [*John Stubs, John Burnet,
William Edmundfon,* and my felf] I think fit to tell A great
the Reader what a *preparatory Conflict* the moft holy private
and only *Wife Lord,* was pleafed to exercife me with, *Conflict.*
before I came to the *Publick.* before my
publick.

My former antient Neighbour and friend *J. T.*
being bit by fuch *infectious Teeth* himfelf, fell on
me, as a man would fall upon *a Toad* or *Serpent,* and
fent me this following *Letter,* notwithftanding he
was but newly bitten by them; and for forty yeares
pretended no fmall love and refpect to God and
me.

He

He firſt *gave fire* upon me in this following *Letter.*

Providence. 18. 5. 72.

Roger Williams

J T. his Letter to me uPon the ſight of my *Propoſitions* to *G. Fox.*

THy *Scurrilous* Paper *in thy* Propoſitions to G. Fox. *and others (who in ſcorn are called* Quakers) *I adviſe thee to refrain any further pub-liſhing thereof, and as, it is written keep thee far from an evill matter, thy* paper *being full fraught with* impudent Lyes *and* Slanders, *with high flown airy imaginations, which if thou ſhouldſt live the dayes of* Methuſelah, *thou couldſt not per-form. In Love to thy* Perſon *and* Name, [6] *which ought to be precious, I adviſe thee not upon a* ſud-den motion *(as thou termeſt us to act by) but from the* ſpirit of Truth *and tender love unto thy ſoul, which* Spirit *by thy writing appears thou art a ſtranger to. Conſider thy latter end, leaſt with*

A Note of Card *Mazarin*

Cardinal Mazarin, *thou cry out in* a dying hour *Oh my poor* Soul, *what will become of thee? whi-ther art thou a going? And ſaid if he ſhould lon-ger have lived, he would leave the* Court, *and be a* Capuchin. Time *is precious,* Repent, Repent, *and mind the* manifeſtation *of the* Spirit, *which is given to every one to profit withall., and knocks at the door of thy* Heart, *for entrance, which being* rejected *will be thy* Condemation. *If thou reject-eſt this my faithfull witneſs for the* Lord, *I then ſay with* John *in the* Revelation, *let him that is filthy be be filthy ſtill, and ſo remaines*

thy friend and Neighbour *J. T.*

Having

Having read this Letter, and knowing this my
Neighbour of late to have declined much from his
former profeſſion of *Godli,neſs*, and many wayes by
his *Looſneſs* had grieved my *Soul*, I wondered not
much at his Lines, (though now much unexpected
of him) as knowing the Quakers ſpirit, to be a
ready Ditch or *Gulfe*, that readily ſucks and draws
into it Soules *afrighted* eaſily to ſkin over their
Sores; *P*roud and Self-conceited ones, who gladly
cloſe with the *Spirit* of, and Children of *Pride*, and Fuel *for*
Looſe fading *Profeſſors*, of which ſort the *Quakers* the Quakers Fire *of*
Meetings do much conſiſt, as not being able to walk Hell.
cloſe with God, not daring to turn wholy *Profane*,
or *Atheiſts*, and ſo daube up the breach with *untem-*
pered Morter (the wild and fooliſh notions of the
Devils *Whiſperings*, under the cloak of the immediate *Inſpirations* of Gods holy and heavenly *Spirit*)
Many thoughts I had to paſs by his Affronts, and
Inſultations: But conſidering that it was not my
Name (not worth the while) but the moſt High,
Eternall *Majeſty*; and his moſt *holy Spirit* thus fouly
pierced and debaſed, I return'd this *Anſwer* following.

My ancient loving Friend, My *Anſ-*
wer to the
  IF you *pluck out the eyes of your* Underſtanding, fore-going
  Profeſſion, *and* Experience, *yet* (*through the* Letter
mercy of the Father of Lights *and Mercyes*) I from *J.T.*
cannot do ſo with mine. You tell me my Paper *to*
G. Fox, *is* Scurrilous, *&c.* full fraught with [7]
Impudent Lyes and Slanders, *&c. And you ſay*
you write in Love, from the Spirit of Truth, to
which

which (*you say*) I am a ſtranger. *You mind mee of* Death *&c. and bid me* Repent, Repent, *or elſe be filthy ſtill, and be damned.*

To which I will not Anſwer as G. Fox *an-ſwered* H. Wrights *Paper with a ſcornfull and ſhamefull* Silence. *Thus I ſay in generall, you are my* Witneſs, *that I have long ſaid with* David (*and I humbly hope have made it good*) *I hate and abhor* Lying, *but thy Law do I love, for which I have loſt in my time ſomething,* &c *If I had not loved his* Law, *and abhorred* Lyes, *I had long ere this bowed down againſt my* Conſcience, *yea I had fired the Countrey about this barbarous Land (as ſome in this* Colony *have done) I had murthered the* Indians, *and* Engliſh *by the* Powder *and* Liquor *trade, to which you know I had Tempta-tion, as much as your ſelf, or any others in* N. Eng-land, *but I loved the Name of God.*

For your ſelf, if the God of heaven have terri-fied your Soul, (which I believe is the caſe of moſt Quakers, *and of the* Devils *themſelves) and made it tremble at the* Wrath *to come, you muſt not think to run from his flaming* Eyes *and* Hand *(as* Adam) *amongſt the* Thickets; *you cannot talk of* Mercy *without a way of Satisfaction to an infinite* Juſtice. (*Who payes the* Old Score)? *It is im-poſſible that all created* Powers, *in* Heaven *or* Earth, *can diſcharge for one ſinfull* Thought. *There muſt be an Equivalent diſcharge, not by filthy Rags, and menſtruous Clouts of our own* Holineſs; *which muſt be thought of before we can ſay, We can ſin no more againſt* God, *than he*

can

can fin againſt us; *as you know who* Blaſphem-
ouſly *and* Horribly *maintain it.*

In your lines I pray you to Conſider,

Pirſt. Your Irrationality, *for how can you
imagine that a ſerious Chriſtian, in humble Confidence of the of the mercifull Preſence, and gracious
Aſſiſtance of Gods* holy Spirit, *and of no little* Af- The
fliction *and* Suffering, *ſhould be ſo eaſily ſtird (as a* Bruitiſh
Rock *with a* Feather) *by your bare crying* Re- Simplicity
of the
pent, Repent or be Damned, hearken to the Quakers
Light within thee? &c. Spirit.

2. *Can* Reaſon *imagine, that after much* ſtrug-
ling *within my ſelf, and the* Birth *of my* Propoſitions *and* Reſolutions, *that I can ſo* ſuddenly
ſtrike Sail, *and bear up, and immediately* [8] Stifle,
and Smother, *and Burn my* Conceptions *and Reſolutions, as ſoon as I hear your ſimple and childiſh
ſpirit Countermand me?*

3. - Is it not unmanly Childiſh *and effeminate,
to cry out a* Scurrilous paper, Lyes, Lyes, impudent Slanders &*c. and yet give me not one* Reaſon
or one Scripture *againſt any one of them? Is it
not too like the irrationall and brutiſh Anſwer of*
Humphrey Norton *(to a ſober and Sollid Paper of*
Thomas Olnys *ſen.) crying out, Lyes, Lyes,* 224
Lyes, *without any ſerious* Examination *of* Particulars?

2. *I charge your Lines with* Impiety, *where* The Man-
you infer that the moſt holy Spirit *(from that* Scrip- ifeſtation
of the
ture [The manifeſtation of the Spirit &*c.) is* Spirit. 1.
poured forth upon every Individuall perſon in the Cor. 12.
World.

World. Did the Oyl *moſt precious and holy, the holy* Ointments *and the* Blood *in the Law, reſpect the whole world, or the* Meſſiah *the anointed and his Members (Chriſtians or anointed alſo)? Was not* 1. Cor. 12. *written to the* Chriſtians, *or Saints gathered into the Chriſtian flock or Congregation at* Corinth, *unto whome the Father of* Spirits *(as in that place) vouchſafeth thoſe three heavenly Favours.*

1. Gifts *which he ſhews there to be different.* 2. Adminiſtrations, Miniſteryes *or Offices.* 3. Operations, *Works or Succeſſes, all wrought in the Saints by the holy* Spirit, *for the Glory of the ſame* Father, Lord, *and* Spirit, *the mutual comfort and edifying of the* Saints, *yea and for the Convicting and drawing of other poor* Sinners, *out of the World to God.*

The Lord *mercifully awaken your Souls to the* Love *of God, and the Love of his holy* Truth, *for the not beleiving of which but the profane playing with it, the moſt high and righteous* Judge *of the whole world (in a way of Judicial Sentence) delivers up poor Souls to believe Lyes, and that ſo ſtrongly, as to give their bodyes to be burned for them.*

Gods wonderful Juſtice.

The Papiſts *catch hold upon a* Letter [This is my body] *You as ſimply as doe the* Generaliſts *catch hold upon the* Letter [All, every man that comes into the world *&.c.*] *whereas the* Scope *and* Connection *in all writings, and in all matters in the world are rationally to be minded. The* Sence *and* Meaning *is in all* Speech *and* Writing, *(in*

The words *All* and *every one,* Conſidered.

(in our own and other Languages) *the very* Speech *or* Writing *it ſelf. Theſe Words* [All and every one] *in our own and other* Tongues, [9] *are often uſed* figuratively: *it is ſo all the Scripture over, and thrice in one verſe,* Colloſſ. 1. 28. *where Reaſon cannot imagine that* Paul *did literally and individually admoniſh* every *man,* teach *every* man, *and preſent* every *man that comes into the world, perfeƈt in* Chriſt Jeſus *which could not, cannot poſſibly be true without another Sence and* Expoſition, *then the words literally hold out.*

4, *Again, you are dangerouſly bold to ſay that you write from the* Spirit of Truth, *wherein you Father theſe your childiſh* Irrationalityes, *your profaning of the holy* Majeſty of God, *his holy* Scriptures *and writings, and your raſh* Judging *and Examining of others, upon the holy* Spirit of God: *But I do humbly hope to evince, that the Spirit you boaſt of, is ſo far from the* Spirit of God, *that it falls beneath the foot of a ſober and well grounded* Humanity. *At preſent I only Inſtance in that* whoriſh *and* monſtrous *aƈt of your* Women *and* Maidens, *ſtripping themſelves* ſtark naked, *by your Spirit, and with a face of* braſs *coming into the open* ſtreets, *and publick* Congregations of Men *and* Youths. *This* Spirit *(though defended by* G. Fox *and others) is ſuch a piece of unnaturall and* bruitiſh Impudence, *that I cannot hear of the like amongſt* Jews *or* Gentiles, *yea not amongſt the moſt* Savage, Baſe *and* Barbarous *of them all (all Circumſtances conſidered).*

The Impudency and Uncleaneſs of the *Quakers* Spirit.

5. In

5. *In the last place I observe your* Fickleness *and Inconstancy, what, and how often have I heard you speak of the* Chief *of the* Quakers *now at* Newport? *How lately and how much have you uttered of* John Crosman *his Cross and froward spirit (even since he pretended the* Spirit) *yea how* inhumane *and* injurious *to your self in the way of his Calling? now all on a* sudden (*for I heard but little untill I saw your Lines) you are got up into the lofty Chair of* Judging *and ready to say,* God I thank thee I am not as this Publican, *I beseech the Lord to make you savingly to remember that* Word [God resisteth *that is sets himself in Hostility against the* Proud, but he giveth Grace unto the Lowly] *so prayes*

your old unworthy Friend *R.W.*

Providence 18th. 5th. 72.

I had hoped that I had Conjur'd down (at least for the present) that *Waspish spirit*, but he flyes out against me (within a few dayes) in this second *Letter* following.

10]   Providence, 23. 5. 75.

J. T. his second Letter to me. *A*Ncient *Friend and Acquaintance, I read thy Note four dayes after the subscribing it, that so thy Councellors might throughly be informed of thy continued* Zeal *in a dangerous Case. What I write to thee in* Love *hath a contrary effect in thy* Spirit, *being so prejudiced against us; according to the* Proverb, Nothing is well spoken, that is not well taken. *Upon Discourse*

Difcourfe thou didſt ſay the Quakers could not be
believed on their Words or Writings, having a ſecret Reſervation within them, *which gives me to conclude, that wee are Judged before wee Speak. For
my charging upon thee* Slanders and Lyes, *Examine
but thy* Poſitions, *which will make manifeſt what I
ſay. As for the* Terror *which thou ſpeakeſt of* &c.
*I leave it to thee to conſider what thou art about,
leaſt thou be called to Account for it before thou art
ready. As for charging me with* Irrationality *for not
alleadging Scripture for what I write, yet I alleadged
three Scriptures, one of which thou wreſteſt, adding
what I wrote not, ſo that if I had urged more, I ſhould
have had the like Catching :* But we both muſt come to
give an Account of what is done in the Body. *In this
my Letter thou mayeſt ſee my witneſſing againſt moſt of
thy* Slanderous Propoſitions. *Concerning the* Spirits
manifeſtations, 1 Cor. 12. 13. *I freely conſent that
they were the* Saints *by Calling, who are there Conſidered. As thou alleadgeſt the* Papiſts *Catch at a word*
[This is my body] *ſo we catch at a word* [All] *and
miſapply Scripture; ſo that I perceive thou haſt not a*
Guide *to thy mind, but uttereſt thine own Conceiv-
ings.* John. 3.16. *The Promiſe is to them that* Believe, *and not to* All.
Again, *Thou findeſt fault with my raſh judging thee,
and abuſing Scripture: Take it to thy ſelf, for the
word* Damning, *thou foiſteſt in thy ſelf, neither dare I
paſs Sentence of* Damnation *upon any: For Judgment
belongeth to the Lord, and we muſt ſtand or fall to our
own* Maſter. *As for my* Ficklenefs *and Inconſtancy,
Lay thy hand upon thy mouth and Conſider thy Wind-*

4   *ings*

*ings and Turnings, in thy Judgment and Practice, how
thankfull thou waſt to* J. Burnet, *whome thou highly
commendeſt after thou cameſt home, and now reproacheſt
the Truth, which then thou aſſenteſt to: and in thy* 14
*Poſitions, thou hinteſt (by thy wicked Surmiſes) what
the* ſudden ſpirit *of the* Quakers *is, to take away the
Lives of* Kings, &.c. *but I told thee in my firſt Letter,
thou art a ſtranger to that* holy Spirit *we act by.*

   But further thy Malice *appeareth in going to one
thou ſaidſt, that* [11] *if the* ſpirit *of the* Governour
were to cut of his head, *he muſt doe it. Call to mind
what thou didſt to thy peaceable Neighbours ſeeking
their Blood, crying out* Treaſon, *when the* Court *diſ-
cerned thy Blood-thirſty ſpirit, which thy friends at*
Newport *were aſhamed of, and thy Accuſations proved
Invalid. How childiſh didſt thou act to ſwear againſt
One, when another told thee of ſomewhat ſpoken to allay
thy fury againſt* William Harris? *Call to mind thy
Books written, and ſee thy Fickleneſs, wanting a Guid
to thy mind, being for and againſt Perſecution. Thou
chargeſt me to have gotten into the Chair of Judging :
thy two Scripts I return upon thy ſelf,* Phyſitian heal
thy ſelf. *The Wiſdom of man puffeth up; but the
Wiſdom of God humbleth, that God may be all in all.
I deſire thee to look back to thy Lines, and where thou
mentioneſt the Satisfaction of infinite* Juſtice : *who*

The high 'payes the old ſcore? &.c. *Alſo to conſider my* Irra-
Opinion G *tionality, that thy great* Education, *great* Search &.c.
Fox his *as alſo thy great Travels and Struglings to bring forth*
Followers
have of *thy* Poſitions, *all being in thine own will, and in the*
him yet he *Apoſtacy wherin the great Whore hath made all* Na-
faild & run
for it. tions *drunk with her* Fornications, *which the Lord*
                                               will

*will in his Time, confume with the breath of his mouth.
I know thou haft undertaken a great* Burthen *in Challenging* G. Fox *to anfwer thy* Pofitions; I *wifh thee
to provide thy* Armour *of* Proof, *as* Golias *that de-
fied the Army of* Ifrael. G.Fox *is furnifhed with that*
Armour *that thou haft no fkill to make ufe of;* having
alfo the Sword *of the* Spirit *to cut down all thy airy*
Imaginations : *Therefore ceafe from further troubling
thee : a Word to the Wife is Sufficient, if thou haue a
heart to make ufe of it.*

thy Friend and Neigbour, *J. T.*

To this Second Letter *I Replied* in this following

NEighbour, in this your fecond Letter (mifdated
as well as mine) you pafs by many Particulars
which I wrote concerning G. *Fox, Hump. Norton,*
your felf, and the ftripping your Women *Stark naked* in publick, *&c.* you infift upon my Irrationall
dealing.

2. For your charging my *Pofitions* to be Lyes,
and Impudent *Slanders,* without giving me one
Scripture or *Reafon* to prove them fo ; and here you Unreafon-
fay [*For my charging upon thee Lyes and Slanders,* able kind of Reafon-
examine *but thy* Pofitions, *which will make manifeft* ing.
what I fay] But is this any more *Rationall* or Man-
like ? or is it not bruitifh to fay, you are a *Lyar* becaufe you are a *Lyar* ; [12] Or you are a *Lyar*
becaufe you fay thefe *Pofitions* are true, and offer to
prove them. It is a *Man-like fpirit* to lead a *Beaft*
with an *Halter,* but a *Man* with *Reafon* ; but to lead
or drive a *Man* with an *Halter* or Cudgel, and not
with

with a *Reason*, (in *Naturalls* and *Rationalls*, moſt of all in *Spirittalls*) is not the *Spirit* of *God* nor of *Humanity*: For what will my *Chargings*, and Cenſures and Clamors, and Curſings, and Damnings effect and beget upon a rationall Soul, without a proof of Reaſon, but an Opinion of my wicked falſe bruitiſh and irrationall *ſpirit*?

3.   Tis true in your Exhortation to me, you bid me hearken to the *Manifeſtation of the Spirit* which is given to every man *&c.* This I acknowledg *Scripture.* You ſay I wreſted and added to an other Scripture, but you mention it not, ſo I am in the dark what you mean. And for this of the *Manifeſtation of the Spirit*, your ſelf now conſent to me, that it was ſpoken to the Saints or Chriſtians at *Corinth*, and therefore I ſpake true in ſaying, that as to my Poſitions (by you call'd *Impudent Lyes and Slanders*) you gave me not then, nor now any one *Scripture* or *Reaſon* to prove any one of my *Poſitions* to be ſo.

.4.   As to *John Burnet*, I ſaid before him and afterwards, that he delivered many *Truths:* yet withall, I then at the ſame time (in their *Publick Aſſembly* at *Newport*) I told them, that it lay upon them to manifeſt to their own *Souls* and others, 1. That their *Chriſt* was *true* 2. That their *Spirit* was *Gods*, and the rather becauſe they were charged with denying the *Inſtitutions* of *Chriſt Jeſus*, and with the ſetting up of many *Will-worſhips*, as *Preaching of Women &c.* And I went on purpoſe to *Diſcourſe* of theſe matters (this being the time of their *Generall Aſſembly*, and a great *Concourſe*) I

I can give many Inſtances of their abuſing the Ordinance and Name of the *Spirit of Prayer* for a ſudden *Silencing* of their Oppoſites.

was

was ftopt by the fudden praying of the *Governour's Wife*, who alfo told me of her afking her hufband at home (meaning *Chrift* which I had toucht upon) I rofe up and faid, if a man had fo alleadged, I would have anfwered him: But I would not Countenance fo much the violation of *Gods Order* in making a Reply to a *Woman* in Publick: Hereupon *J. Nicols* ftood up and faid [*In Chrift Jefus neither male or female &c.*] I was Replying to him and to *J. Burnets* Speech alfo concerning their *Spirit*, but I was ftopt by *John Burnets* fudden falling to Prayer, and difmiffing the *Affembly*. I refolved (with Gods help) to be *Patient* and *Civill*, and fo I ceafed, not feing a willingnefs in them for me to proceed; which experience made me not to trouble [13] *G. Fox* and the *Affembly* at *Providence*, but rather to make a fair and Solemn offer of *Difpute* about thefe matters: fo that it is notorioufly falfe, that I *Owned* or *Countenanced* any of their *Opinions*.

5 You tell me of my foifting in that word *Damning*, and I tell you that thofe words of *Condemnation* and *Damnation* are all one in your *Greek* and *Latine* and *Englifh* and other Languages: So that in your telling me if I hearken not to you, it will be my *Condemnation*, you (all one) tell mee it will be my *Damnation*.

There are two *Damnations*, one which all Mankind is under, (*He that believeth not is condemned already*) the other, that finall Sentence [*Goe ye Curfed*] my *Charity* bids judge that you meant not the latter: But my *Knowledg* tells me amongft

Jews

Jews and *Turks, Papists* and *Protestants* and *Pagans*
(with all of which I have converfed) I never met
with fuch a Judging Cenfuring Reviling *fpirit* as is
the *fpirit* of the *Quakers.*

6. As to my faying in my 14th *Position,* that
the fpirit of the *Quakers* tends to a fudden *Cutting
off* of people, yea *Kings* and *Princes:* It lyes upon
me to prove it, and you do only upbraid me with
it but offer no difproof, nor can you or any other
evade it, when the *Roots* of *Affairs* and *Actions* are
dig'd up and examined. ·

7. Next you cry out againft my Blood-thirfty
fpirit in *William Harris* his Cafe: and I anfwer
that it is not the fign nor the part of Loyall and
gratefull fubjects having received fuch wonderfull
Favours and *Priviledges* from fo mighty a *Mon-*
arch, fo to Slight and damn, to Null and make void
fuch Royall *Grace* and Favour. Is it not high and
monftrous abominable *Prefumption* for any man to
quarrel with *Soveraign Majefty* for granting Favour
and Mercy to the *Souls* and *Bodyes* of their *Sub-*
jects (which he ought to doe, even in *Confcience* to
God) and for difpenfing with *Laws* made for *Super-*
ftitions and *Oppreffions.* I think you have been an
Officer your felf in a *Corporation* in *England:* I
queftion how you durft then (or durft now) omit
to take *Cognizance* of fuch *Actings,* againft your
Corporations fafety, and the Honour and royall fupream *Authority* of his *Majefty.*

I was in place and ingaged more than others to
maintain the righteous fplendor of the Kings *Crown*
and *Majefty* and *Prerogative,* and the *Colonyes* fafety

peace

*W.Harris
his late
Cafe of de-
nying that
the King
hath pow-
er to dif-
pence with
his Sub-
jects in
Religious
matters.*

peace and Liberty, and yet I acted not without the Counfel and Concurrence of all the reft of the 14] *Magiftrates* who did no more but what belonged to our *Duty* and Alleagiance as faithfull *Officers* to his *Majefty* and this *Colony* under him: nor did we any more then *Neceffity* and common Prudence compeld us to, for who knoweth what *after Reckonings* may befall us? Did not *W. Harris* (when in place) more than juftifie us, by judging himfelf bound to hurry your felf, and about twenty more to *Newport*, to anfwer for Contempt of the Kings *Authority*, though but in an accidentall, peaceable, and (by his Covetous violence) occafioned Meeting. Was not *Mr Clark* (though favourable to *W. H.*) fo amazed at *W. Harris* his defperate *Prefumptions*, that he readily acted with us in *Examination* and *Commitment*? Yea did not *W. Harris* (upon the point) Confefs that we could not but Commit him, and therefore provided beforehand his Bedding, and other Conveniences for a *Prifon*?

8. It is not true that either in *Word* or *Writing* I cryed out *Treafon* againft him. But it is notorioufly known, that he and his *Complices* lay in Wait, and at Catch at every word as *Foxes* and *Lyons* for *Mr Greens* Blood and mine, as *Traitors* againft *King Charles* for our pleading the *Colonyes* proceeding againft *W Harris* in the time of the *Parliament*, and O*liver Cromwell*.

Oh Friend, whither will thy poor Soul next be hurried? Is not the Gap and Gate now left open for *W. Harris* or any man to Difpute openly againft His *Majeftyes Declaration*

the

againſt *W.* Haris his preſump- tious Attempt the *Kings Prerogative,* and tell him that he knowes not, nor his *Councill* nor *Judges* the *Laws?* that he cannot diſpence with *penall Laws* on the *Conſciences* of his *Subjeċts, Papiſts* or *Proteſtants,* at *Home* or *Abroad?* But ſee the Finger of the moſt High! the *Kings Majeſty* (as if he knew all our proceedings againſt *W. Harris* his preſumptions, debaſing the *Kings Power* and *Prerogative*) in the preſent junc- ture of theſe Affairs, ſent forth his *Royall Declara- tion* to the World, aſſerting his *Supream Power* and *Authority* in ſuch matters, and by virtue of many Statutes and Aċts of *Parliament.*

9. In the laſt place, that your ſelf and others may admire your *new ſpirit,* how much, and how often, and how long hath your own *Mouth* and *Hand* (and *Capt. Fenner* and diverſe with you) de- clared and remonſtranced to the *Generall Aſſembly* againſt *W. Harris* (which Aſſembly therefore fined him and outed him) as the reſtleſs *Fire-brand* of *Town* and *Colony* and who hath with all his power now kindled and blown this *Fire* between [15] *Con- eċticut Colony* and our ſelves. Yet now in your, and the Quakers boſom, muſt *W. Harris* be hug'd, as an innocent and peaceable Soul, and the *Kings* faith- full *Officers* reproached and threatned as Blood- thirſty and cruel *Oppreſſors.*

10. You bid me mind my Books, and my being for and againſt *Perſecution:* But through Gods mercy I can look at them with humble *Thankſgiv- ing* and peace; without any recoiling thought to Perſecution (as you falſly intimate) from them.

11. As to *G. Fox* his *Armour, Sword, and Cut- tings*

tings with which you threaten me; I defire to think as low of my felf, *&.c.* as you or G. *Fox* can think high of himfelf. It is infinite mercy that I live, and as a *Living Dog* may wait for *Crums* of mercy, clearly to *See*, dearly to *Love*, uprightly to *Follow*, and conftantly to *Maintain* the eternall *Crown* and *Glory* of the true *Lord Jefus Chrift*, and his moft holy *Spirit* and *Scriptures*, with whofe gracious *Affiftanee* I hope to prove that the *Quakers fpirit*, and *Chrift* have no *Communion*.

Roger Williams.

THe Ingenious and upright *Reader* might now well fuppofe that the Conteft were over: but it is not the *Light* of *Truth* or *Reafon* or *Scripture* or *Experience*, or the *Teftimony* of the *Prudent* or their own *Confciences* that will fatisfie this *white Devill* of this pretended *Light* and *Spirit* within them, and therefore muft I crave the Readers *Patience* while I produce I. T. his third and laftLetter to me and my Anfwer to it.

Neighbour,

COncerning the miftaking the Date of my Letter as J. T *thou writeft*, which could not be, feing I fent it *thee the fame day I writ it, but thine, I heard of it fome dayes before I received it. As for my paffing over many particulars (which did not concern the matter in handling) I willingly omitted them, difcerning thy fubtil fpirit, in no refpect anfwering by fcripture or reafon my loving Admonitions to thee: But in thine own words, is it not bruitifh, irrationall, childifh to affirm*

His
third and
laft Letter
to me.

5   *we*

we are worſe then Barbarians, *which thy* ſordid Poſitions *do hold forth?* How childiſh, yea how fooliſh
doſt thou ſhew thy ſelf in thy firſt Poſition, *for* G.Fox
to prove *what he and all friends diſown, and in ſcorn
thou calleſt* Quakers. And in thy 12th Poſition doſt
affirm, That our Sufferings are no Evidence of the
truth of our Religion, *Thou mighteſt have ſpar'd thy
paines in bringing* [16] *forth this Brat, which is of
thine owne begetting : But we are ſure it is an* Evidence *againſt thee, & all other of thy Spirit, which
perſecute, that they have drunk deep of the Cup of
Fornication, upon whom the Violls of* Gods wrath *are
powred forth in* ſpirituall Fornications.

a *Whore* is as bold in her *whore-doms,* as a ChaſtWife in her Ino-cency.

How dareſt *thou find fault with me in not alleadging*
ſcripture, *nor* reaſon *in declaring againſt thy impious
Charges mentioned in thy railing & impious* poſitions?
Would'ſt *thou have me to take the matter in hand
(which thou challengeſt* G.Fox *to anſwer) to give like
a fool ſcripture & reaſon for what thou aſſigneſt another
to doe? Oh what Serpent-like ſpirit doſt thou act by,
that doſt not own my* plain dealing with thee in owning
the ſcripture & wreſteſt & foiſteſt in, as J meant not,
nor writ : Jf thy ſpirit were reall (as before men thy
words ſeem to import) thou wouldeſt not then ſhew a
ſmiling Countenance when War is in thine heart, in
witneſſing againſt thy Neighbours ſecretly, againſt that
Golden rule,* Doe as thou would'ſt be done by.
*Thou counteſt it open violence for a Woman to ſpeak in
the* Church: *but if thou kneweſt what* Woman *that
ſhould not ſpeake thou* would'ſt *have ſpared me theſe
lines writing, & have eaſed thy ſelfe of thy great
ſtruglings & ſtrivings within thee to bring forth on*
. Abortive.

Abortive. *Thou chargeſt me in making a great Out-cry againſt thy Blood-thirſty ſpirit, concerning* W. Harris, *as though thou dideſt at no time cry out Treo-ſon Treaſon.* Anſw. *how doſt thou ſhift of as one that is guilty, and dare not mention the caſe I writ up-on, ſhufling it to be his laſt impriſonment, which I know not the ground of, but as I had it related by thee: But the Circumſtances conſidered, it cannot poſſibly be par-aleld (as my Letter declareth) with this laſt Caſe of* W. Harris. *Firſt, thy taking Oath againſt my wife upon an other mans word on purpoſe to allay thy furious ſpirit againſt* W. Harris, *he not thinking thou wouldeſt have proſecuted againſt her, as alſo againſt ſixteen of thy peaceable neighbours, Can thou deny that at that* Court *thou cryed not out* Treaſon Treaſon, *making all as guilty as* W. Harris? *Thou ſayeſt I bid thee mind thy Book written againſt* Perſecution, *and yet thy ſelf a* Perſecutor *of thy peaceable Neighbours even unto death.* Anſw. *How canſt thou in peace (through the God of peace, (as thou ſayeſt) look upon thy wicked Travels to murther the Innocent as thou dideſt at* Newport, *cry-ing out* Treaſon *being* Preſident.

Alſo what I have ſpoken againſt W. Harris *touch-ing his firing the* Town *and* Colony, *I thought ſo, and therefore contended againſt him, but I never ſought his life, note that* R. W. *Thou ſayſt* [17] *thou art not conſcious of any recoyling in thy* ſpirit, *ſo much as in a thought. Here thou manifeſt's an impious* ſpirit *that ſeekes to murther the* Innocent: *what* Fury *poſſeſſeth thee to talk of the* God *of peace & yet retaineſt a murtherous mind, not having repented of thy wick-edneſſe, how is thy heart hardned in ſeeking the lives of*

If there were any *Colour* for any of theſe hor-rible *Out-cryes,* I ſhould have heard of them

ſuch

from *W.*
Edmunfon
who rak‘d
up all he
could
againft me
both in the
Difpute at
Newport
and *Provi-*
dence.
*fuch as thou thy felf haft confeft to be the Children of
God? Oh murtherous man that hath not any Re-
morfe for thy long-liv‘d* Wickednefs, *J am forry for
thee, though thou flight all my writings & counfells, &
take all in the worft fence ; yet J befeech thee to confider thy latter end, & my defire for thee is that the
Lord would awaken thy Soul & give thee* Repentance
unto life.

In the laft place thou writeft how highly I efteem of
G. Fox. *and thou defireft to think as low of thy felf:
How will this agree with thy boafting of great* Education, *great* Experiences, *great ftruglings and ftriv-
ings within to bring out thy* Pofitions *and* Conclufions,
*which all my loving Teftimonyes againft (as iffuing from
a diabolicall fpirit) did no more take place with, then a*
Feather *againft a* Rock. *Call to mind the preaching
of* Jonas *to* Ninive, *yet forty dayes and Ninive fhall
be deftroyed (a fhort fpeech) yet they repented and the
Lord pardoned: And fo I defire thou mayeft repent and
find mercy with the God of mercy.*

Thy Neighbour *I. T.*

THus *Reader* it pleafed the Infinite *Wifdom* of
the moft holy and only Wife, to pierce through
my heart with the thrufts and ftabs of a of a foul-
mouth’d *flanderous fpirit*, by the hands of long profeffed *friends* and lovers, yet pretending the name
of God and of Scripture, as wel as my felf. How
doth it behoove us then to make fure that we can
in truth fay as *Jeremiah*, Lam. 3. *Thou art my portion faith my Soul O Lord*; Thou and none elfe,
Thou alone without *Health, Strength, Beauty, Hon-*
our,

our, *Lands*, *Goods*, *Friends*, &c. How fhould we make fure that with *Thomas*, we may fay unto the ·Lord Jefus, *my Lord and my God?* for whofe fake we ought joyfully to bear what *falfe Chrifts, falfe fpirits* and their Souldiers can dart from *Earth* or *Hell* againft us.

My Anfwer was as followeth.

My Anfwer to *J T*. his 3d *Affault* upon me.

MY ancient Friend, it pleafeth the moft High to give to all mankind (his *Children* alfo and them efpecially) many *bitter Cups*, and that oftentimes by the hands of *dear friends* and [18] *dear Relations*, that we might fall more in love with himfelf then ever who isinfinitely more fweet, and even Holinefs and *Power* and Wifdom and Love it felf.

Your Lines(in this your third *Fury* againft me) being full of *Bitternefs* in themfelves, are more bitter to my Spirit upon diverfe accounts. But the *moft High* and *only Wife* will have it fo, and your judgment and Confcience (and mine) will have it fo, yet that will not acquit us, we both fay we muft come to another *Barr*, and there ftand or fall eternally.

In this, *Firft.* You tell me you willingly omitted the *Particulars* I mentioned as not concerning the matters in handling: I am not of your mind, it is an *Eafie* yet a *fufpicious* way of anfwering, and implyes not only unwillingnefs, but a *willing Ignorance* and *Guilt* alfo : For is it not concerning the matter in hand (efpecially when fo perfonally provoked)

A deceitfull way of Anfw.

from *W.* *fuch as thou thy felf haſt confeſt to be the Children of*
Edmunſon God? *Oh murtherous man that hath not any Re-*
who rak'd
up all he morſe *for thy long-liv'd* Wickedneſs, *J am ſorry for*
could *thee, though thou ſlight all my writings & counſells, &*
againſt me
both in the *take all in the worſt ſence ; yet J beſeech thee to con-*
Diſpute at *ſider thy latter end, & my deſire for thee is that the*
Newport
and *Provi-* Lord *would awaken thy Soul & give thee* Repentance
dence. *unto life.*

    In the laſt place thou writeſt how highly I eſteem of
G. Fox. *and thou deſireſt to think as low of thy ſelf:*
How will this agree with thy boaſting of great Education, *great* Experiences, *great ſruglings and ſtriv-*
ings within to bring out thy Poſitions *and* Concluſions,
which all my loving Teſtimonyes againſt (*as iſſuing from*
a diabolicall ſpirit) *did no more take place with, then a*
Feather *againſt a* Rock.   *Call to mind the preaching*
of Jonas *to* Ninive, *yet forty dayes and* Ninive ſhall
be deſtroyed (*a ſhort ſpeech*) *yet they repented and the*
Lord *pardoned*: *And ſo I deſire thou mayeſt repent and*
find mercy with the God of mercy.

                Thy Neighbour *I. T.*

THus *Reader* it pleaſed the Infinite *Wiſdom* of
the moſt holy and only Wiſe, to pierce through
my heart with the thruſts and ſtabs of a of a foul-
mouth'd *ſlanderous ſpirit,* by the hands of long profeſſed *friends* and lovers, yet pretending the name
of God and of Scripture, as wel as my ſelf.   How
doth it behoove us then to make ſure that we can
in truth ſay as *Jeremiah,* Lam. 3. *Thou art my por-*
tion ſaith my Soul O Lord; Thou and none elſe,
Thou alone without *Health, Strength, Beauty, Hon-*
our,

our, Lands, Goods, Friends, &.c. How fhould we
make fure that with *Thomas,* we may fay unto the
Lord Jefus, *my Lord and my God?* for whofe fake
we ought joyfully to bear what *falfe Chrifts, falfe
fpirits* and their Souldiers can dart from *Earth* or
Hell againft us.

My Anfwer was as followeth.

My Anf-
wer to *J*
T. his 3d
Affault up-
on me.

MY ancient Friend, it pleafeth the moft High
to give to all mankind (his *Children* alfo and
them efpecially) many *bitter Cups,* and that oftentimes by the hands of *dear friends* and [18] *dear
Relations,* that we might fall more in love with
himfelf then ever who isinfinitely more fweet, and
even Holinefs and *P*ower and Wifdom and Love
it felf.

Your Lines(in this your third *Fury* againft me)
being full of *Bitternefs* in themfelves, are more bitter to my Spirit upon diverfe accounts. But the
moft High and *only Wife* will have it fo, and your
judgment and Confcience (and mine) will have it
fo, yet that will not acquit us, we both fay we muft
come to another *Barr,* and there ftand or fall eternally.

In this, *Firft.* You tell me you willingly omitted the *P*articulars I mentioned as not concerning
the matters in handling: I am not of your mind,
it is an *Eafie* yet a *Sufpicious* way of anfwering, and
implyes not only unwillingnefs, but a *willing Ignorance* and *Guilt* alfo : For is it not concerning the
matter in hand (efpecially when fo perfonally provoked)

A deceit-
full way of
Anfw.

voked) to vindicate our felves and friends, our Teachers and *Apoftles*, our *Spirits* and Religion alfo?

2. Next you blame my fubtle fpirit, for not anfwering by Scripture or Reafon your loving Ad-monitions: I gave you my Reafon, fhewing how fimple it was for you to give fire upon me, and tell me my *Paper* was *Scurrilous, full fraught with im-pudent Lyes and Slanders,* and yet give me not one *Scripture* nor *Reafon* to prove any of them to be fo. 2. I fhewed you how irrationall it was for you to think, that I fhould fo fuddenly renounce my underftanding and *Confcience* and *Pofitions* upon the fudden found of your Outcry *Repent, Repent.*

The hor-rid Naked-nefs of the Q Women fhews the worfe then barbarous nakednefs of their Spirits. 3. You tell me it is childifh, bruitifh and irra-tionall, to fay that you are worfe then *Barbarians*: *Anfw.* I faid not fo in generall, you and all the world ought to abhor the particular cafe, *viz.* the ftripping *Naked* of your *Women* and Maidens; a cafe worfe then Savage and Barbarous, only prac-tifed by the *Bruites*, and fometimes by *Indians*, and *Whores* in their drink, when all *Modefty* and *Rea-fon* is overwhelmed with more then common *Drunkennefs.* Who can but abhor to think of fuch whorifh and monftrous *Immodefty*, fuch an hellifh *Incentive* to filthy Lufts, and that under the moft holy name of the *Spirit of God.*

4. *A*s to my firft Pofition, you now tell me that *the name* it is childifh and foolifh for G. *Fox* to prove (I fup-pofe you mean, for me to defire G. *Fox* to prove) *Quakers.* what he and all friends difown, and thou in fcorn calleft Quakers: *Anfw.* I know the Quakers
fay

say [19] that name is given them in fcorn, and yet we alfo know it it hath its denomination from thofe great bodily *Shakings* which have been believed to have come in mightily upon them by the power of *Devilliſh ſpirits* (for many Reafons of which afterward) However G. *Fox* in 370th. page of his Book *in Folio* writes thus in the title of each page [*The Quakers anſwer. The Quakers Anſwer*] I know what may be faid; and I know may be faid and juftly to that excufe, and what fhall be faid in the Difpute following.

5. As to my 12th. *Poſition*, of Suffering of the *Quakers*, and you fay it is a *Brat* of mine own, and that is an evidence againft me, and all of my *Perſecuting Spirit*. *Anſw*. I fhall (by Gods affiftance prove that you doe make it an *Evidence* of your *Religion*, and then it muft be your one *Brat* and *Baſtard*.

The Quakers Sufferings.

As to my perfecuting fpirit, the moft High hath been a holy witnefs to my Travels and loffes and hazards and other fufferings, in my vindicating and procuring *Soul-liberty:* and I humbly hope in his mercy, he will preferve me from being like many *Quakers*, fouly fallen from their former *Chriſtan Religion*

6. You fay, *How dareſt thou blame me for not giving Scripture or Reaſon againſt thy railing and impious Poſitions, when thou challengeſt and aſſigneſt another to doe it* G. Fox, &.c. *Anſw*. I only blamed *J. T.* for being fo fierce and furious, fo hot and hafty in crying out *a ſcurrilous Paper fraught with lyes and impudent ſlanders*, and yet gave me not one Scripture or Reafon againft any one of them: common

mon *Modesty* and humane *Sobriety* would have taught a little *Patience*, till G. *Fox* had answered, or untill you had answered something of *Scripture* or *Reason* your self.

7. Nextly you tell me of my *Serpent-like spirit* in witnessing against my neighbour secretly: To which I lay before the most High, I know not what you intend 2. I know it not to be any Crime (much less a serpent-like spirit as your railing pen phrases it) to give a true testimony, and witness in private and publick, even against the *highest* and dearest, in the matters of *God* and *Truth*, which ought to be only *High* and only *Dear* unto us.

Womens Preaching.

8. As to *Womens preaching* in the Church, you tell me that I know not what that *Woman* is, *Answ.* I know the allegoricall Interpretations given of both those Scriptures, to the *Corinths* and *Timothy*, But where the holy *Scripture* is plain, and agrees 20] even with *Nature* it self; where the holy *Spirit* of *God* gives Reasons why Scripture should be so expounded (which is an extraordinary signification of Gods soveraign will and pleasure) where else one part must be *Literall* and an other part *Allegoricall*, (which is most improper and not suiting to the *Majesty* and *Purity* of *Gods Spirit*) what can be soberly in the fear of God and with any sober reason collected, but that the most High, the *God* of *Order* (and all Order and Wisdom it self) is pleased there to set down the *Order* of his *Worship* in the *Christian Congregations*.

9. Concerning *W Harris* you tell me I shift

of

of the matter, for you meant not *W Harris* his laſt Impriſonment: You prove it by my taking Oath againſt your Wife upon an other mans word on purpoſe to allay my furious ſpirit againſt *W Harris*.. Theſe are your words, which may be taken three wayes, but neither of them can I call to mind: God knowes I truly deſire to See, Lament and forſake every Idle word or thought, which my ſoul may be ſatisfied is ſo: for I dare not goe beyond (as you proudly doe) that *Direction* of the *Lord Jeſus, dayly* to cry [*Forgive us our Treſpaſſes*] I dare moſt confidently deny that ſimple Charge, *viz.* that I ſhould cry out *Treaſon* Treaſon, againſt your Wife and others, labouring to bring them into the ſame guilt with *W. Harris.* whoſe facts and courſes others (of no ſmall *Authority* and *Prudence* amongſt us, with whome I adviſed) ſaw to be deſperate high *Treaſon* againſt the *Laws* of our *Mother England,* and of this *Colony* alſo. When *W Harris,* ſent his *writings* or *Books* to the *Main* and to the *Iland,* againſt all *Earthly Powers, Parliaments, Laws, Charters, Magiſtrates, Priſons, Puniſhments, Rates,* yea and againſt all *Kings, and Princes,* under that Notion that the *People* ſhould ſhortly cry out,*no lords no maſters*; and had in open Court proteſted, (before the whole *Colony* aſſembled) that he would maintain his Writings with his *Blood.* Was it my *Fury* (as you call it) or was it not *Honeſty* and *Duty* to *God* and the *Colony* and the *higher Powers* then in *England* to act faithfully and impartially in the place wherein I then ſtood *Centinell*?

W Harris his former practices againſt all Goverment but that of Saints as the Quakers now ſpeak.

And

And it is not true that I fought his life as you
upbraid me, much lefs theirs, who purpofely (as
the moft high God is witnefs) were prefented, that
fome prudent courfe might be taken by the Court
for the preventing of their greater danger, and the
Colonyes alfo. By your reafon the *Kings Majefty*,
his *Judges* (yea all *Judges*) [21] yea the *King* himfelf, yea the *moft High*, and *King of Kings* fhall be
condemned as *Blood-thirfty*, bloody feekers of the
lives (though of high handed wilfull and dangerous
Tranfgreffors) as though *Juftice* and *Mercy*, true
Pitty and juft *Severity* might not harmonize, and
make up the bleffed concord of *Peace* together.

10.   You mind me again of my Books againft
Perfecution, and yet my felf a *Perfecutor* of my
peacable Neighbours to the *Death*, murthering the
innocent, yea that I ftill retain a *Murtherous* mind,
and you cry out againft me, *Oh murtherous Man*
&.c.   To which I fay, I am not better than *Da-*
vid, nor (in this cafe) are you better than *Shimei*,
who rak't up *Stones* and *Dirt*, and flung them with
Railings at *David*, crying out *Come out thou bloody*
Man, and this in the name of the holy *Spirit* alfo.

My Right-
eoufnefs as
to my deal-
ing with
W. H. As to *W. H.* I never appeared In *Town* or *Colony*
againft him for any private matter (although many
wayes extraordinarily provoked and wronged by
him) but always in *Witnefs* (as I humbly appeal
unto God) I fay in witneffing againft his *running*
down and deftroying the *Publick*,(as at this day) for
his *Private Covetous* and *Contentious* Ends.

The hor-
rible Mur-
thering of And for your felf, who cry out fo much of *Blood*
and Murther for my being impartiall to *God*, to the
King

King and the *Countrey*: I heartily wish that your the *Indians*
hands were washed from the bloody trade of by *Liquors* which the
Liquours to the *Indians*, which even the *Quakers* Qu: have
have practised, telling the *Indians* that the *Quakers* notoriouf-
only know God, and therefore would sell them tifed.
Powder and *Liquors* cheaper, and they would not
mix water with *Rhum* as others did: so that by
many sudden deaths, what by *Confumptions* and
Dropfies, the *Barbarians* have been murthered, *hundreds*, if not *thoufands* in the whole Countrey, and
more in this *Colony* than in any part of the *Countrey*
beside that I have heard of, againft which I have
witneffed from Court to Court in vain.

11 You afk me how I can think as *low* of my
felf, as you *high* of G. *Fox*, when I boaft of *Education Experience &.c.*

I anfwer, I boaft as *Paul* did, who confeft himfelf the leaft of all *Saints*, and the chiefe of *Sinners*; and yet reckons up the *Priviledges* end *Favours*, which God had vouchfafed to him, againft
the foule Clamours of his malicious and envious
Oppofites, the falfe *Apoftles*.

12. You conclude with advifing my *Repentance*,
and you propofe to me the cafe of *Nineve*, telling
me that forty dayes is a fhort *Speech*.

22] *Anfw.* I humbly befeech the *Lord* to help
you and me, humbly and faithfully to examine our
true laying of that *Foundation* of a true Repentance,
which is a totall turning of our *Soul* or *Spirit* unto
God; not out of *Fear* or felf ends, as *Diffemblers*
do; but in *Mariage-love* with *God* that it might be
faid unto us, *thy Maker is thy Husband.*

As

As to your special Hint to me of forty dayes, I can say it (through infinite mercy) that more than forty or fifty yeares, I have been acquainted with *Death*, and have (not seldom) familiarly discoursed with the *Grave* and *Pit of Rottenness* : I have desired to be ready at a *minutes warning*, waiting for a wind to transport me (as *Paul* speaks) unto *Christ Jesus* in *Abrahams Bosome* which is best of all. I pray you to know that I believe there is a *black Familiar* that haunts the *Quakers*, it may be he *whispers* to you that within forty dayes you shall be ridd of me except I repent; he may see into the crazy temper of my house of *Clay*. (These *Dog-dayes* not to continue and abide a little of that time) Or God may suffer him by some immediate *Revelation* to employ some malicious soul to *Murther* me, that this foul *Lyar* and *Murtherer* may extoll and predicate himself in print by your *Pens*, that he was a true *Prophet*, applauding and triumphing in the righteous Judgment of God against a *Blasphemer* of your *gods* and *godesses*. I believe that every *Hair of mine head*, and every *Minute* of my Life is in the mercifull hand of the *Father* of *Spirits*. I doe not simply and blasphemously think as G. F. that my Soul is a piece or part of God ; nor can I (as the unbelieving *Quakers*) slight the *Rising* of my body; *Steven* fell asleep, and so (among *Stones* or whatever his holy Wisdom pleaseth) I humbly hope shall I, and rise again in the *Morning*.

They were the Dog-dayes when these hot and doged barkings were made at me.

Death and the Resurrection.

R. W.

Prouidence, July 30. 1672. (so called)

HItherto (gentle *Reader*) have been the *Skir-mishings* of my *Forlorn-Hope*; I haften now to the relation of the main *Battle*, for after this my third Letter and *Anfwer*, I heard no more of that *foul* and *flanderous fpirit* : I fhould rejoice to be in-ftrumentall to his cafting out of my ancient friend *J T.* however he pluckt in his horns as G *Fox* him-felf did, and I have yet heard no further.

Within fome few dayes after that our *Deputy Governour* had [23] delivered my *P*aper to them, the ftrange *Quakers* (as was agreed with G. *Fox*) came to *Providence*. *John Stubs*, *John Burnet*, and others, and came to my houfe fix or feven together : their *Salutations* were (like the meetings of their *dumb fpirit*) in filence. I bid them welcome *&c.* *John Stubs* began and faid, they had received a *P*aper from me, and they came to me to tell me, that they accepted my *Offer*, and that they had appointed (according to the liberty given them by my felf in my *P*aper) the 9th. of the prefent *Au-guft* to be the day at *Newport*. I told them they were welcome, and the more welcome becaufe they brought me tidings of their *Refolution* : for I longed for *Opportunityes* of fuch *Exercifes*, to which I thought the moft High invited us by our precious *Libertyes &c.* I added that my *P*aper was in the firft place directed to G. *Fox* : but they fuddenly catcht at my word, and *John Burnet* told me that G. *Fox* was departed before my *Letters* were opened, and that *G.Fox* never faw my *P*aper (and probably as afterward in the difpute he fpake honeftlie not knowing the Miftery) *John Stubs* added that my

The firft
*Interveni-
ence* at
Provi-
dence of
the *Qu.*and
my felf.

G *Fox* his
cunning
Departure

Paper

*P*aper gave liberty to G. *Fox* or his friends. I faid
therefore I would not fail (if God pleafed) to meet
them at the place, and by nine in the morning, on
the day they had appointed.

They departed (after drink offered and accepted
by fome) but the next morning being the firft of
the Week I fent them word in writing, that diverfe
of our Neighbours were grieved that the *Conference* fhould be carried away from *Providence* to
My care of *Newport* wholly, (as fome of them had alfo fpoken)
ingaging I told them that the accepting of my *Proffer* ne-
them to
my whole ceffarily included the Conference about the latter
Offer and feven at *Providence*: I told them their *Confciences*
of difcuf-
fing the and *Credits* lay on it, and therefore defired them to
latter feven fix on a day for the difpute of the latter feven at
at *Provi- Providence* before their departure hence. This Pa-
dence.*
per was delivered to one of their Company in the
room where they were together, but whither on
purpofe or (as tis poffible) by miftake, they fay the
Paper was loft: fo receiving no Anfwer from them,
I late in the evening fent them another writing,
fignifiing, that I could not hold my felf ingaged to
meet them at *Newport* about the firft feven, without their promife of difcuffing the latter feven at
Providence. Then they wrote to me that I had
feemed willing, and that they had given notice, and
the Countrey would come in, therefore they
challenged me to appear and prove my malicious [24] and bitter charges againft them, and withall promifed that upon the finifhing of the firft
feven at *Newport*, fome of them would give me a
meeting a *Providence &.c.* Upon the receipt of
this,

this, I fent them a third writing fignifiing that I
refted in their Promife, and therefore (if God
pleafed) I would not fail to be with them at the time
and place appointed. And God gracioufly affifted
me in rowing all day with my old bones fo that I
got to *Newport* toward the *Midnight* before the
morning appointed.

Then I fent them a fourth *Paper* (with a Copie
of my firft that mifcaried as they faid) and fignified to them, that it would be convenient to agree
about fome *Order* of *Tranfition*, or paffing from one
pofition to another: as alfo fince they were *many*
and I but *One*, I prefumed their Reafon told them
that I expected but *One at once*, and that if
another defired to fpeak, the firft fhould hold his
peace; as alfo I fignified that fome were fcrupulous
of going into the *Quakers Meeting-houfe*, and ther- Scruples
fore I defired fome thoughts about it: they thought about
it convenient to fend *H. Bull* to requeft me to goe meeting in
to his houfe to them; I went; they urged the *Ca-* the *Qua-
pacioufnefs* and *Conveniency* of their houfe, and I ing houfe
told fuch as fcrupled, that it was one thing to at *Newport*
goe into a *Jewifh Synagogue*, or a *Popifh Chappell* to
worfhip, or countenance their *Worfhips*: another
thing to *Profefs* and *Conteft* againft them, in which
refpect *Paul* difputed many dayes in the *Jewes
Synagogues* againft them, and I could freelie goe into the *Popes Chappel*, to difpute againft the *Pope*
and his *Worfhip*.

I knew our aged *Governour Mr. Nich. Eafton*
& other *Magiftrates* (of their judgment) would be *the way to
there, & fo the Civill Peace* maintained, & I had a *Conquer.*

ftrange

ſtrange *aſſurance* given in to my *ſpirit* from God in anſwer to my poor requeſts *&.c. viz,* that by *Moderation* and *Patience* I ſhould conquer their *Immoderations* and *impatiencies,* I therefore thought it in vain to ſpend time about a *Moderatour* : Tis true they gave me no Anſwer either by Speech, or writing concerning their coming on me one at once, but to their ſeeming great advantage they conſtantly fell on me *all at once,* and one of them *William Edmundſon* with grievous Language and inſulting.

The Per- When I came into the place aforeſaid I found
ſons diſ- three able and noted preachers amongſt them, *viz*
puting *John Stubs, John Burnet, William Edmunſon* ſitting
with me. together on an high Bench with ſome of the *Magiſtrates* of their Judgment with them : I had heard [25] that *John Stubs* was learned in the *Hebrew* and the *Greek* (and I found him ſo) as for *John Burnet* I found him to be of a moderate *Spirit,*
W Ed- and a very able Speaker. The third *W. Edmund-*
mundſon *ſon* was newly come (as was ſaid) from *Virginia,* and
deſcribed. he proved the *Chief Speaker,* a man not ſo able nor ſo *moderate* as the other two: For the two firſt would ſpeak *Argument,* and diſcuſs and produce *Scripture*: but *William Edmundſon* was very ignorant in the *Scripture* or any other Learning: He had been a ſouldier in the late warres, a ſtout portly man of a great voice, and fit to make a *Bragadocia* (as he did) and a conſtant exerciſe meerly of my Patience : he would often *Vapour* and preach long, and when I had patiently waited till the *Guſt* was over, and began to ſpeak, then would he ſtop my mouth with a very unhandſome Clout' of a
grievous

grievous *Interruption*: fo that fometimes I was forc't to play the *Moderator*, and to proteft that fuch practifes were againft the fober rules of *Civillity* and *Humanity*. It pleafed *God* to help me with fuch *Patience* to weather them, that *John Stubs* openly confeft twice, that though fome others had given them fome interruptions, yet that I had not done it. *J Stubs his Inge-nuity.*

I took my Seat at the other end of the houfe oppofite to them, and began telling them that the *moft High* was my witnefs, that not out of any pre-judice againft, or difrefpect to the perfons of the *Quakers* (many of whome I knew and did love and honour) nor any foolifh *Paffion* of pride or hold-nefs (for I defired to be fenfible of my many de-cayes of *my houfe of Clay*, and other wayes) nor any earthly or *worldly ends* I had that occafioned this trouble to my felf and them. *The be-ginning of the Difpute*

I was firft commanded this work from *Heaven*: Why fhould not this Argument be good for mee and for others as well as the *Quakers?* they fay their commands are immediate (for *Interpretations* are *immediate*) but I fay they herein fuffer *Satan* to cheat them; for they fay they pray, they faft, they wait, they liften, they judge of the motions that arife within them, and fo have I done. The great maker and fearcher of all hearts knowes, that none but his holy *Majefty* was privy to the *Conception* of this bufinefs. *The Occa-fion of it.*

1. My end was, the vindicating his *moft holy Name*, which my Soul faw was trodden in the dirt by *Sathan* clothed with *Samuels Mantle*, and the *My ends.*

7   bright

bright garment of an *Angel of Light,* which once he was, but pride deceived him.

26] 2. I had in mine eye the vindicating this *Colony* for receiving of fuch perfons whome others would not, we fuffer for their fakes, and are accounted their *Abettors*: that therefore together with the improvemeut of our *Libertyes* which the *God of Heaven,* and our *Kings Majefty* have gracioufly given us, I might give a publick teftimony against their O*pinions* in fuch a way and *Exercife,* I judged it incumbent upon my *Spirit* and *Confcience* to doe it (in fome regards) more than moft in the *Colony*. I may alfo truly fay that

Nicholas Davis drowned at Newport a little before the Difpute. 3. I had alfo in mine eye, that this exercife might occafion fome *Soul Confideration* in many. I told them that we had a dolefull *Alarum* and inftruction lately, we were taught what *Salvation* and *faving* was, in the late death and drowning of a perfon fo known to us (and all *N. England*) *Nicholas Davis.* I told them our cafe, and the cafe of all mankind is his (in Spirituall and *Soul matters*) *Oh a world for an Oar, a Rope, a Plank*. Only it muft be to all of us our work, to try whether our *Saviour* our *Salvation* be reall, and not failing in fo great a Straight.

Some of thefe bleffed ends it hath pleafed God to propagate by this occafion all this *Colony* over, and all of us round about have put forth our felves in *Difquifitions* and Searchings after the true grounds of the *Chriftian Religion* and *Worfhip*.

What Prayer was ufed. I had many thoughts of beginning fuch an exercife with *Prayer* unto God for his Prefence : but I knew

knew I could not joyn with them nor would they
owne my *Prayers*: I had thoughts (as *Eliah* among
the *Baalites*) to have prayed in the fingular number:
But fome *Confiderations* made my fpirit content
with this kind of Petition unto God: For not only
in my *Clofet* and my heart, but publickly before
them all I faid, *I doe humbly hope and beg of* God
the Father *of Spirits fo to order and direct our Spirits
in thefe our Agitations, that his holy name may receive
glory, and the* Soules *of all of us fome* Soul-profit *and
Advantage.*

I began with the firft Pofition, which I think *W.
Edmunfon* alfo read out of the Paper. *viz.*

That the People called Quakers are not true Quakers The firft
Pofition.
according to the Scriptures.

1. I faid I knew they did not owne that name
Quakers, as impofed on them by God, or taken up
by themfelves, but given them in fcorn and derifion, The name
as G. *Fox*, *Ed. Burrowes* (and I had heard *John* Quakers.
Stubs who joined with them) declared, and that
27] one *Gervace Bennet, a Juftice* in *Derby* firft
fo called them in the year 1650 And yet I had
caufe to judg that the name was given by *Juftice
Bennet* and others to them from that ftrange and
uncouth poffeffing of their bodyes. with quaking
and *fhaking* of their *Bodyes* even in publick Affemblyes and Congregations, which extraordinary motions I judged to come upon them, not from the
holy *Spirit* and Power of God, but from the fpirit
and power of *Sathan* for diverfe *Reafons.*

Firft. Although they pretend that *Mofes* and *David* and *Habbacouck* and *Daniel* were *Quakers*, yet
as

as to the Chriftian Profeffion, and the dayes fince
our gallant fore-Fathers in *Germany* (at *Spiers*) protefted againft the whore of *Rome*, and from that
Profteftation, by the *Papifts*, they were called in
fcorn and wrath the *Protefters*, or Proteftants (about
150 years fince) unto this day. I fay as to the
Proteftant Profeffors and Confeffors, the *Quakers*
are but a new upftart party or *Faction* rifen up
little above 20 yeares fince in the northern parts
of *England, Lancafhire &c*. Tis true, tis probable
they are the Offfpring of the *Grindletonians* in the
fame *Lancafhire* about two yeares before, who held
thofe two grand *Points* (though many wicked paths
of *Doctrine* aud *Practice* were amongft them) *viz.*
1 *That God doth all.* 2 *They could not fin*, taking
it according to the Letter. Thefe *Grindletonians*
were the Offfpring of the late *Nicholaitans*, (as all
of them are in truth juftly fo called) from *Henery
Nichols* who put forth his Books of the fame Poi-
fon in **K.** *James* his time, (which long fince I read)
and were confuted by many, and by Mr *Ainfworth*
and Mr *Robinfon*, precious and powerfull *Witneffes*
of Chrift Jefus. *H. Nichols* aud his *Nicholaitans*
were the Litter of thofe *Spirittualls* and *Libertines*
which fpread in *Germany* and *France* in *Calvin's*
dayes; againft whome that heavenly foul, gave his
powerfull and heavenly witnefs in his Book againft
the *Libertines*. Thefe *Libertines* Satan raifed up
about the *Proteftant Reformation* from the ruines
and rubbifh of the old *Manicheans* and *Gnofticks*,
and other blind Guides who fwarmed in the firft
third and fourth Chriftian *Centuryes*, until the *Pope*
fwallowed

The Rife of the word Proteftant.

The Grin-dletonians.

The Lib-ertines.

ſwallowed up all the leſſer *Serpents*, and ſo became a *Dragon* with ſeven Heads and ten Horns, forcing all with fire and Fagot to deny *Chriſt Jeſus*, and to martch under Anti-Chriſt (the *Anti-chriſt* the man of ſin) his Colours.

Some of these *P*articulars I could not then ex-preſs, but think [28] fit here to remember the for-mer dayes, for Information of ſuch as doe deſire it.

Theſe *P*eople came from *Lancaſhire* and other northern parts to the Southward of *England* and to *London*. I ſpake with ſome of their Chief then in *London*, I knew it was the old proud *ſpirit* which had appeared in ſo many foul lyes in their former deceived and deceiving *Leaders*, and I was the more confirmed in my thoughts when I ſaw their foul *ſpirit* ſo tranſport them, not only in lying *Doctrines*, but lying *Quakings* and *Tremblings*, lying preaching through the Streets *Repent, Repent*: and lying and abominable *Nakedneſs* of men and women, untill their ugly Child and Daughter *Rantiſme* roſe from their Bowels and practiſed *Nakedneſs* of men and women in the Streets and in their religious *Meet-ings*, as *Adamites:* when it is notoriouſly known they fell into many *uncleanneſſes* and *Adulteryes*. To my face and to the world in print they maintaind, there were no ſins in them : Saying *That the Saints could not ſin, and God did all and was all*, and they were *as pure as Adam and God himſelf*, this is known by the Writings extant *&c.*

The Rant-ers *are but* the Quak-ers Daughter

2. Again I ſaid unto my *Antagoniſts* that the manner of theſe *quakings* and *ſhakings* were not as. of those *quakings* and tremblings of *David, Moſes,* and
the

the *Corinths* receiving *Titus* with Trembling, or
True Qua- the working out Salvation with *Fear* and *Trembling* :
king for that may many wayes be proved to be the *Soul*
and *Spirit*, out of a holy Aw and Dread of the
Majesty of Heaven with whome we have to deal,
who only can pitty and help us in our deplorable
and forlorn conditions : Hee it is who worketh
the *Will* and the *Deed*, and therefore with deep
impressions of *Aw* and *Dread* we ought to attend
upon all his holy meanes appointed, wherein (as of
old in the Tabernacle and Temple) he hath promised to come to us. Beside, as it is naturall for the
Body to tremble when the mind doth, as we see in
many Persons in the beginning of a Battle, or going over a deep Water, or going to suffer Death,
or looking over a high *Clift* into the sea &c. So
when the Bodies of those holy men, or any now
doe so tremble *Experience* proves it that it is no
ordinary motion, but extraordinary, and upon
extraordinary occasions, and those holy and heavenly Occasions, as may be instanced.

But the quaking and shaking motions of the
Quakers (as I shall prove) they proceeded not from
The horrid those holie Affections [29] proper to Gods Chil-
shaking of dren, so also they were horrid and monstrous cast-
the Qua- ing their bodies into horrid and monstrous motions
kers. and Gestures which mine eyes have seen : Besides
the abundance of notorious Instances, what strange
horrid motions are those which *Theora John* (as he
madly calls himself) and *John Toldervy* were tost
and tumbled up and down with? which cannot
be

be imagined to proceed from the holy *Spirit of God*, but from Sathan to delude and cheat poor finners with.

To this purpofe I told them at the firft coming of this fpirit to *London* and *Weftminfter*, fome *Parliament men* told me that themfelves went to one of the *Quakers* Meetings about *Charing Crofs*, but were fo affrighted with the *fhaking* of their own bodies, and of their *Chairs* and Stooles under them, that they could never again be got into their *Affemblyes*.

I added, that fuch *Shakings, Motions, Extafies,* &c. were known to be the frequent workings of *Sathan* upon his Servants in all ages, Such were the furious motions of *Baals Preifts*, the motions of the *Poffeffed* mentioned in the *Gofpells*, and other *Hiftoryes*, and known to be amongft the *Barbarians*, our Neighbours about this time. *John Burnet* and *William Edmunfon* rofe up and faid that I had laid many deep and heavy *Charges* upon the people of the Lord, which I fhould never be able to prove: I had denied them to be *Chriftians*, and fo had wronged the good Spirit of God in them, and their Profeffion of worfhipping God in the Spirit: Yea I had taken away their being (as men) out of the World, as a dangerous *People* to *Nations* and *Kingdomes* & *Common-weales*, yea to *Kings* & *Princes*, and fo not fit to live amongft men in the World. Thefe Speeches were often uttered and enlarged by one or other of them, and that with Zeal (and Paffion in *W. Edmunfon*)

I waited patiently till thefe *Gufts* of their angry
Spirit

Satans Counter-feit motions.

The Quakers Anfwer.

Spirit was over, and then I told them I had not wronged them in a tittle: But by the help of the moſt High I would make all good againſt them; & toen leave it to every mans and womens Soul to judge at their own *Perill*.

About this time *John Stubs* alleadged that of *Paul*, Phil 2. *Work out ſalvatson with fear and Trembling.*

Quaking and Trembling I replyed I in no way oppoſed the awfull and moſt ſerious impreſſions of *Gods Majeſty* in all his appearances & ordinances upon the Soules and Spirits, yea and *Bodyes* of Gods Children. [30] But I denied that thoſe places to the *Corinthians* and *Philippians* concerned any ſuch bodily ſhakings and quakings as we now debated.

No Ordinance of God Beſide I ſaid if *Quaking* and *Trembling* were a Command and an Ordinance, and inſtitution of God to. be practiſed, then was it conſtantly to be practiſed (as the *Jewes* ſay of *Cain* that the Mark which God ſet upon him was a conſtant *Trembling*) Or if not alwayes, yet alwayes in *Worſhip*, or if not alwayes in *Worſhip* yet at ſome certain times. But

Counterfeit Quaking and Trembling the plain truth is, the *Devill* will be *Gods Ape* in moſt things: He ſubornes and ſubſtitutes a baſtard *Quaking and Trembling* of the body in Imitation of *David, Moſes &c.* on purpoſe to thruſt out the true Fear and Trembling which ought to be conſtantly in us, raiſing up all our Affections and all within us to a due ſence of the *Terror* of the Lord, the dreadfulneſs of our *Danger*, and the wonder of our *Deliverance* (which we can never make too ſure) from ſin and wrath to come to all eternity.

I alfo declared, that the *moft High* and holy one, was free as he pleafed to caufe the trembling of the *Soules* of his People to over flow with influence upon their *Bodyes* alfo, asin *Mofes, David, Daniel, Habakkuk, Paul, &c.* this is like to be in fome extraordinary cafes and *Converfions* or turnings to God, as *Paul's* was, and that efpecially in bringing of *great Sinners* or *old Sinners* unto himfelf *&c.*.

There were fome few Speeches, fome from the *Governour* and his Wife, and fome few others that fpake, fome in favor of, and fome againft the *Quakers,* but neither did my Oppofites nor I fo far attend them as to engage with them, excepting fome Turnes that were between *William Edmunfon,* and *William Hitchcock* (an Inhabitaut of *Newport*) who (as others did) witneffed againft their upbraiding me with my age (*Old man, Old man* &c.) as alfo for their *Interruptions.*

Mine own Brother Mr *Robert Williams,* SchoolMafter in *Newport,* defired to fpeak : nor he nor others diffenting from them could be permitted, except they would fet their hands to my Paper. A Paper put in of My Brother (unknown to me) put in a paper to them, which he took the liberty to read, defiring two great that two things might be anfwered by the *Quakers.* Confiderations 1· The matter of the true fence of *Sin* as Sin. 2. Of the *Materiallity* of fuch a Perfon as the *Lord Jefus Chrift,* and the materiallity of his [31] *Bloudfhedding.* This Paper they took but waved it. *W. Edmunfon* openly charged me with breach of Covenant, *viz.* That if any would fpeak on my behalf, they fhould fet their hand to my *Propofitions.* Tis

8   true

true it was defired by one of them at my houfe at *Providence*, that if any joined with me, they fhould fubfcribe to my *P*aper.   But I anfwered that I was *alone* in the Bufinefs, I had not confulted with any others but the God of heaven himfelf: fo that I denied vehemently that there was any fuch agreement, or any colour for it. Befides it was ridiculous to put either fuch a *Bar* and Limit upon any mans fpirit, and leaft of all upon Gods *Spirit*, *viz*, that no man fhould defire leave to object or querie *&c.* except firft he would fubfcribe my *Propofalls·* But I took the boldnefs juftly to charg them with palpable and grofs *Partiality* viz. that *W*. *Hitchcock* and others, (oppofing or diffenting) might not fpeak, but *W*. *Harris*, *W*. *Dyar* or any favouring of them might fpeak without exception, becaufe all that fpeak for their ptetended light, it muft be fuppofed that they fpeak from the Spirit of God himfelf: others out of *Ignorance*, *Malice and Envy*: this will appear more afterward.

 However, there were thefe few debates about the liberty of fpeech in the Auditory and By-ftanders, and the *Quakers* deniall and enjoining of *Subfcription*: yet the moft High, *Father of Spirits* did fo compofe all fpirits, that it was wonderfull that fuch *Oppofites* fhould goe through fuch a work and Conflict all day untill night, without more *Interruptions* and *Difturbances*.

 I was ready and waited to put forth my third Reafon to prove they were not true Chriftian Quakers, it was from Ifai. 66. *To this man will I look that is poor and contrite, and trembleth at my* Word. I
told

The unequall Termes of the Quakers enjoining Subfcription.

& their open Partiality·

told them that *G.Fox* in his Book all along was ſo
far from trembling at the *Word of God* in the holy
Writings or *Scriptures*, that he could not endure
they ſhould have that name, or be once called the *The Qua-*
Word of God, Tis true I know his pretence, that *kers evill*
Chriſt Jeſus is called the *Word of God*, Rev. 19. *ſpirit to-*
But I know tis true alſo that he grants the Scrip- *ward the*
tures to be true, and inſpired from the holy *Spirit* *holy Scrip-*
of God, and to be Gods words, though not his *Word*. *tures.*
Well, to paſs by the ſimplicity of the *Diſtinction*,
and let us take what he grants, and is it not prodigious and monſtrous Contempt that theſe holy Words,
this holy Book and Writing of God ſhould be ſo
undervalued and ſlighted, yea vilified [32] and nul- *The Light*
lified, if compar'd with their pretended *new found* *of each*
Light within them, which was (ſay they) before the *man in the*
Scriptures, and gave forth the *Scriptures*, and there- *above the*
fore was above the *Scriptures* and gave forth the *Scriptures.*
Scriptures, and therefore was above the *Scriptures*,
and therefore is not judged or tried by the *Scrip-*
tures, but they by it. Yea, and this light muſt be
in every one of mankind in the whole World :
Hence it was that theſe holy Writings were ſo
diſuſed in their own private Readings, in their
Publick Worſhip, and in their Families. *The Pope*
I told them God was little beholding to the *Pope* *Quakers*
and the *Quakers* for their humble Reverence and *great affec-*
great Affection to his holy *Letters*, *Declarations* and *tion and*
Proclamations. The Pope had his *Infallibility* as *ownneſs*
well as they, his immediate *Inſpirations* as well *holy Scrip-*
as they : They both owned, and yet did not owne *tures.*
the *holy Scriptures*, the *Pope* and they only muſt
interpret

interpret *Scriptures*, they only give the *Sence*, they only judge all *Controverfies*: yea they difpence with the *Scriptures*, and if they were quite loft and burn'd and not a Copy of them left in the World, yet there were no lofs but a good Turn, a good Riddance, for then the *Pope* and the *Quakers Infallible fpirit* and its immediate *Infpirations*, would be more efteemed and fet by.

An In-
ftance of a
long-haird
profane
Qua. flight-
ing *Nature*
and the
Scriptures.
I produced an Inftance of one *Thurfton* an Apof-tle of theirs who came to *Providence* with extraordinary long hair hanging over his fhoulders; It was fo long that an aged Soul (captivated for prefent amongft them) the wife of *C.S.* demanded of him why he ware it fo long fince Nature it felf did teach it to be a fhame for a man to wear *long Hair*, as the *holy Scripture* affirmed? He would not fay, He car'd not what *Nature* or the holy *Scriptures* faid, but he faid as much in effeét (as fhe told me her felf, and may with true fear and trembling ftill think on it) *viz.* when that God that bid me wear it, bids me cut it off, then will I cut it off. As if he would fay, what tell you us of the teachings of *Nature* (as we fee in that monftrous cafe of their womens *Nakednefs*) or what tell you me of Scripture? I have a *Light* within me that made that *Light*, was before it, gave it forth, & is above it. This mans hair was fo offenfive and odious, that meeting of me, and faying, *Fear the Lord God*, I could not but anfwer him in thefe words, *viz. What God doft thou mean a Ruffians God?* alluding to that of *Paul* to *Titus*, *They profefs to know God, but in their Works they deny him.*

[33] I

33| I told them the rage of the Devill in all Ages had been moſt fierce againſt theſe heavenly *Records,* in which the moſt gracious God and *King,* out of the infinite depths of his Wiſdome and Goodneſs, had provided for the Ages and Generations to come the glorious *Appearances* of the eternall *Inviſible King* in the former *Generations* of mankind · from the Creation of the World, as alſo the *Wonders* yet to be finiſhed till time ſhould be no more, all which were in the holy *Scriptures.*

I remembred them of a profane bloudy Wretch in *Ireland* who in the late horrid *Maſſacre,* hunting (among other bloudie Wolves) after the Goods and Lives of the *Proteſtants,* found a *Bible,* and with Indignation (the ſame which I believe is in moſt *Papiſts* and *Quakers*) he flung it into the *Kennell,* and *ſtampt* upon it with his feet ſaying, *A Plague of God take this Book, this hath cauſed all the Quarrels among us.* *An horible Inſtance in Ireland againſt the Holy Scriptures.*

Whether I ſpake all theſe *Particulars* at one individuall time or Turn I cannot clearly remember, only I am certain thus I ſpake and more.

My Oppoſites once and again had Turnes of Speech, but ſtill the only Sum of all was, that they owned the *Scripture,* but yet the *Spirit* that gave it forth was above it, withall they urged that I could not prove where in the Scripture, the *Scripture* was called *the Word of God.*

I Anſwered, That many things were infallibly ſo, and true although not in ſo many Terms and Words mentioned : But yet there were abundance of *Scriptures* wherin the *Prophets* did expreſly ſay, *The Scriptures the word of God.*

Thus

*Thus faith the Lord, The Word of the Lord came unto
me,* and Hebr. 1. *The Lord fpake diverfe wayes, and
at diverfe times in the Prophets, but now he hath fpoken
by his Son.* Sure his Speech is his Word: Hence
the *Word of God* is the Word preached, as *Paul,* 2
Theff. 1. *Not as the* word *of man, but as it is indeed
the* Word *of God, Act.* 19 which preaching· of the
Word & growing of the word were not compe-
tent and proper expreffions to be affirmed of the
perfon of the *Lord Jefus;* efpecially I told them I
would ufe the words of the *Lord Jefus* when he
fought with the *Devil* that famous *Combate, Math.* 4.
No other Weapon did he ufe againft him but γέτραπτοι
It is written, and again, *It is written, It is written,*
here *Chrift Jefus* quotes *Dut* 8. *Man fhall not live
by bread only, but by every word that proceedeth out of
the mouth of God:* where *Mofes* and *Chrift Jefus*
affirm [34] that God hath many words, contrary to
what fome *Quakers* hath affirmed to me faying, *that
God hath no more words but one,* and *Chrift Jefus* here
affirmeth, That every appearance and providence
of God, is a word proceeding out of the mouth of
God, as well as this holy Scripture he alleadged.
Though yet it is true, that *Chrift Jefus* is the *Word,*
or declared Mind of *God,* incomparably above all his
fpoken or *written* or *providentiall* Words and Expreffions: He came out of the *Bofome* of the *Eternal
Father,* and brought the brighteft Revelations of
his eternal *God-head* & *Councels,* and therefore is
moft juftly and eminently ftiled the *Word of God.*
  I urged that the *Word* or *Words* of God were
Figurative Speeches, for properly God had no *Mouth,*
nor

nor *Tongue*, nor *Lips*, nor *Heart* nor *Brains* &c. but
as our *Kings* Majesty his *Declaration* touching *Re-*
ligion, his royal *Charters*, his *Letters* from *Breda* are
often insisted on and urged by the *Quakers* as the
word of a *King*, though his writings contain many
hundred words; so it is with the *King of Heaven* his
Scriptures and writings &c.

I had oft occasion to mention G. *Fox* and *Ed. Bur-*
rowes their *Book* in Folio called *The great Mystery*
&c. upon which *W Edmundson* reproved me for
speaking of G. *Fox* and *E. Burrowes* in scorn and
derision (so his words were) I guest he took me as
if I had scornfully intended G *Fox* in his *Burrowes*, *The Occa-*
but I had openly purged my self, protesting before *sion of the*
the Lord, that I had no such thought, yet this Pas- *Title of*
sage was the occasion of the *Title* of the *Book*: For *this Book.*
the finger of *Gods* most wise and holy *Providence*
is often wonderfuliy seen in small, unexpected & in-
considerable Turns and Occasions: In such poor
shells oftimes may be found the *Kernels* of rich
and usefull *Observations.* Sure (thought I) Gods
holy Finger is in it, that G. *Fox* and *Ed. Burrowes*
(Men so qualified and named) should so notoriously conspire against the true *Lord Jesus Christ* in
their dark and subtle hellish Contrivings and *Imagi-*
nations. It was also Gods overruling hand that
VV. Edmundson should so upbraid me, and first put
the *Conceit* and thought of such a Consideration into me, which I apprehended as *Digitus Dei* the
finger of God directing and pointing me to so proper and pertinent an use and Application.

Thus the only Wise and Righteous *King* catcheth
the

(54)

the craftieſt *Foxes* in their own *Burrowes*, and turns their proud Surmiſes & Cenſures upon their own *Pates*. This occaſioneth me with Amaze- [35] ment and Aſtoniſhment to cry out *O God how deep are thy* Being, *thy* Attributes, *thy* Providences, *thy* Self *and all thy wayes beyond our thoughts and finding out* !

To proceed, I had obſerved and prepared many *Quotations* out of G. *Fox* his Book, but they deſired not to hear them read, as in the following dayes of *Conference* they were read by my continual importunate Urgings: I ſay at firſt I could not get oportunity to infiſt upon ſome Particulars, a Taſt whereof I think now fit to preſent the Reader with.

In *Page* 155. of G. *Foxes* aforeſaid Book he brings in one *J Stallam* their Oppoſite ſaying [*To ſay the Light in every man gave forth* Scripture, *and will open* Scripture *to us, is palpable* Darkneſs, *and contradicts the* Scripture] G. *Fox* anſwers, [*All be in utter* Darkneſs *and know not the* Scripture, *untill they come to the* Light *that every man was in that gave forth* Scripture, *for the* Light *lets them ſee to what it was ſpoken, and* Chriſt *the end of them.*

G *Fox* his prodigious *Folly* and *Impiety.*

The engliſh of that Anſwer is, That every man, that is all *Mankind* Men and Women if they will, can give forth *Scriptures*, or write holy *Scriptures*: I know they call this Light, *God*, and *Chriſt*, and *Spirit*, the *Covenant of God*, the *Life*, *Truth* and *Grace of God*.

Pertinent *Queryes* and unanſwerable.

I aſked them in publick[Since this Light comes into this World in and with all Mankind, whether it comes into them at the *Conception*, or at the *Birth*, or when elſe ?

Whether it was in all *Mankind* before the coming and

and death of *Chrift Jefus* or whether to thofe that
are in the world fince his coming, or both? Whether it be in the *Underftanding, Will,* M*emory, Affec-*
tions in any of them feverally, or lodg d in all of
them jointly? For it was a prodigious *Fable* to
imagine fuch a *Sun* to fhine in every Room of an
houfe, and yet none of the Inhabitants, nor any that
come into the house difcern and fee it: *Chrift Je-*
fus faith, *as the mouth is, the heart is, and before a*
true turning unto God, we are in darknefs, we are
darknefs, we hate the light of *God* and endure not
to fee it, but wifh there were no *God,* no *Father of*
Lights to difcover and plague us for our dark
Courfes *:* yet our *Hearts* are fo *cunning* and *cheating*
that they will tell us that we have *Light* and *Chrift*
and *God* within us, and that we can fpeak and write
holy Scripture, not remembring that (as *Chrift Jefus*
faid of the *Temple*) our hearts are *Dens* of Thieves
and (like-painted *Tombs*) full of dead mens bones
and rottennefs, [36] untill a fecond *Birth* by the
VVord and *Spirit* of *Chrift Jefus.*

  Again, in the fame Page G. *Fox* brings his Oppofite faying, [*And to fay every mans* Light *is the true*
word of Prophecy *is* an old Fable, *no man fhall be*
able to fpell out a fyllable of the Gofpel *by all that is*
written in a mans Heart.] This fubtle Fox anfwers,
[*The Light that enlightens every man is* Chrift, *and*
the fure Word of Prophecy *to him he fhall find it*]
In this Paffage who can but fee their *horrible* and
fimple profaning and wrefting of plain *Scripture:*
Is it not clear as day to him that is not willingly
blind, that this *word of prophecy* in *Peter,* is the
Word

Word which the *Prophets* fpake and writ of *Chrift*
Jefus, unto whome the fpirit of God in *Peter* fends
us, as being a more fure and convincing *word* to us
then that voice which *Peter* and *Iohn* affirmed that
they heard from heaven in the Mount of *Tranffigu-*
ration? But thus *profanely* and *fimply* do others of
them affirm this *Light* to be that *Prophet* which
Mofes wrote of, *Deut.* 18. whereas the *holy Spirit* in
Stephen Acts 7. applyes exprefly that *Prophefie* to
the perfon of the *Lord Iefus*, that *God-man* in one
perfon, whome *Mofes* and *Stephen* preached the
great *Meffiah*, or *Chrift* the anointed *Prophet, Prieft*
and *King* unto all that receive or believe in him.

The tu-
multuous
fpirit of the
Quakers in
Difputing.
    Now diverfe obferving and publickly expreffing
how unfuitable it was that three of the ableft
Speakers amongft them fhould *Confult* openly and
whifper and utter themfelves one immediately after
each other, and fomtimes *all together* as one man
againft me *:* *W.Edmondfon* anfwered and excufed it
faying, that it was mine own *Paper* (which he often
produced) which expreft my Offer to make good
my *Pofitions* againft all *Comers* : But I replyed
(once and again) That as God is a God of *Order*,
and doth all things in *Number, Weight* and *Meafure*,
in moft admirable *Order* and *Method*, fo I had
thought that (according as I writ and fpake to
them) they would have had so much *Ingenuity* to
conceive, that nor I nor any man was fo fimple as
to offer to Difpute with, to oppofe and to anfwer
twenty or thirty or one hundred at once *:* But thus
'Tis hard to
hold the
  like fubtle and impudent *Foxes* and *Iefuites* they
pleaded and practifed from the beginning of the
Conference

Conference unto the end of the *4th* day, refolving to ^{Foxians} make ufe of and (like dying men by drowning) to ^{or any guil-}_{ty difputant} catch at any ridiculous *Advantage* though *unchrif-* ^{to a fair} *tian* and *uncivill*. _{Difpute.}

But the truth is, this and many other *Difcourage-ments* and *Difadvantages* and *Difficultyes* the *Lord Iefus* gracioufly and faithfully [37] (For his name fake) enabled me to cut through, otherwife I faw the *Debate* would not have held on fo many *Hours* as it did *Dayes*, I knew they had as much mind to this work (no nor any guilty *Soul* in the world) as *Bears* to be tyed to a ftake to be baited; and I muft humbly declare and predicate it (to the praife of the *Father of mercyes*, and for the incouragement of others to be *Patient* for *Chrift Iefus* fake) that an hand from heaven caried me through to the end of each day, and to the end of the whole bufinefs.

Sometimes I offered to proceed to an other *Point*, but all this firft day was fpent upon the firft *Point* of *true* and *falfe Quakers*: For though many upon a fudden fpake as *Mr. Coddington Mr. Eafton* (then Governour, who fpake fharply) *VVilliam Dyer*, *VVilliam Harris* and others againft me, yet I minded clofely what my *Antagonifts* vented, who were placed on high in their *Defk* againft me : *Iohn Stubs* and *Iohn Burnet* were more fober and manly, but *VV. Edmundfon* (who was the junior of three) would fpeak all like *Solomons* foolifh woman, *loud* and *clamorous*, *fimple* and *knowing nothing*, being in truth nothing but a *flafh* of wit, a *Face of Brafs*, and a *Tongue* fet on *fire* from the *Hell of Lyes and Fury*.

One

One *Inſtance* here fell out, for when I urged that
it was not what man had *within him* already, and
brought into the world with him, that made a true
Quaker, but the *Spirit of God* accompanying and
bleſſing the *Reading* and *Hearing* of the *writings*
of *God preached* and *opened*: I ſaid the *Heart* of man
was ſhut up lockt and barr'd up in *willing Ignorance*
and *darkneſs* until the *finger of God* in the uſe of
thoſe and other bleſſed meanes, *pick* open in a more
gentle way, or *break* open by great afflictions and
and *terrours* the *Soul* and *Spirit* of man.   I ſaid
that *Paul* preached the *word* by the River ſide, but
the Lord opened the heart of *Lydia*: and while I
was ſaying that, *It was not Paul nor Pauls Preach-*
ing nor the word that he preached----- at this word
VV. Edmondſon clamour'd out, *He ſpeakes Blaſphe-*
my: But it pleaſed God to move the heart of our
Deputy-Governour Capt. *Cranſton* juſtly and ſeaſona-
bly to witneſs againſt this *Interruption* ſaying, *Let*
him have liberty to make out his mind: So I proceeded
and ſaid, it may be *VV. Edmnndſon* is offended as
thinking I ſpoke againſt the *word Chriſt*; but *Chriſt*
Ieſus knowes that I had no ſuch thought, but of the
words which *Paul* ſpake.   And I added that it was
not *Lydia* nor all her *Light* within her, nor *Paul*
nor [38] his *Preaching*, nor the *word* nor *words*
that he uttered, but the Finger of *Gods Spirit* (according to *Election*) that ſet the *word* or *words* of
Paul home, opening her *heart*, and not every heart,
(ſhewingwhat free grace is againſt the *Popiſh* and
Arminian and *Foxians* exalting of *Curſed Nature*)
and then it was that ſhe being by the Lord turned,
ſhe

*W. Ed-
mondſoo
juſtly re-
proved by
the Depu-
ty Gover-
nor Capt.
Cranſton*

fhe turned to attend & apply to her foul the words which were fpoken by *Paul,* as a poor *Rams-horn* made ufe of in the hand of *God.*

Toward the end of the day *VV. Edmondfon* fell into a long *Invective,* how I had falfly flandered the *People of God,* not only in this place, but the whole Body of the People of the *Lord* called *Qua-kers* in all parts: For faid he we are a great people, many thoufands in *England,* many thoufands in *London,* befides in *Virginia* and *Barbadoes* and other places, and *N-England.* And he and they faid, haft thou any more to fay to make out thy *Lyes* againft them. *The Fox-ians boaft of their Number.*

I Anfwered (as at other times) that the *Papifts* the common *Proteftants,* the *Jews* and the *Mahumi-tans* and *Pagans, &c.* fited the world with their *Numbers,* and yet we jointly oppofed them in *Relig-ious matters* notwithftanding their *innumerable num-bers* : And as for more proof that they were not *True Quakers,* and fo truly *Feariug and Tremb-ling* before *God,* I told them I would produce an Argument, that they were fo far from being *Chrift-ians,* that they were a to be *exploded* and *abhorred* of all *Mankind,* as being fallen beneath the com-mon *temper* and *nature* of the *Humanity* of men and women, yea of the Savage and *Barbarous* in the world, *viz.* their ftripping *ftark naked* their *Men* and *Women* and *Maidens* and paffing along in publick places and *Streets* unto the *Affemblyes of Men* and *Youths* and fo were beheld and gazed upon by them! and this under a pretence of being ftirred up by God as a *Service* or *Worfhip* unto God,

God, as an act of *Christian Religion* proceeding from the immediate moving of the most holy *Spirit of God*, most glorious in purity, and purity and holiness it self.

At first *W. Edmundson* seemed to make strange of the matter as if it could not be proved that any of their women should so appear in the *Assemblyes* of People. I told them the matter of *fact* was so notorious that it would be loss of time and *Impudence* to question it, being so fouly and openly *practised* both in *Old* and *New England*.

Two of the Foxian women naked in New England.

39] Also I added further, that G. *Bishop* of *Bristow*, one of themselves, in the second part of the *Persecutions of New-England*, relates in print the names of two women in *N-England* that did so practice: and he complains of *N-England Persecution* because those women suffered *Whipping for* those actions by the *Courts* and *Officers* of *N-England*.

John Burnet said that the People called *Quakers*, were a People known to abhor all *Impurity* and Uncleanness and the *Appearance* of it, and if any of their women should so practice, they should condemn it in them, yet nevertheless if it should please the *Lord God* to stir up any of his *Daughters* so to appear as a *Sign* and *Testimony* against the *Nakedness* of others, they durst not condemn it.

John Stubs said, that they did condemn all immodest *Appearances* in women, both in *Behaviour* and *Gestures* . But if God stirred them up and commanded them to this service to discover the *Nakedness* of others, they could not but acknowledge

Gods

Gods hand, and fubmit to it: And he further added, that it was a great *Crofs* to a fober womans fpirit fo to act, as well as an affliction and fuffering to her body.

John Stubs likewife alleadged the *Prophet Ifaiah*, (as alfo did *W.E.*) and the *Sign* of the Prophet *Eze-kiel*: and *John Stubs* read the 20*th* of *Ifa*. where *Ifaiah* was commanded to goe *naked* for a *Sign* to the *Egyptians* and *Ethyopians*, to prophefie and de-nounce that they alfo fhould go naked with their buttocks uncovered as the words are: and this is (faid they) a proof that the *People* of the Lord might be ftirred up by *God* to fuch actions for *Signs* unto others.   Ifai. 20 *dif-cuffed touching* Nakednefs

I Anfwered, that this was in the dayes of *Fig-ures* and *Signs*, Shadows and *Ceremonyes*: And though this was *G.Fox* his Anfwer (in his Book which I had there by me) yet *G.Fox* throughout all this his Book in *Folio*, turns of the Allegations and Arguments of many of his *Oppofites* with this Anfwer, *to wit*, *The* Subftance *is come*, the Body *is come*, Chrift *the* End *of the* Law, *the* End *of the* Command, *the* End *of the* Scriptures, *the* End *of the* Prophets, *and of all* Signs *and* Shadows *and* Figures.

2.   Although it were fo threatned that the *Ethi-opians* and *Egyptians* fhould fo goe *totally* and *ftark Naked*, and that *Ifaiah* did fo, which is much quef-tioned: yet it is not to be queftioned but that the *Egyptians* and *Ethiopians* in their flight, would cover [40] their *Secret parts* with the firft cloaths or raggs they could get, as it is no queftion but the Prophet *Ifaiah* did.

3.   The

3. The difference of *Nakedneſs* of *Mankind* and *Womankind* is very great in all *Nations*. The *Sex* of *Women* is more fitted and framed by God for a *Covering*, for *Retiredneſs* and keeping at home and for *Modeſty* and *Baſhfulneſs*; nor do we ever read that ever God commanded ſuch a thing to Women, or that ever it came into his heart, or that ever any *Godly Woman* did ſo practice : there is no ſhadow or colour of *Proof* from the holy *Scripture*, nor from any *Civill* and ſober *People*, no nor from the naked *Barbarians* themſelves, who though they ſuffer their *Male Children* to go naked till about ſeven years old, yet cover they their *Females* from their birth : Tis true it is ſaid in *Braſil* and other bruitiſh places ſome *Savage bruits* go ſo, but they are *Canibals*, *Men-eaters*, &c· and other B*arbarians* do not ſo except in *Drunkenneſs* and *Madneſs*.

They ſtill anſwered, that they would not *Countenance* any ſuch *Practice* but if the *Lord God* ſo commanded his *Sons* and *Daughters* it muſt be obeyed.

I demanded of them how it ſhould be known that it was the voice and command of *God*, the *God* of *Holineſs*, and not the command of the unclean *ſpirit* ? for I told them that under that Cover that one of them might be ſo commanded, and ſent of God in ſuch a poſture and behaviour amongſt men, why might not ten or twenty, yea all the women in this preſent *Aſſembly* be ſo ſtirred up as it were by the *Spirit* of *God* to the horror and amazement of the whole *Countrey* yea of the whole *World?*

They ſeemed to me to be *Confounded* with this

The true voice of God, and many falſe and pretended.

Argumnet

Argumnet and weary to hear of it, and not willing to *Immeaiate*
ſpeak to it : I therefore took occaſion my ſelf to ſay *Inſpira-*
that it was true in former Diſpenſations. The Com- *tions and*
mand of God came to *Abraham* to kill his own *tions.*
Child, his ſon *Iſaac*, and this faƈt enjoined him did
ſeem as horrible *unnatural* and *cruel,* as this *Naked-*
ueſs of the Women unwomanly and *unnatural.* But,

1. It was in the day and diſpenſation of ſuch
wonderfull *Signs* and figurative teachings unto men.

And 2. I ſaid *God* did furniſh them with a Spirit of diſcerning the *true* dream from the falſe, the
true voice from the falſe, the voice of *God* from the
voice of *Sathan* : But in our day wherein God had
altered his Diſpenſations and Revelations which
he [41] uſed to the *Fathers*, and had ſpoken to us
by his *Son*, and had left his mind both in the *old*
and *new Scriptures* or Writings : We have the example and Preſident of the *Lord Jeſus*, that is, to
attend to the holy *Scriptures* only, and to uſe the
weapon of | *It is written it is written*] againſt *Sa-*
thans immediate *Inſpirations* and temptations.

Here *W. Edmondſon* fel into a great heat againſt
me and ſaid that I ſpoke *Blaſphemy*, in ſaying that
Abraham and the *Saints* then had a way and Spirit
of diſcerning the Spirits which we had not, implying that Gods Spirit was not the ſame : He added,
that I had kept them long and had proved nothing,
and yet we had not done with the firſt *Poſition.* I
replyed, that I had produced ſuch *Grounds* as ſhould
never be ſhaken, and that I preſumed did appear to
the *Conſciences* of many, and I heartily deſired might
alſo appear unto their Spirits, Soules, and *Conſci-*

10   *ences.*

ences. Some of the Auditors fpake to this Purpofe, efpecially *W. Hitchcocks* who infifted upon the *Water Baptifme.*

And thus by Gods *Mercy* and Patience the Difcourfe of the firft day ended: which very day was notable and *fignificant* as to the created *Sun* in the Heavens, who in the midft of our Conteft was eclipfed, and hid his Face remarkably, and preached aloud to us, that although the true *Lord Jefus Chrift* the *Sun* of Righteoufnefs do fuffer (in his infinite wifdom and and Patience) falfe *Chrifts* and falfe *Prophets* and *Herod* and *Pontius Pilate,* and his enemies of all forts, *Jewes* and *Gentiles,* to cloud his *Face* and *Glory* a little from the World and his own People, yet he will break forth again in his eternal brightnefs, fplendor and glory.

The Eclipfe of the Sun in the midft of the firft dayes Difputation.

When that heavenly young *Martyr* or Witnefs of *Jefus Chrift William Hunter* was burnt at *Burntwood* in *Effex* it was a clofe and gloomy day, but this gallant young Champion of *Jefus Chrift* crying out aloud at the ftake, *Son of God look on me, Son of God fhine upon me!* immediately that moft wonderfull *Light & Fire* of Heaven the *Sun* tore the clouds and brake forth and fhined glorioufly aud remarkably upon the face of this bleffed *Witnefs* at the fuffering of the flames of fire, for *Jefus* his truth fake againft the *whorifh Principles* of both the *Papifts & Quakers:* and thus do the holy writings tel us, that this moft glorious light *the Sun of Righteoufnefs,* vifibly appeared in his glorious and glorified Form and Shape to the vifible eye of his fervant *Steven* while he patiently fuffered for the true

A Note of W. Hunter burnt in Effex at Burnt wood.

true *Lord Jesus* sake the murthering Stones to lay
him down to sleep.

42] THE second day of our Spiritual *Contest &
Battle* being come, (being the tenth of the
sixth Moneth August (so called) I heartily wished
that I might rather have kept my *Bed* then have
gone forth to a whole dayes fresh *Dispute* with such
(reputed) able and noted *Champions*. Not that the
most high Lord *Jesus* whose cause and *Name* I was
that day to manage, for the next point was about
the true *Lord Jesus Christ*) not that I say he faild
me in my *Resolution* to march on against *Men* and
Devils for his Name sake; nor that he faild me in
my cheerfull *Confidence* that he would carry me in
the everlasting armes of his *Power* and *Goodness*
through that dayes Conflict (as he had done the
day before) but that he was pleased to try me with
more than ordinary *Weakness* and mouldring of my *My great
house. of Clay*, that so my strength might be in a *Indisposed-
ness of body*
great respect immediately from Heaven, consider- *to the sec-*
ing my great unfitness for this dayes Service : for *ond dayes
Contest.*
thus it was, My continued *loud Speech* all the day
before had left an impression of *Hoarsness* upon
me, and much *rain* falling that afternoon (after the
Eclipse) I took some wet in my feet that evening,
so that my *Hoarseness* increased, and all that day
my *Head* was afflicted with pain, and my voice with
a painfull *Hoarsness*. I lookt up to heaven, and *Prayer*
desired to wait as a *Begger* at the *Gate*, and as a *Dog* *and
Patience.*
under the table of *Mercy*, and my Spirit was chear-
fully resolved not to give occasion of *Reproaching*
the

the name of God to them who (I knew) waited and watched for it, nor any *Difappointment* to fuch as were refolved to attend the Meeting.

This day I chofe a middle Seat neerer to the Seat of my three *Antagonifts J. Stubs, J. Burnet. W. Edmondfon* that fo I might be heard the better with lefs *ftraining* of my *Voice* and *Breaft*.

I began and ftood up and faid, the holy Scriptures by the Prophet *Jeremiah* told us of certain *Bow-men*, fome that bent their *Tongues* as *Bowes* for Lyes and complain'd that none were *Valiant* for the *Truth* : I told my oppofites that they and I were met as *Bow men*, and I could heartily defire that all our *Arrowes* might fly one way, to wit in the defence of the true *Lord Jefus Chrift* againft the falfe : But fince I had charged them in my fecond *Pofition* to have fet up a *falfe Chrift* in ftead of the *true Lord Jefus* I fhould addrefs my felf to make probation of my fecond *Pofition*. Yet before I enter upon it, I pray the *Readers Patience* to be acquainted with fome *Particulars*.

43] *Firft*. Though my head was ill, and my *voice & fpeech* hoarfe and painfull, yet the Lord gracioufly carried me through the the whole day with little hindrance in my felf, and little difadvantage to the underftanding of the *Auditors*.

Secondly. This dayes Difcourfe was but accidental and additional; for they and I defired to have finifhed the the whole firft feven *Pofitions* in one day at *Newport*, only in my paper I added, that if the whole feven were not finifhed in one day, the *Conference* might continue fome few hours the next

day

Spiritual
*Bowmen &
Gunners*

*The fecond
days
Conteft.*

day following: on this fecond day therefore was a great Affembly, the *Governour, Magiftrates, Inhabitants and ftrangers*, Men and Women, &c. And this dayes Conteft alfo held unto the Evening.

Thirdly. As I had beg'd of God a Spirit of *Patience* to bear all their *Cenfures, Reproachings, Revilings, Vapourings and Infultings*, fo it pleafed God to exercife me with one notorious though private,' *That I was Drunk, and could not fpeak that day as I had done the day before:* But my Daughter *Hart*, at whofe houfe I lodged, and *John Trip* fen. who lodged with me can teftifie that I complained of *Illnefs*, and eat but a few fpoonfulls of milk with Mr. *Trip* at Breakfaft: and though my daughter kindly offered me a *Dram* for my *Illnefs*, but I refufed it knowing it might curdle the milk I had taken, and fo increafe my cold and *Obftruction*: & this the moft holy God knowes, and thefe Witneffes know was all I took that morning which might conduce to that foul *Slander* , of being fo *Drunk* that I could not fpeak plainly that day.

A black and fencelefs Imputation.

Fourthly. This day alfo I encountred with that *Difadvantage* of all the three aforefaid *Difputants* at once with all their might fighting for their *Idolls* and *Images* againft me: I fpake of it, and fo did others again and again; But *W. Edmundfon* ftill bruitifhly

The confufed fpirit of the Quakers.

In the copy of this book belonging to the Library of Brown University, are many manufcript erafures, corrections and annotations, in the well-known handwriting of Roger Williams. They were *poffibly* made with the intention of correcting a fecond edition of the book, if fuch had proved defirable. Thefe alterations will all be noted in this reprint and will be defignated as Roger Williams' Manufcript Annotations.

' though private "Vizt." *R. W. Ms. Ann.*

iſhly pleaded that it was mine own *Offer* to undertake all *Comers*: I anſwered as before, that I took
them to be *rational Men*, and by all *Comers* not to underſtand *ten* or *twenty* or *an hundred* confuſedly at
once, but in a fair and equal way, one after an other:
it was grievous & often expreſt by ſome of the
Audience: But as before on the firſt day I reſolved
not to loſe time, or ſuffer a *Breach*: and the Lord
was pleaſed to make my *Yoke eaſie* and *Burthen light*.

The ſecond Poſition.   Now to the proof of my ſecond *Poſition* which was,
That their Chriſt was not the true Lord Jeſus Chriſt.

44] Here I prayed their patience to ſuffer me to
Concerning true & falſe Chriſts tell them that they were not *Chriſtians*, nor Profeſſors of *Chriſtian Religion*: They might (with *Jewes*
& *Turks* & *Papiſts*) profeſs one God, yet *Chriſtians*
they could not be: but as the true Lord Jeſus told
us, many *falſe Chriſt* aud *falſe Prophets* ſhould come,
Traitors & Rebells againſt the King eter-nal & Murther-ers of him. who like *Mountebanks* inſtead of *true Phyſitians*, and
falſe and counterfeit *Money* inſtead of true, ſhould
with *Satans power* and *policy* paſs up and down and
deceive *Peoples* and *Nations*, ſo I muſt affirm and
declare that for their parts they had cut of the head
of the *Chriſtian Religion*, the true *Lord Jeſus
Chriſt*, and they had ſet up a falſe *Chriſt*, a falſe
King, an *Uſurper* in his ſtead, they had like *Michal*
put a wooden *Image* upon a pillow of goats hair in
Davids bed, but *David* himſelf was gone, the true
David, the true Lord Jeſus Chriſt was not to be
found amongſt them: this I ſpake expreſly and
they did hear me awhile.

My proof was, *Firſt*. Becauſe the *Deſcription* and
Character which the holy Scripture gives to the
            true

true *Lord Jesus*, no way agrees with the *Image* which they have set up. I·told them that it was known that the word *Christ* was a greek word sig- *The true* nifing *anointed*, as the word *Messiah* in the Hebrew *Christ* *Lord Jesus* did. I said this true *Lord Jesus* was one Person made up of two *Natures*, *God* and *Man* united into one person, I said one Individual person, whatever *S Fisher* blasphemously utters against it. That as to his *humane Nature* or being *Man*, all the *Figures* and *Ceremonyes*, al the *Priests* and *Sacrifices* pointed to him as the great *Prophet*, the great anointed King and Governour &c. *His hu-*

2. As to his humane *Nature* and being a man *mane na-* *ture woich* and *One Man Moses* and the Prophets wrote of him: G. Fox *all* of his *Mother a Virgin*, of the place of his birth *night long* *Bethlehem*, of his bringing up at *Nazareth:* of his *so barks* *against.* *Scourging* and other sufferings, drinking *Vinegar* and *Gall*, the piercing of his hands and feet, the numb- ring of him with *Malefactors*, the parting of his *Garments* and casting *Lots*, his *burying*, *rising* and *Ascending* &c. and I said all those *Prophesies* and many more were exactly, literally, and punctually fulfilled in and upon that *Individual Person*: so that I affirm, there is such an exact *material and literal Harmony* between the *Prophesies* and the historical *Narration* of his *Birth*, *Life*, *Death*, *Resurrection*, &c. that he must needs be an Unbeliever, (*Jew* or *Gentile*) that doth not acknowledge the admirable Consent and Musick of [45] them in a *literal* and *historical Declaration*.

On the other hand I affimed their *Christ* was but *The Qua-* half a *Christ*, a *Light*, an *Image* or *Picture* or *Fancy* *kers Christ* of *allegorical and meerly Fancy, de-stroying the History.* of a *Chrift* made up of the *Godhead* and their *flefh*, I faid they had fet up a Chrift within them which was but an *Imagination*, an Image, a Chrift in the myftical *Notion:* but in reality *Nothing* : For as the *Papifts* make ufe of the name *Chrift*, and the *Pope* faith he is *Chrifts Vicar* and *Lieftenant*, and he doth all for *Chrift*, and the *Iefuites* (foaring above all *Chriftians*) pretend the name *Iefus*, and yet the *Pro-teftant Witneffes* have made it to appear that in many refpects the *Papifts* are infinitely againft both *Chrift* and *Iefus*, and fo are not *Chriftians* but *Antichrift-ians* : fo I told them did they, they blew a *Trumpet* for *Chrift Iefus*, God in Man, the everlafting Father, that we are *bone* of his bone and *flefh* of his flefh, that he was fo born at *Bethlehem* and dyed at *Ierufa-lem &c*, And yet all thefe fair *Flourifhes* and Col-ours are but as an *Englifh* Flag in a *Spanifh* or *Dutch* or any other Enemies Bottome : For do not all their Books declare that *Chrift is Spiritual*, that *Chrift, God and Man is within us, that his Birth, his Life, his Death, his Burial, his Refurrection, his Afcenfion are wrought within us*, fo that like the Oracles of *Apollo*, and the *Ecchoes* of the *Iefuites* the *Quakers* fay *Chrift was born at Bethlehem* and dyed at *Ierufalem*, but intend in truth and reallity no other *birth* nor *life* nor *death &c.* but what may be extant and wrought in the heart of man.

Hum-phrey Nor-ton deales plainly againft the Perfon of Chrift To this purpofe I told them that *Humphrey Nor-ton* (one that blew the *Trumpet* and beat up the *Drums* in the Name of *Chrift Iefus* as loud as any of them) exprefly writes openly in his Book printed at *London* after his return from hence, to wit, *Is not Chrift*

Chrift God and is not God a Spirit? you look for a Chrift without you, from what coaft or Countrey fhall he come? what Country-man is he? You ftand gazing up in the clouds after a man, but we ftand by in white chiding of you. So that if you fix now really and truly upon a *Man* the *Manhood* and *Humanity* of Chrift, and that he did confift and ftill doth of body and foul (as we doe) then you are gone from, (and *Chriftopher Houlder* in his late Anfwer to *Nathaniell* Morton) are gone from your former *Religion, Tenents* and *Principles,* or elfe you are miferably bewilder'd in your Souls and Confciences, and fome of you moft fearfully *equivocate,* and others muft be fearfully up to the ears in *Boggs & Swamps* not knowing what to hold between this Chrift without, and the |46] Chrift within which you fo much charge upon all except they be *Reprobates.*

The Equivoca- tion of the Foxians.

    I told them I acknowledged *Chrift* within as much as any of them,& infinitely more, for I did confefs that every believing foul did bring home and apply the power and virtue of *Chrifts Birth,* and *Life* and *Death &c.* according to that clear Scripture *Eph.* 3. 10. *That Chrift may dwell in your Hearts by Faith.* I faid there was a nearer union between Chrift Jefus and a Soul believing on him, then between a *Man* and his *Wife,* and between the *Soul* and the *Body.* That *Union* is *Earthly* and dif- folving: but that between *Chrift Jefus* and the *Be- liever,* it is *eternal* in Gods Decrees and Councells, it is temporary in *Gods* calling of his chofen out of the *World,* to *Repentance & belief* in the Mediator

Eph 3. 10. The true Unton that is between Chrift Je- fus & Be- lievers.

11   Chrift

Chriſt Jeſus, and it perpetuated and continues to *Eternity.*

I told them that (as the holy Scripture ſaith) they preached not *Chriſt Jeſus* but *Themſelves,* yea they preached the *Lord Jeſus* to be *Themſelves*: that whatever were their Pretencſe (as the *Papiſts*) of *God & Chriſt & Holineſs & Mortiſication,* yet *The Qua-* they held not the *Head* (as the Scripture ſpeaks) and *kers paint-* if their head be but a painted and an *Imaginary* *ed Chriſt.* Head, they are but a painted and Imaginary *Body.* Their *Sun* of Righteouſneſs they talk of is but a *Sun* painted upon a *Sign* or *Wall* which is not the true Sun, but the picture of the *Sun* of Righteouſ-neſs.

I told them they ſet up this *Chriſt* within, oppo-ſite to *Chriſt* without, as *Oppoſites & Contraryes, Denying & Deſtroying* one an other : for as it is with *Chriſt* a *King* and his *Palace,* if his ᛫perſon be without, his *within and* perſon at that time is not within, though he be *Chriſt* *without.* within by his *Right, Authority* and *Influence* : if his Perſon be within the᛫Palace at that time it is not without. But the moſt clear Truth ᛫ is though theſe ſubtle *Foxians* ſometimes ſpeak of a Chriſt without that dyed at *Ieruſalem* agreeing with the Chriſt within, yet they preſently declare their mean-ing to be *Myſtical:* For aſk them but᛫theſe two *Queſtions,* and if they make any *Anſwer* you will ſee the *Cheat,* the *Equivocotion* and the *Miſtery of Ini-* *Two Queſ-* *tions to* quity in it. *Quakers.* 1. Do they not hold the *Light* within every man to be *All,* to *doe All* and to *ſuffer All* within which the Chriſt without, *Is* or *Did* or *ſuffered* without. 2. Aſk

2. Ask them now what is become of this *Man,* this perfon that thus fuffered at *Ierufalem,* and they are forced to confefs he [47] is within, and can give no other account of him, as they anfwered to me at *Newport* the laft day of the Conference.

But to return, I told them what I faid I would prove out of their *Writings,* and efpecially out of G. *Fox* attefted by *Ed Burrowes* his large *Epiftle,* and as it was thought by *John Stubs* prefent.

John Burnet declared not, (nor any of them) againft what I fpake: but faid (as faid the reft) if G. *Fox* have fpoken or written any thing that is not right and *truth,* we profefs not to follow him : and they were willing I fhould produce out of G. *Fox* his Book what I could that might make for my proof, *viz.* That they did not profefs the *true Chrift.*

I faid G: *Fox* had pickt out fome particular Lines, Sayings & Sentences out of the Books and Writings of his *Oppofites,* (it is not to be queftioned but to his utmoft *Advantage,* as knowing beft how to *Answer* what he chofe and *cull'd* out) and fince they were free and willing, I would produce fome In-ftances: I took up the Book and read in the 3d. *page,* where he brings in his *Oppofite Samuel Eaton* faying [The Sainfts have not Chrift in the *Flefh*] G. F. his Anfwer is [*Contrary to* Chrift and the Apoftles "*DoEtrine, who faid they were of his* Flefh,*and of his* "Bone, *and fhould eat his* Flefh, *and they that eat his* "Flefh *have it in them.*] Whence I affirmed that Chrift Jefus had fuch a Body as might be really and materially in the Saints, and ii was clear that they were

GF x his *Book in Fo-lio pro-duced. Page 3.*

were one with the *Papifts* in their Sayings and *Doctrines* denying the Flefh, Body and Perfon of Chrift Jefus: For as the *Papifts* in ftead of a *Spiritual* feeding upon his *bloud* and Merits, they fubftitute and bring in a *Real*, *Material* and Carnal, in their horrible and fantaftical *Tranfubftantiation*; fo do the *Quakers* profeffing to eat Chrift *fpiritually*, wholy deftroy his *material* and flefhly being.

The Papifts & Quakers deftroy the Perfon of Chrift.

I proceeded faying, in the 4*th Page* G. *Fox* brings in the fame Oppofite faying, *The Saints do not fee* Chrift, the Heavens contain him.   And G. F. Anfwers "*And the* Apoftle *faith they fate with* Chrift " in heavenly places: *fo he is contrary to the* Apoftle, " *and* Chrift *was in them and walked in them, and* God " *dwelt in them and* Chrift *in you except you be* Repro- "bates.   I faid that as the *Papifts* were up *ridiculoufly & odioufly* with *Hoc eft Corpus meum, This is my Body* &c. fo they with *The Light within you, the Light that enlightens every man,* Chrift *within you except you be* Reprobates *&c.*

The being of Chrift in the Heavens

48] For if the Heavens do contain that Man Chrift Jefus bodily, (as they grant in word) faying They believed he *dyed, rofe,* and *afcended*: then in that fame fence and refpect the Saints cannot now fit bodily with *C*hrift in heavenly places, and therefore to alledge *Chrift* within, and their fitting with *C*hrift in heavenly places, was but irrational *Nonfence* and Jefuitical *Equivocation*:

The truth is they were gravel'd with thefe *Confiderations*, and they were willing that G *Fox* his book and his Anfwers fhould anfwer for them, and although the oppofitions of *G.Fox* his Oppofites

The Quakers endure not trying

were

were mighty, and G *Foxes* were meer fimple *bark-* ^{but are} ings of dogs or foxes compar'd with the rational ^{willingly} ^{ignorant.} and prudential Anfwers of a man, yet when I be— gan to open and compare the *Affertions* of the Oppofite and *Fox* his anfwer, they would cry out (efpecially *W E.* like a *galled horfe* winching) *Why doft thou make thy* Obfervations *upon* G. Fox *his words ?* G.Fox *his words need not thy* Expofitions, *let* G. Fox *his words alone they are able to fpeak for themfelves.*

I told them it was a fencelefs bufinefs for me to alleadge, (and they to be willing I fhould) G.Fox his fayings and his *Anfwers,*and we fhould not debate and difcufs the *Sence,* and I make out my *Proof* out of G. *Fox* his words, and his *Adverfaryes* compar'd together: when they had fpoken they knew their liberty to take of my *Anfwers* with their own, and leave what was fpoke to every ones Confcience in the fight of God.

They were *Obftinately* (that is in *Greek Hereti-* ^{Willing} *cally*) refolved to avoid this Courfe, therefore I was ^{Ignorance.} glad to *hale* my *Tacks* & *Bolings* clofe home, and make my beft of a *bare Wind* and now and then *loof* up into the wind, and get liberty to fay fomething and omit abundance of my Thoughts.

Once I was forced to fay to *W. Edmondfon*: Friend yefterday you quoted the 9 of *Nehem.* how it pleafed God to fend them his good *Spirit* to guide them: I pray remember now a word in the 8 of *Nehem.* ^{Nehem 8} They read and gave the *Sence* and caufed the People ^{they gave} ^{the Sence} to underftand the *Reading.* Without this fearching for the *Sence* and meaning, the *Pith* and Marrow of

the

the holy *Scriptures*, or any other Scriptures or Writings we make ufe of, what are our Readings but the *Papifts Latine*, the *reading Minifters*, the pratling of *Children* and *Parrets*? yet notwithftanding all that I could fay and urge, it is known to all the *Audience* the Song was, *let G. Fox words alone to fpeak for themfelves, if thou haft any* [49] more to bring forth let us have them: fo that as before I was forced to wave my *Obfervations* and *Intentions*, and pafs on to new *Allegations*: Though now I fhall crave liberty to touch and point at (as with the finger) the *Oppofites Affertions* of *Truth* and *G. Fox* his unfavoury and rotten Anfwers

The Quakers nonfenfical Spirit.

In Page 8. He brings in *John Bunyan &c.* faying [*The Lord Jefus Chrift is afar in his bodily prefence*] and *G.Fox* anfwers, [*And yet he faith the Lord is at hand, and the Apoftle faid he was in them and Chrift faid he would dwell with them*] I here obferve and reply, the holy *Scripture* abundantly tells us of a twofold prefence of *Chrift*, 1. His bodily vifible *Prefence*, which *John Bunyan* fpeaks of and the *Quakers* in words grant. The 2. His *Spirituall*, invifible Prefence, of which many *Scriptures* fpeak and that moft clearly. *Eph. 3. 10. That Chrift may dwell in your hearts by believing &c.* Concerning this vifible bodily prefence, of which the Queftion is. *Firft.* G.Fox his impertinent and filly Anfwer is not to the *Point* no more then the *Eaft* and the *Weft* is to one point of the Compafs. 2. He fallacioufly, (moft *unchriftianly* and *impioufly*) denyes the body of *Chrift Jefus* to be any where, and as *Conjurers* do (*Hocas Pocas*) that which all now fee

John Bunyan Chrifts twofold Prefence.

The Quakers Conjure with Chrifts Body.

is

is gone & vanifhed, fo that with the ancient enemies
of *Chrifts Humane Nature*, the *Manicheans*, they *fay*
and *unfay* and at laft affirm a *Chrift* only *God* and
Spirit dwelling in them, and in all mankind alfo.

About this time thefe fubtle *Foxes* minded to
fpin out Time, and wave the *clofe Fight* of examining Particulars concerning *Chrifts* humanity. G. *The Qua-*
Fox his Book was brought forth (the fame with *kers endure*
mine (*John Burinat* took it and went along with me *not Sences*
in the *Quotations*, I read and alwayes endeavoured *or Mean-*
ings juft as
to make my proof out of the *Allegation:* But *W. the Papifts*
Edmundfon kept ftrict watch and ftood Centinel, that *and yet talk*
all of light
no Obfervations of *Sences* or *Meanings* fhould pafs,
refolving to keep out the Fire and Light of Chrift
Jefus with *Stand,* or Ile let fly a *Fire* (from Hell)
upon you. Well, I knew what froward Children
and bruitifh Spirits I dealt with, & refolved to go
foftly and to fpeak *foftly*, and as I could gain ground
by *inches* (at leaft) for liberty to give my witnefs for
the Lord *Jefus*.

In *Page* 9. He brings in *John Bunyan &c.* af- *The old*
queftion of
firming that the Son of *Mary*, God-Man is abfent *Chrifts*
from his Church, G. *Fox* anfwers, but never touch- *Prefence.*
ing Scripture about it. [*contrary to* [50] *Chrifts*
words, I in them and they in me: and I will be with
you to the ends: and Chrift the Head of the Church. &
where two or three are gathered &c. and the Saints are
bone *of his bone and* flefh *of his flefh.*

I Reply, here half an eye may fee as before, how
he gives no other *Prefence* or *Abfence* of a Chrift
but invifible and Spiritual, and fubtilly affirms that
Chrift Iefus hath no bodily Prefence at all, in the
fence

fence which all Chriſtians of what ſort or Sect
ſoever (but theſe *Juglers* (and themſelves alſo in
word and horrible hypocriſie) do acknowledg and
profeſs,

Fox &
Bonnet *no*
difference.
In *Page* 10 He brings in the ſame Author ſaying
[*Chriſt was not in his Diſciples when he ſaid I am the
Light of the world*] G *Fox* anſwers. [*And ſo cor-
rected by Chriſt, I in you and you in me.*

Pag. 12. He brings in the ſame Author, ſaying
[*The Body of Chriſt is out of the ſight of all his
Saints,*] G. *Fox* Anſwers, (they ſat with Chriſt in
Heavenly places, the Saints are *Fleſh* of his *Fleſh,*
and *Bone* of his *Bone,* were the Church which he

The Qua-
kers pre-
tend to
owne
Chriſts
Bloud &
yet in truth
allow him
no Bloud
to ſhed.
is head of his Body:) In which I Anſwer, and all
his Book over (though he own a Chriſt without,
and that died at *Jeruſalem* in word yet he allows in
effect no other Body to *Chriſt Jeſus* but what is
Miſtical and Spiritual : ſo that with notorious *Jug-*
ling, and *Jeſuitical Impudence,* they would make
their ſimple Followers believe that they own ſuch
a *Chriſt* as ſhed his *Blood* at *Jeruſalem,* and yet leave
him in his Body no more Blood to ſhed then is in
a Spirit which hath no *Bones, Fleſh* nor *Blood* to
ſhed at all.

Enoch
Howet.
Pag. 17. He brings in *Enoch Howet* Affirming
[*That it is Blaſphemy to ſay that Chriſt is in Man as
God Man,*] G. *Fox* Anſwers (ſtill like the *Cuckow* in
one ſilly Note) How are they of his *Fleſh* and of his
Bones : And doth not the Scripture ſay, *Chriſt* in
you, and God will dwell in you, and walk in you,
and are not his Saints of his *Fleſh,* and of his *Bones,*
and there is one ſentence added, are they not partakers of the *Divine Nature?*   I

I Reply, this *Participation* of the *Divine Nature* ^{*The divine*} is (faith *Peter*) in the Saints by thofe precious ^{*and humane*} Promifes, that is by receiving Chrift Jefus, by be-^{*nature of*} lieving in him according to that *Ephef.* 3. 10. (That ^{*the Lord Jefus.*} Chrift may dwell in your hearts by Believing) not that the Divine *Being* or *Effence* and *Nature* or *God-head* is communicable to a finite Creature : from hence thefe proud *Simpletons* fancie (and fome have been fuch bold *Bayards* as to fay) they are Chrift and God, as much as he that died at *Jerufalem,* Chrifted with Chrift and Godded with God.

51 | It is remarkable that *Nicholas* the *Deacon* ^{Nicholas} was the Father (as I believed)[1] of the old *Nicholai-* ^{*the* Dea-con *and*} *tans* and *Henery Nichols* in *King James* his time the ^{Nicholas} Father of the new *Nicholaitans* in *London* and other ^{*Fathers of the old and*} places, crying up their perfection, their *Spirituality* ^{*new* Nich-} and *Godhead*, all leading from the purity of *Gods* ^{olaitans.} *Worfhip* and Authority of the *Holy Scripture*, and at laft to carnal *Filthinefs* as the Daughters of thefe the *Ranters* declare evidently.

This Humane Nature, humane Soul and Body ^{So Crifto-} of Chrift Jefus is fo crofs, oppofite and contrary to ^{pher Houlder} their new whimfical Chrift Jefus (the Light within ^{*be boggles*} them) that G. *Fox* in all this Book cannot endure to ^{*at the word*} hear of the word *Humane*, as being a new Name ^{*Manhood.*} and never heard of in the *Scriptures*.

As to the word *Humane*, fuch an odious Word and *Bugbear* to G. *Fox* in all this Book : I faid in ^{*The word*} publick; many Words truely and properly *Englifh* ^{Humane} were well and commendably ufed that were not in ^{*confidered*}

the

---

[1] "believe." *R. W. Ms. Ann.*

the Scripture in *English* : it is true the word *Humane* comes from the word in *Latin Humanus*, fignifying partaining or belonging to Man : fo a *Humane Soul* or *Body* is no more but fuch a *Soul* or *Body* as all *Mankinde* have. Hence I told them, *Ufed in the Scripture,* that the word *Anthropinos peirafmos*, 1. *Cor.* 10. (I *1 Cor* 10. prefumed *John Stubs* knew) might have been turned *Humane*, but is truely turned no *Temptation* or *Trial* but fuch as is common to Men. This *Fox* knows, that if Chrift Jefus be granted to have had fuch a Soul and Body as is *Humane or Common* to Men, down falls their *Dagon* before the *Cheft* or *Ark* of God, *viz.* their *Horrible, Monftrous Idol* of a Chrift called *Light within them.*

We went on thus in alleadging Quotations, though not in a clofe Examination of them which they endured not, though ever and anon I made fome fallies out upon them and had fome *Skirmifhings*, and fometimes fharp *Difputes* before I would retreat from the *Quotation.*

Dan. Gru- In Pag. 282. He brings in *Daniel Gaudry* faying *dry Chrift* [*We fhall not fee Chrift as he is until he comes to* *not feen as* *Judgement, and then and not before we fhall fee him*] *he is until* *the day of* G. *Fox* Anfwers, (You where you are fee him not: *Judgement* nor know him as he is, we do believe you : but the *Saints* the *true Church* whom he is the Head of, in whom he is in the midft and in whom he is, &c.

I was not defirous to trouble the *Audience* with more *Quotations*, but they ftill urged, hafte thou any more, haft thou any more, &c. upon their provocation I Quoted many more (to [52] make up an overwhelming Cloud of Witneffes againft
thefe

thefe *Proteſtant Jeſuites* and *Judaſites*, Betrayers of the Son of God the true Lord Jeſus Chriſt.

In *Foxes* Anſwer to his Oppoſite *Daniel Caudry* it is clear that he affirms the contrary to his Oppoſite, *to wit*, that Chriſt Jeſus is as much now ſeen viſibly as ever he ſhall be ſeen : in which I believe he ſpeaks the heart of all the *Antichriſtian Wolves and Foxes* who quake and tremble at the thought of Chriſts return again to judgment : and therefore theſe deluded and deluding Souls in their dark *Priſons* of willing *Blindneſs*, and the helliſh *Chaines* of the pride and hardneſs and ſecurity of their hearts, they dream they ſit in *Robes* of Glory themſelves & now keep open the high Court of eternal *Judgment* and paſs Sentence upon this Chriſt without as a poor *Outſide Chriſt* and all that worſhip him. *The perſonal coming of the Lord Jeſus.*

2. I obſerve in *Fox* his anſwer that he can not keep out of his *Burrow* of confounding a *viſible* eye and a *Spiritual*, a viſible and inviſible ſeing : you ſee him not ſaith he where you are, that is you that look upon ſuch a real perſon indeed, ſuch an one born living and dying as the Hiſtory ſets forth, you cannot ſee him as he is, but we that look at *Chriſt Jeſus* and the hiſtory of him as *Myſtical, immediate, inviſible,* though we uſe to pleaſe you *children and fools* with the words of *Chriſts dying at Ieruſalem* : we ſee him he is in the mideſt of us : and he is the inviſible *Head* of the *Church* in God, while you talk of *Viſibles* and ſeing him as *Viſible &c.* *A viſible and in viſible eye and objeĉt.*

In *Page* 276. he brings in *Richard Meyo* ſaying, that he did believe in a *Chriſt* that dyed at *Ieruſalem* : *Chriſt ithin & Chriſt without.*
lem :

lem : and that he doth not believe in a Chriſt *within*, and preach Chriſt within, is a Reprobate. *Colloſſ.* 2. 2. *Cor.* 13. And he is not in a true Belief of *Chriſt without*, that doth not, believe in a *Chriſt within*, but is in the *Devils Belief*, and believes as the *Devils* do.

In this his anſwer an humble Soul may ſee how this ſubtle *Traytor* under the golden name of *Chriſt*, and Chriſt within in the heart, he ſtabs at the heart of the true *Lord Ieſus*, who ſuffered for poor Mankind in mans own nature at *Ieruſalem*.

The Pa-
piſts and
Quakers
Chriſt is
no where

2. I obſerve his virulent and venemous *Mind* and *Pen* ſtabbing damning and *reprobating* all that truly believe in the true *Lord Ieſus*, whome he con-feſſeth to have been a real man dying at *Ieruſalem*, *&c.* except they can believe that he is now no where to be found but in every mans heart that cometh into the world, that is no where.

Chriſtoph
Wade.

53] In *Page* 246. He brings in *Chriſtopher Wade* ſaying, [*It is whimſical to ſay Chriſt God and Man, Fleſh and Spirit is in them*] He anſwers, [*Contrary to the Apoſtles Doctrine who ſaid they were of his* fleſh *and of his* bone, *and Chriſt in you, and he would walk in them, and he that hath not the Spirit of Chriſt is none of his, and they are of his fleſh and of his bone, and Chriſt in you the hope of Glory*]

In the ſame Page he brings in the ſame Author ſaying |*Fleſh and bone cannot be a meaſure in one and a meaſure in an other*] He Anſwers [*wheras the Apoſtle ſaith, we are of his* Fleſh *and of his* Bone, *here thou art contrary to the Apoſtle, and that was more then one that had the* Fleſh *of* Chriſt, *and his* Bone *and his* Spirit.   In

In *Page* 248. He brings in the fame Author fay-ing, [*It is a falfe thing to fay Chrifts Perfon is in man*] He Anfwers, [*which is as much as to fay, none are of his* Flefh *nor of his* Bone *nor eat nor had not his Subftance.*

And *Page* 249 *The Saints bodyes are not Chrifts body.* He Anfwers, *How are they Chrifts? How dwels he in them? and how are they of his* Flefh *and of his* Bone *then? and how bruitifh are you become in Knowledge? hath he not bought them with a price, and are they not his?*

And in the fame *Page* he brings in the fame Author faying, *that neither Gods Effence, nor Heaven, nor Chrifts Perfon was in* Peters *holy body.* He anfwers, *but the Apoftle faid God will dwell with you and walk in you, and again, our converfation is in Heaven.*

And once more in the fame page *There is not whole* Chrift God *and man in men.* Answ. *Then how muft men grow in the meafure of the fullnefs of the ftature of* Chrift: *and* Chrift *and* God *will dwel in man and walk in man,* God *that made all things, and* Chrift *by whome all things were made.*

I Reply, this Author *Chriftopher Wade* I know not many of his oppofites (living and dead, whome he here vapours to anfwer in his Book, I know were worthy of Chriftian efteem and honour for the grace and Knowledge of Chrift Jefus in them, and for other worthy refpects: and whither this Oppofite or any other whome he pretends to puffe at or Anfwer, have thought this audacious *Quack-falver* worthy of any Reply, I know not: For certainly (as he commonly concludes his Anfwer in

The Author whome G.Fox *opofeth and in Pride and madnefs rageth againft.*

his

his Book(*Thy many notorious Lyes and Slanders and Blafphemyes are not worth the mentioning*: however for the proof of my *Pofition* I am occafioned [54] to follow this *Fox* into his holes and *Burrowes*, and to hale him out before God, Angls and Men as a moft greedy audacious *Fox* and *Wolfe*, not fparing the Son and Lamb of God, nor his precious Lambs and Sheep.

Thr Qua-
kers Chrift
but a
whimfical
Chrift
Now to all thefe laft *Quotations*, I fay (as the Oppofites to *Fox* faid) that this Notion of Chrift wit hin oppofite to Chrift without is a moft Frantick and Whimfical, Grofs and Blockifh Fancy: For though he grant Chrift Jefus to be a Man which *died at Jerufalem*, yet making him only Spiritual, and fuch a Chrift as is whole Chrift, God and Man in every man in the *World*, he makes Chrift Jefus to be but *Whimfical Chrift*, and that Man that died at *Jerufalem* but a *Babylonian* Fancy.

Hofanna to
the Son of
David
In Pag. 221. He brings in the Author to a Book called *Hofanna to the Son of David*, faying, [*Chrift is without the Sainfts in refpect of his Bodily prefence*,] He Anfwereth, (They are of his Flefh and of his Bone, and eat his Flefh and drink his Blood: and how have the Saints his Mind and Spirit, and he with them and they with him, and fit with him in Heavenly places, and he is the *Head* of the *Church*: how then is he abfent? the[1] poor *Apoftates* from him who feel not Chrift with you, but he is with the Saints, and they feel him.)

I Reply, I obferve this *Viperous Tongue* faying to the unknown, heavenly *Author*, and *Fox* his other
Oppofitee

[1] "Ye" poor Apoftates. *R. W. Ms. Ann.*

Oppofitee [*Ye ·poor Apoftates &c.*] what is it but a heighth of Devilifh Pride going before deftruction and condemnation? this proud fwelling Bladder puft up with a *Timpany* of *Wind* and *Vanity,* what a huge fwelling fhew he makes? what a breadth of confident boldnefs and bruitifh impudencie he carries before him? what a grofs, Frantick *Papift* is he become, that cannot, will not diftinguifh between *Chrifts Spiritual prefence* and his bodily? that cannot, will not confider the difference between *Spirits* and *Bodies,* a *Spirit* that hath no Flefh nor Bones, and a Body which hath both, as Chrift his Body had? that cannot, will not diftinguifh between their finful *Flefh* and *Bones,* and the finlefs *Flefh* and *Bones* of that Man Chrift Jefus? that cannot, will not diftinguifh between God manifefted in the *Flefh* and *Bones* of that Man Chrift Jefus, and manifefted in the *Flefh* and *Bones* of *Believers* in him: O moft Holy and Righteous are thy Judgements, O thou moft High Judge of the World, who art a devouring fire and Juftice it felf, who thus cafteft down the·*Proud* and *Self-conceited* into the Dungeon of fuch *Black* and *Hellifh Ignorance!*

The Spirit of the Papifts & the Quakers but one.

55] Pag. 217, Out of a Book mentioning the *Quakers Caufe,* faying, [*To fay Chrift within is never to mention Chrift without*] He Anfwers, There is none knows Chrift within, but he knows him without: the fame yefterday, and to day, and for ever: And there is none knows him but they know him within, revealed of the Father, which is beyond Flefh and Blood.

I Obferve, This foolifh *Fox* (for all his hiding Craft)

The Qua-
kers notori-
ously dif-
femble, for
they do own
and not
own the
Chrift
that dyed
at Ieriſa-
lem.
Craft) is here found out : He profeffeth (againſt
his Will and Heart) a Chriſt that *died at Jeruſalem,*
and therefore is he forced to name a Chriſt without : but when the *Hole and Burrough* is *Digged* the
Fox is found : For Examine what is this *Chriſt
without?* is he that litteral, real and material Perſon the Son of *Mary* (as all profeffing Chriſts Name
generally agree? Is this he whom the *Quakers* acknowledge to have *lived* and *died* at *Jeruſalem?* and
do they intend a *Material Croſſe,* a literal Death, a
literal and real *Ieruſalem?* ſome of them will ſay yes,
but therein give the lye to others of themſelves,
and alſo to the reſt of their own ſtory, in acknowledging no other Chriſt but ſuch as is in *every man:*
ſuch a Chriſt as really and bodily *died at Ieruſalem,*
they ſcorn and hate and fly from as the *Devils did,*
crying out, *What have we to do with thee Jeſus thou
Son of the moſt High God, art thou come to torment
us before the time?* Hence the former *Arch-deacon*
or *Arch-biſhop* of theſe parts *Humphrey Norton:* he

*Humph.
Norton
more plain
in words
then other
Quakers.*

mocks at an outward Chriſt, he asks what Coun—
tryman he was and ſhall be : He reproves the
Fools that have their Eyes abroad, and gazing after
a man into Heaven, he jeers at the Croſſe, aud asks
what manner of wood it was made of, ſeeing
we muſt take it up dayly? And *Fox* ſaith, this Jeſus Chriſt without and within, is Jeſus Chriſt yeſterday, and to day, and the ſame for ever : therefore

*Chriſt yeſ-
terday and
to day.*

in the *Logick* or *Reaſon* of this *Bruite,* Chriſt had no
body that was born at *Bethlehem,* or died at *Ieruſalem:* For he was born yeſterday, and to day, and
he is born forever : he dyed yeſterday, and he dies

to

to day, and he dies forever, which is a moſt Heavenly Truth relating to Gods purpoſe, Chriſts Merit, and to Forefathers, our preſent times, and ſuch as yet muſt be born and follow after us.

But ſuch Myſtical and figurative Scriptures (which are in themſelves like *Sampſons Lion* and *Riddle*) through *Satans Policy*, and the proud ſimplicity of theſe ſimple *Foxes*, are made the common *Holes* and *Burroughs* where you may be ſure to find them: juſt like the *Jeſuites* (whoſe Coſens, if not Brethren of one belly of Hell [56] they are) who uſually confound clear Scriptures with Spiritual and Myſtical Illuſions, and fly from Diſtinctions and openings neceſſary in places more dark, figurative and allegorical.

In pag. 211. He brings in *John Burton* ſaying, *That the man that was crucified his body is now in the preſence of his Father, abſent from his People as touching his bodily preſence.* He Anſwers. *Doth not the Apoſtle ſay he is the Head of the Church? and doth not the Apoſtle ſay they are of his* Fleſh *and* Bone *and fit it heavenly places, with* Chriſt, *and* Chriſt *ſaith, they muſt eat his fleſh, and he is in them.*

As I remember at the reading of this *Quotation*, I urged that herein G. *Fox* did plainly deny (as indeed in all the reſt I have quoted) Chriſt Jeſus to have had ſuch a body as could be born of a woman, wrapped in ſwadling Cloathes, &c. as could be *hungry, weary, ſleep, diſcourſe,* [1] *apprehended, buffeted, whipped, nail'd to the Gallowes, die, be buried, ariſe*

The Quakers endure not to be ſearched, temer of falſe and thieviſh ſpirits.

[1] Interline " be." *R. W. Ms. Ann.*

13

arife and afcend up vifibly into thefe vifible Heavens, now in the prefence of his Father, and abfent from his *P*eople on Earth, as touching his bodily pre- fence: But one of my *Oppofites,* (I think two of them) bid me not wronge G. *Fox* by my *Obferva- tion,* for his words were not fo. I Anfw. In *effect* and Subftance they were, for G. *Fox* here,(and in all his Anfwers) maintains·the *Negative* to what his Oppofites *Affirm.* And 2. As to the grounds of his deniall it is clear that fometimes they are moft plain and clear, and fometimes moft fubtle, and common- ly fuch as will bear a twofold Sence, on which they commonly ground fome *Jefuitical equivocation.*

The Qua-
kers &
Apolloes
Oracles
the fame.

In Pag. 210. He brings in *John Burton* faying, *Chrift went away into Heaven from his Difciples, and fo not within them.* He Anfwers, *Did not he fay that he would come again to them? Did he not fay he was in them, I in you? And did not the Apoftle fay Chrift was in them except they were* Reprobates? *the hope of Glory?* was he not revealed to the *Apoftle* and fo in him? and did not the *Apoftle* Preach Chrift within, and you preach Chrift without?

Iohn
Burton.

Again in the fame *Page* [*Thofe Believers that are in the body at this day are abfent from the Lord:*] He Anfwers again, Doth not the Apofte fay Chrift is in them except they be Reprobates? and he is in them the Hope of Glory? and they have fellow- fhip with God, and God will dwell in them, and walk in them, and he that believes believes in him, and Chrift and fo notabfent.

If ever
there
Equivoca-
ting Jef-
uites in the
world the
Quakers
are.

Again in the fame *Page,* they fay [*He is abfent from them as touching his flefh,* He Anfwers, *Doth not*
the

the Apoſtle ſay they [57] *are of his* Fleſh *and of his* Bone? *and he that eates not his* Fleſh, *hath no* life *in him, and they ſit in* heavenly places *with him, and he that eates his* fleſh *hath it in him.*

And again in the ſame Page they ſay [*There is not any* Heaven *within into which the Man* Chriſt *is aſcended, or can any man contain a man four foot long?*] He Anſwers [Chriſt *is a Myſtery, and is he not to be revealed within who is a Myſtery?* He who did deſcend to be revealed and made manifeſt in his Saints in fleſh and Spirit, that did deſcend, which is now manifeſted, that the World wonders at: that is aſcended far above the Heavens, who is the Saints life living *Bread* and *Drink*: and where ever uſed the Miniſters of Chriſt any ſuch expreſſion as thou doth, which ſhews that Chriſt to thee is a *Myſtery?*

Reply, In all theſe four Paſſages G. *Fox* expreſly denies that Chriſt is aſcended into Heaven from his Diſciples: That Believers now in the Body are abſent from the Lord: that he is abſent from Man as touching his Fleſh: that there is a Heaven into which Chriſt is aſcended: and that Chriſts Body is not containable in a place according to his ſtature and proportion. *The Quakers wonderful juggling about the true Chriſt*

2. In his Anſwers he notoriouſly jugles and equivocates as if he maintained Chriſt *in Truth,* he that lived and died at *Jeruſalem,* and viſibly aſcended into Heaven though the whole ſcope and the plain open faced meaning of his words, with loud cries tend altogether to another buſineſs, *to wit,* to ſet up himſelf by ſetting up the Image and Picture, this *Imaginary Chriſt* which he calls the *Light within them.* The

The fame *Author* faith, *Pag*. 206. [*A falfe Chrift*
hath a new falfe Faith to apprehend this Crucified
Chrift within,] He Anfwers, [*Which is contrary to the*
Faith of the Apoftles which Preached Chrift that's
Crucified within and not another; *Him that was raifed*
from the dead was rifen that Lord Jefus Chrift
within, the fame yefterday, to day, and for ever, by
whom the World was made glorified with the Father
before the World began: it was he that was manifeft in
the Saints, that was, and is not another, for the other
is Antichrift.]

John
Burton:

Again in the fame *Page*, it is a *Sceipture* of the
Devils making to apprehend this Chrift within:
He Anfwers, Now I fay if there be any Chrift but
he that was crucified wit hin he is a falfe Chrift,
and the *Scripture* holds forth this, and the *Devil*
never made it, but he and his *Meffengers* are againft
it: And he that hath not this Chrift [58] that was
rifen and *Crucified* within is a *Reprobate* though
Devills and *Reprobates* may talk of him without.

This Quotation was read again in their own
Book by *John Burnet*, and they magnified the
Chrift within, but they would not fuffer me to
obferve the fence and argue from it, faying, G.
Foxes *Words were plain concerning the true Chrift*;
And fo indeed I fay they are to any penitent Soul
truly (like *Paul*) unbottom'd from weak and filthy
felf, and his own *Dunghil Righteoufnefs*, and burning with fincere *Affection* to the true *Lord Jefus*:
For thefe fubtle *Foxes*, and their Words difcover (as
the Sun at noon day) that as plainly as ever *Abfa-*
lom, Achitophel, Shimei, Sheba rofe up in confpiracy
and

The Qua-
kers Trai-
tors & Re-
bels againft
the true
Lord Jefus

and Rebellion againſt *David*, &c. as plainly as ever
Judas and *Peter* (for a time) and *Alexander* the
Copper-ſmith, and *Hymeneus*, and *Julian* the *Apoſ-*
tate denied *Davids Antitype* the true *Lord Jeſus* : ſo
under the Cloak and Colour of *Chriſt Crucified* within, do their *Rebellious Traitors* bear Arms againſt
the *Mediator* between God and Man, the Man
Chriſt Jeſus : For although it be *Scripture Phraſe,*
that we are *Crucified, Dead* and *Buried,* and *Riſen*
with Chriſt : yet what a poor proof is this, that
Chriſt was Born and *Crucified* &c. yeſterday, and to
day within us, and there is no other *Birth* nor *Life,*
nor *Death,* nor *Grave* but what is within us, and all
are *Reprobates* and *Devils* that bow not down to this
painted devouring Monſter.

   Still my *Oppoſites* were catcht in their own
Craftineſs they ſeemed well pleaſed that G. *Fox*
ſhould be heard in his Anſwers to his *Adverſaries,*
and I reſtrain'd and ſtopt from making out my
Proofs from the *Senſe,* and *Scope* and *Meaning* : I
was yet glad that ſo much was diſcovered, that I
had (by *Catches*) liberty to give fire ſometimes, and
intended to make uſe of this preſent Advantage
(which I from the firſt intended, when I ſaw I
ſhould be ſtopt, and they would not afford me the
liberty I gave to them without the leaſt *Interrupt-*
ion) as *John Stubs* confeſſed.

   Page 135. He brings in *Thomas Moor* ſaying
[*Chriſt is abſent from us while we are in this Mortal*
Body] He Anſwers contrary to the *Apoſtle,* who
ſaith, *the Life of Chriſt is manifeſted in their mortal*
Fleſh.]

*I have
known the
poor Lob-
ſters catch
the Foxes.*

                        And

And Page 136. The fame Author faith [*Chrift is diftinct from every one of us, and without us in our particular perfons,*] He An- [59] fwers, [*The Apoftle faid Chrift was in them except thed were Reprobates: and they were of his Flefh and of his Bone, and they eat his Flefh and drank his Blood, then it was in them, and he is diftinct from none but Reprobates who hates the Light.*]

The wonderful blindnefs and hardnefs of my Antagonifts

Reply, I wondred not fo much at this *Thunder*, and *Fire*, and *ftinking Brimftone* from this *Foxes* mouth, and that all are *Reprobates* with him that bow not down to his *Carved Image*: but I wondred at my Oppofites, who declared (publickly as before) that they would not follow G. *Fox* but in the Truth, &c. and yet when I read all their[1] plain Evidences to them of *Foxes* denying the true *Lord Jefus*, God and Man; and making only a *Spiritual Chrift*, a *Myftical Invifible Jefus*, &c. that yet they fhould be fo blinded and hardened, as to cover, excufe and plead for G. *Fox* in all particulars, and ftop me from drawing the *Curtain* and letting in the *Light* by Opening and Arguing from the Sence and Meaning.

I do not remember that any one of my three *Oppofites* gave any pofitive anfwer to any of my Obfervations on *Foxes* Principles, Anfwers, and Evafions: All their work was to keep themfelves within their Trenches or Burroughs, and to cry out [*Thou muft keep to Foxes Words*] or, *Wilt thou go on to another?*

Frances Higginfon

In Page 71. He brings in *Frances Higginfon* faying, [*Chrifts Humane Nature*] He Anfwers, [*Where doth*

---

[1] "the plain Evidences." *R. W. Ms. Ann.*

doth the Scripture speak of Humane, the Word Hu- The Qua-
mane where is it written that we may search for it : kers endure
Now we do not deny that Christ (according to the Flesh) word
was of Abraham, *but not the word* Humane : *And* Humane
Christs Nature is not Humane *which is Earthly, for
that is the first* Adam.]

Reply. This ignorant and simple Cavil (as I
have before proved it to be from 1 *Cor.* 10.) is
often brought by G. *Fox* in this Book, in an horrible equivocation to overthrow and destroy that
Humane Nature, that Flesh and Body of the Lord
Jesus, who yet had such a Body they say that died
at *Jerusalem* : These Traiterous Jesuits or *Judas-
ites* tell us *Humane* is of the Earth or Earthly, and
that is the *first Adam,* but Christ Jesus is of the
Seed of *Abraham* according to the flesh, that is, in
their mental Reservation, according to their flesh,
God in their flesh, Christ in their flesh suffering at
a *Mystical Jerusalem* within them : They are *Abrahams* Seed, *Isaaks* Seed in whom all Nations (by
this Christ the Light within them) must be blessed :
And all that are not this Seed, this Flesh, [60] this
Christ (which they are) are in the *Serpents Nature* Acts 13.
and *Reprobates.* But amongst all the most full and Opened of
heavenly *Scriptures* for the *Humane Nature* of the Humanity.
Lord Jesus *:* I shall touch but one at present, *Act.*
13. at *Antioch, Barnabas* and *Paul* in a *Synagogue* of
the *Jews* made the *Humane Nature of* the Lord
Jesus, (as also in other places) the great Subject of
their Discourse and Preaching : and concludes *ver.*
38. *Be it known unto you therefore Men & Brethren,
that through this Man is Preached unto you the For-*
                                                    giveness

givenefs of fins, and by Him all that Believe are Jufti-
fied from all things from which you could not be juftified
by the Law of Mofes. By the meritorious Sufferings, Death and Blood-fhedding of this Jefus (literally in the *Hiftory* born at *Bethlehem* as the *Quakers*
fay, &c.) is only forgivenefs of fin, and juftification,
&c. and not by a *Chimical* and *Diabolical* Chrift and
Fancy within us, begot by the *Devil* on a proud
and lazie Ignorance: Let therefore (as it follows)
the *Proud* Defpifers wonder and perifh, believing
not in him the true Light of the World, the true
Brazen Serpent to all that look up unto him.

In Page 37. He brings in Thomas Collier faying,
[If the very Chrift God Man be within thofe called
Quakers he cannot come down from Heaven] He
Anfwers, [Here he ftands againft the promife of
Chrift, that he fhall come and dwell in you, and
walk in you: I will come again unto you. And he
hath revealed his Son in me faith the Apoftle, and
know you not that Chrift is in you except you be
Reprobates: and the Spirit of the Father fpeaks in
you, and fee how contrary thou art to the Prophets,
Chrift and the Apoftles..

I urged that here G. Fox did plainly deny the
expected perfonal coming of the Lord Jefus: but
they charged me to give none of my Sences and
Meanings to G. Fox his words: but now I have
leave (by Gods merciful hand) here to fay, that
their Hypocrifie and Deceit (whereby they cheat
themfelves and others) is fo much the more grofs
and abominable, becaufe they pretend in words to
own Chrift Jefus Humane defcending, or Afcending

*Tho. Col-
lier*

*The fecond
coming of
the Lord
Jefus*

as

as a Man into Heaven, and Chrifts there abiding until the time of the *Reftitution*, and Chrifts return the fecond time: They know alfo that all thofe *Scriptures* they produce (as *Chrift in you except ye be Reprobates, &c.*) concern an inward invifible and Spiritual prefence, and yet they bruitifhly cry out contrary to the *Prophets, Chrift, & the Apoftles.*

61] It comes to my mind that in reading & urging fome of thefe Paffages concerning thefe *Foxians* denying the *Humane Nature* and *Perfon* of the *Lord Jefus*, one of my Oppofites *John Stubs* infifted upon that 9. of *Ifaiah* where Chrift is called the *Everlafting Father*: and yet he faid, *He was the Son of Man born of a Woman, &c.* I Anfwered, the *Hebrew* word rendred by our *Tranflators*, the *Everlafting Father* is Tranflated by fome, the *Father of an age*, or *the Father of Ages*, alluding to the great increafe and fpreading of Chrifts Name, and the mighty increafe of his Spiritual Seed (as the Lord promifed to *Abraham* and *Ifaac*) as the Stars of Heaven. *John Stubs* faid the *Hebrew word* was [*Abi Haad*, &c.] and it was rendred *Pater Eternitatis*: I replied that it was rendred (and that more near the *Hebrew*) *Pater feculi*, or *feculorum*: But I told him it was not a feafonable time and place for him and me to fpend much time about the Tranflation of the word: he faid he had brought the *Hebrew Bible* with him, and it may be he underftood the *Hebrew* and the *Greek* and other Languages as well as my felf and better too: I was about to fay that they were wonderfully altered and changed from their former principles and practifes, for heretofore they have

The Everlafting Fath r Chrift J fu. & how

The Quakers wonderfully changed & yet but in Diffimulation as to learning & the Scriptures

14

have profeſſed to me that they had no need of Books, no not of the Scripture it ſelf, for they had the Teacher within them that gave forth Scripture, &c. if now they were perſwaded to ſtudy the Holy Scripture and the Tranſlation of it, and to examine the Tranſlations and the Copies of them, then they did err and ſin before, (which they ſay the Saints cannot) in ſo wonderfully neglecting and ſlighting them as uſeleſs and needless things.

Yea the truth is if their Light be ſo Alſufficient as they make it, to bring them to Heaven, to guide them immediately and infallibly &c. what ſimplicity is it in them to ſtoop to *Pen and Ink*, and mens fallible Tranſlations, yea, many wayes charged with many failings.

I know their Pretences of becoming *All to All* to win the more, and of removing the offence and ſtumbling block, *viz.* as if they denied the Scriptures, but the truth is, they look at the *Holy Scriptures* ſtill but as the *Ceremonies* which the *Apoſtles* diſpenſed with for a ſeaſon : they care no more for the Scriptures then the *Papiſts* do, they are forced to make uſe of them for an end, but all their hope is in their *Interpretations*, which both *Papiſts and Qua-* [62] *kers* bend their utmoſt to ſecure, *viz.* the *Priviledge* of *Interpretation*, and chair of *Infallibility* to themſelves, or elſe down they tumble, for moſt ſure it is the *Holy Scriptures*, and both *Papiſts* and *Quakers* are at irreconcilable difference, if the one ſtand the other muſt fall for ever.

Although I deſired to finiſh all the firſt ſeven Poſitions that day, and offered once or twice to
proceed,

proceed, yet *W. Edmundſon* (eſpecially) upbraided W. Edmund.
*leaves the
Diſpute &
is hurried
into
Preaching*
me that I kept them long, and that I proved
nothing, and upon a ſudden a violent, tumultuous
diſorderly *Wind* or *Spirit* filled all his *Sails*, ſo that
he roſe up and fell into a downright *Speech* or *Sermon* to the *People* and *Auditory:* and firſt he declared how notoriouſly I had wronged them, in
laying and publiſhing ſo many falſe, and ſome of
them dangerous *Charges* againſt them. 2 And how
they had been ſo.long patient towards me and ſuffer me to produce ſo many *Allegations* out of G.
Fox his Book, and yet they ſpeak nothing for me,
but G. *Fox* his words cleared him from all my unjuſt challenges and charges. 3. He Appealed to
the People, how willing they had ſhewed themſelves to own the Scriptures, and to have all their
Teaehings and Differences tried by the Scriptures.
4. He fell upon the two Hinges of all the Quakers common Diſcourſes.

Firſt, An Invective againſt the *Prieſts, Falſe
Teacher, Falſe Apoſtles,* who had got on the *Sheeps
cloathing,* and ſold the words of *Scripture* for their
Game and *Lucre* and he amplified this much how
all their care and ſtudy was to get a good *Living*
or *Benifice* of 50. 6c 100. or 200 pounds a year
(more or leſs) and he that complained how I took
up time, now (tediouſly) made us all to hear a Story, which he ſaid he knew himſelf of one of the
Prieſts that lived not many miles from the place w.Ed-
mund.
*his ſtory
concerning
Bentfices*
where *W. Edmund.* lived, who told with his own
Mouth unto *William Edmund.* viz. how that having
a good *Benefice,* another *Prieſt* of his acquaintance
came

came to vifit him, whom he entertained kindly, and this his Gueſt told him, that he was going to the *Biſhop* of *Dublin*, who was his Friend: and the *Prieſt* the *Hoſt* was afterward informed that this treacherous and ungrateful Gueſt, did ufe all the art he could with the *Biſhop* of *Durham* (or *Dublin*) to get his Friends (that had entertained him) his Living from him.

2. The fecond part of his Sermon was (as ufually it is of all their Sermons) an extolling and magni‑ fying of that Light which [63] he faid had ap‑ peared to him, which he advanced as the *Principle* and the *Foundation,* the Light, &c. he added how they had left all the Glory and Pleafures of the World for this Light: and how they had endured and fuffered much for *Preaching* this Light to un‑ godly and ungrateful men, who had ill requited them: for their Meſſage and Work was only to bring good News unto them, to tell them that they fhould be free from fin and have Chriſt Jefus live and dwell in them. I kept filence until this famous *Apoſtle* and *Preacher* of *Chriſt Jefus* had done this Speech or Sermon which he faid *he* was moved in his heart to make unto them & (as he often faid) to give an account of his Faith which he performed with very great zeal and fervency, both of mind and body.

And his vain extol‑ ling of their Idol Light

John Stubs his fermon
I had thought then to have fpoke, but imme‑ diately *Jo. Stubs* ſtood up being moved (as he faid) to Declare his mind and Thoughts unto the peo‑ ple alfo, and fo he began a large *Oration, Speech* or *Sermon* alfo (though not fo long as *William Ed‑ mundfons*)

mundsons) he declared how pleasant a thing the
Light was, and how pleasant a thing it was to behold it? And he said, *are you angry because we bring
you the Tidings of the Light?* This was the principle,
this was the *Foundation* of all, the *Light, &c.* He
added (for *John Stubs* his was but *a* Repetition of
William Edmundsons his *Sermon*) that they had for-
saken all the Glory of Honours and Pleasures of
this World for this *Light*: and they had left their
Wives and *Children*, and exposed themselves to hard
Travels and to many Hardships and Sufferings for
the *Light* sake: I heard him also patiently and
gave him no *Interruption* (as he twice openly con-
fest that I had not interrupted them: but when he
had finished his *Sermon* and I had gained a little
calm and liberty of Speech, immediately before I
could finish one Sentence; that *Pragmatical and Insulting Soul* W. *Edmundson* stopt and Interrupted
me, so that I openly complained of incivility and
inhumanity: that hearing patiently their two Sermons, they were set down, and common Reason
said that it was my turn to speak, and every body
desired what Answer I could frame to hear it, that
then I should be *disturbed* and *stopt* was no way be-
fitting the Societies of Civil and Morral men: I
then Answered, that those very *Sermons* or *Orations*
which they had now made to the *People* were so
far beneath the merit of an Answer to them, that
they ministred and afforded to me a mighty and
invincible *Argument*, that the Spirit of God [64] was
not the *Author of them*: For we all knew that the
Spirit of God was most purely *Rational*, and a *Spirit*
of

*The Qua-
kers unru-
ly and rash
interrup-
tions*

*A short
Answer to
2 Sermons*

of pure *Order,* and did not prompt or move men to break *Hedges* and leap over one *Ordinance* into another : We were engaged in a mutual *Conference* and *Difputation,* we were in the midft of it, how came we then to fall into *Popular* Orations and *Sermons?* is it comely when perfons are *Difputing* to fall upon our knees and Anfwer an *Argument* with a *Prayer* (as it is a frequent practice with the *Quakers,*) is it proper to break off *Prayer* and fall to difputing, or out of Difputation into *Preaching?*

The mo-tions of Gods fpirit not thofe of the Qua-kers

But I faid my Oppofites Spirit was far from the *Holy Spirit of God:* and his movings are far from the *Motions* with which my *Antagonifts* were acted, for they had neither power to keep civil Order, nor to be patient, for not being able to anfwer nor bear my words *W. Edmundfon* faid exprefly what fhould we fit here and fuffer him to vent his *Blaf-phemies and Lies?* he hath kept us here two dayes, and have proved nothing, &c.

The Qua-kers not or-derly nor patient

I took a little boldnefs and told them, that if *Paul* himfelf were prefent, or *Jefus Chrift* himfelf in their bodily prefence which they confeffed he *died* in at *Jerufalem,* yet they would fay unto them, even unto Chrift himfelf, thou haft falfely *charged* but thou haft proved nothing : *Paul* himfelf fhould be an Enemy, and Jefus Chrift fhould be a *Blaf-phemer* and a *Beelzebub* becaufe he brought glad news of the Truth from Heaven to them.

I further faid, that I had more to offer in the name and in the caufe of the true Lord Jefus Chrift, and after I had got liberty of fpeech, I faid that as they which *denied* the perfon of the true

Lord

Lord Jesus denied the true *Lord Jefus* himself, fo ^{The}
they which denied the Offices which God the ^{Offices of}
Father had invefted him with and *defigned him to* ^{Jefus}
fulfil, the *denied* the true *Lord Jefus Chrift.*

They *demanded* of me wherein *they denied the
offices of Chrift Jefus*: I Anfwered, *I had many
things to declare in which they denied the* Offices
of Chrift Jefus (as well as the *Papifts* for which we
feperated from them as *Antichriftans*, not holding
the Head the true Lord Jefus the *Sacrifice and Sacri-
ficer*, the only *Prophet, Apoftle* and *Meffenger*, bringing in *the laft times, the laft Difpenfation and Will of
his Father* : contrary to the *Papifts* who fet up
(fome of them) *the* Pope and (fome of them) *the
general counfel above the* Lord Jefus declaring his
mind in the *Holy Scriptures*: and con- [65] trary
to the *Quakers* who fet up a voice or motion within
them overtopping and over pouring the voice of
Chrift Jefus in the Scriptures, fome of them maintaining that this *Light* within them is that *great
Prophet* that was to come which *Mofes* Prophefied
of, *Deut.* 18.

I faid I would contract my thoughts, and fpeak at ^{The King}
prefent only a little of his *Kingly power and Office*, <sup>ly office of
the Lord
Jefus.</sup>
and I plainly denounced that they were all notorioufly guilty of *High Treafon* againft the King of
Kings, the Lord Jefus, yea as far as in them lay,
they robd him of his Crown, and Life and All.

In particular I told them I had abundant proof
there ready to bring forth from G. *Foxes* Book, that
he and his Affociates denied (yea all of them) that
vifible Kingdome and *Church* and *Inftitutions* which
he

he as *King* over all his *Subjects* hath *Sovereign Right* unto, and moſt faithfully and wiſely ordained to continue until his coming again.

The viſi-
ble Chriſ-
tian
Church
& Ordi-
nances.
I told them that G. *Fox* his Book and all their Books and Profeſſions denied any viſible Church of Chriſt at all : and though they maintained and kept up *Congregations* (of pretended Chriſtan) *Worſhips* and *Worſhippers* (in a direct contradiction unto their own Tenents, yet) they maintained the Church was in God and ſo not viſible : the Officers of the Church were inviſible and immediately made by the immediate and inviſible Spirit. The *Baptiſme* was within, and only the *Baptiſme* of the *Spirit* and of *Fire*: The *Lords Supper* appointed by the Lord Jeſus to be a Spiritual Feaſt remembring him until his coming was with them nothing elſe but Spiritual joy, which they have one in and with another, which they have by the ſecond coming of the Lord Jeſus to them, who they ſaid was come again to the Apoſtles the ſecond time, and unto themſelves alſo.

Upon this (as I remember) there fell out ſome words between my Oppoſites, and ſome of the people called *Baptiſts*: But ſome of them (eſpecially *John Stubs*) demanded of me, why I thus charged them and was my ſelf ſo guilty, not living in *Church Ordinances* my ſelf.

Touching
the ſeveral
Churches
extant.
I Anſwered, that it was one thing to be in Arms againſt the *King of Kings* and his *viſible Kingdome* and *Adminiſtration of it*, & to turn off all to *Notions* and *Fancies* of an inviſible Kingdome, and inviſible Officers and Worſhips as the *Quakers* did: Another thing

66] thing among so many pretenders to be the true *Christian Army* and *Officers* of Christ Jesus) to be in doubt unto which to associate and to list our selves.

After all my search and examinations and considerations I said, I do profess to believe, that some *come nearer to the *first primitive Churches*, and the *Institutions* and *Appointments* of Christ Jesus then others, as in many respects so in that gallant and heavenly and fundamental Principle of the true matter of a Christian Congregation, Flock or Society, viz. *Actual Believers, true Disciples & Converts Living Stones*, such as can give some account how the *Grace of God* hath appeared unto them, and wrought that *Heavenly Change* in them; I professed that if my Soul could finde rest in joyning unto any of the *Churches* professing Christ Jesus now extant, I would readily and gladly do it, yea unto themselves whom I now opposed.

But *Thirdly*. Not finding rest, they themselves knew, there is a *Time* of purity and *Primitive Sincerity*: there is a time of *Transgression & Apostacy*, there is a time of the coming out of the *Babilonian Apostacy & Wildernefs*: there is a time of many *Flocks* pretending to be Chrifts and saying. *Loe here he is, &c.* and a Command of Christ Jesus, goe not into the *Wildernefs*, goe not into the private *Chambers*: There is a time when *Christ Jesus* his Doves and Loves cry out to him, *O thou whome my Soul loveth, tell me where thou feedest, where thou makeft thy Flock to rest at noon; for why should I be as one that turns aside to the Flocks of my Compan-*

Churches nearest to Christ Jesus

This was and I hope is the principle of the N English Church.

The various appearances of Christ Jesus

ions ?

ions? I doe not remember that any *Reply* was made to this by any of my *Oppofites,* nor heard I any more of this *Objection.*

I now praied there[1] patience to hear me a few words: I faid we had fpent two whole dayes from *My offer in the end of the fecond dayes conference* morning to night and had proceeded no further then the Debates of the two firft *Pofitions,* I told them if they were free I would attend them again in the Morning (being the firft of the week) to fall upon the proof of my other five pofitions remaining for *Newport*: or if they were not willing to that, I would (if God permitted) attend them there on the fecond day called *Munday,* in the Morning to proceed upon the reft.

W. Edmundfon faid, they had fpent fo much time *Lying pretenders to Gods fervice* already upon but two of them : and both he and *John Stubs* faid they had other bufiness in hand then to attend unto my *falfe Charges* which in all 67] this time I could not make out: they faid they muft go about the work of the Lord to which he had called them.

I told them I had ufed all diligence, I failed not to meet them about the exact hour appointed, and always before the audience was come. I never withdrew nor abfented a *Minute,* but put my old *Carcafe* to conftant purfuit of my promife which lay on me to fulfil, and to make out my proofs, *The Authors juft Apologie agaiſt* although they had fpoke never a word until I had finifhed: I ufed all poffible brevetie, and oft times fuppreffed my thoughts preffing in upon me for

Utterance

---

1 " their."   *R. W. Ms. Ann.*

Utterance and Audience; I rather chofe thus to *the unjuſt*
Apologize for my felf, then down right to blame *clamors of*
them, on whom (they faw well enough) I laid the *kers* *the Qua-*
blame of our long proceeding. I told them I had
fpoken nothing to them but the *Eternal truth* of
God, which fooner or later would arreſt them,
and uſing aloud the words of the Lord Jefus [*viz.*
The words that I have ſpoken ſhall judge you at the laſt
day.] I withdrew.

Within a quarter of an hour they fent one to
me to defire my coming in again to them, and
William Edmondſon (commonly their proud mouth)
told me that I had deeply charged them and laid
many *falſe Accuſations* upon them, and fome of
them dangerous, both as they were *Chriſtians*, and
as they were men: they had uſed long·patience in
hearing of me, and yet becauſe it ſhould be feen
that they were willing to hear the utmoſt that I
had to fay they would meet and fpend a few hours
with me on the fecond Day following at *nine in the*
Morning, only they would not endure any long and
tedious Diſcourſes.

I anfwered that their own fouls knew, and the *A mutual*
Auditors knew I ufed to be brief: and if they had *agreement*
pleaſed to have given me leave, I would have fin- *for a third*
iſhed the whole feven by noon the firſt day : and I *ference.* *dayes con-*
would now promife them (by Gods help) to finiſh
what I had to fay to the other five remaining in a
quarter of an hour, fo that in five quarters of an
hour I would prefent them with what I had to fay :
W. Edmundſon faid they would expeᷓ I ſhould fo do,
and all of them ſeemed well pleaſed that I offered
                                                    to

to difpatch each Pofition in a quarter of an hour; I faid they muſt not count me falſe& a *Promiſe-breaker* if I was not exaɛt to a quarter of an hour poſſible I might be within a quarter, poſſible I might fomething exceed it, but I hoped not to exceed above a quarter.

W. Edmundſon replied, Nay *Roger* thou muſt be punɛtual if [68] thou wilt be a·Chriſtian : and indeed afterward at *Providence* he unjuſtly more then once upbraided me faying, *Is this your quarter of an hour?* I anſwered that Chriſtians nor any prudent man would be fo curious and critical as. to raiſe Cenſures and Accuſations upon the nicityes and uncertaintyes of a few *Minutes,* for unless we had Clocks and Watches and quarter-Glaſſes (as in fome Ships) it was impoſſible to be exaɛtly punɛtual : however by Gods help I faid I would ſtudy ſuch *Exaɛtneſs,* that I would rather omit much I had to ſay then fail in my promiſe to them.

A quarter of an hour much canvaſed.

After this (as I heard) *W Hitchcock* of *Newport* held diſpute with them about Water-Baptiſme, I was withdrawn being evening and weary.

I was told by many of *Providence,* that I knew them they· would not ſtand a *Diſputation* : or if they did they would not continue without great *Advantages* and be as ſlippery as *Eeles,* and break off abruptly, as their ſpirit hurried them, I therefore ſtudiouſly endeavoured to tole and drive them to the finiſhing of my remaining five at *Newport,* and the other ſeven at *Providence.* And thus by the moſt wiſe and gracious hand of God we came to the end of the ſecond dayes work, and the ſecond Pofition and the end of the Week. It

The Qua-kers ſpirit & policy

It was queried by some why (at *Newport* and *Providence* afterward) they appointed the end of the weeks for the *Disputation*? and why since it was not finished they would not proceed on the first day? It is not immaginable that they cordially owne that day, (for the *Quakers* work upon it) but they wisely resolved to have the whole first day with the People to make up their *Breaches*, stop *Leakes* dress wounds that might be in the foregoing *Agitations* against their *Consciences* & *Credits*. It is dolefull that men of excellent parts, and of great knowledge in the *Scripture*, should yet so ly under a Sentence of *Gospel justice*, that they cannot but *deceive* as they are *deceived*, that they cannot but *believe Lyes* and *tell Lyes*, horrible and blasphemous Lyes, as confidently as the *Purest Truths*, and suck in and, powre out the poyson of Dragons, the great *red Dragon*, the *Father of Lyes*, instead of the sweet *Milk* and *Wine* from the *Breasts* of the *Way, the Truth, and the Life*, the son of *God Christ Jesus*.

The Quakers would not dispute on the first day and why.

69] THe third day of our *Conference* being come, being the second of the Week as was appointed, *W. Edmundson* began and said to this effect, *Roger*, we have waited upon thee two dayes already to hear what thou hadst to say to prove thy false *Charges* against us: we are here according to promise to spend some hours about the rest of the seven which yet remain: we must tel thee that we will not give thee leave to make a long work of it: if according to thy promise thou wilt dispatch each

The third dayes conference at New-port

af

af the other five in a quarter of an hour, we will keep our promise and hear thee.

I knew it was in vain, (as in the other two dayes past I found it) to insist upon their obstinately continued *Advantage* of three constantly engaged against me (beside their accidental speakers who had liberty when others were forbidden) I say notable and *Chief men* in their way and *Sect*: and having just then read a Letter as I sate there directed to my self and all of us to be read in the *Assembly*, I begun with presenting the Letter to them, and told them that just now it was delivered to me *&c.* I knew not certainly from whome it came, nor of one Tittle of the Contents of it: only I judged it to be my Brother *Robert Williams* (*School-Master* of *Newport*) his hand: I read the *Superscription* and offered if they pleased to unseal and read it, or I would deliver it into their hand so to doe.

W. Edmundson answered that they came not thither to hear *Papers*, but to hear how I would make out my false *Charges* against them and this he speaking none would whist against it, and this he did speak because my Brother beyond my expectation and thoughts spake some words the first morning against their *Insulting* and *domineering* over me, as also delivered a paper to them which was with much adoe handed and delivered to them but never read, containing these two great *Points* in every true penitent Converts eye, *viz.* the fight of *Sin as Sin*. And 2. The fight of the material *Lord Jesus* as the true *Messiah* or anointed, these

were

A Letter sent in to all of us.

were the two *Daggers* which they knew ftab'd at the heart of their feigned *Chrift* and *Light* within them.

I knew my Brother patiently waited there the two firft dayes, and was (with others) filenced : and now I guefled he had fent them his mind and would trouble them no more. I told them [70] the whole *Affembly* had Intereft in the Letter, as di- rected to us to read to the reft. *The Let- ter refufed to be opened by the Qua- kers*

W. Edmundfon and the reft defired. the *Auditors* to fpeak if they defired to have it read : fome of the *Quakers* faid it might be read when the bufinefs was over : fo I to make no breach put it up, and in the end of the day offered it again, claiming their *Promife*, but they regarded it not, fo that after the *Conference* ended (we of *Providence* being called away by a Boat preparing to depart) I ftept to my Brothers houfe and acquainted him with Paffages, who faid that not only the *Superfcription* was his hand but the Letter alfo, and I might open and read it, and (if it might be) prefent it to the intended *Affembly* at *Providence :* of which we fhall hear when it pleafeth the mercifull hand of the Lord to bring us to thofe Tranfactions. In fhort, it was refufed there alfo, & therefore I have judged it fit, fince it was fo folemnly flung out both at *Providence* and *Newport* that it fhould have as fol- emn a *Publication* to the whole world, and the rather becaufe it is a *witnefs* of Truth as to the two firft dayes tranfactions, impartially reproving my *Oppofites* and me alfo where he conceived we were failing : It is true I am not of my .Brothers *The Sum of the Letter*

My felf reproved in the Letter in 3 par- ticulars

Confcience

Conscience as to the *Discipline* of Christ, *viz*. that I ought to have admonished the *Quakers* in private, before I had so publickly *&c*. since they proclaimed their sin like *Sodom* on the house top: and it is preposterous to run from *House-top-sins* to closet *Concealments* and *Admonitions*.

2. Nor can I own the *Quakers* in their wayes and worships to be Servants of the Lord (as my Brother calls them) any more then the greedy *Wolves*, devouring the souls of the *Ephesians, Act.* 20. were the meek and innocent *Lambs* and sheep of Christ.

The differ-ence of the Quakers

3. Nor doe I think I charged them too deep or too sharply, as my Brother speaks: I knew the *Foxes* and *Wolves* (the able Leaders amongst them) do not run away with *Pigs* and *Worldly Swine* only, but that some *Lambs* and *Chickens* of *Christ Jesus* are carried away in their (Soul bloody) jaws also, whom I beseech to remember themselves, and I humbly beseech the God and Father of mercies to pull them out, and help all that love his Name, to help pull them out as *Brands* from the *Eternal*

Sharpness sometimes a duty.

Burnings. As for the *Wolves* and *Foxes* the *Blind Leaders*, the *Chapmen* that by feigned words make *Merchandize* of Souls (2 *Pet.* 2.) their [71] mouths must be stopped, and the *Prey* rescued from their Jawes, and because we ought to save what is saveable, and to recover poor sinners Leaders and Followers from their corrupt and rotten Profession we ought to use *Sharpness, Tit.* 1. *Reprove them sharply* (*Apotómoce*, cuttingly) that they may be found, or recover in the Faith of *Jesus.*

These

These three words I thought fit to say as to my self, let the Quakers answer for themselves, who I fear will answer to my Brother as they did to me [*Lyes, slanders, faise Accusations, &c.*] However the Reader is here presented with the Copy of it.

The Superscription.

To his Loving Friends Roger Williams *and the* Quakers *now assembled at* Newport   *deliver,*

Humbly desiring the reading of it to publick *The Letter* Audience *for the Truths sake of* Christ Jesus.   *it self.*

Loving *Friends, though the Lord in his Wisdome hath denied me from* Nature *the gift of utterance, yet in his infinite mercy he hath vouchsafed to me his free gift as to* writing, *whereby the private motions arising between* God *and my own Soul (without knowledge unto any) may be declared, being moved hereunto out of a sensible sadness, which is upon my Spirit in beholding the* Cloudings *and* Vailings *of the most precious Truths of my Lord and Master* Jesus Christ: *But* (Loving Friends) *herein mistake me not at first: This is no charge nor discharge, but an appearance unto my Soul, even unto the moving of my Bowels within me: For my* Beloved *at his putting in his hand at the hole of the door, when all my* Lovers, Priests *and* Elders *gave up the Ghost in the City:* (*for gladness*) *is taken away, and joy out of the pleasant field, and in the Vineyard there is no* (*true*) *singing, and the* Tread-

16   ers

ers *tread out no (pure) Wine, for the Lord hath made
the* Vintage *shouting to cease* : *But to avoid Prolixity,
I write not to charge nor admonish, neither for* contending Argumentation, *it being against my understanding, and as the taking of a* Dog *by the ear* : *But
sincerely unto edification, in signifying the appearances
unto my Soul in what I have gotten from these your
so earnest and tedious* Debates.

72] *Therefore I am humbly bold to speak, unto all the
contending* Disputants *in the plainness of my heart.*

And First *unto the* Complaining Disputant *it appears unto my Soul, that you have not dealt as a faithful Servant of the Lord Jesus, with your fellow Servants, for you should have admonished them both first
and second time in private, and if they would not have
heard you then to have told it to the Church, the great*
Congregation *of God.*

2. *It doth appear unto my Soul, that you have
assumed and presumed too much, being so large and
high proposals, which do appear unto me not as charges,
but in this first Appearance as Proposals, until they
are maintained as charges by sufficient proof, wherein
they may be molified* : *But in truth herein I am at a
stand, for against whom were the true* Apostles *more
bitter than against the* False ? *which if the* Defendants *be so (which in charity I have reason to hope otherwise) your Conscience will be more cleared in your Lord
and Masters service* : *yet know there may be a zeal
without true knowledge, therefore let true zeal appear
that is not in persecution, but for the Glory of God and
truths sake, as it is in* Jesus.

2. *Unto the* Defending Complainants (*the loving*
Quakers)

Quakers) *which I pray take not as a charge, but as appearances unto my Soul in that you never dealt faithfully in your Lord and Masters service, for both* Complainants *and* Defendants *are all but Servants unto one Lord and Master, and you must do that service which is ordained by your* Lord and Master *to do in your several stations (either in truth or falshood) there is no hindring of it, and when you have done all you can, you are but unprofitable Servants, falling short of your* Lord and Masters *infinite Glory, and in the end of your service, you shall as the Grasse wither, and as the* Flower *fade, but unto our everlasting comforts the word of the Lord shall stand and for ever.*

First, *That you have not done your Master faithful service by assuming and presuming beyond the bounds of* Moderation and Christianity : *but as I said before take not these as charges, but as proceeding from your own* Expressions *and* Behaviours *in your late actings which have not been for that solid edification of the* Auditors *which was expected but for defending and advancing of self, which appeared* :

1. *By your limiting the Holy one of* Israel, *contrary unto your* Lord and Masters *Commission.*

2. *By breaking an* Apostolical Command (*so far as in you lay) as not to quench the* Spirit.

73] 3. *You have not dealt faithfully and Christian like with your elder fellow servant, and then what would you do with the Heir.*

To the first appearance you would not begin before you had stated by forced Covenant that none should speak (though with leave in modesty and sobriety) but those that would joyn issue with the complainant, and
that

*that under·hand writing. And herein (loving friends)
you have infringed upon thofe great Liberties and Mercies which God hath beftowed upon thefe parts, and
which you do enjoy, and cannot enjoy elfe where : And
will you now fhut up your common Wine-preffes that we
can have no fruit nor refrefhing but what comes from
your private Preffes? Know* (Loving Friends) *this
is a fad grievance that lies upon us. Yea, you do in-
fringe not only upon our Souls but upon our* Temporal
Liberties.

·*For in our Courts of Judicature there is a fundamental liberty ftated for any to fpeak freely for Confcience fake in any Caufe in the Bounds of Sobriety
and Modefty. But this appears againft the Rules and
Practifes of all* Chriftianity, *not practifed by the*
Judicial Convocation, *nor by the high* Commiffion
Court *in our Native Couutry, where often I have been,
and the* Metropolitan *with the reft of the* Bifhops *in
Gravity and Chriftianity (though their pleadings were
by Proctors, yet) gave liberty efpecially for Relations
to fpeak: As in one Inftance of a perfon whom you
all have heard of, when he was to come upon Examination, his wife being big with Childe came with him,
the* Arch-Bifhop *(though otherwife he might be improper, yet herein fhewd great civility by confidering
the Womans condition, and gave liberty for fpeaking to
the full, with replying no difcomfortable Words, yea in
Chriftianity delayed further profecution until fhe was
delivered, though afterwards they acted their improper
perfecution.*

*But into what a condition fhall we be brought (I
hope ·not into an high* Commiffion· *nor* ·Inquifition
Court)*

Court) *if this* Imprimator *goes on, that none shall
speak, no not so much as suffered to desire to speak,
though they are great with Childe with the Man
Chrift Jesus: But I hope the People will see their
Liberties, and your selves know this was not the true
Apostles practises.*

2. *Your sad quenching of the Spirit when the mo-
tion of it arose in any for Soul-satisfaction in any to* Quenching
speak, you would not suffer them to be expressed but of the
stifle them in their coming forth: O dear Friends con- Spirit
*sider, you would not be so dealt with: For what did you
know but* [74] *the Lord might bring forth from any of
the Auditors for witnessing his* Eternal Truth *and*
Glory? *therefore as your* Heavenly Master *is bounti-
fully free, be not you* Niggards *in shutting up his Boun-
ties and suffring none to pass but through your own
Purses: I speak as the Apostle did after the manner of
men.*

3. *Your Indecorum Behaviours both in words and
gestures unto your elder* Fellow-Servants & *aged Father complaining as not performing your duty as young* The
men according unto Rule of honouring gray hairs insulting

1. *But by unseemly smiles of Derision, saying often* Spirit of
(*for a time*) Thou old Man, *thou old Man, thereby* the
appearing to provoke to passion: Quakers

2. *When that would not move his exceeding great
patience, then charging of him with Blasphemy, and to
prove his Blasphemy:*

3. *Again (not* Apostle *or Gospel like) seeking and
taking advantages against the* Aged, *and contrary to
Covenant by three or four baiting him at once, unto the
confounding of his memory, or stopping of his utterance,*
under

under the pretence of challenging all comers (when reasons considers of coming in Order.) But your defence was that you were but one Man, then you should have been but one Mouth.

Again your improper charging of the complainant with mispending of time, when in Truth it was your *The true* selves (in not suffering of him orderly to proceed) But *cause of our* by your often Iterations, Tautologies, Indecorum *long dis-* Behaviours and Expressions, with improper Preach- *course at* ments at that time, and yet lay the defect upon the *Newport* aged, and would not be satisfied with his substantial Proofs, divine Reasons and Argumental Demonstrations. And herein your Conscience (if unsatisfied) had liberty in timely Order, to have made your substantial Defence, if patience had been suffered to have had her perfect work. It is acknowledged by Auditors, that as the Complainant brought substantial proof (for so far as he proceeded) so you the Defendants also brought substantial defence (in what was substantial) but now who shall judge? ye will not suffer the Gospel rule, that the standers by, the Spirits of the Prophets shall judge. Then both of your own private Interpretations doth aim to be judges, and so will be endless and true judgeless: And by proceedings, the cause of Christ Jesus (being now at stake) much dishonoured unto the sadness of my Soul and unsatisfied Conscience, and also the expectation of the Auditors which was for Soul-edification frustrated, and unto publick shame (as yet) only self contendings hath the supream Appearance. Therefore (Loving Friends) [75] pleading and defending for your Lord and Masters sake, shew your selves faithful Servants of Christ Jesus in all Humility, *self-denial, self-denial, Love, Charity, Tendernefs, in bowels of compaffion, in Gofpel Peace and Unity: only unto your Mafters praife and Glory: that the Auditors may receive the plain naked Truth of the Lord Jefus unto their Souls Edification, even the real Truth as it in Jefus, and not as words of man which is only* Vanity and vexation of Spirit under the Sun *of* eternal and univerfal Righteoufnefs, *whofe infinite glory is witneffed by*

Robert Willams.

Newport Auguft. 6.
1 6 7 2.

THis was that poor Letter (condemned unheard by thefe high Saints who now keep Judgement day) to the fire and everlafting filence: this was the two edged Sword which fmote in the hon- *The modefty of this letter* eft upright intentions of the Author every way reproving me, reproving them, and yet having fo much Sugar with his Vinegar and Honey with his bitter *Powder*, that had it been unfeal'd and read at *Newport*, or read at *Providence*, whofe tafte could it have offended, but theirs only who like the men of *China*, judge all the World to have no eyes but themfelves excepting the Men of *Europe* to whom they will grant one eye, and that is more then our proud *Pharifees* will do to any that bow not down to their moft groffe *Phylacteries*.

But from this finger of God this providential Letter appearing upon the Wall before us: I return to the work of the day, which was the Difcuffion and

and *Probation* (on my part) of the other five Proposals remaining.

I therefore (after the Letter was put up unread into my pocket) requested their Patience, while I produced my Proof of the third Position, which was, *viz.* [*That the Spirit by which they were acted was not the true Spirit of God:*] Tis true I had many things in my mind and memory) some of them I here express) but I was forced to pick and chufe and lay by: for I told them that according to my promise, and their expectation I would present them with the Substance of my proof of this Position in the compass of about a quarter of an hour.

The third Position against the Quakers spirit Discussed

76] I reminded them first of the nature of the Word Spirit in Latine *Spiritus*, in Greek P*neuma*, in the Hebrew *Ruch* and *Ruach*, signifying sometimes *Breath*, sometimes *Wind*, and from thence applied unto God himself, unto Angels, unto Men, as denoting a spiritual, powerful, invisible fine Substance distinct from flesh and earthly Bodies: Hence God was said to be a Spirit, not properly but that his Being was pure, powerful, invisible, &c.

The word spirit

1, Whether God was properly a Spirit (as the Quaker affirmed) we had some controversie at *Providence* of which hereafter.)

2. Concerning Spirits, I observed two great Sects: 1 Those of the *Pharisees* (who were accounted the most Orthodox, Sound and right, holding such a Spiritual Substance in Angels and Spirits and a Resurrection. 2. The Sadduces which held neither Angel, nor Spirit, nor Resurrection, as at this day, &c.   3. It

3. It is clear there is a two-fold Spirit: 1. Holy and pure : fuch a Spirit is God himfelf, and the *The quality of Spirits* Holy Spirit proceeding from the Father by the Son, fuch are the Spirits of the Angels, the Spirits of Gods Children in part, and the Spirits of juſt men made perfeƈt (the *Quakers* fay here, we fay in the life coming.)

The other Spirit is a wicked Spirit, a lying and a murtherous Spirit in Sathan and his Children, yet often counterfeiting the Holy and pure Spirit, like the Oile and Ointment which God prefcribed and forbad the like of it to be made on pain of death. Therefore we are commanded not to believe every Spirit, but to try even the very Spirits, not only of men but of *Doƈtrines, Churches, Religions,* pretend- *All ſpirits muſt be tried* ing the Name of God, (as do the *Turks, Jews* and *Chriſtians*) and of the Son of God, as do all the Antichriſts and Antichriſtians extant.

4. The Holy Spirit of God (being the *feven Lambs of Fire, the feven Eyes, and feven Horns,* Rev. 5.) he is pleafed to work variouſly.

Firſt in an ordinary way of Regeneration and Sanƈtification, &c. common to all the loweſt and youngeſt of Gods Children, (*John 3. that which is born of the Spirit is Spirit*) Hence we read of the Spirit of Prayer, and of Holineſs wrought in the Soul by the finger or power of God: fo that the knowledge of God, the fear, the love, the truſting to and in God, the calling upon God is natural to all Gods Children, *Gal. 5. Abba Father,* &c.

77⌋ The fecond is extraordinary and immediate, fuch as was pour'd upon the Lord Jefus, *Ifai.* 11.

fuch

such as Chrift breathed upon the *Apoftles*, and by the *Apoftles* hands upon others when they fpake with *Tongues*, fortelling things to come, and penning the Holy Scriptures or Records, as did the Prophets of old, and the firft Meffengers the Apoftles of Chrift Jefus.

I told them I had many things to fay as to the falfe Spirits of the falfe Chrifts, and falfe Prophets, the Spirits of Devils as well as the Spirits of God (in the *Revelation*) and the three wayes of deceit mentioned, 1 *Theff.* 2. by Spirit, by Word, or by Letter: but I would contract my felf, I fay that their Spirit by which they were acted was not Gods Spirit.

1. Becaufe the Holy Spirit of God was given *Gods Spirit* by means, but the *Quakers* pretended all along in *given by* G. *Fox* and other Books, that their Spirit was im- *Gods* *means* mediate or without means: I faid in the 8*th* of the *Romans* was a *Golden Chain* of *Gods Order* or *Method* of *Working* from *Predeftination* to *Glorification*: In the 10*th*. to the *Romans* was a *Golden Chain* of the *Means appointed*, &c. How fhall a Man be faved? *The Spirit* by calling upon God? How fhall he call on him *of God working by* except he believe in him? how fhall a Man be- *means* lieve in him except he hear of him? how fhall a Man hear of him except fome Preach? how fhall a Man Preach except he be fent, &c, Hence *Peter* Preaching Chrift Jefus to the firft Converts, they were fome thoufands brought to Chrift, when they were pierced to the heart, and cried out *what fhall we do?* *Peter* fends them nor to a light within them, but bids them *Repent and be Baptized*, Act. 14.

14. *Paul* fo fpake that many believed, *Act.* 16. *The Qua-kers at* Newport *appealed too pub-lickly* while *Paul* fpake the Lord opened *Lydias* heart: and I appealed to the Confciences of thofe called *Quakers* at *Newport* there prefent, whether in a contradiction this Spirit they now profeffed, de-fcended immediately upon them from God (as they fpake) or was not conveyed unto them by the Min-iftry of the former Preaching *Quakers* that came unto them: fo that thefe now are but the waterers and confirmers of this Doctrine of the Spirit in them.

2. As Believing and Converfion comes by hear-ing, &c. fo thefe extraordinary gifts and powrings forth of Gods Spirits was generally by means alfo: Chrift ufed Breathing upon the *Apoftles*: the Spirit of God defcended, *Act.* 8. 19. in the laying on of hands: in *Peters* Preaching, *Acts.* 10. the miracu-lous Spirit of [78] *Tongues* and *Prophecy* defcended upon *Cornelius* and his company, and not before, yea, and what is that waiting in filence ufed in pri-vate, and in the publick Affemblies of the *Quakers*, but a confeffed means in which they wait for the Spirit of God (as poor Souls they think) defcending on them.

I was then forced to omit the *Allegations* out of G. *Fox* his book then by me and ready, but I will now recite a few of them.

In page 6. of this Book in Folio, G. *Fox* brings Samuel Eaton in *Samuel Eaton* faying [*The Prophets and Apoftles drew people to an outward Word*] He Anfwers, Now is that which lives and endures forever, outward?

and

and did not they bring them to Chrift the power of God, which is the end of words which is immediate.

Again in the fame Page *Samuel Eaton* [*Is not the Gofpel an External way*] He Anfwers *No*, the Gofpel is a Living way which is revealed within, and is the power of God to *Salvation*.

In the fame *Page Samuel Eaton* [*Are not they feduced who are drawn off from the External means by which the Spirit is given and Faith wrought, to wait for the receiving of the Spirit without any Word to convey it to them, which Spirit when they have it is not the Spirit of Truth but of delufion*] For Anfwer, [The Spirit and Faith is not conveyed to any Man without the Word, and they are feduced which refts in the *External* from the Eternal, and the Spirit is not given by Eternal means, neither is Faith wrought.]

I Reply, and obferve how the wifdome of Men is enmity againft God, and how witty this *Fox* is to catch himfelf and others in the Traps of eternal Howling? how doth he here confound the audible words or preachings of Gods mercy in Chrift Jefus, with the inaudible, invifible, myftical and metaphorical word, Chrift Jefus himfelf.

2. Who fees not his grofs and impudent denying of the *Spirit* and *Faith* to be conveyed by means from God unto us.

In Page 15. G. F. brings in *Henoch Howet* faying [*There is nothing in Man to be miniftred to but man*] He Anfwers, How then miniftred the Apoftle to the Spirit? and Chrift fpake to the Spirits in Prifon :

Henoch Ho vet

and

and *Tim.* was to ſtir up the Gift that was in him
and the Spirit of the Father ſpeaks within them :
and the Light ſhines in the Heart : and the Son
of God is revealed in me ſaith the *Apoſtle* : that
which may be known of God is manifeſt in man,
for God hath ſhewed it unto them, *Rom.* 1. and the
Apoſtle was [79] manifeſt to every ones Conſcience
in the fight of God, and that was of God which
the Children diſobeyed.

I Reply, 1. (As in his late Book exalting his
Heathen Light above the *Holy Scriptures*) he ſimply
and prophanely joyns the *Philiſtian Prieſts*, and
Egyptian Conjurers with *Holy Job* and his Friends,
&c. ſo here he confounds and jumbles together the
natural powers and faculties and *Humane Light* in
all Mankinde with the Grace and Spirit of God
both ordinary and extraordinary as may be ſeen at
the firſt view.

2. His Scope is (abominably and horribly,) to
make the holy Spirit of God capable of being
preached unto, to be converted and turned unto
God, yea to refuſe and be damned, for it is not *Man*
he ſaith that is preached unto.

3. How *Sottiſh* and *Blind* doth this *Deceiver* pro- G. *Fox*
claim himſelf in the *Chriſtian Doctrines* of Preach- *ignorant of*
ing, *Converſion*, *Faith* and the *Grace* and *Spirit* of *ſpirit of*
God confounding *Gold* and *Droſſe*, *Pearls* and *Peb-* God
bles, *Harps* and *Harrows* (as all one) altogether.

In Page 136, 137. He brings in *Thomas Moor*, Tho.
ſaying [*Nor are we to wait for a further Revelation* Moor.
to be given forth then the Scripture for the Word of
God came not firſt immediately to the Gentiles but to
the

the Apoſtles :] He Anſwers, The Apoſtles that Preached the Word of God, it was immediate to whomſoever they preached it, for they had read it immediately, for the Word it ſelf is immediate with more that follows to the ſame ſenceleſs and abſurd purpoſe.

Reply, As if all that receive G. *Fox* his Book ſimply pretended to be from the Spirit of God re- *The uſe of means* ceive it without G. *Fox* his *Brain* and *Hand*, and *Pen* or *Paper*, *Printing* and *Letters* : or becauſe a King delivers his minde to his Secretary, and commands him to *Pen it* in a *Proclamation*, *Declaration*, &c. therefore the Kings Word or Will comes to every man immediately without any ſuch means, as the Secretaries compoſing his *Clarks* Tranſcribing, the uſe of *Printing*, *Letters*, *Paper*, *&c.* to talke after this ſort, what is it but to talk Frantick and Bedlam, and without the guidance of a common rational Spirit.

In *Page* 5. he brings in *Samuel Eaton*, ſaying [*Though all the Saints have the Spirit of Chriſt dwelling in them, which is Eternal and Infallible, yet that this Spirit ſhould do all which Saints do, and ſhould ſay all that Saints ſay, and ſhould judge for them, both per-* *Fox and the Qua-* *ſons* [80] *and things after an infallible manner, and* *kers above* *that they ſhould neither ſay nor do any thing by any* *all Kings and* *underſtanding of their own but the Spirit: all this we* *Princes,* *deny*] He Anſwers, [Which is contrary to the Apoſ- *Popes &* tle, who ſaith, as many as are the Sons of God are *Emperors* *Saints and* led by the Spirit of God : and Chriſt acts all in *Angels* them and for them : and the fruits of the Spirit, &c. and the Spiritual man judgeth all things : And that

that is it which leads the Saints to divide and dis-
cerne all things both temporal and spiritual; the
spiritual Wisdome of God which gives them a
spiritual understanding, which men must rule
withal, but not with their own which comes to
nought: and you that have not that which is infallible to judge in you, know not the Spirit of
Christ, neither can you judge of persons or things
that have not the infallible judgement, nor have
the Spiritual man: neither have you the Word of
God in your hearts, nor Christ which is eternal
and infallible all which the *Quakers* have to judge
persons and things.]

I Reply, *Mahomet* the *Grand Segnior*, or *Elder*,
and *Prophet* transcending *Moses* and *Christ* (as he
and his followers *Mahumetans* say) he pretended *The Ma-*
that he had the mind of God by immediate Reve- *humetans*
lation, and that by Revelation of the *Holy Spirit* *& Qua-*
in the shape of a *Dove*, he wrote the Minde, the *sidered and*
Word or Scriptures of God the *Alcoran* : But poor *found one*
silly Souls were *Mahomet* and all his Disciples compared with the *Seraphical Doctors*, the *Foxians*, who
neither say nor do any thing with any understanding of their own, but the immediate and infallible
Spirit of God says and does all in them: who are
fit to be *Kings* and *Princes*, Governours and Judges,
Masters of Ships and Families, &c. indeed of any
place of power or trust, but these walking *Gods*,
and *Christs*, and *Spirits*, even the meanest of the
Quakers ? May not the meanest Youth or Wench, *The Qua-*
if but a pretended *Quaker* (according to this rule or *kers Gods*
rate of being immediately inspired in all they do *upon Earth*
or

&all other Beaſts Re-probates & Devils or ſay) tranſcend all other *Teachers, Tranſlators, In-terpreters, Kings* and *Counſellors, Navigators, Hiſtori-ans, Geographers, Rulers* and *Judges*, &c. It is true that *Thomas Munſter* and *Becold,* and *Knipperdoling,* and *Fifer* pretending immediate *Revelations,* and ſo have other Leaders of theſe *Nicolaitans* in *France* and *England,* &c. but none were ſo large and open hearted as to communicate ſo freely and bounti-fully to all their followers, the immediate Inſpira-tions of their pretended holy ſpirit, as theſe [81] fooliſh and filthy Dreamers do: for ſo ſaith *Fox* [*All the Quakers ſay or do is by the infallible and eternal Spirit*] but how horribly their Spirits, Prin-ciples, Diviſions, Miſcarriages (in many ſinful prac-tiſes) and Apoſtacies amongſt themſelves give the lye and contradict this their infallibility is notoriouſly' proclaimed on the houſe top: and I may ſay ſome-thing more to this Head afterward.

At preſent I return to my *Antagoniſts,* who (while I was Arguing againſt their immediate Spirit) could not hold until my quarter of an hour, and this Head *The lead-ing of the Spirits debated.* (about their Spirit) was finiſhed but brake ſilence, and they ſaid (*eſpecially John Stubs*) doth not the Scripture ſay, if any man have not the Spirit of Chriſt he is none of his: And as many as are led by the Spirit of God they are the Sons of God, and ye have an unction, and need not that any man teach you, and you know all things?

I then anſwered that there was a leading of a *Beaſt* by an *Halter* or *Bridle,* and there was a. lead-ing of a Man with a *Reaſon* when his underſtand-ing and judgement is ſatisfied, and if ſo, I preſumed

they

they intended, that the leading of the Spirit did not lead them as *Beasts*, but as Rational, satisfying *The tryal of Revelations* their Reasons and Judgements: and if so Reason grants that there are false Spirits, lying *Prophets*, Seducers and Deceivers, &c. *Reason* therefore further saith, that every Soul must be satisfied, whether this *Leading*, or *Anointing*, or *Teaching of the Spirit* be by means of *Praying, Preaching, Reading,* *Reason sanctified* *Meditating, Conferring,* &c. or immediate without the use of these: if motions without the use of *and rightly improved* these be pretended *Reasons* tells us that a *Rational Soul* must be able to try whether the Spirit pretending to be a true or lying Spirit, and that it must have some *Rule* or *Touch-stone* to make their Tryal by, that the Rule must be my own Reason, or some Testimony of unquestionable Witnesses satisfying my Reason, or some heavenly inspired Scripture or Writing which my Reason tells me came from God: *Reason* also tells each rational creature, that it is very suspicious to be a false, lying and develish motion, which slights the *Holy Scripture* and other holy means wherein the *Holy Spirit*, *Presence* and *Power of God* hath appeared to Gods People formerly Reason tells me, that if I finde my self weak (as who doth not) to fight against the Devil (the roaring Lion and old Serpent) and I am bound to seek out for help, and what help more powerful [82] and proper then that of the eternal and all powerful Father of Spirits: and that it is best to take *James* his *Counsel*, if any Man wants wisdome let him ask of God who gives to all Men liberally and upbraideth not: if so, then *Reason*

18   tells

tells us, that except we fuffer our felves to be led as *Beafts* by *Sathan* (as the poor *Quakers* are) we muft come to the ufe of Means, or a mediate leading and teaching, and then what is become of thefe hellifh fancies of only immediate *Teachings* and *Infpirations?*

I told them that befide this *Counfel* and *Command* of God in *James,* the Lord Jefus tells us by an admirable fimilie, *that the holy Spirit of God is given in the ufe of means,* Lúk. 11. *If you who are evil give good gifts unto your Children, how much more fhall your heavenly Father give the holy Spirit to them that ask him?* and that is *Ifa.* 11. the Spirit of Wifdome, the Spirit of Knowledge, the fear of the Lord and all the Graces of the holy Spirit. It is clear that the Pen-men and holy Scribes of Gods will unto us (in whom God did fpeak, and by whom he wrote immediately and infallibly thofe bleffed chofen pens of his were not infallibly guided by an immediate Spirit in all that they faid and did about this Scripture, as thefe poor *Dreamers* fay of themfelves, and therefore muft neceffarily dafh againft the *Holy Scriptures,* and all holy means formerly ufed by the firft Chriftians, yea and all rational means to pieces; for all that they fay or do is the immediate Spirit, and Chrift and God himfelf as *Fox* here affirmeth.

I anfwered further, that if that *Scripture* alleadged by *John Stubs* [*To know all things*] be to be expounded litterally, and (as G. *Fox* in this Book) *viz.* that the Saints know all things as God, then why are not the *Quakers* Omnipotent and *Almighty*

The Spirit gotten of prayer

The Quakers Spirit

The omnifciency of the Quakers

Almighty as well as *Omniscient* : yea as it is said of the *Pope*, if he can deliver all Souls out of *Purgatory* (if he please) without *Money*, surely he is very in-humane, impious and cruel that he doth not : so I said what impiety is it, what cruelty and inhumani-ty is it in the *Quakers* said I, so infallibly knowing all things as God, not to reveal unto Men, and especially in their publick Assemblies so many deep points of the Godhead, of Creation of the Holy Three in Heaven and Earth, (which they con-fess) and all the deep Mysteries and Prophecies in the *Holy Scripture* especially in *John* and *Daniel* their *Revelations*, &c. the *Most Holy*, *Omniscient*, and *Eternal Jehovah* knows that the *Pope* and his *Purgatory*, the *Quakers* and [83] their *Omnisciency* are but *Childrens* and *Frantick Persons Dreams* and *Phantasies*, and that the Saints knowing all things is the same with their doing all things through Christ which strengtheneth them that is not all things litterally, (for that were ridiculous and blas-phemous to affirm it) but all things *figuratively* and *Comparatively*, which his holy Wisdome thinks fit to require them to know and do in order to his *Glory* and their *Salvation*.

But *John Stubs* insisted how they knew the *Mysti-cal number* of 1260 dayes, the 42 Months, the *Time and Times* and *half a Time*, and that the *Woman* was come and coming out of the *Wilderness* in them, and that now they were *Preaching* the *Everlasting Gospel* to them that dwell upon the Earth.

I Replied, it is notorious how many excellent men have been bewildred, and missed in the open-ing

ing of thefe *Myfteries.* I faid that if their infalli-

The Light within. ble and their all-knowing *Light* could open all things and was now the *Everlafting Gofpel* or *Glad News,* the Word *Eternal, &c.* and that it was not only in the *Quakers* and their *Saints,* but in all Mankind, I defired to know what they meant by this Word within, whether they meant in the un-derftanding (the eye of the Soul) or in the Will, or in the Memory, or in the Affections, or in all of thefe joyntly : for Light is only feen with the Eye, not with the Tongue, nor Ear, nor Hand : it is true in the 2 *Cor.* 4. it is faid; *that God hath fhined in*

2 Cor. 4 God hath fhined in our hearts *our Hearts,* but there the heart muft be underftood the Underftanding the Minde which is properly and nextly the feat of the Light and Knowledge of God, and this fhining (though *Fox* make it to be natural or born with every Man) is faid to be by *Pauls Preaching* as is there abundantly proved where it is as clear as the Noon day fhining, that *God fhined, Chrift fhined,* and *Paul fhined* before the *Light* or *Notice* of the glad news of a Saviour come to the heart or ears of poor Sinners, and fo thereby are turned from their natural hellifh *Darknefs* to a *Supernatural Heavenly Light.*

Who knows not (with *Jeremiah*) the heart of

The dark-nefs within Man to be naturally dark, deceitful, defperately evil and wicked, & *Gen.* 6. the imaginations of the heart of all men to be *only Evil* and that *continually,* and that it may be faid of all men (as it is faid of the holy God, in him is Light and no Darknefs fo) in them is *Darknefs* and no *Light,* fo that to hearken to, to turn to, to liften to any voice or

motion

motion within in heavenly things, in matters of
fupor- [84] natural light, is as proper as in matters
of law to go for Counfel to a cheating thief or
rogue, in matters of health, to a known cheating
Mountebank, as to turn within to a mans heart
which was the arranteft *Jugler* and *Cheater* in the
world.

At this word *W. Edmundfon* cryed out, *Blafphemy, He fpeaks Blafphemy.* I conceived he meant I
called their *immediate holy fpirit* which they pretend
to, the arranteft *Jugler & Cheater* in the world: *An Evidence that*
My heart was warm, and my tongue breaking *the Quakers fpirit*
filence, and longing to fhew him his willing mif- *and a deceitful*
take, and that I mentioned not nor thought of the *Heart are*
Holy Spirit, but every mans own deceitful heart *one*
(though clearly I have thought and proved their
holy Spirit is no other but Sathan himfelf and every
Mans own deceitful Heart: but I was prevented,
for fome of the Auditory fpake aloud that he mif- *The teftimony of*
took me, and amongft others our *Deputy Governour* *the Deputy*
Capt. *Cranfton* openly faid that *W. Edmundfon* mif- *Governour*
took me, for I exprefly faid that the *Heart* of man *Capt.*
was the arranteft *Jugler & Cheater* in the world. *Cranfton*
This did not fatisfie *W. Edmundfon,* but he re- *and others*
plyed, let the words be read then by him that took *againft W.*
them in fhort-hand: fo they cal'd upon one of *E. flanderous rafh-*
theirs to read what he wrote: now I knowing *nefs,*
what fhort-hand could doe as well as moft in *England* from my *Childhood,* and that it is impoffible for
any to write *Verbatim* fo faft as I then fpake with
vehemency, I concluded he had not exactly my
words : yet I am confident in a faction and partiality

he

he feemed to read fome words favouring my calling their *fpirit* the arranteft *Jugler and Cheater* in
the word, extreamly contary to my certain knowledg of my intentions, and of what I uttered, befide
the fndden and quick exception of our Deputy
Governour and others: but alas this was a fmall
bufinefs: but I was about to fay (as before I did fay)
from the holy Scripture *Pro.* 28. *He that trufteth
to his own heart is a fool,* and till a fpirit of Regeneration and Converfion change the heart of man,
there is no other *Chrift* nor *Spirit* within, but the
fpirit of Sathan, which is the fpirit by which the
Quakers are acted, and is the arranteft *Jugler &*

The great Cheater who cheats all Cheaters. *Cheater* in the world: This *Jugler* is fo cunning
that he out-jugles the *Juglers,* he catcheth the
craftieft foxes that catch fo many others, he takes
Captive and leads away in chains the *Wife* and
Prudent, the High and Mighty, til the holy *Spirit
of Chrift Jefus* difcover and break his fnares and
lead him Captive alfo.

The great Magna Charta xi Ifa. 59. 85] 2. I was adding another Argument from *Ifai.*
59. and I did mention the place where the great pro-
mife, *Grant* or *Charter* is given by God the Father
to *Chrift Jefus* and his Pofterity, *viz.* that his word
and his Spirit fhould be in Chrifts mouth, and in
the mouth of his *Seed,* and in the mouth of his
Seeds Seed from thenceforth and for ever.

I faid that that bleffed *Son of God* and *Son of
Man* the man Chrift Jefus, lived and dyed a *Batche-
lour,* he never had any natural *Seed* or *Iffue:* Be-
lievers are his *Offpring, his Seed,* his *Children* and
Grand-Children and fo downward to as many as the
Lord

Lord fhall call. And that *Fox* fhould not fay the ^{*The true*}
Word and the Spirit are all one (as commonly G. ^{*Seed.*}
Fox doth) and that the Father and the Son are one
without Diftinction (as boldly and Babilonically he
doth) Here is (moft diftinctly and exactly diftin-
guifhing) 1 The *Father promifing*. 2. The Son
the *Mediator* receiving this Promife. 3. The
Promife it felf, which is of a *Word* to the Son
(though that bleffed Son is alfo called the Word)
viz. of the revealed Doctrine, Will and Mind of
God recorded from and by the holy Scriptures, *viz.*
that this Word fhould be in his mouth and in the
mouth of all his *Seed,* or *Chriftian Children* after
him, efpecially his *Meffengers* and *Preachers* to the
end and Confummation of all things.

I told them it was notorioufly known how they
flighted this holy *Charter,* how they joyned not
the holy *Word* and *Spirit* together but trod upon
the *Word of God* under a cloak of advancing the
Spirit, *&c.* But of this I fhall fpeak in the next
Pofition following.

I was alfo mentioning a *third Argument* againft
their fpirit from the *Irrationallity* and Unrulinefs of
it, contrary to the *Wifdome* and *Rationallity* and
Order and *Holinefs* of the holy *Spirit of God* : this
is apparent from their bitter *Reviling,* and often
fencelefs and frantick *Reviling* in fome of them,
Devil, Devil, Devil The devillifh *Inquifitors, Monks* ^{*The rail-*}
and *Fryers, &c.* exceed them not in fpattering^{*ng fpirit*}
out *Diablo, Diablo* againft fuch as dare to op-^{*of the*}
pofe them: indeed they are both *Poffeffed* by one^{*Quakers.*}
fpirit of blafphemous *Railing* and *Reviling* againft
the

the Witneſſes: far from the holy Spirit of the *Goſpel* who in *Meekneſs* inſtructeth thoſe that oppoſe them-ſelves. Was there ever fouler Language given by any poor *Oiſter-woman* at *Billingſgate* than is given by M. F. [86] againſt Capt. *Wiggan* (to be ſeen in print to the ſhame of the *Quakers Spirit*) of all their womanhood? What is all their notorious common cenſuring and curſing even of eminent and learned and holy perſons) for *Cains*, *Judaſes*, *ſerpent Phariſes*, *dumb Dogs*, *Witches*, *Blaſphemers*, *Reprobates*, *Devils*, but a fruit of wicked and rotten fleſh, deny and defying the holy *Spirit of God*.

Their Curſing.

It is true the Holy Spirit of God in Scripture is pleaſed to uſe *Cenſures* & *Curſes* but not to every one, nor in ſuch a manner as this foul-mouth'd Spirit doth: I mentioned before their *Impudency* (which ſtinks up to Heaven and cries for vengeance) in the ſtripping ſtark naked of their Women, and diſcovering of themſelves in the Aſſembly of Men and Youths, under the Cloak and Cover of the Spirit of God: as alſo the unnatural *Preaching* of their *Women* in *publick Aſſemblies* and *Congregations*, contrary to ſo many Reaſons from Nature and Grace, ſo poſitively expreſſed by the *Holy Spirit in Scripture*.

Mens and Womens Nakedneſs

Their Womens Preaching.

What Spirits are their Dumb Spirits in their Dumbe Meetings but thoſe foul dumbe Spirits mentioned in that Goſpel, which the Lord Jeſus will caſt out and tumble down to Hell (whence they came) in his holy ſeaſon.

Dumb Meetings.

What is their monſtrous way of Singing and Toning and Humming many at once, as they often

The monſtrous Singing of the Quakers.

do

do and notorioufly did at *Portfmouth* on *Rhode Ifland* this laft year, when no man is edified, nor underftands what they fay, and it may be not themfelves (and this under colour of finging in the Spirit) what is it I fay but rendring their Tongues which fhould be their Glory and the Glory of God, their fcorn and fhame, and the holy Name of Gods holy Spirit contemptible alfo.

4. I did alfo mention a fourth Reafon againft their Spirit, and had profecuted it but I knew that *The true* (by reafon of my Adverfaries interpofure) I had *Spirit willing to be* exceeded my quarter of an hour: It was taken *examined* from the Holy Spirit of God fubjecting it felf to *by the Scripture* be tried, commanding all men to fearch the Rec- *and every* ords, commending the *Bereans* for examining P*auls* *mans Con-* *Preaching* and *Spirit* by the *Holy Scriptures*, and *fcience.* this is the true meaning of the Spirit of the Prophets are fubject to the *Prophets*, not that a true *Prophet* or *Meffenger* of God can fubject the truth of God (which he believes fo to be and will rather fuffer many deaths then relinquifh) to be fentenced by all the *Prophets* in the Church to be falfe, and he acquiefs or reft in, [87] or fubject his *Spirit* and *Confcience* to that Sentence : but that the true *Prophets of God* are willing to have their *Teachings* queftioned, examined and made clear by the holy *Records* to the Souls and Confciences of all men. *The falfe*

Hence it pleafeth God to give Rules for the trial *and Jug-* and difcerning between the true Spirit and the falfe, *lers endure* 1 *Job.* 3. & 4. *chapters.* *not fearching.*

On the contrary, I would have fhewed (which indeed all men know) that the thief endured not

19   fearching

fearching the *gall d Horfe* endures not rubbing, the guilty Debtor endures not Reckoning, the falfe and jugling Spirits efcape in a Mift, and by the help of dark *Lanthorns,* and under the covert of the night : who may not fee this in G. *Fox.* all along his Book, running into the Thickets and Burroughs of Words of *divers fignifications,* Scriptures notorioufly wrefted, general, and fometimes uncouth and barbarous Lan - guage, which hath been the trade of the falfe and lying Murtherous Spirit in all ages, and will be un- til that fhort time be finifhed wherein the Lord will tread him under the Saints feet, and caft him into the Lake that burns with fire and brimftone.

How oft have I been vifited by the *Quakers,* cry- ing *Repent, Repent, hearken to the Light within thee,* &c. And I never could perfwade them to fit down and examine their fayings by the *Holy Scriptures,* but when their *Cuckoes note* aud *fong* was over, and their *Fools Bolt fhot,* then fell they to *Curfing and pouring out the Thunder-bolts* of Gods *Judgement* : and fo be gone no lefs then *Reve and Muggleton* (pretending to be Gods two laft Prophets and Wit- neffes) about twenty years fince in *London* whofe Curfings were notorious.

But to return, while I was beginning to urge the tryal of the *Spirits, W.Edmundfon* faid the *Spirit of God* was above the *Scriptures* and not to be tryed by them: for it gave out the *Scriptures &c.* And I faid and fay it is eafie to boaft of the *Spirit,* but the *true Spirit* (in a Senfe) and the holy *Scriptures* are one, as the *Father* and *Son* are one, and therefore can not but be willing to be examined by the holy

Records,

The Qua-
kers cry is
Light but
they dare
not come to
it.

The two
pretended
Witneffes
Reeve and
Muggle-
ton.

The Qua-
kers would
fet the Spi-
rit and
Scripture
at odds.

Records, as every man or author will ſtand to his own ſcripture, work or writing; for the Writers were but *Pens of Heaven writing,* and uſed by the hand of the holy *Spirit.* And I remember that I ſaid to *W. Edmundſon,* Friend, You yeſterday in your long Sermon alleadged that *holy Scripture* viz, *Men will not come to the light, leaſt they ſhould be reproved,* [88] becauſe their deeds are evil: This is the true cauſe of your quarrel againſt the *Scriptures,* and of exalting the Spirit above them that is upon a true ballance, your own Spirit, yea the Spirit of Sathan to be God, and Chriſt, and Spirit and all.

After ſome few interchanges and altercations, we deſcended to the fourth *Poſition,* which they read out of the Paper (as they did all the reſt) which was this, viz. *That the People call'd Quakers did not own the Holy Scriptures.* *The 4th. Poſition concerning the Scriptures.*

In one Copy it was written *Really* own, *viz. They did not really own* the *Holy Scriptures.*

I ſaid there was a twofold owning the *Holy Scriptures* or the *Writings of God* as there is a twofold owning the *Scriptures* or *Writings of men,* the *Proclamations* and *Declarations of Kings and Princes:* The one is verbal and literal, *viz. that ſuch a writing or Declaration, or Treatiſe is extant, and that it proceeds from the Kings Authority and Command.* *A twofold owning of any ſcripture or Writing.*

The ſecond is real and actual, when the Authority of it is in all humble obedience ſubmitted to and obeyed: when the Juſtice and Equity, and the excellency and goodneſs, as well as the royal Authority is embraced and magnified.

I ſaid the *Jews* owned verbally and wonderfully
that

that Writings of the *Old Teſtament* and the *Papiſts* owned both old and new but it is known that in many particulars they do in effect deny and damn them. 1. They both ſet up their rotten *Traditions,* their unwritten *Verityes* (as they ſpeak) of equal authority with, if not (in caſes) above the *holy Scripture.*

The Jews and Papiſts and Qua-kers all of them in effect deny the holy Scriptures.

2. They ſet up the Papiſts by the authority of the Council of *Trent,* a moſt defective *Tranſlation,* notoriouſly falſe in many places all over above the firſt Copyes of the *Hebrew* and *Greek* whence all *Tranſlations* as *Counterpanes* and ſecondary Copyes or *Duplicates* ought to flow.

3. The Papiſts ſet up the *Pope* as the only in-fallible Judg & Interpreter in all *Queſtions* about the *Scriptures* and the Jews make their *Rabbies* as ſo many *Popes* alſo.

4. Their *Interpretations* are ſo forraign and ſtrange and many of them ſo abſurd & mon-ſtrous from the genuine & proper Sence of the Scriptures, and adulterated with *Wreſting and alle-gorizings &c.* that is truly ſaid of them that they bring not their *Doctrines, Diſciplines* and *Converſa-tions* to the *Scriptures* but force the [89] holy *Scrip-tures* of God to attend and wait upon their Abomi-nation as a Negro Slave and Lacquey.

I ſaid the Jews and Papiſts did not more diſowne the holy *Scriptures* upon the account of their *Popes and Traditions* and Interpretations than the Quakers did upon the account of their *Light* and *Spirit* and *Interpretations* alſo. Who knows not that in the beginning of their Profeſſion, they generally fell

The Qua-kers ſlight-ing the holy Scriptures

from

from the reading of them by themselves or in their *in many horrible Particulars.*
*Families,*or in their *Publick Assemblyes,* only crying
up the *Light within, the Spirit within, the Scriptures*
within, their Teacher within. They ftil fay *The*
Scripture was not the Word of God, the Scripture is
but a dead Letter, they have no need of *Paper-*
Teachers having the fpirit that gave it forth? Yea
as the Papifts fay, if the Scriptures were loft and
burnt out of the world, the *fpirit* within them
could give new *Scriptures.*

Tis true the *Quakers* in this Difpute profeffed to *A diffembling Show of Quakers refpecting the Scriptures.*
be tryed by the *Scriptures,* which the firft *Quakers*
among us wholly denied, but only by the Spirit
within them : But what avails this *Confeffion?* Is it
not but a fubtle trick of *Equivocation,* when ftil
they profefs to owne *G.Fox* all along, and he profeffeth the Soules of all men to be a part of God
and the divine Effence, and that their is no diftinction between *God, Chrift, and Spirit* and *them-*
felves; what fhould hinder but that the Scripture
is but a *dead Letter,* and (compared with their fpirit)
a weak and needlefs *Paper* unto them that hath
fuch a *light* and *Spirit* within to guide them?

I told them before and now that there was an
Irifh Papift in the late warrs that fpoke the very *An Irifh Papift confeffing the Truth.*
heart and foul of *Jews, Papifts* and *Common Pro-*
teftants, and the *Quakers* themfelves, as to the holy
Scriptures. In plundering and rifling a *Proteftants*
houfe he found a Bible and flung it in the Kennel,
and kickt and trod upon it faying, *The plague of God*
take this Book, it is the caufe of all thefe Quarrels.

My Oppofite faid they owned the *Scriptures* in
their

their place as a *Declaration* of the Saints Conditions, & *John Burnet* took a *Bible* and read publickly that Paſſage in *Luke* 1. where *Luke* calls his Writing a *Declaration*. I urged that this will of God. (for this *Declaration* of what Chriſt ſaid and did, and of all the reſt of the Scripture, was a *Declaration and Revelation* of *Gods* Will to his People and to the whole World) this written and revealed [90] will of God I ſaid was the Judge and Decider of all Queſtions, the tryer of all *Spirits,* all *Religions,* all *Churches,* all *Doctrines,* all *Opinions,* all *Actions.* They anſwered they did owne the *Scriptures,* and would be tryed by the *Scriptures* (which is a new trick, meaning according to their own not to be queſtioned *Interpretations*) I urged that they ſet up their Spirit above the Scriptures, (fathering all their Revilings Curſings and Abominations upon the holy Spirit) I asked whether they owned the Scripture as the ſquare Rule or Guide according to whoſe ſentence all the Knowledge of God and of our ſelves, the Knowledge of Gods Worſhip and Service and our own Bleſſedneſs and Salvation was to be determined, yea and the Spirit within them to be tryed, determined, approved and condemned alſo.

The Scrip-
tures
miracu-
louſly pre-
ſervd to
be Gods
ſtanding
outward
Record &
witneſs.

They ſtill fled to this *Burrough,* the Spirit that gave forth *Scripture* is greater then the *Scripture :* the ſpirit is in us, that Spirit only opens the Scripture *:* the Spirit is immediate and infallible and they only who have this Spirit know the Scriptures. I anſwered that I maintained the inward breathing of the holy *Spirit* more than themſelves,

for

for I quoted before *Luke* 11. *viz.* that we ought in all our *Preachings*, *Hearings*, *Readings*, *Prayings*, &c. to beg the help of the *Spirit* called the Finger and Power of God: and yet I alſo maintained that this Record, this Word Will or Mind of God written and pen'd by choſen Pen-men as *Pens* in the hand of his holy Spirit, and ſo miraculoufly preſerved from the Rage of the Devils fiery Inſtruments, *Babilonian*, *Aſſyrian*, *Romane* and *Popiſh Tyrants* and that much among the Jewes and Papiſts (and much by their meanes also though they hate it) I ſay this Record is the outward and external *Light*, *Lanthorn*, *Judge*, *Guide*, *Rule* by which God witneſſeth himſelf and his Truth in the World, comforteth and feedeth his ſaints in their Diſperſions, diſcovers and reforms the defects and wanderings of his People (as in *Joſiah* his finding this Record, and *Ezekiel* & *John* eating the Book, out of which the holy Spirit inſpired them to propheſie to Kings and Peoples &c.

Tis true who doubts it but that God and the Spirit were before the Scriptures, and ſo he was before the Creation, before Chriſt Jeſus was born, and his Redemption actually accomplished: are the works of God therefore, and the ſeveral Diſpenſations and Inſtitutions and Inſtruments of God in their ſeveral times and [91] places of any whit leſs power or eſteem becauſe the moſt holy *God* and his moſt holy Spirit were before them? *John the Baptiſt* ſaith that Chriſt Jeſus was preferred before him, for he was before him and he was not worthy to unlooſe the Shoe-latchet of Jeſus the *Lamb* of God ;

God; and yet for the fulfilling of all Righteoufnefs the *Lord Jefus* muft come to *John* to be baptized of him, and the holy *Spirit* of *Light* will declare himfelf to be true by the holy *Scriptures,* and dif-cover all other Spirits to be fpurious falfe and Baf-tards and notwithftanding their cracking and prat-ing of *Light* if they flight this outward ftanding *Record* and Witnefs of God in the World it is be-caufe there is no light in them,

One of thefe two muft be done either we muft fubfcribe to the *Papifts* and by their pretended Spirit and Church find out and authorize the Scrip-tures, juft as the *Foxians* fay, or elfe we muft with *Luther* and his Affociates, *Calvin* and his followers maintain Learning ftudy the Scriptures, fearch the Originals, Copyes and Tranflations, and vindicate their *Purity* and *Perfection,* their Authority and fole external Direction how to judge of all pre-tending *Chrifts and Prophets* and *Doctrines & Churches* and Spirits.

The holy Scripture the only outward ftanding Rule & Record like the Records in the Tower

While we were thus difcourfing *W. Edmundfon* propounded this Similitude, ·if I fhould write a letter to a friend and fubfcribe my name *W. Edmundfon,* doth it follow therefore that the Letter is *W. Ed-mundfons?* I anfwer that the Quakers do affirm that the Scripture is within them, what is the eng-lifh of that? but that the Light which they and every man in the World hath within them (the Chrift the Spirit which every one hath) is Scrip-ture, and in a fence I faid it was a Truth that *W. E.* his letter to his friend was *W. Edm.* not only a *Declaration* of his word, mind or will to his Friend,

The Holy Scriptures are Gods Love-let-ters

but

but in a refpect his mind and will it felf that he
fent in Writing to his Friend, and fo the Scripture
in a Sence is Gods mind and Will to us.

Upon this occafion I told them that the Scriptures were the *Love Letters of Chriſt Jeſus* to his
Church, as the *Love-Letters* of fome mighty *Monarch* to his Betrothed Queen or Empress, they are
dear, not as common *Paper* and *Ink*, but as the
Good-Will, the deareft Love and heart of the King
and Emperour himfelf: and thus are holy *Scriptures* highly prized and embraced, and laid up in
the heart and bofome of the true *Children of God,*
92] believed liftned to, and followed as the voice of
Chriſt Jeſus to his true fheep and Spoufe: the
Baſtard Children and the *Wolves* covered only with
the *fheepskins* : they have other *Words, Letters &
Spirits*, 2 *Theſ.* 2. whatever they prate of Scripture,
and fpeak brave fwelling empty words as *Jude*
fpeaketh.

Tis true as G. *Fox* all along in his Book vapours
that the Spirit was before Scripture, and gave forth
Scripture : but I proved before, that their Spirit,
their Light, their Chriſt, were but hellifh *Darkneſs*, the fpirit of Sathan, and a falfe lying Chriſt,
&c. 2. The Difpenfations of God were many and
divers (as before the Law and after (but in this laft
and third difpenfation, he hath fpoken (that is his
word, mind and will whatever) the *Quakers* as well
childifhly as Blafphemoufly prate to the contrary
by his Son: And as the Son himfelf the Lord Jefus in his own perfon, when he perfonally maintained that famous combat with the Devil ufed no

*The admi-
rable ex-
cellency of
the Scrip-
ture*

20   other

other weapon but Prayer and Fasting and the Holy
Scripture, so he left written this holy patern and
example, that we through *Patience* and Comfort
of the Scriptures might have hope, *Rom.* 14. *Lu-*

Luthers
Light

ther being demanded how he gain'd such knowledge and abilities in such blind *Popish darkness*, he
freely confessed that the holy Scripture was his
first help, the second Meditation, the third earnest
Prayer to God to vouchsafe his Spirit to bless the
two former unto him. The Lord Jesus therefore
not only ordained his Messenger or *Preachers* of

Job 20.2. his glad Tydings to *Jews* and *Gentiles,* but his Pen-
considered men also, *Joh.* 20. for those two great ends (as to
us) to wit,

1. These things are written that you may believe
that Jesus is the Christ (to wit, that that individual
person and man called Jesus was the *Christ*, the
Messiah so long promised and expected (contrary to
the Blasphemous Fancies of the *Quakers.*)

And 2. That Believing in him (that individual
person called Jesus, and not in a Fancy within) we
might have Life and Blessedness.

It is no wonder therefore, that the *Devil* (the
great *Thief*) as he compasseth Sea and Land with
the *Pharisees, Jesuites* and *Quakers* to make *Prose-*
lytes, so wherever he comes he labours to blow out
the *Candle of the Holy Scripture.*

It is the Spirit Breath or wind of the *Devil* in
the lips of *Atheists, Jews, Papists, Quakers, Ranters,*
&c. that puffs and blows [93] against this Holy
Light (more precious infinitely then the Sun in the
Heaven :) it hath been most wonderfully to amazement,

ment preferved like the Sun in the Firmanent, and
fhines moft glorioufly again and again, after the
blackeft and longeft ftorm and night of *Apoftacies*
and *Perfecution*.

The *Turkifh Hyftory* tells us of a Woman appear- *A famous vifion in Turkey*
ing in the Heavens with a Book open in her hand,
fome of their *Mahumetan Priefts* dared to·fay (for
which one greatly fuffered) that the Woman was
the Chriftian Church, and the *Book* was their *Bible*
or *Scriptures* which threatned ruine·to their *Mahomet* and *Alcoran*:   *John* was not commanded
(and in him the *Proteftant Witneffes*) to ftand ftill
and liften to a Light, to a motion or voice within,
but to eat úp the little Book open (once again) in
the hands of Chrift Jefus, *Rev.* 10. and after this
eaten up to prophefie to *Peoples*.and *Nations*, to
Tongues and *Kings*.

Whether this Book be the Book of the *Revela-* *The two Witneffes eat up the book of Script.*
tion or the Book of the whole·Bible or Scripture,
it is apparent that during the 42 Months of the
the *Papal Reign* and *Darknefs*, *Chrift Jefus* hath
given Authority and power·to his Witneffes to
fearch after the Holy Records in the *Original*,·*Hebrew* and *Greek* Copies, and to bring them forth by
Tranflating and *Preaching* the *Doctrine* of them,
&c. for.which.they have fuffered Death and Burn- *Tindal the firft heavenly Tranflator burned*
ing, as *Tindal*· and many other· excellent ·men of
God.   The Walls of *Rome*, yea the Gates· of .*Hell*
have. fhaken and felt the.might.of.this· Heavenly
Artillery: It lies therefore.the Devil and all .his
                                                    Meffengers

Meſſengers in hand to break to pieces, or to nail up their[1] heavenly Ordinance.

It hath been obſerved that there never were any *The Jews outward reverence to the Script.* (more than others) famous for Chriſtanity, but they firſt were famous for an admirable Love kindled by God in their Hearts to the *Holy Scriptures*: It is true the *Jews* (to whom the Oracles of God were committed, *to wit* in the *Old Teſtament*: how ſtudious have they been in it, even to every Word, and Letter? they accounted it a crime for any Book to ly upon it, but this alwayes to lye uppermoſt. My ſelf have ſeen the *Old Teſtament* of the *Jews* moſt curious writing whoſe price (in way of trade) was threeſcore pound, which my Brother a *Turkey-Merchant* had and ſhewed me: But I ſpeak of an inward love, a *Soul-love*, &c. It is wonderful what *The firſt Proteſtants affection to the Scripture* *Luther* relates of that bleſſed *Duke of Saxony*, whom [94] God ſtir'd up to favour and cheriſh *Luther*, &c *viz.* that he cauſed his ſix *P*ages each of them to read to him daily everyone his hour in the Holy Scripture. This was the affection in all the firſt Witneſſes the *Waldenſians, the Bohemians, the Engliſh, French, Dutch, Scotch*, &c. who together with the Scriptures had mighty Affection to the ſtudy of the *Hebrew* and *Greek* in which golden *Cups* and *Bowles* the *King of Kings* was pleaſed to convey the Wine (like *Ahaſhueroſh*) of his Eternal Majeſty and Goodneſs to us.

It is wonderful to conſider how much the ſtudy of the *Scriptures* and of the *Hebrew and Greek Tongues*

---

[1] "nail up this." *R. W. Ms. Ann.*

Tongues confounded and put to flight the *Papifts,* and forced them to ftudy the *Scriptures* and the *Tongues* alfo, both which the barbarous dark Spirit of the *Quakers* hate, as darknefs hates the Light.

It is no wonder this Spirit of Lying cries out fo fiercely againft the Schools of Learning in *Old and New England*, it knows that the right and regular propagation of natural, of civil, and efpecially of *Divine Knowledge* fcatters the thick Fogs of the *Quakers* affeĉted hellifh ignorance.

The bleffed *Martyrs* and *Witneffes* of Jefus in all ages have been ravifhed with holy delights like *Da-vid* in the holy Scripture, in *Q Maries* dayes, that famous *Ridley* (called *Bifhop of London*) he had got moft of the holy Epiftles in *Greek* by heart, even before he left *Pembrook Hall in Cambridge*: and as the fire of perfecution grew hotter, fo did thofe bleffed Witneffes (like Jefus with *Mofes* and *Elias,* and *Paul at Troas*) fpend hours and nights in *Prayer* and holy Conference upon the Scriptures, and thofe things which the Lord Jefus fhould and hath now accomplifhed according to the Scriptures.

It is true (in print) *James Parnel* fpake like a *Papift* an *Atheift,* and a *Quaker* of the holy Mar-tyrs or Witneffes of Jefus Chrift, and of the book of Martyrs it felf. It is no wonder that the moft Righteous and jealous Lord left him not to dye the common death of all Mankinde, but to Murther himfelf by a proud prefumptuous attempt of de- claring himfelf to be Chrift by fafting 40 dayes and 40 nights, I believe this to be a Truth from the Teftimonies I have feen of *Parnels* cafe (being my

felf

felf then in *London*) whatever, *Fox* & the *Quakers*
impudently affirm to the contrary.

95] It is true that *James Parnel*, and *Fox*, and all
of them fometimes miferably (and after the Devils
Method) make ufe of *Scripture* as a Shield or Buckler to fence themfelves againft the Scripture, and
as a Sword to run through the Heart and Bowels
of the Scripture, the Saints, and Chrift, and God
himfelf: they make ufe of it as *Stirrops, and Lad-
ders*, and *Scaffolds* for their counterfeit Chrift (in
pretence but in reallity themfelves) to mount up
into their *Saddles* and *Thrones of the Eternal power
and Godhead* that fo the Earth may be theirs by
Authority: So that as the Lord fpeaks of the
Jews Sacrifices that they were not his: and of *Je-
hoiakim that he did not know the Lord*, Jer. 22. and
of the *Corinthians*, 1 Cor. 11. *that they did not eat
the Lords Supper* though *they did eat it*: fo I affirm
(from all the premifes alleadged) the *Quakers* do
not own, that is truely and Chriftianly (as they fay
Bonâ fide and *in reality*) but flight, and villifie, and
abominate, and nullifie the holy Scripture, that
their unwritten Lies and lying Spirits may be
exalted.

We have a great word in ufe amongft *Merchants*
and others, to wit the word [*Effects*] they defire to
fee *effects* of money or Goods, for want of a real
and effectual prizing and loving & obeying and
magnifying the *holy Scriptures*. The *Jewes* &
Pharifes, the *Papifts* and *Quakers* do not owne
the *perfection* & *Authority* of the holy Scriptures,
but fet up their *Traditions and Popes Councils* &
Spirits

*How the
Quakers
own Scrip-
ture*

*2. King.
17. the
Samaritans
feared the
Lord and
yet feared
him not.*

*The word
Effects*

Spirits above them, and therefore the *Jewes* & *Papisfts* and *Quakers* do not owne the holy *Scriptures.*

I freely acknowledge that many of thefe Particulars I could not then exprefs becaufe of my Confinement to a quarter of an hour, and fometimes the *Interpofure* of my *Oppofites:*

I remember I urged that dead and rotten efteem that both *Papifts* and *Quakers* fling as dirt in the face of the holy *Scriptures,* calling it *a dead Letter,* *a Nofe of wax, a leaden Rule* which may be pincht and bow'd to every mans Opinion : But *Firft,* They horribly bow and pinch that *holy Scripture,* 2. Cor. 3. which meddles not with all the *Scripture* but with the *Covenant* of the *Law* and *Juftice,* oppofite to the *Covenant* of *Grace* & *Mercy,* & calls the *Law a killing Letter* compar'd with the Grace & Mercy of an offended God now reconciled by *Chrift Jefus.* *The Papifts and Quakers call the holy Script. a dead Letter.*

But *Secondly,* Thefe poor *Foxes* fly to their *Burroughs* and confound the matter of the *Scripture* or *Writing*; being *P*aper [96] and ink, &c. with the contents the purport, and (as I may fay) the matter contained in the matter : we ufe to fay what have you to fhew for it? what evidences have you? what Records, and fometimes when no Witneffes are living or can be had, an old poor Record is produced which proves the life and fpirit of the bufinefs : what *Simpletons* do thefe (only) wife ones fhew themfelves in affairs of men that know not, that (as *Solomon* fayes of the *Tongue, Life* and *Death* is in the power of the *Tongue* fo) *Life* and *Death* is in the power of a piece of Paper : what hath an *Executor* (yea many thoufand Executors to fhew for their *The power of Writing in all Affairs.*

their Eſtates ſometimes of hundreds, yea thouſands years but a little paper, and ink, and wax from the Teſtators? what gives life to a condemned ſoul but a *Pardon* or *Reprieve* in a piece of *Paper?* who knowes not that a Writ or Paper ſigned by his *Majeſty, the Lord Chancellour, the Lord ceief Juſtice* hath Death in it, and fetcheth off the heads of many, yea the *higheſt Offenders?*

The *Quotations* out of *G. Fox* which then I could not inſiſt on, I ſhall preſent a few and then paſs on to the *fifth Poſition.*

Joſh.
Miller.

In the 47*th.* Pag. *G. Fox* brings in *Joſ. Miller* ſaying, *It is an Errour (if not damnable) to ſay Chriſt is the meanes, and that there is no other meanes of Salvation.*

He Anſwers, *And Chriſt ſaith no man comes unto the Father but by me: and he is able to the uttermoſt to ſave? and he ſhall be my Salvation to the end of the Earth ſaith the Lord: and ſaith the Apoſtle, God is in Chriſt reconciling the World to himſelf, and he that hath the Son hath Life, and the Father and the Son are one, and there is no ſalvation in any other.*

I reply: I ſhall now freely declare to the Sence cf this *Allegation,* though in the Diſpute my *Adverſaryes* would not ſuffer me to meddle with the Sence of *G. Fox* his words, contrary to our Coven-

The Qua-
kers notor-
ious Cove-
nant-
Breakers.

ant in my Writing, *viz.* that each *Party* ſhould ſpeak as long as they pleaſed, which Liberty they enjoyed without my *Interruption*: and firſt I doe not think that *Joſ. Millers* words run ſo looſely in his own Book: I do not think that a man of Wiſdom would call it an error to ſay that *Chriſt is the*

meanes

meanes of Salvation : But to the fecond part, to which G. *Fox* oppofeth, I believe it is an *Error,* and a damnable *Error,* and a Doctrine of *Devils,* to fay there is no other meanes of Salvation : for this wretched *Jugler* fubtilly confounds the *Inftrumental Caufes* of *Salvation* with [97] the *Efficient* in God the Father, and *Meritorious* in God the Son, Chrift Je- fus. 'Tis true, there is no *Redemption* and Forgive- nefs of fin, but in his Blood, *Ephef.* 1. though I know this *Jugler* (as before) means not a Chrift, nor his Blood, nor Death as we do mean, but *Imaginary within,* &c. And yet as *Means* and *In-ftruments* : Chrifts Meffengers are faid to fave them- felves and others : The holy Scriptures are faid to *make wife to Salvation* : A man may be *Gods means* or *Hand* to fave his *Wife* and the *Wife* her *Huf-band* : *We are faved by hope* faith *Paul,* and faved by *Baptifme* faith *Peter,* yea, Women are faved by Child-bearing, as God bleffeth thofe *painful Curfes* to be bleffed means of bringing to, or growing up in Chrift the Saviour. All thefe fubtly and wicked- ly G. *Fox* fets at variance with the *Meritorious Sal-vation* by Chrift Jefus, between which there is an *Heavenly Union* and *Concord,* as between a man fav- ing his Brother by throwing a *Rope,* or *Oar,* or *Board* unto him, *&c.* or a *Midwife* faving both Wo- man and her Birth in *Child-bearing* by the Means of Women, and Helps which her Skil and Labour adminiftreth to her. To talk of this *Immediate Chrift* and *Spirit* without Scriptures, without *Preach-ing,* and other holy means, is as filly, as Impious,

Means of Salvation.

A Union between the Meritorious Caufe and means, and the Inftrumental and Effici-ent or worker.

as Blockifh, as Blafphemous, and as Bedlam, and Frantick, as wicked and *Anti-Chriftian.*

Would not every body laugh at G. *Fox*, if he fhould fay, that becaufe the *Kings Majefty* gracioufly pardons *Condemned Rebels* at the *Mediation* of the *Prince* his Son, therefore the Compofing the writing, the proclaiming of the pardon, the bring- of it to the *Rebels hands* written and fealed with the *Kings broad Seal*, are no means of their Salvation and Deliverance ?

Hofanna to the Son of David. In *Pap.* 221. he brings in the Author of *Ho-fannah to the Son of* David, faying, [*The fure Word of Prophefie the Apoftle fpeaks of, is the Prophefie of Scriptures.*]

He Anfwers, Doth the Scripture fhine in a dark place until the Day dawne? Are they them them that muft be taken heed unto as to a Light? Can any fee the Scripture, and know the Scripture, but with the *Light within*? Can not a *Cain*, a *Baalam*, a *Core* bring Scripture that is gone from the Spirit of Prophefie within, and then put the Letter for it?

The more fure Word of Prophefie. 98] I Reply 1. I know that *Fox* makes their *Idol within* called *Light*, to be the more fure word of Prophefie, and his ufual proof is, [*The Teftimony of Jefus is the Spirit of Prophefie,*] But firft, why muft all the Prophets or Meffengers of God, who from the beginning of the world were Gods mouth and Pens, Concerning the *Birth, Life, Death, Burial, Refurrection, Afcention* and coming to Judgement of the Lord Jefus be here caft out from the Word of Prophefie? Is it nothing, *Luk.* 1, that God fpake (furely Gods fpeaking is his word) *God fpake*
by

by the mouth of his holy-Prophets, which have been **ods** *since the World began.* And *Heb.* 1. *God ſpake ſun-* **ſpeaking** **by His** *dry times and in divers manners in Time paſt unto the* **Prophets** *Fathers,* but how did God thus ſpeake or utter his **is his** **Word.** word, but by the Prophets: And *Rom.* 16. But now is made manifeſt, and by the Scriptures of the Prophets, according to the Commandment, &c. Therefore how oft is it written concerning the Lord Jeſus. *Theſe things were done that the Scriptures might be Fulfilled,*] in which regard, (as to our ſatis-faction and belief) the written word of Propheſie of the Prophets are a more ſure Word and Evi-dence to us concerning the Lord Jeſus then the *Miraculous Appearance* from Heaven of *Moſes* and *Elias,* and the voice from Heaven of which *Peter* here ſpeaketh; though in it ſelf a true Teſtimony, yet not ſo ſure, ſo firm and pregnant as the Word that God ſpake by the mouth of his holy *Prophets* from the beginning of the World, &c. Hence the Anſwer of *Abraham,* and indeed of Chriſt Jeſus: If they, hear not *Moſes* and the *Prophets, neither will they believe though one ſhould riſe from the Dead.*

2. How ſure is the *Quakers Light,* their Word of **The mad-** *Propheſie?* A ſober mind can not but admire that **neſs of** **leaving** Face and Forehead of Braſs and Adamant with **the Scrip-** which God the Righteous Judge of the whole **tures and** **turning to** hath plauged Satan and his Followers, ſo that they **a Spirit** bluſh not to prefer ſuch a ſimple Image, a *meer Ba-* **within.** *bie* and *Childs Puppet* of their *Immediate Word* of *Propheſie* before the Word, the mind and will of God by the mouth of all the Prophets?

For is it not known in the holy Scripture, in all
Hiſtories,

Hiftories, in all Ages, in all Nations, what Curfed
Opinions, horrible Uncleanneffes, Bloody Murthers
and Slaughters have been Conceived and brought
forth from the Spirit within, and Revelati- [99] ons
from *Divilifh Lights* and *Spirits*, and the horrible
End that generally the Authors and *Promoters* of
fuch Spirits and Infpirations have come to?

The workings of Satan by Spirits and Infpirations in all Ages.

3. This Scripture, *Revel.* 19. *The Teftimony of
Jefus is the Spirit of Prophefie,* what is it but *Goli-
abs Sword* to fetch off the head of this proud *Phi-
liftin,* for, doth not the *Angels* forbid *John* worfhipping of him upon this ground, *viz.* that the *Angel*
was his *Fellow Broker, Fellow Servant, Fellow Wor-
fhipper, Fellow Witnefs?* Is not this the Argument
whereby he prohibits him, *viz.* that one Teftimony
of Jefus was the work of Gods Spirit in the *Angels,*
in their way, as well as in *Iohns* and *Peters* in theirs,
&c. and fhall we fay that the Angels too are
Quakers, and Chrift hath enlightened them alfo, as
well as every man that comes, *&c* And *Revel.* 22.
Doth not Chrift threaten the *Adders* to, and *Dimin-
ifhers* from the word of this Book of this Prophefie: what *Affinity* hath a written Book a written
Prophefie with *Immediate whifperings* and *Infpirations?*

The Devil and the Quakers alleadging Scriptures

2. Why fhould G. *Fox* here mention *Cain, Balaam,
Core?* what Scriptures could they bring? what Scriptures were written in their times? I think it no
breach of Charity to guefs that the *Quakers* and G.
Fox are fo ufed to Curfing and Cenfuring their *Oppofites* (at the firft dafh) for *Cains, Baalams, Cores,*
that they could not well tell how to mifs them:
Such

Such perfons no queftion, and the *Foxians*, and the
lying Spirit, the *Old Fox* and *Serpent*, bring Scripture: But doth the Divel cordially prize and love
the word of *Prophefie*, the *Teftimony* and *Witneffes*
of Jefus? However he plainly here Confeffeth that
the holy Scripture is fo powerful that the very
Counterfeit, the picture and Name of it will do
him good Service, with fuch whom he defires to
cheat and Ruine. And yet *fecondly* this fhews the *Quakers horrible wickednefs*, that although they love the
holy Scripture (for the general of them) as well as
doth their *lying Father*, yet turn they the Truth of
God into a lye, and with the ugly Spider fucks that
which he turns into poyfon, even from the fame
Flowers of Paradice, the holy Scriptures, from
whence the *hony Bees*, the true Believers, fuck the
pure hony of Eternal Truth and Comfort.

   3. Again, what madnefs is it for this *blind
Dreamer* to ask his Oppofite, whether the Scripture fhines in a dark place until the [100] dawne?
& whether they muft be taken heed unto as to a
Light? For, how often is the holy Scripture even the
very Law before the Gofpel, or glad News was No Light
preached, adorn'd and beautified with the *Illuftri-* in the bold
ous Title of Light? and all the *fubtle Foxes* in the pretend-
world muft know that if they attend unto whif- much) the
perings and peepings, *Ifai.* 8. and leave the written Quakers.
Law, the Word, and other Prophefies of Scripture,
or written Prophefies, Words and Oracles of God!
For all their Childifh Vapourings and pratings of
their Light, the *Eternal Father of Lights* proclaims
them to be Children of *howling darknefs* and that
                           there

there is no Light within them : I fpeak it with horrour and Amazement, and alfo with forrowful Confidence that he that fhall find a fpark of true Light either of the knowledge or grace of the true Lord Jefus in this their *Fantaftick Light*, he fhall find the Living among the Dead, he fhall prove the Prophets that fpake, and the Lord God of the *Prophets* whofe word was fpoke, to be Lyars, for faying there is no Light within them.

But *Fox* again demands, (*Can any know the Scripture but with the Light within?*] And I ask him what Light have the *Papifts* and *Iews*, and the *Divel* himfelf, when they and he bring Scripture to Chrift himfelf? I know very well what he means in his *Iefuitical, Diabolical Refervations,* by the *Light within* and by knowing the Scripture, his meaning is known and Common, *viz.* except he be one of thofe dark Souls called *Quakers*: But did not the Devil bring a pertinent Scripture and promife to Chrift Jefus as ever *Papift* or *Quaker* could have alleadged, though pointed and directed as are the *Papifts, Iews* and *Quakers Allegations* to a *Venemous* and *poyfonous End.*

He brings in *Henoch Howet* faying, [*The Scripture to be the only Weapon whereby Chrift overthrew the Devil.*]

He Anfwers, who bruifeth his Head, and was before Scripture was, yet the Scripture is for Correction and Doctrine, furnifhing the man of God in his place, and Chrift the Seed was before the Scripture was: And all them that hath Scripture and not Chrift cannot overcome the Devil, you and the

Marginal notes:

The pure Scripture filthily abufed.

Pag 14: Henoch Howet. By the Weapon of the Scripture only Chrift Conquered the Devil-

the *Papifts* doing his work: for they that overcome him that is with the *P*ower, and thofe have
the Scriptures of Truth, which the Devil is out of.
101] I Reply, How doth Chrifts bruifing of Satans Head, and being before Scripture was, difprove
Fox his Oppofites faying, *viz.* the only weapon
whereby Chrift Jefus overcome the Devil was the
Scripture? what is this to the point of the Compafs? may not half an Eye fee what a *fimple
Sophifter* this is, to make fuch Yawes as not to come
near the Ships Courfe and point in hand.

2. Who fees not *Fox* in his *Burrough* of the divers Acceptation of the Word Chrift? For in the
Senfe of his Oppofite that man Chrift Jefus who
fought the Devil, and *Fox* Confeffeth died at *Ierufalem*: was not before the Scriptures, But his Birth,
and Life, and Death, &.. were Proppefied and declared by the *S*cripture long before he was born.

3. As for this faying, [*They that have the Scripture
and not Chrift can not overcome the Devil*] What
News doth *Fox* tell the World, which no Body
denies? and how doth this deny that Chrift Jefus
overcome the Devil by the Scripture?

4. Is all Scripture or writing given by Infpira- The
tion of God, *and is profitable* (though *Fox* alleadg- Scripture
eth this Scripture by halves) *for Correction and Doc-* and pro-
trine, &c. then it clearly follows, that as Chrift per Wea-
Jefus overcome the Devil by the Scripture, fo by pon
the fame Weapon this *fubtle Fox*, and all other of De.
Satans Foxes muft be Corrected, Confuted Catcht
and deftroyed, (except they repent) for ever: But
what is this Confeffion that the *Scripture is profitable*
                                                    for

for Correction, &c. but a kind of grant to his Oppofite that Chrift did overcome the Devil by this
Weapon, for he Confeffeth it profitable for Correction, *&c.* though yet all this running about in
and out into his holes in this Anfwer is a whisper-
ing, and yet loud enough to be heard, *viz.* that
Chrift did not overcome the Devil by the Scripture,

The Dev-il a Fox too Crafty for all the Foxians.

5. As for the *Quakers Power* here pretended in
Oppofition to the Scripture, as being thofe that
have Scripture within them, and fo overcome the
Devil? How doth the Devil deal as one that pretends to Fight, with Children who lies down and
Cries as if those poor Childifh Souls had Overcome
him? Thus fometimes a Devil of Drunkennefs,
of Swearing, of Stealing runs away from the Sermons of the *Quakers,* as a *naughty Devil,* fometimes
at the Chiding and Conjuring of a *good Witch!*
That he may get the fafter hold by fpiritual pride,
hypocrifie, [102] felf Conceit, and Contradiction
to the Scripture, by will worfhip and Superftitious
Inventions againft the holy Inftitutions and Commands of the true Lord Jefus Chrift.

Francis Duke.

Pag. 289. He brings in *Francis Duke,* faying,
[*When Chrift told the Devil that man fhould not live
by Bread alone, but by every Word that proceedeth out
of the mouth of God, that was believing the Scripture:
And this Word of God in the Scripture was the Ground
of Chrifts Faith, and fo to all that are his*

He Anfwers, Many may have the Scripture and
never hear the voice of God, as the Jews in the
fifth of *John,* and they faid they believed the Scriptures though they were out of the true belief

But

But receiving the Word from God, is, as they that
gave forth the Scriptures: which man lives by and
not by bread alone, and so knows him who was
before Scripture was given forth: And for faying
that the Scripture was the Ground of Chrifts Faith,
he was afore the Scripture was writ, and fo fulfils
their Words, and is the Author and the Finisher of
the Saints Faith, which was before the Scripture
was given forth, him by whom the World was
made, and is the Author of the Saints Faith,
that bruifed the Serpent under his feet, which was
before the Scripture was.

1. I Reply, How Notorious for *Tautologies* are
thefe *brutifh* C*lamours*? Thrice in this fmall Anfwer have we of Chrift, which was before Scripture
was, who was before Scripture was, &c. fhall we
believe their Notorious Lyes, *viz.* that the Light
within them gave forth Scripture, and that they
fpeak and write as they are moved by the moft
holy and Infallible Spirit, when their writings are
fo weak, lame and Childifh, juft like the talk of
Aged doting Women, and fo full of Idle Repetitions?

The Qua-
kers Ricĩ-
culous for
and in
their *Tau-*
tologies.

2. What Anfwer is this, how brutifh and Impious, *viz.* that a man may have the Scripture and
yet not be in the belief, therefore the Word of
God was not the Ground of Chrifts belief, fo again,
the Devil and wicked men may have the Scripture,
and yet believe not in them, therefore Chrift Jefus
and his faints believe them not neither: this Inference is clear, you fay Chrift was before Scripture
was, &c.

22

I Reply,

I Reply, He was, and he was not,: But let Hea-

The Qua-kers mad Fancies as to Chrift and the Scripture. ven and Earth Hear and abhor the *Sophiftry* of thefe *Deceivers*, they would fain [103] have no fuch Chrift as man, a Chrift without, an *out-fide Chrift*, but a *Spirit* and God only, and that in their Flefh: yet again, (for fhame of the world) they are forct to Confefs that there was fuch a man or perfon, *&c.* and yet to Cloak and Cover that Confeffion from Croffing their Principle, they fay; that before Scripture was Chrift bruifed the Serpents Head, that is Chrift that made the World, Chrift the Light, the Word,: But this again., we fay is falfe alfo, for the Promife is, *Gen.* 3. that the *Seed of a Womau* which was Chrift in his Manhood, born in the Fulnefs of Time, *Gal.* 4.

And let G. *Fox* or any of their *Juglers* Anfwer If they fpeak honeftly, and (*bona fide*) if there was really fuch a man called Jefus at *Jerufalem*, &c. as there was fuch a man called G. *Fox* lately in *New-England*, was there not fuch a man called Jefus,

The Hu-manity of Chrift. after the Scripture was written or penn'd? was dot this ma*n* *forty dayes tempted of the Devil*, and did not this man called Jefus Chrift Overcome the Devil by the Weapon of the writing or Scripture: and was not the holy Scripture the Ground of his Faith, as he makes the Will or Word of God declared in this holy Writing or Record the Ground of his faints Faith alfo?

Pag 16 John Timfon He brings in *Iohn Timfon* faying, [*The Scripture is the Rule of Life.*]

He Anfwers, Contrary to Chrift, who faid, *the Spirit fhould lead them into all Truth*: *And they that are the*

Sons

Sons of God are led by the Spirit of God: and the Churches was to hear what the ſpirit ſaid, for the ſpirit lead them to ſpeak forth Scripture.

I Reply, If among the ſeven things that God hates, he is an Abomination that ſoweth Diſcord, what is he that would Oppoſe and ſet at Odds the moſt holy ſpirit, againſt the holy ſcriptures Inſpired by him? and in Effect declares that Gods Children are not to attend to the voice of God in theſe his holy Inſpired writings, but to a ſecret Voice or whiſpering within them : Contrary to the ſcrip-tures Voice both before and ſince Chriſts coming, as I have and ſhall further manifeſt. *The holy Scriptures the Rule*

2. As to the ſpirits leading into all Truth, and the ſons of God are led by the ſpirit of God: Is not *Fox* here in his *Burrough*, not diſtinguiſhing between the Extraordinary leading of the holy Apoſtles Appointed to be the Eye Witnyſſes of Chriſts Death [104] and *Reſurrection*, &c. and the firſt Meſſengers or Apoſtles to the Nations, in which Reſpect, the one Author of thoſe three Gifts, Adminiſtrations, Operations, 1 *Cor.* 12. peremptorily asks the Queſtion, *Are all Apoſtles, are all Prophets, have all the Gifts of Miracles?* and yet all Gods Children are Regenerated, are ſanctificd, are guided and built up an habitation of God through the Spirit: and yet alſo the gracious preſence and working of the holy Spirit, may be hindred and quenched, by neglecting of the holy Fuel of the holy Scriptures and other holy means appointed. And therefore the Lord Jeſus Commands us to pray for the Spirit: and *Daved* cries out, *Thy Spirit is good* *.... leading of the Spirit. Gods Spirit given by means.*

lead

lead me, &c. *and take not thy holy Spirit from me.*
And this is the Devils (the *Old Fox*) his *Devilish Subtlety* to make the Cloak of the Spirit Extraordinary Affiſtance, and the Angels Extraordinary protection, a ground of Chriſt Jeſus, and his Servants flinging themſelves down from the *Pinacle* of the *Temple,* and this I ſay from the God of Truth will be the *Breack neck* of the People called *Quakers,* (without Repentance) every Soul of them.

We now deſcend to the proof of the fifth Poſition with their Conſent, which was, their *Principles and Profeſſions are full of Contradiction and Hypocriſies.*

I told them, that they knew well, that the Spirit of God had given us abundant Warning againſt *falſe Gods, falſe Worſhips, falſe Chriſts, falſe Spirits, falſe Prophets*: He Commands us in Scripture not to believe them, *&c.* but to try them, to try all things, as we do with *Touchſtones,* and with *Ballances,* yea, with Fire it ſelf. For, ſome *Counterfiet Coyne* hath been ſo like pure gold, ſo double guilt in the middle, and the Ring round about pure gold, that it hath deceived the *Touchſtone.* The Devil himſelf as black a *Fiend* as he is, the Spirit of Darkneſs, yet he knows how to wear *Samuels Mantle,* and the white Robe of an *Angel of Light,* &c. I told them it was Common for *Spaniſh, Turkiſh,* or any other Enemy in Time of Warr to hang out *Engliſh Colours,* the more easily to deceive & Catch the poor Merchant man, and *Judas* the Traitour gave no other ſigne to the *Jews* in his betraying of his *Lord* and *Maſter,* the Lord Jeſus, *but God ſave my Maſter* and a Kiſs.   Moſt

The fifth Poſition

The danger of being deceived

Depths of Hipocriſy

105 ']   Moſt of this I Remember I ſpake, and then Lies in Hipocri-ſie.
I told them that *Paul* tels *Timothy* of ſome that
ſhould ſpeake Lyes in Hipocriſie : I told them of
theſe, there were two ſorts.

   1 Such as knowingly (for wicked and Deviliſh
Ends of Profit or *Preferment*) take the *Leading Staff*
in hand, as 'tis more then probable, that the *Miſleader*
of ſo many Millions of *Mahumetans* did : and as
one of the *Popes* in Merriment to his *Cardinals* Confeſt it, ſaying, *Quantum Lucri fecimus ex hac Fabula
Chriſti*?   What gain have we made of this Fable
of Chriſt?   Thus *Judas* knowingly, for his Gain Two ſorts of Soul Deceivers
ſought Opportunities to betray Chriſt Jeſus.   Thus
the *Schechemites* (and Millions are their *Succeſſors* as
they are to *Nebuchadnezzars Idolaters*) underwent
that painful and ſhameful Ordinance of *Circumciſion*,
partly to pleaſe their *Princes*, and partly for that
hope as (*Schechem* told them) that all that I*ſrael*
had ſhould be theirs.

   A *ſecond Sort* of *Soul Deceivers* that are, and yet
know not in their Conſciences that they are *blind
Guides* or *blind Followers*, but for not loving Truth
God hath given them up to believe Lyes, for Truths :
falſe Chriſts and Spirits, for true Chriſts and Spirits ;
yea, and with *Paul* to think that they verily ought
to do many things againſt *Jeſus of Nazareth*, yea,
and as the Lord Jeſus *Poſitively Foretold* they ſhall
think to do God Service to kill himſelf, in killing
his Servants.

I told

---

   1 In the copy in poſſeſſion of Brown   his autograph acroſs the outſide edge of
Univerſity, Roger Williams has placed   this page.

I told them my Charity, bid me hope that the
Quakers and themfelves prefent were not of the *firſt*,
but of the fecond fort, and I prayed them to be as
patient as they could while I muſt prove that their
Principles and Profeſſions were full of Lyes and
Contradictions, and of Hipocrifies, and Diſſimula-
tions. I wondred that my *Oppoſites* and *Auditors* bare
all this Load fo filently? But at this word *W. Edmundfon* and the reſt brake out faying, We regard
not what thou thinkeſt and fayeſt of us, nor do we
need thy Charity, but go on to thy proofs, &c.

*The Qua-
kers of late
have
Changed
much of
their Spi-
rit, or elfe
more no-
torioufly
Equivoca-
tors.*

I then faid, that their many Books, and G. *Foxes*
(that thereby me) and their Profeſſions, did fo exceedingly Claſh one with another: and fome of
their latter Books (as *Chriſtopher Houldsworths*) and
fome of theis latter Profeſſions and Practices were
fuch that many of their Obfervers Conclude, that
either they had altered their Religion in many of
their Principles [106] and Practices, and were
turned from what they formerly held, and were
amongſt us: Or elfe their Hipocrifies and Diſſimu-
lations were more and more prodigiously Abomina-

*The Jug-
ling of the
Quakers
about
Chriſt.*

ble. I came to Inſtances, and told them that when
they were Charged to deny that man Chriſt Jefus,
they profeſs and preach they are wronged, for they
believe in that Chriſt which was born of a *Virgin*,
and died at *Jerufalem*, and yet for all this, it is but
in Truth a *Spiritual,* and *Miſtical,* and *Allegorical
Chriſt,* which under boord andin the bottom) which
they hold.For,in *New-England* (before G. *Fox* came)
H. *Norton* and others fay, is not Chriſt God, and is
not God a Spirit, and is there not a *Spiritual Virgin,*
a **Miſtical**

a *Miſtical Bethlehem*, an *Heavenly Ieruſalem*? And do
not G. *Fox* and *Ed. Burroughs* all along hold out
ſuch a Chriſt, whoſe Body is not now to be found?
and ſuch a man as is in every Saint, or *Quaker*? and
in every perſon in the world except he be a Reprobate?

Again, 2. They ſay, they hold the Chriſtian Church, About the
the *Chriſtian* Ordinances, the *Christian Miniſtry*, the Church
ChriſtianBaptiſme,&*Supper* the *Reſurrection*, the *Iudge- and Ordi-
ment*, the *Life Everlaſting*, but ſearch their Books, nances.
Examine their preachings and profeſſings, and you
ſhall ſee, and may admire their Juglings and Diſ-
ſimulations: Do not *Fox* and *Burroughs* all along
diſclaim any *Church Miniſters, Baptiſme,* &c. but
what is *Immediate* and *Inviſible*? Do they really own
any Supper but Chriſts inward Supping with them,
and they with him? Or any *Reſurrection* but the
tiſing of their *Bodies* to *perfect Holineſs*? or any
Iudgement and *Eternal Life*, but what they have now
attained, and are now paſſing Judgement upon the
world?

3. Again, though they do deny any Church but
Inviſible, yet their Churches and Congregations are
known and *Viſible* and ſtated (not attending *Inviſible
Motions*) both firſt day and other dayes with prayers
and *Preachings*, and ſingings, and real joyninigs or
Addings to them & Caſtings out: Theſe things ne-
ceſſitty forceth them to practice, or else they cannot poſſibly keep together, although in *Monſtrous
Diſſimulation* they diſclaim it.   Inward

4. They profeſs that their Saints have an *Unction*, and out-
yea, that every perſon in the world is ſo enlightned Preachers.
                                                         by

by Chrift Jefus, that he hath Chrift and Spirit, and
the Kingdom of God in them, [107] (as the *Pharifees* had, and the very fame the Saints have) and if
they will, they have Teaching enough to Juftifie,
Sanctifie and fave them : and yet again what a noife
is there in the Worid about the *Quakers, Teachers,
He Apoftles,* and *fhe Apoftles,* fnch as the Lord Jefus
never fent either the *Twelth* or the *Seventh,* or their
Succeffors. How do they boaft to be the only Minifters of Chrift Jefus fent into *Old England* and
New-England, into *Scotland* and *Ireland,* yea, into
Italy and *Turky,* and other Nations as diligent and
zealous as the *Pharifees* to pervert and poyfon Souls
with a falfe Converfion and Salvation.

As to the
Scriptures
5. You profefs the Scriptures to be the words of
God, but not the Word of God, and yet now you
profefs to be tryed by them : Anon again, you need
not the Scriptures, you have that Light and Spirit
within you that gave out the Scriptures, and if all
G Fox his
laft Book
Exalting
the Hea-
then
the Copies in the World were burnt yet you have
the Scriptures within you, therefore you not only
(as the Spirt of God faith) deceitfully handle the
Scriptures by deceitful Interpretations, but by deceitful owning, and not owning, and as G. *Fox* in
his late Book in Exalting *Heathens* above *Chriftians*
owning them, and yet Exalting the Spirit in the
Philiftian and *Egiptian*Sorcerers above them.

As to Mag-
iftrates
6. As to *Magiftrates,* how full are their Books
and Sermons againft Perfecution and Perfecutors,
and yet how plainly do their Principles perfecute
all others that fubject not to their Light, when they
have attained fuch *godly Magiftrates* as they arc (as
they

they fpeak) in the Light. I told them I was Concerned to make this out more fully in the proof of
my *Fourteenth Pofiition*, and therefore at prefent I
would trouble them but with one *Quotation* out of
G. *Fox, Pag.* 170. where I Read, and *Iohn Burnet* Pag 170
Read alfo, how G. *Fox* brings in *Iohn Stallam* fay- John
ing, [*And the Magiftrate is not to Level the Law with* Stallam
the Light in every mans Confcibnce, Again, if the
Magiftrate be in the Light and difcern the mind of The Qua-
Chrift, and difcern his Law, is he to Compel all the Na- ciples are
tion and Common-wealth to come to the practice of his for Perfe-
Light ?] cution

G. *Fox* Anfwers, the Magiftrate of Chrift, the
help, Government for him, he is in the Light and
power of Chrift: and he is to fubject all under the
power of Chrift, into his Light, elfe he [108] is not
a faithful Magiftrate: and his Laws are agreeable
and Anfwer according to that of God in every
man: when men act contrary to it they do evil, fo
he is a Terrour to the Evil doers, difcern the precious and the juft from the vile, and this is a praife
to them rhat do well.

I urged from hence, that the *Quakers* (and G, *Fox*
in his Book in many places) owne no Magiftrates The Qua-
but fuch as are godly that is in their dark Sence, kers Zeal-
that be Magiftrates for their Chrift, be in the Light ous Perfe-
and *Power* of Chrift, for then fay they, their Laws cutors.
are agreeable to that of God in every man.

2. Thefe their Magiftrates (in the Light) ought
to fubject even the Confciences and Souls of
all that be under them, by *Corporal punifhments* to
coine under the Power of Chrift into the Light.

23   3. This

3. This is Confirmed and fealed with a *peremptory Doom* upon the neglecter and failer, *viz.* [*Elfe he is not a Faithful Magiftrate.*]

4. I obferve the Reafon and Equity which they alleadge of this fubjecting all Subjects to the Light of Chrift, becaufe fuch *Magiftrates, Laws* and *Edicts* are witneffed by God in every man, and therefore he fins againft God himfelf who breaks fuch a *Magiftrates Command,* and therefore is juftly punifhed, *&c.*

Upon my urging of fome of thefe particulars fome of them defired to hear the *Quotation* read again: fo *Iohn Burnet* read the whole paffage again, and faid, that G. *Foz* fpake not there of matters of Religion and Confcience, nor of the Magistrates compelling men to be of his Religion and Confcience, but of punifhing them for matters of wrong between man and man, which are againft the Light in every mans Confcience, as *Drunkennefs, Whoredome, Murther, Stealing,* and the like.

Yet will not own it.

I Replyed, the Terms were fuch both of the Queftion by the *Oppofite,* and the Anfwer by G. *Fox* which argue and Comprehend the matters of Religion and Confcience, *viz.* If the Magiftrate be in the Light, and discern the mind of Chrift, *&c.* and G. *Fox* his Terms are the fame about Chrift and the Light and bringing them fubject to Chrift.

2. It is not Imaginable, that the Oppofer would queftion whether the *Civil Officer* ought not to punifh fuch incivilities and [109] Incivilities and Inhumanities as *Drunkennefs, Whoredome, Stealing, Murther,* &c. Therefore G. *Fox* muft intend that their Magiftrates for Chrift muft Fight for their
Chrift

Chrift againft all their *Oppofites*, though they cry
Perfecutors, Perfecutors, &c. .

In *Pag.* 221. *G. Fox* brings in the Author of the The Quakers Per-
fection,
Book called *Hofanna to the Son of* David, faying,
[*They know not abfofolute Perfection that are admitting* and yet in
of Meafures and Degrees, nor come to the Day and the Meafure
Pag.221.
bright Morning Star,is not Rifen.] Hofanna

He Anfwers, did not the Apoftle fpeak that they to the Son
nf David.
were Children of the Day, and the night was over,
and knew the whole Body,and yet faid, he would
not go beyond his Meafure ? And doth he not fpeak
of the *Stature and Meafure and Fulnefs* of *Chrift?*
and were they not come to Perfection, and fpoke
wifdome among them that were perfect?

I Reply: As to their *Monftrous pride* I fhall fpeak,
when I come to Compare the *Pope* and them in the
Tenth Pofition: At prefent I Ask them, whether
Paul fpeak of his Meafure in Holinefs and Grace,
or no? Some of them fay that they are not only
perfect as God in Holinefs, but alfo in Power *Om-*
nipotent, Omniprefent, Omnifcient, &c.But if *Paul* be The Old
Romans
with their
not brought in to fpeak of fuch a *Perfection* in
Holinefs as is in God, G. *Fox beats the Air*, & comes Dii Min-
not near the Queftion: to fave their Doctrine of Per- ores or leffer Gods
fection from being a perfect Contradiction & Lie, and the
and they would fain make themfelves &others be- Papifts
lieve that they are as truly perfect in their Holi- and Quakers all
nefs as God is,though their Holinefs be not fo much: one.
As if they were perfectly Gods, (though but little
Gods) as God himfelf being a great God, and fo are The Per-
forct to fhow their Contradictions, and wheel about fection of
the God-
to Perfection of parts as a Child is mankind though head

not

not a perfect man, and a drop of water is true water, and may be as Salt as any drop in the *Ocean*:
having the Quality of, but not the Equality with the
Ocean   As otherwise G *Fox* foolishly & blasphemously speaks of God in this Book, Moreover, since
these high minded Souls dare to say that they are
as pure as God, and (some say what they think)
that they can no more sin against God, then God
can sin against them, *&c.* I Ask them whether
there be any Measures and Degrees in God? whether
his Perfection in Holiness be not Holiness it self?
Wisdom it self, goodness it self, unto which there
there can be no Addition or [110] growth as we
are Commanded *to grow in the grace and knowledg
of Christ Jesus.* To talk therefore of *Measures* &
Perfections, is as silly as for G. *Fox* when he hath begun
to sow a Shoo, and hath as yet taken but a few stitches,
yet to boast Confidently that the Shoe is perfect.

The Qua-
kers Falla-
cious Per-
fection.

We deny not, but a Dram Cup may be as perfectly full of wine as a *Pipe* or Butt, and so *Johns
little Children* as perfectly, that is, as truly Gods
Children, as his strong men or Old men: But to
say this Cup or Spoon is equal in quantity to a *Pipe*
or Tun, a Child is equal to a strong man, much
more for a *poor Potsheard* to say he is equal with his
Porter, and a *Worm* of the *Earth* equal to his *Maker,* what is it but a *bloccish* and *blasphemous Fallacy*
and *Contradiction?* and a wheeling about to a Perfection of parts which none deny.

Hosanna
to the Son
of David.

In 222. He brings in the same Author saying, [*Christ
is without his Saints in respect of his bodily presence.*]
He Answers, How are they of his Flesh, and of
his

his Bone, and how do they eat his flesh, and drink
his Blood? And how have they his mind and Spirit?
And he with them, and they with him? and sit in
Heavenly Places: And he is the Head of his Church,
and how then is he absent? yea, *poor Apostates* from
him feels not Christ, but he is with the Saints, and
they feel him.

I Reply, and Ask, is this Eating of his Flesh,
and drinking of his Blood after a *Corporal, Bodily*
manner, visible and real as to other Senses Or is it
Miraculous and Spiritual? Or is it *Spiritual* & *Misti-*
cal by Faith, and by believing as the *Protestants* say?
After the first *Corporal way* the very *Papists* affirm
not: After the *second way* you will not say it is:
Nor would you be thought to be so *grofs Papists*
as to hold *Transubstantiation*? and therefore must
it be the t*hird way* which is by believing: and then
you *poor Jugling Souls*, what is it to a *Bodily pref-*
ence, that you Eat him by believing?

2. Whereas you say, you *fit with him in Heavenly*
Places, you are one wiih him, *&c.* he is Head of the
Church, *&c.* Here I must Ask you you hold him
to be such a *Visible Head* of the Church, as the *Pope*
faith He is, and if you say yea, I then Ask you where
will you direct us to such an *Individual Man*, or
person as the *Pope* is, and may be directed to, as we
know from so great Art all the World over, If you
say No, what is this then to talk of a *bodily* |111
presence of Christ (which is the point) and then
Flap me in the mouth with a *Fox Tail*, and tell me
(in a *Childish* and *Equivocating Contradiction*) that
you mean not a *Bodijy presence* but a *Spiritual*.

3. As

G Fox
his Falla-
Presence
of Chrift
Visible
and Natu-
ral or Mi-
raculous
and Super-
natural
Eating of
Chrift.

Chrift
Head of
the
Church

3. As for the *poor Apoſtates*, and your feeling of Chriſt, which the *poor Apoſtate's* do not.

I Reply, An *Adulterous Wretch, Accuſed* Ioſeph of *Whoredome*, who was a pattern of *pure* and *holy Chaſtity* : For, whom do this *Whoriſh Brood of Fox-ians* thus brand for *Apoſtates*, and fling among them *Firebrands, Arrows* and *Death ?* Are they not all the Children of God that are, or ever were, or ſhall be called ? Are they not the Souls under the *Altar* who have been ſlain *Thouſands* and *Ten Thouſands for the Teſtimony of Ieſus* againſt theſe *horrid Delu-*

His Bodily preſence. *ſions ?* Are they not the very *firſt Churches*, and the *Apoſties* of Chriſt Jeſus, from whom Chriſt in his *Bodily preſence* was departed, as he often Forewarned

The Qua-kers Count all Gods Children Apoſtates. them, and (as the holy Scriptures abundantly Re-cordeth) is Fulfilled ? For, ſee the Jugling of theſe Deceivers, when this *Bodily preſence* is Ex-amined, they mean no ſuch *Individual Man* and perſon, but a mind and Spirit, and ſuch a Chriſt as hath no *Individual Bodily Preſence*, as we and all men have.

G Fox his Juglings and dreams about the perſon of Chriſt If G. *Fox* when he is in *New-England* ſhould ſay he is in *London* in his *Bodily Preſence*, and that his Friends feel (as he ſpeak) his *Bodily Preſence* there, becauſe they feel his Love and his Affections in their minds and Spirits : What *Hocas Pocas* and *Iugling Chriſtianity* is this ? All the Saints and Chil-dren of God muſt all be *Apoſtates*, fallen from God and Chriſt, and Grace, that cannot Skill and Feel this *Horrible Egiptian Canting Language.*

I will turn my Thoughts higher. O thou moſt *glorious Sun of Righteouſneſs, Truth* and *Holineſs*
ſhine

shine forth, and let it be seen, how the Devil called
the Lord Jesus *Beelzebub* : The *Treacherous Revolters* and *Apostates* from thee, they call thy self, and
thy Saints *Revolters* and *Apostates*.   They boast
with the *bloody Papists* and other *Traitorous Rebels* An Apos-
against thee, of their Right and Interest in thee, of trophe or
their possessing and feeling of thee, feeling thy Pe tion to
Scriptures and thy *Bodily presence* within them : Oh Jesus
let thy *glorious Light* declare, who these *poor Apos-*
tates and *Revol-* [112] *ters* are, *who break down thine*
Altars, burn thy Temples, scoff at thine Institutions,
Cry up a false and *Hellish Christ* within them,
Christen him with the Name of *Light,* though he be
thy *Conquered Slave* the *Devil,*telling us he is thine
Angel of Light, who with his *Counterfiet Souldiers* of
Light, Crucifie thee and pierce thee, and mock and
Curse thee, (the only true Son of God and Son of
man) as ever *Herod* and *Pilate,* the *Preists* and *Iudas,*
the *P*eople and Souldiers did.

In *Page* 259, he brings in *James Browne* saying, 259 James
[*the Kingdome that is in the Saints, is not in the* Brown
Pharisees.]

He Answers, [That is, in the *Saints,* is in the
Pharisees in a *Measure,* though it be but as *a Grain
of Mustard Seed,* which is like to *Leaven little.*]

I Reply, 1. What If I should send you to some of
your *Margents,* where the Greek word [*Entos*] is Christs
rendred amongst you : that is, unto you, upon you, Kingdom
as *Luke* 11. *If I by the Finger of God cast out Dev-* among the
ils,surely the Kingdome of God is Come upon you? Pharisees
The Pharisees expected (and so did all the *Iews,*
and *Christ Disciples.*were not free) I say look for a
glorious

glorious Temporal King that should make his *Ingress* with *Pomp*, and [*Meta pur oteresio*] as the Scripture speaks with Observation, but he came in as some Kings in disguize, and (as they speak) *Incognito*, and yet his Kingdome was among them, in the midst of them, by his *per onal presence*, his *powersulp each-ing*, and his *glorious Miracles*.

2 Since (in Opposition to *Chrifts Visible King-dome* his Church) you predicate a *Kingdome within, Consisting of Righteousness, peace, and joy in the holy Spirit*: do you think indeed that the Hipocritical Cursed Pharisees were snch Righteous, peaceable and joyful Souls as your selves: As sure as God is Light: They and their Successors your selves, will find your selves when you wake, in *horrid Quaking*, and except you repent HellFlames about your Ears, as the Lord Jesus told those *whited Walls* and *painted Sepulchres*.

Horrible and hipo. critical Chistiani- ty

3. Must you take Measure of the Pharisees, and tell us that the Pharisees in a Measure as a grain of Mustard Seed and Leaven are the same with your selves ? Do not you Cry out that you are perfect, not in Measures and Degrees, but that you are all one in *Quality* and *Equality* of Power and Glory with God? and must [113] this must be the same with Christ Jesus and his Saints, and you and the *Phari-sees* all together ? *Can two walk together*, live and love together, board and bosome together *and not be agreed* together, no other wayes then *Light* and *Darkness*, *Christ* and *Belial, Righteousness* and *un-righteousness* ? What stinking work do these *provd Pharisees* make of *Christianity* ? How justly doth the Son of God give them their proper Titles, *Ye Fools and Blind?*

4. If

4. If it be the fame Kingdome in Chrift Jefus
and in Saints, and in the *Pharifees*, and every wicked
man in the world,though but *as a grain of Muftard* A Mon-
Seed, and *Leaven*, what is the Reafon this *Muftard* ſtrous King and
Seed grows not up, this *Leaven* ſpread not in them? Kingdome
Can a Nation be ſubject to the King of *England*,of of the
Spain, or any oſher Ptince or *Monarch*, and yet not Quakers.
know how, nor have no knowledge nor feeling of it
at all? Can there be fuch a God, fuch a Spirit, fuch a
Fire? yea, but fuch a *Muftard Seed*, or *Levven*, fuch
a *Teacher*, and yet not grow, not prevail, not prof- Abomina-
per, nor be perceived? ye *Fools* and *Blind* are all ble lyes in
your *Muftard Trees* ſtunted all the world over, no hipocrifie.
Shelter for the *Heavenly Birds*, your pure flowre of
Holineſs and ſincerity,mixt and- blended with the
black Weeds, Cockle and *darnel* of *open Idolatries* and
prophaneneſs, and *Pharifaifme*, and *Hipocrifie*: What
abominable *Contradictions* and Lyes in *Hipocrifie*
are here? The *Pharifees* have Chrift and his Kingdome of *Righteoufneſs,'peace* and *joy* in the *Holy Spi-*
rit within them, and yet live in pride and Covetouf- The Phar-
neſs, and Extortion, and Exceſs, and Cruelty, and ifees and Quakers
Hipocrifie, and Blasphemy, and all this *Rottenneſs* hipocrifie
and *Dead mens bones* ſtinking and ruling all within, wonderfnl
notwithſtanding all the *white* and'*paint*, and *garniſh-*
ing without your felves, (their *Hipocritical Offſpring*)
have, and live in, you fay, this Kingdome of Chrift
Jefus, this *Kingdome of Righteoufneſs and Joy in the*
holy Spirit, as perfect and pure as God himſelf: all
one with us, Infinite in *Majefty, Holineſs, Power* and
Glory, not only in *Quality*, but *Equality*, &c. (as this
wretched G. *Fox* affirmeth) And yet within and
24   withont

withont *Idolatrous* and *Superſtitious,* *Inhumane* and *uncivil,* *paſſionate* and *fierce,Cenſorious* and *Curſing,* and moſt *Impudent* and worſe then *Barbarous,* in ſome *of your Impudently, monſtrous and avowed prac-tices*

Having diſpatched our Agitations about the *fifth* *Aſſertion,* [114] and the *Quotations* out of G. *Fox*

The ſixth which I could not then Inſiſt on in publick, I de-
Poſition. ſcended to the *ſixth Poſition* which was, *viz.* [*The* *Religion of the Quakers is not only an Hereſie in the* *matters of Gods holy worſhip, but alſo in the Doctrines* *of Repentance, Faith,&c.*

This *Aſſertion* hath two main Branches: *Firſt,* that the Quakers Religion is an *Hereſie,* and them-ſelves *Hereticks* in the matters of Gods worſhip.

The Her-
eſie of the 2. Not only ſo, (about the Circumſtances of
Quakers. which Gods own dear Servants themſelves greatly differ) but alſo (which is more Lamentable and dan-gerous) in the Doctrines of Repentance and Faith, and the reſt of the graces of Chriſt Jeſus.

I told them *firſt,* that the word *Hairefis* Hereſie, in *Greek,* (from whence the word *Hairetikos* an Heretick) ſignified an O*pinion* or O*pinions,* choſen and ſtood in by one or more againſt the *Chriſtian Religion.* I ſaid the matter mighr be aggravated, and a ugmented from the Greatneſs and *Vitallity* of the matter of the Opinions, but the *Formality* and *Nature* of it lay in the will and obſtinacy thereof.

John Stubs ſtood up and ſaid, that *Hereſie* was de-
Hereſy fined by ſome to be an Opinion obſtinately ſtood in
what againſt the *firſt Chriſtian Purity*:· I Anſwered, yea, and the Opinion of ſome was, that *Hereſie* was an

Error

Error in the *Foundation* obstinately stood in: But I said we had not time to enter upon a Dispute about the word or thing at this time, the Substance of my *Affirmation* was, that their Religion, Sect or way was false, and gone from the *Institution* and *way* of the Lord Jesus delivered by himself and his Apostles, or *Messengers*:

1. As to worship, they denyed the Converting and gathering of the Saints into *visible Assemblies*, or *Congregations*: affirming the Chnrch to be *Invisible*, the *Ministers Invisible*, the *Baptisme* and *Supper Invisible*, &c.

The second (which was aur *Position*) was in those *two great Fundamentals*, the *Beginning*, or *A. B. C.* of the *Chrstian Religion*, viz Repentance from dead works and Faith towards God: As for those two Doctrines of laying on of hands, and of *Baptismes* they concerned the Church, and worship, (concerning the Circumstances of which God is pleased to permit his [115] Children to be lovingly differing and discussing; the other four *Repentance, Faith, Resurrection* and *Judgement* (in which generally Gods Children agree) in these also as well as in the matter of worship, these wandring Souls are *Hereticks*, that is, obstinately maintaining *Notoriously false* and *Anti-Christian Abominations*, In so much that the many Sects amongst the *Protestants*, yea, and the *Papists* themselves do not so differ from *a true Protestant* and *true Christian* as do these *wilful, ignorant*, and *wandring Souls*.

The Quakers Hereticks against all the Christian Principles, and more Heretical against the first Christian Religion then any Protestauts or Papists.

1. Then as to Repentance, I said it was the first heavenly and saving work of God upon the Soul, *The Quakers Here.*

wherein

fy in mat- wherein he turned back home again the whole
ter of Re- Soul unto himfelf, being revolted and run from
peutance.
him into the Arms of Rebellion in the Fall of our
firſt Parents.

This was the great point preached by *Moſes* and
the *Prophets*, and more expreſsly by *John the Bap-*
tiſt, and by the Lord Jeſus himſelf: and when he
fent abroad his Apoſtles or Meſſengers into all Na-
This 24th. tions, they were to preach the Goſpel or glad News
of Luke I of the Forgiveneſs of fins according to *Luke* 24.
earneſly viz. that Repentance and Remiſſion of fins ſhould
Infiſtedon. be preached in his Name unto all Nations, beginning at *Jeruſalem*.

Here about I remember they told me that it was
known that they preached the Doctrine of Repentance and of turning from all fin unto God, *&c.*

I Anſwered, that the *Papiſts* and they made a
ſhew and Colour of Repentance, but it had not the
Life and Subſtance of Repentance in it: It was no
The Pa- more but an *empty Title* and *ſhadow* of Repentance:
piſts and we know the *Papiſts* define their Repentance by
Quakers
Repent- theſe three. *Firſt*, Contrition, *Secondly*, Confeſſion,
ance. and *Thirdly*, Satisfaction or Reſtitution.

But I ſaid the *Proteſtants* proteſted againſt this
Repentance of the *Papiſts*, and ſo againſt the *Qua-*
kers, for, who knew not the ſorrow and Confeſſions
of *Saul*, and *Ahab*, and *Pharaoh*; and the *Philiſtins*,
and *Judas*, yea, and alſo the Reſtitution which *Judas*
made, (not daring to keep in his hands that which
he had unjuſtly and wickedly gotten) and yet who
can truly aſcribe unto theſe mens Repentance, the
Character and bleſſedneſs of a true Chriſtian returning and coming home to God.   2. I

2. I said it is known in daily practice, that when some times [116] *Notorious* and *openly Flagitious Perfons* profefs to be *Quakers*, (for all their craking of fear and trembling and Quaking) there hath appeared no Senfe of godly forrow, of godly Contrition and brokennefs of heart in them, for their finful Nature and Life againft fo *Infinitely pure* an *Holinefs* and *Majefty*? but immediately (upon their bowing down to Satan, and owning him as a *Light*, and *Chrift*, and *Spirit* within them) they are, having lefs Prophanenefs now pure and holy as God is, they can no more fin then Chrift can! *the Miftery of godlinefs is God manifefted in their Flefh*, I know fome of them fay they come to perfection by degrees, yet they fay the leaft of their *new-born Quakers* can not fin, and what is that but Perfection? yea, they are Chrift and God: and therefore why fhould they give refpect to any *King*, or *Kings*, &c. why fhould they not *Thee* and *Thou* the *Aged, Learned, holy, and High*, why fhould they not fit filent even fcores and hundreths of them (poffeffed with a dumb Spirit) as in a Form and Order of Chriftian worfhip waiting for this Spirit, and then be perfect Chriftians?

The Quakers Converts.

3. The *Proteftants* both *Englifh*, *French* and *Dutch*, &c. have manifefted againft the *Papifts*, and therein againft the *Quakers*, that Repentance is a turning of whole Soul from all fin as fin to all of God as God: from the fin of Nature, and that *Heart filthinefs* which we bring into the world with us, and from whence, even from within, as Chrift Jefus tells us? what ever Satan and the poor Quakers

The Proteftants true Repentance.

kers

kers prate *proceed our evil thoughts, Adulteries, Forni-cations, Murthers, Thefts, Covetoufnefs, Wickednefs, Deceit, Lafciviousnefs, an Evil Eye, Blafphemy, pride, Foolifhnefs,* Mark 7, *&c.*

4. I urged that their *Profelites* and *Converts* are but like the *Pharifees* of old, though oftentimes dearly bought by Sea and Land, I fay, but tnrned from one fin to another, from one Image to another, from one Devil of Drunkennefs or Swearng; *&c.* to a Devil of *Pride, horrible pride,* the worft of all prides in Earth or Hell, to wit, a *Spiritual Pride* fwelling with the *Dropfies* and *Tympanies* of their *Conceited knowledge, Conceited Repentance, Conceited Faith, Love, patience, joy, holinefs, Juftification, Sanctification, Mor-tification* and *Salvation.*

2. How horribly do they defpife the *true broken hearted Pub-* [117] *licans,* who can fee nothing but

The Qua-kets defpi-ling fin and D'amnation in themfelves, and cry out for mercy and Forgivenefs? How do they *Supercilioufly* and *Pape-like* belch out as from Hell, *God I thank thee that I am not like thefe Publicans?*

AndRevili others. 3. How bitterly do they Inftantly raile and re-vile, Condemn and Curfe, breathing out Fire of Damnation as Fire and Brimftone from the Moun-tains in *Sicily,* or elfe Hell it felf againft all that op-pofe them? as far from the Teaching of Chrift and his *firft Meffngers* as *Lambs* and *Doves,* are from the *Ravenous, popifh* and *Devilifh Lyons* and *Eagles.*

4. To name no more at prefent, How doth the Devil of worldlinefs and Covetoufnefs domineer

Their Covetouf-nefs. over many of them? By a ftrict Profeffion all per-fons are taken off from Drunkennefs, Whoredome,

Swearing,

Swearing, &c. und put on *Theiftinefs* and *Induftry*,
and if their hearts Centre and fix not on Chrift Jefus, and the *Heavenly Records* of Chrift, the Scriptures: and on the Life to come, but upon *Self, Exalting felf, a felf Chrift*, and *Spirit*, and *Heaven*, and
Refurrection, &c. which is the Truth and bottom
of the Quakers Religion, what can the moft of
them run in but a Courfe of *greedy gaping* after,
and getting, and raking, and gathering the *muck*
and *dung* of this *prefent Life*?

It is true, that many that hold the fame *Fanciful
Notions* with the *Quakers*, yet are of *Ranting, jovial,
fpending Spirits*, but the Spirit that haunts the *Qua-*
kers moft is a *foure, proud*, and *Melancholy Devils*,
and his Commiffion is to turn fuch perfons into the
Gadarens Swine rooting up all that ever they come
at for their own Ends and Belly: How many are
the Inftances even in this *Colony* in fome efpecially,
as able and as active Souls as any in this *Colony* or
Country, and as guilty of murthering the *Natives*
by the *Liqour Trade* as any: and as fuddenly and
ftrangely fnatcht away by the hand of *Gods Power*
and *Iuftice*, as any ufually can be, but being departed
I will touch no more upon this ftring.

From their Doctrine of, and their Herefie or Ob-
ftinacy in a *falfe Repentance*, I touch next npon
their *falfe Faith*: I faid it was true they fpoke much
of Faith and Juftification, &c. as the *Papifts* did,
and as G. *Fox* in his Book (by me) did: yet if they
pleafed, I would demonftrate by Inftances out of
his Book all along that he Confounded and made
all one, both Faith and Ju- [118] ftification, yea,

and

*A fowre
Spirit is
the Com-
mon Spirit
of the
Quakers.*

*The Qua-
kers Falfe
Faith.*

and Sanctification, and made believing in Christ Jesus but a *meer Babel* and *Chaos* of *Nonsence* and
Cnnfusion. For although (which is *Foxes Common
Burrough*) he that Faith hath Repentance, hath
Justification, Sanctification, and all *Christian graces*,
yet to Confound and make them all one, is as to go
into a *fair Garden,* and say a Rose is every Flower
in the Garden : or to say, that the Letter *A*, or *O*
is every Letter in a *Printers Box*, or Book : Or to
say, that a *Rebels* receiving the *Kings pardon*, that is
the *King himself* : his receiving it is the pardon it
self, that is the *Rebels* Conviction, *Conversion, Condemnation, Execution, Resurrection, Acceptation, Ex-
altation*, and *Adoption* into the *Favour* and *Communion* with the *King* for the Future. All this *Mon-
strons* and *Nonsensical Language* is the Tongue or
Speech of the *Quakers*, and G. *Fox* especially.

G Fox his horrible confounding of Faith and all other Chistian Virtues and Graces together.

   2. I told them that although (with the *Quakers*
and *Papists*) G. *Fox* talkt much of Faith in Christ :
yet I had proved and further should, that the *Quakers* put out and obliterate the true Christ or Object
to be received and believed on, as before in the
matter of Faith, they put out the true living Eye
of Faith, and put in a painted, or *Glass Eye* in the
Room of it.

True Faiah what it is

   True Faith is a Receiving of Christ Jesus as my
only King, Priest and *Prophet* : It is a believing
on, or receiving of Christ distinct from God, *Iohn*
14. You believe in God, This true Lord Jesus
Christ the *Quakers* turn into a *meer Fiction, Dream,*
or *Imaginary Christ* in the mind of a man, or Woman : a *Popish Transubstantiated Christ*, all Spirit
and

The Quakers Transubstatiarion worse then the Fantastick

and no Body, and fo not confifting of Flesh and Tranfub-
ftantian
of the Papifts
Spirit : He hath no Flefh of his own, as you make
him : and yet Flefh of his own, becaufe your Flefh
is his Flefh, and yet your Flefh you fay alfo muft dye
and rot, and never rife again, and fo you have blown
up and Jugled away the Flefh of Chrift Jefus, both
his and your own alfo altogether.

This is a Trick of *the Father of Lyes*, and *Iuglings*
beyond that *Monftrous* Fancy of the P*apisfts Tran-
fubftantiation*, for although they turn the Bread into
the Flefh of Chrift, yet they turn not the Bread of
Chrift, nor the Flefh of Chrift into their own
Flefh : The *Quakers* can give no Account what is
become of the Flefh or Body of that man Chrift
Jefus, thefe *Foxes* have devoured the Lambs of God.
Miraculous and Monftrous is [119] the Papifts *blaf-
phemous* and *Bloody* Fancy of *Tranfubftantiation*, but
not more miraculous and monftrous, *&c.* then that
of the *Quakers*, which granteth Chrift Jefus to have
been born, lived and dyed as We,&c and yet now
Tranfubftantiated into a Spirit, and the *Quakers
Flefh*. So that in the Upfhot, the Chrift in whom
they believe is vanifhed (by an *Hellifh Chimiftry*)
into themfelves, and it is moft certain, (the Lord
open in great mercy fome of their Eyes to fee it)
they do believe on themfelves, and that lying Spirit
within them.

I remember, that hereabouts *Iohn Burnet* faid, that
it was not true that they preached not true Repent-
ance, and herein he fell into a Speech or Sermon to John Bur-
net his
Sermon
the People, profeffing that the *Quakers* maintained
Repentance toward God and Faith in Chrift and

25   Godlinefs,

Godlinefs, and Righteoufnefs, &c. and he continued
I Judge above half an hour, (though not fo long
nor fo furious as *William Edmundfon* the day before.

I liftned carefully and watcht his Ending (being

And my
Anfwer

defirous to fay fomething leaft another of them
fhould fall into a Sermon alfo and put me by) and
I fpeedily faid (to this Effect) Friend you have here
delivered many holy Truths of God (at this there
was deep filence, as if I had turn'd a Profelite, at
leaft it pleafed them to be applauded, I went on and
faid concerning Repentance and turning from all
fin, of the Blood of Chrift, and of being faved by
his Blood, *of living foberly, Righteoufly, and godly in
this prefent World*, &c. but withal I faid, they did
not reach me nor any thing that I had fpoken as
proof againft them, for I and all their Adverfaries
the Proteftants preached Repentance and Faith,
&c. but theirs was an *Anti-Chriftian Repentance,*

The Qua-
kers and
the Papifts
general
Faith and
Repent-
ance

and Faith, &c. becaufe either not true Repentance
and Faith as Proteftants argue againft the Papifts
and Quakers, or elfe in general Terms not diftin-
guifhing between true Repentance and falfe, and
fhewing the difference between the true Faith and
the falfe: So that I faid you might have preacht
this Sermon even in *Rome* before the *Popes* face in
his own Chappel, yea, the Pope and the *Cardinals*

The Jug-
lings of
the Papifts
and Qua-
kers

and *Friars,* and *Iefuits* deliver the fame Doctrines
(in general Terms) daily: But as *Thieves* I*uglers,*
and *Counterfiets* when they come to Examination,
their Impudent fayings and Swearings prove but
the paints of *Whores* and *Har-* [120] *lots?* So do
the Devilifh Doctrines and Devilifh Conceit and
Fancies

Fancies of *Papiſts, Quakers,* and all Fantaſtick, Formal, Carnal Proteſtants, who Cry *Lord, Lord,* &c. but are Anſwered by Chriſt Jeſus with I *know ye not, Depart from me ye that work* Iniquity.

I cannot Affirm that I ſpake all theſe Individual words, nor have omitted ought that I or they ſpake: yet I remember no more, though being Confined (by their great deſire and my ſelf) to a puarter of an hour, for each point I was forced as all may judge to omit many Amplifications and Illuſtrations which now I crave the Readers patience, while I preſent him with ſome of them.

I intended to have Charged them with the falſe- neſs of their Hope, and Love, and Peace, and Joy which they often Crake, (though they pretend quak- ing and Trembling) their Heaven conſiſteth, and all the Eternal Life to come, they look for, they are now in preſent, full Poſſeſſion of. *^{*The Hope peace and Joy of the Quakers}*

What Scripture is more common in the mouths and pens of the *Quakers,* then that of *Paul* to the *Coloſſians, Chap.* 1. which is, *Chriſt in you the Hope of Glory:* whereby they Inſinuate two of their grand Deceits and Lyes, *Firſt,* that their is no other Chriſt but what is in every man in the World. *Secondly,* That there is no other Glory to be hoped for in, or by, or with the Lord Jeſus, but what the Saints, that is the *Quakers* enjoy, and are already poſſeſſedof within them in this Life. *^{Chriſt the Hope of Glory}*

To which I ſay, how many painted Anchors and painted Hopes are there? How many Hopes as in *Iob* like the Spiders web ſwept away to Eternity?

If

If there be e're a painted Anchor or e're a Spiders web in the world[1] this of the *Quakers*.

Hope is one, as in time I may furthet demonftrate.

For, do they not overthrow the very Nature of Hope which they prate of, and give rhe Spirit of God *Rom.* 9. the Lye, which tells us that Hope is not of things in poffeffion, or which we fee? doth not *Paul* there tell us almoft in plain Terms, that it is fimplicity and Non-Senfe to talk concerning Hope after fuch a Rate? Doth not 1 *Pet.* 1. tell us of a *Living Hope* (oppofite to painted and dead Hopes) and this *Living Hope* called in other places *the Hope of Righteoufnefs, the Hope of the Redemption of our Bodies?* the Hope as of Heirs for an Inheritance? of the Glory that [121] fhall be revealed in us, which is a ftate of the manifeftation of the Sons of God, though faith *John, We are now the Sons of God,* 1 John 3. we know not what that is, all that is now enjoyed is but as the *firft Fruits* to the *Harveft,* as the Spirit fpeaks.

The Sim-plicity as well as Impiety of the Qua-kers Hope

2. Again, what Ignorance and fimplicity is it to call Chrift or God, the Glory or the goodnefs, or good things which we hope for, Literally and properly upon the Promife, and the Power, and goodnefs of God, no Chrift Jefus? Can the *Eternal God* in any *Literal Senfe* be called the Hope of *Ifrael,* Jer. 14. but in the fame *Figurative Senfe* whereby *Mofes* cals him *Our Life and the Length of our Dayes?* and we in *Common Speech* call fuch a man, or his
Promife,

---

[1] Interline "it is" after world. *R. W. Ms. Ann.*

Promife, or any Creatures dear to us, *Our Hope, our Love, our Joy,* &c. that is the Ground or the Object of our Hope &c

Their *great Blunderer Humphry Norton* he deals as plainly and roundly as G. *Fox* (his *æmulous Corrival*) falfly and fraudulently, when that holy Scripture [*If in this Life only we have Hope,* &c.] was here objected to *Humphry Norton*, he clapt his hand on his Breaſt ſaying. He had it there already, that is oppoſing it to (and denying the Hope in) the Life to come, eſpecially, as to their Bodies which are not raiſed up (they ſay) *Spiritual Bodies,* being (though of late) more ſubtly and hipocritically all one with thoſe deceived Souls that ſaid the Reſurrection was paſt already. It is true, they will pretend to owne the Scriptures, Chriſts humane Nature, the Reſurrection, and Judgement, and Faith, and Hope, ahd Repentance, *&c.* as true and found as any Proteſtant: but ſtill it is no otherwiſe, but as G. *Fox* and *Ed. Burroughs* ſay in this Book, that is, (as I have and ſhall open) in a moſt *Jugling* and *deceitful Senfe* and meaning.

It is reported that ſome of them at their Death have uſed thoſe words [*Lord Jeſus receive my Spirit,*] ſome have Charitably thought that they intend thereby their going preſently into the preſence of Chriſt Jeſus, but as the Truth and bottom, however they blind the world, and the weakeſt of their Followers, (until they be fit to wean and fall to ſtrong meat) others of them Covertly ſay & write, and others of them more plainly ſay, *viz.* That they believe no more Riſing of their Bodies then the
riſing

Humpry Norton his Hope

The Quakers Hope of life to come

rifing of a Dog: and as to their *Spirits* they believe
Souls are [122] patts of God, and go unto God and
into God: and therefore their faying, *Lord Jefus
receive my Spirit*, is no more then Lord Jefus receive thy felf, according to fome of their plain Expreffions: To whom fhould I pray? my felf? to
whom fhould I give Thanks? my felf? wherein
their *woful*, *black*, and *filthy Spirit* Contradicteth
it felf amongft themfelves, though they agree in

The Qua- the *Devils Bait*, (which Catcht himfelf, and with
kers bait which he Catcht our *firſt Patents* and all his *Pofteri-*
by which *ty*) viz. *Ye fhall be as Gods*, live as God, know as
Satan takes God, be Gods and Chrifts for Evermore.
them

    I fhall now crave the Readers patience to hear
fome fewQuotations out of G. *Fox*, which my quar-
John
Bunyan ter of an hour would not then permit) declaring
thcir *Apoftacie* and *Herefie* in the matters of *Repentance, Faith*, &c.

In *Pag.* 127. he brings in *John Bunyan* faying,
[*It is a Counterfietlng of the New Birth for men to
follow the Light wherewith men coming into the World
are enlightned.*]

G. *Fox* Anfwereth, [*which none comes to the New
Birth, but who comes to the Light, wherewith every man,*
&c. *which believing in is a Child of the Light: believing and receiving comes to receive power to be the Sons
of God.*]

The new   I Reply, none are truly Converted, born again,
Birth of
the Qua- &c. but in a true Senfe they come to Chrift Jefus:
kers For the Scripture faith, *he gives Repentance to Ifrael*,
He is the Author and Finifher of our Faith: But that
Jefus Chrift as God, (fo the *Quakers* owne him) and

as

as man (for fo they alfo owne him) fhould be in
every man, and Woman, and Child in the World,
I have proved and fhall prove it to be a *blockifh* and
Devilifh Fancy.

2. If this Light, this Chrift the Mediator between God and man be only a Spirit and not man,
why do the Scriptnre, why do the *Quakere* madly
fay there was fuch a man, though they cannot tell
now what is become of him except he be (as they
fay) within, *&c.*

3. If this Light, this Chrift, this Mediator be
in every man, what fhould be the Reafon that fo
many *Thoufands* and *Ten Thoufand* of *Millions* fee
him not? Only a few perfons Curfing and Reviling
all the reft, and that fay all but the *Quakers* are deceived? Can the Sun be in a Chamber and perfons
not blind, but [123] feeing and awake, and ufing his
Light and yet not fee it. Certainly it is but a *painted
Sun* that doth not fhine equally on all, it is but a
painted Fire that doth not burn, and the *Quakers* are
but *Pictures* of *Chriftians,* and pictures of men to
argue aftet fuch a Rate, that Chrift not only as
God, and Creatour fhould be in every man, but alfo
as the Mediator, as the Spirit, and yet not operate
according to the Nature of the Sun and Fire: It is
true, the Lord Jefus came into the dark world, and
their darkness comprehended him not to be He
that was to come, the *true Meffiah*: but when Chrift
Jefus as Mediator, the true or only Light fhall
dwell in the Undeftanding and Will, and Memory,
and Affections of a man or Woman; and thofe perfons be favingly inlightened by him as you write,
and

and yet not Converted and faved by him, it can be the Language of none but thofe that peep and mutter *Ifai.* 8. but have no true Light, but a falfe and painted Light within them.

The true and falfe new Birth. Laftly, faith *Fox* this turning to the Light within is the New Birth: But the *Holy Record* faith, that till the preaching of the Word, or Gofpel, or glad News come to the mind of a man, (ordinarily by the Ear, and hearing, and preaching, *Rom.* 10.) there is no *Faith,* nor *Covenant,* nor *Chrift,* nor God in the Soul, *Ephef.*2. and we are not only in darknefs, but darknefs it felf, *Ephef.* 5. and only by the holy Word and Spirit preached¹ the blefling, *Ifai.* 59., God fhineth in our hearts, and not by any fuch *Immediate Fantaftick Faith* or Spirit, as the *Anti Chriftian Quakers* dream of, yea, againft the Light of a twofold Experience in their own Souls.

The Quakers put out the Eyes of their own Experience. 1. That many of them being enlightened and formerly Convicted by the reading or preaching of the Doctrine, Word or Will of God revealed in the holy Scripture.

2. That of their new Light (as they falfly and foolifhly prate) pretended to be brought unto their Ears and knowledge by the means of thefe *new Apoftles, Preachers,* and *Minifters,* fo pretended of Chrift Jefus.

When God hides (that is by *Spiritual Judgements*) the Light of Scripture, of the Spirit of Reafon, and of Experience, &c. who can find it out? No man, no nor Devil can fubfift one minute without the power of *Chrifts Eternal Power and Godhead*:

¹ Interline "is" after preached. *R. W. Ms. Ann.*

head: [124] but when Chrift Jefus comes into the
Soul as *Mediator* of the *new. Covenant*,and be thus
idle and not operative in all mankinde in the
World, and not to Convert,and work belief in them,
which muft be either becaufe he cannot, or becaufe
he will not, as the *Leaper* faid, is as black and blafphemous a Fancy as any *Atheiftical* or *AntiChriftian
Soul* can harbour.

He brings in *George Willington* faying, [*He is Iuf-* Pag 44.
tified by Faith alone without good works]He Anfwers; George
[*What without Faith that works by Love.*] ton

I Reply: In this paffage, and in many others, this
fubtle man clearly difcovers what he makes true
Juftifying Faith to be, *viz.* not one hair breadth
more then the Faith that may be to God in the
firft Covenant, the Covenant of works, and a looking
to be Juftified and faved be God for a mans own
Abilities, performances and Righteoufnefs, far from
the Faith of the Gofpel, which though good works
in Love follow it, yet not one good work in the
world goes before it: Nor one good work in the
world goes with it in the point of Juftification, or The Qua-
pardon of our Tranfgreffions: and therefore G. Jewifh and
Fox hath not only *George Willington* his Oppofite, Popifh
but the exprefs word and Declaration of the Spirit
of God faying, [*Rom.* 3. *Therefore we Conclude that
a man is Iuftified by Faith and not by the works of the
Law.*]

The dole-
Alas *porr Bankrupts* who owe more Infinitely to ful ftate of
God then we are worth: who are over head and all men
Ears in Debt to God, to our own Souls,to Men and till mercy
not juftice
Angels,and the whole Creation, having finned againft pitty them

26 Heaven,

Heaven, &c. that have not one farthing toward the discharge of so many *Infinite Millions* of *Talents* God of his rich Infinite mercy convinceth some of the proud Sons and Daughters of men of their *deplorable Condition*, makes them cry for mercy, and for Christ Jesus sake and Mediation, he freely Iustifies and forgives them. Thus saith the Scripture all along, and that our Faith, our believing or receiving of this grace though it be followed with *Mary Magdalens Love*, contributes not one farthing toward the payment *of our Infinite Millions*, no not so much as one good Thought.

Pag 47 Joseph Miller He brings in *Ioseph Miller* saying, [*It is an Errour to say, we are Iustified by that which Christ doth in us.* He Answers, Contrary to the Apostle, who saith, We are Iustified by Faith in his Blood: [125 And the Faith is in the Heart, and the Blood is in the Heart that purifies it, and held in a *pure Conscience*: And the Word of Faith is within, *Rom.* 10.

The Quakers Justifiratson within us. And Faith gives Victory over the World, and that which gives Victory Justifies, And Christ is within you who is *Justification, Sanctificotion* and *Redemption*: either of them is found within, and thou art in the Errour, and not fit to talk of these things thou understandest not.

I Reply: Grant that in a true Respect and Sense, Faith is within, and the Blood within, and the Word of Faith within, and Christ within, and *Justification* and *Sanctification* within, will it therefore follow I say, will it therefore follow with any Colour

Fox his Babilonish tumbling of Common Reason, that therefore in one and the same Sense they are all within, and they are all

one,

one, and they were not without before they were of all in a Croud and Heap to-gether. within? I know this *fubtle Fox* and he that helps his deluded pate to bind up fuch a *Bundle* of *wrefted* *Scriptures*, would have it fo, that he may *jumble* and *blend* all together in a *Babilonifh Myftery*, and fubtly deny the Truth of the holy Scriptures Hiftory.

It is true,*Cheift dwels in our Hearts by believing,* Ephef. 3. and Confequently his Crofs, yea, his *Man-ger*, yea, his *Blood*, yea, his *Grave* are within, *&c.* But that Chrift Literally fhed his Blood within us, as a *Ranfome* to his Eather for the fins of the whole world, is as *Fine* and *bruitifh a Fancy*, as that the *Crofs*, the *Spear*, the *Soulders*, the *High Priefts*, *Scribes* and *Pharifees* and *People*, *Pilate*,the *Romans*, *Ierufalem*,*Iude*,& the whole world (as fome of them have idly & ofteuprated) are Literally within us.

It is true in a Senfe, the King and his pardon, and Counfellours and Scribes, and writings, and Seals, *&c.* are all in a *Rebels heart*, as he believes and ap- Juftifica-tion opened. plies all thefe within him, and his belief works by love: But if they be within otherwife then we Af-firm, *&c.* and as G. *Fox* would have it, then they are not withont alfo, (which is the mark all thefe *Arrows* from *Hell* fly at,) and Confequently Chrift Jefus and his Blood fhedding, and a *Literal Ierufa-lem*, and a *true* and *real man* Chrift Jefus, and the holy, real Literal Scriptures are blown up and van-ifhed altogether.

Pag. 10. He brings in I*ohn Bunyar* faying, [It *is not Faith and works that juftifies a man before God, but it is Faith and good works which juftifie in the fight of men only, and fuch works will not* [126] *juftifie in* *the*

the fight of God: and he faith, that works is only to justifie their Faith to be true before men.]

G. *Fox* Anfwers, *Abraham* was not Juftified only to men by his Obedience, but to God : And where there is *Faith* there is *Iuftification* which works by Love : And the *Saints Faith* and *works* were not only to Juftifie them in the fight of men. For the work of God is to do what he faith,& the will which who doth not is not Juftified by fo doing, but to be beaten with ftripes : who feek to be Juftified by their Faith and works in the fight of men are dead, Faith and works both.

The Quakers Popifh Juftification by works.

I Reply, He that reads this paffage may without doubting Conclude that G. *Fox* and his *Foxians* are as *perfect Pharifees* (*Iewifh* and *Popifh*) as ever burroughed in *Rome* or *Ierufalem*, maintaining a Covenant of works, Juftification by works, and renouncing Chrift Jefus his Blood and merits : For if *Abraham* was Juftified and received his pardon by his Obedience to God what need was there for him and us, to look out for a *Surety*, a *Redeemer*, a *Mediator* to pay his Blood for our Ranfome, and to fetch us out of the *miferable ftate of Sin; Death*, and *Hell*,&c.

The Papifts and Quakers fee no need of Chrift.

2. Whereas G. *Fox* asketh what is the work of God, but to do what he faith.

The Papifts and Quakers know not the difference between the two Covenants

I Reply, 1. The work of God (according to Chrifts Doctrine) is to believe on him whom God fent. It is true, it is the Command of God to keep his Commands, but fince the deadly Fall of man, none, not one being able, *Rom.* 3. (though *Fox* deny it,) it is the work, the *great work* of God to fly

to

to that *bleſſed Propitiation* for poor ſinners,(throughout the world :) But G. *Fox* cannot diſtinguiſh between the *Covenant of works*, of *Iuſtice*, and of *Debt*, .
and that of *mercy*, and of receiving all as a *Beggar*,
and Condemned Rebels, *poor ʼproud Souls* they know
not any difference between the Blood of Chriſt
Ieſus and their own Blood, as we ſhall ſee afterward.

   3. Whereas he ſaith, that they do not Gods will
are not juſtified in ſo doing :

   I Anſwer, therefore it follows ronndly as his Con-
cluſion, that they that do Gods will are juſtified in
ſo doing : that is their ſins are pardoned as *David*
and *Paul* by pardon of Sin deſcribe juſtification,

127] Who ſees not the ſubtlety of this *Fox* cheating himſelf and others with the divers ſignification
of this *Latin word Iuſtification*? It is true, a man
can not be juſtified or defended for *Thieving, Whor-*
ing, Murthering, &c. Doth it follow therefore, that
they that do not *Steal, whore, murther,* &c. by this
abſtaining from Sin, and by this their work they
obtein the pardon, and ſtand by this their work,
legally right and juſtified in the *Court of Heaven!*

  Fox his playing with the word Juſti fication

   I Conclude, that by theſe hints a broken hearted
ſinner, who hath ſeen Sin as Sin, the ſin of his Nature, his chief ſin, *&c.* will ſee how far from the
Doctrine of true Repentance, true Faith, &c theſe
mens Teachings be, and (for all their boaſting) what
need they have to Examine themſelves whether
they be in the Faith, and whether there be any other
Chriſt Ieſus within them then a *Counterfiet* and ʼpainted *Meſſiah*, and whether their *Counterfiet* and ʼpainted
Faith, Repentance and *Hope* will yield them another
Fruit then a *dolefully Counterfieted and periſhing Sal-*
vation.   At

At laſt by Gods merciful held I come now (with their glad Conſent) to the ſeventh and laſt Poſition propounded to be diſcuſt at *Newport*, viz. that their Religion was nothing elſe but a mixture of *Popery*, *Arminianiſme*, *Socinianiſme*, *Iudaiſme*, &c.

The laſt of the ſeven Poſitions at Newport

Herein I knew I was not to exceed my quarter glass, and there.fore I take liberty now a little to inlarge, to remember the Reader of the old Proverb, *that where God hath his Church, the Devil will have his Chappel*. And that where Chriſt Ieſus hath his Field of *good Seed*, while the Servants ſleep, the Enemy will ſow the *Tares*, of *rotten Doctrines*, and *rotten Profeſſors*, who like *Windefals*, and *Revolting Rebels* fall from the *holy Truths* they have profeſſed, being looſe aud weak believers or only *affrighted* and *Terrified Hipocrites*, by Gods righteous Iudgement delivered over to liſten too, and believe Lyes as the only *heavenly Truths* of Ieſus.

The Quaker Religion pieced up o many old Hereſies

I had purpoſed to have ſhewed how in matters concerning God, the Son of God, the Spirit of God, &c. the *Quakers* have followed, the *Cerdonians*, the *Priſcillians*, the *Valentinians*, the *old Gnoſticks*, and *Manicheans* : but I Confined my ſelf to the Terms of the *Poſition*, and declared that the *Quakers* were *downright Papiſts* in many points, ſome I then Inſiſted on, and the reſt [128] intended, I ſhall now mention. *Firſt*, In magnifying the *rotten ſtrength* and *Arm* of *dead* and *rotten Nature* : when it is Objected to G. *Fox* in his book, that *by Nature we are all dead in ſins and Treſpaſſes* :

G· *Fox* Anſwers, by d,viding all men into three ſorts: Some are born holy from the wombe, as *Ier.*

Some

Some the Saints that is, only their Children born Of Na-tures its Impurity holy without any sinful corruption. *Thirdly,* the wicked who will not turn to the Light within them, and they are only the *Unbelievers dead in sin.* But the *Protestants, David* and his *Followers* Confess their *Natures, Births,* and *Conceptions* to be all de-filed with sin, and with a *sinful proneness* to all Ini-quity, though *miraculously* some are Sanctified, or set apart to God from the wombe as *Ieremiah, Iohn the Baptist,* &c. Some after a more peculiar and mi-raculous manner, as the Lord Iesus : Some by *New Birth,* and the *wonderfal Supernatural Power* of the holy Spirie *Changing, Regenerating,* and as it were *New Creating* the *Soul* and *Spirit,* in *Everlasting, Unchangeable Holiness* and *Righteousness* after the Image of his first and second Creatour.

It is true, that the *Papists* come nearer the Truth as to *Birth, Corruption* and *Defilement* then the *Qua-* The Pa-pists righter then the Quakers *kers,* acknowledging all *,o be Conceived and born in Sin,* not that the Devil or the *Papists* care to ac-knowledge this Truth, but that they may use it as a *Cridge* over which they may pass to the Necessity of Baptisme on pain of *Damnation* : on which they may also build many other *Superstitious Fanciee* as to the holy Ordinances.

But the *Quakers,* although they hold only their own Children to beConceived and born holy &with-out Sin, yet they jump into one step with the *Pa-* The pow-er of Natu e in Spirituals *pists,* as to the Power of Nature in Spirituals, ane that every man and woman in the world hath a sufficient Light within him to see God and Christ, &c. and to turn themselves unto them to *Eternal Life.*

Life. Contrary to the *Proteſtants,* who from the holy Scriptures maintain mans Natural Blindneſs and Darkneſs, *Epheſ. 5.* Mans Natural Deadneſs, *Epheſ. 2.* and that our wiſdome can not diſcern any Spiritual thing, that is, Spiritually, 1. *Cor 2.* That our *Quinteſſence* of *Nature,* our very *wiſdome is Enmity to God:* He hates us as we hate him, and are at *deadly fewd* and *mortal Hatred* like two men of War [129] giving Fire one upon another, we re-

The way of Converſion both of the Papiſts and the Quakers

ſolving to ſink by *Ejods ſide,* rather then to yield to God: but God in *Infinite pitty,* ſeeing our weakneſs and madneſs, and certain Deſtruction hangs out a *white Flag* and offers a P*arly,* on purpoſe to ſave us from our deſperate minde & Ruine, which by many heavenly means of *Free mercy* he Effecteth? The *Papiſts* ſpeak more like Men, and at laſt yield that men and Women have left them (ſince *Adams Fall*) power to liſten too, and obey *Moral Perſwaſions,* and offers which God makes : The *Quakers* talk only (like *Bruits*) of no means, no means but *Immediate Revelation* of the Spirit : and yet in Contradiction to themſelves they make the Spirit an inward means, and their *Apoſtles* or *Meſſengers* an outward means, or elſe they make themſelves *idle Embaſſodors,* in vain and to no purpoſe. The *Pro-*

The way of the trne Proteſtants

teſtants affirm from 2. *Cor· 3.* that we have not one good Thought but from God, that it is God, not we, that turns the will, *Phil. 2.* that when the Word of Faith is preached, *Rom.* 10. and Faith or Belief is wrought by hearing,: yet is it *Gods free Grace* that makes the difference, 1 *Cor.*4. when ſeveral Hearers are Aſſembled, and God opens *Lidiahs heart* and

not

not others, *Acts* 16. the *learned Academians* mock, and only *Dionifius* and *Damaris*, and a few believe, becaufe *God fheweth mercy on whom he will, and whom he will, he hardneth.*

Acts 17. Rom. 9. 2.

The *Papifts* and *Quakers* both maintain that *dole-* fully, *uncomfortable*, and *defperate Doctrine* of falling away from *true* and *faving grace*: The Truth is, neither of them feem to know *Experimentally* what *true* and *faving grace is*: It is true, they differ, the *Papists* make *Saving Grace* the. Property only of the *Regenerate*: The *Quakers* fay it is in every man and Woman in the world, they have it, though they know it not, and will not turn to it, and believe in it: yet both agree that they loofe it, whereas the *true Proteftants* though they grant great Failings and Falls, and Defertions of Gods Children, yet they hold the *Seed of God*, the *holy Spirit* and Word of God, I*fai.*59. and 1 *Cor.*3. that *Incorruptible, Eternal Seed*, of which they are begotten, never *Final-* [130] *ly?* nor *Totally* to be Ecclipfed, and they juftly account that Doctrine of *Interceffion*, viz. when *Son-fhip* or *Childfhip* is cut off by Sin, and Renewed by Repentance, to be a *fimple Fantaftical Notion*, as if *David* were a Child of God to day, a Child of the Devil to morrow, a Child of God this hour, and a Child of the Devil the next, *&*c. only they fix this impiously upon mortal and great fins only, as if *Adam* Eating of an *Apple* were not fufficient to his and our Deftruction, as well as *Davids* finning with *Bathfheba* and *Uriah, &c*

3. I muft be briefer, though not fo brief as I was

Falling from Grace

The true Proteftants Doctrine as to Falling away.

forced

The Pa-
pifts and
Quakers
agree
againft the
holy
Scripture

forced to be in our publick probations : I told them that the *Papifts* and the *Quakers* were *great Confede-rates* in their Endeavours to raze the *Records of Heaven*, and to rob the Saints and the world of this *Ineftimable Jewel* and *Treafure* of the holy Scrip-tures.

1 The Papifts own it not to be all the word or will of God revealed, but that there be unwritten Verities, that is, Gods mind revealed from Father to Son, by Tradition.

The Quakers will not vouchfafe it the Name of the word of God, out of a fimple pretence, becaufc Chrift is the word of God, that is, he isindeed the chief manifeftation of all the Appearances of God.

2 The *Papifts* horribly abufe it, calling it a Nofe of wax, a *Leaden Rule*, a *dead Letter*, *&c.* and fo do the Quakers triumphing over it with base Infultations, as over a *dead Letter*, a *Carkafs*. &c.

3. The whole world of *Papifts* affembled in *eighteen Years Labours*, (& *Chymical Laboratories*at *Trent*)at laft thundred out their *Anathamaes* and

The Pa-
pifts and
Quakers
Enmity
againft the
Hcbrew
aud Greek

Curfes againft all that fhould not prefer the *Vulgar Latin Copies* before the *Hebrew Copies* and the *Greek* (in which it pleafed the holy Spirit of God firft to write his mind and will or word unto us:) And do not the *Quakers* as *fimply* and *bruitifhly* bind themfelves to the bare Letter of the *Common Eng-lifh*? Though they know the *Hebrew* and *Greek Cop-ies* are the *Foundation* and *Touchftone* of all other (though millions of) Tranflations: Though they know there be more *Englifh Tranflations* then one ; Though the Englifh Tranflations *wonderfully* [135
differ

differ; Though *Ravius*(that *Famous Oriental Hebrician*, &c.) proclaims above a *Thousand Faults*, and some grofs in our laft Tranflation : though fome of them (as *John Stubs*) boaft of their humane Learning produced his *Hebrew Bible* in our Conference: yet will thefe Ephefians cry out (like *Frantick mad*) great is our *Latin Tranflation*, great is our *Englifh Tranflation* : Yea, one of them boafted to my felf, that the Spirit of God would teach them Scripture without the *Hebrew* and the *Greek*, or the *Englifh* either.

4. The *Papifts* fet up a Judge in Controverfies above the holy Scriptures, who can difpenfe with Scriptures and do all that God can do. And fay not the Quakers the fame of their Spirit which is above the Scriptures, for it gave forth the Scriptures, and is in every man

[margin: The Papifts and Quakers Judge of Scripture]

5. The *Papifts* though they will not deny to make the Scriptures the Rule, and profefs to be tried by it, yet their Church, and the head of it the *Pope muft Interpret* : And do not the *Quakers* herein the fame concerning themfelves, though fome think more bruitifhly, for they will allow no Interpretations, nor meaning at all, but you muft take the words as the *Tranflators* have given them us (right or wrong) and you must not enquire either into the meaning of words, or the meaning of mind of God in the place. Oh what a *black, deaf* and *dumb, Lazie Spirit* hath poffeffed the Souls of thefe great pretenders too and *Monopolizers* of the holy Spirit of God, both *Papifts* and *Quakers* ?

[margin: Interpretation of Scripture]

6 The *Papifts* generally ufe not, nor have the
holy

holy Scripture, (no not in their Devotions) in their own Tongue, but in the *Latine*, (the *Whores Tongue of Italy :*) therefore no wonder they prize it not: but even the *Lights* or *Luminaries* ſo pretending,

The Pa-
piſts and
Quakers
ſlighting
holy
Scripture

amongſt them diſuſe it, Care not for it, read it not, *&c.* many have it not: So that *Luther* tels us that in *Thirteen years* or more he ſaw not a Bible in his College at *Erford*, until by Gods merciful providence he came to ſee one, to his own & the Comfott of *Thouſands*, & *Luther* tels us that at one great Aſſembly of the *Emperour* and *Princes*, the *Proteſtants* of *Germany* had Conveyed a Bible on the Table: The *Cardinal* being firſt come he opened the Book, and read here and there in it, (it is like he had not ſeen [132] it before in his Life,) In comes one of the *Popiſh Princes*, and askt the *Cardinals Eminency* what Book he had there?

He Anſwerred, I know not: but I am ſure it is agaiuſt us, and it is laid here for that purpoſe. Oh the *I*nfinite mercies of God to us in our times, and our Infinite Debt to his Infinite goodneſs, and our Infinite guilt in neglect of it:

The Pa-
piſts and
Quakers
would be
rid of the
Scripture

The *Quakers* at firſt took off themſelves, *Families* and *Aſſemblies* from any uſe of it: Their Spirit they Crake that made the Scriptures ſupplies all, *&c.* The *Papiſts* and *Quakers* both have ſaid and printed, that if the Scripture were conſumed & quite taken out of the world, there would be no Loſs, ſo long as they have the Spirit. The Truth is I could by Arguments many make it appear that the *Papiſts* and *Quakers* love the holy Scriptures no better than *Goliah* loved *Davids*

Davids ftone and fling? nor no better then the Devil
loved *Chrifts Gegraptai, It is written : It is written*
for the *Papifts* and the *Quakers,* and the Devil
knows that if the holy Scriptures be Exalted, as
the revealed will or word, or Declaration of the
mind of God, down-falls their pretences of *Traditions* and *Revelations,* whereby the *Devil deceivs* themfelves and *himfelf alfo.*

4. The *Papifts* and *Quakers* fhake hands in the
moft *hellifh Doctrine* of Juftification by what is
within us, by what Chrift works within us, in fhort,
by what is called Sanctification put for Juftification,
and the forgiveness of fin, in and for the merits of
the Lord Jefus freely imputed and given to us :
The *Papifts* ufe the word *Inherent Righteousnefs,* but
the *Quakers* bogle at the word not finding it in the
Englifh Bible, yet they agree that by the works of
Obedience, yea, and alfo by the Acts of their own
Inventions and *Superftitions,* they can make a pardon
under a hedge to themfelves, and Crake that they
have received a pardon and Juftification fealed under the *Broad Seal of Heaven* to them, but it is
againft the glory of *the King of Heaven,* and againft
the glory of *the Son of God,* and his *glorious Sufferings,* and their own *Salvation.*

5 The *Quakers* are *Papifts* in that Spirit of *Infallibility* which they arrogate to themfelves, pretending that the holy, Spirit *fhall lead them into all
Truth,* fpeak *Immediately* in [133] them, *&c.* though
herein they differ, the *Pope* infallibly expounds
Scripture, but the *Quakers* fpeaks Scripture, and his
word is Gofpel, *&c.* yea, all men have this Spirit,
and

The Pa-
pifts and
Quakers
unite
againft
the Blood
of the
Lord Jefus

Tne Infal-
libility of
Papifts and
Quakers

and need no *Teacher*, and yet what an *horrible Contradictious noise* is there of the *Quakers, Apostles, Messengers, Ministers, Preachers* He and she sent into *Old-England,* and *New-England, Scotland, Ireland, Turky, Italy,* to bid people hearken to the Immediate *Spirit* within ?

6. The *Quakers* are *Papists* in that high lofty Conceit of their Perfection, when *Calvins time* this Spirit came from Hell under the name of *Spirituals,* and when of latter years in *Lancashire* under the Name of *Grindletonians,* all their Religion turned chiefly upon these two Hinges.

The Quakers Popish Perfection.

1. They could not sin, were perfect, &c.

2. They did nothing, said nothing, but God and the Spirit did all.

The Popish Revelations of the Quakers

7. The *Papists* and *Quakers* are great Friends in their Notions & practice of *Revelations, Visions, Dreams, Impulsions* and *Inspirations* : He that hath known so much as I have known of both their Spirits this way, and hath read their *Legends* as I have done, and can Instance in particulars as I can, will say, it is a *foul, Popish, Devilish Spirit* that haunts them (both under this fine pretence) to turn *both off from the words of Jesus,* Luke 10. How readest thou ?

Pbpists and Quakers one in Ceremonies and Inventions

8. What *Cart Loads* of *Traditions* and *Ceremonies* have the *Papists,* and I believe if the *Quakers* have opportunities and means (as the Papists have had) they will not be behind them : what a noise is made about uncovering or bowing the Head, Knee, for

Courses

Courſes of wearing of Lace, (yea, *Bands* and *Hat-bands* by ſome of them :] Of ſaying you or *Thou*, of uſing *Muſick, Carving, painting*, of *ſitting ſilent*, (ſome hundreths together) of *ſighing* and *ſhaking* of the Body? all which, as relating to *Religion* and *Chriſtians*: &c they are but *ſimple, Inſignificant*, and *Idle, popiſh Traſh and Trumpery*.

9. The Papiſts and Quakers are Biethren in Iniquity in their Affirmations that the Pope is not *Anti-Chriſt*, and that [135] the Church of *Rome* is not the *great Whore*: The Papiſts Affirme that *Anti-Chriſt* is not yet come, and that he ſhall come juſt in the end of the world, and ſhall finiſh all thoſe wonders in the *Revelations* in three years and a half: The Quakers though they hold Papiſts and Proteſtants (all except the Quakers (to be *Anti-Chriſtians*; (& as *Fox* doth) caſt back all the Propheſies of falſe Chriſts, falſe Prophets, and *Anti-Chriſt* to the time of the Apoſtles themſelves: yet the *great Whore* and the Devil, and ſin, (upon the point) they ſimply Confound and make all one; as may be ſeen in *Fox* his Title to this great Book, and other of his and their writings.

The Quakers and Papiſts agree that that hge Pope is not Anti-Chriſt

10. It may be wondred why the Popes when made or created by an hnmane & Deviliſh *Fiat*, they change their Name, and why the Quakers guided by the ſame *Helliſh Spirit* and *Fancy*, are ſo dainty and tender about owning their Old names: The Hiſtories ſay, the *Original* with the Popes was with him who was *Os porce*, or Swines ſnout, by Name, and was not thought fit being raiſed ſo high to bear

The Quakers not owning freely their Names.

ſo

fo low and fordid a Title. If it were fo then, yet it is nothing now but their *horrible pride* being in their Conceits fo high, fo Infallible, fo perfect, to fcorn to be like other men that are but Hogs Snouts, &c.

The Quakers and Popifh Monksand Munns all one.

11. The Papifts andQuakers are led by one Spirit of feigned holinefs, Devotion, monkifh Solitarinefs, &c, Their Monks and Friers and Nunns muft be fequeftred from the world, medle with no fæcular and worldly bufinefs, which is no more but the Beggars Life, and therefore juftly called *Fratre Mendicantes* Begging Friars, and the Indians Life, formerly the men laying all Labour upon the women; and all this is no more than hunger and Eafe, the Dogs Life alfo. It is true, the Apoftles by a true Light ought to have *worldly maintenance*, but *Paul* wrought day and night with his hands,which I never read of any of thefe lying Apoftles, Quakers in all their Travails to have done.

The Papifts and Qnakers Curfing

12. The Papifts and Quakers tongues are both fpitting and belching out Fire from one Fire of Hell: All that have [136] not the Church their *Mother*, our Church fay the *Papifts* have no God to their Father: the *Proteftants* hope and fpeak Charitably of theSalvation of many among the *Papifts*, but the *Papifts* have no Charity for any that bow not to the Image: and the *Quakers* (as G. *Fox* for the reft) Judge all that differ from Chrift that is themfelves to be in the *Delufion*, in differing from them, and if they dare to oppofe them, *Dogs, Serpents, Reprobates, Vipers, Cains, Pharifees, Devils*, &c.

13. The

13. The *Papiſts* and *Quakers* are *Firebrands* both in the matter of Perſecution or hunting ſuch as differ from them.   It is known that the *Papiſts* cry out that they perſecute none but the *Tares,* (the *Lot-tards,* the *Hugenots,* the *Wolves,* the *Hereticks,* &c.) That the *Quakers* as do all *Papiſts* and *Proteſtants* cry out againſt all Perſecution when it is their own Caſes, I ſay the *Quakers* moſt vehemently cry out againſt violence, againſt Creatures, but againſt their Corruptious and Corrupt *Principles* : And yet as for the *Papiſts* let it be conſidered whether there be any one *Religious ſtate* known in the world that Anſwers that woman drunk with the Blood of the Saints, and *Witneſſes of Jeſus* Comparably ſo near as doth the Eſtate of the *RomiſhChurch* and *Pro-feſſion.* *The Per-ſecuting Spirit of the Papiſts and Qua-kers*

And for the *Quakers* two things I ſay :

1: Their Tongues are the moſt Cutting and bit-ter of any that I can hear of profeſſing the *Pro-teſtant Reformation,* and it is certain, where the Tongue is ſo, that the Heart is ſo firſt, and where the Heart is ſo, the Tongue and Hend do never part Company : and therefore they will be as bitter and Cutting in Hand alſo, where God pleaſeth to per-mit a Sword to fall into it. *The Qua-kers Tongue and hand.*

2.   I have proved, and ſhall prove in this dif-courſe, that G. *Fox,* Ed. *Burroughs* and *John Stubs,* &c. maintain in their writings not only a *Magiſtra-tical Power* in the *Quakers,* and in none elſe, raſhly not only to puniſh by the *Material Sword* Tranſ-

28

greſſions

greffions againft men, but alfo fins againft |136 God, his Church, his Chrift, his worfhip and Religion.

2, As for the Agreement between the *Arminians* and the *Quakers,* I told them that the Papifts and the *Arminians,* the *Pelagians* and *Semipelagians,* and the Quakers were fo Confederate and one, that in naming one I named the other

1.   As to the *P*ower of Nature and Free Will in heavenly and Spiritual matters

2.As to the loofing of *true Saving Grace.*

The Qua-kersOne-nefs with the Ar-minians.

3. As to *Election* and *predeſtination* in time, upon *Obedience,*& *Rejection* and *Reprobation.*upon *Rebellion* and *Diſobedience.*   Contrary to the true Proteftant Doctrine of a *Certain Number* of Gods Elect or *C*hofen drawn by mercy, out of the Lumpe of Loft Mankind according to Gods Appointment from *Eternity,* by his Call in Time, by his holy Word and Spirit : and all from this Grace and Spirit of *Regeneration,* or *New-Birth,* it was not, it is not poffible that *David* or *Peter,* or any Child of God be *un-Childed,* can *Finally* or *Totally depart* and *Fall.*

3. The Quakers are Brethren with *Socinas* and the *Socinian*s following him, in making Chrift a *Type* and *Figure,* a *pattern* and *Example* how Chrift-

The Qua-kers and Socinians Onenefs

ians ought to walk· Not that the Blood which he fhed upon the Crofs at *Jeruſalem* was a *ſufficient price* and *Satisfaction* unto God for the fins of the whole world.

Thus all the Quakers more *Explicitly* or *Implicitely* fpeak, and *Humphry Norton* in print, *viz. Can one man s O bedence and Suffering pay a price to God*
for

for another mans fins? It is true, *Socinus* magnifies the *Free Grace* of God in *pardoning Sin*, and fending that man Chrift Jefus to be a *pattern* and *Leader* to all that will follow him.

But they endure not to think that the Flefh and Blood of one man being *Finite* fhould be able to fatisfie *Gods Infinite Juftice*, and to pay a price of *Infinite worth* and *Value*. What is this but the Summe and Snbftance of all the Quakers Teachings? For although they preach Gods mercy and Grace, and talk of fuch a Thing as the Blood of Chrift Jefus: Yet upon the point, that *Body*, that *Blood*, that Chrift Je-
Death &c. is nothing but a *Fancy*, and Chrift Jefus sus but a
his *Birth*, his *Life*, his *Dcath*, his *Burial*, his *Refur-* the Qua-
rection, his *Afcention*, his [137] *Return again to* kers
Judgement are all but a *Miftical* and *Allegorical*, and not a *Literal*, *Real* and *Subftantial matter*; And when they are forced to Confefs fuch a man to have been (though the Term *Humane*, G. *Fox* doth bogle and ftart as at a *Rattle Snake*) yet then examine them (as I have done) what is become of him: then he is vanifhed into a *Spirit* and *Ghoft*, and there was never any fuch thing as a Man you talkt of: And this is a *Devilifh Jefuitical Trick* the *Quakers* have beyond the *Socinians* concerning the Body and Sufferings of Chrift Jefus.

I might here Infift upon the *Quakers Notorious Sabellianifme*, taking clearly away (with *Sabellius*) The Sa-
the diftinction of the *Father* and the *Son*,and Con- bellians
founding *Father*, *Son* and *Spirii* in *One*, as G. *Fox* kers all
in all his Book doth. At prefent I Infift upon the one.
Pofition in my *Paper*, viz. that there is much *Judaifme* in the *Quakers Religion*. 1. In

1. In that great point of *Righteoufnefs, Reconcili-ation* with God, and *pardon* of Sin: They were *Zealous* (as the *Quakers* are) in the works of *Right-eoufnefs*, thinking thereby to pleafe and pacifie God, and to fatisfie his Juftice, putting their own *dirt* and *dung, Swines Blood* and *Dogs necks* upon *Gods Altar*, inftead of that *One fpotlefs Lamb of God,* that Man Chrift Jefus who alone *Expiateth*, and *taketh away the fins of the World.*

2. The *Jews* were *Zealou*s for their *Additions,* The Qua-*Traditions* and *Superftitious Inventions,* which (as the kers Ju- Lord Jefus fpeaks) they pteferred before rhe Com- daifme. mands of God: as the wafhing of their hands, and of their Bodies, and of *P*ots and Cups, and Beds, and Platters, and other things upon a *Confcientious* and *Religious Account.*

The *Quakers* (if they had their Scope) fcorn to come behind the *Jews*, or *Papifts* for *Ceremonies* and *Traditions*, which it was neceffary for them both to add (as *Apples* and *Nuts*, &c. to ftill poor Children from Crying after Gods Worfhip.

1. I named fome of the *Quakers Traditions* and *Inventions* in our *publickConference*, (unto which I fhall now name [138] fome more) I told them, and The Qua- now do, of the *Un-Chriftian* and *unnatural Inven-* kers Tra- ditious and*tion* of *Women Minifters*, *Women Apoftles*, *Women* Ceremo-*Embaffadors* to all *Nations* : a bufinefs that all the nies *Apoftolical firft Chriftian practice*, and all *fober* and *modeft Humanity* abhor to think of.

2. Their *dumb* and *filent meetings* (their *dumb* and Dumb *deaf* Spirit) without Colour of *Common Humanity* or Worfhip *precept* or *practice*, or *promife* of Chrift to fuch a worfhip. 3. Their

3. Their *bruitiſh Salutations* of ſtrangers, yea, and of acquaintance, Foes or Friends : It is true that ſome of them will admit of thoſe two words, How do you, and Farewel, as if there were ſome holineſs in theſe two, and in none other, and they might practice this holineſs toward the world, &c. Either none or Immodeſt Salutations

4. Their *New Way* of *feeling* and *grabling* the *hand* in an *uncouth, ſtrange* and *Immodeſt way*, and this inſtead of kiſſing, called the *holy Kiſs* amongſt Chriſtians, and a token of Love and Reverence to men alſo in ſober and Civilizd Nations.

5. Their *bruitiſh* Irreverence to all their Superiours either in Age, or in any other way of *Prehemi- nence*, a moſt *proud* and *monſtrous Beſtiality* againſt ſo many Commands and Examples of holy Scripture, and againſt the very Light of *Barbarous Nature* it ſelf, for the *Indians* uſe both Reverent words and Geſtures towards their *Sachims, Wiyouhs* and *Rulers.* Contrary to which, ſome of us have heard the Children of the *Quakers* brought up and taught to ſay to their Fathers *George* thou lyeſt : *Mary* thou lyeſt to their *Parents*, a Language which deſerved little leſs then Death by the Law, which God delivered to the *Jewiſh Nation*, and ſurely deſerveth ſevere Puniſhment at this day. The Quakers diſreſpect to all Superiours.

6. Their Crying down of *Muſicians* ond muſick, (ſo Excellent a gift of God) as a *fooliſh* and *Deviliſh practice*, though confirmed by ſo many Reaſons from, and before Chriſts time in Scripture, and in all ſober Nature and Civility, though it is abuſed, as all the gifts of God are. The Quakers againſt Muſick.

7. Their

Fantaſtical ſinging 7. Their own *un-Chriſtian, Fantaſtical, abſurd,* and *unprofitable way* of *Toning* and *ſinging.*

Carving, painting 139] 8. Their Condemning of the Commendable and Ingenious Arts of *Carving, Embroydering,* and *Painting,* ſo approved of, and Commended by God himſelf in Scripture, *&c.*

Orna-ments 9. Their Crying out againſt Ornaments of Gar-ments, and otherwiſe, againſt that Order God hath ſet in his works, and that Variety of his gifts for neceſſity, for Conveniency, for delight, even to *Aſtoniſhment* and *Admiration* in all his glorious works.

All theſe particulars (and more) I had not time, nor have I now to reckon up and amplifie, I re-member no *Material Exception,* or Objections I had from my *Antagoniſts.* Only *Iohn Burnet* ſpake againſt my great charging of them, and *William Edmundſon* he thundred out continually how deep my Charges were, and how weak my proofs, and that I had proved nothing.

The Con-cluſion of the Con-ference at Newport I told them that if *Paul* or Chriſt Jeſus himſelf were there in preſence, they propably would be Anſwered as I was, *viz.* that they made many deep and falſe Charges againſt the people called *Quakers,* but they could prove nothing: but I ſaid, I ſubmit-ted the *Examinatoon* and *Conſideration* of all paſ-ſages unto every mans Conſcience, and the praiſe and Iſſue only unto God.

The quickeſt and laſt turn about where Chriſt is After ſome turns of this ſort, *&c.* I praid their patience to Anſwer me one queſtion, *viz.* where is now that Man Chriſt Jeſus which they had Con-feſſed to me was born at *Bethlehem,* and died at
Ieruſalem,

Ierufalem,&c. At this they were all a while filent, and then *Iohn Burnet* Anfwered faying, he is where the Scriptures fay he is.

I Replied, where do the Scriptures fay he is, *Iohn Burnet* Replied, the Scripture fay he is *within*: I rejoyned to this purpofe: Then muft his Body be *Ubiquitary,* (as the *Tranfubftantiators* and *Confubftantiators* are forced to hold:) Then muft he have Infinite multitudes of Bodies, then muft his *Monftrous Body* or Bodies come from within his Saints, yea from within all mankind to Judgement, *&c.*

Juft here it pleafed God fo to Order it, that from the *Boat* (ready to fet Saile for *Providence*) I and others were [140] called upon to depart: So I was ftepping down, the Lord opened the mouth of *Elizabeth Williams* my *Brothers wife,* one of the Society of the *Baptifts* in *Newport,* who hearing their Clamours, their only Refuge, he hath proved nothing and faid aloud: The man hath difcharged his Confcience: He hath fully proved what he undertook to prove againft you, and the words that he hath fpoken fhall Judge you at the laft day. And thus the *Father of Lights, the firft and laft, the Alpha and Omega* gracioufly carried me through all alone thefe three dayes Contefts, as in a fhadow of Death with thefe *Deceived,* and *Deceiving Souls*: through my Labours of making out my proofs, the burthen whereof lay wholly upon me though they had been filent, (through their

An Unexpected yet Seafonable and true Teftimony from Elizabeth Williams

'Cenfures

Cenſures Reproaches, Falling on me ſo many at once, their *Interruptions*, and other *Diſadvantages* and *Provocations*, his *holy Name* be ever *praiſed* and *magnified.*

Our

141] *Our Conferences and Disputes at P R O V I D E N C E upon the seven other Positions mentioned in my Paper sent to G. Fox and his Associates.*

Fter we were thus (as above said) parted: They Remembered their Promise to me of discussing the other seven at *Providence*, and accordingly I*ohn Stubs* and *William Edmundson* sent me a Note of their willingness to come to *Providence* the last day of the next week being the 17*th*. day of the sixth *Moneth* called *August*.

The Con-
ference at
Provi-
dence·

I Returned them from the *Shoar side* another Note signifying, that (if God permitted) I would then and there be ready to Receive them.

That day it pleased the goodness and patience of God to bring us to, and being met thus at *Providence*, I first presented them with the Letter which was sent to them and me (God knows) without my thought or knowledg, at *Newport*, in publick Assembled. But there they thrice refused it, and here at *Providence William Edmundson* Answers, that
they

they came not to *Pro-* [142] *vidence* to hear P*apers*, but to hear me make out my Charges againft them: One of my Neighbours *Thomas Olny Senior* an able and *Leading man* amongft the People called *Baptifts* at P*rovidence*, moved alfo for the Reading of the Letter, *William Edmundfon* faid to him who art thou? Art not thou a *Baptift*? haft not thou feen it already? and further faid to him, Thou art an *Envious* and *filthy man*, upon no other *Provocation* but his *Rational defire* the Letter might be Read. *William Edmondfon* thongh he had on either fide of him an *able Iohn, viz. Iohn Stubs* and *Iohn Cartwright* fpake all, and at laft was forced to fay that if the Letter Contained matter tending to prove my *Pofitions* it fhould be read. But in the End I put up my Letter again, at the motion of *Captain Holden* of *Warwick*, as I did at *Newport*, in the morning of our *third dayes Conference,* for I obferved that for all their *bruitifh* Clamour of *Diana*, their *Light* or *dark Lanthorn,* rhey could not endure to be *Informed, Admonifhed, Counfelled,* leaft of all Reproved by any: and I alfo refolved to wait upon Gods mercy for a Seafon of publifhing it on the *Houfe Top*, and therefore the Reader hath it *Faithfully prefented* in the *Eighty feventh* Page in the beginning of the *third dayes Conference* at *Newport,* this time ftood up *Captain Iohn Green* of *Warwick* one of our *Magiftrates,* who obferving the *Infulting Carriage* efpecially of *William Edmundfon,* he defired leave to propofe one Query, which being granted he faid, he fpake not as a *Magiftrate* with *Authority,* but as an *Auditor* and fitter by, and he faid, I defire ro know whether

Mr.

Paffages about Reading the former Recited Letter. Thomas Olny

About a ftrange Query put to my Autagonift by Captain Green.

Mr. *Williams* be here as a *Delinquent* Charged to Anſwer at the Barr, or as a *Diſputant* upon equal Terms.

This *Query* they waved as well as they could, and I waved it alſo, and bore what ſeemed *Intollerable* to ſome that we might not be discouraged to go on in our buſineſs, about this time Mr. C*averly* of *Warwick* deſiring leave to ſpeak, motioned for the Choice of a *Moderator* between us, *William Edmund-ſon* Anſwered that *Roger Williams* had himſelf pro-vided a *Moderator*, and he produced and Read my P*aper* of *Poſition*,, wherein I deſired that all matters might be left to every *man*s *Conſcience* and *Iudgement*. &c.

A Mode-
rator
motioned.

143]

I knew with whom I had to deal, and therefore purpoſely waved, what ever I thought they would bogle at,& purpoſely gave them all *poſſible Advantages*, &c. and I humbly waited on God for patience for his ſake to bear with all Inconveniences,Inſultings, Interruptions,&c.and then,*I knew there would be no great need of a Moderator.*

The firſt
of the
Poſitions
debated
at Provi-
dence

Having thus cleard the way, I told them, I would briefly fall on my proof of the *firſt*, of the *ſeventh Poſitions* to be debated at P*rovidence*, *William Edmundſon* took forth his *Paper* and Read it, *viz.* [*The People called Quakers in Effect hold no God, no Chriſt, no Spirit, no Angel, no Devil, no Reſurrection, no Iudgement,no Heaven,no Hell, but what is in man.*

I told them that it was true, that in words and Terms they profeſſed and maintained all theſe, as other *Proteſtants* did, but if their writings were Examined, and eſpecially this of G. *Fox* which I had
there

there by me it fhould appear that what they profeffed in one place they overthrew in another: I
told them that they had there *George Fox* his Book
as well as I, and if *Iohn Stubs* would turn to them I
would name the *Quoted* P*ages,* and read them and
he might read them alfo.

I named *Pag.* 273. where *George Fox* brings in Alexander
Alexander Rofs faying, ⌊*It is horrible Blafphemy to* Rofs
*fay the Scripture is not the Word of God, and to fay
the Soul is a part of* God.⌋

He Anfwers, ⌈The Scriptures are the words of
God, *Exodus* 20. and the *four Books* of the *Revelations,* but Chrift is the word in whom they End.
And it is not *Horrible Blafphemy* to fay that the Soul
is a part of God, for it comes out of him, and that
which comes out of him is of him, and Rejoyceth G Fox
in him, I faid here what *George Fox* meant by the his Non-
four Books of the *Revelations,* I knew not, and if Senfe
they did they fhould do well to declare.

145⌋ But they paft it by and fo did I and I infifted
on the matter which was that G. *Fox* imagined fuch
a *God* and *Godhead* as is partible and divifible, which Quakers
might be divided into parts and pieces, and by this ous opinion
ftrange communication of his Effence, made him about Goa
diffolvable, and fo corruptible, &c. againft the *Puri-* Soul
ty & Majefty & Eternity of *God* : For this renders
the *Effence* or Being of God capable of falling
from his purity as man hath done and doth, and
capable of punifhment and condemnation in *Hel-
Fire* as the Soul of man is; all which and more
neceffary Confequences of of that opinion are horrible and blafphemous to imagine, much more to
be

be uttered of the eternal invifible and infinitely
and only *Wife God.*

John Stubs here read the words of G. *Fox* and faid,
the reafon was to be weighed which G. *Fox* ufed
which was;. For it came out of him, and that
which came out out of him is of him, and rejoyceth in him. To this end he defired the word in
Gen. 2. might be viewed, which he turned to and
read, viz. *God breathed into him the breath of life
and man became a living Soul.*

About this time *Sam. Gorton* fen. defired to fpeak,
and faid, If it be affirmed that God can be divided,
& that man was a *Part of God,* the *God-head* was
deftroyed and the *Soul of man,* and upon this *Bafis*
all the reft would follow which was afferted in this
Pofition. And whereas *John Stubs* read it as it is in
our *Tranflation,* viz. *God breathed into him the breath
of life,* Mr. *Gorton* faid it was *Lives* in the Margin,
the breath of *Lives,* which *John Stubs* acknowledged.

It is frequent in their Books, (when they will
fpeak plainly) for them to confefs that God breathed
forth himfelf into *Adam,* and that ther fore mans
Soul or *Spirit* is a part of the *Divine Effence,* that
the Soul is an increated fubftance : that as for the
Body, it comes from the *Earth,* and returns to the
Earth, and duft and rottennefs, and however they
fometimes preach and print hat the *Body* fhall rife
again, yet others again of them fpeak plainly, that
as the body of a dog or beaft fo it vanifheth : But
as for the *Spirit,* they fay that returns to God, that
is into God. And although they talk to blind our
eyes of a *Refurrection and Judgment,* and of *Souls*
being

being punished with the Devil and his Angels, yet others of them affirm that all Souls return into God, and that the soul of *Judas* is now as happy in God as the Soul of *Peter,* yea others of [146] them speak plainly that they are *Chrift & God*: therefore one of them being defired to give thanks at dinner, asked roundly, *to whome should I give thanks? to my self?* and *Calvin* relates how (long ago) one *Quinitinus* in his time a Leader this way, being demanded how he did? refolutely anfwered, *How can Chrift doe but well?* and yet at that time he was very fick.

Their high blafphe-myes.

About this time *W. E.* faid, what doft thou tel us of ftoryes what this man faid and that man faid we will not believe thee! But juft here rofe up a neighbour *Jofeph Jinks,* who faid he had no prejudice againft the Quakers, yet he could witnefs to the truth of thefe fpeeches of the Quakers, for one of them had fpoke as much to his face lately at *Newport* on *Rhode-Ifland*: but I ftill laboured to keep down heat and therefore I told them I would not trouble them with *Proofs* from elfewhere, but from their own *writings,* and from that of G. *Fox* there prefent, and therfore I prayed them to turn to *Pag.*39. where G. *Fox* brings in *Magnus Bine* faying, *The Saints are neither in the fulnefs of the God-head nor part, away with this Blafphemy which faith this is,* &c. *Fox* anfwereth, The work of the Miniftry was to bring People to the Knowledg of the *Son of God,* to a *perfect man,* to the unity of the *Faith,* to the meafure of the ftature of the fullnefs of *Chrift*: and *Chrift* will dwell in the *Saints,* and God will dwell in them : and thou fayeft they have

Pag. 89. *Magnus Bine.*

no

no part of the *Fulnefs* of the *Godhead*, and *John*
faith, *of his fulnefs have we all received, in whome
dwels the Godhead bodily*, and ye be all in the *Blafphemy*, that be out of this part of the *Fulnefs*.

I faid, that *G.Fox* rofe up contrary to what *Magnus Bine* affirmed, to wit, *That the Saints are not in
the* fulnefs *of the* Godhead. But *W.E.* bid me let

G.F. his words alone, his meaning alone, and keep
to the words. I told them the fubftance of my
proof lay there in the fubftance of *G.Fox* his anfwer
to his Adverfaryes : I took *Fox* his own word for
the *Quotation* out of his Adverfary, which may be
thought to be taken with as much Favor and advantage to himfelf as may be : and therefore if

they ftopt me from opening and comparing the
words in a rational and juft way, they ftopt me in
the bringing forth of my *Proofs and Arguments*.

I think here it was that *W.E.* faid further, If
thou goeft on to make out *G.Fox* his Sence and
meaning, we tell thee that we will ftop thee, *&c.*

147] But fince our bufinefs is with *G. Fox*, as well
if not more than with *W. E.* efpecially becaufe of
his *Book*, we fhall now more freely inlarge upon the
words *&c.* and Sence and *Meaning* alfo.

For the *Fulnefs of the Godhead* is one thing, and
another thing our (and all his works and Creatures)
partaking of that *Fulnefs*, in fome mercifull like-
nefs and coformity, as *Mofes* and we behold his
Back or dark *Refemblance*, and by Reflection, (as we
behold the Sun) take in fome weak low thoughts
and conceits of the Eternal and Invifible incomprehenfible and inconceivable *Power* and *Godhead*.

Thus

Thus to partake of some drops of the Ocean of *The great temptation of knowing* his *Wifdom, Power, Goodnefs, Holinefs, &c.* is not to *and holy* become an *Ocean* of *Power, Wifdom, Goodnefs, Holi-* *People.* nefs, yea *Wifdom it felf, Power it felf, Goodnefs it felf, Holinefs it felf* as God is. This devilifh *Pride* was the Sin of the *Devils,* or *wicked fpirits,* this was the Sin of our firft *Parents* unto which the Devil beguiled them; and this is *Sathans* bait ftill to catch all *Wife & Rich & High,* and efpecially *Holy People* with, *viz.* to be as God, to be in the fulnefs of the *Godhead,* to be *God himfelf.*

2. However this *Jugler* fpeaks here of the *Ful-* *The Quakers make themfelvs* nefs of the *Godhead bodily* in *Chrift,* yet if he be ex- *God and* amined and fearched it is clear that by *Chrift he* *Chrift.* meanes the *Body,* the *Quakers* and every one of their *Bodyes* is *Chrift* in whome the *Godhead* dwels bodily : and the great Myftery of which the *Holy Scripture* fpeaketh, 1 *Tim.* 3. Is God manifeft in their flefh, and therefore *Sam. Fifher* ufeth in his Writing, *Chrift Jefus*) as *Peter* did in his denying of him faying [that Perfon whome you call *God-Man*] is as high Treafon againft the *King of kings,* and *King of Saints,* as hath ordinarily been acted fince God moft wonderfully gave life to a lump of Clay, which now perks up to the eternal *Power* and *Godhead.*

Pag. 90. G. *Fox* brings in the fame Author fay- *Magnus* ing, *There is a kind of Infinitenefs in the Soul, and it* *Bine.* *cannot be Infinitenefs it felf,* He anfwers, *Is not the Soul without beginning, comeing from God and returning into God again which hath it in his hand? which hand goes againft him that doth evill, which throws*

30 *down*

down that which warrs againſt it, and Chriſt the Power of God, the Biſhop of the Soul which brings it up into God, which comes out from God, hath this a beginning and ending, and is not this infinite in it ſelf, and more than all the World?

148] I Reply, in theſe few lines, let him that hath his ſences make common ſence and Engliſh of ſome of them.

However this is expreſs that the Soul is without beginning or ending, coming out of God, and returning into God : ⌊*Hath this* (ſaith *Fox* (*a beginning or ending, and is not this infinite in it ſelf and more than all the World*⌋

I know I have had better Opinions and better Reaſons from theſe poor Natives of *America* then this poor ſelf conceited God and Chriſt. *G.Fox* expreſſeth concerning the Soul and Spirit of Man : what is here but a bruitiſh notion of the Spirit of man, and a bruitiſh notion of the Eternal *Power* and Godhead?

Among the ſix or ſeven Opinions of the Soul of man, this is one (and one of the groſſeſt) *viz.* that Mans Soul is an efflux, efflation, that is a flowing or breathing out of the Eſſence of eternal and infinite Godhead. This worſt and moſt Blaſphemous Opinion of the reſt, the old Serpent hath taught theſe *Foxians,* in ſo much that theſe bewitched Souls ſay and print, that this World is God, and the Godhead, manifeſt no[1] variety of appearances, and returning all again into the center of the Godhead :

in

---

[1] Change " no " to " in," *R. W. Ms. Ann.*

in which they fhew horrible ignorance and Block-
ifhnefs in heavenly or earthly matters : for reafon *Municheus*
tells us that Finites be innumberable and yet nu- *his 2*
Principles
merable in time, but Infinite is but one. The *Qua-*
kers and *Manicheans* are but one in many particulars *Manicheus* held two infinite powers or princes :
One infinitely good, the other infinitely as bad,
which they fay is the reafon (in fome Difputes I
have had with them) why God nor the Devil, good
nor evil gets the final victory one over another in
this World. But this notion of two infinite or
boundlefs Beings, is foon found fimple and bruitifh
for an infinite or boundlefs Being, cannot poffibly receive a Neighbour a Competitour, or fecond infinite
or boundlefs, for then the fecond would terminate and
bound the firft and it felf alfo and fo not one infinite
at all be granted. Beware of *Dogs* faith *Paul* & the
Holy Spirit faith (*Cant.2. beware of Foxes* [*take us the* *The infin-*
foxes] fure it is : we are to fly from bruitifh fellow- *ite patience*
of God
fhip, with them in thefe bruitifh Fancyes, fo alfo to
fly from thefe their brutifh Barkings and Blafphe-
·mings againft the infinitely Glorious and inconceivable Excellencies of God, and among the reft
his incomprehenfible patience, which could not bear
fuch horrible provocations were not his patience
himfelf, infinite and incomprehen- [149] fible :
Alas poor lump of clay and duft and afhes : poor
finite vapours we are, that are fo far from being infinite that (in a fence) we are infinitely Blocks and
Beafts, and not able to give a guefs at what Infinity, *The Qua-*
and an infinite Majefty and Godhead is. *kers obfti-*
nate in hor.
 I quoted *Pag.* 67. where againft *Fr. Higinfon* he
faith

faith [*Again thou makeft a great Puddir that one
fhould witnes he is equall with God*] G. *Fox* anfwers
that the *Englifh Divines* in their *Catechifme* fay [*that
Holy Ghoft and the Son are equall in Power and Glory
with the Father*] yet if any one come to witnefs the
Son of God revealed in him: or come to witnefs the
Holy Ghoft in them as they that gave out Scriptures to witnefs the mind of Chrift and witnefs that
equality with the Father, that equality which you
fpeak of you *Priefts* deftroy, that which you have put
forth to the Nation, and cry out horrible Blafphemie.

I Reply, let thefe horrible Blafphemous lines be
examined, and when the black and hellifh juyce is
preft out of them, will it not be this, *viz.* [*The
Quakers fay that they are equal in power and Glory
with God the* Father, Son, and Holy Spirit?

Pag. 182. I will adde to this *Pag.* 282. where G.
Fox brings in *Daniel Gaudry* faying, *furely they cannot be perfect here nor hereafter in equality but in quality.* G.F. anfwers, *Chrift makes no diftinction in his
words but faith,* be ye perfect as your heavenly Father is perfect, *and be you Merciful as he is, and as he
is fo are we in this world.* &c.

I Reply, whether it be G. *Fox* his Ignorance
of the difference between *Quality and Equality*, or
whether it be his *flinty Impudence*, or both, fure I
am there is an horrible, monftrous Brat of hellifh
Blafphemy hatcht amongft them, *viz.* that poor
duft and afhes may not only (by infinite Grace) be
like the King of Glory in Holinefs, &c. but he may
be (and the Quakers are) cheek by joll with him
as great a King, Prince and Monarch as he, equal
in

in *Power, Wifdome, Goodnefs, Juftice, Holinefs, Mer-cy,* and all thefe *Eternal, Infinite and Incomprehen-fible.*

G. *Fox* would not endure this in his own ftinking Dignity and *Preheminence:* for although he fuffer his Inferiour and petty Saints to be like him in (his pretended *Holinefs, Goodnefs, &c.*) yet he is fo great a *Diotrephes,* and fo jealous of his Crown, that *Humph. Norton* himfelf muft not dare to touch that *fimple Bable,* but himfelf and blind followers muft all adore the Godhead, and [150] none muft dare to be equal; or Corrival with him.

Unto this I adde, *Pag.* 248. where *G.Fox.* brings in an unnamed *Author* faying. *To fay that God is fubftantially in man, and effentially one with him, can be no other but the Man of Sin, the Devil himfelf hath transformed himfelf into an* Angel of Light, *and if it were poffible would deceive the very Elect.* G.Fox. Anfwers, *That God will dwell in man, and the Saints had unity with the Father and the Son &c.*

In which Anfwer it is plain, 1. That *G.Fox* maintains that the Godhead is effentially and fub-ftantially in man.

2. That his *Proof* is only fome *Myftical* and *fig-urative* Expreffion, as *viz.* of *Gods dwelling in Man, and walking in man, &c.* whence he impioufly & ignorantly confounds that relative union by be-lieving in the Son of God, into an *Effential* or *Union* of *Beings* with the eternal *Creator* himfelf: a Union of *finite and temporal fhadowes,* with the moft *Infinite and Eternal Creator;* of vifible and vanifhing and foolifh duft, with the invifible immortal

immortal and only wife God, which no truly humble Soul can but tremble to hear and think of.

The Quakers make themselves Father, Son & Holy Spirit It is clear in these Paſſages, 1. That the *Quakers* make themſelves *Father, Son* and *Holy Spirit.*

2. They make no other work of *Redemption* on *Juſtification, &c.* but what is wrought in their *ſpirits, minds* and *fancyes,* called *within them.*

3. They make no other ſtate of *Heaven, Reſurrection, Judgment or Life to come,* then is in them and their Bodyes at preſent.

Now concerning their bold and blaſphemous aſcending into the Throne of God we ſhall hear a little more in *G.Fox* making no Diſtinction between the *Father* and the *Son,* with that known Heretick *Sabellius.* and 2. In his making no diſtinction between Chriſt Jeſus himſelf, and his Saints or Believers in him.

Chriſt. Wade In *Pag.* 246. He brings in *Chriſtopher Wade* ſaying, *God the Father never took upon him humane Nature.* G F. anſwers, *God was in Chriſt reconciling the world unto himſelf And art ignorant of the great myſtery, God manifeſt in the fleſh; and his name is called the everlaſting Father.* As for the word *Humane,* which is *from the ground,* it comes from thy own Knowledge which is *Earthly, And Chriſt took upon him the ſeed of* Abraham *and* David *according to the fleſh,* and this is *Scripture-Language.*

H. Nortou more plain then G F. 151] I reply, in the former part of this *Narrative* I have ſhewn how ſimple & irrational G.F. his clamour is againſt that word *Humane,* and that the bottome is their impious, unchriſtian and hypocritical denying of Chriſt Jeſus to be a man, one individual

individual perſon as every man is : therefore *Humph.*
Norton (G. *Fox* his Corrival) is more plain and down
right,ſaying,is not Chriſt God, and is not God a
Spirit, and chiding us for gazing after a man, &c.

I ad to the former page 293. where G. *Fox* *Fergiſon.*
brings in one *Fergiſon,* ſaying, *that Chriſt and the*
Father and the Spirit are not one, but are diſtinct, &c.

G. *Fox* anſwers, this is a denying of Chriſts Doc- G F
trine, who ſaith, *I and my Father are one*: and the *againſt the*
Holy Ghoſt proceeds from the Father and the Son : *myſtery of*
Father
and he was conceived by the Holy Ghoſt, and they *Son and*
are all one and not diſtinct, but one in unity : that *Spirit*
which comes out from him leads the Saints into
all Truth that ever was given them from the Spirit
of truth, and ſo up unto God the Father of truth,
and ſo goes back again from whence it came.

Again the ſame *Author* ſaith, *it is Blaſphemy to*
ſay the Son is not diſtinct from the Father, &c.

G. *Fox* Anſwers, the Father and the Son are one,
the Father in the Son, and the Son in the Father :
ſo that which is in him is not diſtinct from him,
and they Blaſpheme which ſay, the Son is not in
the Father, and deny Chriſts Doctrine.

I reply, G.*Fox* all along his Book calls that blaſ- *The Quak*
phemy which the moſt holy and eternal *Lord* calls *blaſphe-*
heavenly *Truth.* He hath like ſome *Witches* and *myes as to*
the moſt
other notorious wretches ſo inur'd himſelf to poyſon, *holy Spirit*
that it is all one to him to ſwallow down the moſt
ſenſual and ſenſleſs *Dreames,* even concerning the
fearfull myſteryes of the *Father, Son,* and *Holy Spi-*
rit, when the *holy Scripture* tels us concerning theſe
Myſteryes, that in this life we know but in part, as
through a glaſs darkly *&c.*   2.   For

2. For his *Proof*, it is *the Childs song in the streets*, they are one and therfore not diftinct: I fear he knows, but will not know the nature of feveral refpects and accounts, *viz.* that in one refpect *Chrift Jefus* faith, I and my Father are one, and in another refpect my Father is greater then I; thus in one fence *a Father* is one with his Children, an *Hufband* with his *Wife*, a *Captain* with his *Souldiers*, a *Skipper* with his *Sea-men*, a *King* with his *Subjects*. And yet in another refpect, the Son is not the Father, the Wife is [152] not the Husband, the Mafter is not his Servants, the Captain is not his Souldiers, the Mafter is not his Sea-men, and the King is not his fubjects.

And thus though *GF.* and *MF.* be one in marriage, and one in a *fpirit* of notorious railing, yet she her felf will not fay but fhe is the *Woman* and he is the *Man*, fhe the wife and he the husband, and this Diftinction God in Nature the Law of our Countrey and all Nations will force them (will they, nill they) to acknowledge: otherwife (like the man poffeffed in the Gofpel) I fear no Chains of Humility nor Modefty would hold them from throwing off all Chains of Confcience, and from flinging all upon heaps of confufion without all due refpective refpects and diftinctions.

Tee Quak rs Chaos & babel.

There are four great points of the *Chriftian* Belief:

The Quak. dig up the root of al Chriftianity in the 4 great Doctrines thereof.

1. The Doctrine of the Father, Son and Spirit, and thefe they will not diftinguifh but make all one, and all to be in man.

2. The

2. The Doctrine of the Fall, Redemption, Justi-fication, Sanctification, &c. and these are all in man by their Tenents.

3. The Doctrine of the Church, the Officers, Baptisme, the Lords Supper, and these (say they) are all invisible, and within man.

4. The Resurrect on, eternal Judgement, Eter-nal Life. Heaven and Hell, Angels, Devils, & these their Professions and Printings proclaim to be in Man also : yea, so within him that they are only within him, and that without [1] there is no God, no Christ, no Heaven nor hell, &c.

In Page 38. G. *Fox* brings in *Tho.* Collier, saying *Tho Col-lier* [*The Kingdome is not come, nor the refreshing from the Spirit of the Lord.*

G. F. Answers, *which shews they are unconverted, gadding here and there, :* And Christ tells them *the Kingdome was in them. And they that are not turned to the Light which comes from Christ the Refresher where-by refreshing might come, and so are not come to Re-pentance yet.*

Reply, Who sees not that G. F. speaks not here of the Kingdome of Christ (so often promised in the future and to come, and the time of refreshing, *Act.* 3.) but that he cuts off all future hopes and expectations to come, and appropriates aud con-fines and fixeth, and stakes down all to the present moment of this vanishing life, and to what is (in this moment) in the minds of Men and Women ?

153]   The Holy Scripture tells us, and Experience tells

---

[1] Interline " man."   *R. W. Ms. Ann.*

The
Quak. bold
no Heaven
nor Hell
to come tells us that *Hypocrites* have no folid peace and joy here, nor folid hope of joy or glory to come : and yet (to ftill the deen and clamour of Confcience) abhorring the thought of a judgement and reckoning to come, they foolifhly and atheiftically pleafe themfelves with a childifh *Dream* of no Heaven nor refrefhing, no Hell nor torment but what is now within us.

Pag. 101 he brings in *John Clapham,* faying [*To
witnefs Heaven, and Hell, and Refurrection within is*
the *Myftery of iniquity.*] G. *Fox* Anfwers, [*which
fhews thou never knew Heaven in thy felf nor hell
there, nor Chrift the Refurrection and the Life, which
they are bleffed that are made partakers of the firft
Refurrection, on them the fecond Death fhall have no
power; and the Scriptures do witnefs Heaven within,
and if Chrift that was offered up, the Refurrection and
the life be not within thee thou art a Reprobate*]

John
Clapham

I Reply, If G. *Fox* would fpeak of Heaven, and Angels, and Hell, and Devils, and of the Refurrection and Life to come, by way of allufion and fimilitude, or by way of firft Fruits or Taft of them, he might profitably do it, but to fpeak of them in oppofition to a rifing again, an Heaven, an Hell, &c. to come, what is it ?

I fay, what is it but to proclaim their Revolt from, and their Rebellion againft all the Chriftian Faith and Religion, and their wonderful hardening againft whatever is yet to come, either here or in the eternal State approaching ?

Pag. 214. He brings in fome (namelefs, faying, [*To fay Heaven and Glory is in man, which was be-*
fore

fore man was, they are fottifh and blinde.] He Anf-
wers, |*There's none have a Glory and a Heaven but
within them, which was before man had a Being.*]

Unto this I adde, *Thomas Pollard* faying, for a ^{Tho Pol-}
perfection of Glory to be attained to on this fide ^{lard}
the Grave, I utterly deny.]

G. *Fox* Anfwereth [*Where Glory is (in the leaft de-* ^{The epi-}
gree) it is in perfection, and who have not Glory, and ^{curian Phi-}^{lofophers &}
doth uot attain to Glory on this fide the Grave they are ^{the Qua-}
in a fad condition : for the Saints rejoyce with joy un- ^{kers one}^{Sect.}
fpeakable and full of Glory, &c.]

I Reply, as the Swinifh Epicures and *Dives*'s of
this World, what ever they formally and loofely
profefs) have no folid hope of peace and joy to
come after this life, and therefore (like Biuit
Beafts) practically confefs it faying, (in their hearts
and Life) [154] let us eat and drink for to morrow we fhall dye: fo do this cynical and doggid
kind of Philofophers (the Quakers) profefs plainly
(though fome would cover it) no hopes of a rifing of
the Body but what they have here, no hopes of a
Heaven but what they have here, no hell but what
they (in their minds) have paft through : no Judgement but what (as Saints) they are now executing.

I know that fome of the *Quakers* will not believe that G. *Fox* and others of them deny the
Refurrection, &c. but (if they will not willingly
fifh[1]) let them read and confider thefe my *Quotations* from G. *Fox, Ed. Burrowes* and *John Stubs*
their Book in Folio, and let them alfo know that
whatever they profefs againft this that I have faid,
that

[1] Change to "err." *R. W. Ms. Ann.*

that is but horrible Hypocrifie and Deceit, for they would not in all our Difputations depart one hair from thofe horrible and monftrous *Blafphemies, and bruitifh Reafonings in* G. *Fox and* Edward *Burrowes.*

The 9th Pofition proved

We came to the ninth Propofal, the fecond in order to be debated at *Providence,* viz [*all that the Quakers Religion requires externally and internally to make* Converts *or* Profelytes, *amounts to no more then what a Reprobate may eafily attain to and perform.*]

I did not (the Father of Spirits is my holy witnefs) fling this in as a Firebrand of *Reprobation* againft either Teachers or Followers called *Quakers* : it is true they do fo againft all that ever were not or are not or fhall not be in their Opinion, but my hope is, that many amongft thefe mifled and wandring Souls may come to *Abrahams Bofome,* &c. yet this I affert, that thoufands and ten thoufands may be of their Religion, and may have gotten all that their Religion requires or performs, yea, all that their *Principles* call for outwardly or inwardly, and yet not be accepted but rejected from the holy and gracious prefence of God.

I told them that I had this notion from a man famous in his day (Mr. *W. Perkins*) who having been a deboift young man in *Cambridge* after the call of God to him he proved famous in *Preaching* and Writing, and (with a lame Club hand) he wrote admirably againft the Papifts, and maintained that all *Popery* preacht to the making of Converts or Profelytes amounted to no more then what *Reprobates* may eafily attain unto.

Mr. Perkins faying of the Papifts and mine of the Quakers.

I fay the fame of common Proteftants, and of the
Quakers,

Quakers, they may have a great meafure of forrow for fin: great refolu- [155] tions, great Reformations, great Rejoycings, great and wonderful performances endure great perfecutions, endure burning of the Body in the Flames, and yet be far from the true Proteftant Religion either in the true Doctrine and Principles, or in the true life and practice of it.

For the Foundation both of the *Papifts* and *Quakers Faith* is laid upon the Sand of *Rotten Nature* which they (both) only adorn and trim as the dead *Carcaffes* and *Coffins* with Rofes and Lillies and other *Flowers and Garlands*, their own penances fatisfactions, Alms, *Prayers*, Faftings, Suffrings, which are but Womens filthy Clouts, and Dung of Men and Beafts put into the ballance of Gods infinite Juftice, inftead of the infinite Righteoufnefs and Satisfaction of the Son of God : poor Souls, they know not that the whole Creation (vifible and invifible, feen and unfeen, known and unknown, cannot reach Gods moft holy and inconceivable juftice, for the leaft evil word or thought. Neither of thefe (nor millions of *Proteftants*, much lefs millions of millions in one evil word or thought, then in all the forrows and calamities felt in this life, or juftly feared in the life a coming. *Neither Papifts nor Quak skil bow to pay Gods juftice*

With the *Quakers* 'tis known, that if a notorious Drunkard,&c be convinced, and come to hearken to a Spirit within him, to fay, *Thou and Thee*, and think himfelf equal and above all his former Superiours, &c. he is Juftified, he is Sanctified, and fo *The Character of a Quaker*

Holy

Holy that he cannot fin in Thoughts,[1] Words, and from this high Mount looks down on all others (efpecially if oppofite) as *Pharifees, Publicans, Cains,* &c. Thus they pretend *Repentance, Faith,* and a change of heart becaufe they have changed their talk, their Garments, &c. But,

1. I told them that true Repentance lay in a difcovery of fin as fin, as greater than the greateft filthinefs in the world: no poverty, no fhame, no lofs like unto it, &c.

What true turning to God is. 2, In an utter inability to contribute one mite, either from felf, , or from the whole Creation toward fatisfaction to infinite Majefty and Juftice for the leaft evil thought or imagination.

3. That as bleffed *John Bradford* faid to God : *Lord thou art Heaven, I am Hell,* viz. that in the beft natural Soul in the World, there is nothing but a *Kennil,* an *Hogftie,* a *den of Atheifme, Murther, Theft, Fornication, Adultery, and all kinde of Wickednefs.*

156] 4. That I have not fo much in me as to defire *Deliverance,* nor to be fenfible of any need of it.

5. That it is only mercy and rich free Grace *Jacobs Ladder of true Chrif-tianity.* that worketh in me or any Soul a Sence of my Condition a Sence of Juftice a Sence of Mercy.

6. That it is Mercy only worketh a willingnefs, a new defire, new Affections towards my Maker, towards my Ranfomer, who paid his *Bloud,* his *Heart-Bloud,* the *Bloud of God* to ranfome and redeem me.

7. That in this work, Mercy not only worketh

a

[1] Interline "or." *R. W. Ms. Ann.*

a Sence, a thirſt after *Pardon* and Peace with my
Maker, but alſo after a *Conformity* and *Likeneſs* unto
God.

8. Becauſe I cannot reach this, the Mercy and
Pitty of God worketh in my Soul a longing after
God, and after the turning of the whole Soul unto
God, and after thoſe ſeven Evidences of true Re-
pentance, 2.*Cor.*7.

9. This is in true Chriſtian *Repentance* and turning of the whole Soul unto God, *viz.* to receive
every *thought*, every *motion*, every *deſire* upon the
account of Mercy and Pitty, as ever poor Dog received *Crum* or *Bone* under the Table.

Much of this I ſpake publickly, as alſo that no
Papiſt nor *Quaker* by their grounds could get up
this *Jacobs Ladder,* much leſs upon thoſe higher
grounds and ſteps of caſting off *Self,* of doing all
purely for God, and in Gods eye: of meekneſs and
Mercy to other poor drowning Soules, of pure Love
to God for *Himſelf* for his *Holineſs, Mercy, Goodneſs,* The Qua-
yea for his *Juſtice* : of quiet and patient and thank- *kers ond
moſt mens*
full reſting in his holy Pleaſure, whatever he take *Shipwrack*
from us or bring upon us.

I ſaid and ſay, that neither the teachings of the
Papiſts or *Quakers* will help them to get up one
Step of this heavenly *Ladder*; for by the utmoſt
ſtrength and activity of *Nature* no man can advance and climbe higher then to love *God* and *Chriſt*
and *Heaven* for it *Self,* and *Self-ends,* which is no
more but *Flattering* of God, baſe and dog-like
Fawning and *Hypocriſie.*

I cannot call to mind ought that was oppoſed by
my

my *Antagonists* against these Considerations : but *John Stubs* said, Dost thou count our *Religion* an easie *Religion*, for my part said he, we have not found it so easie to forsake all the glory and pleasure of this world, to forsake wife and children *&c.* to goe about the work of the Lord in strange Countreys, *&c.*

157] And *W. E.* said thou sayest our Religion is an easie Religion : For my part said he I have not
found it so, I have not found it so easie to forsake all the glory and honour and pleasures of this World, and to expose our selves to hardships, to forsake our Wives and Children, Friends and Relations, and to goe about in strange Countreys *&c.* And *W. E.* further said in that thou saist our Religion is an easie Religion, it is a plain evidence that thou that talkest so much of Religion, and of the Religion of the *Quakers* thou yet never knewest what Religion is, with more to this effect : and they (according to their wild spirit) insisted vehemently on the wronge which I did them, and the People called *Quakers* : and that as for themselves they were but a few, but the people called *Quakers* were a great *Body* : they were many thousands all over *England*, they were many thousands in *London*, as also in *Barbadoes*, and *New-England* and *Virginia*, and other places.

I replyed, that my time would not give me leave as they knew, to say much to their greatness and
number, yet I said their Religion like the *Papists*, was easie and agreeable with *Nature*, they had the wind and tyde of *natural corruption* to joyn with their *spirit*, which knew this well enough.　　　　1. It

1. It was eafie to perfwade the *Quakers* to change
one fowle *Spirit* and *Devil* for an other, a Devil *One Devil changed for another.*
more grofs and ugly, for a Devil more refined
painted and guilded: their pride in *Cloathes* and *yea fome-*
fantaftical Ffhions, to pride in *felf conceit* and *fan-* *times one for feven*
taftical Opinions, their Drunkennefs and Gluttony,
with Wine and Flefh to Intoxications, with high
and proud Vapours: How many millions travel on
the broad way to Deftruction, and yet prate of a
ftrict and narrow *Path*? What wonderfull hard-
fhips doe both *Turks* and *Papifts* endure in their
religious *Pennances*? How doe they *macerate* and
whip themfelves, even till the bloud of their tender
Women hath ftreamed down upon the ground from
them? Yea how zealoufly (in the caufe of their
Religion) have the very *Jewes* themfelves caft away
their Lives, as *Spain* and *Portugal* can witnefs.

Befides, I told them it was a poor lame thing to
talk of *numbers* when the Council of the only
Wife was fo clearly revealed concerning his *Little
Flock,* oppofed to the vaft and monftrous *Herds* both
of civiliz'd and wild *Nations.*

158] I put them in mind of the innumerable
multitudes that followed after that ftupendous *The Qua-*
Cheater Mahomet, even *thirteen* parts of the world, *kers fimple boaft of*
divided into *thirty,* as very knowing *Cofmographers* *numbers*
or *Defcribers* of the World have computed. And
if fo be that the *Pope,* and Church of *Rome* be the
eight *Head,* the great *Whore* that fits upon many
Waters, Kingdomes and *Nations,* what a poor Slut is
the *Quakers Fancy* compar'd with the *Baals Priefts,*
the

the *Romiſh Proſelites*; the Beaſt whome the whole world wonders after?

3. Again it is to me and may be to all men, wonderfull that ſince the *Religion* of the *Quakers* is ſo eaſie *&c.* that ten thouſands more of people in old and new *England, Scotland, Ireland* and other parts, have not lifted themſelves under this new *Mahomet,* pretending ſo much from the *Dove* from Heaven as *Mahomet* did.

The carnal weapons   Tis true G. *Fox* and *Foxians*, pretend the two horns of the *Lamb,* and that their weapons are not *Jehues* nor *Baals Prieſts,* but that they have forſaken all *Carnal Weapons*: but this I ſhall ſhew to be an horrible Lye when I come to the laſt *Poſition.*

The *Devil* and the *Papiſts* and the *Quakers* know that the *Quakers* only want a *Sword* to ſubdue as many *Proſelites* as either *Mahomet* or the *Pope* hath done. The *Quakers* ſome prate ſubtilly, others childiſhly againſt *Carnal Weapons, Carnal Weapons &c.* but I ſhall ſhew (if God pleaſe) in my 14*th.* and laſt Poſition, what a *Devil* of *Pretence* this is.

At preſent the *Devil* knowes they want but a *Sword* (not *Hearts* nor *Hands* nor *Principles*) whereby to ſubdue as mauy *Proſelytes* as the *Pope* or *Mahomet* hath, and literally and materially *thraſh* the *Mountains* with *Flails* of iron, and make the *Nations* turn (in an eaſie *Hypocriſie* and *Diſſimulation*) *Diſſembling Quakers.* I wonder and adore the *Councels* of the *Eternal,* that any of theſe three ſhould be *Cheated* by this *ſpirit.*

Firſt, Any of thoſe truely fearing *God;* for their *Principles ſpirit and practices* being ſo notoriouſly
oppoſite

opposite to the meek and patient *Spirit* of true
Purity and *Holiness*, and evidencing them to be lead
by a dumb and dogged *Spirit*. 1. Their high and
shameless *Pride* and *Vapouring* is notoriously known,
of which in the next Position. 2. Their mouth
full of *Curfing* and *Railing* above any or all that
profess to march under the *Christian Name* and
159] *Colours*. 3. They spit not out their *Venome* so
fiercely against any as against the most conscientious *Preachers* and *Professor* of the *Protestant Faith*,
as appears all along in this railing of *Fox* in Folio
against them.

*The Qua-
kers Spirit
far from
purity and
Holiness.*

4. They easily fall in with openly profane and
ungodly *persons*, and with carnal and luke-warm
Laodiceans, who can swim with the tyde, sail with
every wind. If they can but say *Thee* and *Thou &c.*
5. It is wonderfull how their spirit (professing to
be *Protestants*) can so wickedly strike in with the
bloudy spirit of the *Papists*, against the Witnesses
and Martyrs of Jesus, compiled by that heavenly
J. Fox. in the Book of *Martyrs* which this bloudy
spirit (in *James Purnels* Watcher) upbraidingly
calls [*Your Record*] as if it were none of theirs, nor
the bloudy Papists, against whose bloudy practises
under their *Popes*, and the old proud *Romans*, the
Romane Gods and *Emperours*, that heavenly Book
shews how those heavenly *Martyrs* or *Witnesses* over
came by the *Bloud of the Lamb*, the word of their
Testimony, and not loving of their *Lives* unto the
Death.

*The Spight
og the
Quakers
Spirit*

6. That most Savage and worse then *Indian
Spirit* of their stripping their women stark naked,
and

and fo to enter into the *ftreets* and *Affemblyes* of men and youths, which *Piety Chriftianity* and common *Womanhood* and *Modefty* abhor to think of.

Secondly. As I wonder how any *godly Soul,* fo how any *Learned Soul,* who hath ftudied the primitive Copyes of the *Hebrew* and *Greek Scriptures,* can yoke with fuch rude *Bablings* and Repetitions of fimple ignorant *Praters.* Tis true the Lord Jefus and his Embaffadors were not all traind up as *Paul* was at the feet of *Gamaleel,* yet had they before the whole World the miraculous effufions of *Fiery Tongues,* and heavenly Oyl upon them, which thefe poor *Simpletons* ridiculoufly like *Puppets* in a Shew pretend too. Befide, the *Commons* among the firft Chriftians were as learned if not more then our primeft *Academians,* the *Hebrew* being their Mother Tongue, and the *Greek* and *Latine* familiar, by the *Greek* and *Romane Conquefts* over them, all which Helps the moft of the Leaders of the *Quakers* want, only pretending to underftand fupernatural and miraculoufly (in a trice and immediately) what is to be gotten by honeft and faithful Labour and induftry, the holy will and mind of God from the true Original Copies.

160] *Thirdly,* I do admire that any fober, modeft *Woman* (made fo by nature, and much more by Grace (fhould ever dare to come into their Affemblies: it is certain that the *Ranters* is a Sifter or Daughter of them: though they quarrel, and fight, and fcratch one the other: The *Ranters* more plainly (according to their *Principles* make the *Nakednefs* of Men and Women, a part of *worfhip* unto God,

The ignorance of the Quakers

The abominable Spirit of the Quakers nakednefs

God, unto which they fay they are reftored by *Chriſt Jeſus* the fecond *Adam*. This *Adamites Fowle ſpirit* is no *New-come ſpirit*, I have know nit almoſt fixty year, and what a motion was made and urged by ſome (whome I can name) for *P*lantations in warmer *Countreyes*, where they might practice that *Ordinance of God* viz, *Of Nakedneſs of men and women in Gods worſhip*.

Theſe our *Adamites* are led by a more Savage and Barbarous, and Monſtrous Spirit, the which under the vizird and mantle of Religion deceives them, and of being a ſign to others : And this very bruitiſh practiſe have kept ſome Women (too much inclin'd to them) from falling into their filthy puddle, and of returning ſome which were left by Gods Juſtice to go too far amongſt them ſure we are the holy ſpirit of God (all along) abhors the appearance of uncleanneſs, and commands the vailings of Women (eſpecially in Chriſtian Meetings) *Quakers driven on by the old Spirit of the Adamites*

I have been too long upon the eaſineſs of their Religion, and of the agreement of it with corrupt and rotten Nature which ſlides into it as eaſily as Brooks and Rivers ſlide and run down into the Ocean.

There be two other cauſes of falling into falſe Religions or ways of worſhipping God.

1. Hope of Gain, which was the *Sechemites* Bait : (the ſweet Muſick propounded by *Nebuchadnezzar*.) &c.

2. The fiery Furnace, &c.

Theſe moderate times have not driven the *Quakers* to bow down to their Spirit for fear of perſefecution,

The rising of the Quakers cution, and the fiery Furnace but Sathan knew well enough that the Corruption of Nature, and the hope of Gain and Glory would cheat to purpose (as all may fee it hath done.) Sathan knows that some have a moving and travelling Spirit, and cannot reft in a fedentary or quiet life.) Some are of a rifing, afpiring Spirit (though neither from Birth nor Breeding, nor abilities) and therefore cry down all Honour or refpect to be given to any (but themfelves) fome are falfe and [161] rotten in their *Profeffion*, and ready to fall and tumble when any *ftrange wind* of Temptation blowes upon them.

7. Some may be *Sincere* and upright to God in the *Root*, but *Weak*, and not fo rooted in the *Holy Scriptures*, as the Difciples themfelves, who wondered for a time what the *Rifing* from the dead *Diverfe Sorts fuf-* fhould mean, and had need of their *Lord* and *Maf-* *fered by* ters *Take heed and beware* of the *Leaven* of the *God to fall* *into the* Scribes, and *Pharifees*, and *Sadduces*, &c. Some *Quak* truly fear God, but have neglected the purity and *Ditch.* chaftity of *Gods holy Worfhip*, and have referved in a weak Confcience a liberty of playing the *Whore* againft a jealous *God* and *Husband*.

But generally they that are taken by the *Quakers Bait* are fuch as never loved *Chrift Jefus* in Sincerity as the Scripture fpeaketh, neither within nor without, and therefore fuckt in *Nicolds* and *Nailors*, *But efpeci-* and *Foxes* dreames of a *Chrift*, within them oppo- *ally* fite to *Chrift* without: of a *Chrift* a *Light* a *Spirit* *for Male* within, which had no *Humane Body*, or if he were *and Fe-* *male Pro-* humane, or a man they know not now what is be- *teftants.* come of him.

The

The *Lord Jesus* tels us that some will plead with him at the last day, that they have heard him *Preach*, that they have been at his *Table*, that they have prophesied themselves, *cast out Devils* in his Name, and in his Name done many *Wonderfull things:* should not this make every Soul that calls it self *Christian*, startle and look about them, especially when they hear Christ Jesus say, *depart from me I know you not ye workers of Iniquity.*

I told the Quakers that their *Theora John* pretended to write after the *Spirits* Dictate, a volume in *Hebrew, Greek, Latine, Arminiack*, &c. which he confessed he understood not: what if it should please Gods infinite Wisdom, to suffer the Quakers or others to speak and understand all *Languages*, to work great *Miracles*, yet if they come under the Note Christ gives them, of *Workers of Iniquity*, they fulfill the termes of my *Position*, and prove but *False* and *Reprobate*.

This is the true and infallible distinguishing *Character* between the true *Legitimate* and the *Bas-* *The great distinguishing Character of true and false Pretenders* tard and false *Christian*: The soul of the *True* is broken for Sin, as Sin, as opposite to God, as filthy in his eye: The soul of the *False is* broken for Sin as bringing temporal Loss or shame, or pain, and beside temporal, Eternal. The soul of the true, is broke off from Sin, from the least Sin, [16z from the appearances of sin from the occasions of Sin, from the thought of Sin as worse then all the Afflictions of this life, or the Torments of Hell to come. The soul of the False, hath secret Friendship and Correspondence with Iniquity (as *Church-Papists*

Papifts with *Popery* &c) in the fecret chambers and
Clofets of the heart, at which they willingly wink,
and to find it (when they are put to it, yea and feem
to doe it) they are willingly remifs and negligent.

Hence it was a famous Principle of the firft *New-
Englifh Reformers*, viz. to be Chriftianly carefull
that their Members gave *Chriftian Evidence*, (fo far
as godly eyes of Charity could reach) of the truth
of their Converfion and turning unto God, which
for ought I know is not changed by their Succeffors.

It is dolefully true that many feemingly *Elect*,
prove *Reprobate*, and many truly *Elect* fall into many
great *Sins* and *Sorrows*. How black and dolefull
then is their Condition (fuch as the *Papifts* the
Quakers and others) whofe *Religion Principles* and
Practices, arife no higher then what a *Reprobate*
may attain unto.

*The 3d
Pofition
debated at
Provi-
dence.*
We came to the tenth *Pofition*, (the third in order to be difcuffed at *Providence*) which they read
out of their paper, viz. *That the Popes of* Rome *do
not fwel with; and exercife a greater* pride *then the*
Quakers *have expreft; and would afpire unto, although
many truly humble Souls may be captivated amongft
them.*

*Two great
Competi-
tors the
Popes and
Foxians.*
I have here two mighty *Fields* to expatiate and
walk in, viz. The pride of *Chrift Jefus* his pretended *triple-crowned Vicar*, and the pride of the
new *Papifts* pretending to be *Chrift himfelf*: of
which the holy *Spirit* fpeaketh, *There is a Generation, oh how lofty are their eyes and their eye lids are
lifted up?* In publick Difcourfe I knew I was but to
take

take a ſhort turn of a quarter of an hour, I am now at more liberty of inſerting what I intended, but was forced to abbridge wlth all poſſible brevity at that time.

I told them there was a *pride* in *outward* and external things, in P*arentage*, in *Perſon*, in *Beauty*, *Strength*, *Wit*, *Aparrel*, *Houſes*, *Money*, *Shipping*, *Land*, *Cattle*, *Offices*, *Relations*, *&c.* this I now paſt by : All theſe (like *Diogenes* on *Platoes* carpets) the *Quakers* ſay they tread on *&c.*

There was 2. the devils *pride*, and the devils *Condemnation*, a pride in Spiritual *Knowledg*, ſpiritual *Gifts*, ſpiritual *Priviledges* and *Excellencies* : This was the Devils *Break-neck*, and will be [163] of the *Popes* and *Quakers*, and of all tha*t* aſpire to the *Eternal power* and *Godhead*; for God or they muſt fall to all eternity. *Spiritual pride the devils pride*

I named then diverſe *Parallels* between the *Popes* and *Quakers*, I will now name all I can remember I named, and will name ſome more at this preſent,

Firſt, The *Popes* have exalted themſelves above all that is called *God*, above all *Civill powers*, *Kings* and *Princes*, riding upon their backs, diſpoſing of their Crowns, making them lead their horſes, hold their ſtirrups, kiſs their toes, yea lye down under their feet bodyes and ſouls, and ſubmit their neck to this abominable foot of pride, as the *Scripture* calls it. *The Popes & Quakers pride compared*

As to the *Quakers* they know it is not yet time to put on the *Lions* and the *Eagles*, but the *Sheeps* and the *Foxes* Skin : but no man need queſtion that if God ſhould pleaſe to let looſe the *Quakers* ſpirit

to

The Qua-
kers boaſt
of their
number.

to the full length of its tedder, as he hath done that of the *Popes*, the ſpirit of the *Quakers* would ſcorn to come behind the *pope*: For who ſees not how at the firſt, *fledging* and creeping out of the *Shell* how they boaſt and vapour of their numbers? We (ſaid W. E. to me in publick at *Newport*) are a great *People*, many thouſands in *England*, many thouſands in *London*, beſides *Virginia, Barbados, N-England* and other places : what would they ſay and doe if they had the *popes Univerſality*, and could boaſt of the many *Waters, Peoples, Nations, Tongues* and *Multitudes* upon which the *Whore* ſitteth?

Beſide, W. E. (a man fit to make a *Bonefacius* or a *Hildebrand*) *John Stubs* alſo though of a more prudent and moderate ſpirit) was up with the ſame boaſting of their *Numbers,* and all of them are ready to cry up their *Diana* whome all *Aſia* and the *world worſhippeth.* But,

The audn-
cious & im-
pious faces
of the
Foxians

2. In their firſt creeping (like Hercules out of the Cradle, how doth this Spirit dare the Spirits of Kings, and Keyſars, and Popes themſelves (under the pretence of Tranſlations and acceptations of words) to *Thou* and *Thee* to the faces of mighty *Monarchs*? with what *Braſen Faces* have they ad- dreſt the *Royal preſence* of our *Gracious Dread Sove- raign,* without either bowing the knee, or baring the Head (ſigns of Engliſh reverence and civility) and this out of an horrible and lying pretence, that Chriſts amity (even in Civil things) reſpecteth no mans perſon, that they may trample as Gods on all man-kinde, &c.

3. I

164]   3. I can fay what mine eyes and ears have *Pope Ed-* feen and heard, *viz.* our Honoured and Aged Mr. *mond com-manding* *Nicholas Eaſton, Governour* of this Colony under his *& filenc-* *Majeſty,* offering to fpeak once and twice in our late *ing the Governour* Conteſts at *Newport* (and no queſtion would have fpoke for the *Quakers* againſt me, yet) *Pope Ed-mundſon* put forth his hand imperiouſly toward the Governour, faying, *Whiſt, Whiſt,* which whiſting and filencing Language if they ufe to their Friends in Authority, what will they fay or Thunder to their Enemies if ever they get up into the *Papal Chair* ?

   2. The *Pope* fits in the *Temple of God,* as over *A ſecond* the Churches and Confciences of the Chriſtian *Paralel be-* Name and Worſhip, giving *Canons* and *Decretals* to *tween the Pope &* be obferved by all Chriſtian *People* on peril of lofs *Quakers* of *Earth and Heaven,* &c.

   And do not their[1] new *Popes* (not regarding as the *Apoſtles* and *Bereans* the Holy Scripture) lay on the common *Quakers* Confciences and Congrega- tions their *Decrees* ? tis true G. *Fox* in his Book in Folio gives the immediate Spirit of Infallibility to all his Saints : yet muſt they (in a ridiculous con- tradiction) fit ſtill poſſeſt with a *Dumb Devil,* ex- cept fome He or She *Apoſtle* come amongſt them, who fend word of their coming to call the Coun- try in many dayes before, and feem to have a Com- mand of their *Diabolical Spirit* more then other *Quakers* have, though they (as I faid before) in a ridiculous Contradiction) afcribe it unto all their *Saints* and *Quakers.*

Thus

"thefe"   *R. W. Ms. Ann.*

Thus did *Humphrey Norton* (a Pope) in his day in
The Pope and Qua- kers usurp over the Souls of all men thefe parts) overtopping and rating *W. Brand* at *Newport*, he confirmed the *Decree* for the *weekly Meetings* not only on the firft dayes, but on the week dayes at *Newport* and *Providence*: he ordered their fitting and departing Dumb, unlefs a He or She Apoftle came amongft them, he left in writing (which I can produce) an overthrow of all civil Order and Government except in the hands of his Saints, entituling his *P*aper thus, the Saints Law and the Sinners Law as G. *Fox*. his decree under the title of the Law.

Hump b Norton & G Fox compared. G. *Fox* fucceeds (as Pope) *Humph. Norton* in thefe parts, and being angry with his Predeceffour (as fome *P*opes have been) he lets loofe the *Dumb Devil* and gives Liberty to all to fpeak as the Spirit gives them utterance: this fhews what a lying Spirit of Unity they boaft of (fuch an one as was in *Nailors* bufinefs) though they moft proudly deny Unity to all but to themfelves, as [165] the *Papifts* do: G. *Fox*. alfo gave forth his Decree of loofing them from that bruitifh and doggid Behaviour which *W. Brand* and *Humphrey Norton* left them in, and by *Word* and *Example* commanded them to be more fociable and manlike, fo that many of *G P. a fubtler Fox then. Hum. Norton.* them will fpeak in Salutations, and fhew fome reverence by bowing the Heads, or uncovering it, as *Fox* himfelf did after his Sermon at *Providence*, uncovering his Head and bowing to the *P*eople, and paffing through the midft of them (his Hat in his hand) with much refpect and civility. And he blames thofe (as I hear) which violently and madly
                                        have

have flung themfelves upon unneceffary temptations
and dangers : whence follows (in the eyes of the
whole World) that either the latter or the former
Spirit was not Gods, and perfeƈt, and the Spirit of
Unity of which they childifhly fo crake and vapour, as the chiefeſt Flower in their Crown of
Pride.

3. The *Pope* lifts up himfelf as God over the *A third*
Holy Scriptures : He is the fole Judge and Inter- *parallel*
preter of them, and the fole decider of all contro- *the Pope*
verfies in Religion about the expounding of them : *& Quak.*
yea, he hath power to difpence with *Peter* and *Paul,*
&c. yea, what Chriſt and God can do that gave
forth Scripture, that can the *Pope* their *Lieutenant*
do : hence all this *Difpenfations* of Oaths, of Marriages, &c.

Do not the *Quakers alfo tread* this Holy Scripture,
this ineſtimable Jewel of Gods Writing and Book
under their proud feet, as formerly I noted upon *Both Pa-*
the fourth Pofition of their not owning the Holy *piſts &*
Scripture ?   Do they not (upon the point) fay that *their Pride*
they made, they wrote and gave out the Holy *above the*
Scripture ? and though in our late Conference they *Scriptures*
faid they would be tryed by the Scriptures, yet (as
the *Papiſts*) they admit no Interpreter but themfelves, for the Spirit within them they fay gave forth
the Scripture, and is above the Scripture, and both
they and the *Papiſts* have faid that there would be
no loffe if they were gone out of the World, for
the *Papiſts* fay their Traditions, and their infallible
Spirit would fupply the lofs : and the *Quakers* fay
the Scriptures is within them (in effeƈt) they fay
that

that all that they do and fay is Scripture : fo far
are both *Papiſts & Quakers* from a Chriſtian and
Candid Profeſſion of being tried by the Holy Scripture : that they moſt Horribly and moſt Hypocritically trample it under their proud feet.

166] 4. Theſe *Romaniſts* or *Proud ones* (as the *Hebrew* fignifies) both *Papiſts* & *Quakers* moſt infultingly lift up themſelves againſt the Servants and
Children of God all the world over that bow not
down to their Images : be a Soul never ſo humble
and penitent, never ſo holy and mortified, believe
the Scriptures, &c and give his life for the truth of
of them, yet he is damned if he believes not the
Pope to be the head of the Church : and ſay not
the *Quakers* the ſame of all that believe not in their
pretended Lights : your Repentance is nothing,
your Holineſs nothing, your Zeal, Praying, Preaching, Faſting, Suffrings nothing : and they think
they have reaſon to ſay ſo, becauſe you believe not in
the true Chriſt, and therefore you are in *Cains* Nature, in the *Satanical Deluſion*, Reprobates, &c. ſo
that all the bleſſed Souls under the Alter calling
for vengeance againſt the ſhedders of their blood
the *Roman Emperour*, or ſince the *Roman Popes*, they
are all branded with a black cole of damned Souls
and Reprobates by G. *Fox*, becauſe they profeſſed,
preacht and died for a Chriſt without them though
that Chriſt without them dwelt in their hearts
(*Epheſ.* 3.) by believing *and for his ſake they loved
not their lives to the Death.*

I told them that the *Pope* and they were one in
the great point of the Infallibility : they both pretended

The Pope aad Quakers horrible revilers Slanderours & curſers of the Righteous

The 5. parallel

tended the Spirit of God as did the *Apoſtles*, &c.
but I have proved their pretence is as true as that
of *Apollo's Worſhippers*, by whoſe *Prieſts* the Devil
gave Oracles (*Extripode*) from their threefold ſtool, *The infal-*
and that ſo ſubtilly and cunningly that whatever *libility of*
Oracle or *Voice* it was, and whatever the event were *the Popes*
yet the Devil would ſave his own: *Apollo* ſhould *and Qua-*
be the true God of Wiſdome, and *Apollo's* Prieſts *kers Oracles*
true *Prophets*.

At laſt when Chriſt came *Apollo* being conſulted
and failing to give anſwer, the Devil was forced to
anſwer that there was an *Hebrew Childe* borne that
ſtopt his mouth: I am ſure this *Hebrew Childe* (the
true Lord Jeſus Chriſt) hath often alſo ſtopt the
mouthes (in one ſenſe) of *Pope & Quakers*, for their
Prediⱸions have not come to paſs, (though ſome
which the Devil could gueſs at) have: and he will
ſhortly ſtop their mouths forever.

It was truely ſaid of (that long eighteen years *The Holy*
hatching) Deviliſh Junto of *Trent*, that the Holy *Spirit in a*
Ghoſt, (that is the P*opes* Holy Ghoſt) came every *Cloak-bag*
week from the *Pope* at *Rome*, &c. to his *Legates* at *Councel*
Trent, in a Cloak-bag: and do not G. *Fox* his *at Trent*
Books [167] and all their writings declare for their
corrivality and competition with the *Pope* for this *The Pope*
their pretended Holy Ghoſt: do they not upbraid *and Quak*
all other Miniſters and *People* for being out of the *the two*
infallible Spirit: Do they not ſay their Miniſters *great pre-*
and their Commiſſions are inviſible becauſe imme- *tenders and*
diate and infallible? do they not aſſigne this to be *corrivals*
the cauſe of all the Seⱸs and Diviſions among the *tended*
Proteſtants, becauſe they have not the infallible Spi- *Holy*
rit as the *Quakers* have?   Here *Ghoſt*

Here (as I remember) *John Stubs* ſtood up and alleadged that place in 1 *John* 4. Hereby we know that we dwell in him, becauſe he hath given us of his Spirit.

And again, you have the unction and know all things. And *W. Edmondſon* boaſtingly, and proudly ſaid, that they had the ſame immediate and infallible Spirit which the Apoſtles had, and that *John & Peter* were but their elder Brethren.

The Quak pretending to be Apoſtles Unto which I anſwer, *Peter* I know, and *John* I know, but who are you? For 1. They were *Eye-Witneſſes* of the Lord Jeſus his *Life* and *Death* and *Reſurrection*. 2. They were immediately endowed with *fiery Tongues*, and *fiery hands* to preach in all *Languages*, and to pen from Gods mouth his holy word and Pleaſure and to work real Miracles, not metaphorical ones only (as G. *Fox* ſaid at *Providence* the *Quakers* did, that is open the eyes of the *Blind* by *Converſion* &c.) I added that it might pleaſe the infinite Wiſdom of God to ſend higher Pretenders to *Apoſtleſhip* then the *Quakers*, who ſhould ſpeak all *Tongues* [1] doe *Miracles*: But as Gods Servants had a *Rule Iſa.* 8. the written Law and Teſtimony, and were not to believe their *Dreames* though they came to paſs, *Deut.* 13. So have Gods Servants now, *viz.* The *Doctrine of Chriſt Jeſus* both concerning *Faith* and *Order*, and to ſtrive earneſtly for the Faith once delivered.

F F. his Counterfeit mirrcles

A 6. Parallel between the Pope & the Quak. The *Pope* like *Baalam* ſayes, he is the *Mouth* of God: whome he bleſſeth, they are bleſſed, and whom he curſeth &c. therefore ſendeth he his

Curſes

---

[1] Interline " and." *R. W. Ms. Ann.*

Curſes like *Thunderbolts,* yea among *Kings & King-domes* in other Nations, and our own as *K. Henery 8th. K. Edward. 6th. Queen Elizabeth* experimented *&c.* and is there any *People* bearing the name *Chriſtian,* ſo like the pope their Father as theſe, whoſe *Mouth* (ſaith *David*) is full of *Curſing* and *Bitterneſs,* like Floods out of the *Dragons Mouth,* and *fire-brands arrowes* and *Death* crying out againſt the moſt *Humble* and *Con-* [168] *ſcientious* Cain, Saul, *Judas, Viper, Serpent, Reprobate Dragon, Devil* (yea one of their *Shee-Apoſ-tles, Devil, Devil, Devil,* all at once to one that op-poſed her amongſt us) and ſuch foul ſtinking expreſ-ſions (like the *Quakers* in *London*) about the Dung of Mankinde, that modeſty eſpecially the baſhfulneſs and modeſtyof Women would have been far from.

A ſeventh is that great point of horrible Pride *47 paral-* in both *Pope & Quakers,* exalting the Dung and *lel between* Dirt of their own Qualifications, Excellencies, *the Pope* Graces, Labours, Faſtings, Satisfactions, Believings, *and* Sufferings as a price and ſatisfaction to Gods Juſtice, *Quakers* as a *Merit* or *Deſert* for the pardon of their ſin, for though they both Sophiſtically and Hypocritically mention the *Blood of Chriſt;* yet they count the buſineſs of this *Chriſt* (as the Pope ſaid) but a *Fable,* and indeed and truth through the *Pride* of their high ſpirits they think God is beholding to them: I have ſpoken to this already, and of that devilish *8 Parallel* Pride of their being without ſin: yet in this Doc- *as to the* trine of *perfection* the Quakers exceed the Doctrine *ſinleſs con-* of the Papiſts: for generally the *popes* attribute this *dition of* purity but to ſome of their rare Saints. And 2. *the Qua-* Generally the Popes themſelves confeſs themſelves *kers*

34   to

to be finners.   3. They give refpect and civill honour to all eftates, although in *Spirituals* and *Civills*
too they overtop them : But the high and lofty
Devill of the *Quakers* *pride* tranfcends all this :   G.
Fox makes all his *Saints born of God*, that (literally
expounded) they cannot commit fin ; yea, G. *Fox*
tells us that the Saints (that is his *Foxians*) are as
holy and perfect as God, not only like to God in
quality, but in equality alfo.   They have the ful-

G F his nefs of the Godhead in them bodily.   That the
proud Blaf- myftery of godlinefs is God manifeft in their flefh!
phemy as to Hence he faith there is no diftinction between God
God and Chrift, and the Spirit and themfelves.   Hence
himfelf it follows, that they are the Father, Son and Holy
Spirit (which by Devilifh Chymiftry) they can
prove *:* and that they are the *Three that bare Rec-*
ord in Heaven, and the *Three that bare Record in*
Earth : The Scripture is within them : They made
it, and all that they fay and do is Scripture, what
they fay God faith, what they advife God advifeth,
what they do God doth, &c.

 It is true, this is not believed (no not by fome
Novices among them but this and more, many of
their lying *Foul mouths & Books* exprefs, which may
make a Soul that is truly humble to quake and ⌈169

H B the rend his heart at fuch *Blafphemy*, the firft Perfectift
firft Per- in thefe parts was one *H. B.* who came from *Bof-*
f fift in *ton* to *Providence*, who affirmed that what he fpake
thefe parts, God fpake, what counfel he gave God gave, &c.   It
and moft pleafed God to leave him (though a fubtle man) to
notorious
for Imper- ridiculous Folly amognft us, and at *Barbadoes* and
fections. *London* fince, to worfe practices : as commonly God
                                                    punifheth

punifheth fuch height of *Pride* even in this prefent
life before Death feize upon them.

I remember while we were declaring their proud
Difrefpect to all men, *John Stubs* faid, That it was
their practice to pay tribute to *Cæfar*, and to give
Honour to whome Honour belonged. And I anfwered to this effect, that it was againft their *Principles* and practices to fhew refpect to any mans
Perfon in the World. As for tribute they paid none
but what neceffity and policy forced them to, and
notorioufly backward here: But they knew that I
and G. *Fox* knew, and all the world might know
out of *Fox* his *Writings*, that the *Quakers* are the
Higher powers, the *Dignityes*, the *Moft High God*,
and ought to have all Honour and Tribute paid to
them by all the whole Creation. Tis true there
feems to be a Change and fome relenting and *Giv-*
ing of the *Weather* in G. *Fox* his own practice of
Courtefie, and others from him: but while they
own what G. *Fox* hath written, and that he writ it
with a perfect fpirit: I fay untill they do make
fome *Recantation* or *Retractation*: or fhew the Reafons why they doe not, *H. Norton* who keeps more
plainly to his *Principles* is to windward of them,
and the *Foxians* do but ftrip themfelves naked to
be more derided and fcorned as the more notorious
Juglers and *Diffemblers*.

*The differ-
ence
amongft
the Qua-
kers as to
thefe
things.*

We came eafily (with their Good-will) to the
4th. *Pofition* of the latter feven, which they read out
of the *Paper* (as willing to be out of ther pain) viz,
*The Religion of the Quakers is more obftructive and
Deftructive to the Converfion and Salvation of Soules*

*The 4th of
the feven
laft Pofi-
tions.*

                                                                    of

of People than most of Religions that are at this day
extant in the World.

I said for the proof of this it was requisite to take
a short view of *Religions* and *Worships* in the world.
We knew that the Sons of Men were justly divided
all the world over into two Sorts,

The In-
dians
Religion.

First, The wild and *Pagan*, whome God hath
permitted to run about the world as wild Beasts all
this great fourth Part of the World, and in some
of the other three.

170] They acknowledge a great supream God
and Deity, Maker of all things, yet they acknowledge (as other famous *Civilized Nations* formerly
have done) that there be many other *Petty-Gods*
and Deityes in Heaven and Earth, yea within their
own Bodies, yea whatever is extraordinary, excellent or strange to them, they are presently apt to
ascribe a Deity unto it, though it be but *Beast, Fowle*

A Deity or
higher
Power ac-
knowledged
by Indians.

&c. and say it is a *God*. It is commonly known
that as their garments hang loose about their
Bodyes, so hangs their *Religion* about their Souls:
So that (to my knowledge) they are so far from
hindring any to come to God, that when they have
seen the grave and solemn *Worship* of the *English,*
they have often said of themselves and their own,
that they are all one *Dogs* in comparison of the
English.

The second sort of men are the *Civill* brought to
Cloaths, to *Lawes &c.* from *Barbarisme*: these also
the infinite Wisdome of God have pleased to leave
to variety of wayes of *Worshipping* the *Heavenly*
Majesty,

Amongst

Amongft others we find four moft known and eminent,

Firft, The *Jewifh Worfhip* famous from Gods own appointment by *Mofes &c.* 2. The *Turkifh*, famous for fpreading from *Mahomet* to moft of thirteen parts of thirty in the World. *The four chief Re-ligions of the World.*

3. The *Popifh*, famous for fpreading over *Europe* and other weftern parts of the world. 4. The *Proteftant* famous for fo wonderfull a *Revolt* and Seperation from the Popifh. All thefe four profefs one God and fupream *Deity* : but they differ in two things, 1. In the *Prophet* or Meanes by whome God fpeaks to man; the *Iews* cry up *Mofes*, the *Turks Mahomet*, the *Papifts* the *Pope*, the *Proteftants Chrift Jefus* in the Scriptures,

The fecond great difference is in the *Form* of Worfhip, which every one of thefe four great Partyes practice in various and different wayes as they are perfwaded.

Our felves the *Proteftants* are divided into two Partyes,

The firft is entituled *Epifcopal* and *Prefbyterian* in Parochyal or Parifhional Affemblyes.

The fecond is *Seperate* from thofe National and Parochyal Affemblyes, fome more fome lefs, and thofe are now known to be Firft, the People called *Independants.* 2. The people called *Baptifts.*

We that pretend the Chriftian Name againft the *Jewes* and the [171] *Mahumetans*, we mainly differ; 1. In matter of *Doctrine*, as *Repentance, Faith,* &c. 2. Of *Worfhip, Difcipline* &c. And we generally agree, that as the *Mahumetan* and *Jewifh* *The religious Diff r-ences among the Proteftants*

Worfhip

Worſhip have little in them to tempt a Soul to
turn into them compar'd with the *Chriſtian*, ſo thoſe
Chriſtians that differ each from other in point of
Doctrine and Worſhip both, as the *Papiſts* and the
Quakers doe to be farther from the truth of the
Profeſſion of *Chriſt Jeſus*, and more obſtructive
and deſtructive to the Souls of men then the other
partyes; yea and the *Papiſts* not ſo much as the
Quakers, who wildly profeſs all *Ordinances* and
Miniſters to be inviſible, and yet are hypocritically
and ridiculouſly found to be as viſible and open as
any.

    If the true *Foundations* of *Repentance* and *Faith*
Fundamen- be caſt down it is in vain to talk of ſaving of *Soules,*
tal Differ- it is in vain to talk of Worſhipping of God. The
ences.
Quakers(for all their craking of *Quaking* and *Trembling*) their way is more eaſie of *Worſhipping God,*
and of bringing perſons to their *worſhip of God,*
then the way of *Jewes* or *Turks* or *Papiſts,* who to
my knowledge take more paines in *Religion* then
do the common Proteſtants: I confeſs they all do
but paint and guild over natures old and rotten
Poſts, only the real Proteſtants have and profeſs the
greateſt care of any in the world for true *Faith*
and *Repentance.*

    The *Quakers* came not neer that care of *N-Eng-
land*(I am ſure at firſt) for the perſonal true *Repentance* and *Holineſs* of their *Church s* and *Congregations*: For it is notoriouſly known, that if perſons notoriouſly *Deboiſt,* come but to acknowledge
The Qua- a *God and Chriſt within them,* that is in *Engliſh,* that
kers eaſie themſelves are *God* and *Chriſt,* and can practice *Thou*
                                     and

and *Thee*, and *Cheek by Joll* with all their Betters, *Converſion and Churches,*
and can rail at and curſe all that oppoſe them, and
can come and bow down to a dumb Image and *not compa-rable to the way of* N-Eng-land.
Worſhip without any great buſineſs of *Contrition* and
Brokenneſs and *Godly Sorrow*, they are enrold and
canonized for *Saints* and *Gods* &c. they are free
from Sin, born of God and cannot ſin, they now
ſit upon the twelve thrones and judge the unbelieving *Jews* and *Gentiles* in their *heavenly places*.

The wound lyes here (as it is with *Papiſts*, *Arminians*, and indeed with all mankind) in the ſooth-
ing up and flattering of *rotten Nature*, from whence
(from within the *Lord Jeſus* tells us) proceed all
the rotten and helliſh *Speeches* and *Actions*.

172]   I told them it was in this caſe as it was with
Kings and *Princes*, there were two great Enemyes
that haunted the Pallaces of *Kings* and *Princes*. 1.
Traiterous Spyes &c.   2. *Traiterous Flatterers.*

Juſt here it was (as I remember) that *W. Ed-* *Flatterers of Kings*
mundſon ſtopt me ſaying, thou haſt here been tell-
ing us Storyes of *Turk*s and *Jewes*, but what is that
to thy Charge againſt us? we are none of thoſe
that flatter *Kings* and *Princes*, we deal plainly with
all men.

I ſaid they miſtook me: for I did not ſay they
flattered Kings, I uſed a ſimilitude only, viz. that as
Flatterers, &c. of *Kings* and great men, were their
deadlieſt Foes, ſo ſuch Religions and Doctrines as
moſt flatter and ſooth up our rotten hearts and natures they are moſt dangerous and deſtructive to us:
I intended to add that the *Quakers* pretended to be
as fine Flower ſifted out from the *common Proteſtants,*

The whor-ish Quakers, and whore of Rome. ants, yea, from the *Independants & Baptifts,* that Sathan was too fubtle for the fubtleft *Foxes* of them all, for he knowes that by pretence he more eafily & dangeroufly conveys the Poyfon of exalting corrupt and curfed nature in the room of true Soul-faving Humiliation.

I did fay as the *Whore* of *Rome* deceived whole Towns, Cities, Nations and Kingdomes with her glorious Trimmings, and her Golden Cup :· fo that the *Painted Quaker* (as a Drunken Whòre) fhould follow the *Drunken Whore of Rome*) drunk with the blood of Jefus, &c.) for the obtaining of (the fmoak of a *Tobacco-pipe*) the Riches and Honour of this World.

There are two forts of godly Soules catcht up a while by the Devils Craftinefs.

1. Weak and unftable (for there are Children, ftrong Men, & old Men in Chriftianity.)

The Devil a roaring Lion 2 The unwatchful and fecure. The holy wifdome of Gòd difcovers in Holy Scripture, what the Devil, that Sathan an old Serpent is, *viz.* not only a *Roaring,* but a *vigilant Lyon.* *David* (Gods beloved as his Name is) he fails in his managing of Government, therefore the Devil ftirs up *Joab* and *Achitophel* to help (the grand Rebel) his Son *Abfolom* : and afterwards *Sheba,* and all in wonderful Figures, in all Ages, and in this our age and day.

A famous *Jefuit* prints it, that all the Religion in the World lies in competition between the *Jefuits* and *Puritants,* &c. About [173] this time *John Stubs* told me that they (and I fay fo do the *Jefuites* pretend to do) had left the Glory and Pleafure

fure of this world their Wives and Children, Friends and Relations, to Preach the Everlafting Gofpel; For the Woman had been 1260 years 42 months in the wildernefs, and fhe was now come and coming forth, and they were now preaching the everlafting Gofpel, and therefore they advifed me to make hafte and difpatch and not to hinder the Lords work.

I fpake what then I thought fit, and now adde *The Quak* that the *Pharifees*, the *Apoftles*, the *Quakers* and *pretences to outgo* *Jefuites* do compafs Sea and Land: but the *Phari-* *all pre-* *fees*, *Jefuites and Quakers* will be found at laft to be *tending* the *Apoftles Meffengers*, *Heralds*, *Envoys*, *Embaffa-* *Preachers* *dors*, and *Emiffaries* of Sathan fent out from Hell to predicate the goodnefs of rotten nature, hell and damnation, and that falfe and hellifh Gofpel (or good news) of poor rotten Natures *Righteoufnefs*, *Satisfaction*, *Penances*, and to the damning of Souls, &c.

The Devil knows that after the witneffes have *True* done their work againft Antichrift, and after their *Preachers* *or meffen-* flaughters! the Lord Jefus will fend abroad his *gers* *Meffengers* to other Nations (*Jews & Gentiles*) and *New Jerufalem*, or a new vifion of peace fhall then come down from Heaven among the Sons of men: but for the prefent he ftirs up thefe Jefuites and Quakers (with brave titles and pretences) like fo many *Mahomets* (under pretence of *Diogenes* tread-ing on *Platoes Carpets*) to fifh for the fmoak of this Worlds *Sodome*, and no doubt but the *Quakers* will ufe the Sword as much as *Mahomet* or the *Jefuites*,

under

under the cloak and colours of love to Jefus and faving of Souls.

. I confefs that Charity hopes and believes all things, and yet I fay, curfed is that charity that puts out the eye of Reafon, the eye of Experience, the eye of true affection to Chrift Jefus, his Father and his Wife to the Souls of his followers, and. the Souls of poor finners *Jews & Gentiles*.

The Earthly & Heavenly Sword As to the faving of Souls, it was a Thunder from the heavenly mouth of Chrift Jefus. They that take the Sword fhall perifh by the Sword: as if he fhould fay, *the Sword is not a faving but a deftroying Tool*, in Soul-humbling, and Soul-faving: making worlds of *Hypocrites*, but not true *Proteftants*, true *Chriftians & Followers* of the true Lord Jefus, and of his Father, and of his Holy Spirit.

174] The *Spirit* fay the *Quakers*, why thats our *Weapon*! the *Sword of the Spirit* the *Word of God*, why thats the word of God Chrift Jefus our Wea-pon: So faith G. *Fox* and all our *Fantafticks* out of weaknefs and madnefs, not weighing what a perfon *A great myftery amongft Papifts and Proteftants* the holy Records defcribe Chrift Jefus to be, but as foolifh Children and Anticks in the Lord Mayors fhews, they cry out Chrift and the Spirit only for a fhew and colour, I know it that the true Lord Je-fus his holy Father, and Holy Spirit is as odious both to *Jefuits*, and moft *Papifts & Quakers* as the Devil, yea infinitely more then the Devil himfelf, as with Gods help I have and fhall make it as clear as the Noon dayes Sun.

O you confidering . *Proteftants*, fee you not how the Devil would rob you of that Sword with which Chrift

Chrift Jefus overcame him [*The Holy Scripture*] under the colour and cloak of the Spirit in the
mouths of the *Quakers?* how, if the Holy writings
muft yet live, why he hath *Fifher*, and *Stubs*, and
Pennington, and *Bifhop*, and others that skill Tongues,
and yet own the *blockifh* Spirit of the *Quakers*: how
if you blame the *Popifh Devil* for a Blockhead, he
can puff up his Bladders the *Jefuites*, to a late wonderful fwelling of Tongues and Hiftories, and all
kinds of Knowledge, as in *Bellarmine* and his Affociate and Followers and of late in thofe great Writers *Petavius* and *Morinus.*

The eternal Word, and Son, and Sun of God the
true Lord Jefus will more and more difcover who
are his true friends, his true Loves (that love *Alexander* more than the *King*) that are true Chriftians,
true *Jefuites*, and that truly love and pity poor
Souls: he will difcover who are the great *Farmers*,
who having a minde to the *Farm* themfelves confult and fay, *come, this is the Heir* (that is Chrift Jefus in his true Meffengers) *let us kill him*: kill him
with Tongue, and Pen, and Sword, &c. the *Inheritance* of Heavenly and Earthly Glory fhall then be
ours, &c. and to this end only they talk of Souls, &c.

We now defcended to the fifth and forrowful
point of fuffering which they read, *viz.* [*That the
fufferings of the Quakers are no true evidence of the
Truth of their Religion.*]

At the reading of this they told me, that although
their *Sufferings* were great in all places whither the
Lord had fent them, yet they made not their *Suffering* an Evidence of the truth of their *Religion*, &
therefore

therefore I might have been better advifed then to
175 | put this in among the reft of my *Lyes* and
Slanders as not confiderable, and now not worth the
mentioning, *&c.*

I Anfwered, that I underftood what they faid, and
I undeftood mine own affirmation alfo; and defired their patience alfo while I offered my *Proofs*
to two Particulars,

1. That in their *Books* and *Writings &c.* they do
make their *Sufferings* a great Evidence to themfelves and others of the truth of their *Way* and
Spirit.

2. This their *Suffering* is not valid as to the
proof of their *Religion*, *Way* and *Spirit* to be of
God. So then they bid me prove it if I could.

I told them that I could find no *Jewes*, no *Papifts* no *Proteftants*, that did fo magnifie and fo exactly infift upon their *Sufferings* as the *Quakers* did.
Tis 'rue that *Paul* did more particularize his Sufferings then other Saints in Scripture; but it was
alfo true that they were fo exceeding great that
Paul feemed a *None-Such*; but befide that it was
upon fome great *Infultings* of the *Falfe Apoftles*
againft not only himfelf, but againft the Truth of
Chrift Jefus: neither of which is the *Quakers* cafe.
Befide, the *Quakers Sufferings* generally were not to
be compar'd with *Pauls*, and yet they fet down fuch
exact accounts of every *hour* in prifon every *Stripe*
*The Quak.
fufferings
in Hyftory
of G. Bif-
bop re-
corded.*
in *Whipping*, every pound loft: and this publifhed
to the world in print, as if it were a Sign hung out
with this Infcription, *Loe people thefe are the* Evidences *of Gods holy* Truths, *and Gods holy* Spirit, *of*
our

our Perfecutors wickednefs, *and our* Chriftian Faith
and Patience, *who for his Truths fake can endure all
this.* I faid it was not rational to think, that men
profeffing fuch high *Wifdome* and *Confcience,* fhould
declare fuch *Lyfts* and *Catalogues* of *Sufferings* (as
G. *Bifhop* doth to the world, of the *Quakers Sufferings in* N. *England,* in his firft and fecond *Hiftory*)
only in a childifh Vapour, Oftentation and Vain-
Glory, much lefs in hopes of *Reparation* or any
worldly advantage, either in *England* old or new,
Scotland or *Virginia,* &c. and therfore Reafon per-
fwades that thefe Sufferings are held forth (as the
holy Spirit fpeaks of the Sufferings of the *Theffa-
lonians,* 2. Theff. 2.) as a manifeft Token of the
righteous judgment of God rendering *Tribulation* to
their Perfecutors, and *Reft* to themfelves fuffering
for the *Kingdome* of *God.*

As I remember, *John Stubs* faid, they did not
boaft of their [176] Sufferings, but bare them patiently for the Truths fake which they preached
and profeffed.

I faid I did not charge them to fay in exprefs
terms, We have loft fo much outward *Gain, Favour,
Friendfhip, Worldly Advantage* for the Name of
Chrift within us, can you fay the like for the Chrift
without you? We have endured *Imprifonments,
Whippings, &c.* have you done the like? only this
I fay, that as all *Religious Jewes, Papifts, Proteftants
&c.* are confirmed in their Perfwations by their
Sufferings, and do predicate them to others as *Arguments* and *Signs* of the truth of their *Doctrines,*
and of Gods prefence and Affiftance with them; fo
do

do the *Quakers* and that with more Particular and exact *Accounts* then moſt of all the reſt have done.

I told them, I had obſerved much to this pur-poſe in G. *Fox* & *E. Burrowes* in the Book by me.

They bid me alleadge what I could out of them : I took up the Book, and they theirs, I directed them to the 12*th.* Page of *Ed. Burrowes* his large *Epiſtle* to G. *Fox* his Book in Folio where I read this paſſage viz. *And this we did with no ſmall oppo-ſition and Danger : yea oftentimes we were in danger of our Lives, through beating, abuſing, puniſhing, hal-ing, caſting over walls, ſtriking with ſtaves & Cudgels, and knocking down to the ground : Beſide,* Reproach-ing, Scorning, Revilings, Hooting at, *Scornings and Slanderings, and all abuſe that could be though ht or acted by evil hands and tongues, and oft carried before* Magiſtrates *with grievous Threats, and ſometimes put in the Stocks, and whipped, and often impriſoned, and many hard dealings againſt us, the worſt that tongues or hands could execute, ſparing life. Of this all the* North Countreys *can witneſs. And all theſe things are ſuſtained and ſuffered from People and Rulers be-cauſe of our* Faithfulneſs *to the Lord, and for declar-ing againſt the falſe Deceivers. For nothing ſave only the hand of the Lord and his power, could have pre-ſerved us and carried us through all this : neither for any* Reward *outward whatſoever, or advantage to our ſelves would we have expoſed our ſelves to ſuffrings, violence and dangers which befel us daily. But the Lord was our exceeding great reward through all theſe things, and kept us in the hollow of his hand, and un-der the ſhadow of his wings, and gave us dominion in*

Spirit

E. Bur-rowes *his Epiſtle quoted.*

*Spirit over all our enemies, and subdued them before us :
and though Rulers and People were combined against us,
and executed their violence and in-* [177] *justice against
us, yet the Lord made us to prosper and grow exceedingly
in Strength, Wisdome and Number, and the hearts of
the people inclined to us, and the Witness of God in
many stirred for us : for to that in all Consciences,
Words and wayes we did commend our selves to be known
and approved.*

Hereto they suddenly said, What canst thou
make of this, but that *Edward Burrowes* said the
truth, that the Sufferings of the people called *Quakers* were very great, & that he acknowledged the
powerfull hand of the Lord toward them in sup-
porting and delivering them : But this was far
from boasting or making it any *Evidence* of the
truth of their *Religion* and *Principles.*

I replyed, I prayed them to consider why pious
and conscientious Souls (as they would be reputed)
should give so large a *Catalogue* of their *Sufferings.* *The Quo-*
2. Profess it was only for their *Faithfulness* to the *tation*
Lord.   3. Declare that it was the hand of the Lord *weighed.*
that kept them,   4, That he only could do it : I
sayd the *Weaving* and *inter-weaving* of these Particulars, speak plainly that for their *Faithfullness* to
the Lord and his Truth in declaring and suffering
for it, the Lord had been faithfull to them in sup-
porting them and comforting them in all these Suf-
ferrings for his Name sake. Why should wise men
use all these words but to this end, of *Evidencing*
their *Faithfulness* to God, and Gods *Faithfulness* to
them.

After

After fome words had about thefe kind of paffages in *Ed. Burrowes* and other of their Writings,
What true I told them that we muft come to that ancient and
Suffering true Maxime, *Caufa facit Martyrem*, not the Suf-
is. fering of *Burning* it felf that is the evidence of a
true matter. I therefore told them that as it was
in the cafe of Signs[1] Wonders *Deut.* 13. though
they be Signs which falfe *Prophets* give, which
come to pafs, yet God commands his Children not
to be moved from his written word, and his holy
revealed and recorded *Ordinances* and *Inftitutions*.

I told them that I had other places which I had
turned down in *Edward Burrowes* to produce; but
thefe I had fuppreffed in my thoughts for expedi-
tion fake, and would if they pleafed pafs on to my
proof of my next *Pofition,* to this they readily af-
fented : but being now out of my Shackles of a
quarter of an hour (to which I wink'd to draw
them on) I crave the Readers Patience and leave to
hear me fay fomething now which then I could
not fay.

True 178] Firft. To what I have faid before of *E.*
Scripture
Language. *Burrowes* infifting fo largly on the *Sufferings* of the
Quakers, and yet my *Antagonifts* denying them to
make their Sufferings an *Evidence* of their *Truth*, I
prefent the Reader with a witnefs of *G.Fox* his
words in his *Pag* 64, [*And there is a Proof to thee
that the* Quakers *are fent of God who fpeak to thee of
the Scripture right as they are*] He that reads the
place fhall fee that *G.Fox* ufeth thefe words againft
his Oppofite *Jeremiah Jewes,* becaufe that his Oppofite

---

[1] Interline "and"   *R. W. Ms. Ann.*

pofite had faid, viz. That the *Word of God* was contained in the *Scripture* : and *G. Fox* checks him for
it and faith if he had faid [the word which it fpeaks
of] he had fpoken right *&c.* And this G. *Fox*
makes an *Evidence* of the *Quakers* being fent of
God, that they only can fpeak *properly.* How
much more is what I have produced (and have
much more to produce) a *Proof* that they do roll
their Souls upon their *Sufferings* as an *Evidence* and
Confirmation that they are fent of God?

2. It is wonderfull what the *Jewes* and *Papifts*
have fuffered for their *Lyes* and *Blafphemyes* : What *The won-*
a wonderfull Story doth *Manaffeh Ben-Ifrel* relate *derfull*
Sufferings
of a Noble man, a *Portugal*, turned *Jew*, burn'd *of Here-*
in *Portugal* for the *Jewifh Faith*? What *Devotion* *ticks*
and *Zeal* have many of the *Popifh* Party fhewn at
Tiburn? Sure it is that a natural *Valour* and *Mag-*
nanimity, a natural *Melancholy* and *Stoutnefs*, a natural *Pride* and *Vain-Glory* will give wings which fire
and Burning cannot fcorch and conquer.

3. I doubt not but that tis poffible for not only
Chriftians, but alfo *Jewes* and *Papifts* &c. like *Paul*
in his mad *Confcience*, to be zealous for his *Con-*
fcience, and to put others to death for their *Con-*
fciences, and yet neither of them to fin againft their
Confciences, but ignorantly as *Paul* did.

4. I believe that not only *Paul*, and fuch as he, *Great faith*
in Unbelief may fo practice, but even the true *ings of*
Gods Chil-
Saints and Children of God. He that fhall ponder *dren in*
the Fathers *Poligamy*, the beft Kings of *Judah* fuf- *this life.*
fering the *High places, Davids* flaying *Uriah, Afahs*
imprifoning the *Prophet, Peters* rafh ufing the Sword,

36 *Davids*

Davids and *Nathans* unadvifed *Advife* to build God
a Temple, the *Difciples* calling for Fire from Heaven, and fhall fee caufe to reprove the *Quakers* for
their rafh damning of others from whome they
have fuffered. For,

5. As tis poffible for Gods own Children to hold,
and that [179] obftinately, falfe *Principles*, fo it is
poffible for other of Gods Children as obftinately
to afflict and punifh thofe others to *Death*, and fo
bring *Affliction* and *Deftruction* one upon an other
which is that the Devil aimes at.

6. Becaufe the *Quakers* do fo abundantly glory
in their *Sufferers*, and (in comparifon of them)
flight the *Saints* under the *Altar* (in our *Book of
Martyrs*, as *James Parnel* impioufly calls it) cafting
all that differ from them into the *Satanical Delufion*, and *Serpentine nature*, as *Fox* doth, *Pag. 5. and
253. and* 99. Who forbids to receive into their
Houfes, no not *Kings* and *Princes*, nor to bid them
God *fpeed* that are not in their Light. I think it
fit to obferve at this Turn fome Differences between
true *Sufferers* and falfe, both pretending the Name
of *Chrift Jefus.*

True and Falfe Sufferers for the Name of Chrift.

Firft, The Perfons whome the heavenly man
John Fox defcribes, they were men and women
known to be of holy and heavenly Spirits towards
God, and of low and meek Spirits towards all, yea
their very enemyes. I would I could fay fo of the
Quakers (though no queftion but a *a gold Ring* may
fall into the *Channel*, and[1] *Jewel* into the *Dirt* of
worldly and *Antichriftian errors*) But for the *Quakers*

The Quakers defcribed.

kers I have cauſe to fear that generally they are *Proud, ambitious,* and *Worldly-minded* Wretches. Some of them have literal *Knowledge* of the *Scripture,* and ſome ſtirring *Affeƈtions* with the ſtony Ground, others with the thorny Ground have ſuffered formerly, but the Cares and luſts of this world have drild them into this way of Antichriſtian Worſhip. others are *Fierce, Pragmatical, Diſcontented &c.* and they muſt travel and be *Apoſtles* to preach and bring in Proſelites.

The Cauſe of *John* Foxes and G. *Foxes* Martyrs differ as much as Day from Night, and Light from Darkneſs: For it is known that *J. Fox* his *Martyrs* or *Witneſſes* (thoſe bleſſed Souls under the Altar) were ſlain for maintaining the Authority and Purity of the *Holy Scriptures* as the revealed word or will of the *Eternal God* againſt the *Traditions* and *Inventions* of men.

J Fox & G Fox their Martyrs the contrary cauſes of their Sufferings.

But *G.Foxes Sufferers* have generally ſuffered for their *Childrens Baubles,* fantaſtical *Traditions* and *Inventions,* for ſetting up a *Dream* of a *Light* and *Chriſt* within all Man kind, above the *holy Scriptures,* above the *Son of God,* above all *Earthly Dignityes,* and all their *Betters* : endeavouring (with the Pope) to trample all *ſouls* and *Bodyes* under their proud feet.

180] 3. The carriage of theſe two Sorts of Sufferērs differ as much as *Eaſt* from *Weſt,* and *Heaven* from *Hell.*

1. The ground of *Johns* Sufferers was that which *John* ſo much writes of,*viz.*love to the Heavenly Bridegroom, without which *Paul* ſlights burning

Heavenly love carried on. ing it felf: this appears in their wonderfull Love to the holy Scriptures, (the Love-Letters of *Chriſt* *G Foxes* *Jeſus*) and unto all that loved *Chriſt Jeſus* alſo. The *even ſelf,* Quakers are known to be Fierce, Heady, Proud, *God and* Self-conceited, Stout, Bold, and driven on by an *Chriſt &* Audacious and Deſperate *Spirit* (which G.*Fox* and *Spirit.* ſome ſubtle *Foxes* with him have of late blaired in *H.Norton &c.*) No queſtion but ſome of them have a notion of *Wrath* yet to come, and therefore rather then to endure *Hell Fire* they will give up their lives to the Flames, others of them faſt 40 *Virgin* dayes, and yet be far from true *Virgin Love* to the *love to* Son of God. *A Virgin* that loves a man for *Him-* *God, &c.* *ſelf,* will not ſlight his *Love-letters,* nor his *Near Relations* (leaſt of all abhor them, and ſink and burn them as theſe *Foxians* doe.

2. The carriage of *J. Foxes Witneſſes,* though (in reſpect of Gods holy Truth) it was couragious and gallant, yet their lowlineſs and humility did ſhine forth glorioufly alſo.

1. As to God, being more ſenſible of their ſins then of their ſufferings: confeſſing with many tears that although God did turn their ſufferings *The hu-* unto his Glory, and although ungodly men (like *mility of* Foxes and Wolves) hunted them like innocent *Chriſts* *ſufferers* Lambs and *Chickins*) yet they had deſerved and calld for this Storm by their unthankfulneſs for their former peace and liberties, by their drowſineſs and ſleeping upon the Earthen bed of worldly Profits and Pleaſures.

Contrarily it is known to all, that although ſome-times the *Quakers* will ſay we come in love to your
Souls

Souls yet (the *Quakers* are far from confeffing their ^{Devilifb} fins, as having no more fin then God hath, and^{pride} (according to their Principles and fome of them fay it) they can no more fin againft God then God can fin againft them.

As to Men Chrifts fufferers were meek, patient; refpective, contented, thankful.

But as the *Quakers* hearts have an infenfible brawninefs and hardnefs (like frozen Rivers come over their hearts) in matters of God fo as to men. 181] 1. Was there ever a People (Men and Women profeffing fuch an height of Chriftianity) fo fierce fo heady, fo high-minded and though generally not hardned) fo cenfuring, reviling, curfing and damning: and fo favage and barbarous as in the ftark nakednefs of men and women, &c.

2. As to Revenge, how patient, and pitiful, and praying for their Enemies were *J. Foxes Martyrs* or *Witneffes*, and G. *Foxes*, how fpitting *Fire & *The pre-* Brimftone* ? (witnefs the fecond part of *N. England* ^{dictions of} judged by G.·*Bifhop*) becaufe Chrift in them is _{kers} come to judgement) wherein he pronounceth *Deftruction* to Bodies and Souls of *N.England men*, faying in his Epiftle, *that their judgement lingreth not, nor doth their damnation flumber.*

Tis true fome of their Predictions have and may come to pafs as do many alfo of *Conjurers & Witches*, for the Devil knows the Complexion of perfons and things, and·what is like to come to pafs (as in *Sauls* cafe·and in other events) and ftill the poor *Quakers* (and other his Captive Slaves) with fuch Bables as·thefe. I told you what weather ·it would

be,

A bleſſed ſaying of bleſſed Mr. Dod. be, I told you where the Wind would blow : I told you what would come to paſs,] and yet as bleſſed Mr. *J. Dod* uſed to ſay, *though the Devil was up early, God was ſtill up before him* : for the Proverb is here true, *God hath ſent curſt Cows ſhort Horns* : his infinite Wiſdome, Power and Goodneſs is pleaſed to put an Hook into the Jaws of Sathan : he ſhews himſelf the pitiful ſparer and preſerver of men : When the Devil is a *Fiſher* longing for troubled and bloody waters, yet God hath graciouſly proved many of the bloody propheſies of his waſpiſh Pro- phets and Propheteſſes, (as I can prove) to be lying and falſe already.

We now deſcended to the thirteenth Propoſal *The 13 po- ſition diſcuſd.* (the ſixth to be diſcus'd at *Providence*) which was read by them, and is this, *viz.* [*Theſe many Books and Writings are extreamly Poor, Lame, and Naked, ſwelld up only with High Titles and Words of Boaſt- ing and Vapour.*]

I told them that I had not ſhun'd (as in the preſence of the moſt High) to read any of their Books or Letters I could come at : but the truth is, I could never pick out any Wheat (of ſolid, rational and heavenly Truth) out of their heaps of Chaffe, and Dreams, and Fancies of new Chriſts, new Spirits, &c.

It is true that *W. Edmund.* ſaid, that the Word of the Lord [182] was a Fire, and a Hammer, &c. But I ſaid the word they meant was but a painted Fire, and a painted Hammer, and that never broke nor burned up ſin as ſin.

Let a man read the Works of the *Papiſts, Lu-* *therans,*

therans, Arminians, and amongſt our ſelves, the *Epiſ-*
copal and *Preſbyterian* Writings: a man ſhall have
wherein to exerciſe his Judgement, Memory, &c.
he ſhall have Scripture propoſed, Arguments alleadged, yea he ſhall read Anſwers and Replies,
whereby to ſatisfie a rational Soul and Underſtanding.

But in the *Quakers Books & Writings, Peter &*
Jude tells us (what I have found) clouds high of an
imaginary Chriſt and Spirit: high ſwelling words,
ſtrange from the Holy Scripture Language, and all
ſober and Chriſtian Writers and Speakers.

Let *Jo. Chandlers* Writings, and the Writings of
Theora John (that Monſter of Deluſion) be viewed,
whoſe bodily Raptures, and frantick Writings of
the *Quakers* Principles, and of the *Jews* (in *Hebrew,*
Greek, Latin & Arminiack Writings (which he con-
feſt he underſtood not) and let the reſt of their
Writings be brought to the *Touch-ſtone,* and ſee if
an honeſt *Goldſmith* can find ought elſe but the
Droſs, Dreams and Fancies, in ſtead of the ſolid
Gold of Heavenly Scripture.

I have read *Nichols,* and *Nailor,* and *Howgel* and
Burrows, and *Parnel,* and *Farnworth,* and *Fox,* and
Dewsbury and *Pennington,* and *Whitehead,* and *Biſhop,*
&c. And I could readily and abundantly prove my
poſition out of all of them, but my deſire and intention was (as by my *P*aper to G. *Fox* appears) to
have made it good to G. *Fox* himſelf, and to all
Chriſtians, how poor and lame, and naked G. *Fox*
his writings are, who ſeems to be as *Pighius* and
Echius amongſt the *Papiſts,* and as *Bellarmine* the
greateſt Writer amongſt them.

I told

I told my *Oppofites* I would therefore Anfwer
G F. his
book in fo-
lio confide-
red this *Bellarmine*, and I would not fay *Bellarmine* thou
lieft: but I would by Holy Scripture fhew *G.Fox*
and his deluding *Foxians*, how the old *Fox* the old
Serpent was too crafty for them all, and had brought
them and their Followers to the brim of the Lake
that burns with fire and brimftone.

Firft. then I faid, let who will that underftands
true Englifh, and are able to read and write true
Englifh, (though he know no more) take G. *Fox*
his Folio Book in hand, and tell me whether ⌊183
(through his whole Book) he writes like an *Eng-
lifh-man*: And though he upbraids all his Oppofites fcornfully and ridiculoufly (as poor Children
that know not the Bible nor their Accidence in
faying *you* to a fingular, &c.) whether in many fcores
of places in his Book he confounds not the fingular
and the *P*lural: I confefs when I urged this in publick, my Oppofites defired of me no proof of this
out of *Foxes Book* and therefore (remembering my
quarter hour Glaffe) I fpared Quotations, but now
(through Gods patience and my Readers) my Tedder being longer, I fhall give·one or two brief
Proofs and Inftances.

In page 282. in G. *Fox* his fecond Anfwer he
faith, [*You where you are fees him nor*] where it
fhould be the *P*lural fee him not, if this *Proud
Bruit* had known either his Accidence or the Bible.

In Page 300. he faith [*The Scriptures is able to
make wife unto Salvation*]. which fhould be are
able, &c.

In Page 16. [*The Churches was to hear*] for, were
to hear.   In

In *Page* 110. [*As thou doth*] which ſhould be, as ^{*G F his ig-*} thou doſt: And abundance more of this Boyes ^{*norance of*}_{*common*} Engliſh all his Book over, which I cannot im- *Engliſh* pute to his *Northern Dialeƈt* (having been ſo long in the South, and London, and read and anſwered (as he dreams) ſo many Engliſh Books: nor to the *Printer* (the faults of that kinde being ſo numer- ous) but to the finger of the moſt High, and moſt Holy, whoſe property it is, and therefore delights to run thwart and croſſ the ſhins of proud and inſult- ing Souls and Spirits.

2. I obſerve throughout his Book a Devilliſh *Black Line* of deſpiſing thoſe that are Good (as the Scripture ſpeaketh) He counts none Godly but him- ſelf and his *Foxians:* yea there is no *God,* no *Chriſt,* no *Spirit,* but what is in him and them feelingly, though they ſay he is in every man and woman in the world, and *Chriſt Jeſus the Sun of Righteousneſs,* ^{*Horrible*} and the *Holy Spirit,* and the Kingdome of God, ^{*contradic-*} which they confeſs conſiſts in Righteouſneſs and ^{*tion*} peace and joy in the Holy Spirits,[1] and yet (as they impiouſly and ſimply ſpeaks) theſe Inhabitants and Hoſts to all theſe Gueſts know nothing of their lodging and dwelling within them.

G. *Fox* gives a ſhrewd ſuſpition that he never knew what the true fear, and love, and peace, and joy of ^{*The ex-*} God mean; if he did, is it poſſible that he could ^{*cellent*} puff at ſo many Writers (excellent for great Know- ^{*men.*} ledge and godlineſs, denying any thing of God or ^{*Whom*} 184] Chriſt, or Spirit, or Grace to be in them: ^{*G F in his*} ſome

---

[1] "Holy Spirit." *R. W. Ms. Ann.*

37

book in fo-lio tramp-leth 'n as Diſhclouts Dogs & Devils

ſome of them (eminent ſervants of God) I have known : of others of them I have ſmelt the *ſweet Odour* of an Heavenly report from the mouthes of others and in their Writings.

But as *G.Fox* will be found to adore an *Image & Crucifix* for the true Lord Jeſus, ſo whatever he ſay of others will his Faith, his Love, his Spirit of Diſcerning, and *Hope of Glory* and *Salvation* prove (without Repentance) dolefully falſe in the latter end.

For, doth not this *Proud Cenſor* know that men may be true Saints in their perſons, and yet be ſub-ject to ſudden *Epileptical & Falling Fits?* may not *David* walk with God with a perfect heart, and yet in the matters of *Bathſheba* and *Uriah* (and many other particulars) fall down like a Jewel into the Dirt? that Chriſt Jeſus owns *Peter* and his *Confeſſion*, &c. and yet in another caſe, *get thee behind me Sathan?* That *Peter* reſolves to dye for Jeſus, and yet denies with Curſing and Swearing, that he never knew him, and after *Chriſts Reſurrection* and *Aſcention*, even *Peter* plays the *Hypocrite & Diſſembler*.

A differ-ence of Sinners

Yea did not the high Fathers in Godlineſs, fa-mous Kings in Gods Church live long in the incivility of many Wives, and the impiety of Wor-ſhipping in the High places, &c. to what purpoſe doth the Lord inſpire his holy Pen-men to write theſe holy Hiſtories : was it to ſhame his Saints de-parted, or to ſhame his own Holineſs, and to caſt a ſtumbling block, and a protection for after ſinners and tranſgreſſors? or amongſt other holy ends to teach us (like *Moſes*) to diſtinguiſh between an *Egyptian*
whom

whom he flew and the *Ifraelites* whom he chid for
wronging each other, fince they were their Bre- G. Fox no
thien; fo that he is a poor Chriftian Goldfmith, that true Goldfmith.
knows not to difcern the Gold of Holinefs, and the
Copper of Hypocrifie; yea, and to give the beft
Gold in the World its due allowance, with which
it will pafs currant in Earth and Heaven with God,
and fuch who truly know and love him.

. But with G. *Fox.* in all this great Book, the moft
humble and able, godly and confcientious are with
him but *Vipers, Serpents, Cains, Judaffes, falfe Prophets, Pharifees, dumb Dogs, Sorcerers, Witches, Reprobates, Devils, &c.*

3. In this Book of G. *Fox* (all along) he denies
the *Scripture* to be the Word of God : and he faid,
that every man in the world hath that Spirit that
gave forth *Scriptures,* and that all Saints are [185
acted by the fame Spirit immediately that moved
the Prophets and Apoftles and holy Pen-men of
the holy *Scriptures,* all tending to *vilifie* and *nullifie*
the *Holy Scriptures.*

Befides, his *Impiety* in thefe Affertions (which
half an eye of *Mahumetans, & Jewes, & Papifts, &* Fox his
Proteftants will fee) I note his Simplicity (for a F*ox* fubtilty
though he be crafty is but a Beaft ftill) For out of and yet fimplicity
his *Piety* he grants the holy Scriptures through all in granting
his Book to be the *Words of God,* though not the the Script.
Word of God: and for this his Grant he quotes to be the words of
Exod. 20. *God fpake all thefe Words,* and the four God.
Books of the *Revelations,* which I nor my Oppofites
could tell in publick what to make of : But if they
are the *Words* of God, and fome of them fearfully
written,

written by the inconceivable Finger of God once
and twice, then every particular *word* of thefe *words*
muft needs be the *Word* or *Will* or mind *of God*
every grain of gold is gold, and every drop in the
Ocean is Water and Salt too, as I urged to them
before concerning every word that proceedeth out
of the mouth of God) elfe the *Words of God* when
brought to particular examination, they are not the
word of *God*, but of *Angels* or *Men* or *Devills*.

How fweet are (not Words but) right Words:
every man fhall kifs his lips that gives a right Anfwer, how dirty then, how filthy and bloudy are
thofe Lips that in fo many places, debating with fo
many wife and learned and pious men, drop not
Honey and *Milk*, but *Wormwood* and *Gall* the *Venome*
and the *Poyfon* of Afps to them that lick up fuch
deceitfull and deftroying *Doctrines*.

4. In G. *Fox* his Book I obferve that all along
he notorioufly nibbles ar *VVords* and quarrels at
VVords, which he faith are not *Scripture*, as that
wicked word [*Humane*] relating to the Perfon of the
Son of God and man.

The word Humane abominable above all words to the Qua-kers
Alfo the word *Trinity* and *Sacrament*. Oh how
zealous is this *Fox* for the purity of *Language*?
Why may not the word *Humane* be ufed as well as
the word *Sabboth* and *Sabbaoth*, and *Bethlebem* and
Ierufalem which are Hebrew words, and as well as
the words *Baptifme* and *Jefus Chrift* which are
Greek words, *Scribes* and *Scriptures* and *Pretorium*
which are Latine words. That word *Humane* is
odious *&c.* for *Chrift Jefus* fake, and therefore the
more I love and honour it, as expreffing the ap-
peafance

pearance of God in Flesh, in that personal, Individual Flesh of *Chrift Jefus* the [186] *Mediator* petween God and Man, the Man *Chrift Jefus.*

5. I obferve the loofe and wild Spirit of *G.Fox* in dealing with fo many heavenly *Champions*, the Leaps and Skips like a wild *Satyre* or *Indian*, catching and fnapping at here and there a Sentence, like Children fkipping ore hard places and Chapters, picking and culling out what is common and eafie with them to be paid of and anfwered.

6. Any fober Soul may read in moft of their *The fimple* Books, and in *G.Fox* his Book fuch *Tautologies* and *tautologyes of the* needlefs *Repetitions* that may even *Turn* his Stom- *Quakers.* ach, and make him abhor to touch a *Quakers* Book more. How many hundred times have you, *Chrift is within you except you be Reprobates* : Flefh of his Flefh and Bone of his Bone *&c.* and I prefume neer a thoufand times if not a full thoufand times repeated [That lightens every man that comes into the World, that lightens every man that comes into the world] &c. *G.Fox* had many *Bullets* flying about his eares, and therefore at every turn (like a man fighting for his life) he is forced to hold out a *Pretence* a *Buckler* a *Breaft-plate*, fimply called *Light*, and at every turn to cry *Oh the Light, the Light that enlightens every man that comes into the World.*

7 Through all his Book like fome great *Commanders* or *Generals* by Land or Sea, yea like the *The infult-* *Emperors* or *Dictators* among the *Romanes*, fo doth *ing &* this wild devouring Soul give forth his high and *wild im-* *perioufnefs* haughty *Sentences* : this proud Bladder is big with *of G.Fox.* *Simon Magus* his thoughts of being Some Body.

I fhall prefent one Inftance,   *Pag.*

Hen.
Haggar.
Pag. 253. His Oppofite *Henry Haggar* faith, you call [*all men Dead and Carnall, in the Serpents na-ture in what form foever they differ from you*] this proud Soul Anfwers, [*All that be not in the Light that enlightens every man that comes into the World, which is the way to the Father, differeth from us, fuch be dead, fuch be carnal in the nature : for none comes to the life but who comes to the Light, in what form fo-ever they be, and fuch as differ from us differ from Chrift, for none comes from under the Satanical nature but who comes to the Light*] what *Julian* the Apof-tate, what Duke *D'Alva*, what *Wolfey* could have fpoken more imperioufly, infultingly & bloudily then this *wild Fox* hath done againft all the true Servants & *Witneffes* of the *Moft High* that ever have been or fhall be to the end of this world? they differ from *Fox* & therefore are *Devils &c.*

Bloudy and devillifh Pride of the Foxians.

187] 8. I obferve that *G.Fox* all along his Book powres forth a flood of *Fire & Brimftone* againft all his Oppfites and tells us that it is not *Railing &c.* for (his chief *Adverfary*) the holy Scripture gives In-ftance of Chrift Jefus himfelf giving fuch Lan-guage; and alfo it is no other then the Oppofites to the *Quakers* give unto them : but Godly and Sober Souls will confider,

1.   That *Mofes* and the *Prophets,* and *Chrift Jefus* and his *Apoftles* do not univerfally abfolutely and promifcuoufly fling out *Fire-brands,* and fhoot *Ar-rowes* and *Death* into the Sides and Souls of all that differ from them, as here *G.Fox* doth.

Fox his horrible railing.

We may obferve in the holy *Scripture,* that gen-erally they were *high handed hypocritical* and *hardned*
Sinners

Sinners againft whome the holy Spirit thundred
out fuch *Titles,* threatnings and Judgments: But
Fox in this place makes no Diftinction, but as boldly as *Blind Bayard* faith all that differ from us *&c.*

2. This is no rare bufinefs, but *Fox* and his *Foxians* common *Language* and *Barkings* : .Thou *Cain,*
thou *Serpent,* thou *Devil,* (*Devil, Devil, Devil,* as
one of their *She-Apoftles* have faid amongft us. ·

3. It is *G.Fox* his bruitifh and ridiculous Song
in the clofe of his *Anfwers* (and fometimes in the
beginning) without any *Truth, Humanity or Modefty,* to cry out faying [*And as for the reft of thy
Lyes and Slanders, they are not worth the mentioning*] Fox *his*
when he hath pickt out a few *Sentences* or pieces of *bruitifh and ridicu-*
Sentences (eafie for himfelf to carpe at &c.) his con- *lous Song.*
clufion and Burthen of his bruitifh ridiculous Song
is [*As for the reft of thy Lyes and Slanders*] inftead
of holy Scripture, or folid *Arguments* with *Anfwers* to his Oppofites *Reafons* and *Replyes* and *Re-
jonders* that an humble foul may fee fome footing
to reft on.

4. As we fay in the death of the *Martyrs* or
Witneffes of *Jefus,* it is not the *Suffering,* but the *What*
Caufe & Spirit & Cariage is to be confidered: So *Railing is*
in bitter Language, it is not lawfull to call every
Prince or *King, Fox,* as Chrift called *Herod:* nor
every Oppofite *Viper & Serpent, Fool* and *Blind* and
whited painted Wall and *Sepulchre* &c. They feemed
to fpeak *Reafon* to Chrift upon his Crofs [*Thou that
faveft others, thou that deftroyeft the Temple* &c. *come
down now fave thy felf*] &c. and yet Gods Spirit
calls this *Reviling* and *Railing* at him.

9. All

9. All may fee what a fimple *Craking* Sound of vapouring and [188] boafting runs through all this *Foxes* Book: Doubtlefs *Syfera* and his *Mideanites, Goliah* and his *Philiftines, Rabfhekah* and his *Affirians* were types of of thefe Children of *Pride,* whofe *Vapours* whofe *Prophefies* (fo me notorioufly falfe, already proved) whofe promifed *Victoryes, Spoils, Threatnings* lye like black foul Blots of ink or greafe over all his *Papers* and the *Papers* of moft of them, far from that Clofet *Content* and *Sincerity* of the true Saints who are content with the eye of God alone in fecret.

Inftances out of G. F. his Book

10. For a more full proof of the *Lamenefs* and *Stark nakednefs* of their Writings, I fhall felect and mention fome *Particulars* out of this *Grand Alcoran* of G. *Fox* 1. His Oppofites Words, then his Anfwer. And, 3. My Replyes *&c.*

Page 1. He brings in *Sam. Eaton* faying, [*He doth not believe that there is Subftantial, Effential or Perfonal Union between the Eternal Spirit and Believers.*]

Sam. Eaton.

G. *Fox* Anfwers [*Though the Scripture faith the Spirit dwells in the Saints,* 1 Cor.6. *And he that is joyned to the Lord is one Spirit,* 1 Joh. 1. *As though the Saints had not Union with God which the Scripture fay they have.*]

I Reply: concerning the *Effence* or *Being* of the Immortal, Invifible, Infinite, Eternal, Omnipotent, and Omnifcient, and only Wife: we know no more then a Fly knows what a King is, and therefore 1 *Tim.*9.[1] *He dwells in the Light that no man can ap-*

proach

---

[1] "1. Tim. 6." *R. W. Ms. Ann.*

proach to: how fully doth the Holy Spirit in the Book of *Job*, and eſpecially in that dreadful Word or Voice of God in a *Whirlwind* knock out the brains of all theſe proud Fancies? let this proud *Fox*, or any of the ſtouteſt *Lions or Lioneſſes* amongſt them, look but a few minutes upon the glorious Sun in the Heavens, and then tell us how their eyes do: and yet thus like proud and prat-ling Children do they make a noiſe about their *Bibs*, and *Aprons*, and *Muckingers*: and how they are one with God his *Being* and *Eſſence*, &c.

Is it not enough for Sun, Moon and Stars, and Men to be enlightned by his Infinity, but they muſt be God himſelf, and Light it ſelf, in the high-eſt ſence, becauſe God is Light, &c. *Gods being out of our reach*

What impudence would it be in a Wife, becauſe ſhe is one with her Husband in Relation, to ſay, She is the Husband himſelf, and not to keep her juſt diſtinction and diſtance? or in a Subject (be-cauſe the Subjects and the *King* are Relatives, and in a ſence one) [189] therefore to ſay, that they are the *King himſelf*.

Again, we know that the word *Spirit* is taken in *Holy Scripture* for a *Spiritual Nature*. Hence it is ſaid that God is a Spirit, not that God is properly a Spirit, no more then he is Light (though my Oppoſites in our Diſpute affirmed he was) but of ſuch a Heavenly and Spiritual Nature: For the Devils alſo are Spirits, though defiled with ſin and wickedneſs: thus *Joh*. 3. *That which is born of the Spirit is Spirit*, not that Spirits beget Spirits, and *The nature of Spirits*

that

38

that a new Creature is a young holy Spirit or God himſelf, as I told one of the chief of the *Quakers* at *Newport*,

And that 1. *Cor.*6. ſhews us in what reſpect he that is joyned to the Lord is one Spirit : For know *How God* you not (ſaith *Paul*) *that your Bodies are the Temples and Chriſt of the Holy Spirit :* and *Epheſ.* 2. *For an Habita-is in us.* tion of God through the Spirit.

How God and Chriſt is in us.

Thus God dwelt in his Temple of old, as a Man in his Houſe and a King in his Palace : not that a Mans House, or the Kings Palace is of his Sub-ſtance or Eſſence no more then an houſe is of the Suns Eſſence, &c. and no more was Gods Temple of old, nor his Temples his Saints now, after the blockiſh and blaſphemous nonſence of the *Quaker*.

Sam.Eaton In Page 2. He brings in *Sam Eaton* ſaying [*The Scripture is to be judge of Doctrines and Manners.*]

G. *Fox* Anſwers [*The Jews had not the infallible Judgement, that had Scripture but ſtood againſt Chriſt the Light, and judged him to be a Devil, that judge-ment was not infallible, and that Doctrine and Man-ners of theirs was not right which goes againſt Chriſt the Light.*]

The Scrip-ture the Rule.

I Reply, as the Sun in the Heavens is the Epi-tomy or Center of all Natural Light, though ſome eyes are ſore, look a ſquint, or are ſtark blinde.

And as the Rule or Canon (though *Fox* ſimply bogles at that as not a Scripture word) is the ſame, for it is in the Greek, though millions know it not, and millions (as the *Phariſes*) pervert and miſ-apply it.

The Holy Scripture is granted by G. *Fox* to be Gods

Gods Words (though in a subtle fancie, not his *The Holy Scripture a Lanthorn* Word,) but if it be every word of their Gods, then is every Word as *Dovid* faith *a Light to our feet, and a Lanthorn to our Paths,* though we defpife it and wilfully refufe it (as fome fometimes do Lanthorns) and wilfully ftumble [190] into the Ditch Eternal, and other poor Souls after us: Thus the Heavenly Sun-Dial is one and conftant in its guidance and direction to us poor Travellers, though we neglect to look on it, or be ignorant of the figures and *Try all things* lines of it, and be willingly ignorant, &c.

We are not only commanded to read and meditate in the Holy Scriptures, and to fearch them as the *Bereans* did, but we are commanded to try all things, to try the very Spirits. The *Papifts* flap us in the mouth with the infallible Spirit of the *Pope,* and that he is not to be judged: the *Quakers* fay the fame of themfelves, which is no more then as I faid in the Difpute (when *W, Edmund.* interrupted me, crying out *Blafphemy*) for a Man to go for Counfel to an arrant Cheater and Jugler (then cheating moft when he calls all others Cheaters.)

In Page 3. He brings in the fame Author faying *Sam Eaton* [*That God did not intend immediate Teaching, nor to give out an immediate voice in after ages, which fhould direct and guid men in the way of Salvation.*

He Anfwers, which is contrary to the Scripture, which faith, All the people of the Lord fhall be taught of the Lord, and he that is of God heareth Gods word, and that is immediate and living, and doth endure for ever, there is no fallibility nor delufion in the Revelation of God, but all fallibility and delufion is out of it. I Reply,

Gods mediate teachings, his word & voice manifold and specified.
I Reply, it is granted that God ſpeaks mediately unto us by the light of Nature within us; doth not nature teach you that it is a ſhame for a man to have long hair, &c.

2. By his works of Creation.

3. His Providence without us in his mercies and judgements, ſo that every drop of Rain and crumb of Bread, and grain of Corn is Gods word and witneſs:

And 4. The pains of the Body, and Dreams in the night have much of Gods word and voice in them, *Job* 33. God ſpeaks once and twice but man hears it not and is not Gods ſpeaking his Word?

And 5, All grant that the words of· Scripture are the words of God.

And 6. The teachings of men, *Epheſ.*4. are granted to be means, &c. both for the gathering of the Church, as *Apoſtles*, and for the Governing of the Flocks, as *Paſtors and Shepherds*, &c.

191] 7. The Water, the Bread, the Wine, &c. are appointed by Chriſt Jeſus to be means while profeſſion of Chriſt Jeſus is made on earth to hold forth a remembrance of him until his ſecond coming.

8. The private *Prayers* and *Faſtings* and *Meditations* of the Saints day and night, are holy *Meanes* in and by which the Eternal God ſpeaks Peace, Inſtruction, Reproof and Comfort to to them that fear him.

9. Sometimes it pleaſeth God by the Miniſtration of his *Miniſtring Spirits*. (the inviſible Angels) to work by unknown and unſeen wayes to us: thus in

Pauls

Pauls Light and *Voice* and *Blindness*, and the *Jail-*
ors *Earthquake*, but afterward in *Ananias* his fending to *Paul* (as *Peter* to *Cornelius*) and *Paul* to the
Jailor, it pleafed God to ufe his holy means and
inftruments of Men to men (Gods fweet and familiar way to men: the immediate Teachings of
God by *Dreams*, by *Vifion*, by *Voices*, *by* Motion, the
Holy Scripture mentions many before and fince the
coming of the Lord Jefus, the Queftion is not
whether it may not pleafe the moft Holy and infinite *Prerogative* of the moft High, fo to teach
where, and when, and whom he pleafe.

But whether it be Chriftian obedience, or Diabolical lazinefs to fling off all means (as *Fox* all
along teacheth) to fit ftill and liften to immediate
Teachings (that is fay I to the Devils whifperings)
I believe the *Papifts* and *Quakers* would give much
to be rid of the Scriptures: I know alfo, that notwithftanding their pretence of Spirit, yet both of
them are forced to ufe means, *Praying*, *Preaching*,
Congregating, and (in ftead of the holy means
by Gods Spirit) have appointed many Inventions
and Superftitions from a Satanical Spirit.

G. *Fox* faith, there is no Fallacy in the *Revela-*
tion of God?

Anf. True, but will he fay thefe feven things:

1. That all the pretended *Revelations* are the
Revelations of God.

2. That *Revelations* may not pretend *Angelical*
Light, and yet be *Diabolical Darknefs*.

3. That we may receive any *Revelations* and
Teachings

Teachings (as Children and Mad Folks do) without chewing, and rational weighing & confideration.

4. That God hath not appointed his old Scripture and Writing [192] new fince Chrifts coming as a *Standard, Rule* or *Touchftone* to try all our own and others Infpirations by ?

5. That *Mahomets Infpirations* are not one of the moft prevailing Snares, Traps, and Engines, whereby he hath catcht whole Nations and Kingdomes, and the greateft part of this poor world at this day.

6. That when God reveals his word or will in writing (which G. *Fox* grants to be the words of God, and they are flighted) it is not common and moft righteous with God to deliver up proud lazy Souls to ftrong Delufions to believe Lyes (as at this day it is moft wonderfull)

The great business of Revelations
7. Whether there be any way in this world to efcape the fnares of *Sathans Whifperings* but by humble attending to the fearch and Meditation of the heavenly *Records*, by humble cryes to the Father of *Spirits* for his holy *Spirit* and help in all the *Meanes* by himfelf appointed, in Love and Pitty to the Souls of men.

Sam Eaton
A 4th. Inftance of *G, Fox* his lame ftuff is in *Pag.* 4. where he brings in the fame Author *Sam Eaton* faying, [*The Gofpel is the Letter, &c.*] He Anfwers, [*And the Apoftle faith, it is the power of God &c. and the Letter kills, and many may have the Form but deny the Power, and fo ftand againft the Gofpel which is the Power of God.*

I reply, we all know that the word *Gfopel* from the

the old *Saxon* is as ſtrange to us *Engliſh*, as the word *What is the Goſpel*
Evangelium or *Euangelion* (the Latine and Greek)
are: but we all agree that it may be turned (according to its meaning) *Glad Newes*. This wiſe cunning
man tels us the *Glad Newes* is not the *Glad Newes·*
Why ſo? Becauſe it is the *Power* of *God*.who ſees not
here the ſimple ſubtelty of this *Deceiver*? The *Goſpel*
or *Glad Newes* preached is the power of God unto
Salvation to every one that believeth &c. *Rom.* 1.
Therefore this *Glad Newes told, written, printed,
preached,* is not the *Glad Newes* : would he now
perſwade himſelf and us that *Moſes* and the *Prophets* that wrote of this *Glad Newes,* and thoſe four
heavenly *Pen-men* (or *Pens*) which by the finger of
God, (his immediate *Spirit*) wrote the Hiſtory of
the *Life* and *Death* of the Lord Jeſus, &c. wrote
nothing of the Goſpel or glad news, for the glad
news is the power of God.

2. I know the trick of theſe old Cheaters and
Juglers to hide [193] themſelves, and their cheating in the *Buſhes* and *Thickets* of *words* of di- *The horri-*
verſe *Significations*, or figurative Speeches, which all *ble Cheat*
honeſt Reaſon teacheth carefully to diſtinguiſh. I *of the Foxians.*
know it is *Fox* his trick, and all their tricks in his
and their Writing, to make *God* and *Chriſt* and
Spirit & Goſpel & Covenant & Juſtification, (as before I proved) to be all that one cheating Fancy
called *Light* in them and in every one that cometh
into the World. Theſe bewitched ſouls will not *Why the*
owne a *figurative ſpeech* when it makes not for their *Goſpel is*
Idols. 3.Is it not that the Lord calls the preaching *called the Power of*
of the *Glad Newes* the *Power of God,* becauſe of *God.*
the

the wonderfull effect of it to him that believeth
this *Glad Newes*, which few or none believe, as being a foolifh thing to believe (as the *Jews* and
thoufands others fay, to believe in a beggars brat,
laid in a *Manger* and a *Gallowes-Bird* &c. 4. *Paul*

*How it is
called
Pauls
Gofpel.*

calls this *Glad news*, his *Gofpel* or *Glad news*, Rom.
2. Will the *Foxians* therefore fay that either *Paul*
lyed, or elfe it is not Gods Gofpel nor Chrifts, but
Pauls although it is moft true that as *Paul* had
charge of it (as a *Shepheard* of another mans *Flock*,
or a *Mariner* of an other mans *Ship*) it may ¹be
common Phrafe of Speech (though not *literal* but
figurative) be called *Pauls* (or any other Meffengers
of *Chrift*) *Glad news* or *Gofpel*. 5.   There is a wild

*Three
Foxes.*

beaft called a *Fox*, a fubtle and pernicious creature :
there was a famous heavenly Man, a famous writer
of the Book of *Martyrs*, *John Fox*, and there is this
poor deluded & deluding Soul *G.Fox*, to whome I
am now replying, ought not thefe to be *diftinguifhed?* Is there not fuch a mifchievous fubtle
Beaft called the *Fox* becaufe *G.Fox* bears (and that
moft juftly and by a finger of Gods *providence* bears
it) the *wild Beafts* name : or was not fuch a *learned
& heavenly & wonderfully deligent & zealous* man as

*The Scrip-
ture the
word or
glad news
from Hea-
ven
written.*

J. Fox, becaufe *G.Fox* bears that name alfo?   6.
But further, If the Glad news may not be called
the *Glad news* when tis *Scripture* (that is *written*) or
preached, then not *Glad news* when *fpoken*. 7. The
Law denounceth Sentence of Death againft a Traitor &c. this Sentence is written, & in a Sence may
be called a *Killing Letter :* the King pardons this
Traitor,

¹ "by"   *R. W. Ms. Ann.*

Traitor, and this Sentence of *Pardon* is written:
this gracious word of a King is not lefs his *Word*
becaufe it is *Written* then it was when firft fpoken
by him; and this word or pleafure of the King
written may be called Gofpel or *Glad news*, the
Glad news or *Gofpel* of his Temporal *Salvation*:
will any fober man fay as G. *Fox* impioufly and
frantickly, that the writing of the Pardon and
the *Broad-Seal* is a *Dead letter* & a *Killing letter &c.*
becaufe Paper Parchment *&c.* If *G. Fox* from hunting after Souls by Sea and Land, arrive at ⌈194⌉ any
Port in *England* and fend a Letter Poft to his *Wife*
& Friends, containing his many *Deliverances*, many
Experiences, his fafe *Arrivail* and his Purpofe and
Hope fhortly to fee them: fhall now this *Glad news* *Counter-*
(or *Gofpel*) though but a few raggs made (*Paper*) *feits de-*
be ftiled a *Dead letter* yea a *Killing letter* though it *ftroy not*
contain nothing (as the Chriftian *Gofpel* or *Glad* *true heirs*
news doth not) but *glad news* or *Tidings*. 8. Hence *and owners*
it is that we read fo often of *Preaching the Gofpel,* *for ever.*
of *Believing the Gofpel*, and that as before *Paul* calls
it his *Glad news*, or *Gofpel* becaufe it was his work
to tell it.

Yea but faith this Deceiver throughout his Book
A man may have the Letter and Form, without the
Power and Life. &c. I Anfwer Who knows not
that ? and that a *Form & picture* is not the man
himfelf? who knows not that *Judas* notwithftanding his pretended Love and *Kiffing of Chrift Jefus*
that yet he had not the *Life & power* of true *Love*
and *heavenly affection*: but doth it follow that living and moving Bodyes have not Souls & Spirits
39   within

within them, becaufe that *pictures* have not ? That
none preach *Chrift Jefus* truly becaufe that G. *Fox*
preacheth an immaginary and *Allegorical Chrift*,
in order to eftablifh himfelf the only true Chrift,
and the *Eternal Son of God* as many bewitched
Souls call him. 9. What is this but to cheat poor
Birds with the *Chaff & Falacy* of dividing the
Body from the Soul, the *Letter* from the *Meaning*,
the *Inftrument* or *Tool* from the *Workman* or *Huf-*
A word to all Fox-ians. *bandman* ufing it, the *Gofpel* or *glad news* from *Be-*
lieving of it. Ah poor cheated Souls (called *Qua-*
kers all of you) why do you willingly (out of pretended *Enlightnings & Experiences*) fhut your eye of
common *Senfe* and *Reafon*, not daring to call *good*
news, good news, becaufe fome, or the moft will not
Believe it ? was it not fo with the women preaching
or telling the *good news* or *gofpel*, although few or
none were found to believe that *Chrift* was rifen ?
10. The truth is (fearch your cheating *Familiars*
narrowly &) you will find that *your felves* and the
Papifts would make an *Holy Day* of that Day, in
which all the *Bibles* in the world were burnt, that
you may eftablifh your infallible *fpirits & Tra-*
ditions.

I know I wronge you not, I have too much
proof of it, which you would fe if the heart were
Gods won-derful pre-fervation of his word or wil to poor mankind not the arranteft *Cheater* in the World, and your
felves not willing to be cheated. Tis true *Anti-*
ochus attempted the burning of *Mofes* and the *Pro-*
phets out of the world : fome of the bloudy *Empe-*
rours followed on in *Antiochus* his bloudy Steps
raging againft the Scriptures alfo, the *Romane Popes*
in

in theirs, and common reafon may tell all men, and
the *Quakers* themfelves, [195] that if the fame
power come into their hands as *Antiochus* & the
Romane Emperours had the holy Scriptures fhall not
if they can effect it trouble them or others one day
in the world longer. *But of this more in the next
and laft Pofition.*

A 5*th* Inftance is *pag* 10 where *G.Fox* brings in
John Bunian faying, *It is not Faith and works that* John
juftifie in the fight of God, but it is Faith and good Bunian.
works which juftifie in the fight of men only. &c.
He anfwers, *Abraham* was not juftified to men only
by his *Obedience,* but to *God,* and where is *Faith*
there is *Juftification,* which works by *Love :* and The great
the Saints *Faith & works* were not only to *juftifie* Pofition of
them in the *fight of men ?* for the *Work of God* is to tion.
doe what he faith & his *Will* which who doth not
are not juftified in fo doing, but to be beaten with
Stripes *:* who feek to be *juftified* by their Faith and
Works in the fight of men, are Dead *Faith &
Works* both.

I Reply, In this great bufiness of *juftification &
Pardon* of Sin (which *Luther* called the great Wall
of Seperation between us and the *Papifts*) I humbly
hope to fhew how lame this Fox is, and that he
& his *Foxians* agree with the *Papifts, Arminians,
Socinians* againft the true *Proteftants* in this funda-
mental bufinefs. For what is *Juftification* but a
Pardon written and fealed and declared from the
King of Heaven to poor condemned *Traitors.* Juftifica-
That this *Pardon* may be merited by any *Price* that it is
we or all the World can offer, is denied by true
Proteftants,

Proteſtants, but affirmed (in effect) by the proud unbroken Souls of *Papiſts*, *Arminians*, *Socinians*, and theſe *Foxians* called *Quakers*. It is true after a condemned Soul hath received a *Pardon* or *Juſtification* from his *King* freely without Deſert (upon the Princes *Mediation*) he declares his loyal and thankfull Obedience &c. but is this his *Pardon & Juſtification* as our ſubtle *Simpletons* imagine?

Again that *Abraham* was pardoned (or *juſtified*, it is all one) for his Work ſake as this blind Soul ſaith, how doth *Rom.* 3,4. and the *Epiſtle* to the *Galathians* cry out, and the experience of every true broken Heart cry out *Lyar* againſt ſuch proud and *Popiſh Blaſphemies*. Further, If all the *Righteouſneſs* of the beſt of men, that is their good *Thoughts*, good *Words*, good *Actions Aims: Prayers, Preachings, Sufferings*, be but as *Womens Menſtruous & filthy Clouts*, (as the *Moſt High* calls them) what *Popiſh* and frantick *Madneſs* is it in *Fox* to talk of *Juſtification before God by works or by Obedience?*

A *6th.* Inſtance is Pag 16. where he brings in *Henoch Howet* ſaying, *It is an Expreſſion of a dark deluded Mind to ſay that God is not diſtinguiſhed from the Saints.* G.*Fox* Anſw. But God and Chriſt is in 196] the Saints, and walks in the n, and he is is a *Reprobate* and out of the *Apoſtles Doctrine*. I reply to this *Canting Gypſie*, in Pag. 74. He denyes the Poſition of *Ralph Farmer*, viz. *That God the Creator is eternally diſtinct from all Creatures, and that Chriſt being God only in one Perſon, remains a diſtinct perſon from all Men and Angels.* Alſo in the ſame Page, *that God is diſtinct in his Being and Bleſ-ſedneſs*

The proud Quakers affirm no diſtinction between God & themſelves

sedness from all Creatures. - I Anſwer, is it not Sufficient that poor *Duſt* and *Aſhes*, poor *Chaff and
Stubble* may be admitted to a Parly with the *Heavenly Majeſty*, and receive *Smiles* of his *Countenance*,
in the Face of the only begotten *Prince & Mediator?* to be cloathed with the *Virgins diverſe Colours*, and heavenly *Affeɛtions*, but with the Devil
and our firſt Parents, we muſt aſpire to the throne
of the *Incomprehenſible Majeſty* and *Godhead* also?
Beſides, Let mans *Common Sence* be *Umpire*, is there
no *Diſtinɛtion* between *Infinite* and *Finite*? between
the *Infinite Ocean* of *Majeſty power, goodneſs, Wiſdome* &c., and the poor *Droſs*[1] of which Men &
Angels are *Partakers*? The King dwells in *White-
Hall* and in other of his *Royal Palaces*; is therefore
no Diſtinɛtion between the King and his Houfes,
though ſome may be braver then others : And yet
Fox ſaith his *Oppoſite* is a *Reprobate*. I ask why?
The only Reaſon *Fox* gives is, becauſe he licks not
up the filthy and helliſh *poyſon* of *Foxes childiſh* and
helliſh *Blaſphemy againſt the Eternal Godhead.*

A 7th. Inſtance is Pag. 22. where he brings in
Joſeph Kellet ſaying, ⌊*They be all alienated from God,
and Enemies until Faith*⌋ G. *Fox* Anſwers, [*So they
have denied their School-Maſter, which is until faith
which will keep them out of the Alienation which is the
Law.* *Joſeph Kellet*

`I Reply with *Joſeph Kellet*, (and the reſt of thoſe
excellent men whom *Fox* uſeth as *Diſhclouts* that *Our natural Aliena-
tion from
God* by nature our *Alienation* from God is ſo great, that
the fineſt and ſweeteſt nature in the World is ſo
                                                                  alienated

---

[1] "Drops." *R. W. Ms. Ann.*

alienated and *oppofite unto God*,that it refolves like
fome Ships(againft a *Turk or other Enemy*) we refolve to kill or be killd, yea and to fink by his fide
before we will yield to be taken by him : therefore doth the Holy Spirit fo often fpeak of mans
hating of God and Gods hating of him, yea of
mans abhorring of God, and Gods abhorring of
him, and *Rom.*8. that not only mans wifdome is at
enmity but enmity it felf againft God. Hence it
is, few *Kings*, few *Counfellours*, few *Nobles*, few
Schollars, few *Merchants*, &c. (who ufe to be the
Few ex- wifeft of men) relifh the Doctrine of the *Manger*
cellent men and the *Gallowes* for the more natural Wifdome the
faved more averfation from the foolifhnefs of the glad
news to poor, loft, drown'd and damn'd Mankind.

197] 2. Again, I fay as *Solomon, the legs of the
lame are not equal*, &c. for how doth it follow that
we deny the Law to be a School-mafter, pointing
unto Chrift, becaufe we deny the Law can bring us
to Chrift, which is fo indeed in the *Englifh, Gal.* 3.
but is not fo in the *Greek*, yea, how could the Law
of Ceremonies, pointing out the *Lamb of God*, or
the Law of *Do this and live*, keep out of the *Alienation*, do they (more then the Law of Creation)
leave any converting Impreffion from the Soul, until Gods hand open a door of Believing?

The *Dyal* points to the Sun, &c. but who receives benefit by it but he that skills it, and looks
upon it, &c. and yet the Dyal is not the Sun, &c.
but points as all the *Proyhecies, Ceremonies, Commandments*, (before his coming unto that God Man,
the Sun of Righteoufnefs) Chrift Jefus. As to
the

the reſt of his Anſwer, *viz.* [*Which will keep them out of the Alienation which is the Law*] it is a piece of bruitiſh *Nonſence* (as are not a few more in his Book) and it may be taken (like the Anſwer of the Devil at *Delphos*) many wayes : for it may be taken, that Faith will keep them out *Alienation :* or, the *School-Maſter* will keep them out of the *Alienation :* or whether the *Alienation* is the Law, or Faith is the Law, is doubtful, and if his mean- ing ſhould be that thy[1] Law either of Ceremonies, &c. ſhould keep them from being Alienated from God; and ſo being aƈtually to God, how not only will all the Holy Scriptures but all Mankinde, *Jews* and *Gentiles* call him a ſimple ane deſtroying Lyar ? *Our alien- ation from God*

An eighth Inſtance of *Foxes* poor, lame Anſwer is in *Page* 27. where he brings in *Richard Baxter,* ſaying [*To ſay that any is perfeƈt and without ſin is the Devil ſpeaking in man :*] G. *Fox* Anſwers, con- trary to the language of the Apoſtles and Chriſt, who bid them be perfeƈt, and the Apoſtle ſpake Wiſdome, among them that be perfeƈt : and ſaid they were made free from ſin, and it is the Devil ſpeaking in man that ſpeaks for ſin while Men are upon the Earth, for the Devil holds him up that makes men not perfeƈt which Truth makes men free again from the Devil, & ſpeaks in Man, and ſays be perfeƈt. *Richard Baxter*

I Reply, (*whether this willingly ignorant Soul knows or no*) *I know that the Devil knows that there is a Fallacie in this word Perfeƈtion.* 1. Sometime in Scripture, it ſignifies no more then *Sincerity & Up- rightneſs,* *The mat- ters of per- feƈtion*

¹ "Ye." R. W. Ms. Ann.

rightnefs, (and fo is tranflated) fometimes *Compleat-ness & Fulnefs* in its kinde, though but in a fmall Veffel; fometimes *Fortified, Strong & Armed*; and fometimes the *Fulnefs of the Godhead,* to whofe in-comprehenfible *Ocean* not one Drop can be given, nor one Drop taken from him. In *Mat.* 5. *Be ye Perfect,* &c We are not exhorted [198] to be equal with God in Holinefs, for that is to be God our felves, and being fet down in the throne of the God-head, to thruft the Eternal God out, for there can be but one in the Throne of the Godhead: But we are commanded to labour to be like unto God who not only is kinde to his Friends but his Ene-mies alfo: As when we are bid to be like the *Sun* to fhine upon the Bad as well as the Good: will a fober Soul imagine that we are bid to be as *Pure,* as *Glorious,* as *Vaft,* as *Swift* as the Sun is: but the Spirit tells us of a Generation *that are pure in their own eyes, and yet are not cleanfed from their filthinefs.*

Phil. 3. about perfection

Yea, but faith *Fox, Paul* fpake Wifdome amongft them that were perfect, *Phil* 3. I anfwer, what if the *Tranflators* had turned that word among them that be ftrong intelligent, capacious as the word often, and there fignifies, why doth *Paul* alfo fpeak-ing of fuch a ftrength or capacity as the Saints may attain to in this life profefs that he was yet (as it were but clambring up the Hill) this is the vote of all the higheft Saints in Scripture lamenting their Brethren and[1] Inabilities, and the Battle between the old Man and the new: Of which Battle G. *Fox* and his *Foxians* know not: for Sathan having Pof-fef
sion

---

[1] Erafe "Brethren and." *R. W. Ms. Ann.*

feſſion all is in peace. It hath been ever known that all Gods Children are like high and glorious *Queens & Empreſſes* who wittingly endure, not as the Holy Scripture ſpeaks) that ſuch an ugly Fiend as the Devil ſhould touch them, no not in an evil thought. 3. They are like *Fields & Gardens* in which the Husbandman and Gardiner allows not, nor endures not a Weed but with grief and endeavour of their extirpation. 4. And this is far from being Proctors and Advocates for ſin (as G. *Fox* moſt ſimply and impudently urgeth) for the known truth is, that *Fox* and his *Foxians* fall moſt foolifhly and fiercely upon ſuch as profeſs moſt holineſs, moſt ſincerity, and moſt Mortification, moſt love to God, and his only begotten the Spirit of Holineſs, & the Holy Scriptures or written Will of God. *The eſtate of Gods Children upon Earth*

A ninth Inſtance is in page 28. where G. Fox. tells how the ſame Author preached an external word [*Which the Scripture ſpeaks not of, but of the word that lives, abides and endures for ever, and of the Scriptures of Truth that cannot be broken: and of Gods words and Chriſts words, and that is not external: this is not agreeable to ſound words that cannot be condemned: but that is like his Doctrine that knows not the Eternal: but the Miniſters of Chriſt did not tell of an external word, but you being made by the will of man ſpeaks to the People of an external word.*] *Richard Baxter*

I Reply, The word (whether external, internal, or eternal) is a [199] ſimilitude, for we know God hath no Mouth, nor Tongue, nor Words as we have: but as *Kings*, and Generals of Armies or Navies, or any Commanders in chief ſignifie their

40   minds

minds by Speech, by Writing, yea by fign (at a dif-
tance) this Word or will, which was before in the
Kings breaſt, and internal is now outward or external.   Hence Chriſt Jeſus above all other wayes
of Gods manifeſting himſelf externally or outwardly is called the Word of God, and the Word
which was God.   Hence in common ſpeech we
call our Thoughts our ſelves [*So I think, &c. this is
my Word, my Vote, or Mind.*]

The great   And as it is the Field : If a General himſelf who
confequence firſt gave the external Word from his own internal
of a word Thoughts: if he forget the word in the night a
common Sentinel will make him ſtand, or fire upon him : and ſhall men be ſo careful in theſe tran-
ſitory buſineſſes, and ſhall we ſuffer open Enemies
to the true Lord Jeſus preſumptuouſly to paſs without the external word or mind of God, and auda-
ciouſly to deny ſuch a word at all to be ?   When
Chriſt Jeſus *Luke* 4 ſpake out of the *Prophet Iſaiah* :
and when *Paul* diſputed three Sabbath dayes out of
the Scriptures, and when *Apollos* mightily convinced
the *Jews* from the Scriptures that Jeſus was the
Chriſt, did they not uſe external, audible Expound-
ings and Applyings of that written word or mind
of God as the external and outward manifeſtation
of his internal and eternal holy Pleaſure.

Ellis   A tenth Inſtance is in page 32. where *G.Fox*
Bradſhaw brings in *Ellis Bradſhaw* ſaying [*The Quakers Spirit
doth teach them to honour no Man.*]   He Anſwers,
[*That is a Lye: for it teacheth them to have all Men in
eſteem, and to honour all men in the Lord; yet they
are convinced by the Law to be Tranſgreſſors if they
reſpect Mens perſons as you doe*]   I Reply,

I Reply, I have fpoken of their proud and lofty
behaviour toward all men, the *Higheft*, the *Eldeft*,
the *Holyeft*, upon the 10*th. Pofition*, of their Pride &c.
and therefore briefly fay, 1. That all men may fee
how truely they honour and efteem all men in the
Lord, and what Lord and honour it is that they
mean: when G.F. his firft word to his Oppofite is
in that moft provoking Term, *viz.* [*That is a Lye*]
in his very pleading and the very firft words of it. *The honor*
It is true Chrift Jefus and his Servants the Prophets *which the Quakers*
and Apoftles ufed fharp and bitter *Reproofs, Simili-* *give to*
tudes &c. but thus fuddenly at the firft dash to *others*
give fire. *Thou Lyeft, That is a Lye* &c. It fhews neither *Religion* nor *Civility* but a *Barbarous Spirit*, for
they that know the *Barbarians* know how com-
mon that word is in all their mouths. Tis true of
late divers of *Fox* his followers have followed him
in courtefie [200] looking toward you, taking you
by the hand, bowing and half uncovering the head
more or lefs &c. But this is but a *Revolt* and *Apof-*
tacy from their firft *Rigid Spirit* and *Cariage* as *Hum-*
phrey Norton rightly maintains againft them. Yea.
2. it is againft all *Foxes* and their firft Writings,
and this very place of *James* here urged, *viz.* they
are convinced by the Law if they refpeft mens
Perfons.

Again, tis true in Chrift Jefus there is neither
Bond nor Free, Male nor Female, and confequently
no Mafter no Man, no Father no Child no King
no Subjeft, but all are one in Chrift Jefus, and the
fecond Birth: as all are of one kinde in the *firft*
Adam, and the *firft Birth*.

1. Yet

*Civil
respect*

1. Yet firſt how full is the Holy Scripture of
Commands and Examples of Gods Children, giving refpective Words and Titles, aud Bowings, even
to perſons that knew not God? 2. *Fox* grants difference of gifts, and faith that ſome (in comparifon of others of them not ſo grown, &c. are Elders,
& ſure this is ſome refpect of perſons, according to
that of the 1 *Cor.* 12. Are all *Apoſtles*, are all *Prophets*, are all *Teachers*, &c. ·Therefore how ever
they Hypocritically lye, and pretend to honour all
men in the Lord: yet the moſt Holy and only
Wiſe knows how proudly, and ſimply, and barba-
rouſly they have run into uncivil and inhumane
Behaviours towards all their Superiours, the eldeſt
and higheſt, how that they have declared by principle and practice, that there are no Men to be
refpected in the World but themſelves as being
Gods and Chriſts. Tis true our *Engliſh Bibles* and
Grammar (as *Fox* his great Learning often objects)
makes thou to a ſingle perſon, and Thou in Holy
Scripture is uſed in a grave and refpective way unto
Superiours, unto *Kings*, and *Parents*, and God himſelf: But 1. (As I have ſaid) the *Hebrew* and the
Greek ſignifie no more Thou then You, and ſo may
be truely turned. 2. Every Nation, every *Shire*,
every *Calling* have their particular *Properties* or
Idioms of Speech, which are improper and ridiculous with others: Hence theſe ſimple Reformeis
are extreamly ridiculous in giving Thou and Thee
to every body, which our Nation commonly gives
to *Familiars* only; and they are extreamly and in-
ſufferably proud and contemptuous unto all their *Superiours*

*Thou &
Thee*

periours in ufing Thou to every body which our
Englifh Ideom or propriety of fpeech ufeth in way
of familiarity or of Anger, Scorn and Contempt. *Incivilities*
I have therefore publickly declared my felf, that a *ought to be moderately*
due and moderate reftraint and punifhing of thefe *punifht*
incivilities (though pretending Confcience) is as far
from Perfecution (properly fo called) as that it is a
Duty and Command of God unto all mankinde,
firft in Families, and thence into all mankinde
Societies.

201] Having thus through Gods mercifull help
gone through the 13*th Pofition* in publick and this
private fupply of fome few Inftances of their *Lame
writings* of out *G.F,* referving the liberty (if God
pleafe) of prefenting the *Reader* with a further
Apendix or *Addition* of fome few further *Inftances*
out of G. *Fox* his *Writings.* I haften to the 14
Propofition, the laft of the feven at *Providence.*
They read it publickly, viz. *the fpirit of the Quakers tends mainly to the reducing of Perfons from* Civility *to* Barbarifme, *to an* Arbitrary Goverment, *and* *The 14.*
the Dictates *and* Decrees *of that* fudden Spirit *that* *Pofition debated.*
acts them.   3. *To a fudden cutting off of People yea
of Kings and Princes that oppofe them.*   and 4. *To as
fierce and fiery* Perfecution *in matters of Confcience as
hath been, or can be practifed by any* Hunters *or* Perfecutors *in the World.*

I told them I could adde more Branches to this
Head, as unto the peace and civil Societyes of Mankind in the world : but I remembred my promife
of *Brevity,* and *W.E.* was often remembring me
fayinge *Is this thy Quarter of an hour ?* for I believe
                                    they

they ſtood here upon *Coals* and were not willing that I ſhould inſiſt upon it my full *Quarter*; and they haſted me on to prove that their *ſpirit* tended to *Barbariſme*: they ſaid (one and an other) that their *ſpirit* was an *Holy Spirit*, the *Spirit* of God, and the Grace of God had appeared to all men and had taught them to deny all *ungodlineſs* and wordly *luſts*, and to live *ſoberly, righteouſly & godly* in this preſent world.

I told them that in our *Native Countrey*, and in all *civilized Countreys*, the civility, Courteous Speech Courteous Salutation, and reſpective Behaviour was generally practiſed, oppoſite to the cariage of *Barbarous & Unciviliz'd People*. This I ſaid was according to the command of the holy Spirit in *Paul Eph* 4. and in *Peter*, 1. *Pet* 3. Be pitifull, be Courteous, *&c.* Such a Spirit was Chriſt Jeſus of, even to his greateſt *Oppoſites*, and to the greateſt *Sinners*, inſomuch that for his *Courteſie & Gentleneſs & Sociableneſs* with open *Sinners*, the dogged proud and ſullen *Phariſes* counted him a *Drunkard* and *Glutton*, a friend and *Companion* of *Publicans* and ſinners. We *Engliſh* were our ſelves at firſt wild and ſavage *Britains*: Gods mercy had civilized us, and we were now come into a wild and ſavage Countrey, without *Manners*, without *Courteſie*, ſo that generally except you begin with a *What Chear* or ſome other Salutation, you had as good meet an *Horſe* or a *Cow*, &c. And hath not the *Quaker ſpirit* been ſuch a *Spirit* amongſt us? have we not known perſons formerly loving, courteous &c. and as ſoon as this *Spirit* hath come upon them have not our eyes ſeen

them

W E. &c ſtanding upon coals.

Civility and Courteſie.

N. Eng. one work to civilize a Barbarous People.

them pafs by their *Familiars*, their *Kindred*, [202 their *Elders* and *Superiours*, and though kindly fpoken to, not give a *Word* or a *Look* toward them? as if they were not worthy of a *word* or a *look* from fuch *High Saints* &c. How like indeed have they been to the Popifh Saints in a *Proceffion*, they *See not, Hear not, Speak not* &c.? or like thefe very *Barbarians*, and therefore I faid,   2. *G.Fox* in his book affirms that the *Converfation* of thefe very *Barbarians*, in many things were better then his *Oppofites* &c.   I mufed in my felf (being much acquainted with the *Natives*) what G. *Fox* fhould mean, he not having been in *N.England* when he wrote that paffage; but fince I have heard that the *Quakers* have commended the fpirit of the *Indians*, for they have feen them come into *Englifh Houfes* and fit down by the fire, not fpeaking a word to any body: But this cariage of the *Indians* proceeds from a *bruitifh fpirit*, for generally they have boldly come in without *Knocking* or asking of leave, and fit down without any refpect in word or gefture to the Governour or chief of the Family whofoever (juft the *Quakers* general fafhion and Spirit)

Further I told them, that in fome refpect the fpirit and cariage of the *Quakers* was worfe then that of the *Indians*, for if they were faluted by the *Englifh* in the *high-way* or coming into an *Houfe*, they are very ready to receive your *Salutation* kindly, and return you another: But commonly we know that it is not fo with the *Quakers bruitifh fpirit*. 2. The *Indians* morning and evening, and upon all meetings, they give a refpective and

proper

The Quakers monftrous Incivility.

The Indians and Quakers of one Spirit.

proper *Salutation* to their own *Superiours*, and sometimes in gesture as well as speech.   3. Although
the *Indians* are *bruits* in their *Nakedness* both men
and women, yet they never appear (no not in private houses) *stark naked* as the *Quaker men* and
women doe : yea they so abhor such a *bruitishness*,
(except it be in their mad *Drunkenness*, for then
they will be *stark naked*) that as to their *Female
kind*, they will carefully from their birth keep on
some modest covering before them.   *W.E.* rose up
and said they did abhor *Uncleaness* as well as our
selves or any, their women were sober, holy and
Modest, and would not endure (some of them) to
have a Toe to be seen naked : but he said if the
Lord God did stir up any of his *Daughters* to be a Sign

*The Qua-
kers again
maintain
their
womens
Nakednefs.* of the *nakedness* of others he believed it to be a
great Cross to a Modest womans Spirit, but the
Lord must be obeyed.   *John Stubs* immediately
seconded him, and quoted again the Command to
Isaiah, Chap. 20. to go naked, & he added, whereas
I said at *Newport* that it was in the time of *Signs,
Types, Figures &c.* He would now prove that all
Signs were not abolished by the coming of Christ;
for *Agabus Act.* 20. took *Pauls* [203] *girdle* and
bound himself.   I replyed that was indeed one of
my Replyes at *Newport,* and I was yet far from
binding the *sweet Influences* of the holy One by
*Dreams, Visions, immediate Impulses Revelations,
Signs* &c. but withall I said that before the coming
of the *Lord Jesus* and at his coming was the time

*Signs and
Figures
discussed.* and season of such *Appearances* from God : now he
hath fully declared his mind to us by the *Personal*
and

and moſt wonderfull coming of his *Son* out of his
Boſome : who had commanded his Pen-men to
write his *Birth*, his *Life*, his *Life* his *Doctrine* his
Miracles, his *Death*, *Reſurrection*, *Aſcenſion* and
promiſe of *Return* to us : he had alſo preſerved
theſe holy *Writings* & *Records* moſt wonderfully
that (*Joh* 20) we might believe in him, follow him
and live with him. But 2. I ſaid what did this
concern the *monſtrous* ſtripping their *women naked*,
of which we never heard a tittle either at coming
of the Lord Jeſus, or in thoſe proper ſeaſons of
ſuch *Adminiſtrations* before his *Appearance*. *John* ^{The Qua-}
Stubs ſaid he had been a *Quaker* 19 years and yet ^{kers ſpirit}
had never ſeen a woman *Naked*, and ſome of the ^{enraged.}
Quakers ſaid to me aloud, *when didſt thou ſee any of*
our women Naked? and another of them ſaid, *We*
did not think that thou wouldeſt have been ſuch a wicked
man. Theſe two (though of the *Quakers ſpirit*) yet
of long time had been Loving and reſpective to
me, but now they were enraged, ſo that I ſaid unto
my *Antagoniſts*, ſeeing ſome *Heat* is riſen about
theſe matters, I will if you pleaſe go on to the ſec-
ond *Branch* of this 14*th Poſition*. I told them the ^{The Qua-}
2*d. Branch* was, ^{kers ſpirit}
^{tending to}
    That the Spirit of the *Quakers* tendeth to bring in ^{Arbetrary}
an *Arbetrary Government*. I ſaid we all knew how ^{Govern-}
it had coſt the blood of *thouſands* & *ten Thouſands* ^{ment.}
this matter of *Goverment* & *Lawes* : that the Moſt
High & only Wiſe chooſing one *People* and *Nation*
of Iſrael to be his own, he wrote them Laws (ſome
with his own inconceivable *finger* written) and ſome
by *Moſes* his inſpired *Pen-man*, it pleaſed him not

41   to

to leave their *Wifeſt* and *Holyeſt Kings & Gover-nours* without written known Lawes, with *Rewards* and *Penaltyes* annexed. But I argued if that were true that all the *Quakers* were guided in all they ſaid and did by the immediate Spirit of God (as I proved *Fox* maintained) then if they obtain higher or lower Governours of their Spirits, Surely it ſhines cleer that there is no need of Laws for them to rule & act by, for they had no need of Scrip-ture, and ſeing the *Immediate Inſpirations* of God would not ſuffer them to erre in Judgment, for as they ſaid of the holy Scripture, they had no need of it, for they had the holy Scripture within them, their Teacher within them, and all that they ſpake was Scripture, and the voice of God, *&c.* So I ſaid much more [204] might it be ſaid of Mens *Laws & Writings*; that ſurely they had no need of them : for what could be more juſt and equal, more pure & holy in all Caſes Controverſies & Buſineſſes, then the immediate *Voice of God?* *W. E.* ſaid, what doſt thou fill peoples ears with ſtrange *Notions*, as if the People of God called *Quakers* were a lawleſs people and would bring all Goverment and all Laws to nothing ? We are for righteous *Goverment*, and righteous *Lawes*, we are not for any to rule by *Force*, and more he ſpake to this purprſe.

I Replyed, that he miſtook me, by an *Arbetrary Goverment* I did not intend a Goverment ruling by *Force* (for there could be no Goverment in. the world without the *Sword*) but *Arbitrary I* ſaid came from *Arbitrium* which ſignified *Will* or pleaſure : and ſo my *Argument* was, that Perſons immediately

The Qua-kers have no need of Scripture much leſs of the written Laws of men

The Qua-kers & none elſe in the World fit for Govnrn-ment as they judge

ſpeaking

fpeaking from God, it was impertinent and profane to clog and cumber them with *Lawes*, for the Voice of God (the *Law* of all *Laws*) proceeded out of their mouth, then which there could be none more Juft, more Wife, more Holy.

Here ftood up an *Aged man* (and as able as moft in the company, *T. A.*) though much of late adhering to the *Quakers* and faid, Methinks there is *Weight* in Mr. *VVilliams* his *Argument*. He being a noted man, and his voice very audible (and fo heard by all) *VV. E.* was forced to take notice of his fpeech, and faid, wherein is there any weight in it ? *T. A.* Anfwered, why if a *Magiftrate* be *immediately infpired by God*, and fpeaks *Gods Laws & Sentence*, fure there feems to be no need of any other *Laws*. They faw they were in a *Pound*, and I perceived it, and yet (not being willing to *grate* upon them but) watching my time (as I was glad all along) to pafs handfomly from one *Point* unto another, I faid unto them : if they pleafed I would pafs on to the *Third Branch, viz. That the Quakers Spirit tending to the fudden cutting off of People, yea, Kings and Princes that oppofe them.* I here told them that I muft crave their patience whiles I muft profefs my fears, leaft that Spirit by which they were guided, might run them upon their own and others temporal Deftruction. I told them I thought they had no fuch thing in their Thoughts or Eye at prefent : but if power of the Sword come into their hand, it was eafie to imagine that whom their Spirit (infallible) decreed to death, *Peafant* or *Prince*, if it were poffible, he muft be executed,

&c.

T A his Teftimony

The 3d. Branch

&c. *W. Edm.* said, *Thou here makeſt a falſe and lying charge againſt the People of God, who are peaceable and quiet and yielding to Magiſtrates,* &c. I
Replied, I charge them with no matter of Facts:
but I charge them and their Spirit with a tendency,
&c. For why [205] might they not ſay, that *Abraham*, with an impulſe was killing *Iſaak*, *Moſes* the
Egyptian, *Ehud* killing *Eglon* the King of *Moab*,
Samuel hewing *Agag* the King of *Amelech* in pieces,
and *Paul*, *Ananias* and *Saphira*, &c. and why not
Sathan ſtir up his Inſtruments to pretend the like
Spirit, as we know he hath done both in former
& latter days?

My Antagoniſts joyntly bid me ſhew when any
Immediate of the *Quakers* had done ſo: I *Anſw.* They ſpake
impulſes not to the point, &c. for I did not charge them to
have done ſo, but that their Spirit tended to it: I
was ſaying that *Faubord* at *Grindleton* was killlng
his Son in imitation of *Abraham*, if his Sons crying out, and the breaking open of the Houſe had
not prevented: and that *James Parnel* moved by
this Spirit to Faſt forty dayes, &c. periſhed the
eleventh day, &c. but perceiving more than ordinary heats, and that *W. Edm.* charged me that I
had a falſe heart of mine own, and would meaſure
others by my buſhel: I told them of the wonderful actings of *Tho. Munſter*, and *J. Becold*, and *Fiſer
& Knipperdoling*, &c. in *Germany*, and of their Pretences, Murthers, Poligamies, and all by the Spirit,
The Kings &c. I told them that our *Royal Sovereign* his
Grandfa- *Grandfather Henry 4th* of *France* (that famous and
ther H. 4.
of France wonderful Man) he was ſtab'd to death by a Frier
                                                    pretending

pretending a Vifion of Angels on Chriftmas night, *murthered upon pretence of a vifion of Angels*
who commanded him from God to difpatch and
kill the King, which he moft defperately effected.
W. Edm. interrupted me, and fpake (to this effect)
why fhould we fuffer this man thus to wrong the
innocent people of God? we will meafure him
with his own Bufhel: For thy Book declares thy
approving of the killing of the Kings Father, and
faid where is the Book? At which word *W. Harris* (a Fire-brand of *Town*, and *Colony & Country*)
rofe up, and carried a Book (which they faid was
mine) to *W. Edmundfon*: I perceived that *W. Edm. W Edm.
& W.H.* who was for any Religion, and a malici- *& W.
Harris*
ous mortal enemy to all good, had been a plotting: *their mal*
and I faid openly I knew what malicious bloody *lice*
counfel had been between *W. Har.* and themfelves: *towards me*
but they would finde themfelves befooled, for there
was nothing in the matter but ridiculous malice:
for all of us knew that *W.H.* loved the *Quakers*
(whom now he fawn'd upon) no more then he did
the *Baptifts* (whom he till now fawn'd on) but
would love any, as a Dog for his Bone, for Land,
which he had a long Suit for as was known to all
the Country and their coft.   Hereupon Capt.
Green of *Warwick* (Magiftrate) defired that fuch
matters might be forborn, and others fpake to the
fame purpofe: and *J,Stubs* and others are faid to
fpeak to *W. Edm.* to forbear, fo that the Book was
laid afide and delivered again to that [206] malicious bloody Soul *W. Harris*. I challenged them
again and again to read and improve what poffibly
they could, which I knew was no more then fome
words

words applauding the *Parliaments Juſtice* and *Mercy*: which theſe *Bloody Sophiſters* would (like *Wolves
& Foxes* conſtrue as my approving the *Kings* Death,
which God knows I never approved to this day.

Upon this *Occaſion* I may now inform the *Reader*,
how eaſily the malicious Spirit of *W. Edm. & W.
Har.* met in one: formerly no man amongſt us
had ſpoken more ſcornfully of the *Quakers* then *W
Harris*, now he extreamly, privately and publickly
fawns upon them, ſeeing them my Enemies, who
had ever been his Friend, and never his Enemy but
in his outragious practiſes againſt *Town, & Colony &
Country*. He was a *Pretender* in *Old England*, but
in *New* my experience hath told me, that he can
be one with the *Quakers*, yea *Jeſuits* or *Mahumetans* for his own worldly ends and advantage. He
is long known to have put *Scorns & Jeers* upon the
eminent Inhabitants of Town and Country. He
hath been notorious for quarrelling, and challenging, and fighting, even when he pretended with
the *Quakers* againſt *Carnal Weapons*; ſo that there
ſtands upon Record in the Town-book of *Providence* an Act of *Disfranchiſement* upon him, for fighting and ſhedding Blood in the ſtreet, and for maintaining and allowing it (for ought I know) to this
day. Then he turns *Generalliſt*, and writes againſt
all *Magiſt-ates, Laws, Courts, Charters, Priſons,
Rates*, &c. pretending himſelf and his Saints to be
the *Higher Powers* (as now the *Quakers* do) and in
publick writings he ſtir'd up the *People* (moſt ſe-
ditiouſly and deſperately threatning to begin with
the *Maſſachuſets*) and to cry out *no Lords, no Maſters,*

ters, as is yet to be feen in his Writing : this coft my felf and the Colony much trouble. Then (as the Wind favoured his ends) no man more cries up Magiftrates : then not finding that pretence, nor the People called *Baptifts* (in whom he confided) ferving his ends. He flies to *Connecticut Colony* (then and ftill in great Conteft with us) in hopes to attain his gaping about Land from them, if they prevail over us : to this end he in publick Speech and Writing applauds *Connecticut Charter* and damns ours, and his Royal Majefties favour alfo for grant-ing us favour (as to our Confciences) which he largely endeavours by writing to prove the **K.** *Ma-jefty* by Laws could not do. My felf (being in place) by Speech & Writing oppofed him, & Mr.*B. Ar-nold* then *Governour*, and Mr. *Jo. Clark Deputy Governour*, Capt. *Cranftone* and all the Magiftrates, he was Committed for fpeaking & writing againft his Majefties *Honour, Prerogative, & Authority* : He 207] lay fome time in Prifon until the *General Af-fembly*, where the *Quaker* (by his wicked, ungodly, and difloyal plots) prevailing, he by their means gets loofe, and leaves open a door for any man to challenge the Kings Majefty for being too Godly or Chriftian, in being too favourable to the Souls of his Subjects againft his Laws, &c.

I had thought to have declared thus much pub-lickly, and how feafonably the Kings *Declaration* came over againft him : alfo how that one *General Affembly*, and another, and another had been troubled with him, &c. and fined him, &c. but now my *Lord Edmundfon* grew hot, and told me that I *W Edm. his igno-rant and impudent zeal and upbraid-ings*

had

had charged the *People* of the Lord with many
great and grievous Charges, which he said I could
not prove, yea, he said he would speak it before
the Lord, I had not proved one of them, and therefore he warned me, being an old Man, that I
should not carry such a *Burden* on my back to my
Grave, and (among other angry insultings) he said
he heard I had been a Magistrate, and said I was a
fit man to be a Magistrate that would so wrong-
fully charge the Innocent. *Jo. Stubs* spake to the
same effect, and how I had hindred them from going about the work of the Lord: he said also, that
it was only the Light which they had spoke for,
and that some had interrupted them, but he con-
fest that *Roger Williams* himself had not done it:
I saw God in their *Confession*.

And for the last point and Branch of the 14 *Po-*
sition, viz. [*Their Persecuting Spirit*) having spoken
to it before, and finding them unwilling to mention it, I urged it not, having (at *Newport*) shewed
from *Page* 170 of *G. Fox* his Book, [*That the Mag-*
istrate (*that is the Magistrate in their Light*) *ought to*
Subject the Nation to his Light, else he is not a faith-
ful Magistrate.] In *page* 90.&96. *G. Fox* sets up his
Saints (as formerly *W. Harris* his Antagonists) to
be the higher *Powers*, as knowing who Worship
God aright, and who not, and only able to judge
of *Powers, Magistrates, Kingdomes* and *Churches*.
Herein *W.H.* and the *Quakers are one*, &c.   It is
true that *W. Edm.* declared that the People of God
were not to meddle with *Carnal Weapons* : as also
that before time, many of the *People* of God called
Quakers,

The point of perse- cution

So many Quak. so many Popes

The pre- tended meekness of the Quakers.

Quakers, had been Souldiers, *Captains and Colonels*, yet now coming to the *Light*, they had laid down their *Carnal Weapons*: but if *Fox* fay true in his Book, either they *Mope* or *Equivocate*: for *Fox* fpeaks of the Magiftrates for Chrift in the aforefaid Page 170. he difcerns who be I*dolaters*, who not, which true Churches, which not, and are to praife the *VVell Doers*, and terrifie the *Evill Doers* with the Carnal and Material *Sword*, or elfe they talk nothing.

208] But 2. If this *Confeffion* & *Profeffion* of theirs were not; yet if Chrſt Jefus fay true, *viz.* *The Tongue tells to all the World what the Heart is*: was there ever People profeffing the Name of Chrift Jefus (except the *Papifts*) fo Reproaching the *Proteftants*, and amongft the *Proteftants* was there any ever fo *Reproaching* & *Reviling* the Profeffing and Confcientious People as *Quakers do*: was there ever any known (profeffing the fear of God in fo high a meafure) fo fharp and cutting in their Tongues even to eminently, knowing and Confcientious perfons, [*Thou Lyar*, *thou* Serpent, *thou* Cain, *thou* Judas *thou* Hipocrite, *thou* Devil] &c. Shall we rational*ly* queftion whether their hands (like *Simeons* and *Levyes*) will not be as fierce and cruel, if the moft holy and only Wife permits *Whips &* *Halters*, *Swords* & *Fagots* to fall into their Hands? and what did *Sam. Fifher*, & *Ed. Burrowes* write lefs to the Souldiers at *Dunkirk*, that if they received the light they fhould on to *Rome*.

The tongue of the Quakers is the Vipers what will their hand be

The Quakers common language

3. Have we not known the deceitfulneſs of mens hearts fly out into greater matters then *Perfecution?*

42

The cheat- *fecution?* *Hazael* earneftly afked whether the Pro-
ing of phet thought him a *Dog* that he fhould doe fuch
mans
heart matters &c. *Pendleton* vow'd his Collops fhould
fry ere he would to *Mafs* in Q *Maryes* dayes, and
yet to *Mafs* he went and perfecuted others alfo that
would not bow to the Image as he had done.

Juft here Capt *Green* of *Warwick* defired leave
to fpeak to two things,

1. To immediate *Revelations*, fuch as *Abraham*
and *Mofes* and *Ehud* had.

Capt 2. As to the Soul being a part of *God:* I was
Green weary and withdrew, but afterward Capt. *Green*
his 2 points told me that none of them were willing to fpeak
with my
Antagonift punctualy to either of thefe two, but rather defired to wave them as a bftrufe and high *matters*
and *Myfteryes.*

Then *Pardon Tillinghaft* (a leading man among
the *People* called *Baptifts* at *Providence*) he preft
againft them the continuation of *Chrifts* Ordinances
Pardon untill he came. The *Quakers* faid Chrift was come
Tillinghaft
his dif- again to his *Difciples.* He replyed, that after *Chrifts*
courfe with *Afcention* he fpake of another *Coming,* his fecond
my
Oppofite Coming, *Heb* 9. *W. E.* fel to Prayer, (as with me
he ftl to *Preaching*) *Pardon Tillinghaft* (as himfelf
told me) declared to them, that he was free to difcourfe with them, but he was not free to joyn with
them in *Worfhip:* fo he departed, and after *W E.*
his *Prayer,* the whole Affemby.

The Con- And thus it pleafed the *God* and *Father of Lights*
clufion was
ordered by and *Mercyes* to bring us to the end of this 4*th*
the Father dayes Conteft, and the end of the whole matter,
in

in much *Peace* and *Quietneſs*, and the Conſideration *of Mercies with much peace and*
of matters left to every mans *Soul*, and *Conſcience,* *quietneſs*
and ſo doe I this *Narrative*, which God knows is *which had*
the *S*um and Subſtance of all our *Tranſactions:* *not been if*
    Unto his *Eternal Majeſty* therefore I humbly *I had in-*
offer *Eternal Praiſe*, by and in the *Eternal Son of* *inſulted &*
God, the true *Lord Jeſus Chriſt:* whome I deſire *upbraided as W Edm.*
joyfully to expect to return from *Heaven,* as liter- *did.*
ally and perſonally as all true *Chriſtians* hold (*Act.*
1.) he is *aſcended.*

AN APEN-

A N

A P E N D I X

O R

Addition of Proofs unto my thirteenth Po-
ſition,   Viz.

That the Quakers Writings are Poor, Lame and
Naked (not able to defend themſelves, nor comfort
the Souls of others with any ſolidity.)

More
Proofs of
thᵉ Qua-
kers lame
writings
I could produce moſt of their chief extant,
but I have been occaſioned to deal with G. *Fox,*
their great *Goliah,* in ſome Scores of Paſſages of
his Book in Folio, in the *Narrative* aforeſaid.

Unto which I judge fit to adde the Scores
following, faithfully preſenting his Oppoſites,
Words (as he quotes them) his *Anſwers*
and then my *Reply*: let him that
Readeth underſtand.

I Have

Have chosen out the short Assertions of G. *Fox* his *Opposites* as he quotes them, and his short Answer for brevity sake, &c.

1. The first of this Addition I name, is in *pag.* 6. of G. *Fox* his Folio Book, where he brings in *Samuel Eaton* saying [The *Apostle* saying to the Saints, *You know all things*, it is [2] an excessive speech] G. *Fox* Answer [contrary to *John*, and would make him a *Lyar*, the *Minister* of God : so he is in the false spirit gone out into the World, contrary to 1. *Ioh.*2. Who know all things]

1 John 2.
You know
all things.

I Reply, 1. I cannot learn that they litterally hold, that they know all things knowable as God (though G. *Fox* writes that they know all things as God (yet I can not think them so gross as to imagine that they know all things, past. present, and to come, (as the Devil pretends he doth, and offers to reveal so much to some Conjurers) but I judge they must come to some figurative meaning, as their opposite writeth.

For 2. What hinders (as before) but if the *Quakers* be *Omniscient*, and know all things, but they should be also *Omnipotent* and do all things, for so *Paul* writes, *Phil.* 4. *I can do all things* : I know they say, they are one with God and Christ, and they know all things, and can do all things ; and yet this sense which litterally is so Proud and Blasphemous, must be made out by a meaning and by a figure (which they cry out against in others.)

3. Therefore doth not the Spirit of God in *Prov.* 28. open this to us, saying, *Evil men understand not Iudgement, but they that seek the Lord understand all things* :

About
knowing
all things.

things : that is, God anfwers their Prayers, and ina-
bles them to know and do, all that he calls them
to, when the *proud* and *fcornful* are rejected.

4. Therefore I believe it is that the moft Holy
and moft juft and wife Lord leaves thefe poor proud
and fcornful Souls to feek *wifdome* and not to find
it, to be ignorant, *knowing nothing,* (as *Gods Spirit*
fpeaketh,) and to difcover their *Ignorance* in fo
many *Fundamentals* of *Chriftianity,* and in fo many
practices immodeft, irrational, and more then favage, as
I have proved againft them.

The Qua-kers proud of knowl-edge yet knowing nothing.

2. In *pag.* 11. G. *Fox* brings in John *Bunyan,*
&c. faying, [The *Scripture* plainly denies that *Confcience* can *juftifie* though it may *condemn.* [He Anfw.
[which is contrary to Scripture, where the Apoftle
faith Rom. 2. *their Confciences either accufing or excufing.*] And again, *herein do I exercife my felf to
have a Confcience void of offence toward God and toward Men,* and the *Light* condemns, which you
call *Confcience,* &c.

Pag. 11. Joh Bun-yan.

Con-fcience condemn-ing not Juftifying.

I Reply, *Confcience* (in *greek Latine* and *Englifh,*
&c. fignifies a **Knowing** together : a *Reflexion,* or
looking back of a mans mind or *Spirit* upon it *felf,*
in point of *Juftification* or *pardon of fin* [3]. *Confcience* looks upon a curfed rotten Nature, then
upon millions of fins of *Omiffion* and *Commiffion,*
which how to fatisfie an infinite Juftice for, and to
attain a new heart and nature is the high bufinefs
and out of the reach or thought of that poor *Confcience,* which every man *Iew* or *Gentile* Civilized,
or *Pagan* comes into the World with. In the great
Tryal of the three greateft finners that ever were

The Qua-kers con-feft their light to be Confci-ence.

The great Tryal of the 3 greateft actual Sin-ners that ever were

in

in this World, the Devil, and the firſt Man, and
firſt Woman : two of them their Conſciences condemned them, and they confeſt the Faſt (though
with extenuation and Excuſes) could this their
condemning Conſcience (eſpecially with mincing
of ſin as all mens natural Conſciences do) I ſay,
could this Conſcience or Confeſſion pardon their
ſin, reniew their hearts and be their Juſtification
(or clearing) and Salvation?

Tis true *Abimelechs* Conſcience juſtified him
from the Faſt of lying with *Abrahams* Wife, as
well as *Ioſephs* Conſcience juſtified him from the The ex-
falſly imputed guilt of lying with his *Miſtreſs*, or cuſing of
attempting of it : But was this the Pardon of ſcience
Abimelechs ſin, his Juſtification and Salvation after
the *Canting Language* of this poor *Fox*, and all the
Foxians that I have ſeen (and *I* have read all I
could come at &c.)

Oh how little do theſe poor *Beaſts* ſeek what in-
finite Juſtice, infinite Puniſhment, infinite *Payment*
is ! what Conſcience truly pacified is, upon the
Pardon of Sin, and true peace of Conſcience
Sprinkled with the Blood of that only Lambe of
God Chriſt Jeſus.

Amongſt the *Indians* I have known ſome falſely
accuſed of ſtealing *Engliſh* Mens goods, of killing
Engliſh Mens Cattle, yea, of *Murther*; and *I* have
heard them ſay that *Manit*: that is God and their
own Souls know they are Innocent. This *Innocency* who queſtions but that it is their plea and excuſe and diſcharge from that guilt falſly charged on
them : If this be all that G. *Fox* ſaith ! *he beats*
the

the Air and hath no Enemy: No, no, It is a *Con-ſcience* Juſtification within, a *Chriſt* ſhedding his blood within; (in a ſubtle fly oppoſition to the pardon without us from the *K.* of *Heaven* for the ſake of his Son wi thout us) this is the buſineſs which theſe Traitors to the *K.* of *Heaven* aim at : Now they will be perfect and never more admit a ſinful thought ; and this their *preſent Honeſty* ſhall pay the old ſcore of a Curſed Na- [4] ture, and millions of Treaſons, and Rebellions in Commiſſions and Omiſſion againſt the God of Heaven.

A fit Sim-
litude uſed
before Q.
Eliz beth
concern-
ing pardon
of ſin or
Juſtifica-
tion, wh'c^h 1
had from
one
that heard
it being
near the
Queen

It was a pertinent Similitude uſed before *Q Eliz-abeth*. A King ſent for his Lord Deputy of a Province to come home and give account *&c.* The guilty *Deputy* goes to a great friend deſires his Company, *&c.* he ſaid, He was ſent for alſo himſelf, and feard his own *Iſſue*: He goes to others deſires their Company, *&c.* They make excuſe and promiſe to have him or the way, *&c.* Then goes the *Deputy* to an old *friend*, who promiſed to go with him, and what he could ſpeak for him : only, if the *K.* aſked, he muſt ſpeak the Truth, and that will be (ſaid he) your Deſtruction, and therefore adviz'd him to make the young *Prince* his Friend and *Mediator* for whoſe ſake the King would deny no Favour, no pardon, no Honour, *&c.*

Con-
ſcience the
greateſt
Friend or
Foe.

The Application may be large and uſeful : but in ſhort, A Soul Summond to Death and Judgement, looks to Relations, *&c.* they all Anſwer ,they are in the ſame *Caſe*, &c. It looks to *Wordly Eſtate*, &c: they tell us they will go with us as far as the *Grave* and *provide* a *Coffin*, and a *Sheet*, and a *Burial*, &c.   3. The

3. The old *friend is Conscience*, who will go with
us, but can be a *thousand witnesses* against us, *&c.*
It follows then clearly that the *young Prince* is the
true *Lord Jesus Chrift*, not vanifhed away into a
Light in every *dark dungeon* in the World, but Confcience faith he is litterally afcended *up* into *Heaven*, and will as literally *make his speedy Return*
again to Iudgement.

The third Inftance, G. *Fox pag.* 12. brings in the
fame Author, faying, [the Light doth not *shine* ¹n
the *Confciences* of them that be *lost*.] The Anfwer,
[But *Iohn* faith, *he Light shines in darkness but the
darkness cannot comprehend it*, and there is *that of
God* in the *Children of Difobedience* and *Reprobates*,
as in *Rom.* 1. and 2. Chapters.] I Reply, G. *Fox* is
here in his *Burrough*, and takes not the word *Light*
in the fame Senfe his *Oppofite* doth, (the Common
trick of *Cheators*): His *Oppofite* takes it not for the
heavenly Lights Sun, Moon, nor *Earthly Light* of
Fire, Candles, 'precious Stones, nor the *Metaphorical*
Light of mens minds differing them from *Beafts*,
Birds, Fishes: Nor the *Light* of *peace joy* and *Prof-*
perity, call'd in Scripture Light, *&c.*   Nor the
Light and Evidence of *witnefs* or *Reafon* in Cafes
depending : Nor the *Light* of the *holy Scriptures*,
and the *preaching* and offering of a [5] *Saviour* to
poor loft Sinners: But, for that *awakening, faving*
Light, convincing all mens Condition to be miferable and damnable : of *Grace* and *mercy* offered and
applied to a Soul by the *good News* of a *Saviour*
fomeway heard of, and the *holy Spirit* the *finger* or
power of God.

Pag. 2. Jo.
Bunyan,
&c.

The va-
rious
meanings
of the
word
Light

43   G. *Fox*

G. *Fox* faith, this faving Light is in mankind: only perfons don't mind it, and fo *Chriſt Ieſus* is *Crucified*, and flain in them, and God, and Chriſt, and Spirit, and Light, &c. are all captived, hindred from working, yea, altogether killd & flain in them becauſe a Soul doth not mind them, and hearken to Chriſt in them.

Ah poor fimple bruitiſh Imagination that ever it fhould enter into the thoughts of Men profeſſing to be Chriſtians, *&c.* or of men profeſſing to know more than the *Wolves* and *Foxes* in the wilderneſs: I have fpoke to this before, therefore a word only to G. *Fox* his proof, *Rom.* 1. and 2. *Chapt.* From thefe two Chapters he proves that there is that of God in the Children of *Diſobedience*, and *Reprobates*, who denies it. For there is fomething of God, that is from the power and wiſdome of God in the Fallen Spirits the Devils themfelves. But I know by that of God, G. *Fox* means God himfelf (*preſt down as a Cart with ſheaves*) the holy Seed *Chriſt Ieſus*, (under the *Clods*,) the holy *Spirit* in *priſon*, for the Soul is a part of the *Eſſence* or Being of God himfelf.

But that there is here a word or title of Colour to any of this dirt and filth flung in the face of the *Majeſtie* of *Heaven*?

This Scripture fpeaks of the *work* (or working) *of the Law written in their hearts*: but what is this to a fecond *writing* of the holy *Scriptures*, or *writing inſpired* into the heart by the moſt holy *Spirit*? yea, what is this to a third *writing* of their *Names* written in *Heaven* in the *Lambs Book of Life*? yea, what

Marginal notes:
Rom. 1. & 2? Nor favouring Chriſt in all mankind

Four writings confidered

what is this to a fourth *writing*, the *writing* of the
new Covenant Confifting of Sin and a *new heart, a
heart of flefh*, in which his Law is written as formerly *in Tables of Stone*, and yet we poor men of
I*abefh Gilead* muft leave the Teftimony (as *Gilead*
imports) and fuffer *Nahufh* (the *Serpent*) to put out
our *right eyes*, and believe that every man hath the
new *Covenant Chrift Iefus* and the *Kingdom* of God,
&c. with the *Pharifees* in every *mans heart and yet
he never knows of it* ?

4. Inftance : In the fame pag. 12 he brings in
the fame Author, faying, [It is a *Counterfeiting* of
the *new Birth* for men to [6] follow the *Light*
wherewith men coming into the world are inlightned : G. *Fox* Answ. [which none comes to the
new Birth but who come to the *Light*, which every
man, *&c.* in which believing is a *Child* of the
Light, &c.

I Reply: G. *Fox* runs round agren and again, Several
like the *windmil Sails* : It is faith he, no *Counter-* Expofit-
feiting of a *new Birth*, why, becaufe it is no *Coun-* ions of
terfeiting : [none comes to the *new Birth* but who in Jhon 1.
comes to the *Light*, &c.]

As to the words in *Iohn* 1. [1]*Hitchcock* at *Newport*
alleadged, that it was not in his Bible [*enlightneeth
every man*, but lighteth every man, *&c.*] John *Stubs*
lockt in his *greek Teftament*, and confeft it was Pho-
tizes which is not *inlightneth* but *Lighteth*.

2. As to the *Light*, We know there are two
Opinions how *Chrift lighteth every man*, &c. Firft,
as God in the *Creation*. 2. As God man and *Mediatour*,

[1] Infert "W." *R. W. Ms. Ann.*

tour, and that the Greeks word *Erchomenon* doth not relate to the word [*anthropon*] the man or every man that cometh into the world, but [*phoce*] Light, and that it muſt be read in this Senſe, *viz* that *Chriſt Ieſus* the true *Light* cometh into the world lighteth every man that is in the world freely that will receive him : Even as many (whomſoever) look up to him, (as *Iohn* 3.) the ſtung Iſraelites to the *brazen Serpent* : and that *Chriſt Ieſus is* the Light of the world, John 8. and 12. to as many as receive him according to 1 *Iohn* 12. and that the meer phraſe imports no more then a *Light* held forth to all in the world, as the Sun in the *Heavens*, and *Chriſts Followers*, *Math.* 5. are called by *Chriſt Ieſus the Light of the World.* Thus the word *all* and *every man* (as I hinted before) is uſed not abſolutely, but *Comparatively*, and is *figuratively* taken in many places, and four[1] times in that one *ver.* 1 Col. 28. *viz.* warning *every man and teaching every man in all wiſdome that we may preſent every man per-fect in Chriſt Ieſus,* which literally cannot be true.

The World all men and every man

Now G. *Fox* runs into his *Burrough* of the many *ſignifications* of the word *Light*, and the word *all*, and the word *inlightneth*, willingly ignorant that *Chriſt Ieſus* as *Mediator* or the *new Covenant inlight-ens* none but thoſe whom his Father *gives* him : unto whom he gives *Repentance*, to whom he opens the *door* of *Faith*, and gives them to believe and ſuffer, &c.

Chriſt as Mediator enlightens none but the Elect.

So that G. *Fox* Confounds the *Elect* and the *World* together and brings in a Counterfeit new Birth,

---

[1] " 3 times." *R. W. Ms. Ann.*

Birth, a Counterfeit Chrift, and at laft a Counter-feit Salvation.

7] 5. Inftacne: G. *Fox pag.* 20. brings in *Henock Howet*, faying, [It is a fancy to fay the *Covenant* of God is to all men in the world, and the grace of God hath appeared to all men, *&c.* He *Anfw.* [contrary to the *Apoftle*, who faith, *the grace of God which brings Salvation hath appeared to all men*: & contrary to the *Prophet*, who faith, *I will give him for a Light unto the Gentiles, a Light to the people, Salvation to the ends of the Earth*, and a *new Covenant* to the houfe of *Ifrael* and *Iudah*, and they that do not believe this are Condemned :] *Henoch Howet.*

I Reply in thefe Confiderations prefented to the Confcientious :

1. All mankind being fallen from God : He gracioufly gave the Word or call to *Abraham*, and made Promifes both to his *Natural* and *Spiritual Seed*, hence came the diftinction of Jews, (or the Children of *Abraham*) and the Gentiles [as we Englifh it.] *Jews & Gentiles*

2. It pleafed God to make *two Covenants* or *Bargains* with mankind. 1. that of Juftice and due debt, to any man that yielded obedience in all things, *&c. Rewards* according too, yea, above defert. This *Bargain* was made with our *firft Parents*: and with all mankind to this day, yea, even with the moft favage and barbarous. The fecond is of *mercy* and pity, *&c.* The *Labans* of the world change *Covenants* and *Bargains* ten times, and ftill for the worfe, *&c.* but the *Father of mercies* pitying *Mans Mifery* and *Inability* offers a *New*, and Infinitely eafier and *fweeter Bargain* upon the Terms of only *Mercy* and *free grace* and pity.   3. It *The two great Bargains of God with mankind.*

3. It is one thing for God to offer this Covenant or *Bargain*, [wherever the found of this Gofpel or glad News comes] and another thing to embrace and receive it as all the Elect of God do, and another thing to work *freely* and give *freely* the *Means* and *Power* to fulfil this *Covenant*: as God doth by the *Merits* of his S n, and his own *power-ful working* of *Repentance* and belief in the hearts of all his Chofen.

Scripture language 4. It is Common with the *holy Spirit* to fpeak *Figuratively* in the *holy Scripture*. To call the Sign the thing *fignified*, and the *Inftrument* or *Means*, the *work done*. Thus the *Lamb* is the *Paffover*, the *Bread* is *Chrifts body*, the *Cup* is his *Blood*: God and *Chrift* is called the *Hope* of his *people*, and *Chrift Ie-fus* the *Mediator* of the *Covenant*, called the Covenant it felf. The King pardons Rebels for his Sons fake, his Son may in a Senfe be faid [8] [though not *liter-ally*] to be the *pardon* it felf: A man drives a *Bargain* between two Chapmen that are abfent and diftant drives on a *marriage* between a Man and a Woman abfent each from other, and may in a Figurative Senfe be called the *Bargain* or *Covenant*, and yet not *literally* and *properly* as the poor *Quakers* would their *Chrift* to be.

God of-fers the Gofpel divers wayes 5 The grace and mercy of God, the Gofpel or glad News is many wayes offered: fome are invited gently to come to the heavenly Wedding and Sup-per: other Meffengers (more vehement) even force perfons in, and the Kingdome of Heaven is taken by force; many feek to enter, many run; *It is not in him that willeth, nor runneth but in God that fhew-*

eth

eth mercy, and the reſt he juſtly hardeneth that God may be *All in All*.

For as God walketh in the midſt of his (moſt wonderful) *Creation*, with his two feet of Mercy and Juſtice; ſo he hath his two fingers; and with one he wrote the Covenant of Juſtice in the Tables of Stone, and with the fingers of his Mercy and Grace he freely writes his Mind and Will in the Tables of Fleſh and Hearts of his Choſen: Many offers of Bargains and Marriages are made which never are embraced &c. but in the new-Covenant God gives a new heart to his Choſen, and gives not, and is not the Covenant to any but his Choſen all the World over, even to the ends of the Earth. *Two Feet and 2 Fingers of God*

6. For is it not a monſtrous Dream of the *Quakers*, to ſay, that God and Chriſt, Spirit and Covenant is in all Mankinde, and that in a Goſpel ſence? tis true as I ſaid, if G. *Fox* mean that the Knowledge of God in a ſence is offered to each mans Conſcience in the World, though more expreſly and gloriouſly where he ſends his Meſſengers, *Wiſdomes Virgins*, &c. G. *Fox* beats the Fire,[1] I oppoſe him not, but to ſay the Covenant or Bargain & the Mediatour of the new Bargain, and the Applyer of it the Holy Spirit, is in every of Mankinde, and if they will turn to it, &c: and yet perſons know no ſuch thing, nor never heard of it, and none ever had it ſo as to be ſaved by it but theſe *Foxians*; is as wiſe as for a Man to have Fits of the Stone or Gout, or a Woman have Pangs of Childbearing, and yet neither of them know any ſuch matter, *The Quakers monſtrous Marriages*

---

[1] "Air," not "Fire." *R. W. Mſ. Ann.*

matter, no nor how fhe had any fuch Marriage Covenant or Husband nor ever any Word or Thought of it.

7. The Bottome is this, G. *Fox* cares not for the *Jews* nor [9] *Gentiles,* no more then the *Fox* cares for *Lambs* and *Chickins* but to make a *Prey* of them, he pretends Love to all Man-kinde and tells them they have Chrift and the New Covenant and the Spirit within them ; yea, he tells them, he means not the Covenant of works, but the Covenant of Grace, he means that Chrift that dyed at *Ierufalem,* but when it comes too, they mean no other Chrift but a Spirit (as *Humphrey Norton* more plainly then *Fox* confeffeth) and this Spirit will be found to be an *Evil Spirit* by Gods moft wonderful, wife and righteous hand (as one faith) upon them.

A 7*th. Inftance.* G. *Fox* brings in *pag.* 24. *Iofeph Kellet,* &c. faying, [*The Scriptures are the means of Faith,*] He *Anfwers,* and have thrown out Chrift the Authour of it, and God the Giver, and the Scripture is but a Declaration of the Saints Faith : and men had Faith before the Scripture was, as In-ftance *Abraham* and *Enoch.*

I Reply, G. *Fox* Anfwers three things;

Firft, That his Oppofites throw out God, if they make the Scripture the means of Faith.

Secondly, He flights the Scripture with a *But, it is but a Declaration of the Saints Faith.*

Thirdly, He flights the Novelty of it, faying, *There was Faith before there was Scripture.*

I reply, I have had many Occafions to fpeak of the Scriptures already, I fhall therefore briefly fay,

it

G. Fox and the Quakers pretences of Soul kindnefs are Soul cruelties

Pag. 24. Jofeph Kellet

it is wonderful what an aking Tooth againſt the Holy Writings of God: The old Serpent and all the *Wolves* and *Foxes* of this World have had, who hath more or leſs damned and curſed it, and longed to have it out of the World.

The *Jews*, the *Turks*, the *Papiſts*, the *Common Proteſtants*, the *Quakers*, &c make uſe of it for their ends; but none can rightly uſe it, but as a bleſſed *Candle*, *Lanthorn* or *Torch* ſent down from Heaven into this dark *Dungeon* of the *World*, to guid us out unto the Saving Knowledge of God, and Eternal Bleſſedneſs with him.

For how doth this follow, that if God hath ap-pointed the Holy Writings as means that God and Chriſt are thrown out; can there not be an Har-mony between the firſt and all ſubordinate Cauſes? *God is glorious in the means appointeth.* Did *Moſes* throw out God becauſe he took the Rod in his hand, when he wrought all thoſe Wonders? Did *Solomon* [10] throw out God becauſe he uſed (as *Moſes* about the *Tabernacle*) ſo many means in rearing that Wondrous and Glorious *Temple*? Or did *Samſon* throw out God when he made uſe of the Jaw-bone of an Aſſe, &c. Or *Chriſt Jeſus* throw out his Father, when he made uſe of Clay and Spittle? O what a throwing Spirit is this wild *Fox*, and his wild *Foxians* of; who toſs and throw the Eternal, Immortal and Inviſible God, and his only begotten Son in their wild Fancies, as if they were the Wool and Feathers of Lambs and Chickens which theſe *Foxians* have devoured. *The Quakers ſimple and wild boldneſs with the eterna power & Godhead*

Secondly, How is it that G. *Fox* here ſaith, *That the Scripture is but a Declaration of the Saints Faith?*

44   For

For, is it not a Writing or Record of Heaven:

1. Of the Being and Names of the Eternal Power and Godhead.

The wonderful. Revelations of & in the Script. 2. Of his Glorious and Incomprehenfible Works, Creating and Forming the Heavens and all that is in them; the Earth, and all that is therein, the Sea, and all that is therein out of nothing; which Myftery the Quakers have only from the Scripture.

3 Of the fpecial and more particular framing of Men and Women above all his vifible Creatures:

4. Of the Fall of Mankinde from their glorious and firft Making and Creation, which fome talk idly to be every day.

5. Of the gracious Promife of the Father of Mercies, of a Redeemer and Reftorer of undone mankinde. .

1. By his Threatning to the Devil, and promife to the Woman of a Saviour, to be born in time of a Woman.

2 By Erecting fuch a ftate of *Ifrael* (*prevailers with God*) with all their Typical *Lahds, Governours, Worfhips, Wars, Captivities, Deliverances, &c.*

3. Fulfilling of that Promife in the Wonderful Birth, Life Doctrine, Miracles, Death, Burial, Refurrection and Affention of the Son of God, the Man Chrift Jefus, &c.

4. The Eftate of the Believers in him after his Affention, called the *Primitive Church.*

6 Of the great change fince his coming, in the rifing of his many Enemies, or Antichrifts efpecially, of one with feven heads and ten Horns, and of another with two horns, &c.

7 Of the Proteftant rifing and witneffing againft thefe Devilifh *Heads* and *Horns* of which the *Reve-lations* fpeak, and of [11] the burning up of the Whore and of all Chrifts Enemies and Antichrifts.

8. Of the never-ending Joyes of the Righteous after this life, and the everlafting Worm and Fire of the ungodly, which fhall never dye nor be quenched until the Eternal *Power* and Godhead (revealed in the Holy Scriptures) come to a *Period* and Diffolution.

It may be G. *Fox.* will fay, we *Quakers grant all this?*

I *Anfwer,* I queftion whether you fpeak *bona fide,* and in Truth without *I fuitical* or *Foxian* Equivo-cations.

For 1. What means this *But* ⌊*The Scripture is* ^{Wonder-} *But a Declaration of the Saints Faith*⌋ O blinde ^{ful Guids} Guids that undertake (as in *Lincolnfhire, &c.*) to guide men through the Wafhes upon Life and Death, where K. I*ohn* of *Englands* Treafure and Supply perifhed; to guid Souls through Hells Eter-nal *Wafhes!* what is your *But,* but the *Iews,* and *Papifts,* and *Quakers* cry Crucifie him, Hang up Chrift Jefus, burn up the Scriptures, and all Bibles, Old and New-Tements, &c?

2. What is this *Saints Faith?* You acknowledge none but the Faith of the wild Souls called *Qua-kers* or *Foxians!* we poor *Iews,* and *Papifts,* and *Proteftants,* though we own the Scriptures, fome a part, and the reft all, yet we are all but Infidels, Devils, &c.

3. What is this *Faith,* this *Saints Faith,* this *Foxes* ^{Wonder-} ^{ful faith of}
and

the Qua-
kers

and the *Quakers Faith*? is it any thing elfe but (as before I have faid) but a meer *Babel* or *Confufion of God* and *Faith, Chrift and Faith, Spirit and Faith, Light and Faith, Iuftification and Faith, Sanctification and Faith, Salvation and Faith,* &c. and this in every one of Mankinde in the World, if they will believe it, &c.

The third Branch of G. *Fox* his Anfwer is, [*Men had Faith before the Scriptures were.*]

I *Anfwer*, Neither *Abraham* nor ever any Man had Faith before it pleafed the Eternal and Invifible

Gods feve-
ral wayes
of reveal-
ing him-
felf

Deity to difclofe himfelf by Word, or Sight, or Dream, or Motion, or Writing, as *Heb.* 1. at feveral times and wayes *it pleafed him to fpeak*, and laft of all by the beft and cleareft of all, his only Begotten Chrift Jefus.

2. When it hath pleafed the *incomprehenfible Majefty* to Command his *Appearances* by *Words,*

The mad
fancies of
the Qua-
kers as to
the Holy
Scriptures

Vifions, Dreams, &c. [12] to be written to ftand upon *File* and *Record,* (for all Generations) fhall we be fuch *Fools* and *Franticks* as to fay it was his Word when God fpake it to, and in his *Prophets*: but now it is written, it is but *pen, ink* and *paper,* it is but a dead Letter, it is not Gods word, God hath but One *Word, Chrift.* The Scripture is his *Words,* &c. Oh the *audacious brockifhnefs* of the *foul Spirit* in thefe wild *Foxians*: They dare not (though what dares not their *hellifh Spirit* againft the *K.* of Hea-

The word
of a King
and the
word of
God

ven yet) they dare not (they do not deny but predicate) that the *Kings Letters* from *Breda* are the *Kings Word,* that the *Kings Speeches* and *Declarations* are his *royal Word*: fhall a *Bargain,* a *Covenant,*

a *mar-*

a *marriage*, a *Laſt Will*, be our mind, our will, our
Word, when it is ſpokcn! But when it is *written,
fairly drawn*, and *engroſſed, ſubſcribed* and *ſealed*
unto before many *Witneſſes attesting*, then it is not
our word, mind, or will, but words, &c, The bottom and Truth is : The Spirit by which the Quakers are aćted would be glad that there were not
ſuch a perſon called the *Word of God*, nor ſuch a
writing declaring ſo *ſweetly, ſo plainly, ſo fully, and
ſo heavenly of him*

8. Inſtance : In the 25. *pag.* G. *Fox* brings in Pag. 25.
the ſame Author, ſaying, [that the *Power* which Joſeph Kellet &c.
juſtles out the Form is an Error:] He Anſw. which
was the Apoſtles work to bring of the Form into
the *Power*, the ſubſtance Chriſt which was not an
Error, but you bring in the Error, keep people in
the Form out of the *Power*, and not in the Apoſtles work :]

I Reply: G. *Fox* is in his *Burrough* of the vari-
ous Senſe of the word Form : It hath reſpećt to The word Form debated
Nature, to *Art*, to *Civil, Natural*, and *Divine mat-*
ters : Shall I now (like a Fool and a mad man)
Cry down all *Natural, Civil*, and *Divine Beings*?
Are not all the *internal* and *external Forms*, ſhapes,
or Beings of the Creatures in *Heaven, Earth*, and
Sea, of *Angels, Sun, Moon*, &c. *Men, Birds, Beaſts,
Fiſhes*„admirably glorious and *ſtupendious*? G. *Fox*
runs to the Pićture, or Forms of theſe Forms, and
ſaith childiſhly, that the Form or picture without
the Life is nothing: who knows not that, that as to
Life it is good as nothing.

1. But to come to worſhip, was there not a Form,
or

or manner of *Circumſion*, the *Paſsover*, the *Taber-nacle*, the *Temple*, &c.

2. Did ever the Servants of God when they in-veighed againſt the *Cuſtomarineſs*, the Carelefsneſs, the pictures, and the meer ⌊13⌋ Formality of the Worſhippers (Jews or Chriſtians) inveigh againſt the worſhip it ſelf, and the Appointments of God and of his Son Chriſt Jeſus.

3. Did the Servants of God ever labour to bring and hale off Gods people from the worſhip it ſelf, but only from the dead and meerly formal uſing of them, until the time appointed by God himſelf for their withdrawings, diſappearing and abrogation. What a ſhameleſs falſhood is it that any of Gods Meſſen-gers brought Gods people off from thoſe *heavenly Fabricks* which God erected by their Miniſtry or Service all the World over?

Gods Or-diances and Inſtitu-tions

4. May not *Gods Meſſengers* now Cry out againſt the *apiſh* Imitations & *Formalitie*s of the *Papiſts* (ſo horribly and bloodily) abuſing *Prayer*, *preaching*, *Baptiſme*, the *Lords Supper*, *Excommunication*, &c. but (like the *Aſſyrians* or *Babilonians*, Pſal. 74. All theſe *Chriſtian Appointments* muſt be broken and tumbled down with *Axes* and *Hammers*. &c.

5. This is Treaſon and Rebellion in any Athe-iſts or whomſoever, but more abominable Hipo-critical in theſe *Phariſaical Foxians*, who Cry out againſt the *apiſh* Imitators, and yet themſelves prac-tice, *preaching*, *praying*, *Congregations*, or *Churches*, *ſingings*, *Conventings*, and (implicite though real) Ad-dings to *Caſtings out*, &c Full well (as the Lord

The Qua-kers groſs Hypocri-ſie

Ieſus

Iefus (peaks) abrogating the word and Appointments of God, that they may fet up and eftablifh their own Traditions, &c.

6. Tis true, the Proteftants have made feparation from the Church of *Rome,* as *whorifh* and *Bloody* : in order to the Return to the firft Primitive purity, from which the whore of *Rome* hath departed.

7. G. *Fox* Cries out againft all Scripture and Common Senfe, againft all Forms, that is, wayes and manners of Gods Worfhip : Cries up a Chrift within, *Scripture within, Church within, Minifters within, Baptifme and Supper within,* yet practice they moft of thefe [fo many as their Idol requires] and will ferve his turn) as outwardly and vifibly as any in the world.

8. I know it is the obfervation of one of G. *Fox* his Oppofites [a man of excellent knowledge, piety & induftry, M *Baxter*] *viz.* that the Churches of the *Independents,* & *Baptifts* have been the fource and Spring whence have flown the Generation of the Quakers. For my felf I have obferved the contrary in thefe parts, [14] and that [although fome rotten Profeffors, or weak Souls though true] have been bewitched by thofe Soul-witches yet generally [where they have any Liberty] the *National Church* fills up their numbers : My Reafon I gave them in publick, when W. *Edm. Boafted* of their Numbers, *viz.* their Religion is fo eafie, never coming near the *Roots* of *rotten Nature,* but fo wonderfully agreeing with it, and changing one Devil for another, as I have before inftanced, fo that I told them I adored the *Infinite Power, wifdome* and *goodnefs* of God,

Margin notes: A paffage of Mr. Baxters weighed

Whence the Quakers Profelites do arife

God, that they were not *ten thoufand* fold more, and
I fay Millions more, then they are : For, I can demonftrate that if G: *Fox* (for all their *hypocritical
prating* againft *Carnal Weapons*) get a Sword (as
Mahomet did) moft of the Popifh, and Proteftant
and pagan World, will eafily be brought to dance
after him.

9. As to the point of Separation : I pray Mr.
Baxter and others of G. *Foxes* learned and godly
oppofites who are yet (in their Judgement and
Confcience perfwaded to the *National Worfhips*]
to hear me patiently four words.

1. I pray them to remember what the word
Nazarite is in *Englifh.* The word *Nazareth* and the
word [*Jefus of Nazareth*] and in plain Englifh.[1]]

2. Was there ever Child of God in this world
but he was a *Nazarate, feparate* from worldly perfons, worldly practice and worldly worfhips, as he
comes to fee them, *&c. and endureth not that the evil
one fhould touch him* ;

3. Is not *Gods* name *Iealous* in this end of the
World, not the weft-world, as well as fince he firft
proclaimed it in the Eaft.

Confider-
tion touch-
ing fepa-
rate
Churches

4. Hath not his Jealoufie raged againft the *Iewifh whoremongers,* who defiled his *firft Bed,* and will
he wink at the *Chriftian Adulterers* and *Adultereffes*
either in Worfhip or Converfation ?

5. With what good Confcience can I (a national
Proteftant) *feparate* from my *Father* the *Pope* and
my *mother* the *Church of Rome,* and my Brethren
and Sifters the *Papifts,* and yet it muft not be
                                             Chriftian

---

[1] Add " yᵉ faviour of yᵉ feparate." *R. W. Ms. Ann.*

Chriftian for other Souls to fee further degrees of that *Separation* neceffary, and I muft bring up the foot of every mans Light, and *Sight*, and *Confcience* to my *Lafte*.

6. This is the main ground of my Controverfy with the proud Quakers, they ftir up in their Illuminations in themfelves, and [15] Condemnations The Quaagainft others, but they magnify (with the *Papifts* kers Conand *Arminians*) Curfed, rotten Nature: their *Con-* verts *verts* and *Profelites* have but a painted, formal Repentance, Faith, *&c.* Only if they can come to their Church, *&c.* and Thou and thee, and difref- p & all Superiours then are they high Saints, can- .. not Sin, *&c.*

7. This (as before I hinted) was the heavenly N. E. gloPrinciple of thofe many precious and gallant *Wor-* ry the *thies*, the *Leaders* and *Corner Stones* of thefe *New-* very top *England Colonies*, viz. they defired to worfhip God it in purity according to thofe perfwafions in·their Confciences, which they believed God had lighted up.

8. They defired fuch for their *Fellow Worfhippers* as they (upon a Chriftian account) could have evidence that to be true and real *Worfhippers* of God in *Spirit* and *Truth* alfo.

But I forget this is but an Appendix, and therefore I return to another Inftance of G. *Fox* his poor. and lame, and naked Anfwers, *&c.*

A 9th. Inftance, is *pag.* 32. where G. *Fox* brings in *Ellis Bradfhaw*, faying, [*The Spirit of God doth* Ellis Brad*not teach to judge before the time*] and he adds that fhaw others of them fay [*The Saints fhall not Iudge while*
45   *they*

they be upon the Earth.] To which he Anſwers,
[*But the* Spirit *did teach the Apoſtle to judge, and his
Time was come*; And he tells ſome *that they were of
old ordained for Condemnation, and their Damnation
ſlumbred not,* and they went on to Eternal Judgement, *and it is high Time not to judge.*]

I Reply, Some of this his Anſwer, is ſome of his
wonted *Nonſence,* or the *Printers* overſight, *&c.*
But to the point the great Jugler hath taught G.
Fox and his *Foxians* a trick to outface *Death* and
Indgement. They now keep the great Seſſions and
call all the world to their *Bar* and Judgement.
Thus did the poor cheated *Souls in London* lately
Reeves and *Mugleton* thunder out their eternal Sentence of Damnation upon the Souls and bodies of
their *Oppoſites,* & that with ſuch Seriouſneſs, Confidence & Majeſty, that I have known ſollid Chriſtians put into a fright by them.

The two pretended laſt witneſſes Reves and Muggleton

It is true there is a lawful judging not according
to raſhneſs or pride (as the Quakers is) but according to righteous Judgement.

It is true, *the ſpiriturl man judgeth and diſcerneth
all things,* that is, looks into the Cauſes and Natures
of things, Times and perſons : But what is this to
the Natural *Death* of all mankind. [16] *Heb.* 9?
I know the *Foxians* would turn this Scripture, and
that *golden Chain,* Heb. 6. the firſt *Chriſtian Principles* and the Eternal Judgement into *Myſteries,* and
that they now Judge the Secrets of Men, *Rom.* 2.
by *Pauls Goſpel:* (therefore by looking on a man
they can diſcern the inward parts, and what each
perſon is :) For the Lord is now come ſaith *Enoch*
and

The Jugling of the Quakers to make themſelves eternal Judgs

and I*ude* in *ten thousands of his Saints, and now is the Day appointed in which God judgeth the World by that man Christ Iesus* [which man they are] of which the word of God hath approved, in that they are raised from the Dead in Souls and Bodies to keep the *Eternal Iudgement* : This Mystery many of their young Scholars and many that are truely fearing God amongst them will not believe. But they spare not to owne their *high Court* of *Iustice* [when they were put to it] by Speech and writing, and were it not for some obstacles (especially two) this were a fine Colour for their Courts, like a Company of drunken Sots that kept a Court in *Hart-* *ford-Shire*, and feigned themselves Judges, and Justices, and Officers,& had almost brought themselves all to the Gallows,&c. by hanging up one man until he began to look black, and some of them began to fear their own Necks, and to repent of their rash madness.

A danger-
ous coun-
terfeit
Court.

The first Obstacle against this their pretended high Court of Justice, is their own Confession, *viz.* *Christ Iesus was real a Man as any of us, and so continues*, except they can give an account of what is become of him, which at *Newport* they could not do.

Two
great Bars
to the
Quakers
high Court
of eternal
Judgm.

The second is, their own Spirit and Practises, which I have proved to be so far from *Iude* and *Enochs* 10000 Saints, that their *Pride* and Scornfulness, their Rash, Revilings and Railings, their Rash Cursings and Judgings, their Superstitious and New Inventions, their Blasphemies and Hypocrisies, their Inhumanities and Impudencies, such as render them so far from being the high Saints and Judges of the World,

World, that they fall under the Judgement of all
fober end modeſt perſons.

The 10. Iuſtance, is in *pag.* 38. where he brings
in *Tho. Collier,* ſaying, ⌊*All that hath been, are, or
ſhall be Converted ſince the Goſpel Miniſtration are
Converted by the Apoſtles words*⌋ He Anſwers: So
he hath thrown out the Spirit which doth regenerate, and Chriſt the way to the Father, the Word
that Sanctifi- [17] eth, and Chriſt the power of
God to Salvation : who ſaid that they would not
come to him that they might be converted, ſo if
they get all the Apoſtles Words and come not to
Chriſt they are not Converted, and none are Converted ·by the Apoſtles Words, but who comes to
the Life that the Words come from.

*P.*38. T.
Collier

I reply, and aſk G. *Fox* what colour of Truth or·
Modeſty is in his Inference, *viz. That if God pleaſe
to appoint the Words his firſt Apoſtles uſed, to be ſtill
the means of Converſion to he end of the World, that
then he hath thrown out himſelf,* &c.

For 1. Is not this Gods Covenant with Chriſt
and all Chriſtians, that his Word and Spirit ſhould·
be in their Mou·hs to all Generations : wo be then·
to theſe wild frantick In*ferences* which diſjoyn and
ſeparate what the moſt powerful, moſt wiſe and
holy hath joyned together.

·2· For, may there not be as before many Agents
Imployed by one glorious Efficient : as in *Moſes*
building the Tabernacle, *Solomon* the Temple :
Kings in their *Royal Navies* and *Armies, Fights* and
Battels; is *Moſes* here thrown out, *Solomon* thrown
out, and *Kings* thrown out &c? when *Abraham* ſent
his

G. Fox
his throw-
ing God
overboard
and his
own Rea-
ſon and

his Servants or *Kings* their Embaſſadours to Eſpouſe ^{Senſe alſo.}
Brides to their Sons and Heirs, muſt *Abraham* and
all wiſe *Princes* be thrown out, &c. Doth not
rather this mad Soul throw out *Moſes* and *Solomon*,
and *Abraham*, and all *Kings* and great *Efficients* or
firſt Cauſes, yea, and his own *Brains* (in a mad,
proud Frolick) all overboard together?

   3. For, doth not *Paul* tell the *Corinthians, that
they were Gods Husbandry and Gods Buildings*; in-
ferring that under God (not throwing him out) he
was a prime Husbandman, yea, (as himſelf ſaith
further) a Maſter Builder; yea, doth not *Paul* tell the
ſame *Corinthians*, that they were the Meſſengers,
were co workers or Labourers together with God.
Hence *Paul* Preaching, the Lord opened the Heart
of *Lydia* and *Philip* Preaching, the Lord opened
the heart of the *Eunuch*, and *Panl ſo ſpeaking*,
Joh,[1] 14. and *Barrabas*, that a great Multitude
both of *Jews and Greeks* believed.

   4. It is true that without God and Chriſt, *Pauls
Planting*, and *Apollos Watering* is nothing, who denies this? but therefore ſhall not *Paul Plant* and
Apollo Water, though much in vain, as it was with
the Lord Jeſus, his own heavenly *Preaching* and
amazing Miracles.

18]   5. Do theſe *Foxians* themſelves· throw out
God and Chriſt when (as they ſay) they uſe the
Apoſtles words, to gather Stones, and build up the
Church of God ; do they not ſay as much for their
new freſh *Foxian* as ever was ſpoken of the Apoſ-
tles,

*The Har-
mony be-
tween
God and
his Meſ-
ſengers.*

*God doth
all, yet his
meanes
muſt be
uſed by
which he
is pleaſed
to work.*

---

[1] "Aɛts," not "Joh. 14." *R. W. Ms. Ann.*

tles, or any pretending to fucceed them ? I could give many Inftances.

6. There have been many Converfions to the Chriftian Name in thefe parts of the World called *Chriftendome*.

Thefe the Papifts brag to have effected in all the four parts of the World, both in the *Eaft* and *Weft-Indies*, *Afia* and *America*, as alfo in *Africa* and efpecially in *Europe*, where their Man of fin chiefly refideth : thefe Converfions have been wrought fometimes in parts and by degrees, and fometimes of the whole Nations, and this fometimes by the Sword, fometimes by the Marriages of *P*rinces, all which are eafily effected ; becaufe (as in the *Shechemites* and *Samaritains* cafe) whole Peoples, Nations, Tongues and Multitudes will eafily turn to the Beaft with feven Heads and ten Horns ; and that very formidable Beaft alfo for Fear, and Gain, and Hope, &c. will eafily fuffer the Whore of *Rome* to ride him.

The Papifts brag of their Converfions.

7. From thefe Peoples, Tongues, and Nations, &c. it hath pleafed the moft Holy and only Wife, to gather out a Peaple to Himfelf by his Heavenly Witneffes ; the *Waldenfes* in *France*, the *Wicclevifts* in *England*, the *Huffites* in *Bohemia*, the *Lutherans* in *Germany*, the *Calvanifts* in *France* &c. out of the bloody *Romifh Whores* Dominions (144000. Virgin Proteftants thirfting after the Blood of Chrift Jefus only for Salvation)

The Proteftant Converfions

8. The Father of Spirits hath ftirred up fome Witneffes in all Proteftant Nations, to preach againft a Formal, National or *P*arochial Converfion, to
witnefs

witnefs againft the Formality and Prophanefs of theCommon Proteftants, (all one in Life and fometimes worfe then the Papifts,) and to bring thoufands and ten thoufands (even the *one hundred, forty four thoufand Virgins*) to endeavour after purity of heart and Life, purity of Doctrine, purity of worfhip, purity of Churches, *&c.* Thefe the Jefuits call Puritans, and Confefs that they only among the Proteftants, (as themfelves among the Papifts) are fit to be thought on as to pretence of the Chriftian Name and Religion. *The Jefuits and Puritans the two great Corrivals*

9. At the coming of the Lord Jefus there were two great Com- [19] petitours for preaching, *Firft*, the *Pharifees* who by Laud and Sea fent abroad their *Emiffaries* to make Converts to the God of the Jews and their own Traditions, *Secondly*, The Apoftles or Meffengers of Chrift Jefus fent abroad with the glad news of a new Bargain or Covenant of God with the Sons of men, *viz.* this fecond fort; It pleafed the God of Heaven [not to be thrown out as this *Fox* frantickly barks] but to go out wonderfully miraculoufly, yea, alfo with the private labours and preachings of private Chriftians fcattered by Perfecution, as the holy Scripture recordeth. *The two great Corrivals in Chrifts time.*

10. For the flighting of this ineftimable Pearl of this glad News, or Gofpel publifhed by God to the World by writing, preaching, profeffing, Suffering, *&c.* It hath pleafed his Infinite Juftice to plough¹ the World with Popery, a Religion [a baftard Chriftianity,] fuited [as the Quakers is] to *The Jefuits and the Quakers the two great Corrivals abroad.*

rotten

¹ "plague," not "plough." *R. W. Ms. Ann.*

rotten nature, and fit to carry the world after them as *Mahomet* and the *Pope* have done.

11. In this day the two greateft wonders in the world [pretending to be Chrifts Meffengers or Apoftles to the Nations] are the Jefuits and the Quakers: Their Faces look divers, but they both carry Firebrands in their Tails to burn up the holy Scripture, all truly holy Chriftians, yet[1] all the world before them. Gods Infinite wifdome hath Falfe Apoftles figured by Abfolom. fuffered them to be like *Abfolom* beautiful, and plaufible, and fit to play Soul Thieves and fteal away the hearts of thoufands and ten thoufands from the true *David* the Lord Jefus Chrift.

Befide, they are fo fortified with the Faces of Men and hair of Women like the Locufts, *Rev.* 9. The holy Scriptures the great Box both to Jefuits and Qua-kers. fuch pretences, fuch Illuminations and Appear-ances, fuch Affurances and Confidences, fuch feel-ings of Experiences, that it is Gods Infinite *Power* and wifdome, and goodnefs, to preferve the holy Scripture a ftanding Record of what the firft Mef-fengers and firft Churches and firft Doctrine and Chriftians were: or elfe, the world would fall down and adore the Images which the Lord hath fuffered the Devil in them to fet up.

12. I know the Counfels *of the Father of Lights* are very deep, yea the Revelation needs a Revela- Great Conver-fion of · Jews and Gentiles yet expected. tion, the *Prophecies* and *Canticles*, and *Daniel* need Heavenly Meffengers, and the moft holy Spirit or finger of God to untie fuch knots: Sure it is that Millions [20] of Jews and Gentiles muft yet en-quire with tears of, blood after the Blood of a Saviour :

[1] "yea," not "yet." *R. W. Ms. Ann.*

Saviour: Sure they fhall not awake out of their pits of Rottennefs, without fome means & Meffengers fent from Heaven to rouze and wak n them: Sure their fhall be no other words in their Mouths then what were in the mouths of the firft Meffengers according to the *Prayer* of the Lord Jefus on his Death bed to his Father, through whofe Word all that have believed the report ever fince have believed, *Ioh.* 17 and with which bleffed word the Spirit of God will be in the mouths of all true Chriftians, *Ifai.* 59. 20. &c. Surely the true Meffengers of Jefus will fay no other word then what *Mofes* and the *Prophets* foretold and wrought, *Act.* 26. therefore *Fox* and his *Foxians* that tells us they have all by the Spirit and need no Record, are Thieves and Robbers, whom, *Mofes*, and the *Prophets*, and *Paul*, and the *Apoftles* abhor'd to think of. ^{The true Apoftles and Fox and his lying ones Compared}

A 11. *Inftance*, is in *Pag.* 40. where G. *Fox* brings in *I. Deacon*, faying [*The enjoyment of Immortulity is not till they have put off the Body.*] ^{I. Deacon.}

He Anfwers, [Contrary to the Apoftles Doctrine, who faith, *Immortality was brought to light through the Gofpel*: this was when they were upon the Earth, and the Word of God was in them which was Immortal.]

1. I Reply Firft, G. *Fox* affirms an Immortality (that is a not dying of the Soul and Body) As for the Soul, all true Proteftants affirm that the Soul once raifed up to Spiritual Life never dyes, no more than Chrift Jefus, *Rom.* 6. as for the Body Papifts and Proteftants, and the Quakers and all the World grants, that *all Flefh is as grafs*, &c. and the ^{The Quakers dream about not dying or Immortality.}

46   Sentence

Sentence of Death, by ficknefs, Age or Cafualty is impartially executed upon the *Foxians* as well as other C ttel : As to the Soul, who of fober Papifts or Proteftants queftions the Immortality of it : and of the Body alfo, in joy or Sorrow to Eternity.

As for the Body the Quakers fay when the Soul is gone into God, yea, the Soul of *Iudas* as well as the Soul of *Peter* as fome of them fay, and all of them by Argument will be forced to fay, the Body returns to Earth and Rottennefs, never more to be raifed, and no more then Bodies of the Beafts, Birds and *Fifhes*, (though we know who holds the Bodies of Beafts, Birds and Fifhes fhall live again as the Soul mortalifts do) what is it then [21] that G. *Fox* fputters out for Immortality, or a not dying in this Life ? If he fpeak of the Soul who denies it ? If of the Body he fpeaks a Beaftly Contradiction to the doleful Senfe of all mankind, and their own alfo, who die and rot as well as them.

2. It is true, 1 *Tim.* 6. *God only hath Immortality dwelling in the Light which no man can approach unto,* The Doc-what ever thefe *Foxians* bruitifhly fancy of no dif-trine of tinction between God and themfelves their Light Immortal-and his. It is true, yet alfo that *Iefus Chrift*, 2 *Tim.* ity. 1. *hath brought Life and Immortality to Light through the Gofpel.* But what is this but the joyful Condition of the Souls & Bodies of the godly? their Souls and Bodies raifed up with Jefus to a Spiritual holy Life in this World, their Souls going to Jefus, and thcir Bodies *fleeping in Iefus*, and the rifing of their Bodies and uniting to their Spirits in a Life Eternal ?

3. As

3. As to this *Immortality* of G. *Fox*: all that can be kuown of his mind is old H.*Nichols* and the *Ni-* A Chari-table hope of fome Quakers. *colaitans* mad fictions and fancies of their becoming God and Chrift. I hope charitably of many of them, that run in their Simplicity, Ignorance and weaknefs with a true Love to the true Lord Jefus as fome did with *Abfalom*[1] who truly loved *David* but as for *Abfolom* himfelf the Polititians, the fub-tle *Plotters*, and *Ahitophels* who love not the true Lord Jefus in fincerity, I fear inftead of their fan-cied Immortality before the Grave they will meet with a dreadful Mortality, or dearh of Soul and Body to Eternity.

A 12. Inftance is, *pag.* 47. where he brings in *Jofeph Miller,* faying, [*The wife heathen Philofophers* *had a greater Meafure of Light in them* (which is the firft *Adam) then I can think any man hath now*] Jofeph Miller,

G. *Fox* Anfw.which fhews, that he knows nothing of Chrift the *fecond Adam,* the quickning Spirit. He knows no New Creature, for who are *in Chrift are new Creatures,* nor none of Chrift the Covenant of God, of Light, of Life, of Peace, who was *glorified with the Father before the World began,* which is be-yond the *firft Adam,* and hath fhut himfelf forth, not to be as high as his heathen Philofophers. And many witnefs Chrift in them in this Age, as in the dayes of the Apoftles, which is above the heathen Philofophers.]

I Reply, 1. I know it pleafed God (in all Ages) to ftir up the Spirits of fome Men (as the Philofo-phers amongft the Greeks [22] *Socrates, Plato, Ariftotle,* The An-cient Phi-lofophers Confid-ered.

[1] Put " as fome did with Abfolom," in parenthefis. *R. W. Ms. Ann.*

Ariſtotle) to improve that excellent Light of Reaſon which he had given them as Men, and in ſo great a meaſure above other men.

2. This wily Fo*x* he runs to his hole and Confounds this Common Light of Reaſon, with Chriſt and God himſelf, who alſo are called Light by Similies from the Creature.

3. The Queſtion then follows : If this Light of Knowledge were Chriſt, as God, and King, and Mediatour : why is it that none of theſe excellent Men knew nothing of God, nor Chriſt, nor Spirit, (Name nor Thing) but only of the firſt Creation : Can ſuch a Court be kept, a *P*alace furniſhed, and ſuch Royal and heavenly Gueſts be entertaind, and no Body know any thing of it, nor themſelves neither; when Chriſt Jeſus came into *Jeruſalem* (though but in a poor Contemptible way) all *I*oru*ſalem* was moved at his coming : and ſhall this moſt glorious King (now Infininitely more glorious) make his Ingreſs into the Souls of ſuch wiſe and Excellent Men, and neither they, nor others hear of it until juſt now, (twenty years ſince) Some cheated Souls dream of it.

The madneſs of George Fox his Fancy about them.

4. The utmoſt of Reaſon in theſe Excellent Men, it is known I ſay, that the Activity of the higheſt Reaſon in this World falls ſhort in two grand particulars.

1. As to the Creatures : For ſome of them muſt needs fall ſhort, when *Plato* granted a Creation, and a kind of *Father, Son* and *Holy Spirit* in the Creation of it, *Ariſtotle* pretends to ſee further then his Mr. *Plato* and all his Arguments. and aſſerts the World to have no Beginning, nor Ending, *&c.*

The failing of the higheſt Reaſon in this world in many, eſpecially in two particulars

Some

Some of them maintaind the Soul of man to be procreated by the *Parents*: others (as the Quakers) that it was part of the *Divine Essence*, others that it is created and infufed by God, *&c.* Some that the *Center* of the World is the Terreftrial Globe, and that the Sun and heavenly Bodies move about it, others, that the Ceuter of the world is the *Sun*, and that this *Terreftrial Globe* moves about the Sun, and many other fuch, natural Myfteries. ^{The drep knowledge of fome.}

2. However that *Paul* tells us *Rom*, 1. That by the *Creation* fome come to know there is an *Eternal Power and Godhead*, yet 1 *Cor*. 1. he tells us *that the World by wifdome knew not God*, which muft be expounded (or elfe fwallow a Contradiction as the Quakers guife is) *viz.* that by the highth of their wifdome [23] they could not fee God fo as to make him alone their *Summum bonum* and *Bleffednefs*, fo as *to glorify him as God*: So, as the holy Scriptures and the moft holy Son of God from his Bofome hath revealed him, fo that in the highth of Reafons Reafonings the Spirit of God concludes, that the *natural man* can not reach or *perceive the things of God*, (and yet this foolifh Man makes every mans heart in the World the Court of Heaven) a thing which every Kingdom and all men may abhor to think of, but men are vain in all their Reafonings, and *their foolifh heart is darkned*, yea, *their wifdome is Enmity, hating God himfelf*, as the Scripture concludes, *&c.*

The greater depth of the Creator himfelf, the Trinity, the Fall, Redemption Incarnation, Refurrection, &c.

It is true: We re read of *Noah Ark*, of *Mofes* his Tabernacle, *Solomon* his Temple, and we fee many *glorious Fabricks* and Works of the Sons of men

The Ex-
cellent
Gifts of
Nature
reach not
heavenly
and Spi-
ritual
things Spi-
ritually.

men in this world, which argue excellent Gifts of
God to them, both of *wifdome, Prudence, Fortitude,
Patience, Temperance,* &c. but do they all amount
in the Total to more then *Natural parts, good Education,* and *Induftrious diligence* can reach too? What
are all thefe to the enlightning of my Soul, with
my natural undone and damned Condition? to a
fight of Sin as Sin? to a fight of my utter Inability
to pay (or all the whole Creation for me) one farthing to Gods Juftice, or to work my defire to have
any thing to do with him? What are thefe to the
changing of, and a total turning of my whole Soul
unto God? to an humble fight of my Infinite neceffity of the alone Sufficiciency and Excellency of
the Lcrd Jefus the great and only Mediatour, and
of my becoming one with him in *Loves Eternal?*

Befide, what a fingle[1] Confequence doth this
high *Illuminiated Doctor* give to his Oppofite, viz.
that becaufe I magnify the Gifts of God to many
(yea, thoufands of Excellent Men whom *I,* nor G.
Fox are worthy to hold the Candle to) therefore I
fhut my felf out from Chrift and thofe wife men
too: It may be his Oppofite had fomewhat more
in his Affertion, but this is all this high wife man
in his own eyes prints and Anwfers to:

Who knows not how full the World is of admirable Men and Women that are not Chriftians? And
yet what a bafe efteem hath this proud Spirit of
all men, yea of all Chriftians too that dance not
after his foolifh pipe, *&c.*

A 13th. *Inftance,* I mention (though Inftances
are

[1] "Simple" not "fingle." *R. W. Ms. Ann.*

are as Leprofie fpread over his whole Book) is in
pag. 48. where he brings in the [24] fame *Jofeph* Jofeph
Miller faying, [*The Prophets are more certain then any* Miller
other Revelation.] He Anfwers, [*was not the Son of*
God revealed, the end of the Prophets? Did not God re-
veal him which came in the Volume of the Book to
do the will of God? *And fo the Prophets, and the*
Law, and Types, and fhadows, which they that had the
Law, and Types, and fhadows, knew not the Son of
God that was revealed, that was their End fpoken of
in the Prophets, end Epiftles, who is now revealed.

    I Reply, G. *Fox* (to pafs by his un-Englifh Non-
fence obvious to any that underftand publick writings) I fay G. *Fox* either ignorantly or willingly The Pro-
knows not that the Queftion is not here, whether phets wit-
Chrift be the End of the Law and the *Prophets,* in nefs of
a true fenfe: or whether Chrift was not more re- Chrift
vealed at his coming in the Flefh, then before in ftronger
the *Prophecies, &c.* But, whether the written then the
word of the Prophets, of which *Peter* fpeaks and I Apoftles,
have fpoke before be not a more fure word of Com- Speeches:
mand and Comfort to us then any now to be ex- were
pected, yea, then that Revelation which we have
upon that holy Teftimony of *Peter* and *Iohn* themfelves?

    As it is with an Anchor ftrong enough to ride a
Ship in moft weathers, yet fome are as the Seamen
fpake *fecond* and *third Bowers,* and one the beft and Bebaiote-
Sheet Anchor: and as it is in Witneffes fome fpeak ron Iogon
the Truth and Subftance of the matter: and yet a more
others fpeak more plainly and fully, *&c.* So fure
speaks Gods Spirit in *Peter* of the Infinite Fulnefs Word.
                            of

of the *Prophecies* of Scriptures, or the written foretellings and utterings concerning Jefus Chrift.

The Word of God Confidered. Thus the God of Heaven moft holy and only wife ftoops to our weaknefs, and calls his mind his word, his works his word, his *Providences* of mercy or Judgement, his Word, the Lord Jefus his only begotten his word, his writings his Word; and this in a way of Condefcention to our Capacity, feeing that all the World over *Kings* and *Rulers*, Fathers, Mafters of Families, of Ships, *&c.* give the word, that is the manifeftation of their mind and

The Sripture or written Teftimonie. will, and this as the Spring in Clocks and watches turn about all other wheels and motions. Hence it is, that if ancient Records and Deeds with Hands and Seals be produced at the *Bar* of *Trial*, all

Much more their feigned Spirit of Prophecy the Quakers prate of mouths are ftopt at fuch Evidences. Thus the Word of God in the mouths of the Prophets written for after Generations, is (Comparatively) beyond the Report of *Peter* ⌊25⌋ and *John* themfelves is in all Religions.[1] The *Iews* have their *Talmud*, the *Turks* their *Alcheron*, the *Pope* his *Decretans*, and the *Proteftants* the *Written Word*, or *Scriptures*.

The Quakers Sandy Quickfauds When therefore a *Pardon* is written and Sealed with the Broad Seal of a *King* or State, what a fancy is it for a condemned Wretch to hearken firft to a Pardon revealed within : to a voice within, to a *King* within, to a Writing within, a Seal within, and fo flighting the true pardon in the *Kings* way to be conveyed from without to the Mind and Spirit within, to lofe his *Pardon* and Deliverance as thoufands of fuch poor cheated Souls muft do.

A 14.

[1] Erafe "is in all Religions." *R. W. Ms. Ann.*

A 14 *Inſtance* G *Fox* brings in *Pag.* 49. his Oppoſite *Ralph Hall* ſaying [*It is againſt the Light of
Nature for Women to Preach*: &c.

G. *Fox Anſwers* Contrary to the Apoſtles Doctrine and the mind of God and the *P*rophets, who
ſaid, *God would pour out of his Spirit upon all Fleſh,
and his Sons and Daughters ſhould Propheſie* : So that
he is a limiter of the Holy one, a quencher of the
Spirit, and in the Darkneſs, and this is above the
Light of Nature.

I Reply, Firſt, What is the Light of Nature, but
that Light in which every man comes into the
World with (as the *Foxians* ſpeak) a Light differing
from that Light which Beaſts, wilde and tame, and
Birds, and Fiſhes have: And[1] a Second Light differing from what is [2]Supernatural, as that Light revealed from Heaven in the Holy Scriptures, and
infuſed into the Souls of Men by the Holy Spirit
or Power of God.

2. What is the Light of Nature in Man, but
that Order which the moſt Glorious Former of all
things hath ſet (like Wheeles in Clocks or Watches)
a going in ali his Creatures?

Some have obſerved that in the Infenſible Crea-
tures to which the moſt High hath only giving
Beings, that there may be obſerved a Male and
Female amongſt them.

This is more obſervable in Vegetables or growing Creatures, as in *P*lants, Trees, Herbs, Flowers, &c.

More

P. 47.
Preaching
of Wo-
men Ralph
Hall

The light
of Nature
diſcuſſed

Male and
Female

[1] Inſert " there is." *R. W. Ms. Ann.*
[2] Eraſe " Super." *R. W. Ms. Ann.*

47

More yet in Senfitives, as Birds, Beafts, Fifhes.

Moft of all in Rationals: Men and Women, whom the moft High hath fo wonderfully diftinguifhed.

It is true, that in Religious and Chriftian Matters, there is no [26] refpect of perfons with God, as of Man before the Woman: otherwife than to order Natural and Civil.

Men and Women compared

The Woman is Predeftinated, is Called, is Juftified, is Glorified, and wears that Golden Chain as well as the Wifeft and Strongeft of Mankinde.

And it is true, the Wifdome of God perfers fome Women before thoufands of Men, in their being born of Nobles, in excellent parts (as is obfervable in the Lady *Iane*, and Queen *Elizabeth*, &c.) in fome fpecial favour, as Chrift Jefus firft appearing to

The kindnefs of God to women

Mary Magdalen and other Women, and fending them to carry the firft Tydings or Gofpel of his Refurrection to his Apoftles: yea, in effufions or powrings forth of an extraordinary meafure of his Spirit before Chrifts coming, as on *Miriam, Deborah, Anna, Huldah*, &c. and at his coming (according to *Ioels* Prophefie) on his Daughters as well as his Sons (fo that as my oppofites alledged to me in publick: *Philip* the *Evangelift* had four Daughters thus extraordinarily endcwed) yet this favour of God toward Women deftroys not the order which the God of Order or Nature hath fet in thofe Bounds, and Limits, and Diftinctions between the Male and Female, the Man and Woman: though the Holy Scripture were filent, yet Reafon and Experience tell us, that the Woman is the weaker Veffel,

Veſſel, that ſhe is more fitted to keep and order the Womens
Houſe and Children, &c. that the Lord hath given unfitneſs for manly
a covering of longer Hair to Women as a ſign or employ-
teacher of covering Modeſty and Baſhfulneſs, Si-ments
lence and Retiredneſs : and therefore not ſo fitted
for Manly Actions and Employments.

Therefore becauſe of *Ioels* Propheſie, or becauſe
we muſt not limit or quench the Spirit, as G. *Fox*
ſaith, there is no ground in Gods ordinary courſe
of Nature to permit Women to pretend to be
Apoſtles or Meſſengers to the Nation, or *Preach*-
ers and Teachers in the *Publick* Aſſemblies.

1. Becauſe we finde no ſuch Commiſſion given
by Chriſt Jeſus or any ſuch Practice amongſt the
firſt Believers.

2. The Lord hath ſet (as Seamen ſpeak) a pre-And for
venter to ſuch an unnatural boldneſs by expreſs being
Prohibitions, with the Reaſons and Grounds to the Preachers
Corinthians and to *Timothy*: and to anſwer thoſe and poſ-tles eſpeci-
Scriptures with a flam, *viz.* that *Eve* the Tranſ-ally.
greſſor, and Women that be Tatlers are forbidden,
and the Woman *Jezebel*, [27] &c. is all one to tell
us, that *Paul* was not a Man, nor *Timothy* a Man,
nor the Teachers Men, nor *Corinth* a City, but all
ſignifie Metaphorical and Myſtical Buſineſſes.

3. Why may not Women much more be *Lord
Majors*, and *Bailiffs*, and *Sherriffs*, and *Iuſtices*, and
Conſtables, *Captains*, *Colonels*, *Generals* and *Command*-
ers by Sea and Land.[1]

4. That Reaſon the Spirit gives to the *Corinthi*-
ans, for the vailing of Women in publick Aſſemblies,

[1] Change the period to "?." *R. W. Ms. Ann.*

blies, makes much more for their vailing and filence in matters of *Prophefying, Preaching* and *Praying,* viz. Becaufe of the Angels: I know not any fair and fober Expofition of this Scripture (except as the blind *Quakers* who fwallow down a fly & Camel too) but that of the Heavenly Angels and Spirits attending on and guarding the Affemblies of true Chriftians, and rejoycing in the comlinefs, order and beauty of their publick Adminiftrations.

A memorable and doleful ftory

Some few years fince there came to my Houfe two *Maries,* it is faid they came from *London*: they bid me Repent and Hearken to the Light within me, I prayd them 'o fit down, that we might quietly reafon together, they would not; then ftanding, I askt them the ground of their fuch Travel and Employment, they alledged *Ioels Prophefie* ; I anfwered, that was fulfilled, that was not every dayes work ; befides their bufinefs was not Prophetical but Apoftolical, &c. they regarded not my Anfwers nor Admonitions, but powred the Curfes and Judgements of God againft me, and hurried away ; to *Barbadoes* they went, and (being War time, the Ship bound for *England*) they were fet upon by the *Dutch,* and though thefe Women animated the Seamen to fight, and Prophefied *that not an hair of their head fhould perifh,* yet they two were both flain, as afterward came certain Tydings of the whole matter.

What teaching the Lord requirs of Women

I own that it may pleafe the Father of Spirits in cafes extraordinary, he may pleafe to alter his common courfe of Na u e (as in *Abrahams* cafe with *Ifaak*) but we muft not tempt God ; but if God
hath

hath powred forth the gifts of *K*nowledge and Utterance npon fome Women more then other, they
have three large fields to walk in mentioned by the
Holy Scripture, *viz.* of their inftructing their Children, &c. 2. As occafion juftly calls them from
home, of inftructing other women efpecially the
younger. 3. Of confeffing boldly the Name and
Truth of Chrift Jefus, [28] when he fuffers Tyrants to bring Perfecution on them, &c.

A 15*th. Inftance is in pag.* 56. where *George Fox*
brings in *Thomas Higinfon,* faying, [*The fight of the
Godhead without Faith in Chrift is the Foundation of
all falfe worfhips.*]

He *Anfwers,* Can any fee the Godhead? have a
fiht of the Godhead and uot fee Chrift, and have
Faith in Chrift? And who hath Faith in Chrift,
do they not fee *the Fulnefs of the Godhead dwels in
him, Chrift*? And was not their mind turneh from
that of God in them (which declared *the Invifible
things of him from the Creation of his Eternal Power
and Godhead*) which the Apoftle found fault withal
Let all Examine and Judge, and read the Scripture, *Rom.* 1. and try.]

I Reply, In former years I have Converfed
with all the *Indians* of this *New-England* by Land
and Seas, and I have read the 1. of the *Romans*
often, and now once again at *G: Fox* his motion,
and I find that Firft, there is generally in all mankind in the World a Conviction of an *Invifible,
Omnipotent, and Eternal Power and Godhead.*

2. That this Conviction doth arife from the Creation, (though fome of the wifeft of the World as
Ariftotle,

Tho. Hig-
ginfon

The
knowledge
of God by
nature

Ariſtotle, &c. though Confeſſing a Godhead yet) hold the world an Eternal Deity it ſelf, and never to have been created.

3. I find not that ever any man or men (by all their natural Light or wit, or Chriſt within,) could find out how the World or himſelf, Man or Woman were created : Though *Iames Nailour* told us in print, that if never a Letter of Scriptnre had been written, yet their Spirit could tell them all things.

4. I find all men confeſs, that the will or Word, or mind of God is pure, and as they could come to know, it is to be adored, kept, and obſerved : and that it was ever, and is wickedneſs to Sin againſt it.

5. All mankind having the Law or without it are perſwaded that ſome actions are naught, and againſt Gods will, as to ſteal, to Murther, &c.

6. None (for all the Light and Spirit in every one) could ever find out how Sin how Sorrow and Death came into the World : Nor how ſuch Inclinations and Diſpoſitions to Sin came into themſelves, &c.

7. I find in all mankind a Conviction that God is juſt and [29] powerful, and doth bring plagues and puniſhments upon perſons, and Nations for thoſe groſs Sins of Adultery, Murther, &c.

8. I could never lea n (for all that Chriſt in every man *Fox* ſings of) that ever any man living, or all the Counſels of men could ever know or learn four things, but as revealed by God, by *extraordinary wayes,* of *Dreams, Viſions,* &c. or the ordinary of his *holy Record*s, and the *Doctrine* of them opened,
preached,

Marginal notes:

The convictions of nature which the 4 Quakers ſo fooliſhly talk of

The loſs of all men as to God & hravenly things

preached, &c. 1. How to pacifie Gods Juſtice? 2. How to reſiſt the *Devils Tyranny*: 3. How to wor-ſhip God? 4. How to get *true Bleſſedneſs* here, and in the World to come?

9. Hence (according to *Foxes Oppoſite*) all man-kind have invented ſo many falſe Gods, falſe worſhips, &c. all the world over, yet out of no moreLove to God then the Lamb bears to a Lyon: but out of Fear, as the old ſaying is, *primos in Orbe Deos,* &c. Fear made the firſt Gods. Hence the *Philiſtins* ſends the God of *Iſrael* a preſent and offering with Ark or Cheſt: Hence the *Samaritans* (with the *Sechemites*) for fear of Lyons or hope of gain will be of any worſhip or Religion, as moſt this day in the world will be, yea, all and every Soul except to whom (in and from the holy Scriptures) the holy Spirit reveals that Incomprehenſible Myſtery of a Mediatour. *Men natu-rally frame a God as the Devils do but cannot love him.*

A 16*th. Inſtance* of *Foxes* lame writings, is *pag.* 56. where he brings in the ſame Author ſaying, [*The Iuſtification and Redemption by obeying the Light within, is the Myſtery of Iniquity*]

He Anſwers, [*He that believeth is juſtified from all things, and comes not into Condemnation: and he hath the wietnſs in himſelf: and that lets him ſee the Re-deemer, the Saviour, the Light which walking in it he is cleanſed from all Sin, and ſo no Myſtery of Iniquity For the Myſtery of Iniquity is out of the Light. None ſees Iuſtification and Redemption, but with the Light within which comes from Chriſt who hath enlightened him.*]

I Reply,

I Reply, This is fubtle, but being examined it will be a myftery of *hellifh Iniquity*, and lighter then vanity it felf.

Babilonian Jugling, & Egyptian canting

For 1. He ufually, and here (as before I have opened) confounds Juftification and Light, and Chrift, and Faith, and obedience, (after his *Babylonifh wont*) all in a Juglers box within together: So that the Englifh of Faith is Chrift, Obedience is Chrift, Juftification is Chrift, Light is Chrift, &c. It is true, fometimes it pleafed Gods Spirit to fpeak figuratively, and to [30] call Chrift fometimes our Juftification, and fometimes a Curfe for us: Sometimes Sanctification, and fometimes Sin for us: But it is a myftery or fubtle trick of Hell to call Faith Obedience, and Obedience to the Light Juftification and Redemption, and yet mean Chrift. So that *Fox* his words may be in plain Englifh thus rendred, [*None fees Chrift and Chrift but with the Chrift within, which comes from Chrift who hath Chrifted him.*]

Chrifts Name horribly prophaned

The true Senfe, (as Mony) Anfwers all things, but it is a *Myftery of Iniquity* to darken any, much more heavenly matters with Confounding and not diftingu fhing aright when matters are in Examination.

2. It is another Gofpel (or glad News) yet not another, but is a dream and dead picture of an Image or Idol to put in our Obedience and working, though I know they Father this Baftard upon the moft holy God himfelf, faying, it is his Obedience, his Righteoufnefs,& his working,in the Room of the Death and blood fhedding, the Sufferings and merits of the Lord Jefus.   3. It

3. It is a *Myſtery of Iniquity*. (ſubtly and yet churliſhly and ſelfiſhly with *Laban*) to change wages and the Covenant or Bargain ſo often : to pretend (with the Papiſts) great abhorring of the *Jewiſh worſhip* and *Jewiſh Covenant*, the Bargain of, *Do this and live*, the Bargain of ſaving our ſelves, *&c.* and the Bargain of flying out of our ſelves and only to Gods mercy in the Mediation of Chriſt Jeſus : And then again to render our ſelves to be ſo holy, ſo righteous, ſo obedient, ſo loving, ſo Chaſt, ſo meek, ſo patient, ſo Temperate, that in thought word or deed we Sin not, and this our Holineſs is Chriſt, and God, and Spirit, and Juſtification, *&c.* *[The Old and new Bargain to Love. The great Deluſion of Quakers as to pardon of Sin and Righteouſneſs.]*

I know the writers of the Quakers make this high Obedience to be the Crown of ſome high Saints amongſt them as the Papiſts do, and that others come not ſo high, are taken by the fleſhly Spirit, and repent, and Confeſs, and be more watchful as they ſay, in a Contradiction of *I. Naylor*, but this is Contradiction to their general grant, *viz* that every Saint, every one, even the leaſt *that is born again, he can not Sin* : and I know alſo that they have a fooliſh Salve or plaiſter for this ſore too, and Contradict their denying of meanings given to the Scripture, and come to the meanings of the Proteſtants ſaying, they cannot Sin willingly, and ſo, and ſo ; And yet again, (in a horrible Myſtery of 31 | Iniquity) they exclaim againſt the Proteſtants for ſaying, a Child of God can not fall from true grace Finally or Totally. *[The Quakers bewildred as to Perfection.]*

4. Here is a *Myſtery of helliſh Iniquity*, in that

they

The Qua-they Confefs fuch a man Chrift to have been, and
kerr devi-his blood fhedding[1] the Types and real predictions
lifh
Chimiftry and figures of him, a real Death, Refurrection and
Affention, and yet upon the point (by a *Devilifh
Chymiftry*) evaporate all thefe, and leave nothing
but a Chrift within, as God and as Man, whofe
Name is now Light, and our Obedience to the
motions of this Light within this is Juftification,
Righteoufnefs, Salvation, God, Chrift, Perfection,
perfect holinefs, &c.

5. It is a *Hellifh Myftery* of the *Devil* to Cozen
poor Souls with a Notion of the Difficulty and
height of their Profeffion, and of worfhipping God
The   in Spirit and Truth, which they fay no Body in
feined   the World do but they, &c. and yet the Truth is
hardnefs, as I told them in publick, there is an Image in the
but the
real eafi- Bed, but *David* was gone, yea, and that their Re-
nefs of   ligion was one of the eafieft Religions in the world.
the Qua- For, as I have feen pluck but forth a fmall pin or
kers
Spirit.   peg in a *Harpfycon,* and that wonderful Inftrument
will delight your Ear and mind with curious and
The won- various Tunes of Mufick : So if once a poor Soul
derful
Harpficon gives way an Inch, and fets in one thought of
yielding to the voice of a Spirit within them, they
are filled and ravifhed with curious Notions of Juftification, Holinefs, God and Chrift, and Spirit
within them, they can now *Thou* the King himfelf,
The vain
dreams of they need no Scriptures, nor Teachers : and thus
the Qua- as in a dream their great Debts of Thoufands and
kers and
their fools Millions are paid and difcharged. The Cage door
Paradice. flies open, and they are delivered as a Bird, &c.

from

[1] Infert " according to." *R. W. Ms. Ann.*

from Sin and Devil, and Hell, &c. yea, Rapt up into Paradice, and fee, and hear, and fpeak *unutterable Ioyes*, &c. I Confefs as I faid in the Cafe of the *two hundred* following *Abfolom*, I hope there is many a precious Soul fincerely aiming at God, and as precious Diamonds and Jewels fallen in the dirt, &c. As I hope in the Parifhes of Proteftants and Papifts alfo, who being only ignorant as the Difciples were of main points of Chriftianity, yet aim uprightly at God, truly love him, and labour to *increafe in the knowledge and grace of Chrift Iefus.*

A *17th. Inft.* is in *ag.* 63. where G. *Fox* brings in his Adverfary *Ieremiah Ives* faying, [*There may be a Light to Convince of Sin, and yet not within man.*] He Anfwers, there is no people [32] Convinced of Sin, but they are Convinced within themfelves and with the Light within them : It is the Light which makes manifeft to a man when he is Convinced : It Anfwers to fomething, and reacheth to fomething in their particulars, though the words be fpoken without them from the Light. *Jeremiah Ives*

I Reply, *Firft*, it is a doleful Bufinefs to read and hear how *Satan* (in his *Chains of Darknefs*) yet hath Liberty to appear abroad as *an Angel of Light* from Heaven, thus vapouring and fwaggering under the Cloak and Colours of Light, the Light which is Chrift, *the Light by which all things were made, the Light that was glorified with the Father before the World was, the Light that enlightens every man that comes into the World: the Light within you,* &c. the Light which will *guide* you up to *God,* up to *Chrift,* up to *Salvation* and *Eternal Life,* and yet all this *The Devil in Samuels Mantle* *An Angel of Light but a Dragon and Devil of darknefs.*

vapourings

vapourings and Crakings are but Cheatings from *the God of this World* whofe eyes being beat out by Gods moft righteous Sentence, he labours to keep all in *blindnefs*, or to beat out the eyes of thofe whom God hath truly enlightned.

2. As I have faid before, and I faid truly, the word *Light* is a *Similitude* from *Light* and *darknefs* though my Oppofites in the difpute affirmed, that God was Light in a *proper* and not *figurative Senfe*, and it fignifies and intends Truth of all Sorts, whe-

Truth and Light the fame thing.

ther *Natural, Moral* or *Heavenly*: The natural Truth or Light is received within by a natural Light or underftandings: The Civil and moral Light or Truth fuits and agrees with thofe moral and Civil Convictions of the natural Light and underftanding? Hither to Natures Light will reach. But when we mount up to Divine and *Supernatural Truth,* here thefe very *Foxians* Confefs that *the Natural Man perceiveth not the things of God*:. Only they fay, that befide Natural Light, Natural Reafon, *&c.* there is the holy Seed God and Chrift, *&c.* within every Son, and to this Spirit and Seed in Prifon they preach, and *Fox* in our difcourfes al-leadgeth and affirmeth God (in every man) to be a *Cart loaden with fheaves,* preft under, and as it were in Prifon, *&c.* blafphemous wretches if they. keep not, but go beyond *Similitudes* and *Comparative Expreffions*[1] to make ns poor worms creep up to Heaven.

3. All *Light,* or *Truth Natural, Civil,* or *Divine* it comes from without, and is received by the *Internal*

---

[1] Infert " ufed by yᵉ Lord." *R. W. Ms. Ann.*

ternal *Faculty* according [33] to the *Capacity*, *Na-* The way of Truth or Lights goings.
ture and *meafure* of it. All Truth or falfhood,
Light or darknefs is firft efpied by the *watch* or
Sentinel, *Fancy* or *Comprehenfion*, &c. From thence
it is conveyed to the *Court* of *Guard*, where Captain Reafon or his Lieutenant, common Senfe and
Experience taketh Examination, and Memory
keeps a Record of proceedings which go on by
degreen to Actions, &c.

4. When I fay it comes from *without*, I intend
not that Truth or Light comes any other way from Where no Receiver, no Chief.
without, as by force and ravifhment, &c. I fay any[1]
other way then there is a door & Room and Re-
ceptive Faculty within willing to receive, and to
make it welcome: This G. *Fox* urgeth there muft
be a receiver, and fomething that Anfwers. I *Anf-*
wer, Natural Truth, or morals, Civil matters are
foon received by all Natural and Moral Under-
ftandings, yea, in natural Commands and Threat- Natural Under-ftanding in Men and Beafts.
nings, Beafts and Birds are admirably capacious and
obfervant. But when we fpeak of *Supernatural*
Heavenly and *Eternal matters*, of *Spiritual things* to
be difcerned *Spiritually*: What a difference is there
as between *Heaven* and *Earth*, and Infinitely greater?

When the *Lord Jefus* asked his Difciples *how*
many loavs they had, their *Natural Faculty* or *Reafon* An In-ftance of a meerly Rational and an heavenly Power and Faculty.
could give an Anfwer: When he asked them *whom*
do Men fay that I the Son of man am? This was a
Divine and *Supernatural Queftion*, and for the outfide
and Truth of the Fact, the Devils could Anfwer as
well as the Difciples, not ouly that fame faid he,
was

---

[1] Change "any" to "no." *R. W. Mf. Ann.*

was Elias, John Baptiſt, &c. but that he was the
Son of God: All this exceeds not Natural firſt
Birth *Powers* or Faculties: But to give a believing
and an affectionate Anſwer as *Peter* did, this re-
quires a *Faculty* and *Power* which *Fleſh* and *Blood*
could not reach too,[1] but the Spirit or ſecret working
Power of God in the means wrought *Peters heart*
and the *Diſciples hearts,* and to this day all *Believers
Hearts* to receive and welcome all truly Divine and
Heavenly Doctrines.

Whereas therefote G. *Fox* talks of ſomething
within which is preached to: I may Anſwer as they
do, *viz.* that the natural man perceivs no ſpiritual
matter, but when he is born again then he acts and
works, and it is moſt certain, that as an Houſe re-
ceivs his Maſter, as Candle kiſſeth Candle, the
Claſp the Hook, the mortiſe the Tenant, ſo do
Natural or Spiritual Faculties receive *Natural* [34
or *Spiritual Faculties* receive *Natural* or *Supernatural Motions* and *Impreſſions.*

The Proteſtants ſay, that before it pleaſeth God
by ſome word read, preached, *&c.* to ſet up a Candle of wiſdome in the Souls, and to work a ſpiritual
favour in the Soul, all heavenly matters are nau-
ſeous and odious, though as pleaſant, profitable and
honourable, to ſelf Ends they are welcome all the
word over, yet as ſpiritual and heavenly abominable?

G. *Fox* ſaith there is a ſomething, a Seed, though
but as *a Grain of muſtard Seed,* a *Seed of God,* of
Chriſt, of the *Spirit,* to which Chriſt the Word is
preached, and which maketh Anſwer: Hence (horribly

Marginal notes:

A cloſe Companion between all Faculties and Objects.

Nothing truly Spiritual in Nature as now degenerate.

---

[1] Change " too " to " to." *R. W. Ms. Ann.*

ribly abufing *Scripture phrazes*) they fo often fay
God is all (within and without:) Hence they maintain, *&c.* though men be dark and dead, yet Chrift
within is Light and alive in them, and them only.

Hence appears G. *Fox* his lying Cheats of a *Sufficient Light* withiu to lead to God and to Salvation,
a Teacher within all Sufficient, for then no need,
yea, it is a fimple Superfluity, *&c.* to hold a Candle
of outword words to awaken and enlighten fuch a
glorious all-Sufficient Sun within.

5. I ask where this fomething, this fomething of
God, (yea, God and Chrift and Spirit [1]) If he Anf-
About the
wer, in the underftanding he grants it, that[2] is dark, light fhin-
ing in
and perceives no heavenly matters, *&c.* If in the darknefs.
Heart and Affections he Confefieth, all there, is
hard and dead: only he faith, *the Light fhineth in
the darknefs*, &c. Implying that in the dark underftanding there is fome heavenly Light: in the
hearts hardnefs there is fome foftnefs, and *the Light
fhineth in darknefs*, &c.

I Anfwer, *Chrift Jefus tke Sun of Righteoufnefs*
arofe with *faving Rayes* or *wings* of *Salvation*, but
the *blind Jews* could not own him for the *Expected
Meffiah*, what is this G. *Fox* his fomething? a Light
of Chrift *inlightning every man that comes into the
World*, though the man fee it not.

2. What is this to all the Generations of the
World about *four thoufand* years before Chrift came,
and was in that *vifible perfon* as *John* faith of him,
that lightens every man that comes, &c. what is this

to

---

[1] Add " is " after "Spirit." *R. W. Ms. Ann.*
[2] Infert " it." *R. W. Ms. Ann.*

to a mixture of Light and darknefs in the fame
faculty, the eye blind and yet feeing, the man dead
and yet alive ? It is trne the *Lambs wife* confeffeth
that *her Hear t was awae* [35] *while fhe flept.* But
what is this to the heart being dead and no Life
at all and yet waking ?

6. The Conclufion is (as before. I hinted) and
they Confefs, when God in his own Means ordinarily works the will to hear, to turn, to believe, to
pray, he then gracioufly works the work for us,
and being thus turned with *Ephraim*, we mourn and
lament, and fay, *what have we done?* when he turns
our wildernefs (wholly a wildernefs) into a Garden,
then we bring forth his fweet Fruits, Flowers and
Spices : when he turns the Wolf into a Lamb, then
we are meek and Innocent, and patient : but to
talk of preaching to the Spirits in Prifon, yea, of
the Seed of God and the Spirit of God in prifon,
when the Lord fpeaks of his warning and moving
men by *Noahs* preaching in the *old World*, as may
be evidently evinced,) is like the prophane teaching of *Parrots* to prate of Grace and Heaven, like
that *admirable Parrot* in *France,* who could fay her
Pater nofter, her *Creed,* and *Ten Commandments,*
and yet knew as much of grace and the workings
of God in the Soul, as her *Popifh Teachers,* &c.

An 18*th. Inftance* of G. *Fox,* his lame and cheating Anfwers is in *pag.* 64. where he brings in the
fame Author *Jeremiah Jves* faying, [*It is a known
Error to fay, that a man was in Hell and in Heaven.*]
He Anfwers, who in this fhews his Ignorance of
Scripture, for it gives Teftimony of men that did
witnefs

Gods grr-
cious
workings
with and
in the
Souls of
men.

A wonder-
ful Par-
rots
Religion.

Jeremiah
Ives

witnefs that they had been in Hell, in the *Nether-most Hell*, and witneffed again they were in *Heaven*, and *fate in heavenly places in Chrift Jefus*, and fuch were in *Heaven*, as is fpoken of in the Revelations.

I Reply, G. *Fox* and millions more talk of *Heaven* and *Hell* as the *Notable Parrot* (above faid)[1] our *Fore-Fathers*, & fome from the Scripture, and fome out of *Reafons Light* talkt of places of *Ioy Eternal* for the *Righteous*, and of *mifery Eternal* for the *bad* and *wicked*. But the new Light from Chrift Jefus and his pen-men is the cleareft that ever fhined in this world, efpecially, that famous *Parable* or Word proceeding out of the mouth of Chrift Jefus, *Luke* 16. that of *Dives* and *Lazarus* declaring (in fubftance) the ftate of the Life, to Come, and of the two great *Parties* of the poor afflicted Righteous, and the wicked living in pleafures, *&c.*

Heaven and Hell to come.

G. *Fox* is in his *Burrough* of the various fignification of the words *Heaven* and *Hell*: He knows that a ftate of Sorrow and [36] Bitternefs is called *Hell*. That a ftate of *Death* and the *grave* is fet out by the word *Hell* in the fame *Hebrew phrafe*: And to either of thefe he wickedly applies the *thirft*[2] State, of which the Lord Jefus 1. fo clearly fpeaks: *viz.* The State of the ungodly after this Life, in the Life and World to come.

Fox his Hell and Heaven.

2, Again, he knows the vifible State of the true Profeffion of Chrift Jefus is called *Heaven*.

3. Such as have Intereft in Chrift Jefus have fitten

ten

[1] Infert "fo did." *R. W. Ms. Ann.*
[2] Erafe "thirft." *R. W. Ms. Ann.*

49

ten down with him in thofe *Heavenly Manfions* and *glories* into which he is entred bodily and gone to prepare for their Reception and coming.

4. The *third Heaven* (the place of *Pauls Rapture* and *Vifion*) the place of Joy, and Bleffednefs and Glory, when thefe *Heavens* and *Earth* are burnt up and confumed.

It is like G. *Fox* hath been occafioned to thefe thoughts by the *Papifts Fables* about *Heaven* and *Hell*, and *Purgatory*, and their curious Queftions as whether the Torment of Hell be as real and terrible as this *Elementary* and *Kitching Fire*: Whether the pain of Hell tranfcend not all pains of *Childbirth, Stone, gout, Collick, Burning?* &c. Whether it be poffible for a Creature to Continue in fuch Torments perpetually without Intermiffiion? Whether there fhall not be fome end after fome millions of years as well as of the pains of *Purgatory*: G. *Fox* knows how the *Papifts* get a world of Mony by thefe Notions of *Heaven* and *Hell* which the *Atheiftical Foxes* amongft them count but *Fables*, (as the *Pope* fpeaks of Chrift) The *Devils* have a more real Faith or Belief of thefe things and *tremble*: They cried out to the Lord Jefus, *why art thou come to torment us before the Time?* &c. But G. *Fox* not believing (as they think) thefe Fables, he fancies that *Hell* is fome apprehenfions in the mind of wrath to come, and that is *Hell* and wrath it felf, and having had flafhes of *Pride* and *Peace* in their minds, thefe are the Joyes of *Heaven*, whereas the Lord Jefus tells us, that befide the hundred fold

The Papifts Quer es aboutiHell

TheScripture, Hell and Heaven but Fables with G. Fox and other Popifh Foxes

fold of *Spiritual Ioyes* (*viz a hundred Fathers, Mo-* .The Hea-
thers, &c.) there remains for his Followers in the Hell to
World to come *Eternal Life.* come.

They are but fhort Flafhes of *Hell* and *Heaven*
which fome of thefe poor Cheated Souls dream of:
I know they allow time more or lefs before they
come into the perfect and heavenly State of Neceffity.[1]   Death prevents fome from coming to it,
and makes the reign of the reft whom Satan has The Foxes
ticed into thefe [37] *proud Vanities* but fhort, as mad Fancy
Experience hath declared: only they have a mad of the
Fancy of their Souls going into *God,* and becom- next Life.
ing more *God,* and yet this fome of them grant
to the Souls of all men, to *Iudas* as well as *Peter.*

The true Proteftant believes thefe three things,
Firft, that there is a State Eternal of Joy to the
Righteous bodies and Souls after this Life: and a The Pro-
State of Eternal Mifery of Soul and Body to the Faith as to
ungodly: Although the exact knowledge of par- the Life to
ticulars exceed the prefent fight of our *mortal eyes,* come.
the hearing of our *Ears,* and the *Capacity* of our
Hearts, &c.

2. The *firft Fruits* and a *Taft* both of the *hea-*
venly Ioyes and the *Torments of the damned* are given
by God in this Life, to the firft, in that *Solid Peace*
and *Ioy* which they have in God: To the other in
that *Horror* and *Defpair,* and *Enmity againft God,* &c.

3. Three Sorts of men efpecially will feek[2] there Three
is an Hell to come, above other Sinners. *Firft,* The Sorts will
find Hell
Voluptuous

---

[1] Erafe "of neceffity."   *R. W. Ms. Ann.*
[2] Erafe " k " in " feek."   *R. W. Ms. Ann.*

Volnptuous and *Luxurious, whofe God is theii Belly,*
and their *Sences,*&c. *Ars. potenter.*[1]

above
others.

2. The *Devourers of the Poor and helplefs,* potenter,[2] *&c.*

3. The *proud* puft up with *foolifh Confidences,* boldly Crying, *Lord open to us, for we,* &c. alfo the Contrary to thefe three I might inlarge on, *and not
Impertinently, but let him that readeth underftand,* is
in[3] *pag.* 64. where[4] G. *Fox* brings in *Ieremiah Ives*
faying, ⌊*The Pharifeel were far enough from having
the Kingdom of Heaven within them*⌋ He Anfwers
contrary to Chrifts words, who faid it was within
them.

Jeremiah
Ives.

I Reply, G. *Fox* his *Tutor* and *Teacher* within
him knows, that the *Kingdom of God* and the *Kingdom of Huaven* fignifie but one, and not divers
things : and yet alfo he knows that both of them
fignifie (in a Chriftian Senfe) *Firft,* the *Kingdome of
Government* of *God* and Chrift in the Soul. *Secondly,*
The Government of God in his holy Providence in
the World. 3. His Government in the *Congregation* or
Churches of his *Saints* called out of the World.
Fourthly, the *glorious State* to come aft r this Life :
He knowes that his I*ourney man* G. *Fox* is [5](fit Inftrument to deftroy all thefe, and to erect (in their
ftead) a *dull, proud, dogged Confufion,* or *Babel within,*
under the Name of *God, Chrift, Spirit, Light, Faith,
Righteoufnefs, Refurrection.*   The

The King-
dom of
God figni-
fying
divers
things.

---

1 Erafe " *Ars. potenter.*"   *R. W. Ms. Ann.*
2 Erafe " potenter."   *R. W. Ms. Ann.*
3 Change " is in " to " yn."   *R. W. Ms. Ann.*
4 Erafe " where."   *R. W. Ms. Ann.*
5 Erafe the parenthefis, and infert " a."   *R. W. Ms. Ann.*

The Lord Jefus knowing that not the *Phar fees* alone *&c.* but the *Iews* generally alfo, and his own *Chriftan Followers* were leavened [38] with a world-ly notion, *viz.* thar their *Meſſiah* fhould be a *glo-rious temporal King*, that he fhould make his *En-trance*, and *Exalt* his *Throne* with *great Pompe, Solemnity*, &c. The Lord Jefus tells them their miftake and faith, that his *Kingdome* was not fuch a *Kingdome*, but that it was within them: Of which words I find three Expofitions. *Firft*, that the *Kingdome of Heaven* is a *Spiritual, inward* and *Soul Kingdome*, concerning God and the Soul, and Spirit-ual matters, according to the faying of Chrift Jefus, *my Kingdome is not of this World*, &c.

The falfe and true Meffiah.

The King-dome of God with-in you.

Three Expofi-tions.

2. From the word *Entos* within you, or amongſt you, as certainly it was then amongſt the *Iews*, and in the midſt of them in their *Temple Streets* and *Houſes, Hearts* and *mouths* by the moſt *wonderful ſpeakings* of the Lord Jefus, as never man ſpake amongſt them, and the *wonderful power* and *gracious works* which never man wrought amongſt them, nor in the whole World befide

3. The Kingdome of God, that is God and Chrift, and the Spirit were literally in the *Pharifees*, and fo Confequently in every hypocrite in the World, and every wicked and prophane Sinner, though they know it not, yea in all Creatures.

But this is againſt a former, fair Expofition from the Greek word *Entos*, which cannot be refufed (fince fo agreeing with the Truth) except Reafons more prevalent, *&c.*

The Qua-kers Ex-pofition.

2. The Spirit of God asks, *what agreement be-tween*

*tween Chrift and Belial, Light and Darkne/s, Righte-
oufne/s & unrighteoufne/s ?* &c.

And whereas it is moft Improperly and Impioufly Objected, that *the Light fhines in darkne/s,* &c.   I
have faid, that it can not be in the fame Subject or
part predominate, the mind, or will, or Affections :
but the Light is at the window, and the Eye, and the
knock at the door, (by all the wayes and means by
which God vifits poor men) but the Eye, the door
is fhut, *&c.* and the man within is not only afleep,
but dead and rotten in *Natures filthine/s,* and *actual
Tran/gre/fions* and *Abominations.*

3. It is againft all Colour of Reafon to Imagine
that the Lord Jefus fhould tell the *Iews,* the *Pharifees,* and the reft of his *bloody Enemies,* who fome
weakly, fome malicioufly oppofed his Kingdome,
and coming to Rule by his Grace over them, *viz.*
that his *grace* was *King* within them, what ever
their Heart or Tongues faid, or Hands hid, *&c.*

4. It is notorioufly contrary to what G. *Fox,* and
his fo often [39] Clamour that the *Kingdome of God
confifts in,* or its Nature is in *Righteoufne/s, and Peace
and Joy in the holy Spirit* : as oppofite to the Kingdome in the *Pharifees,* and all *Hipocrites* and *prophane,* &c. as Hell to Heaven.

5. The thing is fo notorioufly childifh and ridiculous, *&c.* that a King fhould affirm he was an
actual *King* in his *Enemies Country,* where the
whole is up in Arms againft him : Or for a Lamb
to fay, he was amongft the Wolves and held his
Government in them : Or that a man pretending
Love to a Woman in way of marriage fhould
boldly

The Light
fhining in
darknefs.

'The grace
of God is
offered to
all, but em-
braced by
few that
are freely
chofen

boldly affirm, (though she abhord to hear of the motion yet) that he was in her *Heart* and *Affections*, as an *Husband, Lord,* &c. It is true, the motions of *War* and *Love* are made and offerd from the *King warring,* and the man *suing,* but that their motions and Commands (that is Government and Kingdome) should be in them is nothing but impious and impudent, and childish prating. The frantick fancy of Christs Kingdome in his Enemies hearts.

The 20*th Instance,* is in *pag.* 75. where G. *Fox* brings in *Thomas Weld,* &c. saying, [*How clear the Scripture is, that Faith comes by hearing, and not by minding the Light within*] He *Answers,* Doth any man know Christ but by the Light within? And is not Christ the Word? And can any see without Christ the Word? Doth it not make manifest? Nay, doth it not *give the Light of the knowledge of God in the face of Iesus Christ?* read 2 *Cor.* 4. 1. from whence Faith comes, and so Feith comes by minding the Light within, Christ the Author of it, and brings to look at him, and hear him. Thomas Weld.
Faith how wrought.

I Reply, mine eyes have seen a poor distracted aged woman walking in State, boasting of her *Majesty, Iewels,* and *Crown,* with a Straw in her hand for her Scepter, *&c.* and thus doth this poor mad Soul walk even like *Nebuchadnezzar* upon his *Babel.* All is Christ, and he is Christ, Christ is Faith and all, *&c* & therefore A distracted old woman a picture of the Quakers.

1. He slights this so known and unquestionable Record, *Faith comes by hearing,* and that *heavenly Chain of Diamonds,* Rom. 10. concerning true Salvation, true worshipping, true praying, true believing, true preaching, true sending, which holy writing or Record *Fox* dares not seriously and Rom. 10. The admirable Chain of Diamonds.

impartially,

impartially, and in the fear of the moſt High conſider, as to the various means and wayes of Gods
ſending unto man.

2. For all G. *Fox* his Scepter of Straw, his mad
fancy of a [40] Light that works Faith, *&c.* I ask
what Faith is, and if it be not *Firſt*, a believing the

True Faith what Goſpel, or Glad News to be true. *Secondly*, a receivi-
ving of it and believing in it mine own particular.

As *Firſt*, that a pardon is certainly come, *Secondly*,
that my *Name* is in it, my *deliverance* and *Salvation*
is wrapt up in it The great *King of Heaven* (like
Ahaſhueroſh) his *Angel* is ever : now he hath
thoughts of *marriage Loves* and *Joyes*, and *Secondly*, I (though a 'poor Captive *Jew*, 'poor *Eſther*)
I am ſhe his Eye hath fixt on, and his Soul delights in :

3*dly*, I askt what preaching is, but the publiſhing
or divulging, telling or declaring what the Word

Heb. 1. or mind, or will of the *King Eternal* is, which he
Act. 26. hath revealed or declared to the *Patriarchs Moſes*
and the reſt of his *Prophets*, or *Meſſengers* from the
beginning of the World : And what ſaid the *Apoſtles* or *Meſſengers* of Chriſt Jeſus declare, but what
Moſes and the *Prophets* did ſay ſhould come to paſs?
Act 26. which all was Scripture ? Was not this

The four ſort of Hearers. *Proclamation* of *Good News*, or a pardon to be made
over all the World, and the firſt proclaiming of it
to be at *Jeruſalem*, Luke 24.   And was there not
to be four ſorts of Hearers of this *glad News*.

4. That receive and believe with a falſe and
overly, and looſe, and ſandy Belief: A *fourth*, only
with a deep and rockie Belief, cloſing and uniting

to

to God? Thus the men of *Samaria* told the woman *that they did not believe becaufe of her word,*
(that muft be taken *Comparatively,* for the Hearing
from her this *glad News,* was .he firft means of their
believing) but becaufe they had heard Chrift themfelves,

5. I know thefe poor *Foxians* do hear a kind of The Qua-
Motion within them, but it is but as poor women that kers how
go with *falfe Conceptions* with *Tympanies* of *wind* cheated by
and *water,* or with the *mola* that will refemble the Queen
Motion of a *true Child*: but after all their thoughts Mary was
and fancies by day and night after all their *feeming* of her
feellings perfwafions, *Experiences,* and *preparations,* tion.
this *falfe Conception, falfe Faith, falfe Chrift, falfe
Light* fhall vanifh in fhame and grief, as did *Queen
Maries* after the *Thanks3ivings* and *Ringings* for her
deliverance.

6. For my felf I dare thefe *felf Confidents* to *particularize* any one Scripture where the Spirit of Challenges
God directs any poor Soul to liften and hearken to to the
a *Light* and voice within him, affirming that ⌊41 Foxians.
this is the Hearing by which Faith is wrought? I
dare them to clear Candidly and folidly, this, 10. to
the *Rom.* wherein(as in the *8th* is the *Golden Chain
of Election,* &c.) fo in this *10th Chap.* the *Golden
Chain* of the means of *praying, preaching,* &c.

3. I ask for fome *follid Inftances* where *Souls* have
been truly Converted (the whole Soul unto God)
by any fuch *Notion,* and not by fome *External
means* and outward hearing of this *glad News* and
Gofpel?

4. I ask if it be not a *ridiculous Contradiction*
50   in

in them to fill the World with the found of their
new and only preachers *He Apoſtles* and *ſhe Apoſ-*
tles, &c.

5. I ask if this *Light within* (without and oppoſite to the hearing without which is the queſtion)
be the means of Faith, how is it poſſible, that ſo
many ſerious Enquiring men in all Ages ſhould
not perceive a breath of this wind, no not in their
own boſomes? and that *famous Paul* ſhould be Con-
ſcientiouſly and fully perſwaded that he ought to
do many things againſt Chriſt Jeſus, &c.

If it be ſaid, *Paul* had not only the *Light within* him,
but he had heard of the Doctrine of Chriſt and of
his *Followers*: he heard *Stephens Sermon*, and yet he
believed not: and therefore it is *Grace* doth all. I
Anſwer, this is ſomething, but reacheth not home,
for, if all the men in the world have this *Light*
(which is inſufficient without hearing) why ſhould
not ſome, (eſpecially the wiſe and Enquirours, &c.)
perceive it or ſomething of it, as *Paul* did not, until he had heard ſomething, (and becauſe God had
a purpoſe to make Extraordinary uſe of him, an
Extraordinary hand from Heaven humbling and
preparing him to publiſh or preach unto the Nations.

The 21 *Inſtance*, is in *pag.* 80. where G. *Fox*
brings in *Tho. Pollard*, ſaying, [*To ſay the Officers of*
the Church are Inviſible, It is plain of their Father
the Devil] He Anſwers, The Holy Ghoſt made
the Officers of the Church Overſeers, and that
made the Officers the Overſeers to be Inviſible, for
they ſaw with an Inviſible Eye, and ſo they was in
the

Pauls
famous
Caſe

80 Tko.
Pollard.

the Spirit which is Invisible, and not in the Flesh:
else they could not be Overseers in the Church of
God, and you are the visible apostatiz'd from them. *The Fox*
like and
 I Reply, This is one of the most *impudent Foole-* *dog like*
ries that either *Fox,* or (as the *Proverb* is) *any Dog* *Impuden-*
could be impudent in : For First, *cy of G.*
Fox &c.
42] 1. He acknowledgeth a *publick Affembly* of
Chriftians; as well as of other pretending Worsh p-
pers, *Turks, Jews,* &c. Alſo he acknowledgeth the
Minifters, Officers, and Overseers of their Affemblies.

 2. His Reaſon is notoriouſly filly and impudent, *The viſi-*
viz. becauſe the Church is in God, and the Over- *bility of*
ſeers are made by the holy Spirit : For are the ſe- *Chriſts*
cret works of God alwayes ſecret, and never revealed? *Church*
and her
The *Child* in the *Wombe,* the *precious Stones,* and *Officers.*
Minerals when brought forth, are no more *Inviſi-*
ble then the *Sun* in the *Firmament.*

 3. The Chriftian profeffion and profeffours, however they were wrought and prepared, and by divers means by Gods Spirits : yet the Lord Jeſus
compares them to the moft viſible Conſpicuous and
glorious things and perſons. To the *Sun* and *Moon*
in the *Heavens,* and the *Heavens* and *Stars* alſo, to
Mountains, and *Cities* on thoſe *Hills* or *Mountains* :
To *Kings,* To their *houſes* and *Palaces,* yea, to
Armes with *Banners,* &c.

 4. Although the *Lord Major* of *London,* and the
ſeveral Officers of the City are not made and ordained in the public Streets, nor *Generals* and other
Officers appointed by his *Majeſty,* &c. are they not
therefore

therefore vifible, because their making and appointing was not Solemnized and performed in *Cheap-fide*, &c.

5. It is moſt true and moſt ſweet, that the Church is in God, *&c.* and is it not alſo true, that in one Senſe, we *live in God* and *move in God, have our Being in God,* and yet the *whole* Creation is *glorioufly vifible* in another Sence, the *Saints,* their *Affemblies* and *Officers* are in God *vifible* to the world abundantly, though in an heavenly and ſpiritual Sence, tranſcending the Being of the *firſt Creation.*

The Church in God..

6. G. *Fox* denies not, but that although the *firſt Churches* were in God, and the *Officers* of the *Church,* and ſome of them were appointed immediately, yet they were *vifible* and *audible* by thoſe with whom they Converſed :

7. Yea, G. *Fox* and his *Foxians,* for all their being in God, and ſome of their proud and filly Anſwerings in Courts, that they live in God, and dwell in God, yet they diſowne not their own *vifible Congregatings* and *Affemblings,* their *vifible Teachers, Overſeers,* or *Bifhops,* their *vifible* and *audible* performances and *Worfhips,* ·*praying, preaching, finging,* &c. and wny then doth this [43] poor notoriouſly *vifible Cheatour* thus prate of *Invifibilities efpecially in times of peace and not in* Elias *Cafe?*

G Fox a moſt vifible and idle prater of Invifibilities.

The 22 *Inſtance* is in *pag* 84. where G. *Fox* brings in his oppoſite *Magnus Byne;* ſaying, [*The Scriptures may be underſtood by the help of Tongues.*] He Anſwers, [*All Scripture was given forth by Infpiration, and fo without the fame Infpiration, it is not underſtood again,* Pilate *had the Tongues, yet did not under-*

Magnus Byne.

ſtand

*stand the Scripture, nor Chrift the Subftance of it:
And this you have fet up fince the Apoftacy, your
Tongues, you Raveners from the Spirit.*]

I Reply, Firft, I make ufe of G. *Fox* his *Confef-
fion,* viz. that *all Scripture is infpired,* &c. therefore God hath
fay I, he Confeffeth that every *word, Syllable* and many
Ti:tle in that *Scripture* or *writing,* is the *Word,* or words.
immediate revealed will of God: againft his and his
Foxians common Song: hath God any more words
but one?

2. As to the Scriptures, the underftanding of The un-
them is threefold.   derftand-
                                                       ing of the
Firft, Literal: who underftands not, *Thou fhalt* Scripture
not kill, Thou fhalt not Steal? &c.   threefold.

The fecond is *Metaphorical,* as *I am the Dore, I
am the Bread,* &c.

The third is faving and Spiritual, when it pleafeth God to fet home the *heavenly Commands Promifes,* &c. in particular, *Soul Application.*

3. I obferve the End of G. *Fox* (and efpecially of The Dev-
the *old Serpent* and *Fox* that acts him.) It is to de- Cavilling
ftroy the coming of *Gods holy Records* and *writings* againft the
to poor loft men to their *Salvation,* that he may Scripture
                                                       Tongues,
foift and whifp in what his *hellifh malice* pleafeth yet J.
to their Damnation: For if no knowledge of the Stnbs va-
Tongues in which the moft wife and moft holy he under-
Lord *'pend his Letters* or *writing* to us, then no ftood as
preaching of the Doctrine in them to the world many
                                                       Tongues as
witout fome *new miraculous way,* then no tranflating I, and may
and reading of them, which is, that the Devil in be more.
all Ages and at this day aims at with all his might.

4. I therefore charge upon this *'proud Ignoramus,*
                                                        and

and all his *blind Difciples* and *Followers* the horrible Crime of *Unthankfulnefs*, and *Ingratitude* : for
were it not for *Tindal*, burnt to afhes, and other
heavenly Spirits fet on work from Heaven to dig
out the knowledge of the *Hebrew* and the *Greek*,
and to turn it into *French, Dutch, Englifh*, and now
praifed be God into the very [44] *Indian Language*
of this Country, how would thefe *Seraphical Doctors* know whether there were fuch a *Creation of
Heavens* and *Earth*, or of man and his wife, which
we now fo talk of?

I put this queftion once to a Soul in this Country, who told me although they had no *Englifh
Scripture*, Gods Spirit would teach them *Greek* and
Hebrew : but I can declare to any that ask me the
dreadful End of that party.

5. I Charge upon this *Foxian party* the horrible
Crime of a *proud Lazinefs* for not ftudying the
Original Languages themfelves ; It is a fhameful
Trade and deceitful, when perfons have mony in
their hands, to take up all on truft ! I have known
very *Eminent Men* and *Women Independants* and *Baptifts* , give themfelves up to ferious ftudy of the *Hebrew Language* : I never knew any of the *Foxian
Spirits* fo inclind, but according to the *Lazie fool*
under the *Fig-Tree* which I have feen in an *Em-
bleme* almoft threefcore year fince, they lie down
and cry.

> *Sweet Figs drop down in yielding w fe*
> *For Lazie will not let me rife.*

6. I Judge that G. *Fox* and his *wild Spirit* can
not

not prove that *Pilate* had the *Hebrew Greek* and *Latin*, for though he caused by an *heavenly fin-* ger of God such a Title to be set up in the three then moft known Languages *Hebrew, Greek,* and *Latin*, yet he himfelf might have no knowledge of any more then the *Latin*, which was his *Mother Romane Tongue*: As a *Book feller* may deal in Books of *Hebrew, Greek, Latin, French, Dutch, Italian, Spanifh*, &c. and yet underftand no more then his *Mother Englifh*.

The three Languages upon the Crofs of Chrift.

7. I know the Devil abounds with Tongues, and can fpeak all Languages, and I know, and have feen his *Infpirations*, and three thoufands verfes in fh w very heavenly, infpir'd by him, in an Englifh wo- man of this Country, who had no fuch skill, *ex tempore.* They were taken and written from her mouth, and I have read the n : and do believe from many Reafons which I have to fhew they were from Satan, yet I know alfo that Ignorance is fhame- ful, and that it pleafed God miraculoufly to infufe the knowledge of Tongues to his firft Apoftles, or Meffengers, to the Nations, and what he will fur- ther do in this kind, [45] before this *Worlds glass* is out who can tell? only I am fure thefe *Foxians* talk (like little Children in their grave Confulta- tions) without the leaft knowledge at all (genrally) of any thing, but their *mother Englifh*, and yet as proudly and imperioufly vapouring and triumphing, &c. like *Theora John* proclaming to the *World* his mad *Quaking Revelations, Infpirations*, writing of *Languages*, many which he Confeft, he underftood not, but *Myfteries, Myfteries.*

The Dev- ils skill in Languages and Sub- tlety in Revela- tions.

Theora John

8 G.

8. G. *Fox* is no wiſer in affirming that *Tongues* came in place of the Spirit ſince the *Apoſtacy.* For before the *Apoſtacy* the Lord furniſhed his Servants with underſtanding of ſeveral Languages *miracu-loufly*: with the *Apoſtaſie*, thoſe *heavenly miraculous gifts* ceaſed: In the *Apoſtacy the Father of Spirits* gave to his two witneſſes power, Authority & Ability to prophe*fy*, preach, declare & witneſs to the Truths of Jeſus againſt the *Popiſh Inventions*: with the riſing of *Luther, Calvin,* &c. The Lord raiſed up the ſtudy of the *Hebrew* and *Greek Tongues* in many *heavenly Witneſſes,* who brought to Light the truth of the *firſt Copies* in Oppoſition to the Corrupt *Latin Tranſlation* (bruitiſhly ſettled under a Curſe by the *Counſel at Trent*): This mighty work of the Lord in his *Proteſtant Witn ſſes* drove the *Popiſh Foxes* into their *holes*, and hath driven (for ſhame) the *Jeſuits* to ſtudy the *Hebrew* and *Greek*, and by a *new Stratagem* partly made up of the pretence of their *Spirit* and partly of the pretence of *Corruptions* and *Variations* in the Copies) to aſſault the Camp of the *Proteſtant Witneſſes.*

9. I deſpiſe not, yea, I praiſe God for, and honour the helps and helpers we have in Engliſh: yea, I would not diſcourage the weakeſt *Engliſh man* or *woman* (in Chriſtian humility) to ſound forth the praiſes of God in *writing, ſpeaking* and *printing* in *Engliſh* what they have Experimented of the *Son of God,* No, though they ſhould not *write* or *print,* or ſpeak true Engliſh, as G *Fox* hath not done: But when they lift up their *Horns* on high (or their *bruitiſh Ears* as *Foxes* do, in ſtead of *Horns*) then I

must

The Lord raiſeth his Witneſſes againſt Babel by his Spirit and bleſſing upon Tongues and Tranſlations.

The Papiſts former Ignorance & now their abuſe of knowledge

Engliſh helps a great mercy.

muſt tell G. *Fox*, that although he prat le amongſt A cloſe Query the *Engliſh*, and they be cheated with his *dying Spirit* : yet if he go to other Nations, (as they ſimply pretend to do to *Turks* and *Pope*) they muſt either be furniſhed with the Gift of Tongues miraculouſly, or they muſt fling of their *lazie Devil*, and ſtudy the *Tongues* of thoſe Nations to whom they carry their (*pretended*) *glad News* or *Goſpel*.

46] The 23. *Inſtance*: G. *Fox* in pag.86. brings in the ſame Author, ſaying, [*Notwithſtanding thy paſſing through the firſt and ſecond Reſurrection* (as thou ſaith) *there remains a Torment ſo thee at the laſt day and Woe*.]

He *Anſwers*, They are bleſſed that have part in the firſt Reſurrection : The ſecond Death have no 86, Magnus Byne power over them, but are made free from Wrath that is to come, and are paſſed from Death to Life, and are tranſlated into the Kingdome of the Son of God, and are in union with the Son of God and the Father both ; and ſo thou uttereſt forth Lies.

I Reply, G. *Fox* here Arrogates to himſelf and his *Foxians*.

1. A Paſſing through the firſt and ſecond Reſur- The firſt rection. and ſecond Reſurrection.

2. He triumpheth in their Bleſſedneſs pronounced to their firſt Reſurrection, *viz.* of Communion with God and Freedome from Wrath to come :

1. The Truth is G. *Fox* is in his Burrough of Words of divers ſignifications : He wreſts and winds what is for his wicked ends, but you ſhall never take him in *Diſtinguiſhing* and *Defineing* what the *firſt* and *ſecond Death* is, and what is the *firſt* and *ſecond Reſurrection*. 2. The

51

2. The Truth is, as foon as they hearken to this *familiar Spirit*, they are fo Elevated, that they be in the *heavenly glory*, the *Refurrection* is paft, and (with K. *Agags dream*) the *Bitternefs* of *Death* and *Wrath* is paft for ever with them.

The great Expecta-tion of all the four great Re-ligions. 3. But no fuch *grapes* will be gathered of thefe *Thorns*, nor *Figs* of thefe *Thiftles* : For if we talk of efcaping wrath to come, and of enjoying *Blef-fednefs* : we muft prove to others, as well as to our felves, that the *Expectation* of the *Jews*, and *Mahu-metans* expecting a *Carnal Bleffednefs* to come, is falfe : We mnft prove the *Papifts* and *Common Pro-teftants* (for all their Prayers and Alms, &c.) are under that Sentence, *Depart from me ye workers of Iniquity*.

4. The Lord Jefus being queftioned about the great point of Salvation : he feems to Anfwer two things.

The great point of Salvation. 1. That the moft will hang their Souls upon the *Hedge*, and venture like the *high ways* and *hedges*.

2. Others will *fear* and look after *Redemption*, *Deliverance*, *Salvation*, &c. and of thefe two forts.

Two great Sorts of minders Eternal Life. Firft. Some that will endeavour and feek to en-ter I Judge both ⌊47⌋ of *Pagans* and *Mahumetans*, and. *Jews*, and *Papifts* and *Proteftants*, and fhall not be able.

The fecond is of fuch as fenfible of the *Nar-rownefs* of the way, *ftraightnefs* of the dore, and the *Infinite neceffity incumbing*, and the *Infinite Ex-cellency inviting*, fling away *Preferments*, *Profits*, and *Pleafures*, and choofe to enjoy the *Mediator*, as loft and damned in our felves, and follow him from his
Cradle

Cradle and *Manger* to his *Crofs* and *Gallows*, and labouring to draw other poor drowning Souls out of the pit of *Eternal Rottennefs,* & *howling* with us.

5. The Spirit of God tells us of three forts of perifht Souls.

Firft, Thofe without Law, of which are *Millions of Millions innumerable.* _{Three great forts of Me}

Secondly, Such as had the *Law* or *Word*, or will of God revealed to them in the Covenant of works, *Obedience* or *Juflice*, of which fort were[1] *Millions of Millions* alfo.

A third is of fuch to whom *Infinite pity* hath vouchfafed the *joyful Tidings* of the Son of God, his *Mediation, Interpofition,* and *Interceffion.*[2]

Amongft thefe the *Papifts,* and the Protefters againft the Papifts are chief: of the Papifts the *Jefuits*: of the Proteftant (therefo called) *Puritans* run for it: of thefe the Quakers pretend the higheft, but no otherwife then, *O thou* Capernaum, *which art Exalted,* & *Exalteft thy felf unto Heaven, thou fhalt be brought down to Hell,* &c. For *Tyre and* Sidon, Sodom, *and* Gomorrah, & c. the *poor Jews* and *Mahumetans*, yea, the *Papifts* and common Proteftants fhall have an eafier Cup to drink off then the *Foxians,* &c, that are fo high, & pure, and lofty, and yet abound with *Luciferian filthinefs.* _{Jefuits and Puritans the two great Antagonifts.}

The 24. *Inflance*, is in *pag.* 89. where G. *Fox* brings in the fame Author, faying, [*The Saints are neither in the Fulnefs of the Godhead, nor in part: Away with this Blafphemy that faith this is*] He Anfwers, _{pag. 89. Magnus Bine}

[1] Infert "and are." *R. W. Ms. Ann.*
[2] Add "loft in themfelves but faved by grace." *R. W. Ms. Ann.*

The Qua-
kers in the
Fulnefs of
the God-
head of
their hel-
lifhmouths
and pens
ay bebe-
lieved

Anfwers, [*The work of the Miniftry was to bring people to the knowledge of the Son of God, to a perfect
man, to the Unity of the Faith, to the meafure and
ftature of the Fulnefs of Chrift and Chrift will dwell in
the Saints; and God will dwell in them*;] And thou
faith, They have no part of the Fulnefs of the Godhead, and *John* faith, *of his Fulnefs have we all received, in whom dwells the Goahead bodily,* and ye be
all in the Blafphemy that be out of this part of
the Fulnefs.

I Reply, It was doubtlefs an *horrible Crime* which
the Jews though malicioufly and falfly Objected.

48] 1. Againft the Lord Jefus, *viz.* that he being
a man fhould make himfelf God. What fhall we
fay to thefe *bruitifh* and *blafphemous Foxians,* vile
worms of the Earth, yefterday creeping out of their
holes, flaves and Hellhounds, as we all b Nature
are, fo horribly to fet their faces as *David* fpeaks
again the Heavens, vapouring themfelves to be in
the Godhead, yea, in the Fulnefs of the Godhead,
and that alfo *bodily,* fo that what was applicable and
proper to the *Body* of the Son of God, is proper
and applicable unto them, his *Body in whom the Fulnefs of the Godhead dwells bodily.*

2. See the *horrible Egyptian Darknefs* the Lord
hath juftly poured upon thefe *feigned Gofhenites.*

The Qua-
kers
grutch
Chrift the
Title of
God-man

They exclaim againft us for ufing that Title *God-
man,* and ask where we find fuch a phraze in Scripture : And yet they reft not in that Title *Emanuel
God with us* : nor the Fulnefs of the Godhead *bodily in Chrift,* but Sacrilegious Robbers (in Effect)
arrogate

arrogate the Title, and thing to themſelves to be God-men and God-women, the Godhead dwelling in them *bodily*.

·3. Whereas G. *Fox* here ſaith, the work of the Miniſtry was to bring men to a *perfect man*, &c.

I Anſwer, He groſsly abuſeth that heavenly *Epheſ.* 4. which concerneth the Fulneſs and per-fection of all the Elect of God, *the whole Body, the Church of the firſt-Born,* applying it unto every particular deluded Convert of theirs, as being as perfect, as holy, as much God as Chriſt Jeſus, *God bleſſed for ever* himſelf. Epheſ. 4. The work of Chriſts Miniſters.

4. I may uſe the Exprobations of *Moſes* againſt *Korah, Dathan* and *Abiram. Is it not enough for you,* &c. but will you ſeek the *Prieſthood* alſo. Is it not enough that the moſt *High Potter* made us Men and Women and not Serpents and Toads, *&c.* not *Pagans, Turks, Iews, Papiſts,* &c. but *Engliſh Proteſ-tants,* &c. but we will be alſo *Infinites, & Eternals, Omnipotents & Omniſcients?* Will not the Infinite favour of *Leave* to drink of ſome heavenly drops of the *Infinite & Inconceivable Ocean* of his Goodneſs, ſatisfie and content us, but we will be Gods, with the Devil and our firſt Parents: We will be the *Inconceivable* Ocean it ſelf. Is it not enough for a *Proud Rebel* to be fetcht from the Gallows by a ſmile of his Prince, but he muſt be the *Prince* and *King* himſelf. The horrible pride and Haughtineſs of the Quakers.

5. The *Pagans* of the World as they are *wild* to all *Civility,* ſo to all *Divinity* and *heavenly matters:* They apprehend a *Doity,* [49] as a *Lyon, Whale, Dragon, Giant, Tyrant;* they feignedly will ſtrive to pacifie The Indians baſe eſteem of the God-head.

pacifie him, to make use of his help in Sickness, in
Wars, in Plagues and Droughts : but they will call
Men and Women Gods too, yea Dogs and Geese,
yea any Creature *Manittoò*, God, that is, or doth
any thing strange unto them : And thus the *Meli-
tans* presently cried out of *Paul*, that he was a God,
*And the Gods are come down to us in the likeness of
Men, &c.*

6. Therefore doth it please the most High and
only Wise to meet often with the *Pharaoh's* the
Absolom's the *Nebuchadnezzars*, the *Hamans* the
Herods of this World, yea, with whole Nations,
Cities Armies and Navies for their *Pride*, as he did
with *Sodom*, in signal and remarkable strokes and
Judgements : yea, with his *Iobs*, and *Hezechiah's*,
and *Paul's* in danger to be puffed up, in voices and
questions out of the Whirlwind, till we more and
more come to see how perfect we are in Dirt, and
Stink, and Filth of Death and Hell crawling like
Monsters of Pride and self-conceitedness upon this
Earth his Glorious Footstool.

God and
the great
Adversary
to all
Proud
spirits.

The 25: Instance is in *Pag*. 90. He brings in the
same Author saying, [*There is a kinde of Infiniteness in the* Soul, *and it cannot be Infiniteness it self*.]

He Answers : Is not the Soul without beginning
coming from God, and returning into God again,
who hath it in his hand, which Hand goes against
him that doth Evil, which throws down that which
wars against it : and Christ the power of God the
best[1] of the Soul, which brings it up into God,
which

The *Soul*
of men
horribly
abused

---

[1] Change "best" to "rest." *R. W. Ms. Ann*.

which came out from him ; hath this a beginning or ending? and is not this Infinite in it felf, and more than all the World?

I Reply, More briefly, (having fpoken of the Soul before) That the Soul or Spirit of a Man fhould be boundlefs or without limits, without beginning or ending, is a *Blafphemous Monfter* begotten of *Hellifh Pride* the Father, and *Hellifh Ignorance* the Mother : for Infinity and Infinitenefs in that fence can be no other but the Infinite and Eternal *Power* and Godhead tranfcending the Capacity or Men or Angels to receive it or conceive the nature of it.

2. It is true in a fecondary way (*a pofteriori*) as they fay the Spirits of Angels and men are as a Lamp lighted by the moft high and In- [50] finite Majefty never to go out or be extinguifhed in joy or forrow, This Notion dazles the moft fober and fteady Eye and Braine ; but who can finde a Centre or Clod of ftanding from whence to entertain a thought of no Beginning ; no created finite power can reach to what Infinity is.

3. We fee the mighty Kings and Emperours, their mighty Armies and Navies have Bounds as the roaring Waves of the Ocean have: the moft Glorious Sun and Heavenly Bodies have their limited Motions: the Dayes and Nights, the Summer and Winter, the Light and Darknefs know their periods of beginning and ending &c. All have their hitherto and no further fet by the Infinite, *Eternal* Arm, & no further. But all the ftars of heaven, the drops of the Ocean, the Sand on the Sea fhore, the

The changes of all things created and their Periods

Leaves

Leaves and Grafs of the whole World are all too
fhort to reach to the thought of one Minute of that
which properly is Gods only propriety, *to wit*, Infinity.

4. Among all the Opinions of the Souls Being
and Rife, this of Infinity making it God himfelf,
commits two horrible Murthers :[1]

Two hor-
rible Mur-
thers.
attempts

Firft, It Murthers and deftroys the Soul.

And Secondly, The Infinite God himfelf.

For the Soul of Man by fuch a world of woful experience being fo fubject to change, to fins
and forrows of all forts.   If this fhould be the Infinity of the Soul and fo of God himf lf, there
would be no Infinity at all fo ftopt, fo limited by
fins and forrows.

5. We ufe to fay (hyperbollically) that fuch and
fuch a doing is Infinite Pride, but furely it is wonderful and devilifh lifting up of the mind of a poor
Earthen Pot, though never fo high, fo wife, fo
learned, fo holy to entertain thoughts of being the
Eternal and boundlefs Infinite power and Godhead.

.The bleffed Lord proclaime his Infinite Power,
his Infinite Wifdome, his Infinite Greatnefs, and
Goodnefs, and Patience to poor finners (as he did
unto *Job* out of the Whirlwind) and then for all
Jobs Perfection and their own, (which fo fimply as
well as proudly they prate of) they will with I*ob*
fee caufe to abhor themfelves in Duft and Afhes.

6 Such is the inconceivable Infinity in God beyond the reach of all Creatures, that he is not
only Infinite but Infinity it felf, [51] Eternity it
felf,

---

[1] Add "in its tendency though not in effect."   *R. W. s. Ann.*

felf, Omnipotency it felf, Wifdome it felf, Goodnefs it felf, Juftice it felf in all their eminences and perfe.ctions.

7. Therefore notwithftanding moft gracious and moft glorious Appearances to, and influences from Infinity, upon poor finite Worms below, fure it is not fo fober a Language as that of Birds and Beafts, who keep their Native Tongues and Tones: Only men honoured with fo high Naturals above their Fellow potts, the Irrationals, and in many refpe.cts above other Rationals; yea, in pretence and fome really dignified with Spirituals in the Minde, Will and Affe.ctions by Priviledges, by Promifes. Mankinde I fay fo honoured and degenerating, we are not only like to, but Infinitely (as I may fay) worfe then the wildeft Beafts that perifh.

Mans doleful Degeneracy

The 26. *Inftance* is in Pag. 93. where G. *Fox* brings in *Robert Simfon*, &c. faying. [*The myftical Body may be fometimes fubje.ct to Diftempers, and Humors, and Wants.*]

Robert Simfon the body of Chrifts Church

He Anfwers, Are you Judges? can you judge of the Myftical Body which the Saints are Baptized into? is there Humors, Wants and Diftempers in the Body which the Saints are Baptized into? is not the Wants, Humors, Diftempers in your Body? do you here in this divide the word aright, diftingu fh things in the Ground, and fpeak aright of things, and yet you would not be judged, and fay, *Iudge not* : and is not Myftical Spiritual?

I Reply, In our late Difpute at *Providence, Io. Stubs* and *W. Edm* affirmed that God was a Spirit

52   litterally

litterally and properly, in which for all his boaſt of
Learning, it may be as he ſaid, above my ſelf,[1] he
ſhewed but little Philoſophy or Divinity : and *William Ed.* affi med that properly and really that Scripture of *Wolves coming in Sheeps cloathing,* was to be
underſtood litterally without meaning and expoſitions : but ſober men and aware know how to un-
fold *Parables,* and Similitudes, and Metaphors, and
Allegories *:* they know God is called a Son, and a
Rock, and a Father, and a Husband ; &c. and ſo is
Chriſt Jeſus, and they know how ſuch Similies are
to be expounded.

The Para-
bles & Fig-
urative
Speeches
of Holy
Scripture

They know that Believers in Chriſt Jeſus are
called a Body, an Houſe, a Flock, a Friend, a Center, an Army, and ye are no ſuch properly and litterally but by ſimilitude.

2. The *Papiſts* tell us of an *Univerſal,* or (as the
Greek) a [52] *Catholick Body of Chriſtians :* Amongſt
them are two *great Factions.* The one maintaing
this *Catholick Church* to meet in the *Repreſentative*
of an *Occumenical* or *General Council* of the whole
World : The other in the *Aſſembly* or *Conclave* of
the *Pope* and his *Cardinals :* and in the *Pope* himſelf, while he ſits in *Peters Infallible Chair.*

The Pro-
teſtant
Churches

The *Proteſtants* build alſo a *Catholick* or *Univerſal Body* of true Believers in Jeſus, ſcattered over
the World, &c. the more Reformed affirme this
Un verſal and *Catholick Church* to be viſible in the
Aſſemblies and *Congregations* of *Chriſtian Worſhippers* ſeparate from the Church of *Rome* and her
Abominations.

The

[1] Put " it may be as he ſaid above myſelf." in parentheſis. *R.W. Mſ. Ann.*

The Devil feeing the *Proteſtant Witneſſes* contending about the matter and Form of. the true Churches and Congregations, He (by Gods moſt holy and wiſe permiſſion) ſends out his old and known Spirit of *pure Inviſibles, pure Immediate, pure Worſhippers in Spirit and Truth*, &c. This Spirit being *Cozen German* to, or ſworn Brother in *helliſh equivocation* with the *Ieſuits*, when it ſerves their turn maintain a *Church Inviſible*, and Miniſters and Officers *Inviſible* : and yet when it ſerves their turn practice (as well as *Papiſts* or *Proteſtants*) *viſible Churches* and *Congregations, viſible* and *audible Apoſtles, preachers, Miniſters*, with *audible preachings, prayings, ſingings, Admiſſions, Excommunication*s, (more or leſs profeſſed and Explicite. _{The Qua-kers and Ieſuit Spirits}

The *Qukaers Churches* they are (as they childiſhly vapour) Bodies without wants or diſtempers, *fair* as *the Sun, clear as the Moon, terrible as an Army*, &c. _{The Foxian Churches}

1. But this[1] contrary to the nature of all our *Natural Bodies*, which turning upon the two hinges of Sins and Sorrows, are full of wants and diſtempers, until the daſhing of all in pieces by ſudden or lingring Deaths. _{All bodies liable to Diſtempers}

2. Contrary to all *Figurative* or *Metaphorical Bodies, domeſtick* in Families, *Political* in Cities, Nations, Armies, Navies, *&c.*

3. Contrary to Experience of the Bodies or Churches of Worſhippers in the Scripture *Iewiſh* or *Chriſtian*, who gave up thé *Ghoſt*, through diſtempers) into the hands of *Mahumet,* who brags he hath Conquered *Moſes* at *Ieruſalem*, and *Ieſus* at *Conſtantinople*. &c.   4. Contrary

[1] Add "is."   *R. W. Ms. Ann.*

4. Contrary to the Experience of the World in their daily obferving of the *Quakers Bodies* and *Worfhips.* (befide the Char- [53] ges againft them for their wild Doctrines and Difciplines) what known Divifions and Paffions about *I Nailors* and others Cafes? what Envyings Curfings, Apofta- cies, and moral Idolatry, as that of Covetoufnefs in this *Colony* known notorioufly ?

The sen- dency of the Quak. Spirit But fince G. *Fox* fpeaks fo Rationally to his Op- pofite, Do you diftinguifh things in the Ground? I fhall remember them of the fairnefs of my *four- teenth Pofition* againft them, *viz.* that according to the *Principles,* Roots and grounds of things I have fairly Collected, that the Spirit of the *Quakers* tends to *Incivility* and *Barbarifme,* and to *fudden Affaci- nations, murthers* and *Perfecutions.* &c.

The *Eternal Father* of mercies (I believe that I have, and can further make it good :) ftops mil- lions of mifchiefs in the world daily, which the Natures, grounds and Principles of men (and the Quakers Spirit alfo) now[1] to overrun and over- whelm the World withal.

Jonathan Clapham, &cs A 27th. *Inftance* of G. *Fox* his lame Anfwer is in *pag.* 103. where he brings in *Jonathan Clapham,* faying, [*Men may be called of Men Mafters, and it is but a Cavil to deny it, and they may deny to be called Fathers as well as Mafters*] He Anfwers, Thou haft in this denied that Doctrine of Chrift, and flights it, who faith, *Be not ye of Men called Mafters, for you have all one Mafter which is Chrift, and you all are*

[1] Change "now" to "tend." R. W. Ms. Ann.

are Bretbren, and thou haft fhow'd thy felf out of
the *Brother-hood*.   And there is a Birth to be born
which can call no man *Father* upon Earth which
thou art ignorant of.

I Reply, 1. Amongft other *foolifh paffions* and
Affections haunting all men, and the *Quakers* efpecially, thefe two are notorious, *viz.* pride and a
lazie Ignorance : Thofe two are the *Sire* and *Dam*
of moft of thefe *wild monfters*.

2. For doth not this proud man know how many
of his excellent Oppofites have laid open their
Foxians fcornful. pride in robbing all mankind of
many due refpects and favorable glaunces of Gods
care, of order, and prudent diftinctions and differences amongft the Sons of men in Families, Cities,
Nations, Armies, Navies, &c.

3. Sure he can not but remember, and his own
and all the Light in the *Quakers* (if ferioufly minded) will tell them, that [54] in robbing all the
world of their feveral due moderate, and fober Titles and Refpects, they do but by a *jugling Hocas
pocas*; a *back dore*, &c. rob all others of their *points*, The Pope
Ribbons, and *Laces*, wherewithal only to adorn and and Qua-
trim, and trick their foolifh felves : Juft as the pared.
Popifh party practice to cry up their *Pope, fervus
fervorum Dei*, and yet be *Domine fac totum* your holinefs, *&c.* and yet the *Pope* and *Papifts* herein out
fhoot the *Quakers*, for the *Papifts* give all men their
Civil and Courteous different Refpects, and Ac-
knowledgements, which the *dogged* and *fcornful
Quakers*, are far from their Spirit being prouder
then the *Papifts*,

4. G.

4. G. *Fox* knows how others of his *Adverſaries*
have in print told him that the Engliſh word |*Maſ-
ter*] Anſwers to many words in the *Greek* [*Kathe-
gereſe Didarkalos*, &c.] and that theſe words *Rabbi*
and *Pateer*, all ſhew that the Lord Jeſus only Condemned the *Phariſaical, Popiſh,* and *Foxian Itch* of
being called *Maſters, Fathers, Leaders, Teachers* in
Religion, undervaluing and ſlighting others, *&c.*
Thus amongſt the *Papiſts* their *Magiſter noſter*, their
Patres, &c. their *Irrefragable, Seraphical* and *Angelical Doƈtors*: thus among the *Foxians, James
Naylor, Hoſanna,* &c. and G. *Fox* (at this Town of
Providence) called the *Eternal Son of God. Chriſt
Jeſus.*

Of Fathers and Maſters.

The Popiſh priority an6 the Foxian is of and in their Doctors.

5. Half a *Humane* and *ſober Eye* may ſee that in
all his *Declamations* againſt the *Phariſaical,* or *Popiſh,* or *Foxian Rabbies,* the Lord Jeſus I ſay, comes
not near in a Title, the Civil and Natural Reſpeƈts
of *Inferiours,* to *Heads of Families, Cities, Kingdomes,* &c. all of which, the very nature of man
being *von politikon*[1] a ſociable Creature, and the
holy Scripture is all over (from end to end) full of
moſt frequent Examples, yea, Commands, and
praƈtices.

Meer Civil Reſpeƈts

6. How Childiſhly doth *Fox* Anſwer his *Oppoſite,
viz* that although it be unlawful to call *Maſter*, yet
it is not unlawful to call *Father*, for there is a
Birth which his *Oppoſite* is ignorant of, *&c.* I ask if
G. *Fox* mean not their *Immediate Birth of Light*
(which for a Cover) they call *Spirit* and *Chriſt,* &c.
in Oppoſition to that true *Chriſtian Regeneration* and
Change,

The Quakers Maſters and Fathers.

[1] Change " *von politikon* " to " *animal politicon.*" *R. W. Ms. Ann.*

Change, which it pleaſeth God ordinarily to Effect True Re-
generation
by means, as *Paul* ſaid, though you have ten thouſ-
and Teachers, yet I have begotten you, *&c,* Sure it
is, their Immediate denies the mediate.

55] 7. Where there no *Ordinary means* appointed
by God for *Natural* or *Spiritual procreation* : yet
how ſimple is that Conſequence, that becauſe God
is an *Extraordina y Father,* therefore I may call
men *Fathers* but not *Maſters* ! when God is both
Father and *Maſter,* and both Titles are forbidden in
a true Senſe, by one and the ſame *heavenly Breath,*
at the ſame time.

A 28 h. *Inſtance,* is *pag.* 106. where G. *Fox* brings 106. Wil-
liam
Thomas.
in *W. Thomas,* ſaying, [*Men are ſaved, but not by*
Chriſt within us.]

He Anſwers, [*How is mans Salva ion wrought out*
but by Chriſt within? How is the Juſtification fels
but by Chriſt wit in? And the Seeds we manifeſt that
ſuffered without is made manifeſt within, there . is Re-
demption and Life : He that hath the Son of God hath
Life, Redemption to God out of the firſt Adam, and
who feels Chriſt within, feels Salvation, and who doth
not, are Reprobates, though they may talk of him.]

I Reply, This ſubtle *Fox* is in his *Burrough* Confounding (under the Terms Chriſt) the perſon of
Chriſt, and the *Love,* and *Spirit,* and *Grace* or *Fa-* The per-
ſon of
vour of Chriſt, as if they were all one : As if Chriſt and
where the Name and Authority, and writing of G. the Grace
Fox comes, there of neceſſity muſt G. *Fox* in perſon of Chriſt
diſtingu-
be: Or, to riſe higher, wherever the Name and iſhed.
Authority, of a *King, General,* or *Admiral* is, there
muſt their perſons alſo be. This

Chrifts
perfou.

This *Popifh Ubiquitary Fancy* all *fober Reafons* have long fince laught at, and juftly, as being moft *Fancyfull* and *Frantick*: what,

Not Ubi-
quirary.

2. What is this, but to make the *Kings* of men, yea, the *King of Kings* poor *Mechanicks*, yea, lower, that can do nothing by any *Means*, *Servants*, *Minifters*, *Legates*, *Embaffadours*, &c. except they be perfonaly prefent?

3. The Spirit of God refolves the Quefton, *Ephef* 3. *He dwels in the Heart by Faith*, or believing in

Faith not
Chrift
himfelf.

him, and *Gal.* 2. I *live by believing, or Faith in the Son of God*: This *Faith* is given of God to fome and not to others: This Faith or Belief is wrought by Chrift Jefus, and fin fhed by him, and may with as good Senfe be called Chrift himfelf, as a fhoo which G. *Fox* hath begun and finifhed be called G *Fox* himfelf.

4. With what Colour of Reafon or Senfe is it

K. Charles
King yer
not per-
fonally
prefent in
all his Do-
minions

that if I believe King *Charles* the fecond to be the King of *Englifh Men* and my *King*, I muft of neceffity (becaufe of my belief which He by gra- [56 cious means hath wrought in me) I believe that *K. Charles* is *perfonally prefent*, & *Ubiquitarily prefent* in perfon in all his *Dominions* and all the world over where ever his Loving *Subjects* have their *Refidence?*

Humph.
Norton
yields
Chrift
ubiquitary

5. I grant if we as fome Quakers and *Humphry Norton* by Name refolve Chrift only into a Spirit, and God only he is *Ubiquitary*: But as man, why may not the *General* of an *Army* fay, to his whole Army, and every *Individual Souldier*, as *Paul* to the *Corinthians*, *though I am abfent in Body yet am I prefent*

in

in S*pirit*, Chriſt Jeſus is in his Command, and Courage and Example in every *Regiment*, every *Squadron*, every *Band* and *Troop*, and every Souldier of the m. ny Millions that have, and ſhall believe in him, and that in a Senſe,[1] both as God and man.

6. The *Hinge* and *pinch* of the *Difference* lies in the *Oppoſition*, which the *Quakers* make againſt the *Manhood* of Chriſt Jeſus to be yet Extant, many of them alleadging: *why ſtand you gazing*, Acts 1, *&c.* as if it were but gazing after a *Manhood* and all now were Spirit and Light within. ^{Which word & the word humane they ſtartle ar}

7. Who ever queſtiond, but that the Spirit or power of Chriſt Jeſus worketh in the Souls of his Elect the great ſaving change or regeneration, gives Repentance, opens the heart to Believe, and makes the heart of this Believer a *P*alace for three Kings, yet but one, the Father, the Son and the Spirit, in Holineſs, Love, Meekneſs, *P*atience, &c. and all theſe[2] Royal Attendants. ^{Chriſt Jeſus in the Soul makes it a palace for 3 Kings &c.}

8. Who queſtions but Chriſt Jeſus (as the Sun in theſe Heavens) influenceth all parts of the World in ſeveral reſpects, and nothing is hid from his heat, He is felt in the bruiſed Reed and ſmoaking Flax; in the poor in Spirit, in the hungry and thirſty after Righteouſneſs: ſometimes in the hope of Glory to come, yea, in preſent joy unutterable and glorious; Sometimes the Lambs Wife is viſibly aſleep though her heart wakes, ſometimes ſhe is Alarmed by his knocking and is ſluggiſhly unwilling ^{The varie- ty of Chriſts workings & appear- ances}

ling

---

[1] Add "by faith." *R. W. Ms. Ann.*
[2] Change "theſe" to "their." *R. W. Ms. Ann.*

53

ling to open to him, fometimes fhe rifes and opens but he is gone, and fhe feeks for him by day and night and cannot find him.

9. There is alfo a falfe feeling of Chrift Jefus (as I fpake before of a falfe Conception in a Wo-man) How many are bold to cry *Lord, Lord open ; for we have prophefied in thy Name,* &c and yet I will not fay as G. *Fox.* here faith, of his Feeling *that all that have not my feeling or working of Chrift are Reprobates* : yet [57] this I fay as *Solomon, A Whore is Loud and Clamorous* (not fo the *Chafte,* and *Sober, and Modeft Women*) and the Devil fpake as Holy and Heavenly words as Angels could have fpoken, yet it was but the *Divil* in *Samuels Mantle.*

Falfe Con-ceptions

The 29*th. Inftance* is in *pag.* 117. where he brings in *Giles Fermin* faying, [*Paul Swore after Chrift, and the Angels Swore, I wonder Paul fhould fo forget him-felf and fin fo fearfully in Swearing, fo the Quakers Light that denies Swearing, is of Satan and not the Light of Chrift.*]

Giles Fermin

He Anfwers, Chrift the Light (which Satan is out of) which is the Oath of God, ends all Oathes, Sworn by Prophets or Angels whatfoever ; and who Swares be fallen into the Condemnation of the Devil : And it is no where faid that the Apoftle Swore, but fuch as thou art matters not what thou fpeak ; fo that Spirit that *Preacheth* for Swearing is not the Spirit of Chrift but is the Spirit of Anti-Chrift, &c.

I Reply, firft G. *Fox* dares not deny but that the *Angel* and *Paul* Swore after Chrift, only he keeps
his

his old Song, *viz* That Chrift put an end to Swearing, and that it is not faid that *Paul* Swore.

But 1. He waves that Sweareng of the Angel, ^{Paul &}
or Chrift himfelf, *Rev.* 10. for there he knows the ^{the Angels} ^{Swearing}
very term of Swearing is ufed.

2. As to *Paul*, if the atteftation of the Name of
God be the formality of an Oath, then if ever any
Man Swore in this World *Paul did*, faying to the
*Corinthians, I call God to Record on my Soul, that to
fpare you I came not as yet to Corinth, &c.*

Secondly, It is true that all Nations have ufed to
Swear by, or Appeal to the Gods they owned and ^{Of Swear-}
worfhipped. It is true alfo, that they have ufed to ^{ing in} ^{General}
put Creatures into the room of God, and Swear by
them as the *Jews* did ; and fom write out of a
Superftitious Reverence in forbearing the Name of
God, and indeed the Reafons Chrift Jefus gives,
Mat. 5. look that way.

Thirdly. It is true alfo that for abufe of Swearing
by, and Prophaning the Holy Name of God, a
whole Land may mourn as *Jeremiah fpeaketh.*

Fourthly There feems to be a very fair colour put
on a univerfal Prohibition of Swearing by Chrift
Jefus, and by his Apoftle *James, Swear not,* &c.

58] This Conjuror[1] hath taken with many precious Servants of God former and latter, even with
many of thofe called the *Fathers,* and with thofe
Famous Protefters againft the *whore* of *Rome,* the
Waldenfes, and with *Famous Ufher,* who doth more
then feem to vindicate their not Swearing when ^{Famous}
Convented and Examined by the *Popifh Inquifitors.* ^{Ufher.}

5.

[1] Change " conjuror" to " conjecture." *R. W. Ms. Ann.*

5. Notwithſtanding this, and more which máy be granted, and though I ſhould humbly motion to all *higher Powers* for Chriſtian tenderneſs, (as to the *holy Majeſty* of Heaven his Name, and to the Souls of any making Scruple:) yet I muſt proclaim againſt G. *Fox*, his lame and ſimple Return to the Objection of his Oppoſite concerning *Paul* and the *Angel*.

Moderation as to Swearing.

For, why may not P*aul* and all the *Apoſtles*, and *Chriſt* and all the *Angels* of *Heaven*, and all the *Saints* of *God* upon the Earth (in the words of *Paul*) call God to Record upon their Souls, that this, or this was the Cauſe and Truth, *&c.* Conſidering

1. That neither the moſt holy God nor the Lord Jeſus (who I think is the *Swearing Angel* Rev. 10.) nor the *heavenly Spirits*, the *Angels*, nor *Paul*, nor any of *Chriſts Apoſtles*, or *Meſſeugers* would have practiced a *Ceremony*, or a *Shadow* (like *Circumciſion* or the *Paſſover*) at the[1] time of the Day, *&c.*

2. Swearing or appealing unto God immediately in *Oaths* or *Vows*, or *Lots*, or *Faſtings*, though higher and above the practice of *ordinary Invocations, Supplications, Thanksgivings*, &c. were never accounted *Ceremonies* or *Types* of *Subſtances* to come, but *Real* and *Subſtantial Services* and *Addreſſes* unto the moſt *holy* and moſt *high Creatour* written in the hearts of all mankind before ever *Ceremony* or *Moſes* was born, and therefore as the fear of God is put for the whole worſhip of God, ſo alſo is ſwearing in the holy Scripture: and we may as well deny all worſhip

Swearing no Ceremony.

[1] Change "the" to "yᵗ." *R. W. Ms. Ann.*

worſhip and Service viſible, and all External Acts of *Homage* and *Devotion* of the Body unto God, yea, and all the fear of God is there[1] in the mind, Soul and Spirit, or in any *External Obeyſance* or *Reverence*, as this Service and worſhip of calling upon God, and appealing to his *holy Majeſty*, as *Witneſs* and *Judge* in ſome Caſes, &c

3. Whereupon it follows, that this high point of *Gods worſhip* is as *real*, as *moral*, as *holy*, and *perpetual* as Prayer it ſelf, as *preaching*, yea, as *Baptiſme*, and the *Lords Supper*, and no more *Ceremonial*, though I know the *Foxians* make Baptiſme and the 59] Lords Supper but *Ceremonies* for a time, and ere long if they continue to hearken to S*amuel* within them, they will account Prayer and Preaching (whether *Apoſtolical* or *Paſtoral*) but *Types* and *Shadows* alſo.

4. It is a moſt *ſimple* and *un-Chriſtian* and *Atheiſtical whimſie* that Chriſt was the end of *Oaths*, the end of the *Prophets*, the end of the *Scripture*, the end of *Reghteouſneſs*, (in their Senſe) though as *Mediatour* he was the *End* or *Perfection* of, and fulfilling of the Law of God, which never Soul beſide the Lord Jeſus ever kept in thought, word and deed, what ever the *proud Phariſees* and *Papiſts*, and *Foxians* prate, &c.

5. It is a *groſs Fancy* to imagine that the Lord Jeſus in the 5 of *Math.* gave new Commands, or Contradicted the holy pleaſure of his Father concerning *Revenge, Adultery, Oaths, Prayers, Faſtings,*

but

---

[1] Eraſe " is there." *R. W. Ms. Ann.*

but opened his *Fathers Law* in the *purity* and *Spirituality* of it againſt the *rotten Expoſitions*, *Traditions* and practices of the *Phariſees*.

6. In particular, let all the Reaſons be expended : and carefully weighed, which the Lord Jeſus ſo *wonderfully, exactly gives* why they ſhould not ſwear by *Jeruſalem*, nor the *Temple*, nor their *Head*, nor any *Oath*, to wit of ſuch a Nature, and half a ſober eye may ſee that the Lord Jeſus intends only to reduce them to an holy Swearing, only by God, in Gods way, *&c.* and in their *Common Converſe*, to uſe *yea, and nay*, &c.

The Quakers plainly Confeſs Swearing in Caſe lawful s

7. I have read a *ſober* and *man like Anſwer* of F. H. called a Quaker againſt *A. S.* called a Doctour, concerning *Oaths*, not like G. *Fox* his *bruitiſh barkings* againſt all his Oppoſites and any that prate[1] may ſee F. *H.* yields to *A. S.* that himſelf, (and I preſume he ſpeaks the mind of all the Quakers) could yield to give a Teſtmony in weighty Caſes, by the Name and in the Name of God, as in the preſence of God, and atteſt or call God to witneſs, *&c.* And he ſaith, that they had offered ſo to give a Teſtimony, and that his Oppoſite Doctour *Snalwood*, and I think Biſhop *Gauden* ſo called, aſſented that this was Subſtantial and *Formal Swearing* : only the *Ceremonies* were enjoyned by Law, to which the Quaker could not yield, but ſuffer as indeed they have done upon this Account moſt lamentably in *London* and *Briſtol*, and all *England* over.

Caſes of Swearing

8. I have much to add both as to that *Fancy* of Chriſts end- [60] ing *Oaths* as *Ceremonies*, and of
Caſes

---

[1] Change " prate" to "pleaſe." *R. W. Mſ. Ann.*

Cafes that have befallen my felf in the *Chancery* in *England*, &c. and of the lofs of great Sums which I chofe to bear through the Lords help, then yield to the *Formality* (then and ftill in ufe) in Gods worfhip, though I offered to Swear as *F. H.* mentions they have done, and the Judges told me they would reft in my Teftimony and way of Swearing, but they could not difpence with me without an Act of *Parliament*.

I believe this highly concerns the high Affembly of *Parliament* and all Law makers, to fearch well and to appoint a Committee of Searchers to Examine, if the Laws upon new appearances from Heaven have not need of rectifying and fome of cancelling for fin againft God or the Souls of men eftablifhed by Law, is like *Jereboams* making *Ifrael* to fin, and moft commonly after much patience of God brings double punifhment in the end.

Sin eftab-lifhed by Law, is Sin multi-plied and multi-plied, Judgement here and for ever.

The 30*th. Inftance* where G. *Fox* brings in *Tho* Moor faying [*It is not properly nor in a full fenfe that God is manifeft in the Flefh of his Saints.*]

Tho 30. Tho-mas or Mo.

He Anfwers, The Saints are the Temple of God, and God dwells in them, and they come to witnefs the Flefh of Chrift. And they glorifie him in their Souls and bodies : And the Lord is glorified in their bringing forth much fruit. And the witnefs is the Seed, the one offering for fin to be manifeft within, and fuch are not Reprobates, yet witnefs the one offering Chrift Jefus, and them that have not Him within, they are Reprobates.

I Reply, a great Defigne of the Devil in all Ages hath

The Devils great work in all Ages. hath been to Cavil at, and hinder Gods love to mankind: Hence he plotted and effected *Mans Fall* from God: God Infinite in wifdome and mercy, out-fhoots and out-plots him, and defignes a Reconciliation and a Marriage between the Son of God the *Prince* of Life, and loft mankind: He promifed his coming in our Flefh; prefigured Him, prophefied of Him, *and in the Fulnefs of Time fent Him*, &c.

Sathans Emiffaries to deftroy Chrift Jefus. Againft this Lord Jefus, this old Serpent hiffeth and rageth before his Birth, at his Birth, after his Birth, and in all Ages ever fince, as fearing the crufhing of his Brains, and the downfall of his Throne, if the Kingdome of the Lord Jefus ftand: Hence not long after Chrifts Affention, he ftirred up many *Anti Chrifts*, [61] *Simon Magus* and his *Followers*, the *Arrians*, the *Gnofticks*, *Cerdonians*, *Manicheans*, &c. the great *Anti-Chrift* of *Rome*, and fince the *Reformation*, the new *Manicheans*, thofe in *Luthers* and *Calvins* time called the *Spirituals* and *Libertines*, and in our times the *Adamites*, the

The perfon of Chrift Jefus the Devils great Eye fore. *Ranters*, the *Quakers*, and all in order to his *Dragons war* againft the perfon of the *Arch-Angel*, *Michael*. the word of God, the *Individual perfon*, the Man Chrift Jefus, and after him all that fhould dare to follow him.

Some (as the *Arians*, &c.) have denied him to be fo, but Man, and not God; fome (as the *Manicheans*, &c.) deny his *Manhood*, affirming him to be God, and a Spirit, but, with *Chrifts manhood* and the *Scriptures*, the *Devil* and the *Papifts*, and the *Quakers*, (for moft of them) could with all their hearts make

an

an *Everlasting parting* : The Devils and[1] is to deftroy this Saviour and Salvation to poor loft man :
The *Quakers* pretend their end to be the Exalring
and glorifying of God in the Flefh of his Saints, *The Man-*
therefore fome of thefe *Manicheans* render his Birth, *icheans*
Life and Death to be only *Imaginary*, and *Allegori-* *the great*
cal : a *Figure* of what fhould be done in, and by *Oppofers of Chrifts*
Chriftians : others of them fay it is real, but he *Manhood.*
only lived and died for an *Example*, others, that he
was really fo born, he fo lived and died, but he is
now only within, *&c.* and after his Flefh no
Inquiry.

G. *Fox* here plays upon the various meaning of
the word *Flefh*.   Alfo he plays upon thofe holy
Scriptures, *viz. God is glorified in the Souls and Bodies of his Saints,* &c. *That In-*

This *fubtle Jonadab* he knows alfo, that the *Pro-* *dividual Man*
teftants maintain that the *Godhead* and the Spirit *Chrift Je-*
of God fo dwels not in the Souls and Bodies of his *fus muft*
Servants as in that Soul and Body of the Lord *have the prehemi-*
Jefus.   It is true he was not[2] born of a *Woman,* *nence of*
but againft their wills they are forc't to Confefs *the only Meffiah*
that he was not born of a *Wife*, but a *Virgin,* *and Medi-*
though many Fancies are Coyned about that: They *ator.*
Confefs that no man was *Father* of his flefhly Nature: He knows alfo that the *Proteftants* hold that *The God-*
the *Godhead dwels in him*, and dwels in him as the *head of Chrifts*
great *Mediator* and *Propitiation furety* and *Under-* *Body after*
taker, fo as not in any of the Bodies, or all the *a Tranf-cendent*
Bodies *way.*

---

[1] Change "and" to "end."   *R. W. Ms. Ann.*
[2] Erafe "not."   *R. W. Ms Ann.*

54

Bodies of his Saints, befides, and after a more *high Tranfcendent,* and *Inconceivable manner.*

G. *Fox* knows that his *Oppofite* intends fuch a manifeftation of God in the Flefh that renders the[1] one fingle perfon Chrift [62] Jefus *the Head of his Church,* &c. And that they hold that there is as much difference between that one *Individual 'perfon Chrift Jefus* the *Head* and his *Followers,* as between our Heads and our Bodies, the King himfelf and his Body or Subjects, yea, every one fingly in par-ticular: yea, as between the Foundation and all the building thereon raifed.

Now how poor and lame is it, that becaufe the Saints are Gods Temple, therefore they muft be God himfelf: becaufe 1 *Tim.* 3. *Chrift dwels in his Saints by believing,* Ephef. 3. therefore they are Chrift himfelf: Becaufe God in an holy Senfe, be-came Flefh: Therefore our Flefh is God and Chrift, therefore will they find thofe heavenly particulars, 1 *Tim.*3. affi med of that man Chrift Jefus to be inverted and dreadfully turned upon their proud and divilifh Flefh in this manner, *viz.* The Devil is manifeft in their Flefh, Condemned of the holy Spirit of God: Abhord of the *heavenly* Angels: The world fhall abhor their memory, and except Repentance, they fhall defcend with all the Ene-mies of the true Lord Jefus into the *Lake* that burns with *unquenchable Fire and Brimftone.*

The 31*ft. Inftance* is in *pag.* 136. where G. *Fox* brings

The fix great points.

Dreadful-ly inverted upon the Quakers.

[1] Change " the " to " yᵗ." *R. W. Mf. Ann.*

brings in the fame Authour faying, [*Chrift is dif-* 136 Tho-
tinct from every one of us, and without us, and our mas
particular perfons.]

He Anfwers, [The Apoftle faith Chrift was in them,
except they were Reprobates, and they were flefh of
his flefh, and of his Bone, and eat his flefh, and drank
his Blood, then it was within them, and he is diftinct
from none but Reprobates who hate the Light.]

I Reply, 1. This and the former look face upon
face as in a Glaffe, and yet G. *Fox* herein carries
two faces under one hood: · A Face for God, and a
Face for the Devil; one Face for Chrift another
for Antichrift. For is it not known by all, that
there be divers wayes of eating Chrifts Flefh and
drinking his Blood? Although there be a Myftical
and Spiritual feeding upon Chrift Jefus his Love,
his Paffions, his Merits, &c. which we maintain Eating
againft the bloody Tranfubftantiators of *Rome* and Chrifts
Hell, yet can ought but Hellifh Bewitching and Flefh aud
Impudence conclude, that litterally the Flefh pro-drinking
fiteth nothing, and therefore their Flefh is as good his Blood.
as the Flefh of Chrift, and their Blood (as fome of
63] the *Quakers* have Printed) is of as much virtue
as the Blood fhed of the Man Chrift Jefus: Hence
fo many of them contend that God*s* Blood, *Act.* 20. The Fox-
and Gods Flefh Redeems us, &c. and their Blood ians horri-
and Sufferings are Gods Flefh and Blood Redeem-ble pride
ing, Saving, &c, I know what one of their chief themfelves
faid [*He is a Fool that fpeaks all at once*] and I know to be God
alfo, that in the Bottome (which their *Herods* and[1] and Chrift
Apoftles know better then I) thefe *Foxians* are God,
and

---

[1] Erafe " Herods and." *R. W. Ms. Ann.*

and Chriſt, and Spirit, and Reſurrection, and Life, and Heaven, &c.

2. But for true Believers in Jeſus it is enough for them to believe, *Joh.* 16. That for a little while he muſt leave them, and after a little while he would come again to them, even the ſame Man that left them, *that God man, and the Man Chriſt Jeſus.*

1. I know theſe poor *Foxians* ſay, that he did come again to them, and I know alſo that a Man may feel this Lye with a pair of Mittins: For I[1] know that the *Comforter* came not to them upon his Reſurrection (for then he was forty dayes with them) but after his Aſſention.

2. Who knows not that the *Foxians* maintain Chriſts ſecond coming to be Spiritual, and count all gazing Fools that look after a Man, for he is come anto them in Spirit, and in them he maintains his great Aſſizes, and now paſſeth Judgement upon all the Children of Men by them.

3. If theſe poor filthy *Dreamers* lived without Food and Evacuations, without Phyſick (which ſome cf them cry down, and no Phyſick but Faith) without Procreation, and bringing forth of Children without the filthineſs and ſtinks of Nature; yea without the many thouſands of Holy Words, and Thoughts, and Actions omitted, and the many thouſand paſſionate, impertinent, unreaſonable diſcontented Words and Actions, &c. then might we ſay as the men of *Iconium* (touching *Paul* and *Barnabas*) *The Gods are come to us in the likeneſs of Men,* till then we muſt look upon the *Foxians* (eating ſo

Chriſt

The margin notes read:
Chriſts coming again to them.

The Foxians natural and ſpiritual Defilements therefore not God but filthy Dreams.

---

[1] Change "I" to "We." *R. W. Ms. Ann.*

Chrift his flefh, &c. until they become Chrift himfelf,) as Simple, and Monftrous, and Blafphemous
as the Papifts in their Foolifh, Monftrous and
Bloody Tranfubftantiations.

4. Alas! thefe are old tricks plaid by the *Mani-* The Fox-
cheans in former times, by *Quintinus* and *Pocqueius,* ians in
&c. in *Luther* and *Calvins* time: Did not fome Calvins
thoufands of this frantick fpirit [64] then, fay, *is* time.
Chrift in us? how is he Diftinct from us? what need
you ask me how I do? can Chrift be fick? can
Chrift do but well? fpeaking of themfelves: But,
I obferve Gods ftrokes in the World moft juft & Gods
wonderful upon three forts of perfons 1. *Voluptu-* ftrokes in
ous. 2. *Oppreffors* and *Tyrants.* 3. Ringleaders of this world
Blafphemies,[1] *Opinion*s. Let every Soul confider: I upon
can give abundance of Inftances of former and three
later times had I here time and feafon for it, and forts.
were not all Hyftories full, &c.

The 32*d. Inftance* is in *Pag.* 186. where G. *Fox*
brings in *S*amuel *Hamond* faying [*What warrant* 186. Sam-
have you to go out to the Quakers? fhall a Man go hear uel Ham-
the Iews and Popifh Maffe becaufe Paul bids try all mond.
things? No, No.]

G. *Fox* Anfwers [*Paul* bids us quench not the
Spirit, and where the Spirit is not quenched they
may try *Papifts, Iews, Proteftants,* who quench not
the Spirit: But who quench the Spirit and draws
people from the Light within, they draw from that
they fhould fee withal, then you ftuff them up with
old Authors and lying ftories, as you permit abroad.

I *Reply,*

[1] Change " Blafphemies " to " Blafphemous." *R. W. Ms. Ann.*

I *Reply*, 1. And ask of G. *Fox* and all his *Fox-ians*: Have the *Papifts* the *Iews* or any Idolaters the Holy Spirit of God amongſt them, whom we may go to hear God ſpeaking in his own holy Promiſe, Ordinance and Appointment unto us?

About true bearing.

2. May I hear a *Papiſt*, or *Iew*, or any other Falſe Worſhippers or Idolaters to try them when I am convinced and ſatisfied already that they ſpeak not by the Holy Spirit, &c.

3. May I go to Worſhip God with them who either (as I believe) Worſhip a Falſe God, or Worſhip the true and living God, in Wayes and Worſhips of *Mens* Inventions and Appointments?

4. May I hear a falſe *Prophet*, or be preſent at any falſe worſhip, but with actual reproving of them, and labouring to reduce them to the true God and his moſt holy Inſtitutions and Appointments?

Upon this Reaſon I went to the *General Aſſmbly* of the *Quakers* at *Newport* the laſt year, I queried with them about the true Chriſt, and the true Spirit: but I was ſtopt by a ſudden Spirit of *Prayer* in a Woman, and the unſeaſonable Spirit of *Prayer* in a man, which forced me to ſtop, and occaſioned me to take this [65] way of offering an appointed and ſolemn diſcourſe and diſputation with them.

5. I ask, may any Soul out of Curioſity go to hear a ſtrange Preacher, in whom I have not Faith, that he is ſent from God, &c. eſpecially, if there be not a free liberty for my Queries and Objections, and ſearchings as the *Bereans* did?

6. Are there not two great Cautions given, us by
the

the Spirit of God! *Take heed whom you hear : Take heed how you hear*, and both of thefe in reference to Gods worfhip and mine own Salvation?

7. What do thefe *Foxians* mean by the *Spirits* What the quenching *quenching*? Can the Spirit of God be *really quenched*, of the or put out, any more then the Sun in the Heavens Spirit is. by all the water in the Ocean? Is the Spirit of God *Metaphorically quenched* any other ways then by withdrawing the means or fuel which were to keep the Fire burning that came down from Heaven upon the *Altar*? why then do thefe *proud, lazie Souls* fo horribly flight *reading, ftudying* Books, yea, *Gods Book*, as one of their chief faid to me, (laying his hand upon the Bible of *Junius*, &c. art not thou paft thefe yet? And why do they worfhip a *dumb Devil* in their *dumb meetings*, and ftand ftill and liften, and lie upon their beds of *lazinefs* for *Revelations* and *Notions*, &c.

8. As for G. *Fox* his *fcornful fling* againft *old Authors*, what is it but *pride* and *Ingratitude* : *pride* Old Authors. to undervalne, much more to *fcorn* my *Progenitors* and *Anceftors* : *Ingratitude* to God for fo many helps, *&c.* and to them who have laboured and broke the Ice, and left their Labours behind them for the benefit of *after Commers* : yea, what Injuftice, when I difregard and flight their writings, and reproach them, calling them *Old Authors*, compared with their *new Fancies*, as W. *Edmundfon* did me frequently at *Newport, Old Man, Old Man*, &c.

The 33 *Inftance* is in *Pag*, 206, where he brings John in *John Burton*, fading, [*It is a Scripture of the Dev-* Burton. *ils making, to apprehend Chrift within.*]   He

He Anfwers, If there be any other Chrift but he, who was *Crucified within,* he is the *falſe Chriſt,* and the Scriptures hold forth this, and the Devil never made it, but he and his Meſſengers are againſt it. And he that hath not this Chrift that was riſen and [66] Crucified within is a *Reprobate,* though *Devils* and *Reprobaes* may talk of him without.

I Reply, This is the great difpute between the *Chriſtians* and the *Pagans,* the *Chriſtians* and the *Iews,* the *Chriſtians* and the *Mahumetans,* and the *Chriſtians* among themſelves ſo called, *viz.* Who is the great *Prophet?*

2. To what purpoſe ſhould I alleadge the whole hiſtory of the *Birth, Life, Death,* &c. of the Lord Jeſus, ſince the *Quakers* acknowledge all true, &c.?

3. Why ſhould I alleadge the *Sermons* and *Preachings,* and *Writings* of the *Apoſtles* or *Meſſengers* of *Chriſt Ieſus* after his *Aſcention,* all *harmonizing* with the *four Evangeliſts,* writing his *Life* and *Death,* &c.

4. Certain it is, that he that ſhall turn over all the former Relations and Hiftories, and all the writings and Sermons of the *Apoſtles* ſince, and predicate *a* Chriſt that was *riſen within, Crucified within,* (in *Oppoſition* to that *Ieſus of Nazareth without*) he muſt have the *Forehead* of a *Reprobate and Devil,* (as G. *Fox* phrazeth it)

5. G. *Fox* knows the *Proteſtants* predicate (in Life and Death) the believing in Chriſt Jeſus ſo born, ſo living and dying: And the applying of the *price* of his *Death* and *merits* unto God for *Propitiation:*

The goat difpute about the true Chriſt.

Chriſt without and within

The Proteſtants belief of Chriſt.

tion: And the Applying of the *Promife* and *new Covenant* and *Bargain* in that Blood for a *new Heart*, a *new Spirit*, &c.

6. What fhall then become of G. *Fox*, his be-lieving in a Chrift that was *Rifen* and *Crucified within*, in *Oppofition* to this Lord Jefus fo *Promifed*, fo *Prophefied* of, fo *prefigured*, fo *brought forth*, fo *living* and *dying*, fo *preached*, fo *believed* on, and what a *Forehead* of *Hell* muft he have that calls all thofe *Reprobates* and *Devils* that talk of *Chrift without* ?

The 34*th Inftance* is in· *pag.* 214. where G, *Fox* brings in the *Elders* and *Meffengers* of feveral Churches of *Ilfton*, *Abergevenny*, &c. faying, [*We are Conceived in Sin and brought forth in Iniquity*, &c.] ^{Churches in Wales.}

He Anfwers, |*David doth not fay, you who were Conceived in Sin, but I*, and W. faith, *Iohn was fanc-tified from the Wombe, and the Scriptures fpeaks of fuch as were fanctified from the Wombe, and Children that were clean. And fo you do not fpeak as Elders and* [67] *Meffengers of true Churches, or Men dividing the Word aright, but you are one againft another, though you are all againft them you call Quakers, that be in the Truth.*]

I Reply, 1. In the¹ paffage G. *Fox* difcovers to any *Intelligent* and *Savoury Spirit*, not only a weak and deluded Soul, but a *Popifh* and *Arminian poyfon* about the Eftate of all mankinde in their *firft Birth*, a ftrong prefumption that he never felt what the woful Eftate of all mankinde by Nature is, and ^{The firft Cry of every Child of God.}

what

¹ Change "the" to "this" *R. W. Ms. Ann.*

what to Cry out in his own particular, with *David*, *I was Conceived in Sin and brought forth in Iniquity*, which Cry is one of the *firſt Soul Cries* of every Child of God.

Whence Devils and wicked men come. 2. About 120 years ſince *the Father of Spirits* ſtird up the Spirit of his *Famous Servant Calvin* to batter down the *Babel* of a *Franciſcan Frantick*, who maintained, that God from the firſt Created both *Devils* and *wicked men* in the ſame Condition of wickedneſs wherein we now find them : Contrary to the holy Scriptures Teſtimony (as that *Excellent Soul* proved) declaring their *pure Creation*, their *Fall*, and their *reſpective future Eſtate* and condition to *Eternity*.

The low Countries hazard by the Pelagians. 3. In the Reign of our late *Royal Sovereign* K. *Iames* it pleaſed God to let looſe this *Devil of Pelagius*, who rowzed up the wits of *Arminius* and his *Followers* in the *low Countries*, (during their twelve years Truce with *Spain*) ſo that the Civil Diſcord about this point and other *Pelagian* and *Semi-pelagian Doctrines* had almoſt ruined *Holland*, &c. but that the Lord mightily aſſiſted them. *Firſt*, By the perſonal preſence and Forces of the *Prince* of *Orange*, and *Secondly*, By the *Famous Aſſembly* and *Diſputes* of the *Synod* at *Dort*.

Davids Conceptions vindicated from G. Foxes Aſperſions 4. To follow the *Fox* into his *Burrough*, what if *David* ſay not you but I ? why ſhould the *Papiſts* and *Arminians*, or *Foxians* have a more *holy Birth* then *David* ? Wherein could *holy* D*avid*, Father *Jeſſe* and his mother be charged ? Is not the Engliſh of the word *Devil Accuſer, Reproacher, Slanderer*, Is not Nature that *Law* and *Order* which the moſt

Infinite

Infinite Creator hath fet, in the propagation of all his Creatures, though the choiceft of them Man be degenerated into the *foure Vine*, at firft a *fweet* Vine, Nature or Gods Order goes on, though man-kinde be Corrupted from the Womb, *and the Imag-ination of the Thoughts of mans Heart be only evil and that continually*, Gen. 6. and millions of [68] Ex-periences all the world over Confirm it what the Trade of all mankinde is from the *Birth*. The *Spots* of the *Leopard*, and the *Blacknefs* of the *Ne-ger* comes not by Accident, *&c.*

What Na-ture is

6. The perverfnefs and Crookednefs of the mo-tions of Nature may continue, though Nature and the Courfe of it run on, as we fee in *Rivers* turn'd out of their *Chanels*, in *Clocks* and *Watches*, and *D al* , and *Lutes*, and *Harps* when out of Tune they give their *Natural* and *Artificial* (though dif-tempered) Sounds and operations.

7. Befide the holy Teftimony of *Mofes*, Gen. 6, and *David*, Pfal. 51. and the Lord Jefus declaring what the heart of man is, *Mark* 7. How doth *Paul*, Rom. 5 and 7. declare the Entrance of Sin by the *firft Man*, until by the *fecond Man* Sin and Death, and Hell be Conquered, and at laft Sin in Gods Children fully diffolved, and abolifhed?

8. I end this paffage with *Appellation* to all that kn w what Children are all the world over, the *fweeteft* and the *faireft* born of the *holieft* and *fweet-eft* Parents, how *froward*, how *proud*, how *Revenge-ful* againft their *Fathers*, *Mothers*, and moft *tender Nurfes*.

The pure-nefs of the fweeteft Infants.

1. Thefe rotten and crooked Difpofitions in every
                                                    Childe

Childe bring forth wilde Affes fruits in Youth, of
Rebellion againft Superiours, and of wicked defires
of Wine and Women, and fighting and pleafures
in perfons of greater growth, this rotten Nature
appears in their rooting (like Swine) for earthly
profits, or preferments, or fighting like Lions & Ty-
gers in Wars and Law-conttntions, and oppreffing
of Inferionrs, efpecially if they dare to reprove or
witnefs their Idolatries, Superftitions and Abominations.

The rot-tennefs of nature

2. The experience of all the Saints of God in
the Holy Scripture, who maintained a Battel between the Flefh and Spirit all their dayes, accord-
to *Gal.* 5. A Battel within them, fometimes the
Spirit (or new Man, the new Creature, or the Grace
of Chrift) prevailing, fometimes the Corruption or
Rottennefs of Nature (like the two Houfes of
Saul and *David*) the old Man getting the victory,
as we fee generally in *Abraham, Ifaak, Jacob, Mofes, Aaron, Eli, Samuel, David, Solomon,* &c. till we
come down to the higheft Saints *Paul* and *Peter* :
the one fhamefully again and again vanquifhed,
and the other (*Paul*) crying [69] out, that *the good
he would do he did not,* and yet when he did evil he
had two men within him, the Law of his Spirit
Heavenly, and the Law of fin which dwelt within
him, &c. they that know not and feel not this, they
are either dead or rotten, and fo feel nothing, or if
there be any life of God in them, and yet fay in the
litteral fenfe they fin not, their weaknefs is fuch,
that like very low and far gone weak bodies their
Filth

The ex-periences of Gods Saints in Scripture

Filth and Excrements come from them, but they know nothing of it, nor will believe or acknowledge any fuch matter.

The 35. *Inftance* is in *Pag.* 217. where G. *Fox* brings in *John Jackfon* faying, [*Falfe Prophets and Chrifts, and Deceivers, many fhould come (if it were poffible) to deceive the very Elect.*] ^{217 Iohn Iackfon}

He *Anfwers*, [Yes, Chrift faid they fhould come to the Apoftles, which before their Deceafe they did come, and went forth from them, which Chrift faid fhould inwardly Ravin , and get the fheeps cloathing : which fince the dayes of the Apoftles all the World went after them, as thou maieft read in the *Revelation*s : and now are *P*eople but coming from them to the Rock, and now fhall the Everlafting Gofpel be preached to them that dwell upon the Earth, over the heads of the Beaft and their falfe *P*rophet, and they fhall be taken, and the Lambe, and the Saints fhall have the victory.

I *Reply*, 1. As that great *Fox*, the *Pope of Rome* and his *Foxians* (the Worfh ppers of that Beaft) maintain that Antichrift is not yet come, that fo he may fcape a fcouring, or rather a burning or dafh- ing in pieces, fo doth our little *Fox*, G. *Fox* and his *Foxians* cry out another Lurry, [*Antichrift why he is come and gone long ago*, &c.] As if falfe Chrifts might not be then and now too *:* as if there were no more greedy Wolves to be found then in *Act.* 20 and no more Sheep-skins for them in *Matthew*, 7. &c. ^{The great and little Foxes.}

The Spirit of God proclaims, 1 *Cor.* 11. that
there

there muft be Herefies,, and *Peter* tells us 2 *Pet.* 2.
that *there muft be falfe Teachers, falfe Prophets, and
Damnable Herefies, for the trial of the fincere,* &c.
And were all the *Foxes* hunted out and deftroyed
in the Apoftles dayes, and none left fince *Johns*
time to our times to be hunted after and digd out
of their Burroughs.

70| Are there none found, fincere, and chafte to
be tried at this day to the Lord Jefus the Heavenly
Bridegroom, and to his Eternal King and Father,
God bleffed to Eternity.[1]

2. The Proteftants maintain that the *Pope* or
Papacy is the great Antichrift, the Man of Sin,
with feven heads and ten horns, &c. why fhould not
the Devil be able to raife befides the *Pope,* the *Cere-
donians, Valentinnians* and the *Arians, Manicheans,
Gnofticks,* &c. and fince, or at the beginning of the
Reformation, the *Quintinians,* and *Munfterian* Mou-
fters? why fhould he not be able to raife in our
time the *Nicholaitans* and *Foxians.*

3. It is true that in the times of warm peace,
&c. many Vermine breed, whom the cold winter
of Perfecution utterly deftroyes. I know alfo that in
the late times of Freedome to mens Opinions in
England, Many Opinions and promoters of them
arofe : Sharp times God hath to make difcovery, I
know fome fay that *Judas,* and *Theudas,* and *Bar-
chochas,* and *Rabbi-Iudah,* &c. were the falfe Chrifts
the Lord Jefus fpake of: I know alfo that amongft
the Profeffours of the Chriftian Name, falfe Chrifts
and

[1] Ends with a "?" not a "period." · R. W. Ms. Ann.

and falſe *Prophets*, Apoſtles, *Preachers*, &c. muſt
pretend to the Chriſtian Name, alſo.

4. I know ſome affirm that though the Pope
be Antichriſt, yet that he that letted was not the
Roman Emperour until he was taken out of the
way, but that he that letted was the Holy Spirit to
which the Quakers now pretend, which Spirit being taken away the *Popes* aroſe : But in the dayes
of *Iohn* when thoſe gifts did moſt flouriſh, yet then
there were many Antichriſts, and the gift of the
Holy Spirit did not hinder their riſing ; ſo that all
ages are full of falſe Teachers.

5. What Ignorance doth this little *Fox*, yet
great *Boaſter* diſcover in ſaying [*Now are People
coming forth from them*, &c.] doth he proudly look
over all thoſe Glorious Proteſtant Witneſſes of Jeſus, before and ſince *Luther*, whoſe Names many
of them, God commanded that Heavenly *I. Fox* to
make Record of.

6. Do the *Foxians* juſt now about *twenty years*
preach the everlaſting Goſpel : Now ſaith *W. Edm.*
in our diſcourſe we preach the everlaſting Goſpel to
you, that you ſhall be free from ſin, &c. But Gods
Spirit tells us in *Peter* and *Iude* of pretenders to
liberty, while themſelves are the Servants of Corruption or Rottenneſs.

71] 7. Both Jews and Gentiles have done by the
Name of Chriſt as the Jews and Romans with
Chriſt Jeſus before they murthered him : they
mockd him, &c. and then Murthered him ; that
ſo they might be the *Heir* and *Meſſiah* themſelves :
Juſt as the great *Fox* the *pope* and theſe little

Concern-
ing him
who letted
Antichriſts
riſing

The ever-
laſting
Goſpel

Foxians

Foxians pretend to be the fole great *Heir* apparent to the Crown of Heaven, and all other Rebels and Reprobates againft and from their Heavenly Majef-ties.

John Jackfon

The 36. *Inftance*, is in page 218. Where G, *Fox* brings in the fame Author faying, ⌊*I hope you will not condemn the Generation of the Righteous becaufe they are vot ʻperfeĉt.*⌋

He Anfwers, That which condemneth is Right-eous ; it condemns that which is not perfeĉt, and the Generation is Righteous and not to be con-demned.

I Reply, He Anfwers four things: Firft, ţhat which Condemns is righteous. Secondly, That which is Righteous Condemns that which is not perfeĉt. Thirdly, That which is righteous is per-feĉt. Fourthly, The Generation is Righteous (that is them felves being perfeĉt) and not to be Con-demned, the Summe of his Anfwer is, *Himfelf* and his *Foxian*s are *Gods*, as ʻ*pure*, & *holy*, as God is, and therefore now keep the *Eternal Seffion*s and *Affizes* at the *Tribunal* of their *high* Court, muft all the Generations of the World receive their *Eter-nal Doom* and *Sentence*, I know they know this is the bottom.

1. But ftay, this *Fox* is in his *Burrough* of *Equivo-cation*: for *Judgement* is twofold : Firft, *Judgement Righteous* : Secondly, According to *Appearance*, as the Lord Jefus diftinguifheth : How many are declared by *Appearances* to their Eyes, *Clouded*[1] ʻ*pride*

The hor-rible pride of the Foxians

Falfe ap-pearances

---

[1] Infert " with." *R. W. Mr. Ann.*

*pride, malice, Envy, Lafcivioufnefs, Covetoufnefs, Am-
bition*, &c. And therefore away with the Son of
God, hang him, and give us *Barrabas*, though a
Boutefeau and *Murtherer*, &c·

2. It is not true, that all that is not perfect (in
the *Foxians* Senfe) is not *Righteous*: For 1. (as hath
been before obferved)the words *Tam* and *Tomjin* in
Hebrew, and *Telos* and *Teleios*, and *Teleion* in the
Greek, have divers fignifications, and accordingly,
muft be, and are tranflated and expounded, Con-
trary to the *proud Ignorance* of thefe *Cheators*. The word perfect in the greek and Heqrew

2. The Generation of all Gods Children (in all
the holy Scrip- [72] ture) have ever acknowledged
their weaknefs, folly, pride, and many Tranfgreffions, with *true Quaking* and *brokennefs*, and *bitter
weeping*, &c :

3. In a true Senfe, that which is *Righteous* is *perfect Iuftification* or *Remiffion* of Sin for Chrift Jefus
fake is perfect, it admits (as they fay of no *magis & mi-
nus*) more or lefs, the truely humble *Ethiopian* is as
truly and *perfectly pardoned* and *Iuftified* as *David*
himfelf, and the *bleffed Mother* of the Lord Jefus,
the *Virgin Mary*. The Saints pardon of Sin and Juftifica-tion perfect.

4. We maintain, though pardon of Sin and Juftification, and Acceptation with God before Angels, Men and Devils be perfect, and though a pour
Child of God be born of God, be paft from *Death*
to *Life*, can not Sin in a Senfe, nor fuffer the Devil
to touch him : yet there remains till Death a Combate to be fought between the Law of the Spirit,
and Law of the members, the *old Man* and the *new
Man*, the *Flefh* and the *Spirit*, &c. The Saints bat-tel and daily Combate

56

5. Hence

5. Hence (in an holy Senfe) *Paul* faith, *it is not I, but Sin that dwels in me, that is in my Flefh wherein dwels no good thing,* So that David might fay in one Senfe, It was not I that committed *Adultery,* and *Murther,* and *Peter* fay, It was not I that *denied my Mafter with Swearing and Curfing,* &c. *but the rotten old man and Sin dwelling in me.*

He that knows not to untie thefe Knots, and yet prates of Righteoufnefs and perfection: He is proud and foolifh, and ignorant, and he will proudly and foolifhly fooner or later commit thefe five great evils.

1. He will not difcern what the *Generation* of the *Righteous is.*

2. He will fay Sin is nothing but *Imagination.*

3. He will caft wickednefs upon God, and fay God doth all, and what God doth that is good, therefore no Sin.

4. He muft call David and Peter fools for Confeffing their *Guilt* and *weeping bitterly,* &c.

5. That it is in vain to watch againft Sin, and to cry *Lord lead us not into Temptation,* &c.

In the laft place I Affirm (and have made it good) that the *Generation* of the *Papifts* and *Quakers*: though fo pure in their own eyes, *yet they are not cleanfed from their filthinefs*: The *Papifts* are juftly charged with *Superftition* and *Idolatry* & with drinking the Blood of Saints. And have not the *Generation* of the *Quakers*: [73] their Images and Idols alfo, (as I have manifefted) their pride and Ignorance & Idlenefs in not ufing means, and their paffionate Railings and Curfings? and I believe if
their

Heavenly Piradoxes

Devilfh Tenents of the Spirituals in Calvins time.

The Papift and Quakers perfection

their *Spirit* get a Sword (what ere they ignorantly prate) they will drink the *Blood* of all their *Enemies* as *Hereticks, Idolaters, Reprobates*, and *Devils*.

The 37*th. Inſtance* is in *Pag.* 220. wherein G. *Fox* brings in the *Author* of *Hoſanna* to the Son of *Da-vid*, ſaying, [*Man is not able to diſcern the things of God till he be born again.*] ^{220 Ho-ſanna to the Son of David}

He Anſwers, the Scripture ſpeaks of diſcerning *the Eternal Power and Godhead,* and that was a thing of the *Spirit* of God : and the *Apoſtle* ſaith not that they were born again : And yet I ſay *that none knows the things of God but the Spirit of God,* and that which may be known of God is manifeſt in them, for God hath ſhewd it to them : For that of God in them was of the Spirit, *who is the God of the Spirits of all Fleſh,* which brings them to diſcern the *Eternal Power and Godhead.*

I Reply, 1. With Amazement at the dreadful Juſtice of God hardening this daring Soul for playing away his own Light and the Name of God, and the Light which the Lord hath ſent him from ſo many *Excellent pens* out of which he hath raked nothing but handfuls of Reproaches to fling in the Faces of his beſt Friends, and turned Truth into Lyes, and poyſon to murther himſelf and others. ^{G Fox his Judgment from God}

2. It is clear, that (as in all Anſwers to the *Quotations* of his *Oppoſites* which he picks out) that he holds the Contrary to his *Oppoſite,* ſo here *viz.* That a man may be able to diſcern the things of God before he be born again.

3. He proves his point from two Scriptures, *Rom.*

Rom. 1. *Cor.* 2. As to the firſt, I will not repeat whät I have before written as to the Nature of the *holy* Spirit, his *Godhead,* his *Operations, ſeven Eyes,* & *ſeven Horns, and ſeven Lamps,* his *Common work-ings* in all men! his *ſpecial working* in the Elect, *Regenerating, Juſtifying, Sanctifying, quickning, Com-forting,*: &c. Nor will I repeat matters concerning the power of Nature in the *Philoſophers,* and all mankinde: Only from this *Rom.* 1. I obſerve,

1. That *the Eternal Power and Godhead* cannot be ſeen by *mortal Eyes.*

2. We may reach ſome *mental Light* of this *Eter-nal Power* [74] *and Godhead,* by a ſerious pondering of his works.

3. All mankinde are bound by the Law of their Nature to put forth their utmoſt in ſearching after God.

4. We may gain a great ſight of the Godhead, and yet not ſee him nor glorifie him, that is love him as *Paul,* 1 *Cor.* 8.

5. Natural men until changed and born again of Gods power and Spirit, doe but prate (*as the Devils do and tremble*) *their imaginations are vain, and their fooliſh hearts are darkened.*

6. Yet this ſight of God which men and Devils may get of God by their own Remainders of nat-ural Abilities will leave them without excuſe what-ever *Papiſts, Arminians* and *Quakers* talk of Gods requiring no more then he gives, for in Juſtice God is not bound to give *Sampſon* his Locks or his Eyes when he hath willingly ſuffered *Dalilah* and by her the *Philiſtims* to cut them off, and pluck them out. 2. Beſide

Kom. 1. Diſcuſſed as to the Eternal Power and Godhead.

The natu-ral power of men and Devils.

2. Beſide our wils and wiſdome are now become *Enmity againſt God,* and no man ſpends equal Care and pains for God, until Gods Spirit in free grace ch nge and quicken him with what he does for theſe *temporary Dreams* and *Shadows.*

The ſecond Scripture is 1 *Cor.* 2. *viz* But God hath revealed them unto us by his Spirit : *For the Spirit ſearcheth all things, yea, the deep things of God : For what man know*s *the things of a man ſave the Spirit of a man,* &c. now we have not received the Spirit of the world, but the Spirit which is of God, that we may know *the things which are freely given to us of God.* ^{1 Cor. 2.
as to Gods
Spirit
diſcuſſed.}

In *ver.* 6. the Spirit of God ſpeaks of a twofold wiſ-dome, firſt, the wiſdome of this world, and the Princi-ples[1] of this world which come to nought. Secondly, the wiſdome of God in a Myſtery, even the *hidden wiſdome which* God *ordained before the world unto our glory.* : Again, *ver.* 12. God tells us of two Spirits : The Spirit of the world, Secondly, The Spirit of God. Now this *woful Cheator* finding the word Spirit, Confounds as his Courſe is all together, and becauſe Gods Spirit regenerates the *Corint ians,* and opens to them a glimpſe of the Godheads power and wiſ-dom, and Goodneſs by *Pauls preaching,* and opens their hearts to it therefore he muſt alſo enlighten the world with the ſame Light, *whereas that which is born of the Spirit is Spirit, and that of Fleſh is Fleſh* ; This Change and renewing of the Spirit by the Holy Spirit, I fear G. *Fox* and moſt of his *Fox-ian*s never Experimened, [74] though they enjoy in *Wiſdome.*

^{The Caſe
of G Fox
and moſt of
his Fox-
ian s.}

common

---

[1] Change " Principles " to " Princes." *R. W. Ms. Ann.*

common a Light of Nature, though God hath endowed him and many of them with excellent Natural *Parts*: yea, with a Light from the *holy Scripture*: yea, with a Light of *Experience* and *common Motions* from Gods holy Spirit, and have been lifted
up by their own thoughts and others (as *Capernaum*)
up to the Heaven! and therefore my Soul fears (as to
moſt of them) *that God will bring them down to Hell
with the greater Condemnation.*

222. Ho-
ſanna to
the Son of
David
    The 38*th Inſtance* is in *Pag.* 222. where he brings
in the ſame Author ſaying, [*Salvation and Faith are
the gifts of God diſtinct from Chriſt*]
    He Anſwers, *They are all of him, and from him,
and with him*, And how is he *the Author of Faith in
whom it ends, and from whence it comes.*]

Chriſts
Name
hotribly
abuſed
    I Reply, as *Potiphars wife* cries out againſt *Jo-
ſeph*: and pretends *Chaſtity*, ſo doth this *ſubtle
Whoremonger*, pretending that all is *pure Chriſt*: the
Light is *Chriſt*, their *Hope* is *Chriſt*, their *Faith*, their
Spirit is *Chriſt* himſelf, yea, the *Saints are Chriſt*:
No diſtinction between Chriſt and them, *for they
are all of him, from him, and with him?*

Coloſſians
1. Con-
ſidered.
    In ſhort, I pray the Reader to mind with me the
firſt Chapter to the *Coloſſians*, where *ver.* 1. The Spirit of God declares how Gods Children (poor ſlaves

The Na-
ture and
admirable
Miſtery
and Excel-
len- of
Chriſt
Jeſus
at firſt in *Sathans Clutches*) are *Tranſlated from the
Kingdome of Darkneſs into the Kingdome of his dear
Son*: *In whom we have Redemption through his Blood,
even the Forgiveneſs of Sins.* I know the *Foxians*
turn Chriſt, yea, his Blood alſo into a *Spirit*, a God.
How admirably doth the holy Spirit of God declare

clare the *Godhead,* or *Divinity* of Chriſt Jeſus and
his *Manhood* or *Humanity,* unto *ver.* 21 ? out of
both which I ſhall ſelect two or three Attributes
of the Lord Jeſus.

1. The State of Chriſtianity, amongſt many other
high Expreſſions in the Scripture, is here called *the
Kingdome of Gods dear Son,* which argues a diſtinction from all other Kingdomes, and a diſtinction
from his *Saints,* as a *King* is not his *Subjects,* nor
their *Gifts* and *Honours,* and *Eſtates,* and *peace,* and
Joy though given by him to them,, and procured
by his *great wiſdome* and *love* for them.

Oh *poor Ungrateful Monſters,* not content to be
taken from [76] the *Kingdome,* from the *Dungeon,*
of *Darkneſs* and *Hell,* and that by the *Ranſome* and
price paid and *Blood* and *Death* of his *only Beloved
the Prince of Life,* but we muſt be the *King of
Heaven* and *Prince of Life* our ſelves.

2. I obſerve, The *Inſtrumental* and *purchaſing* The
Cauſe or *price,* is ſaid to be his *Blood,* which argues Blood of
the *Infinite value* of his Sufferings, in which Reſ- Ch i
pect only it is called *the Blood of God* : I know the Blood of
flight eſteem that ſome of theſe *Foxians* have of the God.
Blood of the *Lord Jeſus* ſaying, that *wicked men* the
Souldiers ſhed it; that it was ſpilt upon the *ground,*
that there was no difference between that *Blood* and
the *Blood* of another *Saint* : That by *Gods blood* is
only meant *godly* and *heavenly power,* and *Spirit* by
which God applies Mercy and *pardon, Juſtification,
Righteouſneſs,* &c.   The
I have read the Blaſphemous Diſcanting of the Blood of
Jeſuit concerning *Maries* white Milk, and Chriſts piſed by
Crimſon

The Blood of Chriſt deſ-

Papists and Crimſon Blood, & in the cloſe, his preferring the
Quakers. Milk of the Mother before the Sons Blood.

    I have heard alſo the fooliſh Blaſphemy of one
of my own Neighbours, ſaying, That the Blood of
the Quakers, and by name of *W. B.* was Saving
and Salvation to the World.

Chriſt the   3. But I paſs on, The Lord Jeſus is here called
picture of the Image of the inviſible God: If this ſhould reſ-
God. pect the Godhead only, which is inviſible, how
could Chriſt be a viſible Picture of Inviſibility? If
the Manhood only? is God a Man, and Man his
Image or *Picture*, as the old Heretick, and late in
London, Reeves and *Mugleton fancied.*

    The Truth is, as Chriſts Blood is but figuratively
for an Antitipe and fulfilling of all the Figures
Chriſt foregoing him, and for all his Sufferings, and many
God and Blood-ſheddings both of Minde and Body, ſo this
Man. Image or Picture, this Bleſſed Lamb of God, con-
ſiſting of the Godhead, wonderfully aſſuming ſuch
a *none ſuch Manhood,* both which the *Papiſts* and
Quakers are forced to confeſs, I ſay, it is clear he
was the brighteſt Image or Picture of God to the
World that ever God appeared in, and therefore
called the Word of God the fulleſt and loudeſt of
all the Words of God in which ever he ſpake, &c.

    4. Many more I might inſiſt on, but I muſt ab-
breviate, and only mention *ver.* 18. where the Lord
Jeſus is made the Pallace of [77] the Godhead,
Chriſt that in him as the Head of the Body, his Church,
Fulneſs
filling all. *ſhould all fulneſs dwell,* reconciling and making peace,
through the Blood of his Croſſe, &c. *Iohn* tells us,
that of this fulneſs in him, we receive: all the
                          World

World receives the Mercy and *Patience* of God by
him ; all his Followers receive his Grace and Spirit, Converting, Sanctifying, Comforting, &c. so that
his most holy and glorious Manhood, visible
amongst us, &c. was as a fair and spacious, beauti- A wonderful Conduit, into which the eternal and inconceiv- ful Con.
able Counsels of the eternal *Power* and Godhead duit.
flowed, and from whom by all those blessed means
and Ordinances, as by so many Cocks turned and
let loose, flow and run into poor empty Souls as
Pails and Tankards all sorts of mercies to the whole
World, and especially to the Elect, and Chosen,
his Church and Body that believe in him : what The proud
poor Children and Frantick Souls are we then that phrenzie
cry out (poor Pots, and *Pails*, and Tankards) that of the
we are the Conduit it self; yea, we the Well-head, Quakers.
Fountain and Spring, and (as this frantick *Fox* in
his Book once and again affirms) no distinction between God & Christ & his Saints, yea, though he
often acknowledge that Christ is the *Author and*
Finisher of Faith; So that the Gift of God, the
words of God, which are his *Tokens, Love Tokens,*
and *Love Letters*, they are God and Christ, themselves the *heavenly Father*, and his Son the *heavenly*
Bridegroom.

John the *Baptist* cried out to all such *proud Souls*,
I am not He, I am not worthy to untie his Shoe Latch-
et : He it is that Baptizeth with Fire : He is the
Lamb of God, &c. He, even that man upon whom he The Pa-
saw the Spirit descending like a Dove, &c. and blessed pists and
Paul with Iob, abhors himself, and counts his Holy Christ
Life, his Prayers, his Fastings, his Righteousness

57 *Dung*

Dung and Dirt compared with that of Chriſt Ieſus, in
Oppoſition to that of the Law, &c. In which *mud*
ſtill the moſt zealous *Papiſts* and *Quakers* ſtick, and
talk idly of their fulfilling of the Law now, by
Chriſts Righteouſneſs, Grace and Spirit in them,
which they will at laſt find to be no more but the
firſt Bargain or *Covenant*, let them pride themſelves
never ſo much in their filthy *menſtrous Clouts* and
Rags of Holineſs, that is their *Chriſt within* them.

The 39*th. Inſtance* is in *Pag.* 223. where he
brings in the ſame Author ſaying, [*The Light which
diſcovers Sin and Iniquity* [77] *in Mans Heart is not
Chriſt the dore*] He *Anſwers,* [*The firſt* Adam *was
the Dore wh reon all Sin and Tranſgreſſion entred:
Chriſt the Light, the ſecond* Adam *which doth inlight-
en every man,* &c. *ſaith, I am the Dore, the Way, and
the Life, which finiſh Sin and Tranſgreſſion, and brings
in Everlaſting Righteouſneſs, and the way of Diſe[1] out
of Death, which Light diſcovers Sin*]

I Reply, *Edmund Burroughs* in his *large Epiſtle* to
G. *Fox* thi h s Book, he tells us that this Light
(which they thus boaſt of) ſhews mans threefold
Eſtate, before Tranſgreſſion: in Tranſgreſſion and
what he is by being ſaved out of Tranſgreſſion: It
is true, Chriſt Jeſus doth this by many gracious
means, but not Immediately, nor to every man that
comes into the world: For *the World lies in wickedneſs and Darkneſs.* We are not only bleeding in our
wounds, but we are loſt in the *Wilderneſs*: We are
ſtark dead in Sin, and know no more that we are
dead

223 Ho-
ſanna to
the Son of
David

The
Eſtate of
mankinde

---

[1] Change " *Diſe* " to " *Life.*"   *R. W. Ms. Ann.*

dead then a dead man knows of his Condition:
what do then thefe poor deluded Souls tell us of a
Light and Chrift within every man in the world
difcovering his pure Eftate, his foul Eftate, and his
raifed Eftate, which no man or woman in this world
that I have read or heard of by Nature had any
Spark or fhine of fuch a Light: no nor thefe
proud Ignorants neither, but they have read or
heard of thefe things (more or lefs) from the holy
Scriptures and Records.

2. It is granted, that *Natures Light* difcovers a
God, fome fins a Judgement, as we fee in *Indians*:
Education and preaching difcovers more, as in *Saul,*
Achitophel, Judas: The Word and Afflictions makes
Pharoah cry out *I have finned*: Miracles make *Nebu-*
chadnezzar and *Darius* cry out *There is no God fo*
great as Daniels, and to make dreadful Laws againft
blafphemers of him, though themfelves continue
in their *old* I*dolatries:* yea, doubtlefs *Natures Light*
is able (in felf deceitfulnefs) wonderfully to Counterfiet *true heavenly Light,* and the *Devil* feem an
Angel or *Meffenger of Light* from Heaven!
Convict-
ions of
Nature
one thing,
Conver-
fion
another

3. What is this to a *faving Conviction* which Gods
Spirit worketh in thofe that fhall be faved, when
they cry out as the *wounded Jews, what fhall we do*
to be faved? and as the *Gaolour, what fhall I do to*
be faved?: until this faving Senfe of my Condition,
and Gods Juftice, what is Chrift, a Phyfitian, a Saviour, a Redeemer, *Bread, Water, Wine* and *oil* to
me? All is needlefs, yea, loathfome, (though an
bony C*omb*) to a full Soul: what talk [78] you of a
pardon to an honeft man? or if a *Rope* or *Barr* to
fave a fecure *Epicure* in his *downe Bed*?   4. Again
Saving
Convict-
ions

The State
of Adam
in his Fall 4. Again, how poor a plea is this, *Adam* was the
dore to fin, therefore Chrift is the dore to the difcovery of fin? For, look upon *Adam* in his *Fall.* 1.
He faw his fin? 2. He had horrour of Confcience:
3. He run from God. 4. He hides himfelf. 5. He
He fals to mincing end excufing his fin. All this
is revealed to us, and not a word yet heard of,
Chrift the *promifed See*d, or a *Light*, Chrift Jefus to
Convince him of fin: That was another work, a
faving work, which we may hope the Spirit of God
wrought in him upon the preaching of Chrift Jefus, the *promifed* Seed nd *Mediatour* to come.

Sathans
Cunning
with the
Quakers 5. I know the Song of the great deluder is: Turn
to the *Light*, hearken to the *Light*; thou feeft it
chides thee for thy Stealing, for thy lying, *&c.* Is
not this the Chrift, *&c.* liften to him, be ftill, fink
down, obey him, he will teach thee & fave thee,
&c. But the Bottom is, the Englifh and meaning is,
hearken to Sathan, *the God of this world*, be ruled
and taught, and guided by him,: The Scripture is
but a *dead Letter*, the true Chrift is within thee, he
will turn thee from thefe fins, and make thee per-
Chrifts
coming fect as God is perfect, *&c.* Chrift is come now in
us the *fecond Time without fin to Salvation.* He is
come in us (*Ten thoufand of his Saints*) to Judgement: He within thee is the word of God, the
Chrift of God, the Light of God, the Spirit of
God, God himfelf, and He feeks *Worfhippers in
Spirit and Truth*, for the vifible things are temporal, *&c*
6. But what is there in all this, but the noife of
Fenny

Fenny bitter in *hollow Canes,* &c? What is here but that common Bufineffes may reach to?

1. The Confcience of good and evil which every *favage Indian* in the world hath.

2. The *whifperings,* the *bl ndings* and *cheatings* of the *Devil,* in *Samuels mantle,* pretending *vowing* and S*wearing* to be the word of the Lord to be Chrift Jefus, yea, & that to your feeling *&c.*

7. But what are thefe to Chrift Jefus, *a dore of Hope* to *poor, wounded,* and *damned finners?* God by his Law and Juftice, by outward hearing or reading, and inward Convictions of *Natural Confcience* hath paffed Sentence of *Eternal Death* and *Hell* on them : They feel it they cry out now the Gofpel or *glad news* of a Saviour, a Jefus is *Hony* in the mouth, &c. Now *Luke* 4. he [80] *heals the broken heart, he fets free the Prifoners, ho gives Light to them that fee themfelves blind,* and Cry to him as the blind man did, Chrift medles not with found perfons who have no need of his *Bloud, Righteoufnefs, and Merits,* &c.

Two common Traps and Engines of Sathan in cheating the Foxians

When Chrift is welcome

The 40 *Inftance* is in *Pag.* 224. where G. *Fox* brings in *Ellis Bradfhaw,* faying, [*There is more words then one*]

Ellis Bradfhaw

He *Anfwers,* God is the word, and the Scriptures are the words which Chrift fulfil,.

I Reply, 1. As the defigne of the *bloudy Pope* and *Jefuits* are to kindle wars between the *Proteftants,* that the *Proteftants* may do the *Papifts work* and fave labour and Charges, and fo the *Pope* and his *bloudy Whore* of *Rome* may march away fecurely by the

the Light of the *Proteſtants fires*. So deals the
Devil *the old* Serpent with Chriſt Jeſus, and the holy
Scripture or Records which are but One, in a Senſe,
as the Sun and the Sun-dial: His end is to tear down
the Sun dial the Scriptures, under pretence that the
Sun is within them, and they need no Dials and
Clocks, no viſible thing that are temporal, *&c.* and ſo
to deſtroy the perſon and Commands of the Lord Jeſus, as viſible and fleſhly pretending all to be Light
and Spirit.

*Two great
deſigns of
Saſhan*

2. The words in the *Hebrew Aamar* and *Dabar*,
as alſo the *Greek, Logos* and *Rema* ſignifie a word,
and divers other matters, as I told my *Antagoniſts*
in the diſpute.

*The
Word and
Words of
God*

1. In both theſe Languages, and divers other Languages it ſignifies the will and pleaſure of the Mind
given forth by *Command,* or *Decres,* or *Proclamation*
made by word, or writing from Kings and States,
and *Commanders of Armies, Navies,* &c.

2. In a *Metaphor* or *Figure* it is attributed to
God, though he have no word properly, having no
mouth, no Tongue, no Braine, *&c.* but as Nurſes
he deals with us *poor Infants* and ſucklings, *&c.*

3. It is another *Metaphor* or *Figure* to ſay God
is the word for God is no more a word, then he is
a Man or a Spirit, or a Sun, or Shield, or a Houſe,
or a Fountain, or a Shepard litterally *&c.* For as a
word or Expreſſion proceeds from the mind &
thoughts within: ſo are the Thoughts and mind of
God declared many wayes, but chiefly by that man
Chriſt Jeſus called the Word.

3. The *Inconceivable Godhead* being pleaſed to
vouch

vouch-fafe in Infinite Goodnefs fome back parts
and glimpfes of his *Infinite glori-* [81] *rious Majefty* in the Framing of this world, and in the reftor-
ing of this world, by making a *Marriage* between
his Son and mankind! all his words and Expreffions tend mightily to advance this *marriage* and
great manifeftation, or Word of God.

4. I was once asked by a *'poor Foxian,* whether
God had any more words but one?

Whether God have any more wordsthen one.

I *Anfwered,* (and do now) that God hath a great
many words or Expreffions of his mind and Counfels unto *Men* and *Angels*: and fo G. *Fox,* and all
the *Foxians* Confefs the Scriptures to be the Words
of God, and therein Confefs that all, and every word
of Scripture is a word of God.

The Truth is, when God gives forth a word or
Command by *Angels,* by *Men,* and by other of his
Armies, (wherein his *Infinite Power* and *Providence*
daily appeareth) his word runneth very fwiftly, as
we fee when the word is given in a Kingdome,
Navy or *Army,* (as in *Ahafhueros* his one hundred
and twenty feven *Provinces*: *&c.*) He fends out his
word, that is, his mind or pleafure, and melteth
them, *Pfal.* 147.

5. So that I Affirm, that the *two great Lights*
of *Heaven,* the *Sun* and *Moon,* and all the *leffer Lights*
the *Stars* are *Words* and *Preachings,* and *preacher*s *of*
God to us: Every wind and Cloud, and drop of
Rain and Hail, every Flake of Snow, every Leaf,
every Grafs, every drop of water in the Ocean, and
Rivers, yea, every Grain of Corn, and Sand on the
Shore, is a Voice or word and witnefs of God
unto us.

Infinite millions of millions of Gods word.

6. Hence

6. Hence (as in that *Admirable* 107 *Pſalm*, &c. Every Turn of the *holy hand* of God in *Ruling* and *Over-ruling* all things in the world upon the *two great Hinges* of *Mercy* and *Judgement*, Pſal, 110. are but ſo many Voices or words of God, *God ſpeaks once and twice*, Job. 33. *but man hears it not, in Viſions, in Dreams, in Health, and Sickneſs, in Eaſe, and pain, in wants, in plenty, in dangers and Deliverances, Croſſes, Loſſes,* &c.

7. That the *Hebrew* is moſt full, *viz.* that God ſpake by his *Prophets* (or *Preachers*, or declarers of his will) divers wayes and divers times, *but now he hath ſpoken by his Son: From the beginning of the world*, Luke 1. he hath ſpoken of the coming of this Son *by the mouths of all his Prophets even from the beginning of the World.* Therefore though God have many Sons, yet Chriſt Jeſus (that man Chriſt Jeſus) among the many millions of [82] Sons is ſtiled the only Begotten Son of God, the Head of all the Elect, purchaſed to God out of every Nation by his Blood, &c. ſo by the ſame excellency and eminency (above all the manifeſtations and appearances of God to the World) no word or appearance of God is comparable to that appearance of God in Chriſt Jeſus, and therefore called *the Word of God* as the greateſt appearance of the eternal Power and Godhead.

8. Hence it follows, that theſe poor *Foxians* are ſo much the more ſhameleſs and monſtrous, not only in robbing the Scriptures of their moſt Heavenly and common Title of the Word of God, common to all Gods appearances, but alſo in turning

ing

ing this Word of God Chrīft Jeſus into a Spirit without any body : but what is gone for ever from us, and by their parting him (his God-head from his Man-hood) into a Fancie, a Dream, a meer Whimſie, and Develliſh Imagination.

9 When we deal with *Indians* about *Religion,* our work is to prove unto them by Reaſon, that the *Bible* is *Gods Word,* for by Nature they are much affected with a kind of Deity to be in Writing : That all their Revelations, and Viſions, and Dreams (in which the Devil wonderfully abuſeth them) are Falſe and Cheating.

That this Scripture or Writing we pretend to, is from God by their own experience, becauſe it agrees with their own Conſciences, reproving them for thoſe ſins their Souls ſay they are guilty of : That the terrible Majeſty of Gods Juſtice in pun-iſhing Sinners ſo ſhines in it, and alſo his infinite goodneſs and mercy in finding out ſuch a way of Mediation, and ſuch a Mediator that their Souls cannot but adore Infinite Juſtice and Mercy in it. That the Holy power of God ſo appears in it in working upon the Souls of Millions, turning them from Dogs, and Swine, and Wolves, and Lions, and Sheep, and Lambs, and Doves, &c. in Love, Meekneſs, Patience, &c.

That it could be none but an Omnipotent Arm that hath preſerved the *Holy Scripture* ſo many thouſand years (ſome part of it) through ſo many wonderful changes, through ſo many *Bloody Hunt-ings* of *Kings, Emperours, Popes* ; and this more ſub-
tile

tile Hunting of thefe *Foxians*, to run it out of this World. and by feeming to embrace it to deftroy and kill it.

Tho.
Weld 83] The 41. *Inftance* is in *Page* 228. Where G. *Fox* brings in *Thomas Weld*, faying, [*There lies a Myftery of Iniquity, for to fay the World calls them fo, by fuch and fuch Names or gives them their Chriftian Name.*]

He Anfwers, [There are Names given by the Heathen, the Heathen outward which men are called: There is a new Name which the World knows not written in the Book of Life: Here is the new Man known after God in Righteoufnefs and true Holinefs; Now who is the New Man, and this new Name? the World may call him by the old, fo it is not a myftery of iniquity to fay the World calls him fo.]

As to
Chriften
Names, &
Names to
Children I *Reply*, 1. As to Chriftian or Chriften Names or Things bearing or pretending to bear the Name, Authority or an Uniting of Chrift Jefus (as we know the word Chriftian fignifies) it is incumbent on every Chriftian Soul to fearch into the Root, and Rife, and Practife, and Warrant of them with holy fear and trembling in the prefence of God.

2. But to the myftery of Iniquity here infinuated againft them, Is it not a proud trick of a *Phari-* The
Foxians
fcornful
pride *fee* thus to fcorn the poor *Heathens* and *Publicans*, as not worthy to know the *Foxians* high Names, or take up fuch facred Names and Myfteries upon their Lips? yea, is it not a ridiculous Fancie thus to prate, and (like *Pharifees* to fcold about wafhing of Hands, and *P*ots, and Cups, therein placing invented Holinefs, &c. For,

For, 1. VVhat are the Heathen, this Heathenifh Who are G. Fox his Heathen Soul here ftrikes at? doth he mean the wilde *Savages*, who give Names to their Children, and oft times full of Reafon and Significance, &c. Or doth he account all Nations *Savages* and *Barbarians* that give Names to their Children, and confequently themfelves *Savages* and *Barbarians* alfo, for they give Names unto their Children alfo.

2. It is true that by the word *Heathen* (the *Goj* The Words Heathen in the *Hebrew* and *Ethne* in the *Greek*) the Nations or Gentiles were fignified as diftinct from the Holy Nation or Church of God the *Jews*, but fo it is not common in our Englifh Phraze, to call all the Nations *Heathen* that are not of the *Jewifh Nation*.

3. Did not the Saints before the coming of Chrift give Names to their Children? did not *Leah* and *Rachael* (by *Jacobs* leave) give all thofe fignificant Names unto the *twelve Patriarchs*? and [84] have not the Saints of God (as well as all Nations) ftill fo practifed?

4. Doth *Chriftian Regeneration* or *New Birth* deftroy *Natural Births* or *Marriages*, or *Procreations*, or *Names*, and *Educations*? (Only as *Diamonds* in *Gold-Rings*, and *Aples of gold in pictures of filver*) Chriftianity beautifies and adorns all thefe, *Natural* and *Civil Actions*, with an heavenly Spirit,[1] Carriage in *Earthly matters*.

5 Can there be any Inftances given of any Ser- Chrift deftroys not but beautifies Civility vants of God before or fince the coming of Chrift Jefus, difowning or flighting the Names which their *P*arents had given them: yea, though there were

---

1 Infert "&." *R. W. Ms. Ann.*

were fomé feeming honour to falfe Gods in them, *Fortunatus, Apollo, Phebe,* &c.

6. Why may we not (though we are for[1] his Heathens) call the *Foxians* by the fame Names by which they call themfelves ? for, in this great Book we find G. *Fox* and *Edmund Burrough* fubfcribed ? It is a Query why they fo plainly fubfcribe and yet defend them that do not, Have they a Priviledge ? Or do they thus quarrel with us, (poor Heathens) about ftraws or things Indifferent ? and yet fo weighty as the *new Name, and new man created in bolinefs,* &c ?

The new Man and new Name 7. But what is this *new Creature* and *new Name* they fpeak of ? How fhall the world call them by it if they know it not ? Such are their *Nonfenfical Fancies* of giving no Refpect to any in word or geftures : Such are their *Fantaftical Conceited Anfwers,* when being asked where they dwell, they Anfwer, they dwell in God, and where they live, they Anfwer, They live in God, *&c,*

The Popes flingiug to the world their old Names. 8. Are not thefe *Foxians* a kin to the *Popes* in this Fancy alfo, when raifed to the *Devils Pinacle,* to the *Popedome,* they throw down their old Names to the world, and though they be as fubtle as *Foxes,* yet now they will be called *Leones* Lions, though they be as fierce and Cruel as Lyons, they will now be called *Clement* and though they be as Impious as fwine, even as *Os 'pores,* they muft be called *pius.*

In the laft place, as the *Pope* caft away his net which he ufed as the Remembrance of the Fifherman *Peter* when he had catcht the *Popedome,* fo

G.

G. *Fox* having made his Fortune as it is prophane- ^{G. Fox}
ly called, having attaind a great Marriage : His ^{his great change.}
new Carriage and Courtesie, and Civility condemns
*Humphry Norton*s [85] and his own *former Rigidity*
as I am sure they will do most of them[1] for worldly Advantages, For, as they abuse that *Scripture,* Ecclef. 11.
The World is in their Heart. I may truly use it and
affirme the world and the pride and Advantage of
it, though they deny it as the *Pope* and *Cardinals*
and *Jefuits* do[2] is in their Heart, and is the Body
and Soul, the Root and Branch of all their whole
Religion.

The 42 *Inſtance* is in *pag.* 243. where G. *Fox* ^{243. Rich-}
brings in *Richard Sherlock* saying [*We muſt not look* ^{and}
for an Immediate Extraordinary and miraculous Teach- ^{Sherlock.}
ing from the Lord.]
He *Anſwers,* Yet he ſaith, *all men are taught of*
God, what Confusion is here ? *The grace of God*
which bringeth Salvation hath appeared unto all men
and this he calls an outward Teaching by the Lord
Jeſus Chriſt. Is that *which brings Salvation* outward : All in the Truth may judge this and try thy
Spirit : And the Teachings of the Lord is not mediate, but *Extraordinary* above all yours, which are
men got up ſince the dayes of the Apoſtles.
I Reply, 1. Although I have ſpoken before of
their *Immediate Inſpirations* : yet ſeeing how greed-
ily and boaſtingly this deluded Soul with ſcorn and
Contempt

---

[1] Place " moſt of them " in parenthesis. *R. W. Ms. Ann.*

[2] Place " as the *Pope* and *Cardinals* and *Jeſuits* do" in parenthesis. *R. W. Ms. Ann.*

Contempt of all his *Oppofites*, fucks in the poyfon
of *Devil fh Infpirations* in ftead of the *pure wine*
and *milk* of *Chriftian Truth*, and milks out this poyfon into the mouths of his *poor bewitched Followers*,
I fhall add a few words.

The
Teachings
of God.

G. *Fox* here affirmeth that the Teachings of the
Lord are not *mediate*, but *Immediate, Extraordinary*
and *miraculous*, Contrary to the whole ftream of
Scripture and Experience.

1. Contrary to the *Ordinary* and *daily*, and *mighty
preaching* of the *whole Creation* : Pfal. 9. *The
Heavens*, &c.

2. Contrary to the Teachings of God in every
mans Nature, and making, being taugh*t* of God,
above Gods Teaching, the *Fowls* of the *Air* and
Beafts of the *Field* : Doth not Nature teach you, 1
Cor. 11. as to long hair.

3. Contrary to *Abrahams Teaching* of his Children, and the Command of God to all *Parents*.

4. Contrary to *Ordinary Teachings* of the *Priefts*
and *Levites* Commanded by God, in fo much that
Chrift Jefus Commanded the *Scribes* and *Pharifees
fitting in* Mofes *Chair* to be heard and attended.

5. Contrary to the *Ordinary* and *Conftant feeding*
by *Sheep-* [89] *herds* and *Teachers* in the Chriftian
Flocks and Affemblies.

6. Contrary to the Teachings of the *holy writings*
or *Scripture* written by *Immediate breathing* of God,
for our Inftruction and Confolation, *&c.*

Ob. Yea, but faith this great wrefter of *holy*
writings : *They fhall be all taught of God.*

I *Anfwer*, 1. Who, or how *fhall they be all taught*
of

of God? that teaching in the *Hebrew* applied from
the new[1] *Prophets,* Iſaiah and *Jeremiah* is the teaching of the *new* Covenant, and that is the promiſe of
Grace and Mercy to ſo many as are *predeſtinate* and
called, &c.

2. That is no *Immediate, Extraordinary,* and *miraculous buſineſs,* for this is common to all that repent or turn to God.

3. Many had, and may have the *ſpeaking with
Tongues,* and *working with Miracles,* and yet not
know what the teaching of the Spirit in a *new
Birth* is.

4. In the *Ordinary Teaching* to Converſion, the
Lord owns his Servants as *Fellow Labourers, Workers, Builders, Huſbandmen, Fathers,* &c. wherein he
is pleaſed to open the hearts of *one*[2] *Thouſand* and
Ten Thouſand as he did in the *firſt preachings* of that
glad News, and I hope will do ſo again.

5. The great Promiſe to Chriſt Jeſus and his Outward
Seed is, that there ſhall be a *gracious Continuance* in means.
Chriſts mouth, & the *mouth* of his *Seed,* of both the
word, (that is preached) and the holy *Spirit* more
or leſs) *accompanying* and *Teaching,* Iſa. 59.

6. What is there in G. *Fox* his wild Notion,
[*Can that which brings Salvation be outward?*] Againſt
all the Proofs before I mentioned, and ſo many
others concerning the *Fooliſhneſs of Preaching,* &c.

Object. He ſaith, *The grace of* God *teacheth every
man to deny ungodly Luſts,* &c. And I ask,

1. If every man in the world hath this *Immediate*

---

[1] Eraſe "new." *R. W. Mſ. Ann.*

[2] Change "one" to "many." *R. W. Mſ. Ann.*

mediate work on them? what's the Reafon we find none in the world (no not the wifeft) until they have the Scripture, or the Doctrine thereof fome way opened to them, that have been able to give us the leaft Tidings of any fuch bufinefs.

2. What's the Reafon that fo few in the world have any fhew of Repentance, &c. much lefs a found and and faving turning of the whole Soul unto God?

87] Why do the *Quakers* make fuch adoe about their *Apoftles* Men and Women as if that *glorious Light* the *Father*, *Son* and *Spirit* in every man were not able to teach *Effectually* (by his *Extraordinary* and *miraculous power*) without their outward fpeaking to the *Seed,* that is to *God within* them?

Miracles.

4. If they themfelves teach by fuch an *Extraordinary* and *miraculous power* as the Prophets of old, and the Apoftles of Chrift Jefus did, what fhould be the Caufe why we fee no fuch *miraculous deeds* done by any of them? The Truth is, God is pleafed to chain up *Sathan*: otherwife, the *Foxians* would have their longing (which it may be fome fhall after them) But if they fhall be permitted by God and affifted by the *Devil* to do as the *Magicians* did: yet if their *Doctrine* be other then what is written (as I have abundantly proved it to be) while they cry out *Light, Light,* there is none as *Ifaiah* fpeaketh, not a Spark of *Light* within them.

247.
Chrifto-
pherWade

The 43. *Inftance* is in *Pag.* 247. where G. *Fox* brings in *Chriftopher Wade* faying, [*The written Word*

Word is the Sword of the Spirit :] And he makes
another Rule befide the Scripture[1] falfe.

He *Anfwers*, which we fay is the Spirit which
gave them forth, whereby *P*eace is known upon
the *Ifrael* of God: And the *Pharifees* had the Scripture but had not th*e Sword of the Spirit*, the Scriptures teftifies of *the Sword of the Spirit*.

I Reply, 1. With all *humble Reverence* to the
moft holy Spirit of God, who is God himfelf. I
affirme, the Spirit or God can not here be the *Sword*
intended.

For 1. This *Spiritual Furniture* being a *Similitude* The
taken from *warlike* and *Military Provifion* and *Ar-* Sword of
tillery from *Head* to *Foot*, the *Helmet, Breaftplate,* the Spirit
the *Shield*, the *girdle*, the S*hoes*, and every one applied to gifts and means flowing from Gods Spirit,
as *Faith, Hope, Sincerity,* &c. it were moft improper then to bring in God or the Spirit to be the
Sword, or any of the other pieces.

2. For there is no more Reafon to make the
Spirit or God to be the *Sword*, then the S*hield* or
any other piece.

3. It feems too low to the holy Spirit and God
to be here in this *Similitude*, refembled to a *Sword*
or *Inftrument* in the hands of men to be drawn and
brandifhed and fought withal for *Offence* and *De-*
fence at mens pleafure, though in fome Sence[2] God.

88] 4. This was the Sword, the only Sword, is
called a Sword with which the Lord Jefus fought
and vanquifhed the Devil, *Gegraptas, Gegraptai* :

It

---

[1] Place " befide the Scripture." in parenthefis. *R. W. Ms. Ann.*
[2] Infert " from." *R. W. Ms. Ann.*

It is written, it is written, and we may well fay of it as *David* of the Sword of *Goliah,* by which *David* cnt off his head, *there is none to that,* &c.

The holy Spirit, Chrift and God are Authors of all thefe *heavenly Gifts* and *Graces, the Beginner and Finifher of Faith,* and therefore not *Faith* nor *Hope,* nor any other piece of the *Artillery* themfelves, no more then the *Armorer* is the *Helmet,* or the *Cutler* the *Sword,* &c.

Not the
Spirit
himfelf.

6. In *Revel.* 1. Chrift and the Sword with two Edges (which cometh forth of his mouth) are diftinct, and can not be the fame, as G. *Fox* ufually Confounds and mixeth all together. Hence the the Word of Chrift, *Col.* 3. can not be Chrift himfelf, but that which cometh from him and tendeth to him.

7. Thefe great Interpreters are Confounded in themfelves, for here in *Ephef.* 4. the Spirit muft be the *Sword* and Word of God, But in *Heb.* 4. Chrift muft be the *Sword,* with *two Edges,* being the Word of God, and not the Spirit : So like *Juglers* do they fhift from one hand to another, to Confound and beguile the Beholders.

Object. But the Spirit faith G. *Fox* was before the Scripture, and gave forth the Scripture.

I *Anfwer,* what then, G. Fox is before his Book, and gave it forth, is it not therefore G. *Fox* his word & writing but G. *Fox* himfelf? Or is it not the *Kings Majefty* before his *Declaration,* or *Proclamation* to the world? Is it not therefore the Kings word, or is it the King himfelf? This *Immediate Infpiration* of the holy Scripture from the Spirit

The Immediate
Infpiration of the
Spirit

ma ꝛes

makes it a Word ſo powerful, a *Magazine* & *Store-houſe* ſo full of Treaſury, ſo rich a Standard, *Touch-ſtone* or *Weight*s ſo perfect, for the trial of all Spirits, all writings, all Doctrines, all Religions, Worſhips, Actions, *&c.*

Object. But the *Phariſees* ſaith G. *Fox* had the Scripture, but they had not the Sword of Gods Spirit:

I *Anſwer*, The *Jews* had, and have, and ſo the *Turks* have had much of it, the *Papiſts* and the Quakers, and other Blaſphemors, yea, and the *Dev-ils* themſelves may have the Scripture, the word of God in their Hands and mouths: for may not a true Sword, a choice Sword be in a mad maṇs hand, whereby he may [89] miſchief and wound, and kill himſelf and others: Hence men make merchandize of it, *ſophiſticate* and *Adulterate*, and turn it into a *Lie*, &c.

The Scripture horribly abuſed

On the other hand, the Spirit of God is promiſed to Godˢ Children: Gods Spirit and Word are promiſed to go together in the mouths of all true Chriſtians, *Iſa.* 55. this holy Spirit is to be praid for, *Luke* 11. and is therefore *powerfully preſent* with Gods true Meſſengers, while they *Tranſlate, Expound, Preach* as *Paul* did, *Acts* 26. No other things but what *Moſes* and the *Prophets* wrote of.

The 44*th. Inſtance* is ın *Pag.* 253. where he quotes *Henry Haggar*, ſaying, [*You call all men dead and Carnal in the Serpents Nature, in what Form ſoever if they differ from you*] G. *Fox* Anſwers, [*All that be not in the Light that inlightneth every man*
that

253. Henry Haggar

that cometh into the world which is the way to the
Father, differeth from us: such be dead, such be Car-
nal in the Seepents Nature ; For none comes to the
Life, but who comes to the Light, in what Form so
ever they be : And such as differ from us differ from
Chrift : For none come from under the Serpents head
and Nature, but who comes to the Light.

I *Reply*, 1.   As *David* faid of fome whofe *Teeth*
were as *Swords*, and *Solomon* faith, *there is a Genera-*
tion &c. *of fuch whofe Teeth are as Swords*, and if
ever there were a Generation of fuch in the world
the *Papifts* and thefe *Foxians* are the *Generations*
here intended : For it is in vain to tell them of
Chrift *the Foundation*, and of building *Wood, Hay,*
Stubble, &c. If you come not roundly to the *Pope*
with the *Papifts* : Or to the *Light within*, &c. nothing remains but *Fire and Brimftone, Damnation*, &c.

2.   It is true, in fome of their writings, and in
Edmund Burroughs himfelf there feems to be fome
charitable hopes of fome having fomething of *Sin-*
cerity in them, and of breathing after the Lord,
but I obferve they fall in with G. *Fox* again, *viz.*
except that thofe perfons owne their Idols[1] called
Light within them.

3.   The *Proteftants* overcome the *Papifts* not only
by Scripture and Argument, but in *Charity* alfo,
for they profefs to have *Hope* of many among the
Papifts, as they do alfo of many amongft the *Qua-*
kers, But the *Papift* and *Quaker* like *Fire-fhips* burn
and blow up all, that bow not down to theis
Image, &c.

The Pa-
pifts and
Quakers
of a dam-
ning and
damne
Spirit.

The true
Proteftants
Charity.

4. How

[1] Erafe " s " in " Idols." *R. W. Ms. Ann.*

90] 4. How far are thefe from the Spirit of The Quakers far from the Spirit of Chrift Jefus. Chrift Jefus toward the *poor Woman*, the *Syrophe-nician*, who by her *worſhip* was a *dog*, (and he told her ſo) yet believing in him and content to gather up *Crumbs* (as a *Dog*) under his *Table*, he grants her *Suit*, and magnifies her *perſonal Excellency*! Thus dealt he with the *Centurion* and *Cornelius*, and with every *poor Reed* if truly bruiſed for Sin, and every Lock of *ſmoaking Flax* reaking in truth of Love to God, and the Lord Jeſus.

He proclaims the Kingdome of Heaven to the *poor* in *Spirit*, who ſee themſelves *dead* and *loſt*, and The meek and merciful Spirit of Jeſus. *damned*, and ſeeing no help, no Grace, (not a penny nor a patch of any good in them but) waiting as Beggars at the *gate*, the *beautiful* and *glorious gate* of *mercy*.

He proclaims *Bleſſedneſs* and *Promiſes* to the *bleat-ing Lambs* as the *fruitful Sheep* to the *Infants* and The different ſtate of Gods Children. *new born Babes, that hunger and thirſt for the milk of Righteouſneſs*, that by the Patience and Comfort held forth in the writings or Records they may have hope, although yet they cannot be Confident of any work of God in them, and are not ſo bold to Confeſs Chriſt Jeſus openly, and kiſs him in the Streets, but ſteal to him by night as *Nicodemus*, and *Joſeph*, until they ſaw him bleeding on the *Gallows*.

He bare with his *Diſciples though fooliſh and ſlow of Heart, hard-hearted*, ignorant of his *Death* and *Reſurrection*, and loath to hear of ſuch metters.

The 45th. *Inſtance* is in *Pag*. 259. where he quotes *John Brown* ſaying, [*And them that bring* 259. John Brown
people

people to look at the Light within them, are as Korah, Dathan *and* Abriam.]

G. *Fox* Anfwers, [*All that go from the Light within them, are as* Korah, Dathan, *and* Abiram *amongft the Lords Prophets, Exalting themfelves and Perfecuting.*]

1. I Reply, and Examine unto whom this Famous Hiftory may moft properly be *Applicable*, for fure it was a *Type* and word of God

Number 16. Korah, Dathan and Abirams Revolt applied to the pretended Quakers.

1. Then, that which the Spirit of God chargeth upon *Korah*, is a rifing up, a *Revolt* eud *Rebellion* againft the Lord, his Appointments and Minifters or Officers, *Mofes* and *Aaron*, &c.

I know G. *Fox* chargeth this upon all that pretend to any *Miniftry* and *Miniftration*, and have not the *Immediate Spirit* of |91| God as the *Apoftles* had but as (he fpeaks fimply) are *Ravened* from it, and are ftill *Apoftates*, &c.

The Proteftant Religion Revolted from by the Quakers

But I *Anfwer*, the *Proteftant Religion* is a Religion protefting againft the abominations of that *bloody man* of Sin the *Pope* both in his *Doctrines* and *Worfhips* and Converfations: Thefe Protefters have been fince the *Waldenfes*, in *France* and *Germany*, and *low Countries*, and *England*, *Scotland*, *Denmark*, *Swedland*, *Polonia*, *Tranfylvania*, *Norway*, *Ireland*, &c. Conflicting, Contending with their *Tongues*, their *pens*, and their *Blood* againft the *Bloody Whore* and *Church of Rome*, according to many paffages in the *Revelations*, moft *wonderfully* and *miraculoufly fulfilled* upon them.

From thefe all their holy Doctrines and Endeavours after Gods pure worfhip are the *Quakers*
Revolted

Revolted and set up a *Flag of Defiance* against all but pretended *Immediately Inspired persons, Invisible Worships*, and *Ministers*, and a *sullen, proud,* and *dogged Conversation,* (for the general of them.)

2. As *Absoloms* and *Shebahs Conspiracies* were notable and Signal against *King David,* the *Prophetical* and *Kingly Type* of the Lord Jesus, so was *Korahs* and his *Conspirators* very Considerable and Eminent against *Moses* and *Aaron* Types of the *Prophetical, Priestly,* and *Kingly Office* of the *blessed Lord Jesus Christ:* It is said, *Numb.* 16. that *Korah the Levite,* and *Dathan* and *Abiram the Sons of* Reuben, and *two hundred and fifty Princes* and *Notable Men of Fame* in the *Assembly* thus kindled the *Coals* of this *proud Conspiracy,* which had broke forth into *devouring Flames,* except that the *Sheepherd of Israel (who never slumbers nor sleeps)* had most graciously and wonderfully watcht for the *timeous* and *early Extinguishing* of it.

Conspirators agaiust the Priestly, Prophetical, and Kingly Office and Power of Christ Jesus

As to the *pretending Quakers,* it is known that they are not *Sons of Obscurity,* (as *Bull* and *Farminton, Reeves* and *Mugleton*) but for *Estate* and parts, for Education and Learning, some of them[1] for pretences of *Piety, Conscience, patience, Zeal* and *Mortification,* yea, and also for their Numbers, all which they predicate in their Books, and in my dispute with them with *loud Trumpets*) they are known to be *Confiderable,* and as like to spread as did the *Arrians Papists* or *Mahometans.*

The conspiracy of the Quakers Against Christ Jesus.

3. *Korah* and *Dathan,* &c. they were by Gods righteous Judgement so fixed, and setled, and hard-nec

---

[1] Place "some of them," in parenthesis. *R. W. Ms. Ann.*

ned in their Perſwaſion [92] and Confidence, that they Contemned all *Moſes meekneſs,* and *Anſwered ſtoutly, We will not come up,* when he Cited them _{Korah and the Qua-}before the Lord : yea, ſay they, *wilt thou pluck out* _{kers Con-}*the Eyes of theſe men,* and they daringly and deſ-_{fidence &} perately brought their *Cenſers* to offer *Incenſe* and _{fiercenefs.} *Worſhip* to God : as may be applied to theſe *proud* and *Confident,* and *deſperate Foxians.*

And lying 4. Their Charge was notoriouſly falſe againſt Charges. *Moſes,* as the Charge of the *Quakers* againſt ſuch bleſſed Inſtruments which God hath uſed like *Moſes* to bring the *Proteſtants* out of the *Egypt* of *Popery* :) *viz.* a Charge of Pride and Ambition, *wilt thou make thy ſelf a Prince over us?* a Charge of which the *Foxians* are notoriouſly guilty.

Ingrati- 5. I obſerve their *horrible Ingratitude* both unto tude. the moſt holy God himſelf, and unto *Moſes* and *Aaron,* Gods Servants, by whom he had wrought ſo many wonders for this people in ſo many *wonderful* and *miraculous Directions, Preſervations* and *Deliverances.*

Impa- 6. Their *Impatiencci* and *Unbelief,* &c. *Thou haſt* tience. *not yet brought us unto a Land flowing with milk and hony,* as if God and *Moſes* had only fed them with *Sugred* and *honied Words,* and no Effects and performances.

7. I obſerve their ſubtle and falſe pretences and Suggeſtions : Is not all the *Lords people* holy every one of them, and the Lord is amongſt them, juſt the *Quakers Language,* who ſo advance every one of the people of the Lord : (as they call their *Proſelites*) *viz.* that they are juſt now *born of God,* and

and Literally, *can not Sin*, are *Immediately Inspired*, need no Teachers, no Scriptures, *&c.*

8. I obferve, and I humbly beg of *the Father of mercies* to caufe thefe *poor Foxians* to obferve the *Confpiracy* of the two Elements, *Earth*, and *Fire* to Confume and devour thefe *Famous proud Confpira-* *tors*: I fpare *Applications*, begging mercy from *the Father of Lights* and *mercies*, for their *Humiliations* and *Salvation*: Only I Remember, *that every Plant the Heavenly Father hath not planted, flourifheth it never fo green, fo high, fo long, fhall be plucked up, and caft into the Fire*, &c.

The Wonderful Judgements of God upon the Korathites in this world

The 46*th. Inftance* is in *pag.* 262. Where he brings in *George Johnfon* f ying, [*The Americans were never ordained for Grace and Salvation, and the Grace of God never appeared to the Americans.*] 93] G. *Fox* Anfwers, which is contrary to the Scriptures, which faith, *the grace of God which brings Salvation hath appeared to all men, &c. and I will give him for a Light, and for a Covenant to the Gentiles, a new Covenant to the Houfe of Ifrael and Judah, and that he may be my Salvation to the ends of the Earth; and many in America have received Truth and Salvation.*

62 George Johnfon.

I Reply, 1. To the Covenant or Bargain of God with Man, firft and fecondly I have fpoke, as alfo to the figurative calling of Chrift Jefus the Covenant to *Jews and Gentiles*, and that this blind Soul taking it litterally, he runs upon the Rocks of the Arminian general Redemption, and the *Univerfalifts* general Salvation, and that with a known Con-

Thoughts about America

60

tradiction

tradiction againft their own Foundation of none having any benefit of Chrift, that own not their Light, &c. as alfo with a known Contradiction to all Expeiience, which faith, the whole World lies in Wickednefs, and this *America* in *Barbarifme*, and *Barbarous Wickednefs* of all forts.

Now Chrift a Light & Covenant.

2. I have faid Chrift is the Light, the Covenant, the Brazen Serpent, the Bridegroom held forth as the Sun in the Heavens to all the World: So Chriftians are the Salt, the Light of the World, and the Church the *P*illar and Firmament of Truth, holding it out to all the World; is therefore all the World feafoned, enlightened, converted, faved. yea, doth he not only deny the *Americans*, but the *Europeans*, *Afians*, and *Africans* alfo any Salvation (though never fo holy Profeffour of Chrift) except they bow down to their new black Image of Light within them?

N England's Plantaaion

3. It was a large effufion of the *Holy Spirit* of *God* upon fo many precious Leaders and Followers, who ventured their All to *New-England* upon many Heavenly Grounds, three efpecially.

Firft, The enjoyment of God according to their Confciences.

Secondly, Of holding out Light to *Americans*.

Thirdly, The advancing of the *Englifh Name* and *Plantation*s.

Thefe three ends the moft High and Holy God hath gracioufly helpt his poor *Proteftants* in a Wil-

The Indians of N. England

dernefs to Endeavour to promote, &c.

And as to thefe *Barbarians*, the Holy God knows fome pains I took uprightly in the Main Land and *Iflands*

Iſlands of *New-England* to dig into their Barbarous, Rockie Speech, and to ſpeak ſome- |94] thing of God unto their Souls; and ſurely God hath ſtirred up the Spirit of my ancient·dear Friend *Mr. Eliot* to gain their Language, to Tranſlate them the *Bible*, and many other wayes to bring the ſound of a Saviour amongſt them, which I humbly beg of God to perfect and finiſh for the Glory of his Great Name, &c.

The Indians of New England

4. What G. *Fox* means by ſaying ſome in *America* have received Truth and Salvation I can but gueſs at ; It is known he owns nothing of God in *Indians* or *Engliſh,* until they bow down to their Idol, and that he intends none but ſuch *Engliſh* in *America* as he and others have Poyſoned and Bewitched with Heliſh Sorceries.

5. This laſt Year a *P*aper was ſent me from the Quakers, deſiring me to turn it into *Indian,* that ſo it might be Printed in *England,* and ſo diſperſed amongſt them : it contained two things :

The Quakers deſire of perverting the Indians.

Firſt, *That they had a Light within them which told them that it was evil to Steal,* &c.

Secondly, *That if they did hearken to this Light, it would lead them to God,* &c.

I returned the Paper, and my refuſing in Writing, affir.ning it not to be Truth, &c. and I queſtioned the Quakers themſelves for a falſe Chriſt, falſe Light and Spirit, which they would infect the *Indians with.*

The 47*th Inſtance* is in *pag.* 263. Where he quotes

John
Owen 263 quotes *John Owen*, faying, [*All Truth concerning God and our felves is to be learned from the Holy Scripture, the Word of* God]

G. *Fox* Anfwers, There was Truth learned before the Scriptures were written, and the Scriptures of Truth are the Words of God, which ends in Chrift the Word, and there is no Truths learned but as the Spirit doth lead into all Truth : And many has the Scriptures but know not Chrift and the Truth, &c. fo he hath thrown out Chrift and the Spirit.

I *Reply*, 1. I have more then once before Anfwered this *Childifh Anfwer*. There was Truth, (and the Spirit, and Chrift, and Light,) before Scripture, as alfo that which no *true Proteftant* denies, *viz.* that the Scriptures, nor preaching, nor Baptifme, nor the Supper, nor Afflictions avail except the Spirit (the *Fin-* [85] *ger* or *Power* of God) fet *t*hem home upon us : As alfo that many have the Scriptures yet know not Chrift, which who queftions ? So that his Anfwers are fo loofe and Childifh that none but *Fools* and *Children*, and *Frantick perfons* can find any Savour and taft in them.

Owens
writings
about the
Scripture
Excellent-
ly learned
and Spi-
ritual and
Invincible

2. I therefore further Anfwer to this Quotation, pray the Reader to read fome former paffages, but efpecially, thofe publick difcourfes of this excellently learned and pious Author, wherein he hath admirably (both in *Latin* and *Englifh*) maintained the *Authority* and *perfection* of this *Ineftimable Jewel*, the holy Scripture : both againft *Atheifts* and *Papifts*, and *Jews*, and *Quakers*, &c. and proved (as clear as at Noon-day) the holy Scriptures, and

every

every Tittle of them to be the *holy Word*, or *Will*, or *Declaration* of the holy mind of God.

The 48*th Inſtance* is in *Pag.* 264. where he brings in *Samuel* Palmer, ſaying, [*The State of the Soul in this Life is threefold Creation, Corruption and Regeneration.*]

G. *Fox* Anſwers, [*In Regeneration the Life is changed from the Life which is in the Fall, So Regeneration and Corruption is not one in the new Life*]

I Reply, who ſaith they be? who ſaith that Regeneration and Corruption are one in the new Life? what a foul Trick is this of a falſe man to impute that to his Oppoſite which he abhorreth? I gueſs, or he means that in Regeneration, there is perfection and no Sin, or Corruption left, &c. Hence the plea of ſome of their Spirits for *Adams nakedneſs* being come to the State of I*nnocency*: Hence the poor frantick Souls cry out that the *Proteſtants* preach for Sin, for Tearme of Life, &c,

I *Anſwer*, queſtionleſs the Devil deals with the *Foxians* as the *Pirat* doth with Ships, he makes no Oppoſition againſt ſuch he hath taken, and is poſſeſſed of: So that no queſtion but the *Quakers* may be freed from many Tranſgreſſions and Temptations to them, which others are aſſaulted with.

2. Theſe poor Souls fooliſhly and extream ſimply Anſwer *Pauls* Complaints and Cryes and bewailing himſelf, *Rom.* 7. with *Pauls* giving thanks for his ſudden victory in the laſt words, as if juſt then the Battel had turn d, and *Paul* had not ſpoke of the Conſtant Battel and Warfare, which all the Saints of God (in about four thouſand years together

ther

[margin notes: 264 Samuel Palmer]
[margin notes: Mans threefold Condition in this Life]
[margin notes: The Devil too Crafty for the Foxians]

ther throughout the holy Scripture) [96] Experimented: *Noah, Abraham, David, Peter, John, Barnabas,* &c.

3. It is a miftery which neither *Jews* nor *Turks,*
Atheifts or *Papifts,* or *Quakers* know, *viz.* how the
Seed of all grace may be in the *new born,* and yet
the Seed alfo of all fin (except the fin againft the
holy Spirit) remaining in them: Therefore when
they hear of the Falls of the Saints in Scripture,
and fo great? Some queftion the Truth of the
Scripture: others make a fport of them, and pretend a Cloak for their fins, faying, none are perfect,
why may we not as well as they? Others, (as the
Foxians fay,) We are come to a more perfect and
pure Eftate then *Paul* at firft was in: or *John,* who
faith, *If we Confefs our Sin:* or *Iames,* who faith, *In*
many things we offend all: or the Father that cried,
help my Unbelief, &c. But the *Papifts* and *Quakers*
are fo *perfect* and *Superperfect,* that though they be
full of *pride, Ambition, Unbelief, Unthankfulnefs,*
Intemperancy, Covetoufnefs, full of *rafh Anger, bitter*
Railings, and *dreadful Blafphemies* againft *Heaven,*
yet they can with the *Whore* wipe their mouths,
and fay they are pure from all uncleannefs.

A great miftery.

The Quakers devil-ifh pride.

The 49*th. Inftance* of G. *Fox* his lame writings
is in *Pag.* 275. where he quotes *Richard Meyo,* faying, [*To fay the Gofpel is the Power of God is but a*
Metaphorical Speech.]

275. Rich-ard Meyo.

G. *Fox* Anfwers, [*The Apoftle doth not fay fo, for*
the Apoftle faith, the Gofpel is the Power of God
unto Salvation to every one that believes, in plain words,
Rom. 1.   I Reply,

I Reply, 1. (As before, and as thousands know) that the word *Gospel* is in all *Languages glad News*, the same which the *Angel* brought to the *Sheepherds* of a *Saviour born, and laid in a manger at* Bethlehem, this is the *News*, the *placid good News*, though set forth and beautified in the holy Scripture with variety of Figures and *Metaphors.*

2. The *great Fox* the Devil who thirsts after the Blood of the *Quakers*, and of all mens Souls, he whispers, *viz.* the Gospel is Christ, it is the Spirit, the Light, and God himself, why talk you of a written Gospel? of a preached Gospel the Scriptures are within you, the Gospel is within you, *Translations* & *Interpretations* within you: why gaze you upon pen and Ink, and after a man. *&c.* _{The Devils bloody Craft.}

3. As if the glad Tidings or Gospel to a dying man of a par- [97] don, & of Life, *&c.* founding to his Ear, were not by the *External Dore* of his Ear conveyed (by that Dore) to the *inward dore* and *Closet* of his mind? who but *Frantick Souls in Bedlam* will say, what need you mind the *Kings Declarations* or *Proclamations* of *pardon* or *Liberty*? The King himself is the *Gospel*, the *Declaration*, and the *Librty*, the King is within you, the Gospel or glad News is within you? _{The Kings Declaration of mercy and Liberty.}

4. The Devil hates the *glad News* of Christ Jesus as much as Darkness hateth Light, therefore he hath two sorts of Souldiers. _{The Devils two sorts of Souldiers}

1. Some that say, what tell you us of Reading and praying, and preaching, mind the *Kernel within*, while the second sort are all for the outside, which without the In-side are but *Shels*, and *Husks*, and *Shadows*. _{Anti-Christian-isme.}   5. How

The Fig-
ures in
Scripture.
5. How commonly doth the holy Spirit in the
Scriptures speak *Ridles* and *Figures*, that they that
see not may see, and they that say they see (*Papists*,
Quakers, &c. may be blinded) why is the *Lamb*
called the Passover, Christ the *Temple*, the *Cup* his
Blood, the *Bread* his *Body*, &c.

There were many *hundreds* brought before *King
Henry* and *Queen Mary*, after him, &c. for Insur-
rections with Haltars about their Necks: These
Princes (and others) pronounced their inward mind
by *word External*, the *Heralds* and *Proclamations*,
and *Trumpets* were in a *Figurative Sense* all glad
News and Gospel, and yet the substance of the glad
News or Gospel was the pardon offered and vouchsafed to them?

6. Mine Eyes have seen a Condemned Soul
turned off at the Gallows: a *Post* comes galloping
all drive, waving his hat, which being espied, Exe-
A lively
picture of
the Gos-
pel.cution is staid: the people cried a pardon, the
Post cried a *Reprieve*: The *Sheriff* cried neither no
Reprieve, &c. until he saw the *Kings hand* or *Authority* from him, the Post delivers to the *Sheriff* a
bit of paper, which the *Sheriff* reading He Commanded the *Halter* to be taken off, and the Prisoner
to be delivered to the Post: the Prisoner with joyful lips bid *Death* and his *Fellow Sufferers Farewel*,
and with joyful Legs leaps up behind the *welcome
Messenger* of his *Deliverance*, for, afterward he had
his *pardon* under the *broad Seal of England*. I ask
here how many passages and particulars may *Figuratively* be stiled *Glad News*, or the Gospel to this
dying man.

7. I

7. I ask whether the glad News or Gofpel which this Poft, [98] *Meffenger* or *Preacher* brought, might not *Figuratively* be called his Gofpel or glad Why it is called News, as *Paul* Rom. 2. calls it his Gofpel, and 2. Pauls *Cor.* 4. *our Gofpel if hid, it is hid to them that be* Gofpel. *loft?* It is hid two wayes.

1. When not by writing or preaching it is How it is hid. preached or declared (as it is not as yet difcovered to innumerable millions in the world.)

2. When the *Power* or Spirit of God opens not (as he did *Lidiahs*) the Ears and Hearts and Spirits of men to embrace the Gofpel, or glad News of a Saviour to them : and this outward and inward hearing of this glad News, it is the Devils and the *Jews*, and all *Atheifts*, and (thefe *refined Atheifts*) the *Quakers* work to hinder.

The 50*th Inftance* of G. *Fox* his lame Anfwer is 282. Dan-in *Pag.* 282. where he brings in *Daniel Cawdry* iel Gaw-faying, [*The Saints were come to the Spirits of juft* dry. *men made perfect, but not on the Earth.*

G. *Fox* Anfwers, [*The juft mens Spirits that led them to give forth the Scripture was the Spirit of God, and that was perfect, and was while they were upon the Earth : The Saints were come to, (which was Chrift the End of all words) and fo to God the Judge of all the world.*]

I *Reply*, I have fpoke before, that Spirits are *In-vifible Beings*, both good and bad, Contrary to the S*adduces*, who held neither.

Firft, That, of good Spirits there are three forts. The Vari-ty of 1. The *Increated* God himfelf : 2. The Spirit of Spirits.

61   God

God called (becaufe of his manifold operations) the feven Spirits of God, &c

2. Thofe *Invifible, holy Meffengers,* or *Angels,* called *Miniftring Spirits,* and *Flaming Attendants* upon Chrift and his, *Heb*: Oppofite to thefe are the *unclean* Spirits fpirits of Devils, &c.

3. The Spirits of men, firft, faints, as *Mary* fings, *my* Spirit *hath rejoyced in* God *my Saviour,* &c. and oppofite to thefe are the Spirits of the wicked as *Peter* tels us of the Spirits of the wicked, of the old world now in prifon, &c.

Why it is faid the Spirits made per-fect.

2. I obferve that in this *Heb.* 12. the Spirit of God fpeaks not of the Bodies of the Saints neither Conjoynd, nor a-part. Nor fecondly of the Righte-ous, made perfect, but the Spirits of Firft, the Righteous: Therefore it feems to hold forth not a perfect State of the Saints in this Life, Confifting of Spirits and Bodies, [99] which our proud Boaft-ers fay of themfelves, nor that they are perfect: Nor fecondly, of the Eftate of the Saints in the world to come, where all *true Proteftants* hold, that the Bodies and Souls of the Saints fhall be perfected, and *Everlaftingly* (and as to us now) *Inconceivably glorified.*

But the Eftate of the Souls or Spirits of the Elect, who are (as fome Tranflate) perfected, fome *Confummated* or *finifhed,* fome grounded, or now (*Everlaftingly Eftablifhed,* while their vifible part, *the Body fleeps in Jefus* until the *joyful Refurrection.*

2. Thus it appears the rather to be, becaufe we find in all the *holy Records* the Spirits, Souls, and Bodies of the higheft Saints in this world defective and fubject to great failings, &c.   3. It

·3· It is faid, 1 *Pet.* 3. the Spirits in prifon, not the Bodies nor the wicked, but thofe Spirits of the wicked which believed not *Noahs preaching,* &c. *The Devil*

4. Doth the Scripture fpeak of the Spirit of God *would be* here at all? but of the Spirits of men; or of *rid of* thofe *Penmen* of the holy Scriptures, or of any *and all* prefent ftate of perfection in this Life at all, which *Learning.* might occafion his Anfwer?

Scripture

5. What Truth or pertinency is in thofe words, *Chrift the end of all words*: Doth he mean that now there ought to be no more words or writings? or that Chrift ends all Scripture Words, and there is no further ufe of them? fo they hold out, and yet they fay and practice the Contrary. The Truth is, their horrible unclean and *foul Spirit* would fain be rid of all *Scripture Words,* and all Learning alfo, *&c.* that he may bring the more of miferable man-kinde (under the cheating found of Light] into his *Eternal Darknefs.*

The 51*th. Inftance* is in *Pag.* 325. where he *325 Tim-* quotes *Timothy Trevis,* faying, *God hath ordained to othy* *Eternal Life all that fhall be faved, before they had a Trevis. Being in this World: But none comes to poffeffion of this Salvation, but through Obedience of the Spirit.*

G. *Fox* Anfwers, [*The ground of mans belief and obedience is Chrift, who doth inlighten him to the intent that he might believe and obey the Truth, and who knows the Seed, knows the Election before the World was made.*]

I *Reply,* 1. If he means that Chrift is the Ground or Author, the Giver of Repentance and Faith to
all

all the Elect whom God [100] the Father hath given him, we fay fo, &c. But if he put in their *Invented Light* in the Room of *Gods Election* and *Predeftination*, as the *Efficient* and *firft Caufe*, and of Chrift as the *Mediator* and *Meritorious Caufe* according to the *golden Chain*, Rom. 8. and *Ephef.* 1. and the *fifth Chap.* He fpeaks blafphemoufly of God, and of the Son of God, and of the glorious work of their *Redemption*, and *poor mankinds Salvation.*

G. Fox deftroys the working of the Father and the Son.

2 He is now in the *Burrough* of the *Arminians*, who deftroy *Gods Election* before the world was, and fay, that when a man believes he is Elected, when he is predeftinate, or (being obedient) is Inconftant, he is then *Reprobated*.

G. Fox and the Arminians one as to predeftination.

1 Contrary to all the *precious beds* of *Flowers* and *Spices* in the *Garden* of the *Scripture*, which thefe *rooting Swine* getting in, they root and tear up all the ways and methods of *Gods Councels* and *Salvations*.

2 Contrary to the wit and skill of men, who framing a *Book*, an *Houfe*, a *Ship*, a *Navie*, an *Army*, or any *Sublunary matters*, have all in their *Thoughts*, *Minds*, and *Councels* before they begin their *Enterprize*, they provide their *Materials*, their *Agents*, their means they fit all to their Ends, though all may faile, all mens Affairs being but *Vanity* and *Vexations*. But to whom fhall we liken the *Eternal* and *Infinite Maj fty*, to whom all his works and Events are known (in a moft *Inconceivable way* as to us) even from Eternity to Eternity, his *Juftice*, his *Goodnefs*, his *Power*, all being *Infinite*.

Mans wifdome about his Earthly bufinefs

3. As to the Seed and Election: We know they make

make themselves, the feed and the Election : fec- ondly, They make Christ the feed, that is, (in the End) themselves. And thirdly, They make God and the Spirit of God the feed, the feed in every man which is preached to, by them the *Imprifoned Seed*, and when one turns *Quaker*, then God comes out of *Prifon*: The Truth is, they make no dif- tinction between God and Christ, and *Spirit*, and themselves, as *Fox* in this Book as before plainly tels us, but when this pretended feed of God, or God himfelf is hearkened to, then the foul fo heark ning, is become Goddified, and God with God, whofe *Infinite Being* and Effence thefe poor, proud *Bruits*, have not fo much fight of as the Devils have, who cried out to Jefus, *I know thee whom thou art the holy One of God*, knowing that God and the *Son* of God were *Infinitely diftinct* in them- [101] felves, and all *Created Beings*: Yet fuch is the *Inconceivable wrath* and *Juftice* of the Eternal God u pon thefe fallen Spirits who kept not their *firft Habitation* (as the pretended *Quakers* many of them have not done) that (as *Pharaoh*) they can not but *lye and flander, and kill till the time of their Torment come.*

The 52d. *Inftance* of G. *Fox* his flight dealing is in *Pag.* 326. where he brings in the fame Author, faying, [*The manifeftation of the Spirit is given to every man in the Church to profit withal, and not to every man in the World.*]

G. *Fox* Anfwers, [*The manifeftation is given to every man to profit withal without diftinction, I will* pour

pour out of my Spirit upon all Flesh : For the Spirit of Truth shall lead the Saints into all Truth : And he shall reprove the World, and that which doth reprove the World is manifest to the World.]

I Reply, I spake to this Text before, in Answer to the Letter of my Neighbour I. T. (as is to be seen in the Letters before our Disputes) who declared himself satisfied with my Answers, but G. *Fox* (like a *Cow* with a *Kettle* on her head, giving every one warning to stand clear) he boldly slanders[1] on, and tumbles *Heaven*, *Earth* and *Hell* together, *&c.*

1. This 1 *Cor.* 12. expresly declares three things.

1. That it pleased God to appoint in his Christian Church and Worship the Ministry of *Apostles*, *Prophets*, *Teachers*, &c. according to *Rom.* 12 Ephes. 4, *&c.*

2. He bestoweth several Gifts and Endowments on such persons whom he pleaseth to call unto such Ministrations.

3. He vouchsafeth to give a gracious *Concurrent Operation* of his *Spirit* unto these his Gifts & Ministrations, what now is this gracious promise of *the Father of Lights* to ʰthe Garden of his Church & *Saints*, the *howling Desart* of the whole world, from whence the Garden is taken in, inclosed and separate? Because a *Queen* is a Woman, must therefore all the *Honours* and *kindnesses* of a *glorions Prince* due to his *Royal Consort* be dispensed in Common to all the Women in his Kingdome or Dominions? The Garment in which the Queen is brought, is a

. Garment

Marginal notes:
The mani-festation of the Spirit discussed.

The Garden of Chrisfs Church and the Wilderness, &c. of the World differ as Heaven and Earth

---

[1] Change "slanders" to "blunders." *R.W. Ms. Ann.*

Garment of *Needle work*, richly and moſt curiouſly *embroydered* with the *graces* and *Operations* of the holy Spirit, doth it therefore follow, that thoſe *Heavenly Embroyderies*, &c. belong to every *nnclean* and *Louſie Begger*?

102] Yea, but this prophane Mouth hath ſomething to ſay for it ſelf, three things he ſaith full of *Prophaneneſs* and *Simplicity*.

1. *I will pour out my Spirit upon all Fleſh.*

But, 1. Was this (as he ſpeaks) without all diſtinction done actually? was it, *Univerſally* ſo with all the *Individuals* of mankind in the world at that time?

2. Was not there a *wonderful Wall of ſeparation* between the *Jews* and all other Nations, which the Lord promiſed by the *Prophets* to break down, and at the coming of the Lord Jeſus, and ever ſince hath more and more broke down and aboliſhed? Is not *Gideons Floor* which was dry (the *poor Gentiles* and *we Engliſh* among them) now wet with the *Dews of Heaven*, while the *poor Jews* (which were only wet at firſt) are dry and barren? _{The partition Wall between Jews and Gentiles.}

3. What is that *Extraordinary Promiſe* of *Gods Extraordinary pouring out of his Spirit*, in Fiery Tongues and Propheſyings, fitting ſome to go unto all Nations to carry the glad News or Goſpel, had others and all Believers thoſe Gifts [leaſt of all with any ſhew of Reaſon] belong they to all the Men and Women in the world, who have never ſeen and heard of any Glimpſe of the Sun of Righteouſneſs.

4. Again, I obſerve how vainly and wickedly
this

G. Fox his not cleaving the Hoof though full of Scripture. this deluded and deluding Soul cheats himſelf, and others with this Tearme, *All Fleſh, Every man, All the World*, and ſo with the Terms *Light, Chriſt, Spirit*, his *proud Fancy* playeth, &c. not dividing the *Hoof* by juſt and holy diſtinguiſhing a Crime that he often upbraids his Oppoſites moſt odiouſly with in his Book, not dividing, &c. but is moſt notoriouſly guilty as ever was filthy Camel in this world, or any of the *unclean Beaſts*, &c.

G. Fox his wonderful Confuſion. G. *Fox* his ſecond Anſwer here is, [*The Spirit of God ſhall lead the Saints into all Truth.*] I obſerve here how like a Skittiſh Jade this wild Soul runs in and out, and cannot keep to one *ſteady Affirmation* : Before he brings in the Spirit of God poured out upon the Common of the World, now he brings in the ſpirits leading the ſaints, *Gods Garden and Paradice* : Yet again, in his next words he concludes every man in the World to have the ſpirit becauſe ſaith he, [*The ſpirit reproves the World, and that which doth Reprove the World is manifeſt to the World.*].

The Spirit of God and the world are extream Contraries I *Anſwer*, The holy ſpirit teſtifies that he is the Comforter of the ſaints, but a Reprover of the World, that he Comforts the [103] Saints in the Promiſes, & Aſſurances, &c. that he Reproves the world in his Threatenings and Judgments. That the world knows not, ſees not the Spirit, but mocks at, receives it not, but baniſheth, impriſoneth, murthereth ſuch in whom the true Spirit of God appeareth : Hence it is, that becauſe of this Spirit of God in any ſoul, three are againſt two, & two muſt be againſt three in the ſame houſe, the *Parents* againſt
the

the Children, and the Children betray their *Parents*
unto Death: yea, two in a Bed, and two in a Belly,
and yet he whom Gods Spirit choofeth, fhall be
mockt and murthered by the other' and yet this
lying *Peor* tells us that all the world (without diftinction) have the manifeftation of the Spirit of
God to profit withal.

Prophners of the holy Spirit.

    5. There have been perfons profeffing the Order
of the holy Ghoft, yet far from the favour of the
holy Spirit, there hath been a great Ship in the
world full of Sailors and Souldiers, called the *holy
Ghoft*, and yet fcarce one man in it known to have
any Acquaintance with Gods Spirit: Alas, what
are the *Babilonifh Orders* of thefe pretenders to the
Holy Ghoft or Spirit? what are they but a poor
Ship full of Refifters of Gods Spirit, and Enemies
to the greateft Enjoyers of him in the World, the
true *Proteftant Witneffes*, whom they profeffedly
oppofe under the Name of Profeffors, I hope as I
have often faid, that many of them are of the *two
hundred* that followed *Abfolom* in honefty and fimplicity.

G. Fox, &c. refifting and fighting againft the holy Spirit.

    6. But, Oh what Reproofs of Gods Spirit hath
G. *Fox* and others of their Leaders had in, and by
fo many excellent Oppofites and Scriptures, and
Arguments, which G. *Fox* here proudly tramples
under his prophane feet, without any favour of the
holy Spirit of God!

The ftriving of Gods Spirit.

It is true, it pleafeth God as I faid, to ftrive with
men by preachings, by writings, by their own
Readings, by *publick Judgments* and *private*, and
alfo by *publick mercies* and *private*, for *Acts* 14.

         every

every *Drop* of *Rain* is Gods *voice, word* or *witnefs,*
&c, but what is this *Common grace* to that *Regene-*
rating and *changing Spirit,* John 3. to the opening
of *Lidiahs,* and fo of all faints hearts by his free
and holy fpirit or Finger? what is this to the fame
Power that raifed Chrift Jefus from the Dead,
Ephef. 1. that raifeth any poor finner unto a new
and holy, and fpiritual Cond tion?

The free and powerful working of Gods fpirit.

104]. 7. Excellent and moft heavenly is that fimilitude, *Cant.* 1. *Becaufe of the favour of thy good*
Ointments therefore do the Virgins love thee : Oh how
many prate of this fpirit or Ointment, and yet hate
the true Lord Jefus, hate his *Love Letters,* the holy
fcriptures, and would be glad to fee them in a *Bone*
fire, hate his poor true Quakers that defire to fear
before him, and tremble at his Word, and to mourn
that having received fuch manifeftations of the
holy fpirit of God they have profited others fo little, and glorified God in their Generations?

8. I might Infift upon the End which G, *Fox*
infifteth on, *viz.* to profit withal, and ask why *Da-*
vid, Pfal. 53. Complains that all the Children of
men not one excepted, are *unprofitable,* good for
nothing, yea, *abominable,* that is, to fpiritual matters, heavenly things, the world to come : All even
the *fweeteft Natures,* the *faireft,* the *wittieft,* the
wifeft, the *learnedft,* the *devouteft,* untill the fpirit
of God come and truly change the heart and whole
Frame of Nature. Till then, we as profitable as
Hogs, as *Moles* in a Garden, as *Water* or *Fire* breaking into a fhip, and as *devouring Foxes amongft the*
true Lambs and Chickens of Chrift Jefus.

The whole world unprofitable.

The

The *53d Inſtance* of G. *Fox* his lame Anſwer is
in *pag.* 328: where he quotes *Hugh Archbal,* ſaying, 328 Hugh
[*Chriſt doth enlighten none but them that do receive* Archbal
him.]

He Anſwers, Contrary to John 3. which ſpeaketh of them that hate the Light, and are enlightened, and will not come to it, becauſe the Light
will reprove them : ſo he that hates the Light is
enlightned, and will not receive Chriſt.

I *Reply,* though I have ſpoken much of the
Light and of receiving Chriſt Jeſus, &c, yet ſince
this *proud Boaſter* drags his *Oppoſites* out of *Scotland* alſo *:* I pray the Readers patience while I tell
him of a manifold Light which the Holy ſpirit
mentions under a *Metaphor* or *Figure of Light.*

1. The Natural perceiving of Natural things, as
Chriſt Jeſus ſaith : *The Light of the Body is the Eye.* The manifold Light

2. The Light of *peace* and *joy,* whether Corpo- mentioned
ral or ſpiritual, Temporal, or Eternal : The *Iews* in in the
Hamans down-Fall, and their own Deliverance had Holy
Scripture
Light and Joy, *&c. and Light is ſown for the Right-
eous,* &c.

105] 3. The common offers of the Goſpel as
Light, whence ſome have obſerved that the word
(ſo cried up in *John* 1.) is not *inlightneth* but *lighteth* : but the word *Photizei* may ſignifie both, and
yet be no more then the Common offer, preaching
and ſound of the *glad News,* or Goſpel : The people that ſate in *Darkneſs* ſaw *great Light,* &c, As
the Light of a candle coming in *lightens* or *enlightens* the *Walls* and *Room* but being taken away
again leaves no Impreſſion or change upon the *Wall,*
or

or as the *Sun* shining or guilding the Earth being clouded leaves no *Impression* of shining on the Earth behind it : So is it with the Common offers of Trading or marriages in the world, and so of the *heavenly Offers* of *Merchandize* and *Heavenly Marriage*, &c.

The Common offers of mercy.

⊥. There is yet a *higher Light* which some are *affected*, *Tinctur'd* and *enlightened*, and yet not the *true* and *saving Light* : that in *Heb*. 6. where some persons (as the *pretended Quakers* and G. *Fox* especially) have seen much of the *Nature of God*, his *holiness*, his *Justice*, &c. and had a *Tast* of the *Joyes* of the *next world*, but proudly turned from the *holy* Scripture, from the true Lord Jesus, and the *true, holy, enlightning, humbling and saving Spirit* of God.

5. The *true Lighting* or *Enlightning* of which the *holy Scripture* speaketh, is that of 2 *Cor*. 4 (a place fouly and simply abused by G. *Fox* to prove the Light in every man) where *Paul* shews, how by the preaching of the *glad News* or *Gospel* God had shined in their hearts, (not in the hearts of all the men in the world, nor in the hearts of all the *Corinthians*) and had given them a fight *of the glory of God in the Face*, or from the *Reflexion* or means of the face of the *Mediator*, the man Christ Jesus. Hence all those *Heavenly Appellations* or *phrazes*, or *Names*, Children of the Day : *Illuminated*, or *Inlightned Ones, You were Darkness, but now you are* (not only *Inlightened*, but) *Light in the Lord*, that is, become, (not as *Fox* pretends Christs and Gods and no distinction) but of a *bright Spiritual Nature*, longing *humbly* and *mournfully* in the use of the holy

The true Illumination.

As the first Christians were called.

holy Scripture, and all other means) more to come out of Darkneſs into the Light of holineſs and likeneſs unto God.

Object. G *Fox* alleadgeth *John* 3. They which hated the Light were inlightned :

I *Anſwer*, No queſtion, but with the *general Offer* of mercy, [106] as of the *Candle* or *Sun* to the Eyes of a blind man, which is yet their Condemnation, becauſe if they had power, yet their *wills* and *Luſts*, and *Reſolutions* refuſe and abhor it, and abhor their eyes ſhould be opened to ſee it. <small>The two-fold ſuc-ceſs of the Goſpel.</small>

Whereas the *Goſpel* or *glad News* is publiſhed or preached, there is a twofold Effect of it : as *Acts* 13. and *Acts* 17. and *Acts* 28. and through all Experience in all Ages and in all parts of the world ſome *mock*, ſome *demur*, ſome *perſecute* others, the Spirit or *Power* of God opens their hearts to fear, to believe, to ſubmit, and in Gods time to rejoyce for ever in a Saviour.

The 54*th Inſtance* is in *Pag.* 330. where G. *Fox* brings in *James Dorram*, ſaying [*The Believer is not in ſin as the Unbeliever is, he ſins not as the Unbeliever doth : and in another place he ſaith, the Law is the ſame to the Believer that it is to the Unbeliever.* <small>330. James Dorram.</small>

G. *Fox* Anſwers, Here any may read thy Confuſion, but I ſay unto thee He that believeth doth not commit Sin, but the unbelief is Sin, *Rom.* 11. 20. *And Chriſt is the End of the Law to every one that believes for Righteouſneſs ſake*, Roms 10. 4. and yet thou puts both Believers and unbelievers under the power of the Law.

I *Reply*,

The light of fin as Sin.

I *Reply,* The Devils (no queſtion) know Sin, they fee Sin, but not in the true glaſs of the holy Scrip-ture: They fee fin as *Saul* and *Judas,* &c. in the fire of the Coal, as dreadful in the puniſhment, but not in the blackneſs of the Coale, as againſt their new Life and Nature, and the purity of the *Eternal,* who hath begotten them unto holineſs. The *Robber* and *Murtherer* bewails his offence at the *Gallows,* though yet his heart is not changed, but, (could he) he would murther the Judge, and all that had a hand in his Condemnation and Exe-cution. The Drunkard hates his Sin as a Tyrant over him, only as it brings Diſcredit to him, ſo is it with the unclean perſon, and every other ſinner. But it is not ſo with the *Regenerate* or *new Born,*

The Sins of the Re-generate.

who can no more (unleſs deceived and Circum-vented) touch Sin, then the Devil the Father of it, nor then Fire can delight in Water, nor Light in Darkneſs.

3. It is true, that 7 of the *Romans* is contended for by the *Papiſts* and *Arminians,* and in a great meaſure by the *Quakers,* [107] to Contain not the Combate of the Saints, but of the unregenerate within themſelves: But the true Proteſtants have proved from the Scripture, and the Experience of all true Saints that fin and grace, Fleſh and Spirit,

Whit the Combate between the Fleſh and Spirit in Rom. 7.

the Law of the Spirit, and the Law of fin may, and do continue Combating in the Regenerate, or New born, Contrary to that *proud perfection* of *Papiſts* and *Foxians* in this Life, is more clear then *Pauls Argumentation,* and upon that his Concluſion, *viz.* That with his mind, that is, his Spirit, will,

Affections,

Affections, (renewed by Gods Spirit) *he ferved the Law of God*: *But with his Flefh,* which muft be his *finful Defires* and *Difpofitions* yet remaining in him, *he ferved the Law of Sin?* This was the Reafon of his Cry, *O wretched man,* &c. and G. *Fox* his filly fhifts faying, that in the End of the Chapter, *Paul* was perfect, and gave thanks for victory, it is like that *Fantaftical faying,* of the *Generalifts,* being forced to Confefs Repentance neceffary to Salvation, *viz.* [*In a moment in the Twinkling of an Eye*] wofully abufing that holy Scripture about the *Refurrection.*

4. The fame 7 of the *Romans,* and other· holy Scriptures, and Experience prove that the Sin of the Regenerate, whether of Ignorance, as the *Fathers,* many wives, &c. or of *unwatchfulnefs* as *David* and *Peter's* &c. It is as an honeft man taken prifoner, or as *Souldiers* and Seamen wounded and carried Captive, or as a *Virgin* by force *deflowred,* and crying out, whom therefore both Law and Reafon, and the holy Scripture in a holy Figure declare to be clear and Innocent. *The Sin of the Regenerate as a wound and Captivity.*

5. Hence *Paul* fhews the Sincerity of the *Chaft Will* and *Affections* unto the *Heavenly Bridegroom,* faying, *I delight in the Law of God, in the inner man* : Delight we know is the *Top* and *Flowre,* and *Cream* of all the *Affections,* and the *fierceft hatred* flies in the Face of that which takes away our delight from us. The wicked may defire, and may act heavenly things for his own felf Ends, for his Credit, his profit, his Salvation, but he can not make God to be himfelf, and delight in God. *The Souls delight in God, and Hatred to Sin*

What

Sincerity the Crown of the true Quakers

6. What Confufion is it to affirm that the Saints of God though they fee Chrift fulfilling the Law of works for them, which none in the world could ever do but He, yet they ought to ftrive after perfect holinefs and Righteoufnefs, *to love the Lord with all their Heart, foul, might, ftrength*, &c. as a Child going after his Father, the Scholar or maiden following their Copies and Samplers. [108 though they never come near the full Exactnefs and perfection of them.

338 John Nafmith

The *55th Inftance* of G. *Fox* his fimple and foul Anfwer is in *Pag.* 338. where he brings in *Iohn Nafmith* from *Scotland*, faying, ⌊*Tha the Evil Spirits are both finful and Reafonable.*⌋

He *Anfwers*, This is a lye, for Reafonable is not finful, and unreafonable is finful? 1 *Thef.* 3. *they have not the Faith.* And if the Evil Spirit be Reafonable and the Good Reafonable, they are both one: who is then unreafonable, thou puts no difference between the precious and the vile? Thou haft the mark of a *blinde guide* and of a *falfe Prophet* in thy *Forehead.*

. I *Reply* and obferve *Firft*, the *filthy rafh* Fury of this mind and Pen: Beginning with that's a lye, and after a filly Line and Anfwer: Thou haft the Marck of a *Blind guide* and of a *falfe Prophet* in thy *Forehead.*

2. This *proud Pharifee* will appear to be a *Sadducee* alfo, and to hold no *Angels* nor *Spirits:* It is true, as they pretend to owne Scripture and a Chrift, and *Refurrection*, They with *Jefuitical Equivocations* name *Angels* and *Spirits*, but the bottom as fome

of

of them, and that in print discover is, they hold there is but one Spirit, which is in *All*, and into which *All Return*, and the Soul of *Iudas* is as happy as the Soul of *Peter*.

The Foxians are both Pharisees and Sadduces.

3. G. *Fox* runs into his *Burrough* of the *various significations* of the word *Reasonable*. A man is a *Reasonable Creature* as Oppofite to *Wolves* and *Foxes*, &c. and yet he may be unreasonable in in his Actings, as Wolves and Foxes, who though unreasonable in their Natures, yet are not finful, though a plague to man fince his Fall. Oh happy were it for G. *Fox* that he had been of the wild *Foxes* in the Woods, and had not been fo finful, by fo *horribly abufing* fo great a *Talent* of *Wit* and Reafon which *the Father of Lights* hath given him.

An Item to G. Fox.

4. We know the Admirable Wit and Reafon as well as the Power of thofe unclean Spirits, the Lord Jefus caft out, they did believe and Confefs the Lord Jefus, and made their Requeft unto him: This their knowledge and Ability is from God, though their *finful hardnefs* by Gods juft Sentence, runs them upon fuch mad and defperate Courfes, as it is with the Sons of men, when the moft holy and Righteous Judge delivers them up to the *Councels* 109| and *Projects* of their *proud and deceitful Hearts and Spirits*:

The Nature of the Devils

The 56*th*. *Inftance* is in *Pag.* 345. where he brings in *Henry Forefide* (from Scotland,) faying, [*Concerning thofe words of* Ezekiel 18. 28. *If the Righteous turn away from his Righteoufnefs, his former Righteoufnefs fhall be no more remembred*, and he

345 Henry Forefide.

said

said *the meaning of that Scripture was : They thought they had been Righteous, but were not, but suppofed it had been fo.*]

Ezek. 18
Confider-
ed

He Anfwers, [*Herein thou art a Minifter of unrighteoufnefs thou goeft about to make God a Lyar, and the Prophets, and 'perverts the Scripture : For if he forfakes his Righteoufnefs and commits Sin and Iniquity, and Trefpaffes he fhall dye and not live in the Righteoufnefs : But if he fo fakes his Sins, Trefpaffes and Tranfgreffions, in the Righteoufnefs that he hath done and doth, he fhall live : So Gods wayes are equal, Ezek. 18.*] And thou fayes, they thought they had been Righteous, but it was not fo: And the Lord by the Prophet faith it was fo, *that they fhould live in their Righteoufnefs* and die if they did depart from it and Tranfgreffed: Here thou art a diminifher from the *Prophets* and *Apoftles* words, whofe Name is *diminifhed out of the Book of Life,* read *Rev.* 22. 19

The
Spirit of
Falling
from
Grace.

I Reply, The Queftion is about *Falling away* from *faving grace* and Righteoufnefs, wherein it is notorious, (as I have formerly proved) that the *Quakers* joyn their Forces to the *Standards* of the *Papifts* and *Arminians,* though herein the *Arminians* (though highly abufing an high wit as the *Papifts* and *Quakers* do) yet are they not fo guilty and Infufferable as the *Papifts* and *Foxians* are, becaufe they pretend not to fuch an *Infallible Chair*

The Papifts, Arminians
and Foxians one
in this
point.

as the *Papifts* and *Quakers* do, which is the more *wonderful* and *monftrous,* becaufe the *Papifts* are forced to grant that the Head of their Church the *Pope* may Himfelf fall away and be a Reprobate, and the *Foxians* are forced to Confefs as much, even

of

of divers of their Heads and Teachers, some getting *Saving Grace* again, as they say, and some never. The *Quakers* yet are more gross in this point, because they maintain that the least that hearken to the Light are born again. That they which are born again cannot Sin, that they which can not Sin are pure as God is pure, and therefore they Falling away from them, they must necessarily hold that which is blasphemous of all to be abhorred, that God himself may fall from Grace also, and is kept down as the [110] as this barking *Fox* speaks, as a *Cart laden with sheaves* (perverting the Scripture) by wickedness & wicked spirits which are too hard for God and Christ, and Spirit in all the Men and Women in the world, that do not hearken to their *feigned Light*, and let loose the *Imprisoned Cart* and *Seed*, &c.

Wee may make a stand here and observe three things.

1. The *horrible abuse of Gods Excellent Gifts* of Reason and Acuteness, which these men so grosly defile in handling the Misteries and Parables of the holy Scripture.

2. *Gods Infinite Patience* in bearing with such a *rotten stinking thing* as man is.

3. What kind of Grace it is that so easily persons Fall away away from, and part withal.

2. As to *Ezek.* 18. How doth it follow, that because the word Righteousness in which *Fox* in his *wonted Burrough*, signifies divers things, that therefore in this first place it must signify the Imputed Righteousness of God in Christ, from which a

man

What it is that Papists Arminians and Foxians Fall from.

Necessary Observations.

The Word Righteousness of many significations

man really Invefted with it may really, Totally and
Finally depart. And Secondly the *Sanctifying
Righteoufnefs* of Chrift Jefus adorning a poor finner Juftified and pardoned, and of that true Righteoufnefs, a truly fanctified Soul and member of
Chrift Jefus may make fhipwrack. But is there
not befide thefe a very thirdly, I*ndian Righteoufnefs,*
when a *Barbarian* is Innocent and free from Crimes
falfly charged on him ?

4. Is there not a *C*ivil Righteoufnefs when men
are free from *Grofs* and *Barbarous Courfes,* and live
Civilly, foberly and juftly among their Neighbors ?

5 Yea, is there not a Pharifaical Righteoufnefs
which *Paul* prided himfelf in, *viz* that *concerning
the Law he was blamelefs,* and yet faith the Lord
Jefus, *Except your Righteoufnefs go beyond this Righteoufnefs, you fhall not enter into the Kingdome of
Heaven*

6. Again, Is there not a Righteoufnefs of the
foolifh Virgins, who hath a *fhew* and *Lamp* of *Profeffion,* and make as brave a fhew in building as the
houfe upon the Rock, it may be fairer) and yet no
true work of Converfion of the Soul to God, nor
the Oyle of Gods Spirit in the heart for all their
boafting of it. The moft High and holy will be
clear when he is Judged. *Adam* fhall live if he
keep his *Bargain*: and fo fhall all his Pofterity if
they keep the *firft Covenant.*

God's Covenant with the firft man.

111| If any fhall fay God knows the *Bargain* is
too hard for us: Our *firft Father* did not, how
fhall we ? &c.

I *Anfwer,* what will become then of the *Papifts*
and

and *Quakers,* who say, they can, and the *Papists*
more also then God commandeth?

2. Christ did not mock, but meekly and savingly
teach the young man, when he Answered, *If thou
wilt enter into Life keep the Commandments* : nor doth
he mock the *Jews,* dealing with them upon the
Terms of *Justice* : *Obey and live, Transgress and die.*

It is a pertinent question, why was the holy Law
of God written and given so many hundreds of
years after man was Fallen and not able to keep his
Bargain : The Spirit of God *Gal.* 3, tels us that
four hundred and *Thirty Years* after the Promise to
Abraham, the Law was written by Gods own *Im-*
mediate Finger to shew unto man his Sin, and Judge-
ments, and need of a *Mediator promised.* ^{The Law given so many hundreth of years after mans Fall.}

3. As to G. *Fox* Cursing his Adversary as a
Diminisher from the holy Scripture.

I *Answer,* Doth this Face of Brass, who hath so
horribly flighted the holy Scripture : now adore
them? Is he now zealous for them, and against the
violation of them? Doth he regard the adding to,
or Detracting from them, or the *Plagues* and
Curses therein denounced against the Adders to, or
Detracters from them? Doth he not throughout
all his Book, and all of them in word and writing
deny the holy Scripture to be the word of God,
and only that *Frantick Light* or *Christ,* (imagined
by them to be in all mankinde) to be the only
Word of God? yea, is it of any use or more availe
to them that have the Scripture in their heart, as
they saythen a *dead Letter,* and an *Old Almanack,*
&c. O *hear O Heavens and give Ear O Earth,* did ^{G. Fox making use of the Scripture to Curse his Opposites.} ^{Their horrible Contempt of Scripture.}

ever

ever the Devil vomit out more poyfon (againft God
and the Souls of men by the mouths and pens of
Jews or *Turks*, or *Anti-Chriftans*,) then thefe *Foxians* do in their undermining the holy Scriptures?
Some know it not: Some of them fpeak Reverent-
ly of it: The very *Papifts* Confefs it to be the very
word or Speech of God: But the *Devil* and the
Quakers abhor to hear them *Verbum Dei* the Word
of God.

Thefe bewitched Soules affirme they have a *higher
Teacher*, yea, [112] every man in the world hath
him in them, then the Scriptures are and yet they
fay in horrible fimplicity and hypocrify that they
are the Words of God.

456 A
Book
from
Hollaed

The 58*th*: *Inftance* of G. *Fox* his flight Anfwer,
as in *Pag.* 356, where he brings in a Book from
Holland, faying, [*That God hath put out the Remembrance of your Sins, and of your Corruptions within
you, wherein you muft fight all your Life Time.*

G. Fox
his proud
Ignorance

G. *Fox*, whilft the Sins you are fighting withal
are not blotted out in your own particulars, this is
not the Life of the Saints: They are not fighting
all their Life Time, but come to the Kingdome of
God witneffing fin and Iniquity blotted out, and the
Everlafting Covenant of Peace and Life with God

I Reply, This *fubtle Mountebank* having gotten a
Scaffold, he acts Tricks wonderful in the Eyes of
the fimple, yet as in all his Books he fhews no
knowledge of the *Hebrew* and the *Greek* (whence
our *Englifh Scripture* comes as a *Daughter* from the
Mother) fo falls he fhort of moft *Englifh* writers,
who

who fcorns to difgrace their *Mother Englifh* (by fo
much *baftard* and *falfe Englifh*) as this *poor Mountebank* hath done in all his Books.

If ever any poor empty Soul have talkt of God An Impi-
without God. Of a Chrift, and the holy *Spirit* ous unfa-
within, without them: or any true Savour of them: vonry
Spirit
of the holy writings of God without any true againft the
Reverence and love to them! Of Light without godly of all
any Spark of *true Illuminations!* of fin, without Nations
any true Sence of the *Exceeding Sinfulnefs* of it!
This *Empty Cafk* this loud Boafter and Cenfurer is
one of them.

1. His Anfwer faith three things in Effect.

1, That no fin is blotted out until there be no
more Root nor Seed of it in the Soul to fight againft. The Phar-

I Reply, to this I have fpoke much before, and ifees Perfection
fhewed how clear it is againft fo much holy Scripture: againft the Counfels and purpofes of God as
to his holy ordering of this prefent world, and his 2 Pet. 2 2
Saints in it: and againft the Conftant Experience
of all thofe high Saints in Scripture, and of all that
ever went before us: All which fhews the *Devilifh*
pride of thefe *high Pharifees*

2. He adds, faying, the Saints are not fighting all
their Life Time. The
Saints
I Reply, if there be no Enemies no danger of
Flefhly Lufts *warring againft our Souls,* as *Peter* fpeaks. Continual
warfere
113| 2. Why then doth the holy Spirit fpeak of
the Combate of the Flefh and Spirit, Gal. 5. and
that *Paul did not the things that he would, and did the*
Evil he would not, & of his being taken Prifoner?

3. Why then doth Gods Spirit furnifh us with
all .

all that *Heavenly Artillery*, Ephef. 6. 1. And Commands his Servants (even *Timothy*) *to flie youthful Lufts*, if he were paft wounding by them?

4. And to ftand upon the Guard and watch againft *Gluttonly* and *Drunkennefs*, and *worldly Cares*, which would lull the Souls of the *Difciples* afleep, except they kept the better watch *&c.* Luke 21.

Scriptural dangers and fpiritual Watch.

5. And why then doth the Lord Jefus Command us to pray daily againft Temptations, yea, and to pray daily for the pardon of fin, if his *Followers* be for ever efcaped out of the reach of Sinful thoughts, words and actions, and many *thoufand finful Omiffions?*

Chrifts Difcipline with his Saints and Churches.

6. What was the Reafon of the Cemmand of Chrift Jefus to the *Churches* to *watch*, to *Overcome*, to *repent*, threatning them with *difcharging*, and *Excommunication* which we fee dolefully Effected upon the *Afian Profeffors*, and which was followed with a rich bleffing upon that Ordinance, Executed upon the *Inceftuous Corinthian*, which brought forth thofe *feven Heavenly Fruits*, both in him and that Church alfo, 2 *Cor.* 7.

G. *Fox* his *third Anfwer* is, [*The Saints are come to the Kingdome of God witneffing Sin and Iniquity blotted out, and the Everlafting Covenant of Peace and Life with God.*]

But 1. Take thefe words in his Senfe, *viz.* that all that are in their *Fancied Kingdome* are thus free from Sin, and come to this *Peace* and Joy : why then do themfelves ftill Confefs themfelves to be fubject to *quaking* and *trembling*, as if they were at the *black* and *burning* Foot of *Mount Sinai*, where indeed they are, and not upon the *bright* and *fhining Hill* of *Zion*.

2. Is

2. Is not this Contrary to the Covenant of God *The* Qua-*kers* dole-ful miftake with *David,* concerning *Solomon,* and (in the *Anti Type*) with all Chriftians, *viz.* that if they Sin he will Chaftife them with *the Rods of men, but not take away his mercy,* as he took it from *Saul,* &c.

3. Is there not a *falfe Peace,* a *falfe Joy* as well as a *falfe quaking, a falfe Repentance,* a *falfe mortification,* and *Sanctificatio* , and in Conclufion, a *falfe Salvation* : and therefore the Lord Jefus tels us of the *high pretenders,* Math. 7. yet by him *Everlaftingly rejected.*

114] The 59*th Inftance* is in *Pag.* 365. where G. 365. Rob-ert Tu-chin, &c. *Fox* brings in *Robert Tuchin,* &c. faying, *⌊The moft Faithful Meffengers of Chrift have acknowledged that they have come fhort of their duty.⌋*

G. *Fox* Anfwers, *⌊They that are Faithful Meffengers of Chrift have the Anfwer well done thou good and Faithful Servant : where did* John, *or* Paul, *or* Peter *acknowledge that they came fhort of their duty : Hath not thou flandred the Servants of the Lord, thinking them to be like yourfelves, and falfly accufing them that you may feem Juftified, who are falfe Meffengers and come in his Name, when you have no Commiffion from him : and you come fhort of every good work : But thus it is not with Chrifts true Meffengers, for they fulfil his Will that fent them. It is the Lord that worketh in them, whofe th y are, and whofe duty they perform by his Spirit⌋*

I *Reply,* this *deluded Soul* (as it is written) muft G Fox prouder and prouder, wo fe and grow worfe and worfe (except the Lord *wonderfully awaken* him) to all Eternity: Inftead of feeing any failing againft God and Chrift, the Spirit and Ser-

64   vants

worfe to vants of God, *&c.* he claps his wings upon his
the End of Dunghil, and vapours, that in all thefe Tranfactions
his Book- he hath not faild, no not in a *finful word or Thought.*

1. But he muſt remember that fuch was the *In—
finite, Incomprehenfible Purity* and *Juſtice,* and *wif-*
The Fall *dome* of God, *that the Heavens were not pure in his*
of Angels. *fight, and he laid Folly to the Charge of his Angels,*
and I am fure, their *Natures,* their *Endowments,*
their *Employments,* G. *Fox* comes ſhort of, and yet
they came ſhort of their duty, and are now faſt in
Chains of Darknefs, expecting *Judgement* and *Torment* to come,

2. I prefume G. *Fox* will grant that our *firſt Parents* were *Innocent* and *perfect,* as *highly Gifted* and
Fall of as *highly Employed* as ever G. *Fox* is like to be, and
Man. yet they came ſhort, and We all by them fallen
ſhort of the Glory and love of God into the *Dung-
hill* of *Hellifh Darknefs.*

3. After the *Promifed Reſtoration* by the Son of
God what *Excellent Gifts* had *Noah, Abraham, Lot,
Ifaac, Jacob, Jofeph, Mofes, Aaron, Sampfon, Iepthe,
Gideon, Eli, Samuel, Nathan, Solomon, Afa, Iehofha-
phat, Hezekiah, Iofiah,* and many other glorious
Saints, what *wonderful Affiftance* and *Extraordinary
Appearances of* God had they in their high Services
for God, and yet how grea ly: (fome of them
wonderfully fouly) did they come ſhort of their
115 duty? I remember I was once asked by one
of thefe high Boafters whether I would deny the
Davids Scripture : *viz* that faid, *David* did not fin but in
fin. the Cafe of *Uriah* : unto which I know many full
Anfwers may be given. Here only I obferve how
ready

ready thefe (willingly Ignorant) Souls are to Catch Sacrifice for Sins of Ignorance at any Word that may Fortifie their *proud Fancy,* though againft many other Scriptures and unquef-tionable Examples, &c.

4. Until the coming of Chrift Jefus we know the Command of the moft holy God to private perfons, to the *Princes,* to the Priefts, to the whole Affembly to offer up Sacrifice and Expiation for all forts of failings, yea, for Sins of Ignorance, yea, and for their coming fhort in their holy offerings: Hence *David* cries out, *Pfal.* 143. *Enter not into Iudgement or Reckoning with thy Servant,* &c. and *Pfal.* 19. *Cleanfe thou me from fecret fins, for who knows how oft he offendeth?*

5. I know G. *Fox* ufeth to fay all thefe were Types and Chrift is the body, &c.

I *Anfwer,* There are more *Anti-Types* then the perfon of Chrift, for the *Quakers* themfelves, they make themfelves Kings and Priefts, and the Tem-ple as well as Chrift, &c.

But come to the time of the Lord Jefus, and Great failing of Chrifts Difciples look upon the *Famous firft Apoftles,* who had freely left all to follow him, who enjoyed his *perfonal* preaching and *praying,* his *wonderful Miracles,* his *Heavenly Converfe,* his *holy* and *Powerful Spirit* in their own preaching, healing all Difeafes, raifing the dead, cafting out Devils, &c. and yet how doth the Lord Jefus frequently and fharply chide them for their coming fhort of their duty, for their Ig-norance, negligence, unbelief, forgetfulnefs, Inhu-manity, Ambition, &c.

6. Yea, as to thofe three whom G. *Fox* boafts of,
Iohn,

Iohn, Paul and Peter: Doth not Iohn cry out, 1 Iohn 2. If we Confeſs our ſins, he is Faithful and juſt to forgive us, and to cleanſe us from all unrighteouſneſs? Doth not Paul Confeſs and bewail his coming ſhort, when he cries out, *that the good he would do he did not, but did the Evil he would not, and with his fleſh did ſerve the Law of ſin,* though it was not Paul that ſinned, *but ſin that dwelled in him?* A Miſtery which I more then fear the moſt High hath hidden from this poor *Foxes Eye.*

And as to Peter, to ſay nothing of his ſtupendious failing of his [116] Maſter, &c. even after his *awakening*, after the Lords *riſing*, and Peters *ſeeing* and *talking* with him, his bold profeſſion and preaching of him to the Converſion of *hundreds* and *thouſands*: yet how is he charged by Paul for coming ſhort of his Duty, for Groſs Weakneſs and (in a kind) *Hipocriſy* and *Diſſimulation?* So that ſuch a cloud of wi nneſſes o'rewhelming theſe new Gods, (Papiſts and Quakers) how Righteous is it with God to make their Faces aſhamed with the filth of their own nakedneſs, in the highth of the *pride of their conceited Deities.*

The 60 *Inſtance* of G. Fox his lame Anſwer is in *pag.* 372. where he brings in *Thomas Hodges*, ſaying, [*The Scripture ſpeaks of God after the manner of men.*]
He Anſwers, The Scripture ſpeaks of God after the manner of the Spirit and to the Spirit, whereby men may receive him, and know him by the Spirit which natural men can not.

Marginalia:
Paul, John and Peter, and all come ſhort.

Peters great failings former and latter written for our Inſtruction

372.
Thomas Hodges.

ι. I

1. I *Reply,* This bewitched and bewitching Soul hath all along his Book been picking out fweet Flowers out of his Oppofites Gardens, from whence he hath fuckt, turned the fweet juice of Heavenly Truths into the poyfon and Venome of his proud Conceits. So here he denies this *Heavenly Myftery* of Gods revealing himfelf to us after the way and manner of men, having Head, and Hair, and Eyes, and mouth, *&c.* wherein his Incomprehenfible Goodnefs is pleafed to ftoop to us (even the high-eft and proudeft Souls) as Nurfes do to Children, or as Phyfitians to weak and Crazy and diftempered perfons.

G Fox hath affirmed the Con-trary to all the Heavenly Affertions of his Oppofites which I have produced.

2. But what fhall we fay to all thofe holy Scrip-tures, which not only liken God to a man, a man of war, a Sheepherd, a *Warfaring man,* an *Hufband man,* &c. but alfo to a Shield, and other Infenfibles, Natural or Artificial, as a Sun, a Tree, a Rock, an Houfe, a Fort, a High Tower, *&c.* When God revealed himfelf to *Abraham,* Gen. 15. *I am thy Shield,* &c. will this foul mouth fay that this fimili-tude of a Shield was not a *Familiar Metaphor,* or *Figure,* wherein God fpeaks to *Abrahams weak Ca-pacity?* Or will he fay, that God fpeaking fo to *Abraham,* fpake not alfo in the way the Spirit, Or that God is Litcrally a Shield?

God fets forth to us in Scripture by Natural and Arti-ficial things.

3. It was a late Speech of one of the beft Phi-lofophers, and of the beft Chriftians that *Old Eng-land* or *New* ever had: Then fhall we know (to wit in the next life, in the *Heavenly State* to Come) how to anfwer that great Queftion, *What is God?* But this *poor wild Affes Colt,* G. *Fox* he can refolve

[117 The great Queftion what God is.

resolve the Queſtion : He can gather up the *Ocean* in the *hollow* of his *hand*, he can weigh the *Everlaſting Mountains* and *Winds* in *Scales*, and Incloſe not only the *Sun*, &c. but alſo the *Incomprehenſible Sun of Glory and Purity within his Juglers Box*, &c.

The Devil Gods Ape in Inſpirations.

4. For, what would this *little Thief* and *Fox*, or the *great Thief* and *Fox* the *Devil* have, but blow out the *Candle* and *Torch*, and *Sun* of the *holy Books* and *Records*, that ſo *the Father of Lies* and *Murthers* may be heard, (as he hath been heard in the *Grecian Oracles* in *Mahomet*, and the *Mahumetans*, in the *Pope* and the *Papiſts*) ſo by his whiſperings in the *Foxians*, as if he were the moſt holy Spirit of the *Eternal God himſelf, Immortal, Inviſible, and only Wiſe.* '

The Subtlety of the Devil and his Agenᵗₛ in Catching of men.

5. For, is it not the *Devils Trade* to play the *ſubtle Hunter*, (as do alſo his *Journey-men* who ly in wait to catch men) and to trim his *Pits* and *Gins*, and *Snares*, with *green leaves* and *Boughs*, and *Twigs*, viz : *fair pretences* of the Spirit, the Spirit, the *Immediate Spirit*, the *Infallible Spirit*, the Teachings of the Spirit, the manner of the Spirit, ſpeaking to the Spirit, and Chriſt within you, *Chriſt within you except you be Reprobates, Chriſt within you the hope of Glory*, &c. Theſe are *fair Leaves*, and *ſweet, heavenly green Boughs*, on which the *Old Serpent* twineth, and from whence he uttereth even Scripture it ſelf, and the *ſweet Names* God and Chriſt, and Spirit, in a *frantick purpoſe* to ſtab (for he knows he can not) the holy Scriptures, and *God*, and *Chriſt*, and *Spirit* alſo :

6. More particularly, what doth he mean, that
God

God fpeaks not to us after the manner of men, but What G. Fox means by the mauner of the Spirit. by the way of the Spirit, after the manner of the Spirit? He grants that the holy Scriptures were given forth from the *Immediate Infp ration* of the Spirit: He knows that we maintain from *Ifai.* 59. the great Promife of the Word and Spirit together, to the mouth of Chrift Jefus and his Seed, and his *Seeds Seed.* And alfo that we affirme that no Reading, no Hearing, no Meditation, no Afflictions, *&c.* can do a Soul any good, until God by the *Power* or Finger of his own felf, or Spirit, makes the means *Powerful* and *Effectual.*

All this ferves not, but that which Sathan drives at, and which alone muft ferve his Ends is, *Immediate, Immediate Infpiration* with a *damning,* or changing the means by the *moft Holy, and only Wife God Appointed.*

118] 7. It is one of the *Proverbs* of the *Ancients* G. Fox his proud Simplicity *Sus Minervam docet.* The Sow teacheth the Goddefs of *Wifdome.* It is moft *Infallibly true* here, this *filthy Sow* (that feems to be wafht from Common vices and yet wallows in the *mud & Dunghils* of *Myftical Filthinefs*) He muft teach wifdome it felf how to fpeak, and appoint him his way, and (by wrefting and racing out what he can the *Holy Records*) how to reveal himfelf unto the Sons of men. The Monftrous Ridle of the Foxians Spirit.

8. It is pertinent to Confider the ground of this his only owning the manner of the Spirit, *viz.* [*This Immediate Spirit fpeaks to the Spirit within.*] What is the Englifh of this *Ridle* [*The Immediate Spirit within fpeaks to the Spirit within,*] But their Spirit will tell us that God and Chrift, and Spirit,

and

and Light, and New Covenant, and Faith, and Holinefs, &c. are all in prifon within, in every man,
until the *Immediate Spirit* without means perfwade
a perfon to hearken within to him as to *Chrift,
Light* and *Spirit*, which will bring him to God and
Chrift, (round in a *Conjuriug Circle Chrift* brings to
Chrift, the *Spirit* brings to the *Spirit*,) which though
it be true, after Converfion and *in growth* and *Increafe* of the Grace and Knowledge of Chrift by
the ufe of means appointed by Chrift Jefus, yet I
deny it ever to be done in the *firft turning* of the
Heart and *working of Faith*, that is by any fuch
Immediate Spirit, and *Chrift* and *God* in every of
mankind before, or fince the coming of Chrift
Jefus, efpecially, for they fay, that he is the *true
Light* (of which *John* fpake, then Come, to *Inlighten the World*, &c.

9. I Conclude this *Inftance* and the whole with
a *Reflection* upon Gods wonderful dealing with *Job*:
In the 1. *Chap.* the Lord boafts of his fervant *Iob*
to the *Devil* to be a *perfeit man*, (as the *Foxians*
Job a per-often urge this place) But God Schoold him for
feil man his *pride* and *Impatience*, &c. by *Elihu*, and by his
yet abhors
himfelf own *Voice* out of a *Whirlwind*: and now *Iob* Con-
for his feffeth his *Pride* and *Ignorance*, and profeffeth his
filthinefs. *Rifolution* to prate no more, &c. but to *abhor himfelf* (that is, as fome *loathfome Thing*) *in Duft and
Afhes*, G. *Fox* in this his Book abhors the Term of
Duft and Afhes, as being Elevatedabove *Abraham*
& *Iob* (*punies* to him) with high Fancies of his
Immortality, though we fee they dy, & ftink & Rot
as well as others.

But

But if God pleafe to fhew him, and me, truly what Sin is, What Gods Juftice is, what an *Infinite price* muft pay for the leaft *Evil Thought* and *Natu-ral Difpofition*, on the Old Score: [119] If God pleafe by any of thofe many gracious means he ufeth to Imprint thefe & other fuch *Heavenly Confidertions* upon our Souls! We fhall then for all our pretences cry out with *Peter, depart from me for I am a finful man O Lord*: and with *Iob, Once have I fpoken, yea, twice, &c.* but no more, *&c.* I *abhor myfelf* as a *loathfome, Rotten, ftinking Carrion in Duft and Afhes.* But alas I fear G. *Fox* is fo taken up with his *fitting with Chrift in Heavenly Places,* with *Immediate Dictates* of his fuppofed holy Spirit: That Gods fpeaking thus to his *poor Worms* after the way of Men, and by thefe out-ward means ftinks in his *Noftrils;* which if fo, and fo Irrecoverably, I defire, and defire all that love God and their own Salvations, to flee from him as from *Korahs Pride* and *Korahs Plagues,* for his *Viol* is pouring on him in *fpiritual Indgements,* and fhall be pouring on him in *fpiritual* and *Corporal Tor-ments to all Eternity.*

The Authors humble defire for himfelf and G. Fox.

The Authors fear as to G. Fox his cafe

F I N I S .

Lightning Source UK Ltd.
Milton Keynes UK
UKHW020607120219
337137UK00005B/736/P